WORD BIBLICAL COMMENTARY

Volumes

1 Genesis 1–15 . . . . Gordon J. Wenham
2 Genesis 16–50 . . . . Gordon J. Wenham
3 Exodus. . . . . John I. Durham
4 Leviticus . . . . .John E. Hartley
5 Numbers . . . . Philip J. Budd
6a Deuteronomy 1:1–21:9, 2nd ed. . . Duane L. Christensen
6b Deuteronomy 21:10–34:12 . . . . . . Duane L. Christensen
7a Joshua 1-12, 2nd ed. . . . . Trent C. Butler
7b Joshua 13-24, 2nd ed. . . . . . . Trent C. Butler
8 Judges . . . . Trent C. Butler
9 Ruth–Esther . . . . Frederic W. Bush
10 1 Samuel, 2nd ed. . . . . Ralph W. Klein
11 2 Samuel . . . . A. A. Anderson
12 1 Kings, 2nd ed. . . . . Simon J. Devries
13 2 Kings. . . . . T. R. Hobbs
14 1 Chronicles . . . . .Roddy Braun
15 2 Chronicles . . . . Raymond B. Dillard
16 Ezra, Nehemiah . . . . . .H. G. M. Williamson
17 Job 1–20 . . . . David J. A. Clines
18a Job 21–37 . . . . David J. A. Clines
18b Job 38–42 . . . . David J. A. Clines
19 Psalms 1–50, 2nd ed. . . . . . Peter C. Craigie, Marvin E. Tate
20 Psalms 51–100 . . . . Marvin E. Tate
21 Psalms 101–150, rev. ed. . . . .Leslie C. Allen
22 Proverbs. . . . . Roland E. Murphy
23a Ecclesiastes . . . . Roland E. Murphy
23b Song of Songs/Lamentations . . . .Duane H. Garrett, Paul R. House
24 Isaiah 1–33, rev. ed. . . . . . .John D. W. Watts
25 Isaiah 34–66, rev. ed. . . . . .John D. W. Watts
26 Jeremiah 1–25 . . . . Peter C. Craigie, Page H. Kelley, Joel F. Drinkard Jr.
27 Jeremiah 26–52 . . . . Gerald L. Keown, Pamela J. Scalise, Thomas G. Smothers
28 Ezekiel 1–19. . . . . .Leslie C. Allen
29 Ezekiel 20–48 . . . . .Leslie C. Allen
30 Daniel . . . . John E. Goldingay
31 Hosea–Jonah** . . . . Douglas Stuart
32 Micah–Malachi**. . . . . Ralph L. Smith
33a Matthew 1–13. . . . . Donald A. Hagner
33b Matthew 14–28. . . . . Donald A. Hagner
34a Mark 1–8:26** . . . . .Robert A. Guelich
34b Mark 8:27–16:20 . . . . .Craig A. Evans
35a Luke 1–9:20 . . . . John Nolland
35b Luke 9:21–18:34. . . . . John Nolland
35c Luke 18:35–24:53. . . . . John Nolland
36 John, 2nd ed. . . . George R. Beasley-Murray
37a Acts 1–14* . . . . .Stephen J. Walton
37b Acts 15–28* . . . . .Stephen J. Walton
38a Romans 1–8 . . . . .James D. G. Dunn
38b Romans 9–16 . . . . .James D. G. Dunn
39 1 Corinthians* . . . . .Andrew D. Clarke
40 2 Corinthians, rev. ed. . . . . .Ralph P. Martin
41 Galatians . . . . Richard N. Longenecker
42 Ephesians . . . . Andrew T. Lincoln
43 Philippians, rev. ed. . . .Gerald F. Hawthorne, rev. by Ralph P. Martin
44 Colossians, Philemon** . . . Peter T. O'Brien
45 1 & 2 Thessalonians** . . . . F. F. Bruce
46 Pastoral Epistles . . . . . . William D. Mounce
47a Hebrews 1–8. . . . . William L. Lane
47b Hebrews 9–13. . . . . William L. Lane
48 James . . . . .Ralph P. Martin
49 1 Peter . . . . .J. Ramsey Michaels
50 Jude, 2 Peter** . . . . . . Richard J. Bauckham
51 1, 2, 3, John, rev. ed. . . . . Stephen S. Smalley
52a Revelation 1–5 . . . . .David E. Aune
52b Revelation 6–16 . . . . .David E. Aune
52c Revelation 17–22 . . . . .David E. Aune

**forthcoming as of 2014*
***in revision as of 2014*

30 WORD BIBLICAL COMMENTARY

Daniel

JOHN E. GOLDINGAY

General Editors: David A. Hubbard, Glenn W. Barker
Old Testament Editor: John D. W. Watts
New Testament Editor: Ralph P. Martin

ZONDERVAN®

ZONDERVAN

Daniel, Volume 30

Previously published as *Daniel.*

Formerly published by Thomas Nelson, now published by Zondervan, a division of HarperCollins*Christian Publishing.*

Requests for information should be addressed to:
Zondervan, 3900 *Sparks Dr. SE, Grand Rapids, Michigan 49546*

This edition: ISBN 978-0-310-52192-1

The Library of Congress has cataloged the original edition as follows:
Library of Congress Control Number: 2005295211

The author's own translation of the Scripture text appears in italic type under the heading "Translation" as well as in brief Scripture quotations in the body of the commentary, except where otherwise indicated.

Printed in the United States of America

To
Steven and Mark:
may they stand with
Daniel, Hananiah,
Mishael, and Azariah.

Contents

Editorial Preface

The launching of the *Word Biblical Commentary* brings to fulfillment an enterprise of several years' planning. The publishers and the members of the editorial board met in 1977 to explore the possibility of a new commentary on the books of the Bible that would incorporate several distinctive features. Prospective readers of these volumes are entitled to know what such features were intended to be; whether the aims of the commentary have been fully achieved time alone will tell.

First, we have tried to cast a wide net to include as contributors a number of scholars from around the world who not only share our aims, but are in the main engaged in the ministry of teaching in university, college, and seminary. They represent a rich diversity of denominational allegiance. The broad stance of our contributors can rightly be called evangelical, and this term is to be understood in its positive, historic sense of a commitment to Scripture as divine revelation, and to the truth and power of the Christian gospel.

Then, the commentaries in our series are all commissioned and written for the purpose of inclusion in the *Word Biblical Commentary*. Unlike several of our distinguished counterparts in the field of commentary writing, there are no translated works, originally written in a non-English language. Also, our commentators were asked to prepare their own rendering of the original biblical text and to use those languages as the basis of their own comments and exegesis. What may be claimed as distinctive with this series is that it is based on the biblical languages, yet it seeks to make the technical and scholarly approach to a theological understanding of Scripture understandable by—and useful to—the fledgling student, the working minister, and colleagues in the guild of professional scholars and teachers as well.

Finally, a word must be said about the format of the series. The layout, in clearly defined sections, has been consciously devised to assist readers at different levels. Those wishing to learn about the textual witnesses on which the translation is offered are invited to consult the section headed *Notes*. If the readers' concern is with the state of modern scholarship on any given portion of Scripture, they should turn to the sections on *Bibliography* and *Form and Structure*. For a clear exposition of the passage's meaning and its relevance to the ongoing biblical revelation, the *Comment* and concluding *Explanation* are designed expressly to meet that need. There is therefore something for everyone who may pick up and use these volumes.

If these aims come anywhere near realization, the intention of the editors will have been met, and the labor of our team of contributors rewarded.

General Editors: *David A. Hubbard*
Glenn W. Barker †
Old Testament: *John D. W. Watts*
New Testament: *Ralph P. Martin*

Author's Preface

Faced with the general possibility of contributing to a commentary series, I can't imagine I would have thought first of Daniel as the book to volunteer for; but when the editors of the Word Biblical Commentary made that specific proposal I was intrigued, and I am exceedingly grateful to them for suggesting this project, which has occupied most of my time for research over the past five years. J. A. T. Robinson once said that he never wanted to write a commentary because the genre requires you to have to say something on everything, whether you have anything to say or not (*Wrestling with Romans* [London: SCM, 1979] vii): I have found every aspect of the study of this book absorbing, from matters of text and philology through questions of form, background, and exegesis to consideration of the message of the book and the theological questions it raises.

We live in a period in which vast numbers of commentaries are being produced, and some of my students and friends have asked—in a friendly way!—why I think another commentary on Daniel is worth writing. It is not because one will necessarily say many wholly new things: Rowley ruefully comments regarding a suggestion which a scholar thought was new but which had more than once been anticipated by earlier writers, "in the discussion of the book of Daniel originality is hard" (102). It is thus not because one reckons to have the solutions to all the unsolved difficulties in the book; with regard to many it is still best, as Farrar said was the case a century ago (332), "to obey the wise exhortation of the Rabbis, 'Learn to say, "I do not know." ' "I have felt a commentary worth writing partly because any significant work—and *a fortiori* any part of the Scriptures—deserves and demands ever fresh study by fresh minds and spirits in new generations if those generations are to grasp it and be grasped by it for themselves. It has seemed worthwhile because our period is also one that is seeing the development of a number of suggestive approaches to Daniel, whose fruitfulness for our understanding of the book as a whole I hope emerges in the pages that follow. It has seemed worthwhile because the book has long been treated as "especially fitted to be the battlefield between faith and unbelief" (Pusey, 1): it raises all the central questions about scriptural authority and inspiration, about history and faith, about pseudonymity and inerrancy, about criticism and hermeneutics. It has seemed worthwhile because Daniel thus needs rescuing from at least three kinds of would-be friends who are actually foes that imperil its being heard.

One kind is those who preoccupy themselves with merely historical questions about the accuracy or otherwise of its presentation of sixth- and second-century history, as if the solving of such questions constituted the interpretation of the book. Another kind is those who have turned Daniel into children's stories (the young men in the fiery furnace/Daniel in the lion's den), when the stories are of such deadly seriousness about problems facing adult believers living their lives in a strange land—like ourselves—that they almost require protecting from use in a children's context because of the trivializing this leads to. A third kind is those who treat the visions as mere coded preview of events to unfold in the Middle East, threatening to deprive them of their power to speak to situations when people are not merely exiled in a strange land but faced with the total dissolution of faith and hope. If the commentary contributes to one or two readers of Daniel finding themselves in its stories and reflecting in the light of them on their own lives, or to their looking on past, present, and future in the light of its own visionary perspective on past, present, and future, I shall be happy. I should add, however, that it has been my experience with Daniel as with other books that an appreciation of its inherent significance and its particular meaningfulness for us emerges from close working with the text in all its detailed "irrelevance," and I cannot promise that one hears the Scriptures speak without that close and prosaic work.

I am as ever grateful to Ann, Steven, and Mark for their support, and especially to Steven for encouraging me toward computer literacy and for writing Hebrew and Greek programs for me; to Edward Ball and Gillian Muddiman, my Old Testament colleagues at St John's College, for their criticism and stimulus; to the librarians at St John's and at Nottingham University for obtaining material for me; to Brian Mastin for reading through the manuscript with extraordinary care and for making many valuable comments; and to Rosemary Radford Ruether for the maxim "no theologian can be taken seriously unless he or she can cook" (quoted by E. Schillebeeckx, *Jesus in our Western Culture* [London: SCM, 1987] vii).

JOHN GOLDINGAY

Hanukkah 1987

Abbreviations

Periodicals, Serials, and Reference Works

AB	Anchor Bible (New York: Doubleday)
ABR	*Australian Biblical Review*
AcOr	*Acta orientalia*
AfO	*Archiv für Orientforschung*
AGJU	Arbeiten zur Geschichte des antiken Judentums und des Urchristentums (Leiden/Cologne: Brill)
AHW	W. von Soden, *Akkadisches Handwörterbuch* (3 vols.; Wiesbaden: Harrassowitz, 1965, 1972, 1981)
AJSL	*American Journal of Semitic Languages and Literature*
ALBO	Analecta lovaniensia biblica et orientalia
ALGHJ	Arbeiten zur Literatur und Geschichte des hellenistischen Judentums (Leiden: Brill)
AnBib	Analecta biblica (Rome: PBI)
ANEP	J. B. Pritchard (ed.), *The Ancient Near East in Pictures* (Princeton: Princeton UP, rev. 1969)
ANET	J. B. Pritchard (ed.), *Ancient Near Eastern Texts* (Princeton: Princeton UP, rev. 1969)
ANF	A. Roberts and J. Donaldson (eds.), The Ante-Nicene Fathers
AnOr	Analecta orientalia
ANRW	H. Temporini and W. Haase (eds.), *Aufstieg und Niedergang der römischen Welt* (Berlin/New York: de Gruyter)
AnSt	*Anatolian Studies*
AOAT	Alter Orient und Altes Testament (Kevelaer/Neukirchen: Butzon/Neukirchener)
ArOr	*Archiv orientalni*
ArRef	*Archiv für Reformationsgeschichte*
ASTI	*Annual of the Swedish Theological Institute*
ATANT	Abhandlungen zur Theologie des Alten und Neuen Testaments
AUSS	*Andrews University Seminary Studies*
BA	*Biblical Archaeologist*
BASOR	*Bulletin of the American Schools of Oriental Research*
BDB	F. Brown, S. R. Driver, and C. A. Briggs (eds.), *Hebrew and English Lexicon of the Old Testament* (Oxford/New York: Clarendon/OUP, 1907; corrected ed., 1962)
BetM	*Bet Miqra*
BETL	Bibliotheca ephemeridum theologicarum lovaniensium (Leuven/Gembloux: Leuven UP/Peeters)

BHK	R. Kittel, ed., *Biblia hebraica,* 3rd ed. (Stuttgart: Württembergische, 1937)
BHS	K. Elliger et al. (eds.), *Biblia hebraica stuttgartensia* (Stuttgart: Deutsche Bibelstiftung, 1977)
Bib	*Biblica*
BibOr	Biblica et orientalia (Rome: PBI)
BibS	Biblische Studien (Neukirchen: Neukirchener)
BIOSCS	*Bulletin of the International Organization for Septuagint and Cognate Studies*
BJRL	*Bulletin of the John Rylands University Library of Manchester*
BKAT	Biblischer Kommentar: Altes Testament (Neukirchen: Neukirchener)
BL	H. Bauer and P. Leander, *Grammatik des Biblisch-Aramäischen* (Halle: Niemeyer, 1927)
BO	*Bibliotheca orientalis*
BR	*Biblical Research*
BSac	*Bibliotheca sacra*
BT	*The Bible Translator*
BTB	*Biblical Theology Bulletin*
BWANT	Beiträge zur Wissenschaft vom Alten und Neuen Testament (Stuttgart: Kohlhammer)
BZ	*Biblische Zeitschrift*
BZAW/ZNW	Beihefte zur *ZAW/ZNW*
CAD	*The* [*Chicago*] *Assyrian Dictionary* (21 vols.; Chicago/Glückstadt: Oriental Institute/Augustin, 1964–)
CAH	*The Cambridge Ancient History* (Cambridge/New York: CUP)
CB	*Cultura biblica*
CBQ	*Catholic Biblical Quarterly*
CCSL	Corpus christianorum series latina
CHB	P. R. Ackroyd et al. (eds.), *The Cambridge History of the Bible* (3 vols; Cambridge/New York: CUP, 1963–70)
CHJ	W. D. Davies and L. Finkelstein (eds.), *The Cambridge History of Judaism,* vol. 1 (Cambridge/New York: CUP, 1984)
CJT	*Canadian Journal of Theology*
ClassPh	*Classical Philology*
CML	*Canaanite Myths and Legends* (1st ed., G. R. Driver; 2nd ed., J. C. L. Gibson; Edinburgh: Clark, 1956; 2nd ed., 1978)
ConB	Coniectanea biblica (Lund: Gleerup)
CR	Corpus reformatorum
CSCO	Corpus scriptorum christianorum orientalium
CTS	Contemporary Theology Series
CurTM	*Currents in Theology and Mission*
CW	*Christentum und Wissenschaft*
DJD	Discoveries in the Judaean Desert (Oxford/New York: Clarendon/OUP)

DOTT	D. W. Thomas (ed.), *Documents from Old Testament Times* (London/New York: Nelson, 1958)
DTT	M. Jastrow, *A Dictionary of the Targumim . . .* (New York/London: Choreb/Shapiro, 1926)
EBib	Etudes bibliques
EncJud	C. Roth et al. (eds.), *Encyclopaedia judaica* (Jerusalem: Keter, 1971)
EstBib	*Estudios biblicos*
ETL	*Ephemerides theologicae lovanienses*
EvQ	*The Evangelical Quarterly*
EvT	*Evangelische Theologie*
EWS	T. Muraoka, *Emphatic Words and Structures in Biblical Hebrew* (Jerusalem/Leiden: Magnes/Brill, 1985)
Exp	*Expositor*
ExpT	*Expository Times*
FOTL	The Forms of the Old Testament Literature (Grand Rapids: Eerdmans)
FRLANT	Forschungen zur Religion und Literatur des Alten und Neuen Testaments (Göttingen: Vandenhoeck)
FZPT	*Freiburger Zeitschrift für Philosophie und Theologie*
GBA	F. Rosenthal, *A Grammar of Biblical Aramaic* (Wiesbaden: Harrassowitz, 1961
GKC	*Gesenius' Hebrew Grammar,* ed. E. Kautzsch, tr. A. E. Cowley (London/New York: OUP, 1910; repr. 1966)
HBT	*Horizons in Biblical Theology*
Herm	Hermeneia (Philadelphia: Fortress)
HeyJ	*Heythrop Journal*
HR	*History of Religions*
HS	R. J. Williams, *Hebrew Syntax,* 2d ed. (Toronto/Buffalo/London: University of Toronto, 1976)
HSM	Harvard Semitic Monographs
HTR	*Harvard Theological Review*
HTS	Harvard Theological Studies
HUCA	*Hebrew Union College Annual*
HW	*Hebräische Wortforschung* (FS W. Baumgartner; VTSup 16, 1967)
HZ	*Historische Zeitschrift*
IBD	J. D. Douglas et al. (eds.), *The Illustrated Bible Dictionary* (Leicester/Wheaton, IL: IVP/Tyndale House, 1980)
ICC	International Critical Commentary (Edinburgh/New York: Clark/Scribner's)
IDB	G. A. Buttrick et al. (ed.), *The Interpreter's Dictionary of the Bible* (Nashville: Abingdon, 1962–76)
IDBSup	Supplementary Volume to *IDB*
IEJ	*Israel Exploration Journal*
Int	*Interpretation*
IOS	*Israel Oriental Studies*
IRT	Issues in Religion and Theology (Philadelphia/London: Fortress/SPCK)

ITQ	*Irish Theological Quarterly*
JA	*Journal Asiatique*
JAAR	*Journal of the American Academy of Religion*
JANESCU	*Journal of the Ancient Near Eastern Society of Columbia University*
JAOS	*Journal of the American Oriental Society*
JBL	*Journal of Biblical Literature*
JCS	*Journal of Cuneiform Studies*
JETS	*Journal of the Evangelical Theological Society*
JJS	*Journal of Jewish Studies*
JNES	*Journal of Near Eastern Studies*
JPT	*Jahrbuch für Protestant Theologie*
JQR	*Jewish Quarterly Review*
JR	*Journal of Religion*
JRAS	*Journal of the Royal Asiatic Society*
JSJ	*Journal for the Study of Judaism in the Persian, Hellenistic and Roman Period*
JSNT	*Journal for the Study of the New Testament*
*JSNT*Sup	*Journal for the Study of the New Testament* Supplement Series
JSOT	*Journal for the Study of the Old Testament*
*JSOT*Sup	*Journal for the Study of the Old Testament* Supplement Series
JSS	*Journal of Semitic Studies*
JTC	*Journal for Theology and the Church*
JTS	*Journal of Theological Studies*
JTVI	*Journal of the Transactions of the Victoria Institute*
KB	L. Koehler and W. Baumgartner, *Lexicon in Veteris Testamenti libros* (Leiden: Brill, 1953)
KD	*Kerygma und Dogma*
LAB	Liber Antiquitatum Biblicarum (The Book of Biblical Antiquities)
LD	Lectio divina (Paris: Cerf)
LLA	A. Vogt, *Lexicon linguae aramaicae* (Rome: PBI, 1971)
LumVie	*Lumière et Vie*
MB	Miscellanées bibliques
MGWJ	*Monatsschrift für Geschichte und Wissenschaft des Judentums*
MS	Monograph Series
NedTT	*Nederlands Theologisch Tijdschrift*
NERT	W. Beyerlin (ed.), *Near Eastern Religious Texts Relating to the Old Testament* (OTL, 1978; ET by J. Bowden from *Religionsgeschichtliches Textbuch zum Alten Testament;* Göttingen: Vandenhoeck, 1975)
NKZ	*Neue kirchliche Zeitschrift*
NovT	*Novum Testamentum*
NovTSup	*Novum Testamentum,* Supplements
NPNF	P. Schaff (ed.), Nicene and Post-Nicene Fathers
NRT	*La nouvelle revue théologique*

NTS	*New Testament Studies*
OBO	Orbis biblicus et orientalis (Freiburg [Sw]/Göttingen: Universitätsverlag/Vandenhoeck)
OP	R. G. Kent, *Old Persian* (New Haven: American Oriental Society, 1950)
Or	*Orientalia*
OrAnt	*Oriens antiquus*
OrSt	J. D. C. Pavry (ed.), *Oriental Studies* (FS C. E. Pavry; London: OUP, 1933)
OrSuec	*Orientalia Suecana*
OTL	Old Testament Library (London/Philadelphia: SCM/Westminster)
OTP	J. H. Charlesworth (ed.), *The Old Testament Pseudepigrapha* (2 vols.; Garden City, NY/London: Doubleday/DLT, 1983–85)
OTS	*Oudtestamentische Studiën*
PG	J. Migne (ed.), *Patrologia graeca*
PL	J. Migne (ed.), *Patrologia latina*
Proc	*Proceedings of*
PS	J. Payne Smith, *A Compendious Syriac Dictionary* (Oxford: Clarendon, 1903)
PTMS	Pittsburgh Theological Monograph Series (Pittsburgh: Pickwick)
PTR	*Princeton Theological Review*
RA	*Revue d'assyriologie et d'archéologie orientale*
RB	*Revue biblique*
RechBib	*Recherches bibliques*
RevExp	*Review and Expositor*
RevQ	*Revue de Qumran*
RevSém	*Revue sémitique*
RHPR	*Revue d'histoire et de philosophie religieuses*
RHR	*Revue de l'histoire des religions*
RivB	*Rivista biblica*
RTL	*Revue théologique de Louvain*
RTP	*Revue de théologie et de philosophie*
SBL	Society of Biblical Literature
SBLDS/MS	SBL Dissertation Series/Monograph Series
SBLSP	SBL Seminar Papers
SBS	Stuttgarter Bibelstudien (Stuttgart/Wurzburg: Echter/KBW)
SBT	Studies in Biblical Theology (London/Naperville, IL: SCM/Allenson)
SCO	*Studia classica et orientalia* (FS A. Pagliaro; 3 vols.; Rome [Istituto di Glottologia], 1969)
ScrB	*Scripture Bulletin*
SEA	*Svensk exegetisk arsbok*
Sem	*Semitica*
SJLA	Studies in Judaism in Late Antiquity (Leiden: Brill)

SJT	*Scottish Journal of Theology*
SPB	Studia postbiblica (Leiden: Brill)
ST	*Studia theologica*
STK	*Svensk teologisk kvartalskrift*
SUNT	Studien zur Ümwelt des Neuen Testament (Göttingen: Vandenhoeck)
TBT	*The Bible Today*
TBü	Theologische Bücherei (Munich: Kaiser)
TConnAAS	*Transactions of the Connecticut Academy of Arts and Sciences*
TCS	Texts from Cuneiform Sources (Locust Valley, NY: Augustin)
TExH	Theologische Existenz heute (Munich: Kaiser)
TGUOS	*Transactions of the Glasgow University Oriental Society*
Them	*Themelios*
TLZ	*Theologische Literaturzeitung*
TQ	*Theologische Quartalschrift*
TRev	*Theologische Revue*
TRu	*Theologische Rundschau*
TSF	Theological Students Fellowship
TSK	*Theologische Studien und Kritiken*
TTH	S. R. Driver, *A Treatise on the Use of the Tenses in Hebrew* (Oxford/New York: Clarendon/OUP, 1874; 3rd ed., 1892)
TTP	*Thesaurus theologico-philologicus. . . .* (Vol. 1; Amsterdam, 1701)
TTZ	*Trierer theologische Zeitschrift*
TWAT	G. J. Botterweck et al. (eds.), *Theologisches Wörterbuch zum Alten Testament* (Stuttgart: Kohlhammer, 1970 = *Theological Dictionary of the Old Testament,* tr. J. T. Willis et al. [Grand Rapids: Eerdmans, 1974–])
TWNT	G. Kittel and G. Friedrich (eds.), *Theologisches Wörterbuch zum Neuen Testament* (Stuttgart: Kohlhammer, 1933–78 = *Theological Dictionary of the New Testament,* tr. G. W. Bromiley [Grand Rapids: Eerdmans, 1964–76])
TynB	*Tyndale Bulletin*
TZ	*Theologische Zeitschrift*
UBS	United Bible Societies, *Preliminary and Interim Report on the Hebrew Old Testament Text Project,* Vol. 5 (New York: UBS, 1980)
UF	*Ugaritische Forschungen*
USQR	*Union Seminary Quarterly Review*
VD	*Verbum Domini*
VF	*Verkündigung und Forschung*
VT	*Vetus Testamentum*
VTSup	Vetus Testamentum Supplements (Leiden: Brill)
WA	*Weimar Ausgabe*
WBC	Word Biblical Commentary (Dallas, TX: Word)
WCJS	World Congress of Jewish Studies

WMANT	Wissenschaftliche Monographien zum Alten und Neuen Testament (Neukirchen: Neukirchener)
WO	*Die Welt des Orients*
WTJ	*Westminster Theological Journal*
WUNT	Wissenschaftliche Untersuchungen zum Neuen Testament (Tübingen: Mohr)
ZA	*Zeitschrift für Assyriologie*
ZAW	*Zeitschrift für die alttestamentliche Wissenschaft*
ZDMG	*Zeitschrift der deutschen morgenländischen Gesellschaft*
ZKT	*Zeitschrift für katholische Theologie*
ZNW	*Zeitschrift für die neutestamentliche Wissenschaft*
ZTK	*Zeitschrift für Theologie und Kirche*

Hebrew and Aramaic Grammar

abs	absolute (nouns)
act	active
art	article
consec	consecutive
constr	construct (nouns)
def	definite
emph	emphatic (state)
f	feminine
ha	haphel
hi	hiphil
hit	hitpael
ho	hophal
imper	imperative
impf	imperfect
indef	indefinite
inf	infinitive
intrans	intransitive
juss	jussive
m	masculine
ni	niphal
nom	nominative
obj	object
pa	pael
pass	passive
pf	perfect
pi	piel
pl	plural
plupf	pluperfect
prep(s)	preposition(s)
ptpl(s)	participle(s)
pu	pual
ref(s)	reference(s)
s	singular
subj	subject
trans	transitive
vb	verb
voc	vocative

Miscellaneous Abbreviations

Akk	Akkadian
Apoc.	Apocalypse of, apocalyptic
Aq	Aquila
Aram	Aramaic
BA	Biblical Aramaic
B.Comm.	Bible Commentary(ies)
BH	Biblical Hebrew
C	The Cairo Geniza ms of Daniel
c.	*circa* (approximately)
cj(s)	conjecture(s)
cl(s)	clause(s)
CUP	Cambridge University Press
D	Deuteronom(ist)ic
Diss.	Dissertation
dittog	dittography (written twice)
dl	delete(s)

EA	Eastern Aramaic	n.	note
ed(s).	editor(s), edited by	OG	Old Greek (see G)
esp.	especially	OP	Old Persian
ET	English translation	OUP	Oxford University Press
FS	Festschrift		
G	Greek translation: as published in *Septuaginta,* ed. A. Rahlfs, 1935. In Daniel, G includes both OG and Th, as published in J. Ziegler's ed., 1954.	p	pesher
		perh.	perhaps
		Pers.	Persian
		postex	postexilic
		PRPC	Presbyterian and Reformed Publishing Company
		Q	Qere (the Hebrew text as read out)
Gk	Greek		
gl	gloss(es)	Syh	The Syriac translation of Origen's Hexapla
haplog	haplography		
Heb	Hebrew	Sym	Symmachus
JA	Jewish Aramaic	Syr	Syriac Version (as published in the Peshitta Institute edition, 1980)
K	Kethib (the written text)		
L	Leningrad Codes of MT (as published in BHS)	Tg	Targum
		Th	Theodotion (see G)
LBH	Late Biblical Hebrew	tr.	translator(s), translated by
lit.	literally		
Luc	Lucian	U	University (of)
LXX	The Septuagint	UP	University Press
mg	margin(al)	Vg	Vulgate (as published in Weber's edition)
MH	Middle Hebrew		
ms(s)	manuscript(s)	Vrs	Ancient versions (G, Syr, Vg)
MT	The Masoretic Text (as published in BHS)	WA	Western Aramaic

Biblical Books

Old Testament

Gen	Judg	1 Chron
Exod	Ruth	2 Chron
Lev	1 Sam	Ezra
Num	2 Sam	Neh
Deut	1 Kgs	Esth
Josh	2 Kgs	Job
Ps (Pss)	Ezek	Mic
Prov	Dan	Nah
Eccl	Hos	Hab
Cant	Joel	Zeph
Isa	Amos	Hag
Jer	Obad	Zech
Lam	Jonah	Mal

New Testament

Matt	1 Cor
Mark	2 Cor
Luke	Gal
John	Eph
Acts	Phil
Rom	Col
1 Thess	1 Pet
2 Thess	2 Pet
1 Tim	1 John
2 Tim	2 John
Titus	3 John
Philem	Jude
Heb	Rev
James	

Apocrypha

Add Esth	Additions to Esther	Pr Man	Prayer of Manasseh
Bar	Baruch	Sir	Ecclesiasticus (Wisdom of Jesus the son of Sirach)
Bel	Bel and the Dragon		
Ep Jer	Epistle of Jeremy		
1 Esdr	1 Esdras	S Th Ch	Song of the Three Children
2 Esdr	2 Esdras		
Jud	Judith	Sus	Susanna
1 Macc	1 Maccabees	Tob	Tobit
2 Macc	2 Maccabees	Wisd Sol	Wisdom of Solomon

English Versions

AV	Authorized (King James) Version	NAB	New American Bible
		NEB	New English Bible
EVV	English versions	NIV	New International Version
GNB	Good News Bible		
JB	Jerusalem Bible	RSV	Revised Standard Version
JPS	Jewish Publication Society translation of the Writings, 1982	RV	Revised Version

Pseudepigraphal and Early Patristic Books

2–3 Apoc. Bar.	Syriac, Greek Apocalypse of Baruch	*T. 12 Patr.*	Testaments of the Twelve Patriarchs
		T. Lev.	Testament of Levi
1 Enoch	Ethiopic, Slavonic, Hebrew Enoch	*T. Jos.*, etc.	Testament of Joseph, etc.
		Barn.	Barnabas
Jub.	Jubilees	*LAB* (= Ps.-Philo)	Liber Antiquitatum Biblicarum
Sib. Or.	Sibylline Oracles		

Dead Sea Scrolls

CD	Cairo (Genizah text of the) Damascus (Document)	1QapGen	*Genesis Apocryphon* of Qumran Cave 1
		1QH	*Hodayot* (*Thanksgiving Hymns*) from Qumran Cave 1
1Q, 2Q, 3Q, etc.	Numbered cave of Qumran, yielding written material; followed by abbreviation of biblical or apocryphal book	1QIsa[a,b]	First or second copy of Isaiah from Qumran Cave 1
		1QpHab	*Pesher on Habakkuk* from Qumran Cave 1
QL	Qumran literature	1QM	*Milhamah* (*War Scroll*)

1QS	*Serek hayyahad* (*Rule of the Community, Manual of Discipline*)		*Midrashim*) from Qumran Cave 4
1QSa	Appendix A (*Rule of the Congregation*) to 1QS	4QPrNab	Prayer of Nabonidus from Qumran Cave 4
1QSb	Appendix B (*Blessings*) to 1QS	11QMelch	*Melchizedek* text from Qumran Cave 11
4QFlor	*Florilegium* (or *Eschatological*	11QPs[a]	
		4QDan[a,c]	
		6QDan	

JOSEPHUS

Ant.	*Jewish Antiquities*	*War*	*The Jewish War*
c. Ap.	*Contra Apionem*		

RABBINIC WRITINGS

b. before a tractate indicates Babylonian Talmud; *m.* before a tractate indicates Mishnah.

Texts used for this commentary are:

Biblia Hebraica Stuttgartensia, ed. K. Elliger and W. Rudolph (Stuttgart: Deutsche Bibelgesselschaft, 1976/77, 1984).
Septuaginta, ed. A. Rahlfs (2 vols.; Stuttgart: Wurttembergische Bibelanstalt, [7]1962).
Novum Testamentum Graece, ed. E. Nestle, K. Aland et al. (Stuttgart: Deutsche Bibelgesellschaft, [26]1979).
The Babylonian Talmud, I. Epstein (34 vols.; Soncino, 1935–52).
The Mishnah, H. Danby (Oxford: Clarendon, 1933).

Special note on verse numbering:

In biblical references such as 4:21–24 [24–27], the first is the reference that appears in the printed Hebrew Bible, while that in square brackets is the one that appears in EVV.

Introduction

The Interpretation of Daniel

Bibliography

Only secondary studies of the interpretation of the book are listed here. See the *Main Bibliography* that follows the Introduction for works cited by author's name or short title.

Ackroyd, P. R., et al., ed. *The Cambridge History of the Bible.* 3 vols. Cambridge/New York: CUP, 1963–70. **Albrecht, O.** "Luthers Arbeiten an der Übersetzung und Auslegung des Propheten Daniel in den Jahren 1530 und 1541." *ArRef* 23 (1926) 1–50. **Ashby, G. W.** *Theodoret of Cyrrhus as Exegete of the Old Testament.* Grahamstown: Rhodes U, 1972. **Ashley, T. R.** 213–425. **Audet, J.-P.** "A Hebrew-Aramaic List of Books of the Old Testament in Greek Transcription." *JTS* 1 (1950) 135–54. **Baillet, M.** "Un recueil liturgique de Qumrân, grotte 4: 'Les paroles des luminaires.'" *RB* 68 (1961) 195–250. **Bardenhewer, O.** *Des heiligen Hippolytus von Rom Commentar zum Buche Daniel.* Freiburg: Herder, 1877. **Brady, G.** "Introduction." Hippolyte, *Commentaire sur Daniel,* tr. M. Lefèvre. Paris: Cerf, 1947. 7–66. **Baris, S. D.** "The American Daniel as Seen in Hawthorne's *The Scarlet Letter.*" In *Biblical Patterns in Modern Literature,* ed. D. H. Hirsch and N. Aschkenasy. Chico, CA: Scholars, 1984. 173–85. **Barthélemy, D.** *Les devanciers d'Aquila.* VTSup 10 (1963). **Bauckham, R.** *Tudor Apocalypse.* Abingdon: Sutton Courtenay, 1978. **Baumgartner, W.** "Ein Vierteljahrhundert Danielforschung." *TRu* 11 (1939) 59–83, 125–44, 201–28. **Beale, G. K.** *The Use of Daniel in Jewish Apocalyptic Literature and in the Revelation of St. John.* Lanham, MD/London: UP of America, 1984. Incorporating material from *TynB* 31 (1980) 163–70; *NovT* 25 (1983) 182–88; *JETS* 27 (1984) 413–23; *NTS* 31 (1985) 618–20. ———. "The Use of Daniel in the Synoptic Eschatological Discourse and in the Book of Revelation." In *The Jesus Tradition outside the Gospels,* ed. D. Wenham. Gospel Perspectives 5. Sheffield: JSOT, 1985. 129–53. ———. "A Reconsideration of the Text of Daniel in the Apocalypse." *Bib* 67 (1986) 539–43. **Beckwith, R. T.** "The Significance of the Calendar for Interpreting Essene Chronology and Eschatology." *RevQ* 10 (1979–81) 167–202. ———. "Daniel 9 and the Date of Messiah's Coming in Essene, Hellenistic, Pharisaic, Zealot, and Early Christian Computation." *RevQ* 10 (1979–81) 521–42. **Berger, K.** *Die griechische Daniel-Diegese.* SPB 27 (1976). **Betz, O.,** and **Grimm, W.** *Jesus und das Danielbuch.* 2 vols. Frankfurt/New York: Lang, 1984–85. *Biblia Sacra iuxta latinam vulgatam versionem, xvi. Liber Danihelis.* Ed. Benedictine monks of St. Jerome's Pontifical Abbey. Rome: Vatican, 1981. **Bietenhard, H.** "'Der Menschensohn.'" *ANRW* ii 25, 1 (1982) 265–350. **Black, M.** "The Eschatology of the Similitudes of Enoch." *JTS* 3 (1952) 1–10. **Bludau, A.** "Die Apokalypse und Theodotions Danielübersetzung." *TQ* 79 (1897) 1–26. ———. "Die alexandrische Übersetzung des Buches Daniel und ihr Verhältnis zum massoretischen Text." *Biblische Studien* 2 (Freiburg: Herder, 1897) 1–218. **Bock, D. L.** *Proclamation from Prophecy and Pattern: Lucan Old Testament Christology.* JSNTSup 12 (1987). **Bogaert, P.-M.** "Le témoinage de la Vetus Latina dans l'étude de la tradition des Septante: Ézéchiel et Daniel dans le Papyrus 967." *Bib* 59 (1978) 384–95. **Bonwetsch, G. N.** *Studien zu den Kommentaren Hippolyts zum Buche Daniel und Hohen Liede.* Leipzig: Hinrichs, 1897. **Braverman, J.** *Jerome's Commentary on Daniel.* CBQ MS 7 (1978) **Brownlee, W. H.** *BASOR* 132 (1953) 8–15; 135 (1954) 33–38. **Bruce, F. F.**

Biblical Exegesis in the Qumran Texts. The Hague: Van Keulen, 1959; rev. ed., Grand Rapids: Eerdmans, 1959/London: Tyndale, 1960. ———. *This Is That: The New Testament Development of Some Old Testament Themes.* Exeter: Paternoster, 1968. = *The New Testament Development of Some Old Testament Themes.* Grand Rapids: Eerdmans, 1968. ———. "Josephus and Daniel." *ASTI* 6 (1965) 148–62. ———. "The Book of Daniel and the Qumran Community." In *Neotestamentica et semitica,* FS M. Black, ed. E. E. Ellis and M. Wilcox. Edinburgh: Clark, 1969. 221–35. ———. "The Earliest Old Testament Interpretation." *OTS* 17 (1972) 37–52. ———. "The Oldest Greek Version of Daniel." *OTS* 20 (1977) 22–40. ———. "Prophetic Interpretation in the Septuagint." *BIOSCS* 12 (1979) 17–26. ———. "The Background to the Son of Man Sayings." In *Christ the Lord,* FS D. Guthrie, ed. H. H. Rowdon. Leicester/Downers Grove, IL: IVP, 1982. 50–70. **Buchanan, H.** "Luther and the Turks 1519–1529." *ArRef* 47 (1956) 145–59. **Burrows, E.** *The Gospels of the Infancy and Other Biblical Essays.* London: Burns and Oates, 1940. **Busto Saiz, J. R.** "El texto teodociónico de Daniel y la traducción de Símaco." *Sefarad* 40 (1980) 41–55. **Butterworth, C. C.**, and **Chester, A. G.** *George Joye.* Philadelphia: U Pennsylvania, 1962. 235–44. **Capp, B. S.** *The Fifth-Monarchy Men.* London/Totowa, NJ: Faber/Rowman, 1972. **Carmignac, J.** "Les citations de l'Ancien Testament dans 'La Guerre des Fils de Lumière contre les Fils de Ténèbres.' " *RB* 63 (1956) 234–60, 375–90. **Casey, [P.] M.** *Son of Man.* London, SPCK, 1979. ———. "The Use of the Term 'Son of Man' in the Similitudes of Enoch." *JSJ* 7 (1976) 11–29. ———. "The Corporate Interpretation of 'One Like a Son of Man' (Dan. vii 13) at the Time of Jesus." *NovT* 18 (1976) 167–80. ———. "Porphyry and the Origin of the Book of Daniel." *JTS* 27 (1976) 15–33. **Cohn, N.** *The Pursuit of the Millennium.* Rev. ed. London/New York: Temple Smith/OUP, 1970. **Crafer, T. W.** "The Work of Porphyry against the Christians, and Its Reconstruction." *JTS* 15 (1913–14) 360–95, 481–512. **Cross, F. M.** "Editing the Manuscript Fragments from Qumran: Cave 4 of Qumran (4Q)." *BA* 19 (1956) 83–86. ——— and **Talmon, S.**, eds. *Qumran and the History of the Biblical Text.* Cambridge, MA/London: Harvard UP, 1975. **Daube, D.** "Typology in Josephus." *JJS* 31 (1980) 18–36. **Delcor, M.** "Un cas de traduction 'targoumique' de la LXX." *Textus* 7 (1969) 30–35. ———. "L'hymne à Sion." *RevQ* 6 (1967–69) 71–88. ———. "Le livre des Paraboles d'Hénoch Ethiopien." *EstBib* 38 (1979–80) 5–33. **Denis, A. M.** *Introduction aux Pseudépigraphes grecs d'Ancien Testament.* Leiden: Brill, 1970. 309–14. **Derrett, J. D. M.** "Daniel and Salvation-History." *Downside Review* 100 (1982) 62–67. = Derrett, *Studies in the New Testament.* Leiden: Brill, 1986. 4:132–38. **Dexinger, F.** "Ein 'messianisches Szenarium' als Gemeingut des Judentums in nachherodianischer Zeit?" *Kairos* 17 (1975) 249–78. **Farrer, A. M.** *A Study in St. Mark.* London: Black, 1951. 247–89. **Ferch, A. J.** *The Son of Man in Daniel 7.* Berrien Springs, MI: Andrews UP, 1983. Incorporating material from *JBL* 99 (1980) 75–86. ———. "Porphyry: An Heir to Christian Exegesis?" *ZNW* 73 (1982) 141–47. **Firth, K. R.** *The Apocalyptic Tradition in Reformation Britain 1530–1645.* Oxford/New York: OUP, 1979. **Fischer, U.** *Eschatologie und Jenseitserwartung im hellenistischen Diasporajudentum.* BZNW 44 (1978). 157–83. **Fitzmyer, J. A.** "Further Light on Melchizedek from Qumran Cave 11." *JBL* 86 (1967) 25–41. = Fitzmyer, *Essays,* 245–67. **Ford, D.** *Abomination.* **Fraidl, F.** *Die Exegese der siebzig Wochen Daniels in der alten und mittleren Zeit.* Graz: Leuschner, 1883. **Froom, L. E.** *The Prophetic Faith of Our Fathers.* 4 vols. Washington: Review and Herald, 1950–54. **Fruchtman, J.** *The Apocalyptic Politics of Richard Price and Joseph Priestley.* Philadelphia: American Philosophical Society, 1983. **Gammie, J. G.** "A Journey through Danielic Spaces." *Int* 39 (1985) 144–56. Repr. in *Interpreting the Prophets,* ed. J. L. Mays and P. J. Achtemeier. Philadelphia: Fortress, 1987. 261–72. **Gaston, L.** "The Son of Man." *No Stone on Another.* NovTSup 23 (1970). 370–409. **Gehman, H. S.** "The 'Polyglott' Arabic Text of Daniel and Its Affinities." *JBL* 44 (1925) 327–52. ———. "The Sahidic and the Bohairic Versions of the Book of

Daniel." *JBL* 46 (1927) 279–330. ———. "The Hesychian Influence in the Versions of Daniel." *JBL* 48 (1929) 329–32. ———. "The Armenian Version of the Book of Daniel and Its Affinities." *ZAW* 48 (1930) 82–99. **Geissen, A.,** and **Hamm, W.** *Der Septuaginta-Text des Buches Daniel . . . nach dem Kölner Teil des Papyrus 967.* Papyrologische Texte und Abhandlungen 10 [Dan 1–2; Hamm], 21 [Dan 3–4; Hamm], and 5 [Dan 5–12, Susanna, Bel; Geissen]. Bonn: Habelt, 1969, 1977, 1968. **Gellinek, C.** "Daniel's Vision of Four Beasts in Twelfth-Century German Literature." *Germanic Review* 41 (1966) 5–26. **Glasson, T. F.** "Mark xiii. and the Greek Old Testament." *ExpT* 69 (1957–58) 213–15. **Goldstein, J. A.** *I Maccabees.* **Goodenough, E. R.** *Symbols.* **Grabbe, L. L.** "Chronography in Hellenistic Jewish Historiography." *SBLSP* 17 (1979) 43–68. **Grelot, P.** "Rudolph Meyer, *Das Gebet des Nabonid. . . .*" *RevQ* 4 (1963–64) 115–21. ———. "Les versions grecques de Daniel." *Bib* 47 (1966) 381–402. ———. "Le chapitre v de *Daniel* dans la Septante." *Sem* 24 (1974) 45–66. **Grimm, W.** [See under Betz.] **Gundry, R. H.** *The Use of the Old Testament in St. Matthew's Gospel.* NovTSup 18 (1967). **Hanhart, R.** "Die Übersetzungstechnik der Septuaginta als Interpretation (Daniel 11, 29 und die Aegyptenzüge des Antiochus Epiphanes)." In *Mélanges Dominique Barthélemy,* ed. P. Casetti et al. OBO 38. Freiburg/Göttingen: Editions Universitaires/Vandenhoeck, 1981. 136–57. **Hartman, L.** *Prophecy Interpreted.* Tr. N. Tomkinson. ConB NT Series 1 (1966). ———. "The Functions of Some So-called Apocalyptic Timetables." *NTS* 22 (1976) 1–14. **Hill, C.** *Antichrist in Seventeenth-Century England.* London/New York: OUP, 1971. **Horbury, W.** "The Messianic Associations of 'the Son of Man.' " *JTS* 36 (1985) 34–55. **Jahn, G.** *Das Buch Daniel nach der Septuaginta hergestellt, übersetzt und kritisch erklärt.* Leipzig: Pfeiffer, 1904. **Jellicoe, S.** "Some Reflections on the καιγε Recension." *VT* 23 (1973) 15–24. **Jones, D. R.** "Commentaries on Daniel." *Theology* 66 (1963) 276–80. **Käser, W.** "Die Monarchie im Spiegel von Calvins Daniel-Kommentar." *EvT* 11 (1951–52) 112–37. **Kee, H. C.** " 'The Man' in Fourth Ezra." In *Society of Biblical Literature 1981 Seminar Papers,* ed. K. H. Richards. SBLSP 20 (1981). 199–208. **Kim, S.** *"The 'Son of Man'" as the Son of God.* WUNT 30. Tübingen: Mohr, 1983/Grand Rapids: Eerdmans, 1985. **Knowles, L. E.** "The Interpretation of the Seventy Weeks of Daniel in the Early Fathers." *WTJ* 7 (1945) 136–60. **Köbert, R.** "Zur Daniel-Abhandlung des Simeon von Edessa." *Bib* 63 (1982) 63–78. **Koch, K.** *Daniel.* ———. *HZ* 193 (1961) 1–32. ———. *Int* 39 (1985) 117–30. **Kooij, A. van der.** "A Case of Reinterpretation in the Old Greek of Daniel 11." In *Tradition and Re-interpretation in Jewish and Early Christian Literature,* FS J. C. H. Lebram, ed. J. W. van Henten et al. SPB 36 (1986) 72–80. **Lacocque, A.** "The Vision of the Eagle in 4 Esdras, a Rereading of Daniel 7 in the First Century C.E." *SBLSP* 20 (1981) 237–58. **Lamy, T.-J.** "L'exégèse en orient au *iv*e *siècle.*" *RB* 2 (1893) 5–25, 161–81, 465–86. **Laurentin, R.** *Structure et théologie de Luc i–ii.* Paris: Gabalda, 1957. 45–63. **Lebram, J. C. H.** "Perspektiven der gegenwärtigen Danielforschung." *JSJ* 5 (1974) 1–33. **Liptzin, S.** "Belshazzar's Folly." *Dor le Dor* 7 (1978–79) 119–26. Repr. in Liptzin, *Biblical Themes in World Literature.* Hoboken, NJ: Ktav, 1985. **Lloyd Jones, G.** *The Influence of Mediaeval Jewish Exegetes on Biblical Scholarship in Sixteenth Century England: With Special Reference to the Book of Daniel.* Diss., London, 1974. **Löhr, M.** "Textkritische Vorarbeiten zu einer Erklärung des Buches Daniel." *ZAW* 15 (1895) 75–103, 193–225; 16 (1896) 17–39. **Lust, J.** "Daniel 7, 13 and the Septuagint." *ETL* 54 (1978) 62–69. **McGinn, B.** *Apocalyptic Spirituality.* New York: Paulist, 1979. ———. *Visions of the End: Apocalyptic Traditions in the Middle Ages.* New York/Guildford: Columbia UP, 1979. **McHardy, W. D.** "The Peshitta Text of Daniel xi, 4." *JTS* 49 (1948) 56–57. **Macler, F.** "Les apocalypses apocryphes de Daniel." *RHR* 17 [33] (1896) 37–53, 163–76, 288–319. **Mainz, E.** "Le Livre de Daniel en Judéo-Persan." In *Irano-Judaica,* ed. S. Shaked. Jerusalem: Ben-Zvi Institute, 1982. 148–79. **Mann, J.** "Early Ḳaraite Bible Commentaries." *JQR* 12 (1921–22) 435–526. **Marsch, E.** *Biblische Prophetie und chronographische*

Dichtung. Berlin: Schmidt, 1972. **Méchoulan, H.** "Révélation, rationalité et prophétie." *Revue des sciences philosophiques et théologiques* 64 (1980) 363–71. **Meyer, R.** *Das Gebet des Nabonid.* Berlin: Akademie, 1962. ———. "Das Qumrânfragment 'Gebet des Nabonid.' " *TLZ* 85 (1960) 831–34. **Milik, J. T.** " 'Prière de Nabonide' et autres écrits d'un cycle de Daniel." *RB* 63 (1956) 407–15. **Montgomery, J. A.** "A Survival of the Tetragrammaton in Daniel." *JBL* 40 (1921) 86. **Morrow, W. S.**, and **Clarke, E. G.** "The *Ketib/Qere* in the Aramaic Portions of Ezra and Daniel." *VT* 36 (1986) 406–22. **Müller, K.** "Beobachtungen zur Entwicklung der Menschensohnvorstellung in den Bilderreden des Henoch und im Buche Daniel." In *Wegzeichen*, FS H. M. Biedermann, ed. E. C. Suttner and C. Patock. Das östliche Christentum 25. Würzburg: Augustinus, 1971. 253–61. ———. "Menschensohn und Messias." *BZ* 16 (1972) 161–87; 17 (1973) 52–66. ———. "Der Menschensohn im Danielzyklus." In *Jesus und der Menschensohn,* FS A. Vögtle, ed. R. Pesch and R. Schnackenburg. Freiburg: Herder, 1975. 37–80. **Müller, U. B.** *Messias und Menschensohn in jüdischen Apokalypsen und in der Offenbarung des Johannes.* Gütersloh: Mohn, 1972. **Murray, I.** *The Puritan Hope.* London: Banner of Truth, 1971. **Oliver, W. H.** *Prophets and Millennialists: The Uses of Biblical Prophecy in England from the 1790s to the 1840s.* [Auckland/Oxford]: Auckland UP/OUP, 1978. **Orchard, J. B.** "St Paul and the Book of Daniel." *Bib* 20 (1939) 172–79. **Pace, S.** "The Stratigraphy of the Text of *Daniel* and the Question of Theological *Tendenz* in the Old Greek." *BIOSCS* 17 (1984) 15–35. **Perrin, N.** "The Son of Man in Ancient Judaism and Primitive Christianity." *BR* 11 (1966) 17–28. Cf. Perrin, *Rediscovering the Teaching of Jesus.* London/New York: SCM/Harper, 1967. 164–99. ———. "The Interpretation of a Biblical Symbol." *JR* 55 (1975) 348–70. Cf. Perrin, *Kingdom,* 15–88. **Prete, S.** "Declino e corrompimento morale nella escatologia occidentale: Nota alle interpretazioni su Dan. 2, 31; 7, 3 di Ippolito e Girolamo." *Divus Thomas* 82 (1979) 145–56. **Procksch, O.** "Tetraplarische Studien." *ZAW* 53 (1935) 240–69. **Riessler, P.** "Zur Textgeschichte des Buches Daniel." *TQ* 79 (1897) 584–603. **Rigaux, B.** "*Βδέλυγμα τῆς ἐρημώσεως*: Mc 13,14; Mt 24,15." *Bib* 40 (1959) 675–83. **Rinaldi, J.** "Danielis prophetiae apud S. Augustinum" *VD* 21 (1941) 99–107. **Roca-Puig, R.** "Daniele: Due semifogli del codice 967." *Aegyptus* 56 (1976) 3–18. **Rosenthal, F.** *Die aramäistische Forschung.* Leiden: Brill, 1939. **Rosenthal, I. E. J.** *Studia semitica.* Vol 1. Cambridge/New York: CUP, 1971. ———. "Don Isaac Abravanel." *BJRL* 21 (1937) 445–78. = Rosenthal, *Studia semitica,* 21–54. **Sarachek, J.** *The Doctrine of the Messiah in Medieval Jewish Literature.* New York: Jewish Theological Seminary, 1932; 2nd ed., New York: Hermon, 1968. **Satran, D.** "Daniel." In *Figures,* ed. Nickelsburg and Collins, 33–48. **Schaberg, J.** "Daniel 7, 12 and the New Testament Passion-Resurrection Predictions." *NTS* 31 (1985) 208–22. **Schmidt, J. M.** *Die jüdische Apokalyptik.* Neukirchen: Neukirchener, 1969; rev. ed., 1976. **Schmitt, A.** *Stammt der sogenannte "θ"-Text bei Daniel wirklich von Theodotion?* Göttingen: Vandenhoeck, 1966. **Schmoldt, H.** "Die Schrift 'Vom jungen Daniel' und 'Daniels letzte Vision.' . . . Diss., Hamburg, 1972." *TLZ* 97 (1972) 952–53. **Shaked, S.** "Fragments of Two Karaite Commentaries on Daniel in Judaeo-Persian." In *Irano-Judaica,* ed. S. Shaked. Jerusalem: Ben-Zvi Institute, 1982. **Silver, A. H.** *A History of Messianic Speculation in Israel.* New York: Macmillan, 1927. **Stauffer, E.** "Eine Bemerkung zum griechischen Danieltext." *Donum gentilicium,* FS D. Daube, ed. E. Bammel et al. Oxford/New York: Clarendon/OUP, 1978. 27–39. **Theisohn, J.** *Der auserwählte Richter.* SUNT 12 (1975). **Toon, P.** *Puritans, the Millennium, and the Future of Israel.* Cambridge: Clarke, 1970. **Tov, E.** *The Text-Critical Use of the Septuagint in Biblical Research.* Jerusalem: Simor, 1981. **Towner, W. S.** "Were the English Puritans 'the Saints of the Most High'?" *Int* 37 (1983) 46–63. **Trever, J. C.** "Completion of the Publication of Some Fragments from Qumran Cave 1." *RevQ* 5 (1964–65) 323–44. ———. "1QDan^a: The Latest of the Qumran Manu scripts." *RevQ* 7 (1969–70) 277–86. ———. "The Book of Daniel and the Origin of the Qumran Community." *BA* 48 (1985) 81–102. **Vaucher, A.-F.** "Daniel 8:14 en occident jusqu'au

Cardinal Nicolas de Cusa." *AUSS* 1 (1963) 139–51. **Volz, H.** "Beiträge zu Melancthons und Calvins Auslegungen des Propheten Daniel." *Zeitschrift für Kirchengeschichte* 67 (1955–56) 93–118. **Wegner, M.** "Das Nabuchodonosor-Bild." In *Pietas,* FS B. Kötting, ed. E. Dassmann and K. S. Frank. Münster: Aschendorf, 1980. 528–38. **Wenham, D.** "The Kingdom of God and Daniel." *ExpT* 98 (1986–87) 132–34. **Wieder, N.** "The Dead Sea Scrolls Type of Biblical Exegesis among the Karaites." In *Between East and West,* B. Horovitz Memorial, ed. A. Altmann. London: Horovitz, 1958. 75–106. **Wyngarden, M. J.** *The Syriac Version of the Book of Daniel.* Leipzig: Drugulin, 1923. **Yamauchi, E. M.** "Hermeneutical Issues in the Book of Daniel." *JETS* 23 (1980) 13–21. **Ziegler, J.** *Der Bibeltext im Daniel-Kommentar des Hippolyt von Rom.* Göttingen: Vandenhoeck, 1952. ———, ed. *Susanna—Daniel—Bel et Draco.* Göttingen Septuagint xvi, 2. Göttingen: Vandenhoeck, 1954.

In addition, the works on Daniel by P. R. Davies, R. A. Hall, A. G. Kallarakkal, A. Mertens, J. A. Montgomery, and S. Pace listed in the *Main Bibliography* following the *Introduction* are also especially relevant to the history of the book's interpretation.

The Book of Daniel which this commentary studies is one recension of the varied literature associated with Daniel's name, the work written partly in Hebrew and partly in Aramaic which appears in the Jewish scriptures among the Writings and in Protestant Bibles among the Prophets. It is set in the period of the Babylonian empire and the first years of the Persian era. After the scene is introduced in the opening story, Daniel takes center stage in chap. 2 outdoing the wisdom of the Babylonian sages by the power of God, and thus able to reveal how future political events are to unfold until God sets up his own rule and brings an end to all others. Chap. 2 thus opens up the book's two main themes, the exploits of Daniel and his friends as members of the royal court (chaps. 3–6) and the revelations regarding future events given to Daniel (chaps. 7–12). The revelations are cryptically expressed, but when they are explicitly interpreted within the book they focus on events to take place in Jerusalem itself in the Hellenistic period. Story and vision give the book as a whole a double focus: it describes an arc leading from the dispersion in the sixth century B.C. to the Jerusalem of the second.

The Aramaic of the book (2:4b–7:28) is a form of Imperial Aramaic, the international language of the Middle East through much of OT times (cf. 2 Kgs 18:26). It contains a fair number of Akkadian and Persian words and in chap. 3 three Greek ones, and matches the stories' setting in the eastern dispersion. It is distinguishable from the later Aramaic of Qumran but might be dated anywhere between the late sixth and early second centuries B.C., though the spelling may have been updated later in the light of the ongoing development of the living language (see Rosenthal, *Forschung;* Kitchen, "Aramaic"; Kutscher; Coxon; against Baumgartner; Rowley [see *Main Bibliography*]). The Greek words hardly necessitate a very late date, given the spread of Greek culture in the East, even in Palestine (Hengel, *Judentum,* 108–95 [ET 1:58–106]; also, e.g., Coxon, *TGUOS* 25 (1973–74) 24–40). The Hebrew of 1:1–2:4a; 8–12 also includes some Persian words and a number of Aramaisms. It is written in an idiosyncratic style and idiom with a number of uncertainties about the meaning of individual words and phrases. The Hebrew sections may have been translated from Aramaic (Zimmermann, *Books*), or at least were written by author(s) more at home in Aramaic. The range of possible dates for the Hebrew would be similar to that for the Aramaic (see (Polzin, *Hebrew*).

Over the millennia since its composition, Daniel has been continuously studied and expounded, and a consideration of the stages in this process that are known to us, as well as being interesting in its own right, reveals a series of questions regarding the book's content, background, and meaning that will provide part of the agenda for our own interaction with the book. We will return to some of them in the *Conclusion* to the commentary, in the light of our chapter-by-chapter study.

The first witness to the study of Daniel is the Old Greek translation (c. 150 B.C.?), known only through the incomplete Manuscript 967 of the Chester Beatty papyri from the third century, through Codex 88, the Chigi manuscript of Origen's Hexapla, from about the eleventh century, and through a ninth-century manuscript of the Syrian translation of the Hexapla, known as Syh (cf. Geissen and Hamm; Roca-Puig; Ziegler [see *Bibliography*]). OG is mostly quite close to MT but further from it in chaps. 4–6 and in one or two key passages later. Thus its version of 9:24–27 makes more explicit than MT that the passage refers to events that took place in the time of Antiochus: it dates the events of v 26 after 7 + *70* + 62 years—the 139th year of the Seleucid era being about 172. It also makes explicit—with the benefit of hindsight—that many sevens would elapse after the removal of the desolating abomination and before the End. In 7:13, according to Origen's text, the humanlike figure comes not ἕως παλαιοῦ ἡμερῶν ("*to* one advanced in days"), but ὡς παλαιὸς ἡμερῶν ("*as* one advanced in days"). Lust (*ETL* 54 [1978] 62–69) takes this as original; or it may be a slip; or it may reflect Christian claims for Jesus' divinity. Although Charles saw OG as often a better guide to the original Hebrew than MT, such differences from MT have more recently led scholars to see OG as in part paraphrastic/targumic/midrashic, the last element including both modifications based on other scriptures and other embellishments, in the manner of the Genesis Apocryphon (Ashley, 289–93; cf. Bruce [see *Bibliography*]). Pace, however, argues that at least in chaps. 7–12 OG is a literal rendering of a variant Hebrew tradition, such as the Qumran finds now prove to have existed for other books, plus some later changes in passages such as 7:13 and 12:2, while Grelot (see *Bibliography*) suggests OG is a translation of a second-century B.C. Hebrew version of the original Aramaic.

1 and 2 Maccabees (c. 100–63 B.C.) speak in terms similar to Daniel's of some of the events of the Antiochene crisis: they assume that the original reference of Dan 9:27; 11:31 is to Antiochus's cultic innovation, the βδέλυγμα ἐρημώσεως ("the abomination of desolation," 1 Macc 1:54). The stories in Dan 1–6 provide Maccabees with perspectives on the pressures of the Antiochene crisis (1 Macc 1:41–43; 2:59–60; Goldstein, *I Maccabees,* 44–54, 119–20). But there are ideological differences between 1 Maccabees and Dan 7–12: the former strongly affirms the active measures of the Maccabees and omits reference to the idea of resurrection. Goldstein suggests that 1 Maccabees delights in proving the oracles of Daniel false. 2 Maccabees, whose ideology is closer to Daniel's, is more inclined to tell a story that corresponds to it.

A Greek rendering of Daniel closer to MT, credited to Theodotion (c. A.D. 180), eventually replaced OG in the Septuagint as a whole and is thus better attested. But its renderings are known before Theodotion's time; both OG and Th are reflected in the NT. Thus Th may be based on an alternative "proto-Theodotionic" Greek version from some other part of the pre-Christian Hellenistic/Roman world (cf. Barthélemy; Schmitt; Koch; Jellicoe, *VT* 23 (1973) 15–24; L. F. Hartman, 76–83). Similar uncertainty attaches to the origin of the Syriac translation of Daniel. There are no clear indications that it is of Christian background, nor that it is dependent on OG or Th; it may be an independent translation from a Hebrew tradition related to but different from MT, perhaps deriving from Edessa in Turkey, the "literary capital" of the Syrian world in pre-Christian and Christian times (Kallarakkal; contrast Wyngarden, *Syriac*). There is no targum of Daniel.

Both OG and Th are longer recensions of Danielic material than MT, including another song of praise to God's power and wisdom, another story of false accusation, and another story about the exposure of false religion (involving a lion and an idol). It was naturally this longer Greek version of the book that appeared in the Greek Christian canon of the Old Testament and thus in the Roman Catholic Bible and the Protestant Apocrypha.

The Qumran scrolls, too, contain further "Danielic" material, the Prayer of Nabonidus, who is healed from a seven-year illness through the ministry of a Jewish exorcist, and some apocalyptic fragments, partly in quasi-prophetic form, which have been entitled Pseudo-Daniel (Mertens; Meyer; Milik [see *Bibliography*]). As well as quotations from Dan 11–12 in 4QFlor, Caves 1, 4, and 6 produced fragments of Daniel manuscripts, apparently as we have it in MT (bilingual and lacking the "Additions" present in the Greek versions). Their text differs occasionally from MT, sometimes in agreement with OG (2:5; 10:16) or Th (1:12; 3:23) (cf. F. M. Cross; Mertens; Trever; Pace [see *Bibliography*]). The Caves 1 and 6 material has appeared in DJD, but the major first-century-B.C. manuscripts from Cave 4 are only just being published. There are no real grounds for suggesting that the form of the Qumran manuscripts of Daniel indicates that the book was not regarded as canonical there, though neither for affirming that it was (G. W. Anderson, *CHB* 1:151).

The Qumran community believed that the visions in Daniel, which had patently not been completely fulfilled in the downfall of Antiochus Epiphanes, were about to be fulfilled in their day, and saw themselves as the embodiment of the discerning teachers (משכילים) and the holy ones on high in Daniel (Bruce, *Exegesis,* 27, 63–67, 70). In keeping with their general expository method, they applied prophecies from Daniel to themselves; the Damascus Rule offers "the first of a long line of commentaries" on Dan 9:24–27 (Mertens, 87). 11QMelch alludes to the tenth jubilee with possible reference to this passage (Fitzmyer, *Essays,* 251); words from Dan 9 also underlie one of the Qumran psalms (11QPs[a]: Delcor, *RevQ* 6 [1967–69] 84–88) and the 4Q liturgical text "The Words of the Luminaries" (Baillet, *RB* 68 [1961] 247). Partly on the basis of Dan 9 the Essenes were actually expecting the messiah between 3 B.C. and A.D. 2 (Beckwith, *RevQ* 10 [1979–81] 180). Daniel's portrait of Antiochus as the embodiment of godless wickedness also furnishes them with a portrait of their enemies, especially the Wicked Priest: the framework of the War Scroll "draws its inspiration from Daniel xi, 40–xii, 3" (G. Vermes, *The Dead Sea Scrolls in English* [Harmondsworth/Baltimore, MD: Penguin, 1962; rev. ed., 1968] 122). There already appears here a major theme of

Danielic study. Dan 10–12 seems to promise the coming of the End in connection with the Antiochene crisis. What happens to the book when history continues to unfold? Far from passing into disrepute, the book exercises a growing influence, providing 1QM with a framework for its own picture of the End. What 1QM perceives in Daniel is not merely a falsifiable timetable of events but encouragement to people living in the midst of crisis (Hartman, *NTS* 22 [1976] 5–6, noting also the quotation from Dan 12:9–10 in 4QFlor 174).

During the Persian and Greek eras there had been developing a substantial literature connected with the name of Enoch. This may be dependent on Daniel at a number of points, but current opinion dates much of *1 Enoch* 1–36; 72–108 earlier than Daniel or within the same period, so that in principle it is as likely that Daniel is dependent on *1 Enoch* as vice versa; indeed, many of the parallels (e.g., the use of animal imagery in *1 Enoch* 90) need not require dependence of either on the other. With *1 Enoch* 37–71 (the Parables) the situation is different. The Parables are uninstanced at Qumran, and current opinion regards them as belonging to the Roman period. Their most interesting parallel to Daniel (more likely suggesting dependence on Daniel than on a common source) is their taking up the humanlike figure and the one advanced in days of 7:13. "That Son of Man" (*1 Enoch* 46–48, alongside the "head of days" with hair white like wool; see also chaps. 62; 69), God's elect and righteous one, is eventually identified with Enoch (71.14). Thus Dan 7 is one of the texts that is used to interpret the significance of Enoch and his translation, reported with such tantalizing brevity in Gen 5; and it leads to or justifies a belief in Enoch's functioning as eschatological judge. As in Dan 7, however, the phrase suggests an image, not a title.

This motif appears prominently in the accounts of Jesus' life and teaching that came to be included in the NT, though the historical questions they raise are much controverted. While the expression "Son of Man" may have other background as well as Dan 7:13–14, the NT asserts that Jesus *is* that "Son of Man" who "has authority on earth" (Mark 2:10; cf. Matt 28:18; Farrer, *Mark,* 271–74). It thus uses Dan 7 as *1 Enoch* does, to express the conviction that *its* hero has ascended as "Son of Man" and will return with the clouds. It also connects with Dan 7 its awareness that "the Son of Man must suffer" (Mark 8:31; compare the suffering of the holy ones in Dan 7:21, 25—the Son of Man motif may have corporate as well as individual connotations) before he "comes in glory" (Mark 8:38; cf. 14:62, "with the clouds of heaven"). Further, it qualifies the statement that the Son of Man comes to be served, by declaring that he comes first to serve (Mark 10:45; cf. Dan 7:14). There are indications that a "messianic" interpretation of Dan 7 would not have been seen as a Christian innovation even within mainstream Judaism. R. Akiba (*c.* A.D. 120) refers the passage to David, though others fault this understanding because it plays into the hands of Christians (*b. Sanh.* 38; see also 96; 98 [Joshua ben Levy, *c.* A.D. 250]). (See Perrin; Bock; Horbury [see ***Bibliography***].)

Daniel's effect on the NT is more pervasive than merely the influence of 7:13–14. If apocalyptic *is* at all the mother of Christian theology (Käsemann, *ZTK* 57 [1960] 162–85 [ET in *Apocalypticism,* ed. R. W. Funk]), Daniel certainly contributed to this mothering. Luke *begins* his gospel with Gabriel again appearing at the time of the evening offering, to announce the beginning of a chain of events that will lead to the presentation in the temple as periods amounting to 490 days are fulfilled (cf. Dan 9; Laurentin, *Luc,* 45–63, following Burrows, *Infancy,* 41–42). Mark's Jesus begins his ministry proclaiming that the rule of God that Daniel promised is at hand: the time he spoke of is fulfilled (cf. Dan 2:44; 7:22; Wenham, *ExpT* 98 [1986–87] 132–34). Luke's Jesus sees himself as the stone that crushes, the very embodiment of the rule of God (20:18; cf. Dan 2:44–45). John's Jesus speaks of resurrection in terms that follow Dan 12 (5:28–29; cf. Matt 13:43; 25:46).

Jesus' discourse concerning the End speaks in Danielic fashion of troubling rumors, the final affliction, many stumbling, the need to endure to the end, the deliverance of the elect, the desolating sacrilege, the need to understand, and the coming of the Son of Man in clouds with great power and glory: "the main part of the eschatological discourse is based on a coherent exposition of or meditation on these texts in Daniel [in chaps. 2 and 7–12]" (L. Hartman, *Prophecy,* 158; see table, 172–74; cf. Gundry, *OT in Matthew*). Elsewhere, however, Jesus distances himself from apocalyptic esotericism built on passages such as Dan 2:19–23 (Matt 11:25–27; Luke 17:20–21) (Grimm, *Jesus*).

Daniel influences Paul, too, perhaps partly via the "midrash" that underlies Mark 13. 1 Thess 4–5 reflects Dan 7 and 12; the portrait of "the lawless one" in 2 Thess 2 reflects that of Antiochus in Dan 7–11; 1 Cor 15:23–28 is shaped by Dan 7 (Betz, *Jesus,* 121–43). Daniel thus facilitates Paul's formulating his teaching about the End. Further, no biblical work has greater influence on the Apocalypse of John, a work written for a community under a pressure analogous to that which affected Jews in the second century B.C. (Beale, *Use of Daniel,* 154–305—though the extent of clear influence is overstated). In particular, John's opening vision of Christ and of heaven (Rev 1; 4–5) is shaped partly by Dan 7 and by the description of the angelic appearance in Dan 10. The animals of Dan 7 are an important source for the vision of the animal in Rev 13; 17; the beast terrorizing the people of God is now Rome.

Dan 7 also contributed to the apocalypses of Baruch (see *2 Apoc. Bar.* 39 for the four empires) and Ezra (both c. A.D. 80). Ezra's vision of an eagle, symbolizing Rome (2 Esdr 11–12), is "a midrash on Daniel 7" or "a rereading of Daniel 7" (Kee and Lacocque, *SBLSP* 20 [1981] 203, 237). The interpreting angel explicitly notes that in seeing the fourth empire as Rome he is giving Daniel's vision an interpretation different from that given to Daniel himself (12:11–12). Then in a dream Ezra sees "something resembling a man" emerging from the sea and flying with the clouds of heaven to act as judge (2 Esdr 13). It is God's son; so here too Dan 7 is being used in connection with developing understandings of the messiah, perhaps partly in response to the Christian interpretation of Dan 7:13 as applying to Jesus (Bietenhard, "Menschensohn"). It may also be dependent on Dan 2 as one of the sources of its allusions to a stone-mountain (Beale, *Use of Daniel,* 131–39).

Josephus, too, believes that Daniel wrote of Rome (e.g., *Ant.* 10.11.7 [10.276]. His hesitancy over revealing the meaning of chap. 2 (*Ant.* 10.10.4 [10.210]) suggests that he assumes Rome is the fourth empire. The 490-years prophecy is fulfilled in the events of A.D. 66–70; Vespasian is the "prince to come" of that prophecy (e.g., *War* 6.5.4 [6.310–15]; cf. Bruce, *ASTI* 6 [1965] 148–62; *Exegesis,* 70). But he assumes that chap. 11 refers to Antiochus, and uses Daniel broadly as a source for his retelling of the story of Israel from the exile (e.g., *Ant.* 10.10.1–10.11.7 [10.186–281])—and uses Daniel himself, among others, as an anticipation, a type, of himself. (See Bruce, *ASTI* 6 [1965] 148–62; *Exegesis;* Daube, *JJS* 31 [1980] 28–33; Satran, "Daniel," 36–39.)

For Josephus, as for the Greek Bible, Qumran, Jesus, and the NT writers, Daniel is a prophet and has similar authority to the prophets within the Hebrew canon, though we do not know when the bounds of this canon were established and thus when Daniel became formally canonical. Associating Daniel with the prophets encourages a view of them that sees them as focusing on the End, a view that came to trouble Jews. Josephus, at least, saw this attitude to Daniel as a partial cause of the revolt with its disastrous consequences. The match between its prophecies and the abominations of the Romans perhaps made its place among the Scriptures secure, but in the Hebrew Bible it was finally located in its third section, the "Writings," which suggested a more pedagogical reading of the book. (Wilson, 2:9–64; Audet, *JTS* 1 [1950] 145–46; Koch, *Int* 39 [1985] 117–30; on this aspect of Josephus, Fischer, *Eschatologie,* 180–83; Dexinger, *Kairos* 17 [1975] 265.)

In writings of the Roman period, one can distinguish two types of study of Scripture, what might be called expository midrash and situational midrash. In the former the biblical text sets the agenda, though the text is looked at in the light of concerns and questions of the writer's day. In the latter these concerns and questions set the agenda, and the biblical text is studied and appealed to selectively on the basis of whether it seems to deal with these. The study of Daniel in the period of the Talmud and among the Church Fathers can have either starting point.

The first extant commentary on Daniel is by Hippolytus (? A.D. 170–235). It was written in a context of eschatological ferment, but its concerns are broader, with the historical reference of the book, its parenetic value, and its theological significance—sometimes reached by recourse to allegory (e.g., on chaps. 3 and 6) (Bardy, "Introduction"). The commentary of Origen (185–254) exists only in fragments, but Origen's abiding significance in connection with Daniel lies in his Hexapla, a six-column collation of the Hebrew OT with various Greek versions. During the second century a number of more literal alternatives to OG had come into existence, including Th, a very literal version by Aquila, and a freer one by Symmachus. Greek versions were also translated into Latin and later into Coptic (Sahidic/Bohairic, third century), Ethiopic (fourth century), and Armenian (fifth century). Origen was concerned for the Church to get the OT text right, not least so that it could argue with Jews on a common basis. It was perhaps through his work in the Hexapla that he brought about the supplanting of OG by Th in the LXX: OG Daniel seemed too free compared with the Hebrew as he knew it. At the same time, his Hexapla is our source for the oldest complete manuscripts of OG Daniel, 88 and Syh, as well as for fragments of Aquila and Symmachus.

The commentary of Jerome (?331–420) is our source for a knowledge of Porphyry's work, since he quotes it extensively in order to refute it, and of

Fathers such as Origen, since in undertaking the task of explaining and clarifying the text he seeks to pass on the fruits of earlier commentators' work. Jerome also made a new Latin translation of Daniel (c. 393), as of other OT books, to replace the Old Latin, also made in the second century from the Greek. His version, which came to be called the Vulgate, was made from the Hebrew, but by reference to the Greek, and it is thus not simply an independent witness to the Hebrew text of his day. His involvement with Hebrew is also reflected in his utilization of Jewish exegesis in his commentary (Braverman, CBQ MS 7). The commentaries of Chrysostom (347–407) included Daniel, but this, too, survives only in fragments. From the fourth century we know of two Syriac writers on Daniel, Ephrem Syrus and Aphrahat. From the fifth there are two commentaries in Greek, a fragmentary work by Polychronius, and a historical, exegetical commentary by Theodoret (393–457) in the Antiochene manner, though emphasizing in the preface that Daniel belongs among the prophets (of Jesus) rather than among the Writings.

The Fathers' more situational appeal to Daniel includes the use of the stories for parenetic purposes, but it focuses on the allusive visionary passages. There are occasional witnesses to the view that the four empires are Babylon, Media, Persia, and Greece, or Babylon, Medo-Persia, Alexander, and the Hellenistic monarchies, the small horn being Antiochus and the humanlike figure and the holy ones on high standing for second-century B.C. Jews: see, e.g., Aphrahat's *Demonstration* 5 (cf. Casey, *Son of Man,* 55–59). Similarly, Dan 9:24–27 can be related to the Hellenistic period: thus Eusebius refers the cutting off of an anointed one (9:26) to the suffering of the postexilic priesthood (*Dem.* 8; Bruce, *Exegesis,* 69–70). The pagan philosopher Porphyry (A.D. 233–304) assumes that the latter two empires are Alexander and the Hellenistic monarchies and that Antiochus is the small horn, broken by the Maccabees, and he applies Dan 11 (and 12) systematically to Antiochus, inferring an account of his death from vv 40–45. Porphyry is concerned to demonstrate that there are no grounds for claiming that prophecies in Daniel refer to Christ, or to Antichrist; the visions are quasi-prophecies written after the Antiochene crisis was over (cf. Casey, "Porphyry").

But the interpretation of the empires as Babylon, Medo-Persia, Greece, and Rome predominates among Christians as among Jews, and writers often see themselves and their readers as thus near the End of which Daniel spoke. *Barn.* 4.4 makes this explicit. In the context of persecution and of such expectations of the end of the world, "it is no accident that the earliest surviving complete Greek biblical commentary is that of Hippolytus on Daniel and the earliest surviving Latin one is that of Victorinus on the Apocalypse, the one from the beginning, the other from the end of the third century" (McGinn, *Spirituality,* 100). The belief that Daniel's prophecies pointed to Christ would discourage false expectations of fulfillment in contemporary history. From 300 it became usual to see Dan 9 as pointing to Christ (Fraidl, *Exegese,* 30–98); Julius Africanus worked out that quite a precise 490 years elapsed from the time of Nehemiah to Christ's death (see Eusebius, *Dem.* 8). Such an understanding of Daniel's visions compares closely with Jewish approaches, which saw the four empires and the 490 years coming to a climax with Rome and the events of 70 and 135, though it could also be used in anti-Jewish polemic to prove that the prophecies related to Jesus and not to these events.

There are a number of medieval works associated with the name Daniel (see Denis, *Introduction,* 309–14), such as the seventh-century Greek *Last Vision of Daniel* (ed. Schmoldt) and the ninth-century Greek *Apocalypse of Daniel* (ed. Berger; cf. *OTP* 1:755–70), a quasi-prophecy of eighth-century wars followed by actual prophecy of Antichrist and of Christ's appearing at the End. The assumption that the fourth empire is Greek and the small horn Antiochus is still alive in the Syrian tradition in glosses to the Syriac translation of Daniel that identify the small horn as Antiochus; the glosses perhaps belong to the sixth century (see Casey, *JTS* 27 [1976] 25). But the usual view is that the empires extend into the writers' period, so that Daniel's four-empire scheme provides the framework for understanding world history throughout the medieval period—and beyond, until the view that the empires belonged to the second temple came to predominate and a basis for structuring world history disappeared (Koch, *HZ* 193 [1961] 1–2; cf. Marsch, *Prophetie;* Gellinek, *Germanic Review* 41 [1966] 5–26).

To the Jewish scholarship of the first millennium A.D. we owe the preservation and standardization of the Hebrew Bible, the consonantal text over the first five centuries, the pointing over the succeeding five. Generally this scribal work was concerned to preserve one standard text of the Bible, but a distinctive feature with regard to Daniel is the number of alternative readings retained. These appear in the margins of extant manuscripts as the masora (tradition), and are reproduced in BHS: almost any verse, at least in the Aramaic chapters, provides examples. Some represent expansions or abbreviations of the text; most are matters of spelling, pronunciation, and morphology, though even these reflect an instinct to keep the text up-to-date and readable (see Morrow and Clarke, *VT* 36 [1986] 406–22). It is *a priori* likely that this instinct will also have affected matters of more substance in the text, for example, in the incorporation of explanatory glosses. There is a manuscript of Daniel from about the seventh century among those found in the geniza of a Cairo synagogue, but the work of the Masoretes came to a climax with the work of the ben Asher family. The oldest manuscript from this tradition containing Daniel is the Aleppo codex; BHK and BHS are based on the oldest complete Hebrew Bible, the Leningrad codex (L, located in the Leningrad Library), copied in 1008/9, from the tradition of Aharon ben Asher (c. 915).

The textual work of the medieval period was complemented by systematic production of Hebrew grammars, dictionaries, and commentaries, designed to facilitate access to the text's original meaning; a key figure is Saadia Gaon in Babylon (872–942), whose works included a translation of Daniel into Arabic, the everyday language there, and a commentary on the book. It was another period of eschatological expectation, and this is one aspect of the background to the writing of a number of commentaries on Daniel. There were apparently a number by Karaite authors, of which the most famous is that of Jephet ibn Ali (c. 1000) in Arabic. The Karaites stressed the authority of Scripture alone, questioned the authority of midrashic traditions, and sought to be rigorously literal in their interpretation. Thus Jephet insisted against Saadia that "days" in Daniel means "days" and should not be taken to mean "years" so as to refer it to contemporary events in a way that tends to be proved wrong by events. This does not mean that Jephet in practice avoided following traditional interpretations or avoided what seems to us *re*application of the text, in referring Dan 8 and 11 to events of his own day such as the invasion of Mecca (Mann; Shaked; Wieder [see *Bibliography*]). But the pressure of Karaite interpretation drove mainstream rabbinic scholarship in a literal, historical direction.

In France, Solomon bar Isaac, Rashi (1040–1105), produced a substantial commentary on Daniel combining a concern for the literal sense with a willingness to incorporate traditional midrashic material. Rashi dated the fulfillment of its "messianic" prophecies in the fourteenth century, which was his way of discouraging expectations for his own day. From Spanish Jewry, Abraham ben Meir ibn Ezra (1091–1167) produced a more rigorous literal exegesis, encouraging the reader to avoid attempting to calculate when Daniel's prophecies would be fulfilled, on the grounds that we will not know until it happens (see on 11:31), but referring the prophecies to political events of the Roman period (chap. 9) and of his own day (chap. 7) as well as of the second century (chap. 8). The commentary attributed to Saadia in the Rabbinic Bible dates from the same period as Ibn Ezra. That of Levi ben Gershon, Gersonides (1288–1344), from Provence was also included in some editions of the Rabbinic Bible. The last great medieval exegete of Daniel, or its first Renaissance humanist exegete in his critical scholarly approach, was Isaac Avravanel (1437–1508) (Rosenthal, *Studia,* 21–54). But his מעני הישועה (*Wells of Salvation,* 1496) was written after the Jews' expulsion from Spain, and seeks to enable his fellow Jews to learn from Daniel how to live in exile through the fourth, Roman kingdom, as they await the messianic kingdom on earth; he is not merely a pious exegete trying to unravel the problems of Scripture, but an exile seeking refuge and hope (Silver, *History,* 3).

The medieval Jewish commentaries handle most of the same exegetical problems as modern commentaries, and often the latter can take discussion of such problems little further (see, e.g., 2:1, נהיתה; 6:19 [18] דחון; 7:4 נטילת; 9:21 מעף ביעף). But another stimulus for their work is the pressure placed on rabbinic Judaism by the Christian Church, with its claim that the Hebrew Bible referred to Jesus of Nazareth. Like the patristic commentators, the Jewish exegetes want to understand Daniel in a way that relates it to their own day and is consistent with their theological views (e.g., that the messiah has *not* yet come). For both reasons Daniel's visions are taken to come to their historical climax with the Moslem Arab empire or the Christendom of their day (see, e.g., Jephet's extended treatment of chap. 11). The empires may then be Babylon, Medo-Persia, Greece, and Rome/the Arabs (a view Ibn Ezra refers to), or Babylon, Medo-Persia, Greece-Rome, and the Arabs (Ibn Ezra himself), or Babylon, Medo-Persia, Greece, and Rome divided into Christendom and Islam (Ibn Yachya), or Babylon, Medo-Persia, Greece, and Rome/Christendom (Avravanel). The 1290 days/years were expected to terminate in 968 (Saadia), in 1352 (Rashi), in 1358 (Gersonides and others), while Avravanel promises that the 3½ periods, the 2,300 days/years, and the 1335 days/years will all end in 1503. While Ibn Ezra takes the small horn of 8:9 to be Antiochus rather than Titus (Rashi) or "Ishmael," the

Arabs (Ps-Saadia) (cf. Silver, *History*), the interpretation of all the vision material as relating to Antiochus appears only in Galipapa (c. 1310–80; see Casey, *JTS* 27 [1976] 25, 28). We do not know how he came to this distinctive view. In the next century Albo (*Principles*, chap. 42) takes it up in order to deny that messianic hopes are essential to Jewish faith.

The invention of printing led to the first editions of מקראות גדולות, the Rabbinic Bibles—the Hebrew text with the targums and the commentaries of exegetes such as Rashi, Ibn Ezra, and Ps-Saadia. That work is utilized by Calvin, though it was also mediated through the commentary of Nicolaus de Lyra (c. 1270–1350), and Calvin also indulges in controversy with the more recent work of Avravanel (see on 2:44–45). Even this most sensitive of exegetes reads contemporary questions back into Daniel: chap. 3 shows that kings are justified in punishing heretics (Calvin is following Augustine); 4:24 [27] and 6:23 [22] do not teach justification by works. The influence of the Rabbinic Bible can also be seen in commentators such as Broughton and Willett, and in the AV, which often follows the medieval commentaries rather than the ancient versions (e.g., 2:5 "dunghill"; 4:24 [27] "break off"; both cf. Rashi; see Lloyd Jones, *Influence*).

The centuries of the medieval Jewish exegetes were the centuries of millenarian movements in Christian Europe. Revelation is their key biblical resource, but there is a striking appeal to Daniel in the anonymous *Book of a Hundred Chapters* (Cohn, *Pursuit*, 124). After the death of the German emperor Frederick I during the Crusades, prophets began to speak of a future Frederick as an Emperor of the Last Days. In the *Book*, written near the beginning of the sixteenth century, Frederick is one who will restore Germany to the position of supremacy God intended for her: Daniel's four empires are France, England, Spain, and Italy, while Germany is the fifth and greatest empire, which will not pass away.

The centuries of the millenarian movements were also preoccupied by the figure of Antichrist. Daniel's "small horn" was one important source for such teaching, elaborated in the medieval "Antichrist legend" that tells how this pseudomessiah will come to Jerusalem and enforce worship of himself there for three and a half years until put down by Michael. It was also possible, however, to see Antichrist as a principle of opposition to Christ embodied, for instance, in the papacy or in Islam, as it had been in Antiochus and in Rome (Bauckham, *Apocalypse*, 91–94). Only four years after posting his theses at Wittenberg, Martin Luther published his work on Antichrist (1521), which includes an exposition of Dan 8. Another three years later, Thomas Müntzer, who had been attracted first to Luther, then to millenarianism, preached his sermon *Die Fürstenpredigt* before Duke John, one of the Saxon princes, on Dan 2. The last of the world empires is coming to an end. The challenge to the princes is to take up the sword to slay God's enemies. They are like Nebuchadnezzar and his court; Müntzer implicitly offers to be a modern Daniel to replace the useless sages—Luther and his kind—with whom the princes are currently encumbered. Within a year Müntzer has taken up the sword himself in the Peasants' Revolt and lost his life (cf. Cohn, *Pursuit*, 234–50).

During the 1520s the advance of the Turks in Europe increased, and whereas Luther had earlier stressed that Antichrist was to be broken without hand, his *Heerpredigt wider dem Türken* (1529) not only identifies the Turks with the fourth beast but encourages people to join in the eschatological battle against them (Buchanan, *ArRef* 47 [1956] 157–59). Melanchthon had published an exposition of Dan 7 in this context, and Luther now hastened through his Prefaces to the books of the OT so as to reach this work so relevant to the situation in which Luther and his people lived, and on which he then wrote particularly extensively. In his perception of the true church's final conflict with the forces of evil, then, the latter are embodied in both the Turks and the Pope. While noting the encouragement and example offered by the stories, he gives most space to the visions. The four empires are Assyria-Babylon, Medo-Persia, Greece, and Rome, the last living on in the German empire, currently threatened by the Turks—Mohammed being the small horn—but certain to survive until the final consummation of God's kingdom. Though Antiochus appears in chaps. 8 and 11, these prophecies also point to Antichrist. 11:36–45 refers directly to Antichrist, who is identified with the celibate papacy (cf. vv 36–37).

Luther's exposition of Dan 8 as relating to Antichrist/the pope was published in England by John Frith, writing under the pseudonym Richard Brightwell. Other aspects of continental influence reached the English reformers through their exile in Europe. "Apocalyptic in the early [English] Reformation was primarily a theology of persecution and a theology of history" (Bauckham, *Apocalypse,* 13). George Joye, exiled for his Protestant beliefs for a second time from 1540 to 1547, encouraged himself and others by producing a translation and exposition of Daniel, based on the commentaries of continental reformers, Melanchthon, Oecolampadius, Pellikan, and Draconites (Butterworth and Chester, *Joye,* 235–44). In 1547 John Knox preached his first sermon as pastor at St Andrews, on Dan 7:24–25 applied to the papacy (see his *History of the Reformation in Scotland* [*The Works of John Knox* (Edinburgh: Wodrow Society, 1846) 1:189–92]).

In England's native apocalyptic tradition, too, the mass could be seen as the desolating sacrilege of Daniel: Wycliffe's *Wyckett,* which speaks in these terms, was first published in 1546. In mid-sixteenth-century England the natural way to apply the passages about the small horn was to the papacy. But these years see a decline in the popularity of Daniel. It had been encouraged by Luther's use of it, but it was now discouraged by Calvin's more historical approach that did not apply it beyond the Roman period, though Zwingli's successor in Zurich, Bullinger, continued to maintain Luther's views. The next English commentary on Daniel, by Broughton, denied Daniel's prophecies any historical reference beyond the Antiochene period. The latter part of the century saw both a lively general sense that the End was imminent and a sporadic interest in calculating its actual date, but Daniel does not seem to have contributed to this, though Joye had offered some calculations that pointed to the end of the century in his commentary. There was a spirited disagreement on the interpretation of 9:24–27 between Edward Lively, who accepted the MT punctuation of v 25, and Hugh Broughton, who rejected it in favor of a punctuation open to seeing the passage as a prophecy of Christ (cf. Rosenthal, *Studia,* 152–54).

As ecclesiastical and political events developed, Antichrist came to be seen not only in the Roman church but in the Church of England and in the monarchy. Aspinwall in his *Explication . . . of the Seventh Chapter of Daniel* (1654) sees Charles I as the small horn, England, Scotland, and Wales as the three horns that were broken off, the Puritan parliament as the holy ones, the Puritans' rule as the kingdom Daniel speaks of: the fifth monarchy is now beginning. Harrison justifies the fifth monarchists' violence by noting that Dan 7:18 said that the saints would *take* the kingdom; in 1653 the fifth monarchist Tillinghast redated the beginning of the 1290 years to 366, when the temple was actually destroyed, so that it would now end in 1656 (B. S. Capp, "Extreme Millenarianism," in Toon, *Puritans,* 68, 69). In due course the fifth-monarchy men themselves identified the Protector's dominion as that of the Beast, to be terminated after its due three and a half years in 1657 (Hill, *Antichrist,* 123).

Among others, More (in his *A Trumpet Sounded*) had argued on an exegetical basis with Aspinwall by pointing out that Charles did not fit Daniel's portrait. He killed no kings; it is Cromwell who was the small horn. But history was a more compelling judge of Danielic exegesis. After the end of the fifth-monarchy movement, the eschatological hopes, to whose shaping Daniel made a key contribution, centered on less political events, such as the conversion of the Jews already emphasized by Brightman and Huit. The historical approach to interpretation practiced by writers such as Calvin (*Institutes* quotes Dan 2:34 in this connection) and Broughton did not prevent them from expecting a future fulfillment of OT prophecies of the world's acknowledgment of God, an expectation taken up by the Puritans, with the encouragement of passages such as Dan 2:34–35, 44; 7:26–27; this was to be one important stimulus for the development of the missionary movements of the next two centuries (Murray, *Hope,* with the quotation from Howe, 247).

The seventeenth century also saw developing interest in the two related convictions that underlie the critical study of Daniel characteristic of the modern period: as well as the belief that all the prophecies relate historically to the Antiochene period, the conclusion that this was the period in which the book was actually written. At both points critical study has affirmed what Porphyry declared in the second century. Méchoulan ("Révélation") comments on the way Spinoza, the unapocalyptic unobservant Jew, studies the book in a detached way in the tumultuous seventeenth-century context from which he seems insulated. The main features of the critical argument for the second-century date of Daniel are then already present in the work of A. Collins (1727): the historical problems, the Greek words, the prophecies relating to the second century (Collins is taking up the work of Porphyry), the book's location among the Writings, the late Aramaic.

The systematic working out of such ideas took place in Germany in the nineteenth century, beginning with the work of Bertholdt, von Lengerke, and Ewald. The possibility that the narratives, which make no overt reference to the Antiochene crisis, are older than the visions was advanced by Eichhorn and Meinhold. The critical view was resisted by conservative scholars such as Hengstenberg, Hävernick, and Keil, and in Britain by Pusey, who saw the debate as the key test-case in the conflict between criticism and faith.

The commentaries of Farrar and Driver (following up his *Introduction*) were important in securing acceptance of the critical view in England.

Simultaneously with the development of the critical approach to Daniel, "leading British churchmen and theologians" and "leading British radicals and socialists"—not a mere lunatic fringe—continued to see events of their day as the fulfillment of Daniel's visions and of other prophetic material in Scripture (Oliver, *Prophecy,* 11). A New England farmer, William Miller, decided from Dan 8:14 that the world would end in 1843, 2,300 years after 457 B.C. A Millerite movement gained strength as the date approached, and even continued after 1843 had passed, though it collapsed in 1845 (L. Festinger, *When Prophecy Fails* [U Minnesota, 1956; repr. New York: Harper, 1964] 13–23; cf. Froom, *Faith,* vol. 4). Other writers continued to expound Daniel as they always had, finding edification in the stories, and from the visions finding insight on contemporary history, and making extrapolations regarding twentieth-century history that we now know to have been mistaken and extrapolations beyond the twentieth century that we cannot yet check out: Dan 4:19 [16] refers to the French Revolution (Seeley, 1849); 8:14 refers to the year 1867, when the papacy will fall (Graves, 1854), to a renewed cleansing to come in 2132 (Rule, 1869), to the events of the year 1814 (Murphy, 1885), or to Isaac Newton (Sadler, 1895); 11:36–39 refers to the French Revolution (U. Smith, 1897). The interpreters are Protestant and the interpretations match. A number of these works are American, and a more subtle, more secular use of the Daniel figure appears in the work of American novelists such as James, Melville, and Hawthorne (Baris, "The American Daniel," 173–85).

The approaches that characterize nineteenth-century study continue in the twentieth. Marti, Charles, and Rowley (see *Main Bibliography*) argue for the second-century B.C. origin of the whole, following von Gall (1895). Hölscher, Haller, Montgomery, Noth, and Ginsberg develop the view of Eichhorn; they come to varying conclusions regarding the precise date of the pre-second-century B.C. material, and, as well as the two main stages of composition, tend to see stages of development within the visions as material is edited and updated. Wilson, Boutflower, Young, Wiseman and others, and Baldwin have developed the conservative response. Discoveries regarding Nabonidus and Belshazzar have been taken both to justify a conservative view of the narratives' historicity and to undermine it; research into Canaanite myth has suggested some of the background to motifs in the visions.

The modern period has also seen an explosive growth in study of apocalyptic. After the nineteenth-century discovery of *1 Enoch* and other texts, many were edited and published at the beginning of this century, especially through the work of Charles. But apocalyptic seemed rather alien, and came to be seen as resulting from Persian influence and thus as alien even to Israelite religion. In theology, the approaches of Barth and Bultmann encouraged the neglect of apocalyptic for some years until the work of Pannenberg and Käsemann brought an end to the period during which it could be ignored or dismissed in theological discussion. Meanwhile Plöger's *Theokratie* began a new phase of critical study in which scholars have sought to trace the development of different religious groups and their ideologies in the postexilic period and to identify which of these lay behind Daniel (see Hall). American scholarship has attempted a more broadly sociological approach to apocalyptic, and has been seeking to clarify what precisely we mean by the term (see especially Hanson [see *Main Bibliography*]). Developing interest in literary approaches to OT narrative is overdue for application to Daniel.

Outside critical circles, writers continue to see specific prophecies fulfilled long after Daniel's day, identifying the four kingdoms with Babylon, Medo-Persia, Greece, and Rome, and taking some moment in the life of Christ to signify the last of Daniel's seventy weeks. The most spectacular version refines the approach of Julius Africanus, reckoning the period from Artaxerxes' edict in 445 B.C. to the crucifixion as 483 years to the day. Other expositors see prophecies as fulfilled in their time: the 1967 Arab-Israeli war fulfills both 8:14, coming 2,300 years after Alexander, and 12:12, coming 1,335 years after the establishment of the Caliphate (Filmer). More commonly, however, expositors who believe that many of Daniel's visions are still to be fulfilled avoid associating passages with dated events, expecting their fulfillment in events to come (e.g., Payne, *Encyclopedia*). The most powerful modern exposition of Daniel, however, is that of W. Lüthi in Germany in the 1930s. Earlier in that same telling decade there appeared a more artistic utilization of Daniel, like those of the nineteenth century but in musical form. As Handel's oratorio *Belshazzar* used Daniel to issue a warning to Britain in its ascendancy in the eighteenth century, William Walton's *Belshazzar's Feast* takes up that theme in the 1930s (Liptzin, *Themes*).

The history of the interpretation of Daniel raises issues we will need to keep in mind as we study the book chapter by chapter; we will return to some of them in the *Conclusion*. The history itself, however, suggests some observations at this point.

The first concerns the Hebrew/Aramaic text of the book. We have noted that BHS is based on L, a manuscript copied in the eleventh century A.D., which is thus over a millennium younger than the book itself. That can be only a starting point for study of the text; we must allow for the possibility that over the centuries the book had been affected by both accidental and intentional changes. We may be able to identify some of these by comparing L with older copies of Daniel such as the Cairo manuscript and the Qumran manuscripts. We can also study copies of translations that are older than L, the most important for this purpose being the Greek translations (especially OG and Th), the Syriac, and the Latin, to see if we can infer the Hebrew version utilized by the translators. Our historical study, however, has suggested that some differences between these translations and MT, and between variant Hebrew manuscripts and MT, themselves reflect interpretative activity. They may not indicate that they are mediating to us an earlier text of the book. The trend of contemporary textual criticism is to recognize that biblical books were preserved in a number of textual traditions (e.g., in different geographical areas). A reading suggested by one of the ancient translations that seems to us preferable to the one provided by MT may not actually be nearer to what the author of Daniel wrote. Where MT is more pleonastic than G (e.g., 6:21 [20]; 8:1, 2, 3), or less elegant, or syntactically uneven (e.g., 1:5, 20), or expansive in a way that could suggest glossing (e.g., 7:1, 11), or repeats phrases with variation rather than identically (e.g., 4:9 [12]), in themselves these features cannot be assumed to indicate that MT is not original. My working rule for the commentary, then, is to be rather stringent over accepting a reading other than MT as likely to represent the text as it was at an earlier stage in the Hebrew tradition that underlies MT. This implies a practice that is not as conservative as that in UBS, which invariably advises us to retain MT, but is more conservative than most recent EVV and commentaries. (On the issues raised here, see further Tov, *Septuagint.*)

A second conclusion suggested by the history of the interpretation of Daniel is that it is hazardous to claim that the book directly refers to events of one's own day, or to the key events on which one's own faith is based. It is possible that interpreters who refer Daniel's visions directly to the Christ event or to late twentieth-century events are right, but it is salutary to note that earlier centuries of interpreters of various faiths have been able to relate these visions to events of their day by the same interpretative techniques that such twentieth-century Christian interpreters use, and it seems wise to allow for the possibility that the interpretations of the latter will also be falsified in due course. My presupposition for the commentary is therefore that the forward projections in Daniel were designed to bring a message that was meaningful to people in the postexilic period, and I shall seek to interpret the seer's visions in the light of material in the book itself and in the light of the history of the period as we know it.

This does not mean that interpreters who have related these visions to their own day were simply wrong (see Towner, *Int* 37 [1983] 46–63). Their sense that these visions were relevant to days long after Daniel's was quite valid. Childs has observed that the increase in our historical insight into Daniel in the modern period has not been accompanied by a proportionate increase in our theological insight into the book (*Introduction*, 613). How they speak to days long after their own, and what theological insight they offer, I shall seek to consider in the *Explanation* sections of the commentary.

There is a third issue upon which we need to be aware of a stance as we begin our study. What assumptions should we bring to it regarding the nature of the stories and the origin of the visions? Critical scholarship has sometimes overtly, sometimes covertly approached the visions with the *a priori* conviction that they cannot be actual prophecies of events to take place long after the seer's day, because prophecy of that kind is impossible. Conversely, conservative scholarship has sometimes overtly, sometimes covertly approached these visions with the *a priori* conviction that they must be actual prophecies because quasi-prophecies issued pseudonymously could not have been inspired by God; it has also approached the stories with the *a priori* conviction that they must be pure history, because fiction or a mixture of fact and fiction could not have been inspired by God. All these convictions seem to me mistaken. I believe that the God of Israel who is also the God and Father of our Lord Jesus Christ is capable of knowing future events and thus of revealing them, and is capable of inspiring people to write both history and fiction, both actual prophecy and quasi-prophecy, in their own name, anonymously, or—in certain circumstances—pseudonymously. It was excusable for Pusey (1–4) to think that pseudonymity makes the author a liar and must be incompatible with being divinely inspired. It is less excusable now we know that in the ancient world, and in the Hellenistic age in particular, pseudonymity was a common practice used for a variety of reasons—some unethical, some unobjectionable—for poetry, letters, testaments, philosophy, and oracles, and by no means confined to apocalypses (Metzger, *JBL* 91 [1972] 3–24; Collins, *Vision*, 67–74; Meade, *Pseudonymity* [considering the particular place of pseudonymity within the Bible]; against Baldwin, *Them* 4 [1978–79] 6–12). That pseudonymity is a rarer literary device in our culture, especially in religious contexts, should not allow us to infer that God could not use it in another culture. Whether he has actually chosen to do so is to be determined not *a priori* but from actual study of the text of Scripture. I shall consider these questions in the *Form* sections of the commentary.

Whether the stories are history or fiction, the visions actual prophecy or quasi-prophecy, written by Daniel or by someone else, in the sixth century B.C., the second, or somewhere in between, makes surprisingly little difference to the book's exegesis. One understands the book on the basis of what it says; there are points where its meaning is unclear, but not because of uncertainty over the alternatives just listed. Whether or not we can divide the actual seer and his visionary namesake, the best approach is to take him on his own terms and immerse ourselves in the visionary experience as he describes it (Niditch, "Visionary," 158).

Main Bibliography

The bibliographies list works to which I myself have had access. Works mentioned in the text but not listed in the bibliographies are thus ones that I have not seen.

Commentaries and Other Works on Daniel (cited by author's name)

[Adams, R. N.] *The Jewish Missionary: A New and Literal Interpretation of the Visions of Daniel.* London: Nisbet, 1849. **Anderson, R.** *Daniel in the Critics' Den.* Edinburgh: Blackwell, 1885; 4th ed., Glasgow: Pickering, 1922. **Anderson, R. A.** *Signs and Wonders: A Commentary on the Book of Daniel.* Edinburgh/Grand Rapids: Handsel/Eerdmans, 1984. **Archer, G. L.** "Daniel." *The Expositor's Bible Commentary,* ed. F. E. Gaebelein et al. Grand Rapids: Zondervan, 1985. 7:1–157. **Anonymous.** *Remarks on the Book of Daniel and on the Revelations.* New York: Greenleaf, 1794. **Ashley, T. R.** *The Book of Daniel Chapters 1–6.* Diss., St Andrews, 1975. **Aspinwall, W.** *The Work of the Age: or, The Sealed Prophecies of Daniel Opened and Applied. . . .* London: Livewell Chapman, 1655. **Auberlen, C. A.** *Der Prophet Daniel und die Offenbarung Johannis.* 2nd ed. Basel: Bahnmeier, 1854. = *The Prophecies of Daniel and the Revelations of St John.* Tr. A. Saphir. Edinburgh: Clark, 1856/Andover: Draper, 1857. **Avravanel, I.** מעיני הישועה. 1496. **Baldwin, J. G.** *Daniel.* Tyndale OT Commentary. Leicester/Grand Rapids: IVP/Eerdmans, 1978. **Bar-Hebraeus, G.** [= A. al-F. Grighor]. אוצר רזי. 13th century. = *Scholien zum Buche Daniel.* Ed. and tr. J. Freimann. Brünn: Epstein, 1892. **Barnes, A.** *Notes, Explanatory and Practical, on the Book of Daniel.* Rev. ed. London: Routledge, 1853. **Barr, J.** "Daniel." *Peake's Commentary on the Bible,* ed. M. Black and H. H. Rowley. London/New York: Nelson, 1962. 591–602. **Bayer, E.** *Danielstudien.* Münster: Aschendorff, 1912. **Beek, M. A.** *Das Danielbuch.* Leiden: Ginsberg, 1935. **Behrmann, G.** *Das Buch Daniel.* Göttingen: Vandenhoeck, 1894. **Bellamy, J.** *The Book of Daniel.* London: Simpkin, 1863. **Ben-Ezra** [see Lacunza]. **Bentzen, A.** *Daniel.* Tübingen: Mohr, 1937; 2nd ed., 1952. **Bertholdt, L.** *Daniel.* Erlangen: Palm, 1806. **Bevan, A. A.** *A Short Commentary on the Book of Daniel.* Cambridge: CUP, 1892. **Bickerman, E.** *Four Strange Books of the Bible.* New York: Schocken, 1967. **Bleek, F.** "Über Verfasser und Zweck des Buches Daniel." *TZ* 3 (1822) 171–294. **Boehmer, J.** *Reich Gottes und Menschensohn im Buch Daniel.* Leipzig: Hinrichs, 1899. **Boutflower, C.** *In and Around the Book of Daniel.* London/New York: SPCK/Macmillan, 1923. **Boyle, W. R. A.** *The Inspiration of the Book of Daniel.* London: Rivingtons, 1863. **Brockington, L. H.** *The Hebrew Text of the Old Testament: The Readings Adopted by the Translators of the New English Bible.* London and New York: OUP/CUP, 1973. **Broughton, H.** *Daniel his Chaldie Visions and his Ebrew.* London: Field, 1596. **Bruston, C.** *Etudes sur Daniel et l'Apocalypse.* Paris: Fischbacher, 1896. **Bullinger, H.** *Daniel sapientissimus Dei propheta.* Zürich: Froschouerus, 1565. **Burton, A. H.** *Hints on the Book of Daniel.* London: Carter, 1903. **Calvin, J.** *Praelectiones in librum prophetiarum Danielis.* Geneva: Laon, 1561. = CR 68 (Calvin Vol. 40) 517–722; 69 (Calvin Vol. 41) 1–304. 1889. = *Commentaries on the Book of the Prophet Daniel.* Tr. T. Myers. 2 vols. Edinburgh: CTS, 1852–53. **Charles, R. H.** *A Critical and Exegetical Commentary on the Book of Daniel.* Oxford: Clarendon, 1929. **Chrysostomus, J.** Εὸς ποπ Δανιηλ προφητην. *PG* 56 (1862) 193–246. **Cocceius, J.** *Observationes ad Danielem.* Repr. in Cocceius, *Opera* 3. Amsterdam: Johannis à Someren, 1673. **Cook, A.** *Light from the Book of Daniel.* London: Banks, 1916. **[Cross, J. A.]** *Notes on the Defence of the Book of Daniel.* Dublin: M'Gee, 1878. **Cyril of Alexandria.** *In Danielem prophetam.* Fragments repr. in *PG* 70 (1864) 1461–62. **Davies, P. R.** *Daniel.*

Sheffield: JSOT, 1985. **Delcor, M.** *Le livre de Daniel.* Paris: Gabalda, 1971. **Dexinger, F.** *Das Buch Daniel und seine Probleme.* SBS 36 (1969). **Driver, S. R.** *The Book of Daniel.* Cambridge: CUP, 1900; 5th ed., 1922. **Efird, J. M.** *Daniel and Revelation.* Valley Forge, PA: Judson, 1978. **Ehrlich, A. B.** *Randglossen zur hebräischen Bibel.* Leipzig: Hinrichs, 1914. 7:126–55. **Eichhorn, J. G.** *Die hebräischen Propheten.* Göttingen: Vandenhoeck, 1819. 3:428–515. **Eitan, I.** "Some Philological Observations in Daniel." *HUCA* 14 (1939) 13–22. **Emery, D. L.** *Daniel: Who Wrote the Book?* Ilfracombe: Stockwell, 1978. **Envieu, J. F. d'.** *Le livre du prophète Daniel.* 4 vols. Paris: Thorin, 1888–91. **Ephrem Syrus.** *Opera omnia quae exstant.* Ed. J. S. Assemanus et al. Rome: Vatican, 1740. 5:214–32. **Ewald, H.** *Die Propheten des Alten Bundes.* [1st ed., 1840–41.] 2nd ed., Göttingen: Vandenhoeck, 1868. 3:298–491. = *Commentary on the Prophets of the Old Testament.* Tr. J. F. Smith. London: Williams and Norgate, 1881. 5:152–325. **Farrar, F. W.** *The Book of Daniel.* London/New York: Hodder/Armstrong, 1895. **Filmer, W. E.** *Daniel's Predictions.* London/New York: Regency, 1979. **Füller, J. L.** *Der Profet Daniel.* Basel: Bahnmaier, 1868. **Gall, A. G. von.** *Die Einheitlichkeit des Buches Daniel.* Diss., Giessen, 1895. **Gallé, A. F.** *Daniel avec commentaires de R. Saadia, Aben-Ezra, Raschi, etc.* Paris: Leroux, 1900. **Gammie, J. G.** *Daniel.* Atlanta: Knox, 1983. **Gardner, A. E.** *Nationalists, Theocrats, and Apocalyptists: A Study Illustrating the Inter-relationship of Politics and Theodicy in Daniel and the Texts of the Apocrypha and Pseudepigrapha Which Stem from the Maccabaean Crisis.* Diss., Edinburgh, 1979. **Gaspar Sanctius.** *In Danielem prophetam commentarij.* Lyon: Cardon, 1619. **Gaussen, [? S. R. L.].** *The Prophet Daniel Explained.* Tr. M. Blackstone. 2 vols. London: Mozley, 1873–74. **Ginsberg, H. L.** *Studies in Daniel.* New York: Jewish Theological Seminary, 1948. **Goard, W. P.** *The Documents of Daniel.* London: Covenant, 1930. **Goettsberger, J.** *Das Buch Daniel.* Bonn: Hanstein, 1928. **Graetz, H.** "Beiträge zur Sach- und Wortererklärung des Buches Daniel." *MGWJ* 20 (1871) 337–52, 385–406, 433–49. **Grotius, H.** *Annotationes in Vetus Testamentum.* Repr. Halle: Curt, 1775–76. 1:453–85. **Grynaeus, J. J.** *Explanatio Danielis Prophetae quinque primorum capitum.* Basel: Henricipetri, 1587. **Gurney, R. J. M.** *God in Control: An Exposition of the Prophecies of Daniel.* Worthing: Walter, 1980. Incorporating material from *TSFBulletin* 47 (1967) 10–12; *Them* 2 (1976–77) 39–45; *EvQ* 53 (1981) 29–36. **Hävernick, H. A. C.** *Commentar über das Buch Daniel.* Hamburg: Perthes, 1832. **Hall, R. A.** *Post-exilic Theological Streams and the Book of Daniel.* Diss., Yale, 1974. **Hammer, R.** *The Book of Daniel.* Cambridge/New York: CUP, 1976. **Hartman, L. F.,** and **Di Lella, A. A.** *The Book of Daniel.* AB 23 (1978). **Heaton, E. W.** *The Book of Daniel.* London: SCM, 1956. **Hieronymus.** *In Danielem prophetam.* CCSL 75A (1964). = *Jerome's Commentary on Daniel.* Tr. G. L. Archer. Grand Rapids: Baker, 1958. **Hippolytus.** Εἰς τον Δανιηλ. = *Commentaire sur Daniel.* Intr. G. Brady, tr. M. Lefèvre. Paris: Cerf, 1947. **Hitzig, F.** *Das Buch Daniel.* Leipzig: Weidmann, 1850. **Howie, C. G.** *The Book of Ezekiel, the Book of Daniel.* Richmond: Knox, 1961/London: SCM, 1962. **Huit, E.** *The Whole Prophecie of Daniel Explained.* [London]: Overton, 1644. **Hunter, P. H.** *The Story of Daniel.* 2nd ed. Edinburgh: Gemmell, 1885. **Ibn Ezra.** דניאל. Repr. in מקראות גדולות. [See also Gallé.] **Ibn Yachya, J.** *Paraphrasis in Danielem.* 1528. Tr. C. L'Empereur. Amsterdam: Ioannem Ianssenium, 1633. **Irving, E.** *A Discourse on the Prophecies of Daniel and the Apocalypse.* 2nd ed. Glasgow: Collins, 1828. **Ishodad of Merv.** *nwhr' ddny'yl nby'.* = CSCO 328/*Syr. 146:*101–37; 329/*Syr. 147:*116–58. 1972. **Jeffery, A.,** and **Kennedy, G.** "The Book of Daniel." *The Interpreter's Bible,* ed. G. A. Buttrick et al. Nashville: Abingdon, 1956. 6:339–549. **Jephet ibn Ali.** *šrh spr dny'l.* 14th century. = *A Commentary on the Book of Daniel.* Ed. D. S. Margoliouth. Oxford: Clarendon, 1889. **Jerome** [see Hieronymus]. **Jones, B. W.** *Ideas of History in the Book of Daniel.* Diss., Graduate Theological Union [Berkeley, CA], 1972. **Joubert, W. H.** *Power and Responsibility in the Book of Daniel.* Diss., U South Africa, 1980. **Joye, G.,** et al., ed. *The Exposycion of Daniel the Prophete gathered out of Philip Melanchthon, Johan Ecolapadius, Chonrade Pellicane, + out of Iohan Draconite, +c.* Geneva/Antwerp, 1545. **Junker, H.** *Untersuchungen über literar-*

ische und exegetische Probleme des Buches Daniel. Bonn: Hanstein, 1932. **Kallarakkal A. G.** *The Peshitto Version of Daniel.* Diss., Hamburg, 1973. **Kamphausen, A.** *The Book of Daniel.* Tr. B. W. Bacon and D. B. Macdonald. Leipzig: Hinrichs, 1896. **Keil, C.** *Biblischer Kommentar über den Propheten Daniel.* Leipzig: Dörffling, 1869. = *The Book of Daniel.* Tr. M. G. Easton. Edinburgh: Clark, 1872. **Kelley, W.** *Lectures on the Book of Daniel.* 2nd ed. London: Morrish, 1881. = *The Great Prophecies of Daniel.* London: Pickering, 1897. **Kennedy, G.** [see Jeffery]. **Kennedy, J.** *The Book of Daniel.* London: Eyre, 1898. **Kepler, T. S.** *Dreams of the Future: Daniel and Revelation.* London/Nashville: Lutterworth/Abingdon, 1963. **Kessler, W.** *Zwischen Gott und Weltmacht: Der Prophet Daniel.* Stuttgart: Calwer, 1950. **King, G. R.** *Daniel.* London/Grand Rapids: Walter/Eerdmans, 1966. **Kliefoth, T.** *Das Buch Daniel.* Schwerin: Sandmeyer, 1868. **Koch, K.** *Daniel.* BKAT 22. 1986–. **Kraeling, E. G.** *Commentary on the Prophets.* Camden, NJ/London: Nelson, 1966. 2:19–74. **Lacocque, A.** *Le livre de Daniel.* Neuchatel/Paris: Delachaux, 1976. = *The Book of Daniel.* Tr. D. Pellauer. London/Atlanta: SPCK/Knox, 1979. **[Lacunza, M.]** = J. J. Ben-Ezra. *Venida del Mesias en gloria y magestad.* [1812]. = *The Coming of Messiah in Glory and Majesty.* Tr. E. Irving. 2 vols. London: Seeley, 1827. **Lang, G. H.** *The Histories and Prophecies of Daniel.* London: Oliphants, 1942. **Lattey, C.** *The Book of Daniel.* Dublin: Browne and Nolan, 1948. **Lebram, J. C. H.** *Das Buch Daniel.* Zurich: Theologische, 1984. **Lengerke, C. von.** *Das Buch Daniel.* Königsberg: Bornträger, 1835. **Leupold, H. C.** *Exposition of Daniel.* Grand Rapids, MI: Wartburg, 1949. **Loisy, A.** "Le livre de Daniel." *École pratique des hautes études: Section des sciences religieuses. Annuaire 1925–1926.* Melun: Imprimerie Administrative, 1925. 3–22. **Lüthi, W.** *The Church to Come.* Tr. D. H. C. Read. London: Hodder, 1939. = *Daniel Speaks to the Church.* Tr. J. M. Jensen. Minneapolis: Augsburg, 1947. [Tr. from *Die kommende Kirche.* Basel: Reinhardt, n.d.] **McDowell, J.** *Daniel in the Critics' Den.* San Bernardino, CA: Here's Life, 1979. **Macé de La Charité.** Bible. c. 1300. Repr. [Daniel being Vol. 4 (ed. H.-C.-M. van der Krabben) 44–77] Leiden: Leiden UP, 1964. **McNamara, M.** "Daniel." *A New Catholic Commentary on Holy Scripture,* ed. R. C. Fuller et al. London: Nelson, 1969. 650–75. **Maier, G.** *Der Prophet Daniel.* Wuppertal: Brockhaus, 1982. **Marti, K.** *Das Buch Daniel.* Tübingen: Mohr, 1901. **Mertens, A.** *Das Buch Daniel im Lichte der Texte vom Toten Meer.* Würzburg: Echter, 1971. **Montgomery, J. A.** *A Critical and Exegetical Commentary on the Book of Daniel.* ICC. 1927. **More, H.** *An Illustration of Those Two Abstruse Books in Holy Scripture, the Book of Daniel and the Revelation of S. John.* London: Flasher, 1685. **More, J.** *A Trumpet Sounded: or, The Great Mystery of the Two Little Horns Unfolded. . . .* [London,] 1654. **Murphy, J. G.** *The Book of Daniel.* London: Nisbet, 1884/Andover, MA: Draper, 1885. **Neteler, B.** *Das Gliederung des Buches Daniel als Grundlage der Erklärung desselben.* Münster: Niemann, 1870. **Newton, I.** *Observations upon the Prophecies of Daniel, and the Apocalypse of St. John.* London, 1733. **Nicolaus de Lyra.** *Biblia cum glossa ordinaria.* Repr. 1501–2. 4:293–332. **Oecolampadius, J.** *In Danielem prophetam.* 1530. Repr. Geneva: Crispinus, 1553. **Olyott, S.** *Dare to Stand Alone.* Welwyn: Evangelical, 1982. **Origen.** *Hexaplorum quae supersunt: Daniel. PG* 16, 3 (1863) 2765–2928. **Owens, J. J.** "Daniel." *The Broadman Bible Commentary,* ed. C. J. Allen et al. Nashville: Broadman, 1971. 6:373–460. **Pace, S.** *The Old Greek Text of Daniel 7–12.* Diss., U Notre Dame, 1984. **Philip, J.** *By the Rivers of Babylon.* 2 parts. Aberdeen: Didasko, 1971–72. **Piscator, J.** *In prophetam Danielem commentarius.* Herbornae Nassoviorum: [Raben], 1614. **Plöger, O.** *Das Buch Daniel.* Gütersloh: Mohn, 1965. **Poole, M.,** et al. *Annotations on the Holy Bible.* 1685. "Daniel" is by an unnamed collaborator. **Porteous, N. W.** *Daniel.* OTL. 1965; rev. ed., 1979. **Preiswerk, H.** *Der Sprachenwechsel im Buche Daniel.* Bern: Tagblatt, 1903. **[Ps-]Saadia.** דניאל. Reprinted in מקראות גדולות. [See also Gallé.] **Pusey, E. B.** *Daniel, the Prophet.* 2nd ed. Oxford: Parker, 1868. **Rashi.** דניאל. Repr. in מקראות גדולות. [See also Gallé.] **Reid, S. B.** *The Sociological Setting of the Historical Apocalypses of 1 Enoch and the Book of Daniel.* Diss., Emory, 1981. **Rinaldi, G.** *Daniele.* 4th ed. Turin: Marietti, 1962.

Rohling, A. *Das Buch des Propheten Daniel.* Mainz: Kirchheim, 1876. **Rollocus, R.** *In librum Danielis prophetae commentarius.* Edinburgh: Waldegrave, 1591. **Rosenmüller, E. F. C.** *Scholia in Vetus Testamentum* 10. Leipzig: Barth, 1832. **Rowley, H. H.** *Darius the Mede and the Four World Empires in the Book of Daniel.* Cardiff: U Wales, 1935. Corr. ed., 1959. **Rule, W. H.** *An Historical Exposition of the Book of Daniel the Prophet.* London: Seeley, 1869. **Rupert of Deutz.** *De Trinitate . . . : in Danielem prophetam commentarium liber unus.* c. 1115. = *PL* 167 (1893) 1499–1536. **Russell, D. S.** *Daniel.* Edinburgh/Philadelphia: St Andrew/Westminster, 1981. **Saadia ben Joseph.** Arabic translation and commentary. Hebrew tr. by J. Kafik. Jerusalem: RSG, 1981. [See also Ps-Saadia.] **Sadler, R.** *The Book of the Prophet Daniel.* London: Sheppard, 1895. **Sawyer, L. A.** *Daniel.* Boston: Walker, 1864. **Schedl, C.** "Der Prophet Daniel." *Geschichte des Alten Testaments.* Innsbruck: Tyrolia, 1964. 5:53–90. = *The Fullness of Time.* History of the OT 5. New York: Alba, 1973. **[Seeley, R. B.]** *The Atlas of Prophecy.* London: Seeley, 1849. **Seiss, J. A.** *Voices from Babylon: Daniel's Prophecies.* Philadelphia: Porter and Coates, [1879]/London: Christian Herald, 1881. **Shirres, D. L.** *A Commentary on the Book of Daniel.* Aberdeen: Brown, [1885]. **Slotki, J. J.** *Daniel, Ezra, and Nehemiah.* London: Soncino, 1951. **Smith, U.** *Daniel and the Revelation.* London: International Tract Society, 1897. **Strong, L.** *Lectures on the Book of Daniel.* London: Yapp, 1871. **Tatford, F. A.** *The Climax of the Ages.* London/Grand Rapids: Oliphants/Zondervan, 1953. **Theodoret.** ‹Υπομνημα εἰς τας ὁρασεις του προφητου Δανιηλ. 458. = *PG* 81 (1864) 1255–1546. **Theodorus bar-Koni.** *ktbʾ dʾskwlywn.* c. 792. = CSCO Syr. ii 66–67 (1912), CSCO 431/*Syr. 187–88* (1981–82). **Tiefenthal, F. S.** *Daniel.* Paderborn: Schöningh, 1895. **Towner, W. S.** *Daniel.* Atlanta: Knox, 1984. **Tregelles, S. P.** *Remarks on the Poetic Visions in the Book of Daniel.* 6th ed. London: Bagster, 1883. **Valentinus, B. P.** *Commentariorum in Danielem prophetam libri sexdecim.* Rome: Ferrarium, 1587. **Veldkamp, H.** *Dreams and Dictators: On the Book of Daniel.* St Catharines, Ont.: Paideia, 1978. Tr. by T. Plantinga from *In de Schemering van Christus' Wederkomst.* Franeker: Wever, [?1966]. **Wallace, R. S.** *The Lord Is King: The Message of Daniel.* Leicester/Downers Grove, IL: IVP, 1979. **Welch, A. C.** *Visions of the End.* London: Clarke, 1922. **Willet, A.** *Hexapla in Danielem.* Cambridge: Cambridge University, 1610. **Wilson, R. D.** *Studies in the Book of Daniel* [First Series]. New York: Knickerbocker, 1917. ———. *Studies in the Book of Daniel: Second Series.* New York: Revell, 1938. **Wintle, T.** *Daniel, an Improved Version Attempted.* Oxford: Cooke, 1792; 2nd ed., London: Hatchard, 1807. **Wood, L.** *A Commentary on Daniel.* Grand Rapids: Zondervan, 1973. **Wright, C. H. H.** *Daniel and His Prophecies.* London: Williams and Norgate, 1906. **Young, E. J.** *The Prophecy of Daniel.* Grand Rapids: Eerdmans, 1949. = *Commentary on Daniel.* London: Banner of Truth, 1972. **Zoeckler, O.** *Daniel.* Theologisch-homiletisches Bibelwerk. Ed. J. P. Lange. Bielefeld: Velhagen, 1870. = *The Book of the Prophet Daniel.* Tr. J. Strong. New York/Edinburgh: Scribner's/Clark, 1876.

WORKS CITED BY SHORTENED REFERENCES

Ahn, P. P. *The Distinctive Theological Vocabulary of Selected Jewish Apocalyptic Writings.* Diss., Boston, 1962. **Albo, J.** ספר העקרים. = *Book of Principles.* Tr. I. Husik. 4 vols. Philadelphia: JPS, 1929–30. **Allen, S.** "On Schedl's Attempt to Count the Days of Daniel." *AUSS* 4 (1966) 105–6. **Altheim, F.,** and **Stiehl, R.** *Die aramäische Sprache unter den Achaimeniden. Erster Band.* Frankfurt: Klostermann, 1959–62. **Anderson, J. C.** "Double and Triple Stories, the Implied Reader, and Redundancy in Matthew." In *Reader Response Approaches to Biblical and Secular Texts,* ed. R. Detweiler. *Semeia* 31 (1985) 71–89. **Aphrahat.** *Demonstrations.* 337. Selections tr. by J. Gwynn in NPNF ii 13:345–412. **Archer, G. L.** "The Aramaic of the Genesis Apocryphon Compared with the Aramaic of Daniel." In *Perspectives,* ed. J. B. Payne, 160–69. ———. "The Hebrew of Daniel Compared with the Qumran Sectarian Documents." In *The Law* *and the Prophets,* FS O. T. Allis, ed. J. H. Skilton. [Nutley, NJ]: PRPC, 1974. 470–81. ———. "Modern Rationalism and the Book of Daniel." *BSac* 136 (1979) 129–47. **Atzerodt, I.** "Weltgeschichte und Reich Gottes im Buch Daniel." *Christentum und Wissenschaft* 10 (1934) 241–59. **Augustine.** *De civitate Dei.* 426. = CCSL 47–48 (1955). = *The City of God.* Tr. M. Dods. NPNF i, 2:1–511. **Aukerman, D.** *Darkening Valley.* New York: Seabury, 1981. **Baldwin, J. G.** "Is There Pseudonymity in the Old Testament?" *Them* 4 (1978–79) 6–12. ———. "Some Literary Affinities of the Book of Daniel." *TynB* 30 (1979) 77–99. **Barker, M.** "Apocalyptic." *ExpT* 89 (1977–78) 324–29. **Barr, D. L.** "The Apocalypse as a Symbolic Transformation of the World." *Int* 38 (1984) 39–50. **Barth, C.** *Diesseits und Jenseits im Glauben des späten Israel.* SBS 72 (1974). **Barth, K.** *Die kirchliche Dogmatik.* Zurich: Evangelische, 1932–67. = *Church Dogmatics.* Tr. G. W. Bromiley et al. Edinburgh/New York: Clark/Scribner's, 1936–69. **Barton, G. A.** "The Composition of the Book of Daniel." *JBL* 17 (1898) 62–86. ———. "The Story of Aḥiḳar and the Book of Daniel." *AJSL* 16 (1899–1900) 242–47. **Bauckham, R. J.** "The Rise of Apocalyptic." *Them* 3, 2 (1977–78) 10–23. ———. "Theology after Hiroshima." *SJT* 38 (1985) 583–601. ———. "*Daniel* . . . by John J. Collins," *EvQ* 59 (1987) 164–65. **Baumgartner, W.** "Neues keilschriftliches Material zum Buche Daniel?" *ZAW* 44 (1926) 38–56. ———. "Das Aramäische im Buche Daniel." *ZAW* 45 (1927) 81–133. Repr. in Baumgartner, *Zum Alten Testament und seiner Umwelt.* Leiden: Brill, 1959. **Beegle, D. M.** *Prophecy and Prediction.* Ann Arbor, MI: Pryor Pettengill, 1978. **Berger, K.** "Hellenistische Gattungen im Neuen Testament." *ANRW* ii 25, 2 (1984) 1031–1432. **Betz, H. D.** "Zum Problem des religionsgeschichtlichen Verständnis der Apokalyptik." *ZTK* 63 (1966) 391–409. = "On the Problem of the Religio-historical Understanding of Apocalypticism" (tr. J. W. Leitch). In *Apocalypticism,* ed. R. W. Funk. *JTC* 6 (1969) 134–56. **Betz, O.** "Past Events and Last Events in the Qumran Interpretation of History." *Proc Sixth WCJS* (1977) 1:27–34. **Bickermann, E.** *Der Gott der Makkabäer.* Berlin: Schocken, 1937. = *The God of the Maccabees.* Tr. H. R. Moehring. SJLA 32 (1979). ———. *Studies in Jewish and Christian History.* 3 vols. AGJU 9 (1976, 1980, 1986). **Biggs, R. D.** "More Babylonian Prophecies." *Iraq* 29 (1967) 117–32. **Birks, T. R.** *The Two Later Visions of Daniel Historically Explained.* London: Seeley, 1846. **Bleek, F.** "Die messianische Weissagungen im Buche Daniel." *Jahrbücher für deutsche Theologie* 5 (1860) 45–101. **Blenkinsopp, J.** "Interpretation and the Tendency to Sectarianism." In *Jewish and Christian Self-Definition,* ed. E. P. Sanders et al. London: SCM, 1981. 2:1–26. **Borger, R.** "Gott Marduk und Gott-König Šulgi als Propheten." *BO* 28 (1971) 3–24. **Boyce, M.** *Zoroastrians.* London/Boston: Routledge, 1979. **Braaten, C. E.** "The Significance of Apocalypticism for Systematic Theology," *Int* 25 (1971) 480–503. **Briggs, C. A.** *Messianic Prophecy.* New York/Edinburgh: Clark/Scribner's, 1886. 410–27. **Brownlee, W. H.** "The Servant of the Lord in the Qumran Scrolls." *BASOR* 132 (1953) 8–15; 135 (1954) 33–38. **Brox, N.,** ed. *Pseudepigraphie in der heidnischen und jüdisch-christlichen Antike.* Darmstadt: Wissenschaftliche, 1977. **Buber, M.** "Prophetie und Apokalyptik." *Werke.* Munich: Kösel, 1964. 2:925–42. = "Prophecy, Apocalyptic, and the Historical Hour" (tr. M. Friedman). In *Pointing the Way.* London: Routledge, 1957. 192–207. **Buchanan, G. W.** *To the Hebrews.* AB 36 (1972). **Burgmann, H.** "Die vier Endzeittermine im Danielbuch." *ZAW* 86 (1974) 543–50. ———. "Die interkalation in den sieben Jahrwochen des Sonnenkalendars." *RevQ* 10 (1979–81) 67–81. Repr. in Burgmann, *Zwei lösbare Qumrânprobleme.* Frankfurt/New York: Lang, 1986. **Burridge, K. O. L.** "Reflections on Prophecy and Prophetic Groups." In *Anthropological Perspectives on Old Testament Prophecy,* ed. R. C. Culley and T. W. Overholt. *Semeia* 21 (1981) 99–102. **Buzy, D.** "Les symboles de Daniel." *RB* 27 [n.s. 15] (1918) 403–31. **Calvin, J.** *Quarante sept Sermons sur les huiet derniers chapitres des propheties de Daniel.* La Rochelle: Berton, 1565. = CR 69 (Calvin Vol. 41; 1889) 305–688; 70 (Calvin Vol. 42; 1890) 1–174. **Caquot, A.** "Matthias Delcor, *Le livre de Daniel.*" *VT* 23 (1973) 113–17. ——— and **Leibovici, M.,** ed. *La divination.* 2 vols. Paris: PUF, 1968. **Casey,**

[P.] M. "*Daniel*. . . . by John J. Collins." *JTS* 37 (1986) 478–84. **Charles, R. H.** [*Eschatology*:] *A Critical History of the Doctrine of a Future Life*. London: Black, 1899; 2nd ed., 1913. **Charlesworth, J. H.** "A History of Pseudepigrapha Research." *ANRW* ii 19, 1 (1979) 54–88. **Chary, T.** *Les prophètes et le culte à partir de l'exil*. Tournai: Desclée, 1955. 236–74. **Childs, B. S.** *Introduction to the Old Testament as Scripture*. London/Philadelphia: SCM/Fortress, 1979. **Coats, G. W.**, ed. *Saga Legend Tale Novella Fable*. JSOTSup 35 (1985). **Cohen, D. R.** "Subject and Object in Biblical Aramaic." *Afroasiatic Linguistics* 2, 1 (1975) 1–23. **[Collins, A.]** *The Scheme of Literal Prophecy Considered*. London, 1727. **Collins, J. J.** *The Apocalyptic Vision of the Book of Daniel*. HSM 16 (1977). ———. *Daniel with an Introduction to Apocalyptic Literature*. FOTL 20 (1984). ———. "The Symbolism of Transcendence in Jewish Apocalyptic." *BR* 19 (1974) 5–22. ———. "Apocalyptic Eschatology as the Transcendence of Death." *CBQ* 36 (1974) 21–43. = Repr. in *Visionaries*, ed. P. D. Hanson, 61–84. ———. "Jewish Apocalyptic against Its Hellenistic Near Eastern Environment." *BASOR* 220 (1975) 27–36. ———. "The Court-Tales in Daniel and the Development of Apocalyptic." *JBL* 94 (1975) 218–34. ———. "The Mythology of Holy War in Daniel and the Qumran War Scroll." *VT* 25 (1975) 596–612. ———. "Pseudonymity, Historical Reviews, and the Genre of the Revelation of John." *CBQ* 39 (1977) 329–43. ———. "Cosmos and Salvation." *HR* 17 (1977) 121–42. ———. "Dualism and Eschatology in 1QM." *VT* 29 (1979) 212–16. ———. "Apocalyptic Genre and Mythic Allusions in Daniel." *JSOT* 21 (1981) 83–100. ———. "The Apocalyptic Technique." *CBQ* 44 (1982) 91–111. ———. "Daniel and His Social World." *Int* 39 (1985) 131–43. Repr. in *Interpreting the Prophets*, ed. J. L. Mays and P. J. Achtemeier. Philadelphia: Fortress, 1987. 249–60. ———, ed. *Apocalypse: The Morphology of a Genre*. *Semeia* 14 (1979). Incorporating material from *SBL 1977 Seminar Papers*. **Cook, E. M.** "Word Order in the Aramaic of Daniel." *Afroasiatic Linguistics* 9, 3 (1986) 1–16. **Cook, J. M.** *The Persian Empire*. London: Dent, 1983. **Coppens, J.** *Le messianisme royal*. LD 54 (1968). ———. *Le messianisme et sa relève prophétique*. BETL 38 (1974). ———. "La composition du livre de Daniel." *ETL* 52 (1976) 346–49. ———. "Le livre de Daniel et ses problèmes." *ETL* 56 (1980) 1–9. = ALBO v, 22. = Coppens, *Le Fils d'homme vétéro- et intertestamentaire*. Ed. J. Lust. La relève apocalyptique du messianisme royal 2. BETL 61 (1983) 19–27. **Coxon, P. W.** "Greek Loan-words and Alleged Greek Loan Translations in the Book of Daniel." *TGUOS* 25 (1973–74) 24–40. ———. "The Syntax of the Aramaic of Daniel." *HUCA* 48 (1977) 107–22. ———. "The Distribution of Synonyms in Biblical Aramaic." *RevQ* 9 (1977–78) 497–512. ———. "A Morphological Study of the *h*-prefix in Biblical Aramaic." *JAOS* 98 (1978) 416–19. ———. "The Problem of Consonantal Mutations in Biblical Aramaic." *ZDMG* 129 (1979) 8–22. ———. "The 'List' Genre and Narrative Style in the Court Tales of Daniel." *JSOT* 35 (1986) 95–121. **Cross, F. M.** *Canaanite Myth and Hebrew Epic*. Cambridge, MA/London: Harvard UP, 1973. 343–46. **Davies, G. I.** "Apocalyptic and Historiography." *JSOT* 5 (1978) 15–28. **Davies, P. R.** "*Ḥasidim* in the Maccabaean Period." *JJS* 28 (1977) 127–40. ———. "Dualism and Eschatology in the Qumran War Scroll." *VT* 28 (1978) 28–36. ———. "Eschatology in the Book of Daniel." *JSOT* 17 (1980) 33–53. ———. "Dualism and Eschatology in 1QM: A Rejoinder." *VT* 30 (1980) 93–96. **Delcor, M.** *Etudes bibliques et orientales de religions comparées*. Leiden: Brill, 1979. ———. "Le milieu d'origine et le développement de l'apocalyptique juive." *RechBib* 9 (1974) 101–17. = *Etudes*, 193–209. ———. "Le Dieu des apocalypticiens." *La notion biblique de Dieu*. BETL 41 (1976) 211–28. = *Etudes*, 210–27. ———. "Mythologie et apocalyptique." In *Apocalypses et théologie de l'espérance: Congres de Toulouse 1975*. LD 95 (1977) 143–77. = *Etudes*, 228–62. **DeVries, S. J.** *The Achievements of Biblical Religion*. Lanham, MD/London: UP of America, 1983. **Dexinger, F.** *Henochs Zehnwochenapokalypse und offene Probleme der Apokalyptikforschung*. SPB 29 (1977). ———. *Das Buch Daniel und seine Probleme*. SBS 36 (1969). **Dommershausen, W.** *Nabonid im Buche Daniel*. Mainz: Matthias-Grünewald, 1964. **Driver, G. R.** "The

Aramaic of the Book of Daniel." *JBL* 45 (1926) 110–19. ———. "The Aramaic Language." *JBL* 45 (1926) 323–25. ———. "Sacred Numbers and Round Figures." In *Promise and Fulfilment,* FS S. H. Hooke, ed. F. F. Bruce. Edinburgh: Clark, 1963. 62–90. **Driver, S. R.** *An Introduction to the Literature of the Old Testament.* Edinburgh: Clark, 1891; 6th rev. ed., 1897. Chap. 11. **Duckworth, H. T. F.** "The Origin of the Book of Daniel." *Exp* vii, 2 (1906) 224–33. **Eddy, S. K.** *The King Is Dead.* Lincoln: U Nebraska, 1961. **Eerdmans, B. D.** "Origin and Meaning of the Aramaic Part of Daniel." *Actes du xviiie congrès international des orientalistes.* 1932. 198–202. **Eichhorn, J. G.** *Einleitung in das Alte Testament.* 3rd ed. Leipzig: Weidmann, 1803. 3:382–445. **Eichrodt, W.** *Theologie des Alten Testaments.* Leipzig: Hinrichs, 1933–39. Rev. ed., Stuttgart: Klotz, 1957–61. = *Theology of the Old Testament.* Tr. J. A. Baker. OTL. 1957–61. **Eising, H.** "Die Gottesoffenbarungen bei Daniel im Rahmen der atl. Theophanien." In *Alttestamentliche Studien Friedrich Nötscher,* ed. H. Junker and J. Botterweck. Bonn: Hanstein, 1950. 62–73. **Eissfeldt, O.** *Baal Zaphon, Zeus Kasios und der Durchzug der Israeliten durchs Meer.* Halle: Niemeyer, 1932. ———. "Daniels und seiner drei Gefährten Laufbahn im babylonischen, medischen und persischen Dienst." *ZAW* 72 (1960) 134–48. = Eissfeldt, *Kleine Schriften.* Tübingen: Mohr, 1966. 3:512–25. **Eusebius of Caesarea.** **Εὐαγγελικης ἀποδειξεως βιβλια δεκα.** = *PG* 22 (1857) 13–794. = *The Proof of the Gospel.* Tr. W. J. Ferrar. London/New York: SPCK/Macmillan, 1920. **Ferch, A. J.** "The Book of Daniel and the 'Maccabean Thesis.'" *AUSS* 21 (1983) 129–41. **Fishbane, M.** *Biblical Interpretation in Ancient Israel.* Oxford/New York: Clarendon, 1985. 441–543. Incorporating material from *Proc Sixth WCJS* (1977) 1:97–114. **Fitzmyer, J. A.** *Essays on the Semitic Background of the New Testament.* London: Chapman, 1971. ———. *A Wandering Aramaean.* SBLMS 25 (1979). **Ford, D.** *The Abomination of Desolation in Biblical Eschatology.* Washington, DC: UP of America, 1979. **Frost, S. B.** *Old Testament Apocalyptic.* London: Epworth, 1952. ———. "Apocalyptic and History." In *The Bible in Modern Scholarship,* ed. J. P. Hyatt. Nashville: Abingdon, 1965/London: Carey, 1966. 98–113. Repr. in *The Bible in Its Literary Milieu: Contemporary Essays,* ed. V. L. Tollers and J. R. Maier. Grand Rapids: Eerdmans, 1979. 134–47. **Fruchan, P.** "Sur l'interprétation des apocalypses." In *Apocalypses et théologie de l'espérance: Congres de Toulouse 1975.* LD 95 (1977) 385–440. **Frye, R. N.** *The Heritage of Persia.* London: Weidenfeld, 1962. **Gammie, J. G.** "Spatial and Ethical Dualism in Jewish Wisdom and Apocalyptic Literature." *JBL* 93 (1974) 356–85. ———. "The Classification, Stages of Growth, and Changing Intentions in the Book of Daniel." *JBL* 95 (1976) 191–204. ———. "On the Intention and Sources of Daniel i–vi." *VT* 31 (1981) 282–92. **Garrison, D.** *The Darkness of God.* London: SCM, 1982. **Gese, H.** "Die Bedeutung der Krise unter Antiochus IV. Epiphanes für die Apokalyptik des Danielbuches." *ZTK* 80 (1983) 373–88. **Ginsberg, H. L.** "*In re* My Studies in Daniel." *JBL* 68 (1949) 402–7. ———. "The Composition of the Book of Daniel." *VT* 4 (1954) 246–75. ———. "Biblical Aramaic." *An Aramaic Handbook.* Wiesbaden: Harrassowitz, 1967. i, 1:17–39; 2:16–41. **Glueck, N.** *Das Wort ḥesed.* BZAW 47 (1927). = *Ḥesed in the Bible.* Tr. A. Gottschalk. Cincinnati: Hebrew Union College, 1967. **Gnuse, R.** *The Dream Theophany of Samuel.* Lanham, MD: UP of America, 1984. ———. "Dreams and Their Theological Significance in the Biblical Tradition." *CurTM* 8 (1981) 166–71. **Goldingay, J.** "The Book of Daniel: Three Issues." *Them* 2 (1976–77) 45–49. **Goldstein, J. A.** *I Maccabees.* AB 41 (1976). ———. *II Maccabees.* AB 41A (1983). ———. "The Persecution of the Jews by Antiochus IV." *Proc Sixth WCJS* (1977) 1:135–47. **Good, E. M.** "Apocalyptic as Comedy." In *Tragedy and Comedy in the Bible,* ed. J. C. Exum. *Semeia* 32 (1984) 41–70. **Goodenough, E. R.** *Jewish Symbols in the Greco-Roman Period.* Vols. 1–2. New York: Pantheon, 1953. **Gooding, D. W.** "The Literary Structure of the Book of Daniel and Its Implications." *TynB* 32 (1981) 43–79. **Grabbe, L. L.** "Fundamentalism and Scholarship: The Case of Daniel." In *Scripture: Meaning and Method,* FS A. T. Hanson, ed. B. P. Thompson. Hull: Hull UP, 1987. 133–52. **Grayson, A. K.** *Babylonian Historical-Literary Texts.* Toronto/Buffalo: U Toronto, 1975. ———. *Assyrian and Babylonian Chronicles.* TCS 5 (1975). ——— and **Lambert, W. G.** "Akkadian Prophecies." *JCS* 18 (1964) 7–30. **Grelot, P.** "Histoire et eschatologie dans le livre de Daniel." In *Apocalypses et théologie de l'espérance: Congres de Toulouse 1975.* LD 95 (1977) 63–109. **Gross, E.** "Weltreich und Gottesvolk." *EvT* 16 (1956) 241–51. **Gruenwald, I.** *Apocalyptic and Merkavah Mysticism.* AGJU 14 (1980). ———. "Jewish Apocalyptic Literature." *ANRW* ii 19, 1 (1979) 89–118. ———. "Knowledge and Vision." *IOS* 3 (1973) 63–107. **Guenther, D. A.** *A Diachronic Study of Biblical Prose Syntax.* Diss., Toronto, 1978. **Gunkel, H.** *Das Märchen im Alten Testament.* Tübingen: Mohr, 1921. = *The Folktale in the Old Testament.* Tr. M. D. Rutter. Sheffield: Almond, 1987. **Haag, E.** *Die Errettung Daniels aus der Löwengrube.* SBS 110 (1983). **Hallo, W. W.** "Akkadian Apocalypses." *IEJ* 16 (1966) 231–42. **Hanhart, R.** "Kriterien Geschichtlicher Wahrheit in der Makkabäerzeit." *Fourth WCJS Papers* (1967) 1:81–85. = Hanhart, *Drei Studien zum Judentum.* TExH 140 (1967) 7–22. **Hanson, P. D.** *The Dawn of Apocalyptic.* Philadelphia: Fortress, 1975; 2nd ed., 1979. ———. "Apocalypse, Genre," "Apocalypticism." *IDBSup* 27–34. ———. "Old Testament Apocalyptic Reexamined." *Int* 25 (1971) 454–79. = *Visionaries* [see below], 37–60. ———. "Biblical Apocalypticism: The Theological Dimension." *HBT* 7 (1985) 1–20. ———, ed. *Visionaries and Their Apocalypses.* IRT 2 (1983). **Hasel, G. F.** "The Book of Daniel." *AUSS* 19 (1981) 37–49, 211–25. **Hellholm, D.**, ed. *Apocalypticism in the Mediterranean World and the Near East.* Tübingen: Mohr, 1983. **Hengel, M.** *Judentum und Hellenismus.* WUNT 10 (1969; 2nd ed., 1973). = *Judaism and Hellenism.* Tr. J. Bowden. 2 vols. London/ Philadelphia: SCM/Fortress, 1974. ———. "Anonymität, Pseudepigraphie und 'literarische Fälschung' in der jüdisch-hellenistischen Literatur." In *Pseudepigrapha,* ed. K. von Fritz. Geneva: Hardt, 1972. 1:132–329. **Hengstenberg, E. W.** *Die Authentie des Daniel und die Integrität des Sacharjah.* Beiträge zur Einleitung ins AT 1. Berlin: Oehmigke, 1831. = *Dissertations on the Genuineness of Daniel and the Integrity of Zechariah.* Tr. B. P. Patten. Edinburgh: Clark, 1848. **Herzfeld, E.** *Zoroaster and His World.* Princeton: Princeton UP, 1947. **Hilgenfeld, A.** *Die jüdische Apokalyptik.* Jena: Mauke, 1857. **Hölscher, G.** "Die Entstehung des Buches Daniel." *TSK* 92 (1919) 113–38. **Hommel, F.** "Die Abfassungszeit des Buches Daniel und die Wahrsinn Nabonids." *Theologische Literaturblatt* 23 (1902) 145–50. **Hultgård, A.** "Das Judentum in der hellenistisch-römischen Zeit und die iranische Religion." *ANRW* ii 19, 1 (1979) 512–90. **Humphreys, W. L.** "A Life-style for Diaspora." *JBL* 92 (1973) 211–23. **Hunger, H.**, and **Kaufman, S. A.** "A New Akkadian Prophecy Text." *JAOS* 95 (1975) 371–75. **Isenberg, S. R.** "Millenarism in Jewish Palestine." *Religion* 4 (1974) 26–46. **Jacob, E.** "Aux sources bibliques de l'apocalyptique." In *Apocalypses et théologie de l'espérance: Congres de Toulouse 1975.* LD 95 (1977) 43–61. **Jaubert, A.** *La notion d'Alliance dans le Judaïsme aux abords de l'ère chrétienne.* Paris: Seuil, 1963. **Jepsen, A.** "Bemerkungen zum Danielbuch." *VT* 11 (1961) 386–91. **Jeremias, C.** *Die Nachtgesichte des Sacharja.* FRLANT 117 (1977) 88–107. **Joüon, P.** "Notes sur quelques versets araméens de Daniel et d'Esdras." *Bib* 8 (1927) 182–87. ———. "Cinq imperfaits (*yiqtul*) remarquables dans l'araméen de Daniel." *Bib* 22 (1941) 21–24. ———. "Notes de grammaire et de lexicographie araméenne." *Bib* 22 (1941) 263–68. **Käsemann, E.** "Die Anfänge christlicher Theologie." *ZTK* 57 (1960) 162–85. = "The Beginnings of Christian Theology" (tr. J. W. Leitch). In *Apocalypticism,* ed. R. W. Funk. *JTC* 6 (1969) 17–46. = Käsemann, *New Testament Questions of Today.* Tr. W. J. Montague. London/Philadelphia: SCM/Fortress, 1969. 82–107. **Kaufmann, Y.** *History of the Religion of Israel.* Vol. 4. New York: Ktav, 1977. Tr. by C. W. Efroymson from תולדות האמונה הישראלית Vol. 4, 1. Tel Aviv: Bialik, 1956. **Kitchen, K. A.** "The Aramaic of Daniel." In Wiseman, *Notes,* 31–79. **Klausner, J.** הרעיון המשיחי בישראל. 3rd ed. Tel Aviv: Masada, 1950. = *The Messianic Idea in Israel.* Tr. W. F. Stinespring. London: George Allen, 1956. Cf. *Messianism in the Talmudic Era.* Ed. L. Landman. New York: Ktav, 1979. 200–214. **Klein, G.** "Über das Buch Daniel." *Verhandlungen des xiii. Internationalen Orientalisten-Kongresses.* Leiden: Brill,

1904. 239–41. **Knibb, M. A.** "The Exile in the Intertestamental Period." *HeyJ* 17 (1976) 253–72. **Koch, K.** *Ratlos vor der Apokalyptik.* Gütersloh: Mohn, 1970. = *The Rediscovery of Apocalyptic.* Tr. M. Kohl. SBT ii, 22 (1971). ———. "Die Weltreiche im Danielbuche." *TLZ* 85 (1960) 829–32. ———. "Spätisraelitische Geschichtsdenken am Beispiel des Buches Daniel." *HZ* 193 (1961) 1–32. Repr. in *Apokalyptik* [see below], 276–310. ———. "Is Daniel Also among the Prophets?" *Int* 39 (1985) 117–30. Repr. in *Interpreting the Prophets,* ed. J. L. Mays and P. J. Achtemeier. Philadelphia: Fortress, 1987. 237–48. ——— and **Schmidt, J. M.,** ed. *Apokalyptik.* Darmstadt: Wissenschaftliche, 1982. ——— et al., ed. *Das Buch Daniel.* Darmstadt: Wissenschaftliche, 1980. **Kopf, L.** "Arabische Etymologien und Parallelen zum Bibelwörterbuch." *VT* 9 (1959) 247–87. **Kosmala, H.** *Studies, Essays, and Reviews.* Vol. 1. Leiden: Brill, 1978. **Kutscher, E. Y.** "Aramaic." *EncJud* 3:259–87. ———. "Aramaic." In *Linguistics in South West Asia and North Africa,* ed. T. A. Sebeok. Current Trends in Linguistics 6. The Hague: Mouton, 1970. 347–412. **Lacocque, A.** *Daniel et son temps.* Geneva: Labor et Fides, 1983. ———. "Apocalyptic Symbolism." *BR* 26 (1981) 6–15. ———. "Naissance de l'apocalyptique." *LumVie* 31 [160] (1982) 4–12. **Lagrange, M. J.** "Les prophéties messianiques de Daniel." *RB* n.s. 1 [13] (1904) 494–520. **Lambert, W. G.** *The Background of Jewish Apocalyptic.* London: Athlone, 1975; 2nd ed., 1979. ———. "A New Source for the Reign of Nabonidus." *AfO* 22 (1968–69) 1–8. **Lampe, P.** "Die Apokalyptiker." In *Eschatologie und Frieden,* ed. G. Liedke et al. Heidelberg: Ev. St.-gemein., 1978. 2:61–125. Repr. in *Eschatologie und Friedenshandeln,* ed. U. Luz. SBS 101 (1981) 59–114. **Lebram, J. C. H.** "Nachbiblische Weisheitstraditionen." *VT* 15 (1965) 167–237. ———. "Apokalyptik und Hellenismus im Buche Daniel." *VT* 20 (1970) 503–24. ———. "König Antiochus im Buch Daniel." *VT* 25 (1975) 737–72. ———. "Zwei Daniel-probleme." *BO* 39 (1982) 510–17. ———. "The Piety of the Jewish Apocalyptists." In *Apocalypticism,* ed. D. Hellholm, 171–210. **Lenglet, A.** "La structure littéraire de Daniel 2–7." *Bib* 53 (1972) 169–90. **Lipiński, E.** "André Lacocque, *Le livre de Daniel.*" *VT* 28 (1978) 233–41. **Luther, M.** *Vorrede über den Propheten Daniel.* 1530; revised 1541. = *WA: Deutsche Bibel* 11, 2 (1960) 1–131. = "Preface to the Prophet Daniel." *Luther's Works.* Tr. (from the 1530 ed.) C. M. Jacobs. Philadelphia: Fortress, 1960. 35:294–316. **McCown, C. C.** "Hebrew and Egyptian Apocalyptic Literature." *HTR* 18 (1925) 357–411. **McNamara, M.** "Nabonidus and the Book of Daniel." *ITQ* 37 (1970) 131–49. **Massyngberde Ford, J.** "Jewish Law and Animal Symbolism." *JSJ* 10 (1979) 203–12. **Meade, D. G.** *Pseudonymity and Canon.* Diss., Nottingham, 1984. = WUNT 39 (1986). **Meinhold, J.** *Beiträge zur Erklärung des Buches Daniel.* Leipzig: Dörffling, 1888. **Metzger, B. M.** "Literary Forgeries and Canonical Pseudepigrapha." *JBL* 91 (1972) 3–24. **M'G, J.** "The Chaldee of Daniel and Ezra." *The Journal of Sacred Literature* 12 (1860–61) 373–91. **Milik, J. T.** *The Books of Enoch.* Oxford: Clarendon, 1976. **Millar, F.** "The Background to the Maccabaean Revolution." *JSJ* 9 (1978) 1–21. **Millard, A. R.** "Daniel 1–6 and History." *EvQ* 49 (1977) 67–73. **Moltmann, J.** *Theologie der Hoffnung.* Munich: Kaiser, 1964; 3rd ed., 1965. = *Theology of Hope.* Tr. J. W. Leitch. London/New York: SCM/Harper, 1967. **Momigliano, A.** *Alien Wisdom.* Cambridge/New York: CUP, 1975. **Moran, M. L.** "Notes on the New Nabonidus Inscriptions." *Or* 28 (1959) 130–40. **Mørkholm, O.** *Antiochus IV of Syria.* Copenhagen: Nordisk, 1966. **Müller, H.-P.** "Magisch-mantische Weisheit und die Gestalt Daniels." *UF* 1 (1969) 79–94. ———. "Mantische Weisheit und Apokalyptik." *Congress Volume: Uppsala 1971.* VTSup 22 (1972) 268–93. ———. "Märchen, Legende und Enderwartung." *VT* 26 (1976) 338–50. **Müntzer, T.** *Schriften und Briefen.* Gütersloh: Mohn, 1968. **Muraoka, T.** "Notes on the Syntax of Biblical Aramaic." *JSS* 11 (1966) 151–67. **Murdock, W. R.** "History and Revelation in Jewish Apocalypticism." *Int* 21 (1967) 167–87. **Newsom, C. A.** "The Past as Revelation." *Quarterly Review* 1984, 4:40–53. **Nickelsburg, G. W. E.,** and **Collins, J. J.,** ed. *Ideal Figures in Ancient Judaism.* Chico, CA: Scholars, 1980. **Nicol, G. G.** "Isaiah's Vision and the Visions of Daniel." *VT* 29

(1979) 501–5. **Niditch, S.** *The Symbolic Vision in Biblical Tradition.* HSM 30 (1983). ———. "The Visionary." In *Figures,* ed. Nickelsburg and Collins, 153–79. **Noth, M.** *Gesammelte Studien zum Alten Testament.* 2 vols. TBü 6 (1957; 2nd ed., 1960) and 39 (1969). ET of Vol. 1 *The Laws in the Pentateuch and Other Studies.* Tr. D. R. Ap-Thomas. Edinburgh/Philadelphia: Oliver and Boyd/Fortress, 1966. ———. "Das geschichtsverständnis der alttestamentlichen Apokalyptik." *Geschichtsdenken und Geschichtsbild im Mittelalter,* ed. W. Lammers. Darmstadt: Wissenschaftliche, 1961. 30–54. = Noth, *Studien,* 1:248–73. = "The Understanding of History in Old Testament Apocalyptic." *Laws* [see above], 194–214. ———. "Zur Komposition des Buches Daniel." *TSK* 98–99 (1926) 143–63. = Noth, *Studien* 2:11–28. **Olmstead, A. T.** *History of the Persian Empire.* Chicago/London: U Chicago, 1948. **Oppenheim, A. L.** *Ancient Mesopotamia.* Chicago/London: U Chicago, 1964; rev. ed., 1977. ———. "The Interpretation of Dreams in the Ancient Near East." *Transactions of the American Philosophical Society* 46 (1956) 179–373. ———. "New Fragments of an Assyrian Dream-Book." *Iraq* 31 (1969) 153–65. ———. "A Babylonian Diviner's Manual." *JNES* 33 (1974) 197–220. **Osswald, E.** "Zum Problem der *vaticinia ex eventu.*" *ZAW* 75 (1963) 27–44. **Osten-Sacken, P. von der.** *Die Apokalyptik in ihrem Verhältnis zu Prophetie und Weisheit.* TExH 157 (1969). **Ozanne, C. G.** *The Fourth Gentile Kingdom.* Worthing: Walter, 1982. ———. "Three Textual Problems in Daniel." *JTS* 16 (1965) 445–48. **Payne, J. B.** *Encyclopedia of Biblical Prophecy.* New York/London: Harper/Hodder, 1973. ———, ed. *New Perspectives on the Old Testament.* Waco, TX/London: Word, 1970. **Perrin, N.** *Jesus and the Language of the Kingdom.* London/Philadelphia: SCM/Fortress, 1976. Incorporating material from *JBL* 93 (1974) 3–14 and *JR* 55 (1975) 348–70. **Peters, J. P.** "Notes on the Old Testament." *JBL* 15 (1896) 106–17. **Plöger, O.** *Theokratie und Eschatologie.* Neukirchen: Neukirchener, 1959; 2nd ed., 1962. = *Prophecy and Eschatology.* Tr. S. Rudman. Oxford: Blackwell, 1968. **Polzin, R.** *Late Biblical Hebrew.* HSM 12 (1976). **Prado, J.** "Carácter histórico del libro de Daniel." *Sefarad* 3 (1943) 167–94. **Rad, G. von.** *Theologie des Alten Testaments.* 2 vols. Munich: Kaiser, 1957–60. = *Old Testament Theology.* Tr. D. M. G. Stalker. Edinburgh: Oliver and Boyd, 1962–65. ———. *Weisheit in Israel.* Neukirchen: Neukirchener, 1970. = *Wisdom in Israel.* Tr. J. D. Martin. London/Nashville: SCM/Abingdon, 1972. **Reed, W. L.** "Nabonidus, Babylonian Reformer or Renegade?" *Lutheran Theological Quarterly* 12 (1977) 21–30. **Rhodes, A. B.** "The Book of Daniel." *Int* 6 (1952) 436–50. **Riessler, P.** "Zu Rosenthals Aufsatz, Bd. xv, S. 278ff." *ZAW* 16 (1896) 182. ———. "Die Ursprache des Buches Daniel." *BZ* 3 (1905) 140–45. **Rigaux, B.** *L'Antéchrist.* Gembloux/Paris: Duculot/Gabalda, 1932. 151–73. **Ringgren, H.** "Akkadian Apocalypses." In *Apocalypticism,* ed. D. Hellholm, 379–86. **Rosén, H. B.** On the Use of the Tenses in the Aramaic of Daniel." *JSS* 6 (1961) 183–203. = Rosén, *East and West.* Munich: Fink, 1984. 2:285–305. **Rosenthal, L. A.** "Die Josephsgeschichte mit den Büchern Ester und Daniel verglichen." *ZAW* 15 (1895) 278–84. ———. "Nochmals der Vergleich Ester, Joseph, Daniel." *ZAW* 17 (1897) 125–28. **Rowland, C.** *The Open Heaven.* London/New York: SPCK/Crossroad, 1982. **Rowley, H. H.** *The Aramaic of the Old Testament.* London/New York: OUP, 1929. ———. *The Relevance of Apocalyptic.* London: Lutterworth, 1944; rev. ed., 1963. ———. "The Bilingual Problem of Daniel." *ZAW* 50 (1932) 256–68. ———. "Early Aramaic Dialects and the Book of Daniel." *JRAS* 1933, 777–805. ———. "Some Problems in the Book of Daniel." *ExpT* 47 (1935–36) 216–20. ———. "*Studies in Daniel,* by H. Louis Ginsberg." *JBL* 68 (1949) 173–77. ———. "A Rejoinder [to Ginsberg, *JBL* 68 (1949) 402–7]." *JBL* 69 (1950) 201–3. ———. "Menelaus and the Abomination of Desolation." In *Studia orientalia,* FS J. Pedersen, ed. F. Hvidberg. Copenhagen: Munksgaard, 1953. 303–15. ———. "The Unity of the Book of Daniel." *HUCA* 23, 1 (1950–51) 233–73. = Rowley, *The Servant of the Lord and Other Essays on the Old Testament.* London: Lutter worth, 1952. 237–68. Rev. ed., Oxford: Blackwell, 1965, 249–80. ———. "The Composition of the Book of Daniel." *VT* 5 (1955) 272–76. ———. "The Meaning of Daniel for Today."

Int 15 (1961) 387–97. ———. "Notes on the Aramaic of the Genesis Apocryphon." In *Hebrew and Semitic Studies,* FS G. R. Driver, ed. D. W. Thomas and W. D. McHardy. Oxford/New York: Clarendon/OUP, 1963. 116–29. **Russell, D. S.** *The Method and Message of Jewish Apocalyptic.* OTL (1964). **Saadia ben Joseph.** *The Book of Daniel with Saadia's Arabic Translation. A Babylonian-Yemenite Manuscript.* Ed. S. Morag. Leiden: Brill, 1973. **Sachs, A. J.,** and **Wiseman, D. J.** "A Babylonian King-List of the Hellenistic Period." *Iraq* 16 (1954) 202–12. **Sack, R. H.** "The Nabonidus Legend." *RA* 77 (1983) 59–67. **Saggs, H. W. F.** *The Greatness That Was Babylon.* London: Sidgwick, 1962. **Sahlin, H.** "Antiochus IV. Epiphanes und Judas Mackabäus." *ST* 23 (1979) 41–68. **Sakenfeld, K.** *The Meaning of Hesed in the Hebrew Bible.* HSM 17 (1978). **Schalit, A.,** ed. *The Hellenistic Age.* The World History of the Jewish People i, 6. Jerusalem: Masada, 1972. **Schüssler Fiorenza, E.** "The Phenomenon of Early Christian Apocalyptic." In *Apocalypticism,* ed. D. Hellholm, 295–316. **Schmidtke, F.** "Traüme, Orakel, und Totengeister als Künder der Zerkunft in Israel und Babylonien." *BZ* 11 (1967) 240–46. **Schmithals, W.** *Die Apokalyptik.* Göttingen: Vandenhoeck, 1973. = *The Apocalyptic Movement.* Tr. J. E. Steely. Nashville: Abingdon, 1975. **Schrader, E.** "Die Sage vom Wahrsinn Nebukadnezar's." *JPT* 7 (1881) 618–29. **Scott, R. B. Y.** "I Daniel, the Original Apocalypse." *AJSL* 47 (1930–31) 289–96. **Seeligmann, I. L.** "Voraussetzungen der Midraschexegese." *Congress Volume: Copenhagen 1953.* VTSup 1 (1953) 150–81. **Selby, P.** "Apocalyptic—Christian and Nuclear." *Modern Churchman* 26 (1984) 3–10. **Selms, A. van.** "Temporary Henotheism." In *Symbolae F. M. T. de Liagre Bohl,* ed. M. A. Beek et al. Leiden: Brill, 1973. 341–48. **Shea, W.** "Further Literary Structures in Daniel 2–7." *AUSS* 23 (1985) 193–202, 277–95. **Silberman, L. H.** "Unriddling the Riddle." *RevQ* 3 (1961–62) 323–64. **Smith, J. Z.** "Wisdom and Apocalyptic." *Religious Syncretism in Antiquity: Essays in Conversation with G. Widengren,* ed. B. A. Pearson. Missoula, MT: Scholars, 1975. 131–56. = Smith, *Map Is Not Territory: Studies in the History of Religion.* SJLA 23 (1978) 67–87. Repr. in *Visionaries,* ed. P. D. Hanson, 101–20. **Snell, D. C.** "Why Is There Aramaic in the Bible?" *JSOT* 18 (1980) 32–51. **Soden, W. von.** "Eine babylonische Volksüberlieferung von Nabonid in den Danielerzählungen." *ZAW* 53 (1935) 81–89. = von Soden, *Bibel und Alter Orient.* BZAW 162 (1985) 1–9. **Spinoza, B.** *Tractatus theologico-politicus.* 1670. **Steck, O. H.** "Das Problem theologischer Strömungen in nachexilischer Zeit." *EvT* 28 (1968) 445–54. ———. "Weltgeschehen und Gottesvolk im Buche Daniel." In *Kirche,* FS G. Bornkamm, ed. D. Lührmann and G. Strecker. Tübingen: Mohr, 1980. 53–78. = *Wahrnehmungen Gottes im Alten Testament: Gesammelte Studien.* TBü 70 (1982) 262–90. ———. "Überlegungen zur Eigenart der spätisraelitischen Apokalyptik." *Die Botschaft und die Boten,* FS H. W. Wolff, ed. J. Jeremias and L. Perlitt. Neukirchen: Neukirchener, 1981. 301–15. **Stinespring, W. F.** "The Active Infinitive with Passive Meaning in Biblical Aramaic." *JBL* 81 (1962) 391–94. **Stoebe, H. J.** "Die Bedeutung des Wortes *ḥäsäd* im Alten Testament." *VT* 2 (1952) 244–54. **Streck, M.** "Die Ursprache des Buches Daniel." *BZ* 4 (1960) 247–54. **Szörényi, A.** "Das Buch Daniel, ein kanonisierter Pescher?" *Volume du Congrès: Genève 1965.* VTSup 15 (1966) 278–94. **Tcherikover, V.** *Hellenistic Civilization and the Jews.* Tr. S. Applebaum. Philadelphia: JPSA, 1959. **Thiering, B.** "The Biblical Source of Qumran Asceticism." *JBL* 93 (1974) 429–49. ———. "The Three and a Half Years of Elijah." *NovT* 23 (1981) 41–55. **Tisdall, W. St. C.** "The Book of Daniel." *JTVI* 53 (1921) 206–55. **Torrey, C. C.** "Notes on the Aramaic Part of Daniel." *Transactions of the Connecticut Academy of Arts and Sciences* 15 (1909) 241–82. ———. "Stray Notes on the Aramaic of Daniel and Ezra." *JAOS* 43 (1923) 229–38. ———. " 'Medes and Persians.' " *JAOS* 66 (1946) 1–15. **Towner, W. S.** "The Poetic Passages in Daniel 1–6." *CBQ* 31 (1969) 317–26. ———. "Retributional Theology in the Apocalyptic Setting." *USQR* 26 (1970–71) 203–14. ———. "The Preacher in the Lion's Den." *Int* 39 (1985) 157–69. Repr. in *Interpreting the Prophets,* ed. J. L. Mays and P. J. Achtemeier. Philadelphia: Fortress, 1987. 273–84. **VanderKam, J. C.** *Enoch and the Growth of an Apocalyptic*

Legend. CBQ MS 16 (1984). ———. "The Prophetic-Sapiential Origins of Apocalyptic Thought." In *A Word in Season,* FS W. McKane, ed. J. D. Martin and P. R. Davies. JSOTSup 42 (1986) 163–76. **Vasholz, R. I.** "Qumran and the Dating of Daniel." *JETS* 21 (1978) 315–21. **Volz, P.** *Jüdische Eschatologie von Daniel bis Akiba.* 1903. 2nd ed., *Die Eschatologie der jüdischen Gemeinde im neutestamentlichen Zeitalter.* Tübingen: Mohr, 1934. **Wacholder, B. Z.** *The Dawn of Qumran: The Sectarian Torah and the Teacher of Righteousness.* Cincinnati: Hebrew Union College, 1983. **Wächter, L.** "Apokalyptik im Alten Testament." *Die Zeichen der Zeit* 9 (1979) 334–40. **Wagner, M.** *Die lexikalischen und grammatikalischen Aramaismen im alttestamentlichen Hebräisch.* BZAW 96 (1966). ———. "Beiträge zur Aramaismenfrage im alttestamentlichen Hebräisch." *HW* 355–71. **Walbank, F. W.,** et al., ed. *The Hellenistic World.* CAH vii, 1. 2nd ed., 1984. **Waltke, B. K.** "The Date of the Book of Daniel." *BSac* 133 (1976) 319–29. **Walvoord, J. F.** "Prophecy of the Ten-Nation Confederacy." *BSac* 124 (1967) 99–105. ———. "Revival of Rome." *BSac* 126 (1969) 317–28. **Weisberg, D. B.** *Texts from the Time of Nebuchadnezzar.* New Haven: Yale UP, 1980. **Wenham, G. J.** "Daniel: The Basic Issues." *Them* 2 (1976–77) 49–52. **Westermann, C.** *Das Buch Jesaja: Kap. 40–66.* Göttingen: Vandenhoeck, 1966. = Isaiah 40–66. Tr. D. M. G. Stalker. OTL (1969). ———. *Das Loben Gottes in den Psalmen.* Berlin: Evangelische, 1953. 5th ed. *Lob und Klage in den Psalmen.* Göttingen: Vandenhoeck, 1977. = *Praise and Lament in the Psalms.* Tr. K. R. Crim and R. N. Soulen. Atlanta/Edinburgh: Knox/Clark, 1981. Rev. ed. of *The Praise of God in the Psalms.* Richmond, VA: Knox, 1965/London: Epworth, 1966. **Widengren, G.** "Leitende Ideen und Quellen der iranischen Apokalyptik." In *Apocalypticism,* ed. D. Hellholm, 77–162. **Wiklander, B.** "Begreppet rabbim i Daniel 8–12." *SEA* 39 (1974) 59–73. **Wilch, J. R.** *Time and Event.* Leiden: Brill, 1969. **Wilder, A. N.** "The Rhetoric of Ancient and Modern Apocalyptic." *Int* 25 (1971) 436–53. **Wilkie, J. M.** "Nabonidus and the Later Jewish Exiles." *JTS* 2 (1951) 36–44. **Williams, J. G.** "A Critical Note on the Aramaic Indefinite Plural of the Verb." *JBL* 83 (1964) 180–82. **Willi-Plein, I.** "Ursprung und Motivation der Apokalyptik im Danielbuch." *TZ* 35 (1979) 265–74. **Wilson, B. R.** *Magic and the Millennium.* London: Heinemann, 1973. **Wilson, R. D.** "The Aramaic of Daniel." In *Biblical and Theological Studies by the Members of the Faculty of Princeton Theological Seminary.* New York: Scribner's, 1912. 261–305. ———. "On the Hebrew of Daniel." *PTR* 25 (1927) 177–99. **Wilson, R. R.** "From Prophecy to Apocalyptic." *Sem* 21 (1981) 79–95, 133–35. **Winckler, H.** *Altorientalische Forschungen* ii, 1:210–27; 3:433–57. Leipzig: Pfeiffer, 1899 and 1901. **Wink, W.** *Naming the Powers.* Philadelphia: Fortress, 1984. ———. *Unmasking the Powers.* Philadelphia: Fortress, 1986. **Winston, D.** "The Iranian Component in the Bible, Apocrypha, and Qumran." *HR* 5 (1965–66) 183–216. **Wiseman, D. J.** *Chronicles of Chaldaean Kings.* London: British Museum, 1961. ———. *Nebuchadnezzar and Babylon.* London/New York: OUP, 1985. ———, et al. *Notes on Some Problems in the Book of Daniel.* London: Tyndale, 1965. **Wolf, C. U.** "Daniel and the Lord's Prayer." *Int* 15 (1961) 398–410. **Wycliffe, John of** [?] *Wycliffes Wyckett.* 1381–84. = Wycliffe, *Tracts and Treatises.* London: Wycliffe Society, 1845. 273–84. **Yamauchi, E. M.** "The Greek Words in Daniel in the Light of Greek Influence in the Ancient Near East." In *Perspectives,* ed. J. B. Payne. 170–200. ———. "The Archaeological Background of Daniel." *BSac* 137 (1980) 3–16. **Yarbro Collins, A.** *The Combat Myth in the Book of Revelation.* Missoula, MT: Scholars, 1976. ———. "Numerical Symbolism in Jewish and Early Christian Apocalyptic Literature." *ANRW* ii 19, 2 (1984) 1221–87. **Young, E. J.** *The Messianic Prophecies of Daniel.* Delft: Van Keulen, 1954. **Zadok, R.** *The Jews in Babylonia during the Chaldaean and Achaemenian Periods according to the Babylonian Sources.* Haifa: U Haifa, 1979. ———. "On Five Iranian Names in the Old Testament." *VT* 26 (1976) 246–47. **Zeitlin, S.** *The Rise and Fall of the Judaean State.* Vol. 1. Philadelphia: JPSA, 1962. ———. "The Cryptic Numbers in Daniel." *JQR* 39 (1948–49) 321–24. **Zevit, Z.** "The Exegetical Implications of Daniel viii 1, ix 21." *VT* 28 (1978) 488–92. **Zimmerli, W.** *Ezechiel.*

BKAT xiii, 1–2 (1969). = *Ezekiel.* Tr. R. E. Clements and J. D. Martin. Hermeneia. 2 vols. 1979–83. ———. "Alttestamentliche Prophetie und Apokalyptik auf dem Wege zur 'Rechtfertigung des Gottlosen.'" *Rechtfertigung,* FS E. Käsemann, ed. J. Friedrich et al. Tübingen/Göttingen: Mohr/Vandenhoeck, 1976. 575–92. **Zimmermann, F.** *Biblical Books Translated from the Aramaic.* New York: Ktav, 1975. ———. "The Aramaic Origin of Daniel 8–12." *JBL* 57 (1938) 255–72. ———. "Some Verses in Daniel in the Light of a Translation Hypothesis." *JBL* 58 (1939) 349–54. ———. "Hebrew Translation in Daniel." *JQR* 51 (1960–61) 198–208.

Daniel

Four Young Exiles Gain Wisdom and Prestige without Losing Holiness (1:1–21)

Bibliography

Ackroyd, P. R. "The Temple Vessels—a Continuity Theme." In *Studies in the Religion of Ancient Israel.* VTSup 23 (1973) 166–81. = Ackroyd, *Studies in the Religious Tradition of the Old Testament.* London: SCM, 1987. 46–60. **Alfrink, B.** "Die Gaddsche Chronik und die Heilige Schrift." *Bib* 8 (1927) 385–417. **Berger, P.-R.** "Der Kyros-Zylinder mit dem Zusatzfragment BIN II Nr. 32 und die akkadischen Personennamen im Danielbuch." *ZA* 64 (1975) 192–234. **Bruce, F. F.** "The Chronology of Daniel 1:1." In Tatford, *Climax,* 229–36. **Day, J.** "The Daniel of Ugarit and Ezekiel and the Hero of the Book of Daniel." *VT* 30 (1980) 174–84. **Dressler, H. H. P.** "The Identification of the Ugaritic Dnil with the Daniel of Ezekiel." *VT* 29 (1979) 152–61. **Goldingay, J.** "Nebuchadnezzar = Antiochus Epiphanes?" *ZAW* 98 (1986) 439. **Kohler, K.** "Die chaldäischen Namen Daniel's und seiner drei Freunde." *ZA* 4 (1889) 46–51. **Larssen, G.** "When Did the Babylonian Captivity Begin?" *JTS* 18 (1967) 417–23. **Meek, T. J.** "Translation Problems in the Old Testament." *JQR* 50 (1959–60) 45–54. **Mitchell, G. C.** "The Chaldaeans." *ExpT* 39 (1927–28) 45–46. **Noth, M.** "Noah, Daniel, und Hiob in Ezechiel xiv." *VT* 1 (1951) 251–60. **Rowley, H. H.** "The Chaldaeans in the Book of Daniel." *ExpT* 38 (1926–27) 423–28. ———. "The Chaldaeans." *ExpT* 39 (1927–28) 188–89. **Selms, A. van.** "The Name Nebuchadnezzar." In *Travels in the World of the Old Testament,* FS M. A. Beek, ed. M. S. H. G. Heerma van Voss et al. Assen: Van Gorcum, 1974. 223–27. **Stone, M.** "A Note on Daniel i. 3." *ABR* 7 (1959) 69–71. **Wilson, R. D.** *Studies.* 1:43–95, 319–89. **Winckler, H.** "Daniel und seine Freunde." Winckler, *Altorientalische Forschungen* ii. Leipzig: Pfeiffer, 1900. 1:237–38. **Wiseman, D. J.,** et al. *Notes.* 16–18. **Zadok, R.** "The Origin of the Name Shinar." *ZA* 74 (1984) 240–44.

Translation

[1]*In the third year of the reign of Jehoiakim king of Judah, Nebuchadnezzar*[a] *king of Babylon came*[b] *to Jerusalem and blockaded it.* [2]*The Lord*[a] *gave Jehoiakim king of Judah into his power,*[b] *and he took*[c] *some of*[d] *the articles*[e] *from the house of God to the land of Shinar to the house of his god*[f]*—he took the articles*[g] *to his god's treasury.*

[3]*The king told Ashpenaz,*[a] *his chief of staff,*[b] *to take*[c] *some of the Israelites,*[d] [e]*some of the royal family and some of the nobility,*[e] [4]*young men*[a] *without any shortcoming,*[b] *of good appearance, discerning in all aspects of learning, knowledge, and insight, and capable of taking a place in the king's palace. They were to be taught*[c] [d]*the language and literature of the Chaldeans.*[d] [5]*The king assigned them a daily allowance*[a] *from the king's supplies*[b] *and from the wine which he drank. They were to be trained*[c] *for three years, and some of them*[d] *would take their place in the king's presence.* [6]*Among them were*[a] *some Judeans, Daniel, Hananiah, Mishael and Azariah;* [7]*the head of staff determined on names for them: he determined*[a] *on* [b]*Belteshazzar for Daniel, Shadrach for Hananiah, Meshach for Mishael, and Abednego for Azariah.*[b]

8 *But Daniel determined*[a] *that he would not contaminate himself with the king's*
supplies or the wine which he drank, and he asked the head of staff that he might
not have to contaminate himself. 9 *God gave*[a] *the head of staff* [b]*favor and sympathy*[b]
toward Daniel, 10 *but the head of staff told Daniel, "I am afraid of my lord the*
king, who assigned your food and drink, in case[a] *he sees your faces looking grim*[b]
compared with the other young men of your group,[c] *and you forfeit*[d] *my head to*
the king." 11 *So Daniel said to the guardian*[a] *whom the head of the palace staff*
had assigned to Daniel, Hananiah, Mishael, and Azariah, 12 *"Why not*[a] *test your*
servants over ten days? Let us be given vegetarian food[b] *to eat and water to*
drink. 13 *Our appearance and that of the young men who eat the king's supplies*
will be visible to you: deal with your servants in accordance with what you see."[a]
14 *He heard them on this point and tested them over ten days.* 15 *At the end of ten*
days their appearance looked better and their bodies better-build than all[a] *the young*
men who had been eating the king's supplies. 16 *So the guardian continued to take*
away[a] *their supplies and the wine they were to drink and to give*[a] *them vegetarian*
food.
17 *To these same four young men God gave knowledge and discernment*[a] *in all*
kinds of literature and learning, while Daniel in particular gained insight into
all kinds of visions and dreams. 18 *At the end of the period which the king had set*
for them to be brought in, the head of staff brought them into Nebuchadnezzar's
presence. 19 *The king talked with them, and there proved to be*[a] *not one of them*
like Daniel, Hananiah, Mishael, and Azariah. So they took their place in the
king's presence,[b] 20 *and on every matter requiring learning and insight*[a] *about*
which the king asked them, he found them ten times superior to all the diviners
(the chanters)[b] *in all his realm.* 21 *Daniel was there*[a] *until the first year of King*
Cyrus.[b]

Notes

1.a. The name is spelled in various ways in Dan and elsewhere in the OT (BDB). The most significant variant is נבוכדראצר (Nebuchadnezzar), which predominates in Jer, Ezek; it corresponds to Akk. *nabu-kudurru-uṣur* (with its own variants), a prayer or confession "Nabu protect(s) the eldest son."*Kudurru* also refers to boundary stones which mark grants of land (see Oppenheim, *Mesopotamia,* 206–87; Saggs, *Babylon,* plate 21A), a possible alternative meaning. The name's Heb. spelling can be explained philologically (Berger, *ZA* 64 [1975] 227–30), but van Selms (*Travels,* 223–27) suggests that *Nebuchadnezzar* corresponds to *Nabu-kudanu-uṣur,* "Nabu protect(s) the *mule,*" a corruption devised among opposition groups in Babylon which would naturally appeal to foreigners such as Jews (cf. the malicious corruption of names in v 7). The suggestion that the name is spelled thus to give it the same numerical value as אנטיוכוס אפיפנס (Antiochus Epiphanes) (C. H. Cornill, "Die siebzig Jahrwochen Daniels," *Theologische Studien und Skizzen aus Ostpreussen* 2 (1889) 31) depends on פ = 70, whereas פ = 80.

1.b. בא: "went" might be appropriate to a story set in Babylon.

2.a. אדני (in most mss), not יהוה "Yahweh": see *Comment.*

2.b. The strong expression ויתן . . . בידו "he gave . . . into his hand" suggests a defeat rather than a submission (Driver); so in 2 Chr 36:17, whence it comes.

2.c Taking ויביאם as *waw* apodosis following its obj (Charles, cf. GKC 111h, 143d, so also Mosul ed. of Syr acc. Kallarakkal, 156–57); the construction is frequent in the Heb. of Dan (1:10, 20). EVV imply that Nebuchadnezzar put both articles and king in his temple, which is odd. In 2 Chr 36:6–7, which Dan is following, הביא "he took" refers only to the temple articles: so also here.

2.d. מקצת ("part of the extremity"; BDB 892b, 500b, GKC 20m). "The costliest of" (Ehrlich) is difficult to parallel with קצת or קצה. "All of" (Meek, *JQR* 50 [1959–60] 45–47; cf. NEB) is possible (BDB 892a); pillaging of the temple was not completed until 587, as the OT accounts which Dan is following recognize, but perhaps it is conflating the story.

2.e. כלים can cover furniture, utensils, and equipment generally (cf. the account in Jer 52:17–23) as well as "vessels" (EVV).

2.f. בית אלהיו, without prep. Thus Jeffery "to Shinar, the house of his god" (cf. Hos 8:1; 9:3, 15 for the idea of the land as the god's house); but this is unnatural here with the allusions to temples. OG lacks, but for בית אוצר אלהיו "his god's treasury" has ἐν τῷ εἰδωλείῳ αὐτοῦ, which may cover both phrases; it hardly means OG's original lacked the first (against BHS). On Dan's combining syntactical inelegance (Driver) with careful choice of expressions, see *Structure*. Words such as אלהיו are often ambiguous; JB renders "gods." See n. 3:25.b, n. 4:5.c.

2.g. In emphatic position before the vb (cf. n. 2.c.). The cl explains more specifically where the vessels were put; the *waw* is explicative (see n. 6:29.a).

3.a. אשפנז: apparently a Pers. word for "guest-master" or the like turned into a proper name (see Lacocque). On OG ABιεσδρι see Montgomery.

3.b. סרים comes from Akk. *ša-reši* "he who is the head". It can mean "eunuch" (many oriental palace staff were aunuchs), but it need not. As a term for royal officials, it can apply to members of the Israelite/Judahite court, but it is esp. used for foreign officials.

3.c. להביא, as in v 2: v 2 describes the bringing of the vessels, v 3 that of the young man (Keil); cf the ref in 5:13. EVV give הביא here a different meaning, referring to taking in Babylon, not bringing to Babylon.

3.d. בני ישראל. NEB "Israelite exiles" apparently follows Th τῆς αἰχμαλωσίας Ισραηλ—surely a gl from the similar expression in, e.g., 2:25 (Young).

3.e-e. The sense suggests this qualifies בני ישראל rather than adding extra groups (against Stone, *ABR* 7 (1959) 69–71). Most mss introduce by *waw*—explicative (see n. 6:29.a); hardly "both" (against GKC 154a).

4.a. ילדים covers males from birth to marriage.

4.b. מאום, as in Job 31:7. In both places it is surely equivalent to מום (so Q and many mss), not מאום "something [against them" (against Ehrlich). Each word can denote a moral, not just a physical defect (cf Job 31:7); both connotations may be allowed here (with Ehrlich). Torrey (*JAOS* 43 [1923] 229) takes as a mixed form.

4.c. Taking וללמדם! as dependent on ויאמר "told," (v 3), in parallel to להביא "to take"; though one night ignore MT accents and see וללמדם as dependent on כח "capability," in parallel to לעמד "of taking a place"—hence "and of being taught" (cf. GKC 115e and note). But see n. 5.c.

4.d-d. Two constr dependant on one abs (against MT, OG, and GKC 120a).

5.a. דבר יום ביומו, "the thing of a day in its day."

5.b. פתבג, not hyphenated as most mss, attempting to link the Pers. word with BH פת "morsel." Syr *ptbq* came to suggest rich food, but this is misleading here (against RSV).

5.c. ולגדלם, apparently another vb implicitly dependent on ויאמר in v 3.

5.d. Giving מקצת the same sense as in v 2 and referring the suffix to that of לגדלם "to train them"; cf. OG, Ps-Saadia, NEB (but NEB takes it to mean "all of them" both times: see n. 2.d.). EVV "at the end of them [the three years]" less plausibly gives מקצת the meaning it has in vv 15, 18; שנים "years" is f, though see GKC 135o.

6.a. ויהי followed by pl subj (GKC 145o). A sebir (mg note) has ויהיו.

7.a. MT repeats וישם, Syr has *gr*ʾ rather than repeating *šmy*, G lack it ad sensum; see *Structure*.

7.b-b. The names are difficult. בלטשאצר (with variants), Akk. ?*balaṭsu-uṣur*, "protect his life," presupposes a divine name, presumably Bel (cf. MT's vocalization; see v 2 *Comment*). Abed-nego is a corruption of *abed-nabu*, "servant of Nabu." For suggestions regarding Shadrach and Meshach, see Barr; Lacocque; Montgomery; Berger, *ZA* 64 (1975) 224–25; Zadok, *VT* 26 (1976) 246–47. But the difficulty seems to reflect deliberate corruption to heighten the gross paganism of foreign theophoric names which replaced the Israelite theophoric ones.

8.a. וישם . . . על לב: לב denotes the heart anatomically, but the mind psychologically (as the seat of mental activity and decision making) more often than the emotions (cf. GNB).

9.a. וישם could have been used again (cf. vv 7, 0), but instead the language follows 1 Kgs 8:50; Ps 106:46.

9.b-b. On the pair, see 9:3–23 *Comment* (b). חסד, here without the notion of moral obligation common in secular and religious contexts in the OT, is effectively a synonym for חן "grace," though the former is more a friendship/community/political word, the latter more a family word (Sakenfeld, *Hesed,* 163–64; Glueck, *Ḥesed,* 66; Stoebe, *VT* 2 [1952] 247). Mercy (EVV) is too narrow a translation of רחמים, which suggests the feelings appropriate to brothers or sisters from the same womb or to a mother in relation to the children of her womb (רחם).

10.a. למה (usually "why"), see BDB 554a, and cf. G.

10.b. זעף usually suggests the presence of anger (e.g., 2 Chr 26:19), sometimes worry (Gen 40:6); here presumably Ashpenaz refers to their looking "out of sorts" (JPS). On the basis of a posited Arabic cognate, Kopf (*VT* 9 [1959] 254) suggests "emaciated."

10.c. גיל (only here in BH) means "circle"; it may refer to the circuits of the planets and thus to people born "under the same stars" and consequently of the same "age" (EVV): cf. *DTT* on גיל and גלגל.

10.d. Cf. Bevan; חוב (only here in BH) means "be guilty, answerable, indebted" and thus in pi, as here, "convict, sentence" (*DTT*).

11.a. מלצר, probably ultimately Akk., from a root *nṣr* equivalent to BH נצר; cf Syr *mnṣr*. OG ABιεσδρι (cf. v 3) assumes Daniel is still speaking to the same person.

12.a. נא following the imper.

12.b. זרעים ("seeds"; זרענים in v 16, and in some mss here) would cover vegetables, grain, and non-meat products generally.

13.a. תראה; OG Θέλῃς (cf NEBmg "as you see fit") is a possible nuance of ראה in MH (*DTT*), but here the more usual meaning is suggested by the context.

15.a. Some mss, Th, and perhaps OG omit כל, but this hardly outweighs MT, Syr, Vg.

16.a For the frequentative tr, cf. Judg 16:21; Neh 1:4 (Bentzen; *TTH* 135).

17.a. Taking inf abs השכל to function as noun parallel to מדע, cf. Jer 3:15; Job 34:35, rather than as replacement for finite vb (against Lacocque).

19.a. נמצא: EVV "was found," but ni is commonly used for "be present/appear/prove to be" (cf. 11:19; 12:1). מצא reappears in v 20.

19.b. Vv 19b–20 are consequent/subsequent to vv 18–19a, not a restatement of them.

20.a. חכמת בינה is too unusual to be a corruption (against BHS; G, Vg, Syr are surely translating loosely, like EVV).

20.b. The two asyndetic foreign words interpret each other (Plöger); cf. 5:15. On the terms, see on 2:2

21.a. ויהי; the abs היה reads oddly in Heb. as in English, though היה "be" can mean "live" (cf. חיה: see 1 Sam 1:28 [Charles]) or "exist" (see Lev 25:29 [R. Bartelmus, היה (St Ottilien: Eos, 1982) 188]). Here it picks up the wording of 2 Chr 36:20b and probably refers back to v 19b (Plöger). Cf. Jer 1:3, where אליו is presupposed from v 2. There is no need to add שם "there" (NEB) (cf. Ruth 1:3).

21.b. The order כורש המלך (cf. 8:1) is an Aramaism (e.g., 3:1–5). See n. 2:28.a.

Form/Structure/Setting

The stories in Dan 1–6 combine features of midrash, court-tale, legend, and aretalogy; to oversimplify, chap. 1 constitutes a legend (vv 8–16) in the context of a court-tale (vv 3–7, 17–20) set in a framework of midrash (vv 1–2, 21). The legend, the story of a holy man, exists to exalt its hero and its hero's God in the hearers' eyes; it thus encourages them to take heed of subsequent stories of Daniel and to emulate the hero's faithfulness, confident of his God's power and support. The court-tale entertains by its romantic story of the flourishing of young exiles at a foreign court (cf. Joseph, Esther, Tobit, Ahiqar); it, too, also offers encouragement as it invites the hearer to identify with these exiles. It contains hints of the two forms of court-tale to be exemplified in chaps. 2; 4–5 and 3; 6 respectively, the court contest tale/interpretation story and the court conflict tale/deliverance story (Humphreys, "Life-style"; Davies, 51). In keeping with the nature of the stories, they do not seek to allow the characters of their heroes to emerge in their own right; we discover only those facts that relate to the concerns of court-tale/legend.

In stressing the involvement of God in their triumph (v 17) it manifests the characteristic feature of an aretalogy (on which see Derger, "Gattungen," 1218–31). While the story does not start from the desire to clarify or actualize specific scriptures, it may be described as situational midrash in that it reuses earlier scriptural material in order to establish links between the scriptures themselves and both the extra-scriptural content of the story and the post-scriptural setting of its hearers, who are thus invited to link their story onto scripture's story and to look at their experience in its context.

Midrash, court-tale, and legend are not three separate units. Neither midrash nor court-tale stands on its own; even the legend, which most likely contains pre-existent traditional material, is now inextricably set in its courtly context. Indeed, the formal distinction between the three is not a sharp one. Both court-tale and legend manifest the hyperbole of romance: young men of exemplary appearance and wisdom (vv 4, 17), though of unstated genealogy (v 6), who manifest unparalleled health on an ascetic diet (v 15), unparalleled success in their education (v 19), and unparalleled usefulness in their service in the palace (v 20). The court-tale is midrashic in the sense that it is shaped by earlier scriptural material, especially the story of Joseph, another young man transported to an alien land who proved the superiority of Israelite wisdom over that of pagans, not least as a dreamer and as a dream interpreter. In language, vv 4, 15, and 17 parallel Gen 41 (see *Comment*). The "romantic themes" (Heaton) of beating pagans at their own game and, in the legend, of the friendliness of the court official, already appear in earlier scriptural "romance" (e.g., Gen 39:21; 41; see also Ezra, Nehemiah, Zerubbabel in 1 Esd 3–4, Judith). A Daniel appears in Ezek 14:12–23; 28:3 as a model held before people in the exilic period of a lone insistence on righteousness and of the wisdom to understand secrets—a model such as the stories will describe Daniel to be. The names of all four men appear elsewhere in scripture, especially in the postexilic community (e.g., among its leadership in Neh 8; 10). There are less clear links between Daniel and the Ugaritic Dan'el (*ANET* 149–55; *DOTT* 124–28) and the angel Daniel in *1 Enoch*. The description of the men takes up the royal ideal of 1 and 2 Samuel, Isaiah's prophecy of the exile (Isa 39:7) (cf. Theodoret), and aspects of the account in Jer 39 of the fall of Jerusalem. The legend's concern, defilement, is also a scriptural theme; the treatment here has close resemblances of motif to Ezek 4:9–17. The passages lack verbal parallels, but there, too, in a similar context at the beginning of the exile in Babylon Ezekiel adopts as his diet a loaf of grains and vegetables, and water. He, too, is under pressure to eat food that is ritually unclean—in his case, through the way he was to cook it. He, too, declares his determination to maintain the purity he has always sought. He, too, discovers that the God who put him into a situation where defilement was hard to avoid provides a way of maintaining purity for those who seek one rather than giving in to the pressures that come (ultimately or immediately) from God himself. Ezekiel's loaf of grain and vegetables seems a closer parallel to Dan 1 than the refugees' diet of wild plants in 2 Macc 5:27.

To describe the story in the terms we have is not necessarily to declare it unhistorical. Forms can be used in ways that do not correspond to their origin, and a historical account could use forms that are more characteristic of less factual narrative. Its form hardly suggests, however, that Dan 1 "purports to be serious history" (Young, 25). It is clearly distinguishable in form from OT narrative that does purport to be serious history, such as 2 Kgs 24–25, with its hard facts open to being related to other known historical facts, references to sources, focus on events rather than conversations, chronicle-like shaping by a sequence of events rather than by a plot, and lack of allusion to the miraculous. In contrast, Dan 1 and the subsequent stories are harder to relate to known history, make no reference to sources, let conversations carry the burden of the story, are emplotted tales rather than chronicle, and emphasize the miraculous. It is impossible to establish or exclude the possibility that the story contains factual material on events in the Babylonian period. The exile of young members of the nobility, their provision from the palace, their serving there, and their renaming are historical enough (though royalty in exile did not refuse the king's provision in 2 Kgs 25:29–30) (Bentzen). That all were under pressure to assimilate and that some resisted this pressure at particular points is plausible enough. That some successfully took remarkable risks in order to remain faithful to their religion, and that some proved far more discerning advisers than Babylonian sages, is not inherently impossible. The form of the story, however, suggests that it would not insist on confining itself to historical material if less factual material helped to achieve its concern to hold attention in an entertaining way and to edify. The distinctive and original elements in the story come in vv 8–16, which may constitute traditional material that has become the core of an introduction to the book as a whole.

Structure

Dan 1 forms a chiastically-shaped short story composed of three double panels, the central panels being themselves subdivided chiastically. The story's plot tension builds through the first three panels, which occupy the opening two-thirds of the chapter (vv 1–14). It is (largely) resolved by the latter three panels in the closing third (vv 15–21). Its structure may thus be expressed diagrammatically:

Panels	*Verses*		
1A	1–2	*tension*	Babylonians defeat Israel.
2A	3–7		Young men are taken for training.
3(i)A	8		Daniel wants to avoid defilement
3(ii)A	9–14		and takes on a test.
3(ii)B	15	*resolution*	Daniel is triumphant in the test
3(i)B	16		and avoids defilement.
2B	17–20		Young men are triumphant in the training.
1B	21		Daniel sees out the Babylonians.

The story is dominated by the decision making and activity of its human participants, but each double panel refers once to God's activity, each time using the verb נתן "give/make." Like statements about human feelings and motivation in stories (as here in v 8), such allusions take the hearer behind the action, declining for a moment to leave it to speak for itself. They affirm that God's giving lies behind three events that are surprising for different reasons: Nebuchadnezzar's success in his siege of Jerusalem, Daniel's success in his negotiation with the palace, and the young men's success in their training. (It is noteworthy that no such affirmation is made regarding their remarkable success in the dietary test.)

Thus near the center of panel 1A, the phrase ויתן אדני בידו ("the Lord gave into his power," v 2) stands out from the otherwise movement-dominated context and from its this-worldly tone, encouraging the reader to bring another framework of interpretation to the events the scene relates. The phrase plays an important role in setting up the tension that will be (partially) resolved by panel 1B (v 21). It differs from the subsequent allusions to God's activity in constituting a statement about events in its own right: there is no nontheological description of the fall of Jerusalem, only this theological one. In contrast, the other two such allusions (vv 9, 17) are parenthetic background statements interpreting phenomena that are also described in nontheological terms (vv 10–16, 4/18–20); the story would be quite complete as a story without these comments. The allusion to God's activity in panel 2 differs from the other two in that it occurs in the "resolution" part of the story, panel 2B. The other allusions occur in the "tension" part of the story, in panels 1A and 3A, and thus constitute anticipations or hints of eventual resolution. Panel 2A contains no hint of this kind, though v 4 gives hints in its own way. The phrase נתן להם האלהים ("God gave them," v 17) thus overtly expresses in panel 2B the possible implication of the verse in panel 2A. In panel 3A, ויתן האלהים ("God gave/made," v 9) indicates that the possibility of Daniel's remaining undefiled is based on God's grace as well as on Daniel's determination (v 8), though it does not indicate how either may come to fruition (indeed v 10 all but undoes the hope encouraged by v 9). It differs from the other two occurrences of the phrase because נתן here has a slightly different meaning, closer to those of שים or שית ("put," "set") than to those of יהב or חלק ("give," "allocate"). The three references to God's activity contribute to a series of developments and reversals of movement in Dan 1 as a whole, as the agents and subjects of the verbs change: Nebuchadnezzar . . . (v 1), the Lord . . . (v 2); so the king and the head of staff . . . (vv 2–7), but Daniel . . . (v 8), and God . . . (v 9) [relating to what precedes and to what follows]; again, the head of staff . . . (v 10), so Daniel and the guardian . . . (vv 11–16), and God . . . (v 17). . . . God's giving thus plays a key role in the story's unfolding.

Panel 1A begins by setting alongside each other the autonomous rulers of two independent realms, *Jehoiakim king of Judah* and *Nebuchadnezzar king of Babylon* (Jehoiakim was actually puppet king of a puppet state, but that historical fact lies outside the brackets of the story). No sooner are they named, however, than the former's subordination to the latter, to God, and to the narrator becomes clear. The two verses reflect the straightforward Hebrew narrative style of books such as Kings and Chronicles, and their fulsome repetitiveness ("Jehoiakim king of Judah . . . Nebuchadnezzar king of Babylon . . . Jehoiakim king of Judah . . .") derives from this style, but in this context its effect is to underline the momentous implications of the clash between imperial power and people of God. Two kings and their kingdoms, widely separated by geography and by their location in God's purpose, are brought into harsh juxtaposition, Nebuchadnezzar moving aggressively west and then returning triumphantly east with his plunder.

The movement and violence of the action is conveyed by making Nebuchadnezzar the subject of the four verbs בוא, צור, and הביא (twice) ("he came," "he blockaded," "he took"); בוא and הביא stand at the center of each of the verses and hold the unit together. Jehoiakim, Judah, Jerusalem, and the temple articles appear only in the opening dating phrase and than as the direct or indirect object of the five verbs in the two verses. They are passive objects in the hands of Nebuchadnezzar, the narrator—and God, for he is the subject of the middle of the five verbs. The tension introduced by the reference to the Lord's giving Jehoiakim up is heightened by the further references to deity in v 2. The scandal of what is happening is conveyed by juxtaposing the phrase בית האלהים "the house of God" both with the preceding reference to the Lord's giving over, and with the following fulsome descriptions of the destiny of the temple articles, שנער "Shinar," בית אלהיו "his god's house," בית אוצר אלהיו "his god's treasure house." In making its points, Daniel is characteristically careful in its choice of words and phrases; this often involves fulsomeness and repetition rather than syntactical elegance.

Panel 2A (vv 3–7) takes up from panel 1A by reusing the verb הביא ("he took" once more: there is one further geographical movement to record. With the transition to the court-tale the style becomes simpler (e.g., "the king" or "Nebuchadnezzar," not both). It turns out that the repetition of the ponderous "Jehoiakim, king of Judah" in v 2 constituted a curtain call. Now only one king appears, and panel 2A can assume it is clear who "the king" is (vv 3, 4, 5 three times). The portrait of the Israelites as the helpless victims of enemy power is again underlined by the syntax. Nebuchadnezzar and his lieutenant are the subject of a further series of forceful verbs, with the Israelites as their object: הביא (v 3), למד (v 4), מנה (v 5—indirect obj), גדל (v 5). שים (v 7—indirect obj): take them, teach them, allocate them, train them, name them.

There is some inelegance about the verses' syntax (v 4b and the two clauses in v 5b are rather loosely related to their sentences), partly because, though formally reported speech, vv 3–5 come alive in such a way that we almost hear the king's actual words, catching the irony that he is heard prescribing qualities from the exiles' own scriptures for the young men he plans to reeducate. The pressure of their being swept into an alien environment is also suggested by the appearance of a series of Akkadian and Persian terms and names: Ashpenaz (OP), chief of staff (ultimately Akk.), nobles (OP), Chaldean, supplies (OP), and the four men's own new names. In the context of these foreign-sounding expressions v 4a stands out for its accumulation of expressions from OT tradition, especially the string of wisdom terms. The significance of these lies not so much in their individual meaning (otherwise root ידע "know" would hardly appear three times) as in their cumulative effect set against the foreign terms; heaping up words of related meaning in this way is a further device of Daniel (cf. 2:2. The pen-portrait of the Israelites (vv 3b–4a) set in the context of clauses that put great pressure on them (vv

3a, 4b–7) heightens the tension of the story suggested by panel 1A, yet also hints that things will turn out all right.

The dual theme of panel 3A is stated by the repeated key verbs גאל "defile" (twice in v 8, at the beginning of panel 3[i]A) and נסה "test" (twice nearer the close of panel 3[ii]A, at the beginning and end of the speech in vv 12–13). But first, panel 3A, like panel 2A, links with the preceding panel by repeating a verb, וישם "he determined." It is not the custom of Hebrew narrative to mark an important transition by means of a clearly adversative conjunction; *waw* generally does both for "and" and for "but." So no disjunction is advertised by the *waw*. Then the verb to which it is linked simply repeats the one that had appeared twice in the previous verse; again, no disjunction is overtly indicated. It transpires, however, that the subject of the verb has changed, and so has its meaning. The reappearance of the verb with a different nuance is the more effective after the repetition of it within v 7 itself (cf. the three appearances of הביא "take" in vv 2–3; also subsequent pointed repetitions of words—often in different contexts or with different nuances—in 2:13, 16, 18 [בעא, "seek/ask"]; 2:16, 24 [ועל, "go"; 2:17, 24 [אזל, "go"]). With v 8, for the first time in the book an Israelite becomes the subject of a main verb. Daniel seizes the initiative from the Babylonians, and the story begins that reversal of movement that characterizes chap. 1 and the book as a whole. Daniel is still the object of the verb נתן, God being the subject and the Babylonians the indirect object (v 9, cf. v 2), but there is nothing aggressive or threatening about this giving/making. The initiative of God has Daniel as the grammatical object, but it is Ashpenaz who is now the object of manipulation by Daniel, the narrator, and God.

The earlier scenes have been all action and have moved quickly. The central scene slows the action down and builds up the suspense, reporting on motivation, reflection, and feelings as well as action (vv 8, 9, 10), and relating actual conversations rather than reporting speech indirectly (vv 10–13). The test itself, and the associated move from Ashpenaz to the guardian also serve to slow the action down. Whereas the rest of Dan 1 gives priority to plot rather than to characterization, here it suits the plot to allow Daniel and Ashpenaz to come alive as we are told of their conflicting inner feelings expressed in their outward exchange. The story becomes not merely a lead-in to chaps. 2–7 but a story in its own right (Plöger). Although it slows down, much is happening in these few verses. Daniel's determined action contrasts with that of Ashpenaz (v 8), and God's involvement (v 9) suggests that the story is on the way to a quick resolution. But this turns out to have been a false dawn and the story threatens to collapse; suspense is heightened (v 10). In turn, the threat dissolves as Daniel survives the test of v 10 by offering the test described in vv 11–14. Arioch's goodwill has hinted that a resolution should be possible, and Daniel's proposal of a test period takes up this hint. His accepting of the risk involved in such a test is impressively (under)stated in v 13b. Brave words understated are a feature of the trial stories in Daniel (cf. 3:17–18; also 6:10 and the total absence of words on Daniel's part in 6:10–17), contrasting with the generally explicit and expansive style of dialogue and prayers.

The shorter closing panels of the denouement, vv 15–21, substantially resolve the tension set up by the longer opening ones. Each takes up motifs from the corresponding opening panel; little that is formally new is introduced. Thus vv 15–16 naturally follow on from vv 8–14: v 15 takes up the language of vv 13–14 (at the end of the ten days, their appearance, look, the young men who eat the king's supplies), or reverses it (*good* for *grim*), or goes beyond it (their bodies look better-built), while v 16 follows on from v 15 but takes up the language of vv 8–12 (the guardian, their supplies and the wine they were to drink, give them vegetarian food) or goes beyond it (continued to take away). We were prepared for the test to be successful, so panel 3ii comes to a climax in v 15 with the test achieving more than we expected. Perhaps panel 3i does the same: v 16 may refer to the guardian's imposing the vegetarian diet on the other young men! (but see n. 16.a). The resolution in panel 3B (vv 15–16) is thus simpler and shorter than the statement in panel 3A (vv 8–14); the heart of the story lies in Daniel's determination to avoid defilement, and his bold handling of his masters.

The resolution in panel 2B (vv 17–20), in contrast, is almost as long as the statement in panel 2A (vv 3–7); it dominates vv 15–21 as a whole. It does not follow directly from vv 15–16 but begins resumptively (v 17) by recalling us to vv 3–7 in an asyndetic noun phrase ("Now those four young men: God gave them . . ."). This reference to God's involvement, held back from its "natural" place in v 4, emphasizes the importance of panel 2B. It is not explicit whether v 17 refers to God's original gift of wisdom, which lay behind v 4, to his gift evidenced in the result of their training, or to both; but the verse's concern is to clarify a different point, namely that God (not Nebuchadnezzar or Babylon) is the source of wisdom, whenever it comes. After this opening, vv 18–19a work, as vv 15–16 had, by taking phrases from corresponding earlier verses (at the end, the king said, to bring/take, the chief/head of the palace staff, before the king/Nebuchadnezzar) (v 18), and by using terms that go beyond these, to show that the four did not merely survive their training but triumphed in it (v 19a). In turn vv 19b–20, like v 16, go on from immediate event to further consequences. Once more these are first stated in terms which take up words from panel 2A (v 19b), then in terms which utilize new expressions indicating that results again exceeded expectations (v 20). Yet again, careful choice of expression is combined with some syntactical inelegance: חכמת בינה "insightful learning" is an old construct phrase, החרטמים האשפים "the diviners, the chanters" is asyndetic.

Panel 3D (v 21) in turn briefly closes off (in part) the questions raised in panel 3A by alluding to the moment when it would be possible for people and temple articles to return to Jerusalem (see 2 Chr 36:20–23; Ezra 1:7–11). Thus the chapter opens with Nebuchadnezzar but closes with Cyrus, opens with the beginning of the exile but closes with the beginning of the return, and shows how Daniel links the two.

Setting

The story's motifs and concerns point toward a setting in the dispersion, in a context where Jew and pagan could live together, where the question of service in a foreign court was a significant one (cf. Nehemiah), and where the tension between that possibility and the demands of Jewish faith would be a pressing religious question (Darr, Porteous). The story suggests the aspirations and concerns of upper-class Jews in the eastern dispersion, wanting to succeed in their pagan environment but aware of their calling to remain faithful to their Jewishness (Collins, *Daniel* [FOTL] 36–37; against Steck). Since the close of the story (v 21) presupposes the Persian period and the story itself makes key use of Persian words, the story was evidently composed not before the Persian period. There are no specific pointers to the (pre-Maccabean) Greek period, but neither can this be excluded. Persian culture continued to be very significant then; the period saw a revival of cuneiform learning in Babylon (Wacholder, *Dawn,* 212–15; Frye, *Heritage,* 143). Nor does the story contain specific pointers to the Maccabean era. The concern with assimilation to pagan practices and with dietary defilement could fit that period (Tcherikover, *Civilization,* 460), but no better than any other time from the exile onward. The story's openness to serving in the pagan court, to learning from pagan culture, and to finding favor with the imperial authorities, and its lack of reference to persecution, do not suggest one written with second-century Jerusalem in mind. "The issue is not persecution but the search for a viable life-style amid competing political and religious claims" (Hall, 159, noting also [154–56] that the stories in Daniel concern themselves with the problems of the individual, whereas the visions focus on the corporate experience and crisis). (The acceptance of pagan names does not clash with a second-century date, as this practice was not controversial even then: see Tcherikover, *Civilization,* 346–47).

The story has a setting in the actual book of Daniel; indeed, it provides the setting for it, almost constituting an anticipatory midrash on it (Plöger, Hartman). Panel 1 sets the book in the context of the seventy years of exile covered by the sequence of stories and visions, from the Babylonian kings via Darius the Mede to Cyrus the Persian. It anticipates Daniel's functioning through this whole period (Kock, *TLZ* 85 [1960] 829). It introduces Shinar, the home of idolatry (Zech 5) (cf. chap. 3) and the location of the proud owner of Dabel (Gen 11) (cf. chap. 4), explains how articles from the Jerusalem temple came to be available for Belshazzar's idolatrous revelry (chap. 5), and lays the foundation for considering when Jeremiah's promise of Jerusalem's restoration would be fulfilled (chap. 9). For the self-understanding of what we call the postexilic period, the experience of exile continued to shape the questions that faith had to address. Daniel thus begins from the moment when that exile began, and in anticipation looks to the moment when the seventy years "ended." The whole period is set within the sovereignty of God.

Panel 2 explains how the central figures in the book came to be serving in the palace of Babylon, sometimes using Babylonian names, sometimes Israelite ones, associated with the Babylonian sages but possessing a wisdom far more impressive than theirs, and how Daniel in particular gained his expertise in visions and dreams. As men of discernment (משכילים, v 4, cf. v 17), they model the wisdom of the discerning teachers of the time of final pressure (11:33, 35; 12:3, 10). The panel holds the four young men together yet gives Daniel special prominence, and thus answers questions raised by the way they function largely separately in later stories. Like panel 1B (v 21), panel 2B (vv 17–20) looks beyond the occasion of the immediately following stories: v 17 applies to the book as a whole, vv 18–19a describes the end of their training, vv 19b–20 refers to their position at court through the rest of Nebuchadnezzar's reign.

As panel 3 contains the material that makes chap. 1 a story in its own right, it relates less explicitly to the other stories in the book, though Daniel's insistence on avoiding being tainted through serving in the pagan court answers a question possibly raised by chaps. 2, 4, and 5, while his willingness to stand up to the test in order to maintain his faithfulness introduces the theme of chaps. 3 and 6. The story's central question, then, is "How could these four famous young men have gained such success in the pagan court, without being tainted by it?" And the chapter as a whole thus endorses the lifestyle of the royal courtier and his wisdom (Collins, *Vision,* 30), yet assures us that Daniel and his friends in exile gained success in a way that avoided losing holiness; they proved that holiness was the source of health, and that God was the source of wisdom and the power behind history.

Comment

1–2 Virtually every word parallels earlier material: see esp. 2 Chr 33:6–7; Jer 20:4–5; 39:1; 46:2; also 2 Chr 35:19 (for מלכות, "reign," a favorite word in Chronicles and Daniel); Gen 12:1–9 or Zech 5:5–11 (for Shinar). Daniel replaces the name *Yahweh* in Jeremiah and Chronicles by אדני "the Lord" and האלהים "God." That may issue from reverence, but the effect is also to undermine any hint that he is merely Israel's national God and the temple its national shrine, as Babylon has it's gods and shrines. The titles "the Lord" and "God" belong only to Yahweh; they have absolute implications, hinting that the exile happened by the act of the sovereign God who is also Israel's God, not Nebuchadnezzar's (Lacocque, Plöger).

The Babylonian Chronicle indicates that Jehoiakim's reign saw several aggressive visits to Palestine by Nebuchadnezzar (see, e.g., T. R. Hobbs, *2 Kings* [WBC 13 (1985)] on 2 Kgs 24). Neither biblical nor extrabiblical sources require that Jehoiakim was actually taken to Babylon. Extrabiblical sources do not specifically refer to a siege of Jerusalem. Nebuchadnezzar is perhaps called king proleptically in Dan 1:1, as in Jer 46:2. The invasion is presumably that referred to in Jer 25, Jeremiah's "seventy years" prophecy, though the date there is Jehoiakim's fourth year. The one-year difference arises with other OT dates through the use of different methods of reckoning (Bruce, "Chronology"; Wiseman, *Notes,* 16–18). The years of a king's reign can be counted from the new year before his accession, from the accession itself, or from the next new year; thus the fall of Jerusalem can be dated in Nebuchadnezzar's eighteenth year (3:1 OG; 4:1 OG; Jer 52:29) or in his nineteenth (2 Kgs 25:8; Jer 52:12). Here, however, the difference may mean that the date is not intended as a precise one (and 1:1–2 may be conflating accounts of the subjugations of Jerusalem and the exiles of Judeans). Danielic dates cluster in the first three years of a king's reign (Plöger), and perhaps affirm

God's Lordship at key transition points in history ("first" or "third" can be merely concrete ways of saying "at the beginning" or "not long after the beginning": J. B. Segal, "Numerals in the Old Testament," *JSS* 10 [1965] 2–20). Thus the date probably makes a more than merely historical point. The OG dates just mentioned invite the reader to recall that the image-maker of chap. 3, subjected to God's judgment in chap. 4, is the man who destroyed and pillaged the temple in 587 (Bruce, *OTS* 20 [1977] 27–28). This MT chronological note opens the book with the beginning of Jeremiah's seventy years (cf. Larssen, *JJTS* 18 [1967] 417–23), whose literal end comes at the chapter's close (v 21; cf. 2 Chr 36:20–23), but which in another sense continues through the period the book as a whole is concerned with (cf. chap. 9). It also sets the four young men among the first of the exiles, the elite, the good figs of Jer 24 (Calvin).

For the temple "articles," see 2 Chr 36:7, 10, 18; lists related to 587 in Jer 52:17–23 and to 537 in Ezra 1:9–11. Many were made of precious metals (cf. Dan 5:2–3) and would be worthwhile plunder; cf. the references to tribute in the Babylonian Chronicle. They are also of religious significance, being the Jerusalem temple's nearest thing to images. Removing them is thus a sign of the victory of Nebuchadnezzar and his god over the Israelite king and his god. Wars were fought in a god's name and plunder thus belonged to him. The temple articles are his booty. They are taboo and are put into the "treasury" that belonged to a temple for this purpose: cf. 2 Chr 5:1, referring back to 1 Chr 18:11 (also Josh 6:19, 24), and more specifically 2 Chr 36:18; Isa 39:2, 4; 45:3; though according to 2 Chr 36:7, Nebuchadnezzar took the articles to his היכל ("palace"?).

Shinar as a term for Babylonia, the southeastern part of modern Iraq, is an archaism in the OT (e.g., Gen 10:10; 11:2; 14:1, 9; then only Josh 7:21; Isa 11:11; Zech 5:11) and outside it (corresponding to Šanhara in second-millennium cuneiform texts: see H. D. Güterbock, "Sargon of Akkad . . . ," *JCS* 18 [1964] 3). In the OT, the name especially suggests a place of false religion, self-will, and self-aggrandizement (Gen 11:1–9; Zech 5:11). "His god" is probably Marduk/Bel (cf. 4:5 [8]; Bel and Dragon; Jer 50:2; 51:44), less likely Nabu (cf. "Nebuchadnezzar"). Both appear in Isa 46:1, but Nebuchadnezzar's inscriptions refer most to Marduk, Nabu being his father's god.

3–5 Taking young nobles to Babylon might have various objects: to bring home Judah's vassal status in realtion to Babylon (not to Egypt now), to discourage them from rebelling, to Babylon-ize their future leadership, to add to the manpower of temple and palace. Educating them in Babylonian learning and giving them a place in the court presumably has the latter aims in mind; the effective contribution they come to offer in the court, however, goes beyond what Nebuchadnezzar would be expecting.

The young men are to be *Israelites:* the term is used in the theological sense, to mean "members of Yahweh's people" (as in Chr, Ezra, Neh), for the qualification "some of the royal family" requires them to be genealogically Judeans (cf. v 6). As their royal background should itself imply, they are to be such as will have already received some education to prepare them for political life. Four substantially synonymous terms are used to describe what this education should have given them (v 4): השכיל "give attention to," "have insight," "teach"; חכם "be wise," "understand"; ידע "know," "acknowledge," "be skilled"; and בין "observe," "discern," "perceive" (see *TWAT;* R. N. Whybray [*The Intellectual Tradition in the Old Testament* (DZAW 135 [1974]) 101–4] notes that in Daniel the second of these roots, the OT's most common term for the wise/wisdom, comes only in chaps. 1–6). The description is reminiscent of that of Joseph in Gen 41:33, 39. In combination the four terms convey an impression of young men well-versed in the practical learning embodied in a book such as Proverbs. While such learning is not overtly directed to the education of palace and court, it would naturally be the special province of the king and others responsible for state affairs, and it is embodied above all in the royal figure of Solomon. In the Mesopotamian court, one may compare the role of Ahiqar as counselor, and his Proverbs-like teaching (*ANET* 427–30). The terms are also later brought into connection with supernaturally endowed, revelatory wisdom, and in this context education in Chaldean learning presumably refers not merely to the Babylonian language itself, a dialect of Akkadian (though they would also need to know that), but to the script and contents of the cuneiform texts preserved among the "Chaldean" sages, which formed the basis of their work as court counselors (cf. the recurrence of ספר "literature" in v 17).

The Kaldu were a people from southern Babylonia to whom Nebuchadnezzar's father Nabopolassar belonged; they were thus the ruling caste in Babylonia during the exile. In the OT, however, *Chaldeans* is the regular word for the people of Babylonia in general, though it was not used with this meaning by the Babylonians themselves. In Daniel, it also refers specifically to the Babylonian sages, though again the word was not used with this meaning by the Babylonians themselves; outside the OT, it first appears in Herodotus 1:181–83. Given the OT's idiosyncratic use of it, however, this hardly rules out its being used in this way among Jews even in the exile, still less in the Persian period (cf. v 21). Strabo 16.1.6 (first century B.C.) uses the term both to refer to the sages and as an ethnic term in its original sense. There is no reason to infer from usage such as Daniel's and Strabo's that the Chaldeans were Chaldean by race (against Rowley, *ExpT* 38 [1926–27] 425–26).

The Babylonian sages combined many of the functions fulfilled by wise men, prophets, and priests in Israel, though they are to be distinguished from those cultic functionaries who were more especially concerned with the temple and its ritual. They were the guardians of the sacred traditional lore developed and preserved in Mesopotamia over centuries, covering natural history, astronomy, mathematics, medicine, myth, and chronicle. Much of this learning had a practical purpose, being designed to be applied to life by means of astrology, oneirology, hepatoscopy and the study of other organs, rites of purification, sacrifice, incantation, exorcism and other forms of divination and magic.

The practice of divination presupposes that supernatural forces sometimes reveal events to come or the significance of events that do happen—either of their own accord or in response to human questioning—in the way they arrange natural phenomena such as the stars or weather or the form or behavior of different creatures. Such phenomena thus constitute warnings of coming events, which the subject can take steps to avoid by apotropaic rites, or explanations of illnesses or other experiences, from which the subject can escape by such means as purification rites, exorcism, incantation, and prayer. The library Asshurbanipal assembled in the seventh century is dominated by divinatory texts that record phenomena of various kinds and the events they had presaged, and by linguistic texts that enabled Akkadian-speaking sages to use such texts in the traditional Sumerian; many further texts consist in incantations, prayers, and conjurations for exorcism and protection. Many of these date from centuries before Asshurbanipal; others continued to be written and collected through the Babylonian, Persian, and Hellenistic periods. By applying their learning in such ways to questions affecting king and nation, the sages fulfilled their role as the king's advisers and protectors whom he would consult before taking any action, and as the servants of the state. The stories in Dan 2; 4; and 5 have this activity as their background (cf. also Isa 44:25; 47:13; Esth 1:13), while Dan 1:3–4 may reflect an awareness of the requirements of descent, physical wholeness, and training that they had to fulfill. (On the sages and their work, see, e.g., Oppenheim, *Mesopotamia; JNES* 33 [1974] 197–220; Saggs, *Babylon;* A. J. Sachs, "Babylonian Horoscopes," *JCS* 6 [1952] 44–75; W. G. Lambert, "Dingir.šà.dib.ba. Incantations," *JNES* 23 [1964] 267–327; E. Leichty, *The Omen Series Šumma Izbu* [TCS 4 (1970); *La divination en Mésopotamie ancienne et dans les régions voisines* (xive Rencontre Assyriologique Internationale; Paris: PUF, 1966)].)

According to Oppenheim, the *palace* included "the throne room in which the king received ambassadors and other visitors, the large courtyard in front of it, and a special hall, perhaps used for official banquets. . . . Living quarters for the king and his entourage, as well as storage rooms, were built around these principal areas" (*Mesopotamia,* 105). Into it "poured the tribute of subjugated and even of distant peoples, the yield of royal estates, and the products of royal workshops. From its storehouses had to be fed and clad, according to their status, the members of the royal family, the administrative officials of country and palace, the personnel of the royal household, the standing army and a host of serfs, slaves, and others who depended on the palace for their living" (*Mesopotamia,* 104). A list of the personnel of Nebuchadnezzar's court pictures him "surrounded by the administrators of his palace and of his realm, by bureaucrats and vanquished kings who lived at his court" (*Mesopotamia,* 101). For the provision for exiled foreigners from the palace, cf. the Babylonian provision records which mention Jehoiachin, other Judeans, and other foreign nationals (*ANET* 308b; *DOTT* 84–86); 2 Kgs 25:29–30, which also uses the phrase "a daily allowance"; and other OT instances from other contexts (Gen 43:34; 2 Sam 11:8; Dan 11:26).

6–7 The Hebrew names are all known from a variety of OT contexts (see *Form*), though not all as the names of priests (against Gammie, *VT* 31 [1981] 283); the four have no specifically priestly traits, and the portrayal in vv 3–5 is royal. Each lacks a patronymic (like the names in Neh 8 and 10) and each is theophoric: Daniel, "God is my judge"; Hananiah, "Yah has been gracious"; Mishael, "Who is what God is?"; Azariah, "Yah has helped." Giving (new) names as a sign of (new) ownership and thus (new) destiny (Lacocque) was common court practice: cf. Joseph/Zaphnath-paaneh, Eliakim/Jehoiakim, Mattaniah/Zedekiah, Hadassah/Esther, Joshua/Jason (2 Macc 4:7).

Zerubbabel's and Mordecai's Hebrew names are not even mentioned in the OT; evidently the use of a foreign name could be quite acceptable (cf. the use of the Babylonian names of the three young men in chap. 3). There is thus a contrast between the giving of a theophoric name to replace a neutral one (Jacob-Israel, Hoshua-Joshua) (cf. O. Eissfeldt, "Renaming in the Old Testament," *Words and Meanings* [FS D. W. Thomas, ed. P. R. Ackroyd and B. Lindars; Cambridge/New York: CUP, 1968] 73–79) and the replacing of an Israelite theophoric name by one of alien significance (see n. 7.b-b). The three friends' two sets of names appear together only here. The Babylonian ones come on their own in chap. 3 (also 2:49), in the apparently older material. The Hebrew names come on their own in 1:11, 19; 2:17.

8 Since Daniel and the other three are not the only exiles undergoing the training (see v 6, "*Among* them were . . ."), Daniel's decision presumably involves standing firm when other Israelites do not; the youths with whom they are compared in vv 10–16, 19 are likewise presuambly other Israelites as well as Babylonian and other foreigners. His concern about defilement corresponds to a characteristic feature of Leviticus and Ezekiel, though one also present elsewhere in the OT. He uses the verb גאל, a mostly postexilic word, but having a similar range of meanings to the more common חלל (Dan 11:31) and טמא.

Underlying references to defilement is the assumption that there are objects and activities that are proper to some groups but not to others (e.g., to the nations but not to Israel, or to laypeople but not to priests). The distinctiveness of the smaller group is preserved by its avoiding the objects and activities in question. Expressed thus, holiness/cleanness/defilement are wholly theological or ritual categories. They are also applied to moral and religious activities: thus murder or worshiping other gods, as well as contact with a corpse or eating pork, defiles a person or a people and threatens their identity. (On holiness/cleanness/defilement, see, e.g., G. J. Wenham, *The Book of Leviticus* [Grand Rapids: Eerdmans, 1979] 18–25 and references.)

Having to live in a foreign country is an inherently defiling experience (cf. Hos 9:3–4; Amos 7:17). Various considerations might lead Jews in exile to fear defilement through what they ate.

(a) The food and drink of the palace would be likely to have come from the temple and thus to have been offered to the deity, as in Israel it would have been offered to Yahweh: cf. 5:3–4; Bel; also Exod 34:15; 1 Cor 8–10; Acts 15:20, 29; Rev 2:14, 20. But this problem would also arise with vegetarian food, which Daniel accepts: cf. the offering of flour as well as meat and wine in Bel 3. This consideration thus leads elsewhere to unease about all pagan food (Jdt 10:5; 12:2; Add Esth 14:17; Tob 1:10–11). But Daniel does not refuse to eat at all from the royal table; in this sense he is no more scrupulous than Jehoiachin (2 Kgs 25:29). (On everyday food and on sacrifices in Babylonia, see Saggs, *Babylon,* 172–76, 351–54; Oppenheim, *Mesopotamia,* 42–45, 188–93.)

(b) The palace would not observe laws in the Torah about which animals can be eaten and how they are to be killed: see Lev 11; Deut 12:23–25; cf. the fear of Ezek 4:9–17 (especially v 14), in the exile; 1 Macc 1:47, 62–63; 2 Macc 6:18–7:42, during the Antiochene persecution (cf. 4 Macc 5; Acts 15:20, 29). But the reference to wine as well as meat suggests this is not the focus. Bevan describes Daniel as exemplifying "the most minute attention to the Divine Law"; this seems to import into Daniel the law-centered piety known elsewhere in the postexilic period. If Daniel is concerned about the law (the term does not appear here), it is only in the broad sense of Israel's religion.

(c) Meat and wine is festival food, and abstaining from it is a sign of mourning or penitence and would be appropriate in exile: cf. 10:3; Isa 22:13; *T. Reub.* 1.10; *T. Jud.* 15.4. Further, meat and wine suggest food fit for nobility, whereas the four young men ask for peasant food. But this understanding would not account for Daniel's reference to defilement.

(d) Abstention from meat and wine was an ascetic practice among various groups, including the Essenes and the hasidim (so Hengel, *Judentum,* 387 [ET 1:213]; cf. C. E. B. Cranfield, *Romans* [ICC, 1975–79] 694). One reason for such abstention is preparation for a divine revelation (2 Esd 9:24; 12:51) (see J. Behm, *TWNT* 2:687–88 [ET 690]). Yet no such ascetic significance is attached to Daniel's self-denial here; contrast 10:2–3, where he takes on a similar diet in the course of seeking a word from God (see also 9:3; cf. Russell, *Method,* 169–73). Daniel is not refraining from something good in order to seek God, but refraining from something incompatible with being committed to God at all; he is not seeking an inner freedom, but an outward distinctiveness.

(e) Accepting the king's provisions would indicate dependence on him, entry into a covenant-style relationship with him, becoming his courtiers, and accepting a commitment to supporting him as he supported them (cf. 11:26) (Baldwin). But it is not clear why this should be spoken of as defilement; and anyway, they *do* accept a position as the king's courtiers.

(f) The Mishnah infers from Lev 11:37–38 that grain does not become unclean through contact with meat as long as the grain is kept dry (*Makshirin* 1:1; *Ugtsin* 3:1; with Danby's notes). But it is not clear that Lev 11:37–38 refers to grain for eating or that Daniel alludes to that understanding of it.

(g) Pagan food and drink may simply epitomize the pagan uncleanness associated with exile (cf. Isa 52:11). This reflects the fact that what we eat and drink, like what we wear and how we speak, generally constitutes an outward expression of our self-identity and commitments. These are particularly significant for groups in exile or under persecution (cf. Lacocque). Daniel's abstinence thus symbolizes his avoiding assimilation.

9–14 The romance and scriptural motif of the hero in exile getting on surprisingly good terms with pagan officials (see *Form*) perhaps contrasted with the usual experience of ordinary people in general and of Jews in particular, and was thus appreciated as expressing what such people would like to experience (cf. O. Wallis's account of a Jewish slave's failure to gain his liberty in Babylon, "Aus dem Leben jüdischen Sklaven in Babylon," *Festschrift für Ernst Barnikol* [Berlin: Evangelische, 1964] 14–20). Daniel was actually risking his own head (Calvin). The reply (v 10) need not constitute a refusal: it raises a problem, but leaves open the possibility of agreeing to Daniel's request if the problem can be overcome. Its implication then is, "Yes, if it doesn't involve me and if it doesn't make the king ask questions." Verses 11–15 meet these conditions. ". . . and you forfeit my head to the king": the statement could be metaphorical (cf. our "on your head be it"), but in the light of the picture of Nebuchadnezzar in 2:12; 3:19–20, it is entirely reasonable to take the fear literally (cf. the Red Queen's "Off with his head" in Lewis Carroll's *Alice in Wonderland*).

"Test your servants" (v 12): there are few biblical references to or stories about people testing other people. For נסה, cf. only 1 Kgs 10:1 = 2 Chr 9:1; but note also בחן in the Joseph story (Gen 42:15–16). "Ten days": ten is not a symbolic number, nor is ten days a common period for a trial (against Bentzen; Rev 2:10 is surely dependent on Dan 1). Ten is merely a standard round number (cf. v 18; 7:7; Gen 31:7; Num 14:22; Neh 4:12; Job 19:3; Zech 8:23; *Jub.* 19.8; *T. Jos.* 2.7; *m. ʾAboth* 5.1–6) and ten days simply suggests a period short enough not to arouse suspicion yet long enough for effects to be seen (cf. Gen 24:55). See H. A. Brongers, "Die Zehnzahl in der Bibel und ihrer Umwelt," *Studia biblica et semitica* (FS T. C. Vriezen [Wageningen: Veenman, 1966]) 30–45; P. Hauck, TWNT 2:35–36 [ET 36–37]. On the nature of, and reasons for, the vegetarian diet, see on v 8.

15–16 This motif appears in *T. Jos.* 3.4 ("I fasted for those seven years, and seemed to the Egyptians like someone who was living richly, for those who fast for God's sake receive graciousness of countenance"). The language itself corresponds closely and uniquely to that used to describe the cattle in Gen 41:2, 18!

17–20 The resumptive opening to v 17 indicates that panel 2B begins here; v 17 does not follow from v 16 as a reward of faithfulness or a fruit of asceticism—indeed the endowments of v 17 may have been given earlier. In v 4 the terms refer to rational/experiential/court wisdom, here they denote supernaturally revealed knowledge ("mantic wisdom"), and in this connection they will be key terms in following chapters. The wisdom ideal of court and school is thus brought into contact with a characterization of Daniel as a man of revelatory wisdom (Müller, *UF* 1 [1969] 86). On dream interpretation, see further chap. 2 *Comment.* The narrative hardly sees visions and dreams as a lower gift than prophecy (against Montgomery); the stress is on the excellence of what Daniel is given, which parallels the experience of Joseph and other patriarchs, and corresponds to the demands of the contexts in which Daniel has to function (cf. Young). Cf. also the description of a prophet in Num 12:6.

21 The reference to Cyrus's first year may indicate that chap. 1 originally introduced not more than chaps. 1–9 (see 10:1) (cf. Jer 1:1–3 in relation to less than the whole of Jeremiah). But the inference is hazardous, as panel 1's concern is to reach from one end of the exile to the other, following 2 Chr 36:20–23; Ezra 1, with their reference to the temple articles being returned at that date. Daniel's continuing at court after this is neither implied (Hammer suggests he was in retirement at 10:1) nor precluded (for the עד "until" cf. Ps 110:1; 112:8 [Poole]). The verse's concern is rather to assure its hearers that Daniel (and the temple articles: see Ackroyd, "Vessels") lived safely through their long exile: and so may hearers through theirs (chap. 9). It thus parallels the encouraging conclusions to other chapters.

Explanation

1–2 The destiny of independent Judah was determined in the reign of Josiah: theologically, when he could not root out the paganism of Judah's religious life; politically, when he could not bolster ailing Assyria's hegemony in Mesopotamia. Assyria was replaced by the Chaldean dynasty in Babylon, under Nebopolassar (625–605) and his great son Nebuchadnezzar II (604–562), who sealed the fate of Assyria (and Judah) by his victory at Carchemish, just before his father's death, and just after Josiah's.

The reigns of Jehoahaz, Jehoiakim, Jehoiachin, and Zedekiah were thus a story of defeat, humiliation, submission, and exile at the hands of Egypt and Babylon. The city that Israel called "the perfection of beauty, the joy of the whole world" (Ps 48:3 [2]) is blockaded, assaulted, defeated, raped, and pillaged, by alien, pagan hands and feet. The shrine that David and Solomon had dreamed of and built, and that Yahweh had undertaken to treat at his house (so that people could be sure to find him at home there), is desecrated and torn apart. Its furnishings are transported if they can be carried (destroyed, if they cannot), and taken to grace and to glorify the shrines of pagan gods hundreds of miles away in a city that prophets had declared was ripe for judgment, and whose name stands for human achievement, glory, power, and pride. The royal line which had reigned in Jerusalem for 400 years, back almost to the time of the first Nebuchadnezzar six dynasties ago in Babylon, that line to which God had committed himself in perpetuity, has been treated as a series of puppet kings to be bullied, maneuvered, and moved about by one whose name will also henceforth stand for worldly achievement, glory, power, and might (so that pretenders after the Babylonian throne will adopt it). To all appearances, the God of Jerusalem has been defeated by the gods of Babylon. Removing the possessions of the Jerusalem temple and taking them to a temple in Babylon encourages this impression.

It is not surprising that this event, potentially as devastating for Judah's self-understanding as it was for its bricks and mortar, challenges its people of faith to a deep and wide-ranging quest after its significance and after reactions appropriate to it. The responses affirmed within the OT agree that the fall of Jerusalem is not to be explained by Yahweh's impotence or inactivity. Nor, as many people today might assume, was it merely the chance outworking of political (and personality) factors. It is the deliberate act of Israel's own God. Often in the OT it is seen as his holy and jealous response to the apostasy, neglect, disorder, and complacency of Israel's life. Yet Dan 1 makes no reference to the sins of preexilic generations, perhaps because it presupposes a postexilic perspective (v 21), perhaps because those hardly explain the presence in Babylon of godly young men such as Daniel and his friends. These young men in exile, and the later generation to which the book speaks as people experiencing an exile far longer than originally envisaged (9:2, 24), acknowledge the sinfulness they share with the rest of Israel (9:3–19), but this sinfulness is not appealed to as the explanation for the exile. That event is given no explanation except in terms of the hand of God (v 2). A mysterious initiative on his part lies behind the extraordinary sequence of events comprised by Nebuchadnezzar's expedition, his blockade of Jerusalem, Jehoiakim's defeat, the plundering of the temple, and the glorifying of Babylonian idols.

For people in exile, as an explanation that was vague, but as a place to be it was secure. Their story looks as if it has come adrift from the story of the people of God, but it has not really done so; they are still within the sphere of his activity, even though it does not look like it. They are not mere pawns on a political and geographical chessboard. To be in the hand of Nebuchadnezzar is not to be out of the control of God. The story of God's acts in history has not come to an end. The presence of the Jerusalem temple vessels in Babylon (safe in a temple treasury there) may itself even offer quiet testimony to the fact that God is still at work, his purpose is intact, even though now being pursued in a surprising way in a surprising place (Koch, *TLZ* 85 [1960] 830). This is an important faith-context for the experiences Daniel and his friends are to go through as they arrive in Babylon and over future years. It is what makes it possible to tell the story at all. The articles from the Jerusalem temple are put into the shrine of the Babylonian gods as if the latter had won them. Actually the God of Israel had given them to Nebuchadnezzar; he is in control.

The affirmation of God's involvement raises questions as well as answering them. Of course the Lord has the right and power to do as he wishes with what belongs to him. Yet to hand over king and belongings to an alien overlord is a puzzling action. What are articles from the house of God (the only real God—the noun has no suffix or qualifier to relativize it) doing in the house of a Babylonian god? The scandal is underlined by the ancient versions referring to it as Nebuchadnezzar's idol-house. What happens here is quite different from what happened on an earlier occasion when symbols of the Lord's presence were taken into exile (1 Sam 5–6; 2 Sam 6:6; cf. the warnings of Exod 19:21; Num 4:15, 20). The incident has opened up questions that will need answers before the story is over.

3–7 When Nebuchadnezzar came to Palestine and went back to Babylon, he took with him not only things but people. A group of young Israelites, for the moment silent, faceless, nameless, helpless objects for manipulating by the Babylonian state, are to be taken, taught, provided for, trained, and renamed in this alien environment. Trundled off to a foreign land, they are placed in the charge of a foreign official with a foreign name, are called by foreign titles, and are allocated a foreign education, foreign diet, and foreign names for themselves, to prepare them to serve in a foreign court. Being propelled into exile is an experience of alienness, incomprehension, and abhorrence. In such circumstances, the commitment of faith might triumph, or at least survive, but it might wilt.

Yet in these events lie seeds of hope, partly encouraged by stimuli toward recollection of earlier events and earlier scriptures, which speak of life under alien pressures. Not long after an Assyrian chief of staff went to Jerusalem, Isaiah told Hezekiah that his sons would end up as eunuchs/members of the palace staff in Babylon (2 Kgs 18:17; 20:18). That prophecy is now fulfilled; it was a word of judgment, but the context of God's judgment is at least a context of meaning rather than one of meaningless disorder. A century after Hezekiah, when Jerusalem fell, a Babylonian chief of staff was among those who released Jeremiah from jail after the capture of Jerusalem (Jer 39:13); acting on Nebuchadnezzar's behalf, Ashpenaz ensures that the fate of the royal family on that occasion (Jer 39:5–6) is not their fate here. Further, long ago at the beginning of Israel's story a handsome young man was taken off against his will into a foreign country and put into the charge of a leading member of the palace staff; Joseph had proved himself a man of wisdom and discernment and had taken his place in the royal court without compromising his faith—and he, too, had received a foreign name (Gen 39:1–6; 41:39–46).

The story that began by raising questions about faith thus goes on to raise questions about ambition, or about life at court in a pagan culture. H. R. Niebuhr once analyzed five views of the relationship between Christ and culture *Christ and Culture* [New York: Harper, 1951]). At two extremes are the attitudes that either totally oppose these or assimilate them. Others see Christ as the fulfillment of the ideals that culture perceives but does not achieve, or see Christ and culture as making legitimate demands that stand in tension with one another, or see Christ as bringing the conversion of culture. The relationship between faith and culture is a question which runs through the OT. In different contexts the people of God acknowledges other cultural patterns without being significantly affected by them, or confronts other cultural patterns that seem destructive and threatening, or lets them influence it, both to its enrichment and to its debasement. The exile is a fruit of that debasement, and naturally gives strength to a purist movement that emphasizes the distinctive features of Israel's culture such as the sabbath, food laws, circumcision, and other topics stressed by Leviticus and Deuteronomy.

Such a purist movement would speak with particular force in Babylon itself, where extra pressures drive Israel into assimilation to a pagan culture. Those pressures are overtly placed on the young exiles among the royalty and the nobility, who are educated in Babylonian religio-political lore in order that they may join the king's staff. That education means sharing in the life (specifically the food) of the palace, and receiving names that suggest the service of foreign gods rather than the God of Israel. The provision of education, food, and names places them under powerful cultural forces. Nebuchadnezzar is attempting to turn the next generation of Israel (in the persons of its royal leaders) into good Babylonians.

Nebuchadnezzar wants Israelites, members of a nation he had defeated and intends to keep under control; members of the royalty and the nobility, able to exercise an influence on Judah in general, by their presence or by their absence; young men, with more potential and less prejudice; flawless and handsome men to grace his court; men whose capability, learning, knowledge, and discernment are already proved. But he is thus insisting on young men who belong to God's chosen people and to the royal tribe to which the Lord committed himself in perpetuity. Handsome and lacking any shortcomings, they resemble David's one-time heir apparent, Absalom (2 Sam 14:25). Learned, knowledgeable, and discerning, they resemble David himself (1 Sam 16:12, 18; 18:5, 14–15) and the son who actually succeeded him and became the paradigm of learning and wisdom in Israel (1 Kgs 5:9–14 [4:29–34]). They possess the attributes as well as the background of royalty. Nebuchadnezzar has thus chosen the best men, but also the worst, to seek to reeducate into men of the (Babylonian) world.

To both Israelites and Babylonians, politics, learning, and religious commitment were interwoven; the notion of value-free wisdom had not been conceived. While both their traditions include many observations on successful living and morality that lack overt reference to God, such observations presuppose a context in the faith of their respective religions. The Israelites were thus to be educated in the wisdom of the caste of priest-counselors who served the Babylonian god into whose temple the trophies from the Lord's temple had been placed. Babylonian diviners would pray to their gods before practicing their craft: they were concerned to discover what the gods were revealing. Worldly learning had many insights, but it was a potential threat to Israelite faith because of its relationship with Babylonian religion. Israelite learning was also a threat to Nebuchadnezzar's policy for court development, for a parallel reason. Nebuchadnezzar was looking for natural intelligence that could be developed by and adapted to his nation's learning. But the foundation of Israelite wisdom is the worship of Israel's God. If the Israelite princes and nobles are particularly wise, learned, and discerning, that marks them out as also particularly committed to him.

At the same time, the description places them in a tradition that had been accustomed to manifesting a discriminating openness to the learning of other peoples. The wise person knows how to learn from the wisdom of other peoples without being overcome by it. The story's stance in relation to Babylonian wisdom is thus different from that of Isa 40–55 (see especially 47:9–13 for terms used in Daniel, though Daniel makes strikingly little specific reference to astrology). The stories do not portray a religious conflict between two purportedly divine wisdoms. Their contrast is between Israel's divine wisdom and the merely human wisdom of Babylon. Babylon is thus as radically belittled as it is in Isa 40–55.

The wise person also knows the power of laughter. The possibility that the outward renaming of the four Israelite young men might lead to their inner backsliding is undermined by the way their new names are reported. Belteshazzar, Shadrach, Meshach, and Abednego are all grotesque, silly names, which make fun of the gods whom they are supposed to honor. Like Zerubbabel and Mordecai, the four can use their foreign names without worrying about them, perhaps on the same basis that Paul can eat meat sacrificed to idols—because the idol is really nothing.

8 By military defeat, geographical displacement, and cultural "flooding" the Babylonians have sought to manipulate the Israelites, as humanly helpless (though not Godless or witless) victims of their will. Ashpenaz has just been deciding on names for Daniel and his friends; but now Daniel does some deciding for himself. We wonder what will happen to Israelite youth and Israelite wisdom when it is thrust into exile and taught Chaldean. We hoped that the qualities of those young men would mean that things would turn out all right; now Daniel gives us the first concrete indication that it will indeed be so, showing himself to be a worthy member of this elite (Plöger). The young exiles cease to be faceless ciphers and helpless victims. Daniel seizes the initiative from the Babylonians, insisting on some determining of his own which counters that of Ashpenaz. At Babylonian food he draws the line. Questions about ambition lead to questions about purity.

Accepting the palace provisions involves a compromise of faith in a way that accepting a share in its life, its work, its education, and its names do not. Believers in other contexts or in other cultures might have identified their sticking point elsewhere. In the context of the exile, when Isa 40–55 is scathing about Babylonian religion, Babylonian food is too trivial for the prophet to mention. Perhaps part of the point is that a line should be drawn somewhere. Total assimilation is to be avoided. Food, in particular, is determinative of identity; it is part of being "embodied." We are what we eat: the English call the French "frogs," the French call the English "roast beefs." It is common for an expatriate community to maintain its distinctiveness partly by maintaining its distinctive diet. Israel's own food laws presuppose that food is determinative of identity; part of their point is to preserve the distinctiveness of Israel over against other peoples. It is difficult to be sure precisely what was thought to be defiling about the Babylonians' food, and this may be because it was nothing more sharply conceptualized than that it was Babylonian.

In Dan 1, then, discipleship expresses itself by insisting on maintaining the difference between clean and unclean food; in this way believers mark themselves out (to themselves and to others, and before God) as belonging to a special people and committed to a specific Lord. Works such as Leviticus and Esther take the same stance; particularly suggestive is Num 22–25, which juxtaposes the futility of pagan divination (22–24) and the danger of idolatrous feasting (25). Rev 2:14, 20 takes up those chapters and reaffirms the association. 1 Cor 8–10 similarly insists that discipleship involves being wary of idolatry and of anything that looks like idolatry, but also being wary of taking too seriously beings that are really no-gods. Most importantly, however, it involves being concerned for our neighbors' edification, and if they do not share our freedom, we are not to insist on exercising it in a misleading way (cf. Rom 14). In Mark 7 discipleship expresses itself by repudiating the distinction between clean and unclean food; in this way believers will demonstrate that the source of moral defilement lies elsewhere. Acts 10 takes the same stance on a different basis: God is now abolishing the distinction between clean and unclean, which symbolizes and reinforces that between Israel and other peoples, because the gospel first preached to Jews is now to be preached to gentiles also.

The gospel word that Daniel proves is 1 Cor 10:13 rather than Acts 10. He emphasizes an aspect of Judaism that may seem unimportant and passing; yet it was in fact the means whereby the Jews maintained their identity, and God's means of ensuring that this happened. There is a freedom with which Christ sets us free, but that is not the freedom claimed by the Hellenizing Jews who eventually abandoned those emphases of Judaism (Porteous). We are reassured that the Daniel who lives at court, stands by the side of the king, and serves the empire, is one who has taken his stand and kept himself pure; and we are challenged about our own willingness to accept an involvement in the world, but to recognize that there are points at which we have to draw a line. We are called to be citizens of two worlds, neither surrendering one citizenship by assimilation nor surrendering the other by forming a ghetto.

9–14 So Daniel took his stand. For him to avoid the risk of defilement, however, is for Ashpenaz to take on the risk of his head, if his royal master spots from their appearance that the four young men have not been eating the king's good food. Yet Ashpenaz is favorably disposed toward Daniel and sympathetic to his position, and does not turn his request down. Daniel's demonstration of his commitments is matched by God's own. It begins to look as if things will turn out all right because of who God is, as well as because of who Daniel is.

For a gentile court-official to be so accommodating was a sufficiently remarkable and unusual experience to require explanation. Through the centuries believers had to take their stand knowing that it might well mean loss, perhaps suffering and martyrdom. Whatever is meant by God honoring those who honor him (1 Sam 2:30), it is not that he always grants safety and protection to them. Yet sometimes it does happen, and their faith sees the hand of God at work. So it had been once for Joseph, and for the Israelites on the eve of the exodus, and so Solomon prayed it would be in exile (Gen 39:21, cf. *T. Jos.* 2.3; Exod 12:36; 1 Kgs 8:50; also Gen 43:14; Ps 106:46). He can inspire quite unexpected attitudes in friends or foes (Calvin). Biblical precedent and prayer are once more being followed and fulfilled. Those who have to hold together the claims of the world and the claims of faith are encouraged to remember that God has been known to make it possible for people to life in this world in accordance with faith's claims.

Daniel's purity is not secure yet, however, and sympathy cannot be translated into support until it can be shown that Ashpenaz himself is not about to be endangered. Perhaps Daniel will after all be driven into compromise, or into despair? Divine aid (v 9) does not mean there is no need for the exercise of human responsibility and initiative (v 11): rather it opens the way to it (Joubert).

Daniel proposes a period of testing to demonstrate that the vegetarian diet he seeks, free from the risk of uncleanness, can be as healthy as the official provision. What gave Daniel the idea and what he expected to emerge from it we are not told. The bold and bald wager, even fixing the terminus ad quem, is out of his mouth before there can be talk of thinking it over or seeking God's guidance (Jerome, against Calvin). Before Israel reached Palestine, God tested her by depriving her of regular provision, to show her that people do not live on bread alone but by the word that God speaks (Deut 8:2–3; 29:5 [6]). After Israel has left Palestine, Daniel submits to a similar test (and in a sense tests God in the process) to prove the same point (cf. Hippolytus). The person who can do that is the one who has already discovered how to live with both plenty and poverty (Phil 4:12) (Calvin).

15–16 All the questions have now been opened up: questions about how to believe in a God who lets Jerusalem fall, about what will happen to young men educated in the learning of a foreign court, about whether they can avoid defilement and satisfy their overlords that there is nothing to be lost by allowing them to do so. Now the answers that have been hinted become more overt.

First, the test is successful; indeed, the four Jews look better after ten days of vegetarian food than the young men who eat the royal provisions. Perhaps vegetarian food is better for you, perhaps God intervenes to prove that people flourish at his word and not merely because of what they eat; the story does not tell us why or how this remarkable event takes place. It only declares that it does. So the young men are permanently excused from the royal provision, and their purity is assured for the future. It is possible to be faithful in a pagan court.

17–20 Indeed, it is possible to be successful there. The OT is not opposed to divination (and associated purificatory, exorcistic, and apotropaic rites) as such—though dreams and casting lots are almost its only forms of (approved) divination, and they appear rarely; the OT tends to claim that Yahweh has more distinctive, more direct means of communicating with his people (Deut 18:15). Yet in demonstrating his understanding of visions and dreams, Daniel earns the title "prophet" which later generations give him (4QFlor 2.3; Matt 24:15; cf. Num 12:6). The Bible's overt attacks on divination are attacks on the practices of alien religions (Deut 18:9–14; Isa 47). God, the true God of Israel, is the source of the young men's insight and of Daniel's achievements in the Babylonians' own areas of expertise. There is no positive theology of pagan or secular learning here, but rather the assurance that it can be triumphed over. If there were two main attitudes to foreign wisdom in the postexilic period, Daniel belongs ultimately with the more exclusive, not the more open (against Lebram *VT* 15 [1965] 234–37). By allowing the young men to be open to alien wisdom but then portraying theirs as superior, Daniel makes the same points as Isa 47, perhaps more strongly. It asserts that there is insight about life, history, and politics (the affairs the young men will be concerned in) that only God endows. God is the giver in connection with their destiny, even when it does not appear so (v 2), the giver in connection with their relationships, even when these are most threatening (v 9), and the giver in connection with their character and abilities, even when these are under most pressure (v 17). His involvement thus relativizes military power, political power, and the power of human wisdom (Joubert). " 'God gave'—that is the gospel of this chapter" (Lüthi).

This being the case, it is hardly surprising that the young men's counsel turns out to be not merely comparable with but ten times better than that of the king's other advisers—even if this seems a bold claim, whether in a Babylonian, a Persian, or a Greek context. If the God of Israel is God, it is to be expected that he will enable his people to offer better counsel than those who seek their wisdom from other sources. This is not only pious hope (as in Daniel's visions) but is foretasted as present reality. The God whom Nebuchadnezzar was seeking to eliminate (vv 1–7) is triumphing (Calvin). The Israelite kingly family has been taken into the service of the Babylonian king but it has found itself in a position of leadership in Babylon, and not through military or political achievement but through wisdom (Boehmer, 62–63).

21 Nor is this triumph a single belated event or one relevant only to the lives of individuals. We started on the broad canvas of a defeat by Nebuchadnezzar, a plundering of the temple, and an exiling of the flower of Israel's manhood, which threaten a breaking off of the story of God, his purpose with Israel, and their relationship with him. But Daniel lived through the seventy years of submission to Babylon prophesied by Jeremiah, on to "the first year of Cyrus, king of Persia," who encouraged Jewish exiles to return with the temple articles to rebuild the temple (2 Chr 36:22–23; Ezra

1). Daniel is still there when Nebuchadnezzar, who had brought about Israel's exile, gives way to Cyrus, who will bring about its end.

Daniel offers no answer to the question "Why are we here in exile?" It was simply God's will. It can be accepted, partly because it is not without end. A beginning in "the third year of Jehoiakim" can be acknowledged and recorded because it contains the seed of an end in "the first year of King Cyrus," not by forces immanent in history but by those immanent in the word of God that decides both beginning and end. "Nebuchadnezzar" spells invasion, siege, defeat, plundering, exile. "Cyrus" spells the end of each of these. "Nebuchadnezzar" brings the day of Yahweh's abandoning his people to darkness and wrath, a historical experience and at the same time a pointer to ultimate Darkness and Wrath. "Cyrus" suggests deliverance and freedom, restoration and rebuilding, the joy of going home. It, too, is a historical experience yet at the same time a pointer to the deliverance, freedom, restoration, and joy of the End (cf. Isa 44:24–45:7).

The fact that the exile does not go on for ever and that Daniel sees it out does not provide an intellectual answer to why it happens, but it provides some practical help for living in exile. On the basis of it, those who wait for Yahweh can find new strength (Isa 40:31). Their faith survives and grows.

The God of Heaven Reveals the King's Dream to Daniel and the Empire's Destiny to Nebuchadnezzar (2:1–49)

Bibliography

Alt, A. "Die Deutung der Weltgeschichte im Alten Testament." *ZTK* 56 (1959) 129–37. **Anklesaria, B. T.** *Zand-î Vohûman Yasn.* Bombay: privately published, 1957; repr. Bombay: Cama Oriental Institute, 1967. **Baumgartner, W.** "Zum Traumerraten in Daniel 2." *AfO* 4 (1927) 17–19. ———. "Zu den vier Reichen von Daniel 2." *TZ* 85 (1960) 17–22. **Bergman, B. Z.** "*Han*ʿ*el* in Daniel 2:25 and 6:19." *JNES* 27 (1968) 69–70. **Birks, T. R.** *The Four Prophetic Empires.* London: Seeley, 1844. **Brooke, G. J.** "Qumran Pesher." *RevQ* 10 (1981) 483–503. **Bush, G.** *The Prophecies of Daniel: Nebuchadnezzar's Dream.* 2 parts. New York: Harper, 1844. **Caspari, W.** "Eine neue Tiergestalt in Daniel (Kap. 2)." *NKZ* 34 (1923) 676–87. **Clerget, J.** "L'énigme et son interprétation." *LumVie* 31 [160] (1982) 36–47. **Collins, J. J.** *Vision.* 34–46. ———. "Persian Apocalypses." Collins, *Apocalypse,* 207–17. **Davies, P. R.** "Daniel Chapter Two." *JTS* 27 (1976) 392–401. **Düsterwald, F.** *Die Weltreiche und das Gottesreich nach den Weissagungen des Propheten Daniel.* Freiburg: Herder, 1890. **Eddy, S. K.** *King.* 16–35. **Ehrlich, E. L.** *Der Traum im Alten Testament.* BZAW 73 (1953). 90–113. **Finkel, A.** "The Pesher of Dreams and Scriptures." *RevQ* 4 (1963–64) 357–70. **Flusser, D.** "The Four Empires in the Fourth Sibyl and in the Book of Daniel." *IOS* 2 (1972) 148–75. **Geffcken, J.** *Die Oracula Sibyllina.* Leipzig: Hinrichs, 1902. **Ginsberg, H. L.** " 'King of Kings' and 'Lord of Kingdoms.' " *AJSL* 57 (1960) 71–74. **Glasson, T. F.** *Greek Influence on Jewish Eschatology.* London: SPCK, 1961. ———. "Visions of Thy Head" (Daniel 2[28])." *ExpT* 81 (1969–70) 247–48. **Gruenthaner, M. J.** "The Four Empires of Daniel." *CBQ* 8 (1946) 72–82, 201–12. **Hanson, J. S.** "Dreams and Visions in the Graeco-Roman World and Early Christianity." *ANRW* ii 23, 2 (1980) 1395–1427. **Hartman, S.** "Frågan om eventuellt iranskt inflytande på kristendomens och judendomens apokalyptik och djävulsföreställning." *STK* 52 (1976) 1–8. Cf. "Datierung der jungavestischen Apokalyptik." In *Apocalypticism,* ed. D. Hellholm, 61–75. **Hasel, G. F.** "The Four World Empires of Daniel 2 against Its Near Eastern Environment." *JSOT* 12 (1979) 17–30. **Hawkins, J.** *A Treatise on the Second Chapter of the Prophet Daniel.* 2nd ed. London: privately published, 1833. **Heller, B.** "Das Traumerraten im Buche Daniel." *ZAW* 43 (1925) 243–46. **Höffken, P.** "Heilszeitherrschererwartung im babylonischen Raum." *WO* 9 (1977) 57–71. **Hoonacker, A. van.** "The Four Empires of the Book of Daniel." *ExpT* 13 (1901–2) 420–23. = [revised] "L'historiographie du livre de *Daniel.*" *Le muséon* 44 (1931) 169–76. **Horgan, M. P.** *Pesharim.* CBQMS 8 (1979). **Irmscher, J.** "Die hellenistische Weltreichsidee." *Klio* 60 (1978) 177–82. **Jones, B. W.** 292–314. **Lattey, C.** "Sovereignty and Realm in Dan. 2, 44." *Bib* 4 (1923) 91–94. **Lebram, J. C. H.** "Die Weltreiche im jüdischen Apokalyptik." *ZAW* 76 (1964) 328–31. **Löwinger, S.** "Nebuchadnezzar's Dream in the Book of Daniel." In *Ignace Goldziher Memorial Volume,* ed. S. Löwinger and J. Somogyi. Budapest: Globus, 1948. 1:336–52. **Mastin, B. A.** "Daniel 2:46 and the Hellenistic World." *ZAW* 85 (1973) 80–93. **Mendels, D.** "The Five Empires." *American J Philology* 102 (1981) 330–37. **Momigliano, A.** "The Origins of Universal History." In *The Poet and the Historian,* ed. R. E. Friedman. Chico, CA: Scholars, 1983. 133–54. **Newton, B. W.** *Aids to Prophetic Enquiry.* 3 vols. London: Nisbet, 1848–49. **Niditch, S.,** and **Doran, R.** "The Success Story of the Wise Courtier: A Formal

Approach." *JBL* 96 (1977) 179–93. **Oppenheim, A. L.** "Dreams." *Transactions of the American Philosophical Society* 46 (1956) 179–373. **Pope, M. H.,** and **Tigay, J. H.** "A Description of Baal." *UF* 3 (1971) 117–30. **Prete, S.** "Declino e corrompimento morale nella escatologia occidentale: nota alle interpretazioni su Dan. 2, 31; 7, 3 di Ippolito e Girolamo." *Divus Thomas* 82 (1979) 145–56. **Rappaport, A.** "המלכות הרביעית בספר דניאל." *BetM* 10, 1 [22] (1964) 10–25. **Reichel, H. L.** "Die vier Weltreiche des Propheten Daniel." *TSK* 21 (1848) 943–62. **Resch, A.** *Der Traum im Heilsplan Gottes.* Freiburg: Herder, 1964. 117–23. **Rowley, H. H.** 61–185. **Rundgren, F.** "An Aramaic Loanword in Daniel." *OrSuec* 25–26 (1976–77) 45–55. **Schreiner, J.** "'. . . wird der Gott des Himmels ein Reich errichten, das in Ewigkeit nicht untergeht' (Dan 2, 44): Gestalt und Botschaft apokalyptischens Redens von Gott—am Beispiel von Daniel 2." In *"Ich will euer Gott werden": Beispiele biblische Redens von Gott,* ed. H. Merklein and E. Zenger. SBS 100 (1981) 123–49. **Siegman, E. F.** "The Stone Hewn from the Mountain." *CBQ* 18 (1956) 364–79. **Stevenson, W. B.** "The Identification of the Four Kingdoms in the Book of Daniel." *TGUOS* 7 (1934–35) 4–8. **Swain, J. W.** "The Theory of the Four Monarchies." *ClassPh* 35 (1940) 1–21. **Wallace, R.** "Tyrant, Kingdom, and Church." *Int* 15 (1961) 431–38. **Walton, J. H.** "The Four Kingdoms of Daniel." *JETS* 29 (1986) 25–36. **West, E. W.,** tr. *Pahlavi Texts.* 5 vols. Oxford: Clarendon, 1880–97.

Translation

1 *In the second year of Nebuchadnezzar's reign, Nebuchadnezzar had a dream.*[a] *His anxiety was aroused*[b] *but sleep came back over him.*[c] 2 *The king ordered the diviners, the chanters, the charmers, and the Chaldeans to be summoned to explain to the king what he had dreamed. So they came and took their places before the king,* 3 *and the king said to them, "I have had a dream and I am anxious*[a] *to know what I dreamed."* 4 *The Chaldeans spoke to the king (in Aramaic):*[a] *"Long*[b] *live the king! Tell your servants the dream, and we will explain the interpretation."*[c] 5 *The king answered*[a] *the Chaldeans, "I have made a firm decision:*[b] *if you cannot tell me the dream and its interpretation, you will be torn limb from limb and your houses will be turned into rubble.*[c] 6 *But if you can tell me the dream and its interpretation, you will acquire from me gifts, a reward, and great honor. Now*[a] *tell me the dream and its interpretation."* 7 *They answered a second time, "Let the king tell*[a] *his servants the dream, and we will tell him the interpretation."* 8 *The king answered, "I know very well that you are buying the time,*[a] *because*[b] *you perceive that I have made a firm decision* 9 [a]*that if you cannot tell me what I have dreamed, there is a specific ordinance for you.*[a] *You have arranged with each other*[b] *to make a lying, base response before me, hoping the situation may change. Now*[c] *tell me the dream, and I will know you can explain its interpretation to me."* 10 *The Chaldeans responded before the king, "There is no one on earth who could make the statement for which the king asks. Hence*[a] *no great king or ruler*[b] *has ever asked such a thing of any diviner or chanter or Chaldean.* 11 *The thing which the king is asking is so formidable, there is no one else who can explain it before the king but the gods, and their home is not among mere human beings."*[a] 12 *At this the king flew into a furious rage and said that all the sages in Babylon were to be put to death.*

13 *So the edict went out that the sages were to killed,*[a] *and search was made for Daniel and his friends so that they could be killed.* 14 *Then Daniel responded with shrewd judgment*[a] *to Arioch,*[b] *the royal chief of police,*[c] *who had gone out to kill*

the sages in Babylon. 15 He replied to Arioch, "Royal marshal,[a] why has this severe[b] decree come from the king?" [c]Arioch explained matters to Daniel, 16 and Daniel went and[a] asked the king to give him a period of time and he would tell the king the interpretation. 17 Daniel went home and let his friends Hananiah, Mishael, and Azariah know about the affair, 18 for them to ask for compassion[a] from the God of heaven regarding this mystery, so that Daniel and his friends might not perish with the rest of the sages in Babylon.[b] 19 Then the mystery was revealed to Daniel in a vision during the night. Daniel blessed the God of heaven. 20 Daniel declared,[a]

[b]May the name of God
be[b] blessed from eternity to eternity.[c]
Wisdom and might are his.
21 He changes times and eras;[a]
he removes kings and establishes kings.
He gives their wisdom to the wise
and their knowledge to those who possess insight.
22 He reveals things deeply hidden;
he knows what lies in darkness,
and light sojourns with him.
23 God of my fathers, I acknowledge[a] and praise[b] you:
You have given me wisdom and might.[c]
You have told me now what we asked of you;
you have told us the king's question.

24 Thus Daniel went[a] to Arioch, whom the king had delegated to kill the sages in Babylon. He went[a] and said to him, "Do not kill[b] the sages of Babylon. Take me before the king, and I will explain the interpretation to the king." 25 With urgency[a] Arioch took[b] Daniel before the king and told him, "I have found someone among the Judean exiles who can tell your majesty the interpretation." 26 The king addressed Daniel (whose name was Belteshazzar), "Are you really[a] able to tell me the dream that I had, and its interpretation?" 27 Daniel made his reply before the king, "No sages, chanters, diviners or exorcists[a] can explain to your majesty the mystery about which your majesty asks. 28 Yet there is a God in heaven who reveals mysteries, and he has let King Nebuchadnezzar[a] know what is going to happen at the end of the era. This is your dream, the vision[b] that came into your head[c] as you lay in bed. 29 To you, your majesty, as you lay in bed came[a] thoughts of what is to happen in the future,[b] and the revealer of mysteries let you know what is to happen. 30 This mystery has been revealed to me, not by means of a wisdom that I possess that is greater than any other person's, but in order for the interpretation to be made known to your majesty, so that you may know your inner thoughts.[a]

31 "Your majesty, you looked, and there before you was a large[a] statue. This statue was big, with an extraordinary brightness, standing in front of you, an awesome sight. 32 This statue, its head was made of pure gold, its chest and arms of silver, its stomach and sides of bronze,[a] 33 its legs[a] of iron, its feet partly of iron and partly of pottery.[b] 34 You watched as[a] a rock broke away[b] without being touched. It struck the statue on its feet made of iron and pottery, and shattered them. 35 Then all at once[a] the iron, pottery, bronze, silver, and gold shattered;[b] they became like chaff from a threshing-place in summer, and the wind carried them off. No place[c] could be found for them. But the rock which had struck the statue became a great crag which filled the whole world.

[36] *"That was the dream. Now we*[a] *will state its interpretation before the king.* [37] *Your majesty, king among kings, to you*[a] *the God of heaven has given royal authority, sovereignty, power, and honor,* [38] [a]*and wherever they live, has given human beings,*[a] *creatures of the wild, and birds in the sky into your control and made you ruler over them all. You yourself are*[b] *the head made of gold.* [39] *In your place another regime will arise*[a] *inferior to yours, and another, third regime of bronze, which will rule the whole world.* [40] [a]*Then there will be a fourth regime as strong as iron—because iron shatters and smashes anything.*[b] [c]*Like iron crushing things,*[c] *it will shatter and crush* [d]*all these others.*[d] [41] *But in that you saw the feet and toes*[a] *made partly of clay*[b] *pottery and partly of iron, it will be a split*[c] *regime, though it will have some of the toughness*[d] *of iron. In that you saw iron united with the earthen*[e] *pottery,* [42] [a]*and the toes of*[a] *the feet partly iron and partly pottery, to some extent*[b] *the regime will be strong, but in part it will be fragile.* [43] *In that you saw the iron united with clay pottery,* [a]*human beings will unite,*[a] *but they will not hold together, just as*[b] *iron does not unite with pottery.* [44] *And in the time of those kings the God of heaven will establish a regime which will not be destroyed*[a] *through the ages, nor will royal authority*[b] *pass to any other people. It will finally shatter all those regimes but will itself stand through the ages,* [45] *insofar as you saw that a rock broke away from the crag without being touched, and shattered the* [a]*iron, bronze, pottery, silver, and gold."*[a]

"God Almighty[b] *has let your majesty know what is to happen in the future. The dream is true. Its interpretation is trustworthy."*

[46] *Then King Nebuchadnezzar fell on his face, prostrate,*[a] *before Daniel. He said that an offering and fragrant oblations*[b] *were to be presented to him.* [47] *The king declared to Daniel, "Your God is indeed* [a]*God among gods, Master among kings, and Revealer of mysteries,*[a] *since you have been able to reveal this mystery."* [48] *Then the king elevated Daniel. He gave him many great gifts and would have made*[a] *him governor over the entire province of Babylon and chief officer over all the sages in Babylon;* [49] *but Daniel asked the king to appoint*[a] *Shadrach, Meshach, and Abednego over the administration of the province of Babylon, Daniel being at the royal court.*[b]

Notes

1.a. Pl, perhaps taking up the double dream in Gen 41; but cf. v 28, also 4:2 [5]; 7:1; and GKC 124. Thus the ref. is to the one dream discussed by vv 2–49.

1.b. Lit., "his spirit was agitated."

1.c. EVV tr נהיתה "left," assimilating to 6:19 [18], which has the same Aramaic-style word order and the same use of על (cf. G. R. Driver, review of *CAD* vol. 16, *JSS* 9 [1964] 349); but there is no parallel for this meaning of the vb. נהיתה looks like ni היה (cf. Aq, Syr, JPS)—or is it intensive (G. S. Ogden, "Time and the Verb היה in O. T. Prose," *VT* 21 [1971] 466)? cf. 12:1. But this will not do for 8:27, where the most plausible explanation is to connect the word with היה "fall." Then so also 2:1 and 12:1 (Rashi)? See Gen 41:4–5 for the motif of going back to sleep after being wakened by a dream.

3.a. Cf. n. 1.b., though the vb is now ni, not hit.

4.a. On the presence of ארמית in 1QDan[a] see Snell, *JSOT* 18 (1980) 36; an explanatory gl commenting on the change of language in the text.

4.b. עולם/עלם signifies the furthest possible time; here pl of extension (GKC 124b; cf. colloquial

English "for ages"). A standard hyperbole from courtly style, it appears on the lips of the nobles at Nabopolassar's consecration (Grayson, *Texts,* 3). See further n.20.c below.

4.c. פשרא (only in Dan 2–7; cf. Eccl 8:1; BH פתרון, only in Gen 40–41). The root means "unloose, resolve, or explain, esp. by supernatural means." For the connection with unloosing, cf. 5:12. Thus פשר does not denote interpretation generally, but interpretation by magical means or by supernatural revelation, with specific reference to what something presages (see *AHw* on *pišru;* Oppenheim, "Dreams," 217–25; Horgan, *Pesharim,* 230–37; I. Rabinowitz, " 'Pesher/pittaron,' " *RevQ* 8 [1972–75] 219–32). Some mss here have פשרה, the alternative emph form; others פשרה ("its interpretation"). MT, Vrs show such variation through Dan 2; I follow L (and K rather than Q) throughout.

5.a. ענה could be ptpl or pf; MT points as ptpl, but when pl. the unambiguously pf ענו is more common, and perhaps the s should be taken as pf too.

5.b. מלתא מני אזדא, "the matter has been determined/proclaimed by me." On אזדא see F. Rundgren, *OrSuec* 25–26 (1976–77) 45–55; H. Happ and W. P. Schmid, "Zu ἀσγάνδης . . . ," *Glotta* 40 (1962) 198–201, 321.

5.c. נולי. "Forfeit"/"dunghill" (cf. NEB/mg) may ultimately be guesses. Something fairly extreme is required to match being torn limb from limb; BDB's connection with Akk. *nawâlu* provides this.

6.a. להן is an adversative (cf. Th πλήν). It does not mean "therefore" (EVV) in BA or BH (see G. R. Driver, "Problems in Aramaic and Hebrew Texts," *Miscellanea orientalia* [FS A. Deimel; AnOr 12; Rome: PBI, 1935] 64–66; against Eitan). Cf. 2:9; 4:24 [27].

7.a. Juss replaces imper: the sages become less peremptory.

8.a. The meaning is less clear than the familiar English 'buying time' suggests. Like BH עת, עדן denotes not time in general but a specific time during which to concoct an answer to the conundrum, or a specific time when they will come back with this answer (cf. vv 9, 16).

8.b. כלקבל: on form and meaning, see BDB 1110.

9.a-a. JB "Your intention is not to interpret my dream" apparently presupposes that די הן is equivalent to BH כי אם ("surely"), and that דתכון means "your purpose," not "the law which applies to you": hence lit. "Surely you will not make the dream known to me. You have a single purpose . . ." But דת (OP) elsewhere always means an actual law (human or divine); cf. v 13, also the similar phrase in Esth 4:11 (Ehrlich).

9.b. Taking הזמנתון as reflexive (hitpeel or hitpaal; cf. Q and many mss הזדמנתון), not as ha הַזְמִנְתּוּן.

9.c. See n. 6.a.

10.a. כלקבל די (lit., "because"); see n. 8.b.

10.b. So Th; NEB. Cf the Assyrian title "Great King," still used in the Persian period (Jeffery). JB takes both רב and שליט as nouns ("no other king, governor, or chief"), but רב used as an abs noun would be unique in BA/BH (contrast the constr in v 14). MT accents, Vg take both as adj ("no king, however great and powerful"), but שליט is a noun in v 15 (cf. 5:29; Gen 42:6).

11.a. בשר, humanity in its creaturely weakness (cf. Isa 31:3).

13.a. Cf. OG, see BL 81o; or "and the sages were being killed" (cf. Th, Vg): this underlines the drama of what follows and fits v 18, though perhaps not v 24, and one might expect a ref. to the killing being halted.

14.a. עטא וטעם: the latter can mean "deference" (3:12; 6:14 [13]), but Daniel is not deferential here; more likely the two nouns are near-synonyms, like other pairs in this chapter. "Took counsel with" (Ginsberg, *Handbook*) fits less well in the context.

14.b. Cf. Gen 14:1; Jdt 1:6; probably Persian (P. Grelot, "Ariok," *VT* 25 [1975] 711–19; Zadok, *VT* 26 [1976] 246), though known as a Babylonian name, and cf. Sumerian Eri-aku (servant of the moon [god]) (Jeffery).

14.c. טבחיא, etymologically "slaughtermen," which is just what they were on this occasion! But elsewhere the word simply means "guard/police."

15.a. MT accents link with לאריוך "to Arioch" (cf. EVV), but Th more naturally takes it as opening the actual speech (cf. NEB).

15.b. חצף seems to mean "barefaced/hardfaced," thus "peremptory, uncompromising, arrogant" (cf. 3:22). Commentators look for a more polite translation if they take טעם to mean "deference"; but see n.14.a.

15.c. אדין (EVV "then") appears at the beginning of the clause: it is a standard linking particle, used like ו in BH, and hardly requiring translation. באדין (vv 14, 35, 46) is less usual, though hardly a marker for a new section (against Charles).

16.a. Montgomery omits על ו "went and," following Th, Syr, on the grounds that Daniel cannot have gone straight in to the king without being taken in (cf. vv 24, 25). Perhaps the narrator tells the story briskly here (or presupposes that a person of Daniel's [later!] stature may not need that mediation?) and more slowly/dramatically in vv 24, 25. But does v 16 require that he actually saw the king? This would normally involve using the term קדם מלכא "before the king," as in vv 24, 25. See also n. 24.a.

18.a. EVV "mercy" is too specific a tr of רחמים: see n.1:9.b-b.

18.b. It is not clear whether Daniel is hoping to save all the sages or only himself and his friends.

20.a. ענה . . . אמר: the first word (lit., "answer") commonly conveys no suggestion of "response"; it simply adds force to אמר "say": cf. vv 5, 7, 8, 10.

20.b. I.e., "may Yahweh be." "The name of God" is a surrogate for Yahweh himself, as in later Jewish usage. Cf. 1:2 *Comment;* also the preference here and elsewhere for להוא or even להוה ("may . . . be," an EA-type impf) to avoid the form יהוה which is identical with the divine name.

20.c. Or "from age to age": while both meanings of עלם (furthest possible time, past or future) apply here, the word does not suggest a transcendent idea of eternity (see n. 4.b). That only emerges when עלם is linked with God/his dominion/his salvation (e.g., 4:31 [34]). Even then, the idea of unchangeable certainty is more important than that of mere temporal continuance (cf. B. Long, "Notes on the Biblical Use of עד-עולם," *WTJ* 41 [1978–79] 54–67). As v 20 also implies, to say God is eternal is not to make him timeless or outside time, but to affirm him lord of all time and unlimited by it (see E. Jenni, "Das Wort ʿōlām im Alten Testament," *ZAW* 64 [1952] 197–248; 65 [1953] 1–35; cf. J. Barr, *Biblical Words for Time* [SBT i 33 (1962)], 69–70, 117 [rev. ed. (1969) 73–74, 123–24]; G. Gerleman, "Die sperrende Grenze: Die Wurzel *ʿlm* im Hebräischen," *ZAW* 91 [1979] 338–49).

21.a. זמניא. EVV "seasons" gives the wrong impression; there is no great difference from עדניא "times."

23.a. ידה/ידא can have sin as well as God (and human beings) as its obj, esp. in postex. writings (see *Comment* [h] on 9:3–23); "acknowledge/confess" brings out its meaning in these different connections better than EVV "give thanks."

23.b. שבח, too, is not an essentially religious word; it means "to recognize the value of" (cf. *DTT*).

23.c. JB "intelligence," following OG, produces the kind of hendiadys Daniel is fond of, but the chiasm "wisdom and might" in vv 20, 23 (developed in vv 21–22) looks original. Th has a parallel variant in v 20.

24.a. Some mss omit the first "went" (על); one ms, G, Vg the second (אזל). But both are picked up from vv 16, 17; the omissions (the first being haplog) more likely reflect simplification of an inherently expansive style than a shorter original.

24.b. תהובד: perhaps "stop killing."

25.a. Or "with excitement" (cf. *DTT*), NEB "in trepidation": בהל suggests strong feelings, not just speed of motion.

25.b. הנעל: formed by analogy with the antonym הנפק (5:2) (so Bergman, *JNES* 27 [1968] 69–70).

26.a. איתי followed by ptpl is emphatic/confirmative (*EWS* 81).

27.a. גזרין: see *Comment* on v 2.

28.a. The word order מלכא נבוכדנצר is unusual (contrast, e.g., 3:1–9) and seems to be a Hebraism (so B. A. Mastin, "Appositional Kingship in Daniel" [see *The Society for Old Testament Study Bulletin* 1986, 3–4]); see n. 1:21.b.

28.b. חלמך וחזוי: explicative *waw;* on s and pl see n. 1.a.

28.c. The OT usually associates mental activity with the heart, not the head (cf. n.30.a; n. 1:8.a; Jer 23:16). The reference here may be to the head as containing the eyes. But Glasson (*ExpT* 81 [1969–70] 247–48) finds here the influence of Greek thinking, which did regard the head as the seat of consciousness and thought.

29.a. סלק "come up," uniquely in BA; see *DTT*, also BH עלה (BDB 749a).

29.b. The cl is epexegetic to רעיונך "your thoughts" (Montgomery), not indirect obj of סלק (against JB, NIV).

30.a. רעיוני לבבך "the thoughts of your heart": see n.28.c. The sentence as a whole is slightly elliptical; Daniel's point is that the reason why he has the revelation is not his wisdom but the divine purpose to make it known to the king.

31.a. JB omits, with Th: but Th may be abbreviating because of difficulty in construing the awkward sentence (cf. Syr's paraphrase). Perhaps Daniel is portrayed as not quite coherent before the vision.

32.a. Or copper; but the alloy bronze is stronger and thus more commonly used.

33.a. שק (BH שוק) denotes the leg as a whole (cf. *DTT;* OG σκέλη), though excluding the hip, which belongs to the bronze section. Th *κνῆμαι*, Vg *tibiae* imply the lower leg only (shin/calf). So BDB 1003, but its refs do not necessitate this for human beings and exclude it for animals.

33.b. חסף: not "clay" (the raw material); cf. טינא, v 41. The word suggests decorative tiling or potsherds (Th ὀστράκινον), tatty decoration when strength of structure is really needed. Contrast the description of Bel as clay inside, bronze outside (Bel 7).

34.a. עד די in the visions (also 6:25 [24]) often means "as" not "until" (BL 79i).

34.b. G, NEB, GNB add מטור "from a crag," cf. v 45. But interpretations often contain more detail than the original vision: cf. vv 33, 41–42 (n. 41.a, 42.a-a); 7:7–8, 19–21. O. Eissfeldt ("Die Menetekel-Inschrift und ihre Deutung," *ZAW* 63 [1951] 112–13) compares with the scriptural interpretation in 1QpHab, e.g., 12.1, 7, as well as the omen interpretation in Dan 5:25–28.

35.a. כחדה suggests suddenness more than simultaneity; cf. BH יחד[ו] (e.g., Isa 43:17; 45:16) more than כאחד (e.g., Ezra 3:9; Isa 65:25).

35.b. If דקו (pointed as from דוק, not דקק; both occur [*DTT*]) is intr/pass (BDB). But it may be the common Aram. impersonal act ("they shattered the iron . . ."), to be tr by the pass (KB).

35.c. Possibly "trace" (EVV, cf. KB); but "place" fits regular usage of אתר, fits the context (v 35b: there was no room left for them), and fits the allusion in Rev 20:11 (Charles; Jones, 257).

36.a. While the pl might denote deference/meekness (cf. v 30), less plausibly reference to the divine council or use of the "royal we," the incidental but deliberate emphasis on including the friends in vv 17–18, 23, 49 suggests that this is also the point here.

37.a. די . . . לך, lit., "to whom": the main cl comes in v 38b.

38.a-a. MT accents suggest "and wherever human beings live, he has given . . ." (cf. RV); but more likely human beings are mentioned as among those Nebuchadnezzar rules. Cf. G, though there is no need also to omit ו "and" (against JB).

38.b. אנתה הוא: see GKC 141gh.

39.a. תקום: "will stand" in v 44, but "will arise" is more natural here.

40.a. Vv 40 and 41 are repetitive, and ancient and modern versions often have shorter texts; see following notes. The structure of the sentences, too, can be understood in varying ways, and in v 41 I have not followed MT (for which cf. RV) (cf. n. 45.a-a).

40.b. כלא. Not "wholly," against J. A. Montgomery, "Adverbial *kúlla* in Biblical Aramaic and Hebrew," *JAOS* 43 (1923) 391–95. See Fitzmyer, *Aramaean*, 205–17.

40.c-c. NEB, NAB omit, following G, Syr.

40.d-d. MT takes כל אלין as obj of the previous vb, which it directly follows (cf RV). Th, Syr omit אלין (OG ἡ γῆ being surely explicative of אלין, not grounds for emendation—against NEB). Kaufmann (*Religion* 4:582) follows Th, Syr on the grounds that MT nonsensically has the feet breaking the statue: but here surely the interpretation influences the vision and refers to the historical fact of the fourth empire destroying its predecessor(s).

41.a. JB omits, following OG: but see n. 34.b.

41.b. פחר can mean "potter" (EVV, cf. Vg) or "clay" (cf. OG); the latter fits better. Adding the word emphasizes the weakness of the material.

41.c. פליגה could suggest "divided" (EVV) into smaller kingdoms, as happened to the Greek empire (Ginsberg). But it could equally suggest internally divided *(DTT)* or composite, and therefore vulnerable, which fits the context here better (Montgomery).

41.d. So EVV, but נצבתא would usually mean "seed/planting" (cf. G, *DTT*), hence perhaps "mineral" *(GBA)*, "core" (NEB).

41.e. טינא, "wet clay" or "mud" *(DTT);* cf. EVV "miry."

42.a-a. JB omits—cf. n. 41.a, but here OG includes it.

42.b. מן קצת: perh. "as a whole" (Meek: see n. 1:2.d).

43.a-a. The phase could refer to a combining of two races generally, but more naturally denotes intermarriage (cf. Ezra 9:2; Ps 106:35).

43.b. Probably האך [= היך] די, not as MT הא כדי; a strong form of כדי (= BH אשר). See BDB.

44.a. חבל can mean "be corrupted," but this hardly fits the context here; for the parallelism cf. 6:27 [26]; 7:14.

44.b. "*Its* sovereignty" (RSV, cf. Th, Vg) would require final הּ and repointing, not ה—which is, however, unusual as emph state ending (Lattey, *Bib* 4 [1923] 91–94).

45.a-a. The order is odd (contrast vv 32–33, 35), but G's "pottery, iron, bronze . . ." is surely secondary. Possibly the original omitted "pottery" (one ms lacks it) or it was lost at an early stage and then (re)inserted variously. This phrase is the end of a sentence begun in v 44b (cf. G); MT punctuation (cf. RV) makes poor sense.

45.b. An overtranslation of אלה רב, but using this expression makes it possible to avoid using either the def art (most EVV), even though אלה is abs, or the indef (RSV), which might be misleading (cf. Keil).

46.a. סגד "[and] prostrated himself" is usually taken to refer to a physical action which suggests homage, so that it repeats the content of the previous phrase; it is used in the papyri of prostration before a man. See *TWAT* חוה. But S. Kreuzer ("Zur Bedeutung und Etymologie von *hištaḥ*ª*wāh*/*yšthwy*," *VT* 35 [1985] 39–60) thinks both expressions signify "do homage" without implying a physical gesture.

46.b. ניחחין, a term only used of offerings to God (e.g., Gen 8:21).

47.a-a. Again the second term in each construct chain is abs, not emph; cf. n. 45.b.

48.a. V 49 suggests that והשלטה in part expresses a possible, not an actual act (cf. in BH Exod 9:15; 1 Sam 13:13; GKC 106p).

49.a. See BL 106e.

49.b. Lit., "gate"—i.e., originally where the king's servants awaited his call (Esth 2:19, 21; 3:2–3), though the term came to denote the chancellery. See H. P. Rüger, "Das Tor des Königs," *Bib* 50 (1968) 247–50.

Form / Structure / Setting

Form

See chap. 1 *Form:* chap. 2 also combines features of court-tale, legend, aretalogy, and midrash, blending these into a formally more compact whole than chap. 1. It shares a basic structure and some verbal formulae with traditional tales that tell "the success story of the wise courtier," including Ahiqar and Gen 41. With these, it shares motifs which also appear in other Jewish court-tales in OT and apocrypha (Esther, Tobit, 1 Esd 3–4) and elsewhere: the interrupted sleep, the puzzled king, the ineffectual experts, the angry tyrant, the imperiled hero, the victorious outsider appearing last, the king open to insight and change, the victor rewarded (Niditch and Doran, *JBL* 96 [1977] 179–93; Humphreys, *JBL* 92 [1973] 217; Redford, *A Study of the Biblical Story of Joseph* [VTSup 20 (1970)] 94–97).

As elsewhere in Daniel, Tobit, and 1 Esd 3–4, such motifs are reworked as the court-tale is taken into a religious context; it becomes a legend. Daniel is a model of Israelite wisdom (v 14) and a model of Israelite piety, in his prayer (v 18), his vision (v 19), his praise (vv 19–23), his witness (vv 27–28), his self-effacement (v 30), his conviction (v 45); the fruit of his work is not merely rewards and promotion (v 48) but obeisance and recognition of his God (vv 46–47).

In turn this last motif reflects the fact that in Dan 2 "the God of Daniel is the central figure and not the courtier" (Humphreys, *JBL* 92 [1973] 221); contrast Josephus *Ant.* 10.10.3 [10.200] where it is out of regard for Daniel's wisdom that God reveals the dream to him (Ehrlich, *Traum,* 112). When the situation looks hopeless, it is redeemed by divine intervention: God's revealing things to Daniel, despite the sages' assertion that deity's home is not among humanity (vv 11, 23, 28–29, 45, 47), gives Dan 2 the features of an aretalogy (Hengel, *Judentum,* 205–6 [ET 1:111–12]; cf. Berger, *ANRW* ii 25, 2:1210–31 and references). Daniel's praise and his revelation emphasize God's sovereignty in events (vv 20–21, 37–45), reinforcing this; indeed, court-tale, legend, and aretalogy are subordinate to the theme of the recognition of God's authority over the king (Davies, 52).

The court-tale's structure, plot, motifs, words, and phrases so substantially parallel one involving Joseph and the Egyptian ruler in Gen 40–41, that it can be described as a haggadah or midrash on that chapter (Farrar, Lacocque). It is not merely following the same traditional form as that story (against Niditch and Doran [see above]; it has a more rhetorical and literary, less traditional character, and its midrashic aspect is indicated by its detailed points of contact with the Joseph story. In both a heathen king has his *anxiety aroused* by dreams. He summons *magicians* (the word comes only in Gen 41, Exod 8–9, and Dan 1–2) and other sages, but none can offer an interpretation (פתר, the BH equivalent to פשר in Dan, appears only in Gen 40–41). Both stories refer to the king's *anger* with his advisers, which leads them to be entrusted to the attention of his *chief of police.* Eventually a young Israelite who has been in exile in the king's custody for two years and who may be able to interpret the dream is discovered and brought hastily before him. In response to the king's inquiry about his ability as a dream interpreter, he denies possessing such ability in himself; it is God who must give any explanation of the dream. The dream, he declares, concerns future events affecting the king, which the young man explains, adding that the message is certain to come true. As a consequence the king determines to put the young man in a position of honor as prime minister over the whole land.

Dan 2 has points of contact with other OT passages. It has links with Gen 11:1–9 (Barr). The story's moral parallels Proverbs' promises of success and long life to those who fear Yahweh (e.g., 9:10–11; 10:27; 14:27). The opening of the interpretation of the dream (vv 37–38) reflects Ps 8:6–8 and/or Jer 27:5–7, passages which seem to have been an important stimulus to the content of the vision (see *Comment*). Gold, silver, bronze, and iron are listed together elsewhere (e.g., Josh 6:19, 24; 22:8; Job 28:1–2), though commonly stone and timber are added (e.g., 1 Chr 22:14–16, 29:2; 2 Chr 2:6–13 [7–14]; Isa 60:17; cf. Dan 5:23). The broadest influence on the chapter, however, is that of Isa 40–66. The chapter's major theme is the contrast between the helplessness of the Babylonians' spiritual resources and the power and wisdom of the God of Israel to effect and to interpret history, and this is also a major theme of Isa 40–48 (e.g., 41:1–7, 21–29; 44:25–26; 47:9–15). Those chapters, too, suggest that silver and gold, bronze and iron, end up useless as clay (40:19; 45:2; 41:25), crushed and blown away like chaff (41:15–16; also 41:12, cf. v 35). They, too, see Israel's God as Lord even of things hidden in darkness, Lord of light and darkness (45:3, 7; cf. v 22).

They, too, picture the nations and their kings doing obeisance before the exiles and their God (45:3, 14; 49:23; 60:6–7, 14); in Dan 2 this happens (vv 46–47). They, too, promise an ultimate realization of the Lord's kingship (44:6; 52:7).

Many motifs and expressions in Dan 2 parallel subsequent stories: the explaining of a royal dream about the future (chap. 4), the lists of sages (4:4 [7]), their greeting to the king (e.g., 3:9), the requirement to be told both dream and interpretation (5:7, cf. the wording of 4:6 [9]), the issuing of solemn and unalterable royal decisions (6:9 [8]), the threat of dismemberment and destruction of property (3:29), the king's fury (3:19), the severity of his edict (3:22), Daniel's coming before the king after the other sages have failed (4:5 [8]), Daniel's going home to pray and give thanks (6:11 [10]), the term *mystery* (4:6 [9]), the identity of three other faithful Jews (3:12), God as the one who deposes and sets up kings (4:14 [17]; 5:20], Arioch's urgency (3:24; 6:19 [20]), Daniel's description as one of the Judean exiles when he is introduced to the king (5:13), his Babylonian name (4:5 [8]), the king's question regarding Daniel's ability to fulfill both parts of the interpretative task (5:16), the expression "the vision that came into your head as you lay in bed" (4:7 [10]), the statue and its gold (3:1), Nebuchadnezzar's being given royal authority, sovereignty, power, and honor (4:27 [30]; 5:18), his ruling over the animals of the wild and the birds of the air (4:18–19 [21–22]), the eventual inheriting of sovereignty by a joint empire (5:28), the regime established by God which lasts for ever (3:33 [4:3]), Nebuchadnezzar's falling prostrate before Daniel (the phrase comes six times in chap. 3), Daniel's position as head of the sages (4:6 [9]) but having no role in the administration of the affairs of the province of Babylon, for which his friends were responsible (3:12). It might be that these later chapters depend on chap. 2, but it is simpler to assume that chap. 2 was written in the light of those other chapters, as it reflects other parts of the OT. A fuller way of describing its midrashic aspect, then, is to see it as a rereading of Dan 3–6 in the light of Gen 41, Isa 40–66, and other passages; or as a reaffirmation of fundamental themes of Isa 40–66 on the basis of the stories told in chaps. 3–6 (cf. von der Osten-Sacken, *Apokalyptik,* 23–25; Gammie, *VT* 31 [1981] 287–91; Collins, *Vision,* 44–45).

Daniel's thanksgiving (vv 20–23) parallels those of the Psalms and utilizes their phrases and motifs, though composed for its context in Daniel's experience rather than reflecting actual use in worship. It is an imitation of a thanksgiving, like the wisdom psalms (Towner, *CBQ* 31 [1969] 318–24; cf. S. Mowinckel, *The Psalms in Israel's Worship* [tr. by D. R. Ap-Thomas from *Offersang og sangoffer: Salmediktning i Bibelen* (Oslo: Aschehoug, 1951); Oxford: Blackwell, 1962/Nashville: Abingdon, 1963] 2:104–25). The content actually recalls Job (e.g., 1:21; 12:22; 32:8; 38:19) more specifically than the Psalter. The psalm begins with a very liturgical blessing of God, like those at the end of the books of the Psalter (especially 72:18–19). The twofold reason for this blessing is briefly stated in the opening formula, in the accustomed fashion. It is expanded in vv 21a and 21b-22 in a series of participles, the two divine characteristics being taken up in reverse order. Verse 23a corresponds to v 20, praising the "God of my fathers" as one who has shared with his servants the two gifts on which vv 20–22 focuses. Verse 23b further narrows the focus to the particular event that prompted this psalm, and thus resolves a formal ambiguity about the psalm. Internally, it has the fundamental feature of a hymn: it is concerned to acknowledge God's characteristic attributes and actions, rather than to confess what God has just now done for the speaker. Yet it lacks the hymn's characteristic imperative call to praise. The blessing formula, and the concentrated acknowledgment of the reasons for praise which follows it, are characteristic of that praise which confesses how God's love and power have been personally applied to the worshiper's needs (e.g., Gen 24:27; Ps 28:6; 66:20; 68:20, 36 [19, 35]; also Luke 1:68); and this is the context the psalm presupposes. The content of the praise (vv 20b–22) relates to the fact that God has answered Daniel's prayer, and to the content of that answer. The psalm is not a liturgical piece but (in the setting of the story) a confession arising from experiencing God's action in the midst of life in the world. The relationship between praise and context is made explicit by v 23a. Daniel's psalm makes for an interesting comparison with Ps 113 (also Ps 66). After declaring in very similar terms "may the name of Yahweh be blessed from now to all ages," it bases this affirmation in Yahweh's continuing majesty and condescension to meet his people's needs (mostly in participles). Here too, the general statement is closely related to a confession of particular experience. (See further Towner, *CBQ* 30 [1968] 386–99; Westermann, *Lob,* 61–102 [ET 81–135].)

Although in this rather literary narrative the report of the dream and its interpretation are reshaped through the delaying of the actual dream report, they have a similar form to those in Gen 40–41 and Dan 4 (see Oppenheim, "Dreams"; Hanson, "Dreams"). The introduction to a dream report commonly identifies dreamer, place, time, and the dreamer's mental state. The dream may be visual (so here) or audio-visual (Dan 4) and may also include words addressed to the dreamer (Dan 7). The dreamer's awed reaction is usually described, when dream figures appear and/or when the dream is over. The dreamer expresses his need to have the dream interpreted; its reference is to the immediate or more distant future of the dreamer or his people. Both the dreams' content (their concern with God's control of history as this affects his people's lives) and their framework (the theme of the revelatory gifts of the Jewish seer) link the dreams with their narrative context in the Book of Daniel; they are integral to it and it to them. The account of the dream's interpretation, also used for that of the omen in Dan 5, compares with the form of scriptural interpretation in the Qumran literature; successive features of the dream are quoted, identified, and explained (Brooke, *RevQ* 10 [1981] 403–503; Finkel, *RevQ* 4 [1963–64] 357–70; Silberman, *RevQ* 3 [1961–62] 323–45). Interpretations commonly contain more or less detail than the original revelation, or fail to correspond to it in some other way. This is not a sign of textual development but of the fact that interpretations stand on their own. They are not mere mechanical translation of a coded message but revelation in their own right (Mertens, 117; cf. n. 34.b).

The dream's contents and its interpretation have a more substantial extra-biblical background (Koch, *Buch Daniel,* 102–5).

(a) Dreams, oracles, and prophecies with implications for the future of the state appear in Akkadian texts relating to Zimri-Lim, Esarhaddon, and Asshurbanipal (*ANET* 449–51 [cf. 605–6], 623–26). A number of Akkadian texts offer descriptions in predictive form of the reigns of (unnamed) kings. These are apparently quasi-prophecies, at least until their closing sections where they come to express the hopes of the prophet's day (*NERT* 118–22; Grayson, *Texts;* Grayson and Lambert, *JCS* 18 [1964] 7–30; Biggs, *Iraq* 29 [1967] 117–32; Borger, *BO* 28 [1971] 3–24; Ringgren, "Akkadian Apocalypses," 379–86; Baldwin, *TynB* 30 [1979] 77–99; Hunger and Kaufman, *JAOS* 95 [1975] 371–75; Lambert, *Background*). Further such quasi-prophecies come from Egypt and elsewhere in the Hellenistic period (Hengel, *Judentum,* 386–89 [ET 1:184–86]; McCown, *HTR* 18 [1925] 357–411; Osswald, *ZAW* 75 [1963] 27–44; see chaps. 10–12 *Form*). Collins believes a Babylonian political oracle from the Hellenistic period underlies Dan 2 (*Vision,* 36–43), Davies a Jewish oracle from the sixth century (*JTS* 27 [1976] 399–400).

(b) Royal dreams occur within the OT (e.g., Pharaoh, Solomon); extrabiblical texts refer to the dreams of Sennacherib and Esarhaddon and include detailed accounts of dreams and other communications received by Nabonidus (see *ANET* 309–11, 606; but especially Oppenheim, "Dreams"). It has been argued that Dan 2 reflects factual or folk material concerning Nabonidus, not Nebuchadnezzar (von Soden, *ZAW* 53 [1935] 84–85; McNamara, *ITQ* 37 [1970] 145–148). Herodotus tells of dreams attributed to a series of Median and Persian rulers relating to their political or military future, some interpreted by the Magi (1.107–8, 209–10; 3.30; 7.12–19).

(c) The statue motif has a background in colossi at Rhodes, Memphis, and elsewhere, but not least in palace and temple at Babylon itself; the motif appears in other stories (see Herodotus 1.183; Dan 3; Bel; references in C. Kuhl, *Die drei Männer im Feuer* [BZAW 55 (1930)] 6–7). Statues made of a combination of materials are instanced: e.g., statues of Baal at Ugarit (Pope and Tigay, *UF* 3 (1971) 127; *ANEP* 481–84). Greek philosophy pictured the body-politic, headed by the king, corporately (cf. Flusser, *IOS* 2 [1972] 170), and Iranian sources picture the world as a huge man (Bentzen).

(d) The theme of metals symbolizing eras appears first in the eighth(?)-century Greek poet Hesiod (*Works and Days* 106–201). He divides humanity into five ages, the first three and the fifth being golden, silver, bronze, and iron. It also features in Zoroastrian texts, medieval in the form known to us but containing material that may well derive from the Hellenistic period or even that of Zarathustra himself (discussion in Hellholm, *Apocalypticism*). In Denkard ix 8, the world's spiritual history is divided into gold, silver, steel, and "mixed iron" ages, which take it from the age of revelation to the age of apostasy and wickedness. In Bahman Yasht i, Zarathustra dreams of a tree with branches made of these four metals, which Ahuramazda interprets to denote the reigns of a sequence of kings, and later of a tree with branches made of six or seven metals, denoting a longer sequence of rulers. None of these versions of the motif speaks of a final, ultimate age to succeed the iron/mixed iron age.

(e) The periodization of history into a sequence of empires reflects the shaping of the political history of the ancient Near East by a succession of empires, Assyria, Media/Babylon (respectively to the north/east and to the south/west of the old Assyrian empire), Persia, Greece, and Rome. Ancient writers were quite aware of the outline of this history. It appears in Chronicles in the OT as Assyria, Babylon, Persia; in Herodotus 1.95, 130 as Assyria, Media, Persia; and in the Akkadian "Dynastic Prophecy" as Assyria, Babylon, Persia, Greece, which may also picture good and bad reigns alternating (Grayson, *Texts,* 6–37). By c. 300, this historical outline has become a formal scheme of four empires, Assyria, Media or Babylon, Persia, and Greece, to which Rome is later added (see *Sib. Or.* 4: cf. Collins, *OTP* 1:381–89). Each scheme can work either to a climax that takes a positive view of the last empire in the scheme, or to a negative climax and the hope of a new empire—though not necessarily a final, ultimate one (but see Hallo, *IEJ* 16 [1966] 231–42, for an eschatological reading of Akkadian prophecies; cf. also Höffken, *WO* 9 [1977] 57–71).

Parallels between such sources and Daniel are sufficiently clear to establish that they provide some of the background to the dream, and to chaps. 7–12, but Daniel's distinctiveness is sufficiently clear to locate it one step from them, through the mediation of other cultures (Hengel, *Judentum,* 331 [ET 1:181]) and/or through the author's creativity (Hasel, *JSOT* 12 [1979] 23) and/or his theological and ethical distinctiveness (Baldwin, *TynB* 30 [1979] 92–99).

Interpreters disagree over whether at heart Dan 2 is a court-tale (which happens to contain a dream report) or a dream report (the court-tale being mere framework). The two features are both prominent, and this corresponds to Gen 41. There, however, the two are more integrally related: the insight which is proved by the court contest qualifies Joseph to deal with the crisis revealed by the dream. Dan 2 follows Gen 41 in including both features, but they do not interrelate. The contest and Nebuchadnezzar's recognition of Daniel are unrelated to the content of the dream; the latter's importance is independent of its context. One has to conclude that the chapter simply has two facets, not wholly integrated, but both original. It is not to be assimilated to narratives in which the content of the dream/vision is less significant, or to dream/visions where the narrative element is merely framework. It has a theme within a theme. It thus parallels other ancient works that combine story and didactic material (especially Ahiqar). Both facets (and the whole chapter) reflect the unique sovereign power of the God of Israel, simultaneously unveiled to and concealed from Nebuchadnezzar, relied on by Daniel, revealed through and in the dream/vision, and recognized by Nebuchadnezzar. Only God controls history, and only he reveals what it holds.

Structure

The opening verse unveils the issue the chapter as a whole is concerned with, the significance of a dream of Nebuchadnezzar's. The first major scene (vv 2–12) describes an abortive attempt to deal with the matter. A brief narrative opening introduces the Babylonian sages, at the king's command (v 2). The body of the scene comprises a conversation between the two parties, each speaking three times and becoming more anxious and hysterical (vv 3–11). A brief narrative closure then reports a second royal command, which provides the sages with a fatal exit (v 12). Ironic references to the times changing (v 9) and to the impossibility of divining the actual contents of a dream without divine help (v 11) point to later features of the story (vv 21, 37–45; vv 18–23, 26–30). The second scene (vv 13–23) promises to deal with the issue that has been left unresolved, though it does not yet actually do so. Conversation between Daniel and Arioch/the king (vv 14–16) leads to a report of Daniel's words with his friends and God (vv 17–18) and of God's response and Daniel's song of praise (vv 19–23). The length and exalted tone of this last make it the high point of the scene. It prepares the reader for vv 37–45 (Jerome), anticipating the outcome and the dream's contents, without revealing it as a whole at this point. The scene in fact takes matters round in a circle (from Arioch to prayer and back), like the opening scene, and further builds the suspense of the story.

Verse 24 thus picks up from vv 13–16, verbal parallels indicating the links between the two. But the third scene (vv 24–30) yet further delays the actual resolution of the opening problem, by requiring Arioch to introduce Daniel to Nebuchadnezzar (which for opposite dramatic reasons was not required in v 16), Nebuchadnezzar to quiz Daniel about his ability, and Daniel to draw attention to the theological background to and implications of the situation (taking up the sages' words from vv 10, 11). Daniel thus further teases the reader with the dream's general significance without actually relating it. The slowing down of the story reaches virtual standstill in the chiastic repetitiveness of vv 28–29. The fourth scene (vv 31–45) consists solely in a speech of Daniel recounting the dream and its prophetic meaning, and asserting the certainty of its fulfillment. In the dream, the focus is on the fearfulness of its subject, and on its destruction. In the interpretation, which receives twice as much space, the focus is on two specific parts of the statue, one of which relates directly to Nebuchadnezzar, and on what displaces it. The closing scene (vv 46–49) largely ignores the content of the dream. Nebuchadnezzar reveres Daniel and his God for the resolution of the original issue and puts Daniel in a position of power over the imperiled empire and the discredited sages.

Comparing Dan 2 with Gen 41 brings out important distinctive marks of the former, as well as important features it shares with Gen 41. (a) In Daniel the king requires to be told the actual contents of the dream as well as its significance. The terms of the contest between the sages and the Israelite hero are thus higher, as in Daniel's challenge and his achievement greater than Joseph's. (b) The varieties of sages are listed at length (vv 2, 27) and their helplessness before their challenge is dwelt on at length. (c) Nebuchadnezzar, the angry tyrant, also raises the stakes in the contest, threatening an unpleasant death if the sages cannot fulfill their task, but offering rich rewards if they can. Daniel thus saves their lives and receives rich rewards. (d) Daniel is not a humiliated prisoner, like Joseph, who needed to wash and change before entering the king's presence, but a man of initiative and shrewd judgment. He marches in to request what the sages were denied, and gets it; he marches back with the solution for the king, and the king's Lord High Executioner jumps to attention and scurries to lead him in to the king. (e) Daniel is portrayed as a model for spirituality in his attitude of trust, expectancy, and gratitude, expressed in his practice of prayer and praise in the fellowship of his friends. (f) The contents of his praise expresses key affirmations about God's sovereignty over human affairs and his revelation of the secrets of history which he alone knows; these affirmations reappear in his introductory words to Nebuchadnezzar. (g) The dream refers not merely to the immediate future within the king's reign but to the end of the era. The story thus overtly shifts the locus of God's saving acts from the past to future (even the hearers' future), more radically than the prophets do; its readers can look to a new act of deliverance for themselves (Jones, 86–88, commenting on von Rad). The dream's content and message are distinctive. Unlike Joseph, Daniel offers no practical suggestions arising from the dream. (h) As a result of Daniel's request regarding his friends, Nebuchadnezzar does not merely give Daniel administrative responsibility, like Pharaoh, but instead makes him head over the sages, allowing him to remain at the court. Instead of giving him state honor, he offers sacrifice to him. Instead of giving him a pagan priest's daughter in marriage, he acknowledges his God as sovereign and revealer.

The effect of these distinctive features is to give Dan 2 a more heightened tone. It is like Gen 41, only more so. This feature, combined with Gen 41's context on the eve of the exodus and Dan 2's in the exile, when Israel stands in need of a new exodus, means that Joseph could be seen as a type of Daniel. Some otherwise puzzling features of Dan 2 (e.g., vv 1, 46, 48b) find their explanation in this relationship of correspondence or contrast with Gen 41, rather than in their relationship with the concrete historical actuality of the exile (Ehrlich, *Traum,* 103).

The characterization of the main figures in the story is effected by means of cartooning so as to polarize them: Nebuchadnezzar in the extremes of his original violence and anxiety and of his later reverence and gratitude, the sages exposed in their pretension and incompetence, Daniel as the model of wisdom and piety. Among the chapter's stylistic features are (a) accumulating expressions of related meaning: many terms for sages (vv 2, 10, 27), rewards (v 6), rulers (v 10), power (v 37), shattering (v 40), homage (v 46). The effect of these is to increase the force of a phrase, emphasizing what manifold opportunity was given to Babylonian wisdom to prove itself (v 2), how great its opportunity for self-advancement (v 6), how unprecedented Nebuchadnezzar's challenge to it (v 10), how total its defeat (v 27), how vast Nebuchadnezzar's power (v 37), how devastating the destructiveness of the fourth kingdom (v 40), how complete Nebuchadnessar's obeisance (v 46). Further combinations of terms feature in the hymnic parallelism of vv 20–23. (b) Hendiadys, often with assonance: perverse lies (v 9), furious rage (v 12), shrewd judgment (v 12), deeply hidden (v 22), acknowledge and praise (v 23), visionary dream (v 29), finally shatter (v 44). Such usage stems from BH/BA's relative preference for nouns and verbs over adjectives and adverbs; it adds emphasis by lengthening phrases. (c) Alternating words or forms of similar meaning: four words for "tell" (e.g., vv 2, 4, 5), two for "kill" (e.g., vv 12, 13), three expressions for "pottery" (vv 33, 41), three for "partly" (v 41); two forms of פעם (vv 1, 3), of רעע (v 40), and of ערב (vv 41, 43); also the change in the order of the components in the statue (vv 34, 45). These alternations seem to be simply stylistic. For the chapter's major themes, more significant is the recurrence of expressions related to time, especially עלם "age" זמן "time," עדן "time" (vv 4, 8, 9, 16, 20, 21, 44); other expressions in vv 28, 29, 45. (d) Reusing words in fresh contexts or with different nuances. The root זמן itself is used both nominally for "time" and verbally for "arrange" (vv 9, 16). על and אזל recur in connection with Daniel's going to see the king and going home, then returning with his revelation (vv 16–17, 24–25). נפק records first the ordinance going out, then the executioner going out (vv 13, 14). בעא relates the executioners' inquirty after Daniel, Daniel's inquiry of the king, then Daniel and the friends' inquiry of God (vv 13, 16, 18, 23, also 49). A noticeable verbal feature of vv 1–23 is the nine occurrences of מלה ("word, thing"; cf. BH דבר). The story trades on its range of nuances, by means of which it can make and at the same time deny links through the story, and keep jolting and slowing up the reader. The chapter makes little use of repetition for the sake of economy of expression such as characterizes more traditional narrative (cf. Niditch and Doran, *JBL* 96 [1977] 188).

A further striking rhetorical feature is a change from Hebrew to Aramaic within v 4. Aramaic was the international language of the Middle East and the transition to this foreign but related tongue conveys the sense of foreign sages' using their alien language (Plöger). The transition thus comes at a natural point, like that in Ezra 4:8.

The chapter contains some repetitiveness (e.g., vv 28–30) and apparent discontinuity (e.g., over whether Daniel is a sage and is well known to the king). This might suggest that the chapter has undergone conflation or expansion, e.g, in vv 13–23, 28–30, 36–45, 48–49 (Hartman; Davies, *JTS* 27 [1976] 392–401; Steck, "Weltgeschehen," 53–62; Schreiner, "Gestalt und Botschaft," 133–37). But repetitiveness or discontinuity may as likely be the responsibility of an author as a redactor, and I have preferred to seek to interpret the chapter as it stands.

Setting

Like chap. 1, Dan 2 presupposes a setting in a dispersion community where Jews are a religious and ethnic minority. It is commonly assumed that the four empires are Babylon, Media, Persia, and Greece, and that 2:41–43 reflect expansion of the chapter in the third century; Ginsberg (7–9) seeks to specify the date more precisely. But such views are not compelling, and see *Comment:* it is doubtful whether there are grounds for dating the chapter in the Greek peirod, though it might belong there. The title "Lord of heaven" would perhaps have been avoided in a story developed in the second century (see *Comment*).

In its place in the book as a whole, the chapter introduces the four stories that follow, with which it has many links of motif and phrase (see *Form*). Thus v 49 locates three friends in the provincial administration for chap. 3, and Daniel at court for chaps. 4–5 (Eissfeldt, *ZAW* 72 [1960] 134–48). Chap. 2 holds the friends and Daniel together, even though the former play a rather nominal role, whereas subsequently they only appear separately. While court-tale and vision both lead in to chaps. 3–6, the vision of God's final reign which replaces human kingdoms sets their concerns in a broader and more far-reaching context from the beginning (Plöger) and also introduces chaps. 7–12, where Daniel himself dreams of such kingdoms and subsequently perceives further aspects of history to come.

The chapter's relationship with Dan 1 is ambiguous. The story gives substance to 1:20, though the king's failure to consult Daniel and his needing to have him introduced is odd after 1:17–19. The important motifs of the successful sage appearing last, and his being spectacularly rewarded at the end, are perhaps allowed to recur notwithstanding the formal tensions between stories that this produces (see also *Comment* on v 1).

Comment

1 On such dates, see on 1:1. This date may specifically suggest the period just after Nebuchadnezzar's great triumph at Carchemish: the story then cuts the victor down to size (Hammer). The date seems to clash with 1:5, 18. If it is not a fictional note designed to add to the impression of actuality rather than to convey historical information, so that the question of its relationship to chap. 1 need not be raised (Plöger), it can be harmonized with chap. 1 by assuming it uses the Babylonian reckoning (cf. *Comment* on 1:1) (Driver). The denouements in 1:18–20 and 2:45–49 might then refer to the same events.

2 In OT, NT, and elsewhere in the ancient world, dreams feature both as ordinary human experiences and as means of divine communication. Of the latter, some bring a straightforward, verbal message, while in others the message comes in symbols that require interpretation. For their interpretation, one could look to further divine revelation, to a diviner's intuition, or to the collections of oneirological omens that might provide a relevent precedent. Neither Israel nor other cultures give dreams a central place as means of divine communication, but neither do they take a negative attitude to the phenomenon as such (though see Jer 23:9–40; *b. Berakot* 55–57 offers an interesting discussion) (see further Oppenheim, "Dreams"; Onuse, *Currents* 8 [1981] 166–71; Resch, *Traum;* Ehrlich, *Traum*). Nebuchadnezzar's summoning of the diviners implies that the royal dream is assumed to be of state significance, not that he is troubled by an ordinary private dream. It is the diviners' responsibility to interpret omens of various kinds for him and to advise him on how to avert misfortune threatened by them. Their role in Babylon paralleled that of prophets in Israel (e.g., 2 Kgs 23).

Diviners is by origin an Egyptian word denoting priests/magicians skilled in cuneiform. It is used for dream interpreters at the Assyrian court and in the OT for the magicians of Egypt to whom Joseph proved superior; both usages make it appropriate here. (See Oppenheim, "Dreams" 238; Müller, *VT* 20 [1970] 473). *Chanters* (Akk. *âšipu*) is a more common Babylonian term for magical practitioners skilled at interpreting signs in people who are ill and (presumably) at conjurations and rituals designed to influence how matters turn out for them (Oppenheim, *Mesopotamia,* 289–305; Saggs, *Babylon,* 303–28). It may be cognate with BH אסף, "cure" (2 Kgs 5): cf. the names of Asaph, the head of a guild of musicians and prophets, and of the diviner Joseph (E. C. D. MacLaurin, "Joseph and Asaph," *VT* 25 [1975] 27–45).

Charmers (Akk. *kašapu*) is another word for people skilled in charms and incantations, a more common OT term used to denote the not merely pathetic but sinful practitioners of alien magic and divination (e.g., Isa 47:9, 12). On *Chaldeans* see on 1:3–5; it is also used (e.g., v 4) to denote the groups as a whole, as are *sages* (e.g., v 12) and *diviners* (4:6 [9]). The "sages," then, are not wise men such as Proverbs speaks of but experts in esoteric wisdom and mantic arts (as sometimes in BH: see Müller, *UF* 1 [1969] 79–85). They are people who can resolve mysteries. A further term, גזרין, appears first in 2:27. "Exorcists" is suggested by its use in 4QPrNab 1.4. גזר means "cut" and thus "determine": cf. Symmachus *θύτοι*, Vg *aruspix*, perhaps implying hepatoscopers; perhaps determining the future (KB); perhaps making decisions regarding spirits (A. Dupont-Sommer, "Exorcismes et guérisons dans les écrits de Qoumrân," *Congress Volume: Oxford 1959* [VTSup 7 (1960)] 256–58); perhaps "cutting" the way off for evil spirits (J. Carmignac, "Un équivalent français de l'araméen *'gazir,'*" *RevQ* 4 [1963–64] 277–78).

The terms are thus used randomly and interchangeably; the author was not referring to specific groups and consciously excluding ones that happen not to be mentioned (there was, indeed, no Babylonian group specifically concerned with interpreting dreams). They are all variant synonyms for the Babylonian diviners whose role was central to Babylonian religious and political life, though the author uses a number of the terms in combination to convey the impression of the various guilds (on which see Oppenheim, *Mesopotamia*, 81–82; Saggs, *Babylon*, 346–48; Driver, 12–16). Cf. the further collections of exotic foreign terms in chap. 3.

3–16 There is a suggestion that Nebuchadnezzar has forgotten his dream or at least has only a vague idea what it was about (cf. v 29a) (on the motif of the forgotten dream, see Heller, *ZAW* 43 [1925] 243–46; Ehrlich, *Traum*, 93–100; *b. Berakot* 55b). The verses are ambiguous, however, and this facilitates the motif of the sages' misunderstanding of the king's request. As the dialogue develops, he keeps them in suspense over how much he remembers and how far he is thus capable of telling whether their account of the dream is correct, or how far v 9 is bluff. Parallels with Nabonidus's conflict with the Babylonian priesthood (*ANET* 312–15) and with Darius I's slaughter of Magi (Herodotus 3.68–79) are not very close, but may underlie the story. The sages' "lying, base response" (v 9), uttered in the hope that the "situation may change" (more literally that the *time* may change—i.e., a more propitious day arrive) is the undertaking to provide the interpretation if the king provides the dream: they are seeking to evade facing a challenge to show whether they have supra-normal knowledge by revealing what the actual dream was (which the king may be able to check). For the king's rage (v 12) cf. 3:13, 19; Esth 1:12; 7:7; Prov 16:14; 19:12; 20:2; 2 Macc 7:3. Historically, entering the king's presence (v 16) demands protocol that is ignored here (contrast vv 24–25; Esth 4:11; Herodotus 3.140; Josephus *Ant.* 10.10.3 [10.198]), perhaps partly to underline the contrast between Daniel's confidence and the sages' confusion (Plöger). The king's response to Daniel's request is also unmentioned, however, and v 16 seems to be deliberately brief, hastening on to vv 17–18. See also n. 16.a.

17–19 The title אלה שמיא ("God of heaven," v 18) appears only in chap.

2 (also Ezra, Nehemiah). It parallels the expression אלהא עליא "God Most High" used in Dan 3–7 both in general meaning and in resembling gentile titles for God of the kind that Jews sometimes could feel appropriate for Yahweh. Thus it is reminiscent of the Canaanite title *baʿal šāmēm* ("lord of heaven": cf. 5:23, also 4:34 [37]), which —like "Most High"— was apparently an epithet of the high god El (so R. A. Oden, "*Baʿal šāmēm* and *ʾEl*," *CBQ* 39 [1977] 457–73). Worship of "the Lord of heaven" was widespread throughout OT times. He was later equated with Zeus; hence, perhaps, it was avoided in the Antiochene period, as it seems to have been before the exile. Its popularity in the Persian period has been attributed to the influence of Zoroastrianism. (See D. K. Andrews, "Yahweh the God of the Heavens," in *The Seed of Wisdom* [FS T. J. Meek, ed. W. S. McCullough; Toronto: U Toronto, 1964] 45–57; Eissfeldt, "*Baʿalšamēm* und Jahwe," *ZAW* 57 [1939] 1–31 = Eissfeldt, *Kleine Schriften* 2 [Tübingen: Mohr, 1963] 171–98). Here it takes up the sages' confession that the gods' dwelling is not among mere humanity (v 11), yet denies that this makes God inaccessible; Gos is in heaven, but he reveals things on earth (v 28). At the same time, the title may be a reverential substitute for "Yahweh" (see on vv 20, 23) as "heaven" is later a reverential substitute for "God" (cf. Ahiqar 94–95; *OTP* 2:499). Avoiding the name Yahweh hardly means that no need was not felt to distinguish Israel's God from those of pagans; it is doubtful if any of the titles for God in Daniel implies a less particularist understanding of God than other parts of the OT (against Delcor, *Etudes,* 227).

"Mystery" (רז, OP, v 18) appears in the OT only in Dan 2; 4:6. At Qumran it becomes almost a technical term for an enigma that can only be interpreted by God's revelation, and particularly for God's hidden purpose at work in history despite its sin (e.g., 1QpHab 7.5, 8, 14) (cf. NT *μυστήριον*, BH סוד (E. Vogt, " 'Mysteria,' " *Bib* 37 [1956] 247–57; R. E. Brown, *CBQ* 20 [1958] 417–43 = *The Semitic Background of the Term "Mystery"* [Philadelphia: fortress, 1968] 1–30; I. Willi-Plein, "Das Geheimnis der Apokalyptik," *VT* 27 [1977] 62–81). For such revelatory visions taking place at night (v 19a), cf. especially Zech 1–6 (also 1 Sam 3; Job 4:13; 33:15). Daniel's "vision" is not a superior means of revelation to Nebuchadnezzar's "dream": in v 20 both words are used of Nebuchadnezzar's experience. But only Daniel has things "revealed" to him (see vv 28–30).

19b–23 "Blessing" comes to be a cultic expression, expecially when used in the Psalms for human beings blessing God. Yet its original life-setting is in the everyday world, the realm of human relationships and, as we find it here, the experience of God acting in providence and grace toward his people, to which they respond in praise and thanksgiving. To bless someone is to express in solemn words one's appreciation, gratitude, honor, recognition, or live; it suggests an acknowledging of communion with the one who is named as the object in the light of what that one has come to mean to you (see *TWAT* "ברך brk").

"The name of God" (v 20) is a further reverential substitute for "Yahweh" (cf. v 19). A person's name expressed something of their character, calling, religious commitment, or personal significance. The name stood for the person. The same was true of the name by which a deity was known: God is revealed in his name. To bless the name of God is thus to bless Yahweh himself; but the expression makes it possible to avoid actually uttering the name and perhaps misusing it (Exod 20:7). "The God of the fathers" (cf. v 23) is a title for God as he was known to Israel's ancestors before the revelation to Moses (Exod 3:13–16), but it came into increased usage after the exile, especially in chronicles (1 Chr 5:25; 12:17; 2 Chr 33:12), where it suggests adherence to Israel's own traditional faith rather than resource to novel or alien alternatives. The title here may, then, suggest a recognition that God is acting in his faithfulness to the character he has revealed to Israel in the past. At the same time, it may function as yet another reverential substitute for Yahweh.

The "wisdom" of vv 20–23 is again supernatural insight rather than empirical, rational knowledge. It is not something human beings achieve but something they receive from God by revelation, equivalent to the knowledge of God's purposes that prophets receive from being admitted to Yahweh's council. References to deeply hidden secrets and to light and darkness correspond to other allusions in the OT (Gen 1:4; Deut 29:28 [29]; Isa 45:7; Ps 139; Job 12; 28; 30:16–20) more than to those in the Qumran literature (especially light and darkness in 1QM) or gnosticism. The content of the revelation (v 21a) relates to God's lordship in history (cf. *might,* v 20); vv 37–45 will expand on it. Its talk of "times and eras" is taken further in the Qumran literature and in the periodizing of history in, e.g., *1 Enoch* 91:12–17; 93:1–10; cf. Dan 9:24–27, as a means of structuring the understanding and presentation of history (cf. J. Licht, ". . . תורה הותים," *Erets-Israel* 8 [1967] 63–70, 70*). In Dan 2 the phrase has more general reference; any structuring of history presupposed is that provided by the external course of political events, the fall and rise of dynasties referred to in v 21 and developed in vv 37–45.

24–30 Daniel apparently implies that the king's own thoughts (vv 29a, 30b) had turned to the future, and perhaps that he knew his dream related to the future of his empire—so that he ha some check on purported reconstructions and interpretations of his dream. That people's dreams relate to their current preoccupations is a common enough experience; for the motif, cf. Xerxes' dream (Herodotus 8.12–14). The king was thus not indulging in a pointless test of the sages; he knew he had dreamed about his own future but the dream had "hidden itself" (because of its unwelcome content) as dreams do.

The king's thoughts concern what will happen "in the future" (אחרי דנה, "after this," v 29). Etymologically, "at the end of the era" (literally "the days"; v 28) could also simply mean "in the future." אחרית "end" denotes not a single moment (contrast קץ "end") but the last part or the aftermath of something (8:19, 23; 10:14; 11:4; 12:8), and אחרית יומיא thus could mean "the last part/aftermath of the [present] days"; cf. Akk. *ana ah-rat ūmū* meaning "in the future" (*CAD* A, 1:194). The fourteen OT occurrences of "at the end of the era/days" (see BDB 31), however, suggest that in BH/BA the phrase has a more precise meaning. "The days" are a possibly long, but not interminable, period that will or must elapse before certain predictions, promises, or warnings are fulfilled. The phrase thus refers to "the time of fullfillment." This may come at the End of the Age, though the phrase itself is not of eschatological meaning; it only acquires this association through being used in such contexts (cf. 1Q CD 4.4; SA 1.1). In vv 28–29, then, “in the future” will denote the whole period from Nebuchadnezzar onward (cf. v 45), while “at the end of the era” refers more specifically to the events that bring that whole period to a close (cf. v 44). (On “the end of the days,” see H. Seebass, *TWAT* “אחרית ʾachᵃrîth”; J. T. Willis, “The Expression *beʾacharith hayyamim* in the Old Testament,” *Restoration Quarterly* 22 [1979] 60–71; W. Staerk, “Der Gebrauch der Wendung הימים באחרית im at. Kanon,” *ZAW* 11 [1891] 247–53; G. W. Buchanan, “Eschatology and the ‘End of Days,’ ” *JNES* 20 [1961] 188–93; J. Carmignac, “La notion d’eschatologie dans la Bible et à Qumrån,” *RevQ* [1969–71] 17–31; H. Kosmala, “At the End of the Days,” *ASTI* 2 [1963]27–37 = Kosmala, *Studies* 1:73–83; J. P. M. van der Ploeg, “Eschatology in the Old Testament,” *OTS* 17 [1972] 89–99; O. Rinaldi, “Nota,” *BibOr* 7 [1965] 60; Jones, 220–39; Y. Hoffmann, “ ‘ההוא יביום ו הימים אחרית,’ ” *BetM* 22 [1976–77] 435–44, 529).

31–35 A variety of extrabiblical backgrounds have been posited for the five-part statue (see *Form*). For its materials, the OT background is at least as significant (see K. H. Singer, *Die Metalle Gold, Silber, Bronze, Kupfer und Eisen im Alten Testament und ihre Symbolik* [Würzburg: Echter, 1980]). Gold and silver are standard symbols for what is majestic and precious, in political and religious contexts, bronze and iron for what is strong and hard. The four metals together sum up the variety of valuable natural resources or valuable booty (Josh 6:19, 24; 22:8; Job 28:1–2). There is no implication of deterioration as we move from head to trunk to hips to legs; nor are these four “the metals of idolatry” (cf. 3:1; 5:2, 23) (against Collins, *Vision,* 44). So far, the statue embodies a many-faceted power, splendor, stength, and impressiveness. Clay, however, suggests weakness and transience (Job 4;19; 13:12). Pottery is thus a quite alien element, the antithesis of the political power and strength implied by the four metals (see Isa 41:25 in the context of 40:19; 45:2). It theatens the stability of the otherwise uniformly overpowering edifice that towers above it. All that is needed for the edifice to collapse is a chance rockfall that hits the statue at its weak point. The logic-suspending fantasy of dream then appears at its strongest as the awesome statue is not just toppled but in an instant turned into mere wheat husks as they are blown away from the threshing floors exposed to the wind (recalling Isa 41:12–16), while the rock grows into a monumental crag that dominates the whole world (recalling Isa 2:2–3; 11:9).

36–43 The statue’s four parts signify four regimes. מלכו can denote royal authority (5:18), realm (4:15 [18]), individual reign (6:29 [28]), or empire (7:23). The four מלכותא have usually been interpreted as four empires, but Nebuchadnezzar personally is the head, so it is more natural to refer them to the regins of four kings over a single empire, destroyed at a blow by the “rock.” In contrast to the dream, the interpretation gives special attention to the first and last elements in the statue. Nebuchadnezzar’s empire was indeed the most powerful of his day, and it was of course the one that dominated the people of God for several generations. The understanding of Nebuchadnezzar combines an anticipation of Dan 4 (especially vv 7–9, 17–19 [10–12, 20–22) with a recollection of Jer 27:5–8 // Ps 8. Underlying these passages (and thus less directly Dan 2) are conventions of asserting humanity's dignity and lordship by attributing to them authority over the animal creation. These conventions also underlie Gen 1–2, and perhaps also eastern monarchs' establishing of game parks for caputred wild animals (Oppenheim, *Mesopotamia,* 46–48). Verse 30 thus expresses Nebuchadnezzar's worldwide rule metaphorically, as the description of him as king among kings (cf. Ezek 26:7, and common with reference to Persian and Seleucid kings) does so more straightforwardly. Dan 2 emphsizes that Nebuchadnezzar rules by the gift of God. Even the might, authority, and glory of Nebuchadnezzar come not from himself but from the God of heaven, the Lord even of the king among kings (v 47).

Jeremiah speaks of the rule of Nebuchadnezzar's son and grandson after him, until after seventy years "the time of his land" comes (25:12; 27:7). The perspective of Dan 4 is thus extended beyond a particular context in Nebuchadnezzar's own lifetime to God's activity as Lord of the future history of Nebuchadnezzar's empire (Müller, *UF* 1 [1969] 86). In recalling Jeremiah's words and his figure of speech, Daniel adapts them to another figure, *four* kings suggesting completeness (cf. four quarters of the world, four seasons, and especially the four horns/smiths of Zech 2:1–4 [1:18–21]). Possibly this itself reflects the historical fact that Nebuchadnezzar was to have more than two successors before the seventy years would elapse.

In Dan 2, the second regime is inferior to the first, the third equal to it in power, the fourth of devastating might but ultimate vulnerability. The sequence thus manifests no consistent pattern of degeneration, as in Hesiod, or of contrast between the first three and the last, or of a good-bad-good-bad sequence like that of some Babylonian quasi-prophecies (see *Form*). Daniel passes quickly over the second and third regimes, however, in order to focus on the fourth, elaborating on the dream's brief description (e.g., adding the toes), as he had on the first. The fourth regime has a crushing power (v 40) but an unexpected fragility (vv 41–42: see n. 41.c). It seeks to repair this, but cannot do so in a lasting way (v 43: the reference is probably to intermarriage). Daniel thus emphasizes an arc drawn from Nebuchadnezzar's empire, when the story of the world-powers' direct hegemony over Israel begins, to that manifestation of the world-empire under which the book's implied readers live. It characterizes the world power in originally positive terms, impressive and deserving of admiration in its God-given might. In its final manifestation, however, its power has become crushing—though not explicitly wicked—yet strangely vulnerable and needing to be buttressed by desperate and doomed means.

Chap. 2 does not identify the second, third, and fourth regimes. In chap. 7 the motif of four regimes recurs in the context of the setting of chaps. 7–12 in the Greek period, but one should not assume that that motif is used in the same connection in chap. 2. The characterization of the fourth (vv 40–43) has been connected with events in the Greek period (e.g., Torrey), but it could as easily apply to the Babylonians or Persians. Historically, Nebuchadnezzar II (604–562) was followed by Amel-Marduk (Evil-merodach) (562–560), Nergal-šar-uṣur (Neriglissar (560–556), Labaši-Marduk (556), and Nabuna'id (Nabonidus) (556–539), whose son Bel-šar-uṣur (Belshazzar) was regent in Babylon when Cyrus conquered the city. The four reigns might thus be those of four of these kings (Eerdmans, "Origin," 198–202; Beek, 38–54; Davies, *JTS* 27 [1976] 392–401, or—less plausibly—four Assyrian kings (Löwinger, "Nebuchadnezzar's Dream," 1:336–52), Persian kings (Schedl, *Geschichte* 5:79–80), or Ptolemaic kings (Gammie, *JBL* 95 [1976] 197–202). The possibility of these various interpretations raises the question whether the text's unspecificness makes it inappropriate to attempt to identify the rulers referred to after Nebuchadnezzar, as Jer 27 refers to no specific actual descendants, but simply has them in prospect (Stevenson, *TCUOS* 7 [1934–35] 4–8; Bickerman, 61–63). Perhaps even the symbolic number "four" cannot be pressed historically. There are, indeed, hints of five regimes in vv 32–33, 45, and a five-regime scheme might have been brought into conformity with a four-regime one (cf. Jepsen, *VT* 11 [1961] 388; Schreiner, "Gestalt und Botschaft," 134). There is a similar tension within some of the extrabiblical material.

The unspecificity of Dan 2 means that the four regimes can only be identified on grounds external to it. They can be linked with Nebuchadnezzar and three of his Babylonian successors on the basis of other OT material: the rock then is Cyrus, which fits with the role ascribed to him in Isa 41; 45. The downfall of the empire of Nebuchadnezzar and his Babylonian successors at Cyrus's hand is then linked with the end of Judah's exile, which fits with the promises in Jer 25:12; 27:7.

But Daniel itself does not explicitily describe Cyrus's arrival as the end of Babylon's empire or as the end of Judah's exile. Cyrus's arrival makes no difference to Babylon or to the exiles. The Book of Daniel does, however, refer to four regimes. After Nebuchadnezzar's (2:37; 5:18) came that of Belshazzar (5:28), his "son" (5:2, 11, 14, 18, 22), who was to be "inferior" to him (cf. 5:22–28) (van Hoonacker, *ExpT* 13 [1901–2] 422–23). From Belshazzar this kingship passes to Darius the Mede (6:1 [5:31], cf. 6:29 [28]); he counts the whole world as within his kingdom, like Nebuchadnezzar (6:26–27 [25–26]). The fourth king is the Persian Cyrus, mentioned only at the close of the stories (6:29 [28]), but well known in Isa 41; 45, for his irresistible might. He was said to have been part-Median, part-Persian and to have married a Persian (Herodotus 1.55–56, 107–9; Xenophon, *Cyr.* 1.2.1; 8.5.17–20). Dan 9:1 describes him as ruling over the kingdom of the Chaldeans, the implication being that the Medes and Persians bring a new dynasty but within the history of one kingdom or empire. The perspective suggested by chap. 1 and subsequent chapters, then, is that the four regimes in chap. 2 span the period from Nebuchadnezzar to Cyrus. The advent of the Persians has not brought the end of world dominion as Jeremiah and Isa 40–55 had promised. The implied readers of Daniel in the Persian period, perhaps disillusioned and depressed like those to whom prophecies in Haggai, Zechariah, and Isa 56–66 were addressed, are invited to hold onto the conviction that the Chaldean colussus will not stand for ever. It has feet of clay. This, indeed, is the significance of the statue's message however the parts of the statue are identified.

44–45 Jeremiah's prophecy had not looked beyond the destruction of the Babylonian empire. Daniel's message pictures the establishment of a quite different sovereignty.

The rock, the crag into which it grows, and the crag from which it came, might all be symbols for Israel herself, centered on Mount Zion, and might then indicate the hope that she will be used to bring about the fall of the world empires (Davies, *JTS* 27 [1976] 401). But there is no explicit allusion to the new regime being Israel's (contrast 7:18, 27). It is more natural to take the rock that destroys the regimes and grows into a crag filling the world as standing for God's own sovereignty and power establishing a lasting regime (cf. the mountain that symbolizes and embodies God's rule, in Isa 2:2–3; Ezek 17:23; Ps 2:6; 48:2–3 [1–2]). The crag from which the rock came (v 45) might be a symbol for God himself in his strength and reliability (Deut 32:18; Ps 18:3 [2]; 31:3–4 [2–3]). Again, the elaboration of the dream in the interpretation draws attention to a particular point, the new regime's divine origin (Joubert, 35). The one who was meant to be a source of strength and protection thus becomes a mortal danger to those who build their own edifices and refuges (Isa 8:11–15). But one should be wary of allegorizing the picture.

"Those kings" could signify the succeeding heads of the fourth kingdom, but vv 41–43 have not specifically said that the fourth regime constituted a dynasty rather than just one reign, and they more naturally denote Nebuchadnezzar's three successors. There is no need to infer that all three regimes survive till a moment of simultaneous destruction (against Ginsberg, 6): again, the visions are not allegories. There is no clear assertion that the fourth regime is brought to an end as a judgment on its sin (contrast chap. 7). It falls because of its inherent fragility.

46–49 In a Hellenistic context, Nebuchadnezzar's "worship" of Daniel might be seen as a natural way of honoring a benefactor (Mastin, *ZAW* 85 [1973] 80–93), or as a way of "demythologizing" deified kings (Lacocque), or as a way of honoring the God Daniel represents (cf. Josephus's story about Alexander and the high priest, *Ant.* 11.8.5 [11.329–39]). In a pre-Hellenistic context, the second is also possible (cf. Olmstead, *History*, 217), but the last is most natural (cf. Jerome), and is perhaps suggested by the juxtaposition of v 47. We may compare the acknowledgment of Israel/Yahweh promised in Isa 45:14; 49:23; 60:14; but the acknowledgment of Daniel is more prominent than that of Yahweh (and more explicit than that of Israel). Thus vv 46–49 belong together: Nebuchadnezzar acknowledges Daniel, who has proved himself as a remarkable source of revelatory wisdom (v 46), acknowledges the God who gave him this widsom (v 47), and determines to elevate him to the position of political authority for which it qualifies him (v 48a), as well as to the position of supreme authority over the leaders of the guilds of sages who provided the king with counsel (v 48b), a post perhaps as difficult to accept as the worship of v 46.

Explanation

1–2 Nebuchadnezzar as an individual stood in the background in chap. 1; his figure now comes into sharper focus. It is only the second year of his reign. His prospects are high, his achievements already remarkable (see 1:1–2). Yet he is ill at ease, troubled by nightmares. They are not merely (we shall discover) the reflection of a neurotic felt insecurity on the part of a mighty emperor troubled by inner doubts. They correspond in Nebuchadnezzar's subjectivity to a real insecurity that attaches to his empire. No doubt his Jewish subjects and their descendants who told and heard the story often felt insecure and dreamed nightmares of their own about their future in dispersion. Nebuchadnezzar's nightmares witness to where actual insecurity lies. Nebuchadnezzar's dreams cannot be ignored. They are signs and omens, significant for the destiny of his empire. Dreams, like prophecies, can be manufactured, and need to be tested (Deut 13; Jer 23:25–32). Yet like vision and prophecy, they can be means of divine revelation. They cannot be evaded: they impose themselves, and can testify to the transcendence of God revealing himself as sovereign shaper of earthly events (Gen 37–41; 1 Sam 3). They thus become part of the expectation and actuality of what God does at the climax of the ages (Joel 3:1 [2:28]; Matt 1–2; Acts 2:17) (Resch, *Traum,* 129–37; Gnuse, *CurTM* 8 [1981] 166–71).

Like any powerful administration, Nebuchadnezzar's regime has its back-up agencies and task forces, themselves able to access vast information resources to enable them to interpret the data Nebuchadnezzar provides them with and to suggest what measures need to be taken to counteract any threats to the state that the data portend. Dreams were not the most common sources of such data, but were a familiar enough phenomenon, treated by dream-books. So Nebuchadnezzar summons various of the guilds of his civil servants. The very variety of those he summoned underlines the anxiety built into the situation, and the mockery with which Israelites are invited to view the multiplicity of the Babylonians' toilsome attempts to control their destiny (Isa 47:12–13) (Ehrlich, *Traum,* 92).

3–9 "Explain my dream to me," the king demands. "Long live the king," they begin in reply: there is an irony about the standard courtly greeting, because events are to affirm that the only lasting name and the only lasting reign is the name of God and the reign of God (vv 20, 44). "Certainly we can explain your dream," they go on, "just outline it to us." They have extensive collections of dream omens which they can consult if the motifs in the dream are not of obvious significance. But they have missed an ambiguity in the king's request. In fact he requires them to tell him the actual contents of his dream, not just to look up the meaning of its motifs. The requirements is solemnly proclaimed; failure will mean death and the ruin of their families, success will mean rewards and honour. These alternatives highlight the ambiguous prospects that attach to involvement in the Babylonian court (cf. Müller, *VT* 26 [1976] 340–41]. Nebuchadnezzar is a man of brilliance, achievement, vision, and generosity, yet also mistrustful, angry, arbitrary, violent. The portrait is cartooned, yet consistent with other aspects of Middle Eastern courtly life (Esther, Herodotus, 1001 Nights). Like political life in the modern world, the power and glory of participation in the affairs of state would be attractive and an object of wistful longing for people like Jews who were not part of the secular power structure, but at the same time alien and frightening because of its reputation for contention, betrayal, scandal, humiliation, and moral pressure.

Pardonably, we might think, the civil servants can hardly believe their ears. Their profession is to apply the insights of experience and tradition to data that the king gives them. They are men of sensitivity, imagination, and insight, but they need data to work on, as they patiently and politely point out. In their renewed request, however, the king sees evasiveness and a confession of helplessness that suggests that their whole profession is a sham. All they can offer is textbook answers to set questions. Their inability to move beyond these parameters undermines the validity of the answers they provide within them. They are simply seeking to gain a period of time, in the devious hope that the situation may change in some way. Perhaps they will be able to discover an answer to the apparently impossible question, perhaps sources in the palace will discover for them what the king dreamed or whether he knows what he dreamed, perhaps he will forget the matter (or himself be removed?). Nebuchadnezzar, however, will not let go of the possibility of testing what real access the experts have to resources of insight beyond those available to other people. He requires of them a test Jesus submitted to (Mark 2:1–12): do something that can be checked, whose testimony may carry over into the area that cannot be checked. If they can divine the contents of Nebuchadnezzar's dream, their understanding of its meaning compels respect. If not, the latter is no more than ordinary human opinion.

Nebuchadnezzar's talk of their buying a period of time and hoping the times may change picks up a motif that runs through the chapter. The sages vaguely hope that circumstances may alter, and astutely seek to manipulate them, while Nebuchadnezzar sidesteps their maneuver and declares the hope false. Neitherside takes into account the God who controls circumstances, though unconsciously they prepare us to meet him.

10–12 The sages' third and final attempt to persuade Nebuchadnezzar to be reasonable admits what the king has suspected. After all, he should surely grant, they are only human beings: court counselors, learned sages, expositors of the tradition. The king is treating them as if they were privy to the secrets of the gods. The wistful, sad admission that seeks to excuse them exposes them and judges them. The critique that began by making fun of the toilsome multiplicity of their guilds ends by scoring their futility. It parallels the contempt for the Babylonian sages in Isa 40–55 and the contempt for the Jerusalem prophets in Jeremiah (Isa 44:25; Jer 23:15–32). Jewish exiles might be tempted to find Israelite wisdom and Israelite faith in their God as lord of history looking extremely unimpressive compared with the resources and power of Nebuchadnezzar. Actually, Nebuchadnezzar is helpless. The Babylonians have only earthly techniques that are no heavenly use (in the absence of data) and heavenly beings who are no earthly use. The gods of Babylon are strikingly absent from this story. It is not an account of a conflict between the God of heaven and the gods of Babylon (or Persia) (against von der Osten-Sacken *Apokalyptik,* 18–34), but one between the this-worldly wisdom of Babylon and the supernatural wisdom of Daniel. In the conversation between king and sages, deity is only mentioned in order to be excluded from consideration (v 11).

13–18 Nebuchadnezzar is a man of extreme emotions and actions: in relation to the wise men at the beginning of the story, haunted, fearful, peremptory, tyrannical, violent, suspicious, unreasonable, malevolent, irascible (though all in vain); in relation to Daniel at the end, extravagant in his appreciation, his rewarding, and his promotion of Daniel and in his recognition of Daniel's God. The sages of Babylon descend from a matter-of-fact confidence, via bluster and disbelief, to a bewildered helplessness that faces the guillotine. Our attention now moves from these cartoon portraits to a picture in total contrast, of one who models wisdom and piety, shrewd and astute before Arioch, bold and confident before Nebuchadnezzar, open in fellowship with his friends, believing and urgent in prayer, lofty and profound in praise, decisive and assured when he returns with an explanation of the dream, straight and trenchant in declaring both its origins in God's revelation and its content regarding Babylon's future. Thus Daniel once again embodies both the experiential wisdom of a statesman and the revelatory wisdom of a seer (cf. 1:4, 17–20). The so-called sages have shown themselves fools lacking the diplomatic adroitness to handle the king, but Daniel has it; he gets his way where they could not. They were refused time to devise a solution to the conundrum for themselves; he is granted time to seek a revelation from God. They were dismissed for their self-confessed helplessness; he is accepted for his expectation that he can do something.

His undertaking to provide an answer recalls the instinctive boldness of his earlier offer of a trial period on a vegetarian diet (1:12). No doubt it presupposes that he will seek God and receive a revelation from him, but initially the emphasis lies on Daniel's courageous expectation that he can provide the answer, and on his decisiveness and calm confidence, which contrasts with the sage's incredulous impotence. In relation to the Babylonian authorities, Daniel stands alone. In relation to the people of God, however, he stands in fellowship with his three friends. The importance of that fellowship is that they join with him in laying hold of the divine resources that Daniel needs if his boldness is not to be exposed as foolhardiness.

19–23 The "mystery" is then "revealed" to Daniel. The background of these terms lies in the human experience of keeping and sharing confidence or secrets (see Prov 11:13; 20:19; 25:9; Sir 8:18; 12:11). This experience is applied to a prophet's being allowed to share in Yahweh's secret purpose (Amos 3:7; cf. 1 Sam 3:7; more generally, Deut 29:28 [29]). The theological term revelation, of great significance in recent centuries, has this rather narrow specific biblical background (see F. G. Downing, *Has Christianity a Revelation?* [London/Philadelphia: SCM/Westminster, 1964]).

In receiving visions and dreams that reveal the secret purpose of God in history—apparently understanding history is a divine gift, not a human achievement—Daniel is a prophet in all but name (Num 12:6). But Daniel is the recipient of revelation only in order that Nebuchadnezzar can be (v 28). The God who sends sun and rain to the wicked as well as the good does not stand off from the heathen powers who control Israel's destiny (Jerome; Steck, "Weltgeschehen," 56). He reveals his purpose to them through a prophet, as he had once to Israel's own kings (Anderson).

Having shown himself a man of wisdom and a man of prayer, Daniel also models the response of praise. His praise, and his subsequent confession before the king (vv 27–30), affirm what the dream and its interpretation will later reflect, that the God of heaven (v 19) who is the God of Israel (v 23) controls "times and eras"—the successive epochs ruled by one king or another, one empire or another. He has control of history, and (thus) has insight into history (vv 20–22). The wisdom being referred to here is not the quality of being wise but the possessing of knowledge (about history) that stems from being the deciding factor (in history) and issues in being alone able to grant knowledge (about history). The light and darkness referred to similarly refer to God's capacity to perceive where to human beings all seems dark.

His ability to reveal the secrets of history proves that he does control history. Like Isa 40–55, Daniel denies that history is determined by the planetary forces that the Babylonians studied (cf. Isa 40:25–26). History is under the control of God in his freedom. It is thus his secret. It cannot be predicted, divined by means of techniques, as the sages have now acknowledged. It can only be revealed—hence, in part, the motif of prayer and thanksgiving (Grelot, "Histoire," 105; Ehrlich, *Traum,* 102–3). The civil servants were supposed to know the times (Esth 1:13), but the idea is illusory. The times were fixed by a source to which they had no access. God controls times and eras and his name is blessed from age to age. The words for time that appeared earlier in nontheological contexts (vv 4, 8, 9, 16) now affirm that God alone is Lord of times and ages. Nebuchadnezzar, the sages, and also Daniel himself (v 30) are relativized by him. The pretensions of human magic, of human power, and even of human wisdom, are exposed.

Convictions such as these are characteristic of the OT, though they are expressed here with a universality that is unusual. They may be held to underlie the affirmation in Isa 41 that Yahweh alone is bringing about the victories of Cyrus over the Babylonians and that Yahweh alone is (thus) able to offer insight on the significance of these events. Yet those affirmations concern only specific historical events. Daniel will later speak of particular historical events, but his testimony here goes behind those to God's control of and insight into history as a whole. When Amos speaks of God revealing his secret (3:7), he refers to the secret significance of particular events; when Daniel speaks of God revealing his secret, revelation has as its object future history itself viewed as a whole and viewed from its destiny (cf. v 44) (Grelot, "Histoire," 89). Nebuchadnezzar has been wondering about the future (v 29), and as so often the thoughts suggest the dream (as *b. Berakot* 55b notes). God reveals that the wondering actually relates to events at the end of the era (v 28), the time when God's hand, long unseen, becomes visible bringing the fulfillment of his promises. The range of Daniel's vision and his prophetic role thus extend far beyond anything chap. 1 hinted or chaps. 4–5 parallel. The dream relates not just to a chapter in a man's life or a moment in an empire's history but offers a perspective on the future as a whole (Müller, VT 26 [1976] 338, 350; Plöger). This apocalyptic vision, at least, is one to which an eschatological perspective is integral.

A dramatic effect is achieved by the way Daniel's worship is recorded. First, the structure of his praise is other than one might have expected. The characteristic movement of a Psalm would be from testifying to God's specific recent act of grace, via an acknowledgement of his characteristic activity as revealer and lord of history, to worship of him for his personal characteristics, which these activities reflect. The reverse movement here gives prominence to the particular experience of God's power and wisdom that Daniel himself has been given. A further dramatic effect is achieved by recording this confession here, while reserving the content of the revelation for later. This also has a theological implication. Daniel is to reveal the destiny of Nebuchadnezzar's empire, and that revelation will evidence the power and wisdom of the God of heaven. Most of the time, however, the people of God have to live without revelations of this kind, yet they are still called to affirm that power and wisdom with Daniel on the basis of a revelation in prospect but yet unseen. We do not in fact see much evidence of the might and wisdom of God in international affairs, but we are called to believe in that wisdom to be revealed.

24–30 So Daniel returns to offer his interpretation to the king. There is an ambiguity about his position. He is someone renamed Belteshazzar (v 26) (after the king's god, 4:5 [8]) yet he comes to the king as a Jewish exile (v 25) who has received his revelation from his father's God (v 23). He is able to reveal the mystery to the king, not because he is a more skilled sage (cf v 30), but because he is granted access to supernatural sources of information (cf. Gen 41:16). As in Isa 41 and 47, the reason why Babylonian "wisdom" can be scorned is that something that works is now available. The key assertion of the book is not that there is a God in heaven (against Montgomery): everyone believed as much. It is that, contrary to the despairing assumption of the sages (v 11), this God reveals secrets. The sages were right that a divine revelation would be needed to provide what the king asked for, wrong to assume that this was impossible.

31–35 The awesomeness of Nebuchadnezzar's dream-statue seems to derive chiefly from its size. It anticipates the statue in chap. 3; like that one, it might represent a god or a man. The various metals suggest a combination of costliness and strength. Yet when our eyes reach the bottom of the statue a bizarre feature appears. A single rock is enough to exploit a fatal weakness that lies not in its head, like Goliath's (Anderson), but in its feet.

36–45 The statue represents the empire led by Nebuchadnezzar. It is a single statue, a single empire, passed on from one king to another. The vision focuses not on Israel's history, like the prophets', but on world history, and offers a theology of secular history, not one confined to salvation history (Koch, *HZ* 193 [1961] 3). Yet it does not stand for the whole of history seen as a "single compact phenomenon" (against Noth, *Studien*, 262 [ET 206]). If Daniel knows a scheme that suggests a theology of universal history, such as features in some extrabiblical texts, it turns this into an interpretation of a particular segment of hsitory, that which begins with Nebuchadnezzar (Jones, 250–52; Murdock, *Int* 21 [1967] 170–71). Yet picturing an empire headed by Nebuchadnezzar is not fortuitous, for he had brought the rule of Davidic kings in Jerusalem to an end. He ruled the first gentile empire directly to control the destiny of Israel. Beginning in his day the Jews are part of secular history. This does not means that history is working against God and his purpose for Israel. The Middle Eastern kings under whom the Jews will henceforth live are under God's sovereignty in the same real, though indirect, way as the kings of preexilic Judah had been. He sets their story in motion; he terminates it (Koch, *HZ* 193 [1961] 25–32). The history of the world

(Gen 1–11) had narrowed to become the history of Israel (from Abraham to the exile), but it now broadens to become the history of the nations, on the way to becoming the history of God's rule.

So the golden splendor of Nebuchadnezzar's empire is God-given. God *gave* Nebuchadnezzar not only Jerusalem (1:2) but all his royal might and power (v 37, cf. 5:18), indeed authority over all creation (v 38). based as it is on Jer 27:5–7, Daniel's claim represents the same theology of secular powers as the prophets' (cf. also Isa 10), though it takes that theology further. There a theology of world history was a marginal concern, here it becomes central. Were Nebuchadnezzar himself to claim to be "king among kings" and to hold "the kingdom, the power, and the glory" we would take it as an arrogant appropriation of God's own splendor (cf. v 47; 1 Chr 29:10–11; and the traditional ending to the Lord's Prayer). But it is God's revelation that gives Nebuchadnezzar's rule this very positive theological significance. Daniel makes its affirmations in the context of the domination of gentile peoples over Jews. It asserts that this comes about by the gift of God. Yet this dominion is ultimately destined to be brought to an end and replaced by God's implementing of his kingship. Bowing down to Babylon will not be for ever, but it is necessary now theologically, not merely pragmatically (as in Jer 27; 29).

The regimes that follow Nebuchadnezzar are not identified, nor are the reasons for the transitions discussed. Subsequent chapters may make it possible to infer their identity (see *Comment*), but in the drama of the story the description has to be allowed to remain allusive. People miss the point when they spend time arguing over who the empires were. For the recipients of the book what mattered was that they lived during the fourth regime, and when successive generations have reapplied have reapplied the scheme of empires to the history of their day, in principle they have responded to the vision in the way it sought. If for them the fourth empire is Britain or America or Israel or some other, then the vision applies to it.

The vision looks on from Nebuchadnezzar himself to that; the inferior second and strong third are thus relatively unimportant. It may be that a theological point is also implied. Daniel's understanding of Nebuchadnezzar as Yahweh's agent (1:1–2; 2:37–39) follows the prophetic perception of specific international events such as foreign invasions of Israel or Judah as a fulfilling of God's purpose. Yet when Daniel goes on to describe the development of imperial history after Nebuchadnezzar, no further events of this theological significance seem to be envisaged. Theologically nothing happens, as (or is it "therefore"?) historically nothing happens—though it may be the writer's context in the fourth regime that explains the feeling of nonengagement with real events in the Daniel stories, despite the vision's concern with history (Steck, "Weltgeschehen," 57–58). Nevertheless it is striking that there is no "is given" in vv 39–40, and the message may be that God is not in this history (Atzerodt, "Weltgeschichte," 242).

If the Vohuman Vasht-i pictures the iron-mixed age as the period of domination by demons (so Flusser, *IOS* 2 [1972] 166–68), Daniel's message contrastingly continues on the human plane; it suggests no cosmic dualism. The fourth regime has a remarkable strength. Evidently the readers know that they live under a power capable of awesome violence and destructiveness.

Yet the capacity to crush and shatter is not wicked in itself (God's rule has the same capacity: v 44). The description of the empire's downfall follows an account of attempts to mend its inherent fragility by intermarriage, a practice abhorrent to Jews. They are assured that these attempts will fail. Yet there is no explicit condemnation of the fourth regime, any more than of the others, nor does the vision imply that history has reached such a low point that divine intervention is inevitable (or imminent). History, it hints, is proceeding according to "laws" of its own, neither progressing nor degenerating, but simply taking its changing course, by God's permissive will. But then he acts, for reasons we are not given, though apparently not because history has manifestly reached the appropriate point for this or because a necessary sequence of events has taken place. It is not possible to work out when this act must come; human history always stands before the possibility of his acting (Noth, *Studien,* 263–65, 272–73 [ET 207–8, 214]). His act emerges from his own freedom. But when God's time comes, his kingdom requires the destruction of earthly kingdoms rather than his working through them. They are God's will for now, but not for ever; and when his moment arrives, his kingdom comes by catastrophe, not by development (Atzerodt, "Weltgeschichte," 248, 249).

There is no hint of timing in Daniel's revelation. Whether it is actually comes from the Babylonian period, the Persian period, or the Greek period, it implies that history can be divinely foreknown, but not that it is divinely foreordained. The chapter does not speak of final events fixed since time's beginning, of the whole world under evil's power, of a dualism of this world and the righteous world to come, of judgment in the form of an immutable fate, or of a division of world history into periods determined by God (Moltmann's characterization of apocalyptic, *Theologie,* 120 [ET 133–34]). Indeed, it satisfies von Rad's characterization of Israelite historiography ("Der Anfang der Geschichtschreibung im alten Israel," *Gesammelte Studien zum Alten Testament* [TBü 8 (1958); first published 1944] 148–54 = *The Problem of the Hexateuch* [tr. E. W. T. Dicken; Edinburgh/New York: Oliver and Boyd/McGraw-Hill, 1966] 166–71; cf. Jones, 91–92). It assumes that human beings make real decisions that do shape history, yet that human decision-making does not necessarily have the last word. It affirms the sovereignty of God in history, working sometimes via the process of human decision-making, sometimes despite it.

The end of history promised here is not history coming to its goal (W. Pannenberg, "Heilsgeschehen und Geschichte," *KD* 5 [1959] 220 = *Grundfragen systematischer Theologie* [Göttingen: Vandenhoeck, 1967] 25. = *Basic Questions in Theology* [tr. G. H. Keim and S. C. Guthrie; London/Philadelphia: SCM/Westminster, 1970] 1:18). Nor, however, is it history being broken off (R. Bultmann, *History and Eschatology* [Edinburgh: Edinburgh UP, 1957] = *Presence of Eternity* [New York: Harper, 1957] 29). Nor are the four empires succeeded by a further, fifth empire, but by something wholly other. Daniel promises a new future, one which is not merely an extension of the present (Jones, 102, 113–18). It is of supernatural origin. But it is located on earth, not in heaven. Daniel envisages no dissolution of the cosmos or creation of a different world. His understanding of this kingdom is more like the prophetic idea of the Day of Yahweh than that of some later apocalypses. The problems of politics and history can only be resolved by a supernatural intervention that inaugurates a new kingdom, but this involves changing the lorshsip of this world, not abandoning this world. The new kingdom fills the *earth. History* is not destroyed; other sovereignties are (Barth, *Diesseits,* 93–100; Jones, 253–56). The qualities of this new rule are not described except by saying that it is God's and that it lasts, both of which qualities contrast with those of its predecessors.

The kingdom, the power, and the glory *had* belonged to Nebuchadnezzar for a while by God's gift, but now they are manifested elsewhere "for ever and ever." The motif of time recurs once more: Nebuchadnezzar's kingship cannot last for ever (contrast v 4), but God's regime will, because he himself does (cf. v 20). Whereas the wisdom and power of Israel and her God seemed very unimpressive (as they had to the exiles to whom Isa 40–55 is addressed), in fact God holds and shares resources of wisdom and power beyond Nebuchadnezzar's dreaming (as Isa 40–55, too, asserts in realtion to Babylon and Cyrus). Not that Daniel sees the rock as representing an Israelite empire. His emphasis is that power and wisdom belong to God. It is this, rather than their own status, that is offered as an encouragement to his Jewish readers. Indeed, Dan 2 has no reference to the people of God, the messiah, the eternal destiny of humanity, the remnant, or the temple (Barth, *Diesseits,* 97, 99) God's rule has sole focus. This gives a context to subsequent chapters' references to these other motifs.

Daniel's vision was not fulfilled in the historical periods to which the book refers. In this it parallels the many prophetic oracles that give the impression that the Day of Yahweh is about to dawn, but after which things continue as they have done before: as happens again when Christ comes speaking of the imminent establishing of God's rule (see 2 Peter 3:4). Yet each prophet's words were received as from God, partly in the conviction that they *would* find their fulfillment in time, partly in the awareness that they *had* seen some measure of fulfillment already (hence the conviction that further fulfillment would also follow). So with Daniel's vision. The empires that Daniel and the readers knew did disappear; the rule of the God of heaven was reestablished in Jerusalem.

By NT times, the rock in Daniel had become associated with other "rock" passages, Isa 8:14 (see also 28:16) and Ps 118:22 (see Luke 20:17–18) (Siegman, *CBQ* 18 [1956] 375–79). There is no indication that Daniel understood the rock to denote a personal messiah, but it turns out that (according to Christian conviction) the one who initiated the ultimate downfall of worldly empires and the establishment of God's rule was the man Jesus. His virgin birth makes a parallel point to the picture of the rock breaking off without human involvement (Chrysostom). He came to a people looking for God's rule, and proclaimed that it was now arriving (Mark 15:43; 1:15); though it transpires that the King among kings can also be described as a lamb with the marks of slaughter upon him (Rev 5:6; 17:14), which excludes any triumphalistic understanding of this kingship (W. Dietrich, "Gott als König," *ZTK* 77 [1980] 251–68).

Nevertheless a Christian who lives much later than this has to face the difficulties of Jesus' claim. Calvin attempts to demolish Avravanel's exposition of them, but he is not entirely successful. Daniel's own response to the fact that the exile did not bring the ultimate realization of Yahweh's kingship, as Isa 40–55 seemed to promise, is not to turn that kingship into something nationalistic (Yahweh is [to be] Israel's king) or individualistic (his kingship is [to be] realized in the individual believer's life) or otherworldly (it is [to be] realized in heaven) (Coppens, *Messianisme,* 27–28). He reaffirms the universal, this worldly, corporate persepctive of Isa 40–55. Daniel *is* talking about a reign of God on earth, and that continues to be more an object of hope than of sight. We still pray "may your rule come" (Luke 11:2), and—in the light of Daniel's revelation—have to be referring to a rule which is temporal, worldly, and social. Precisely at moments when such a vision is difficult to believe, Daniel's readers are urged, via his final declaration to the king (v 45b), to take it with utmost seriousness (cf. 8:26; 10:21; Rev 19:9; 21:5; 22:6).

46–49 Nebuchadnezzar is not expected to take any action in the light of this foreshadowed future (contrast 4:24 [27]). He offers the only possible response, an acknowledgment of the revealer—God and his human agent. The experience of God at work leads to an awareness of who God is (v 47). To acknowledge God as Master among kings is to qualify the meaning of his own kingship in a revolutionary way, as to acknowledge him as God among gods is radically to qualify the ascription of divinity to other deities. The story's envisaging of such a response by the heathen king corresponds to the earlier affirmation of his position (vv 37–39); indeed it works out the demand implicit in that affirmation. Both affirmation and expectation correspond to those regarding Cyrus in Isa 40–55 (e.g., 45:1–7). The two belong together. The affirmation (cf. Rom 13) presupposes the expectation that the gentile authority submits its power to God; where this expectation is not fulfilled, the affirmation is withdrawn (cf. Revelation).

The idea of an Israelite's being the head of the Babylonian sages once again suggests a less exclusive attitude to their worldly wisdom than that of Isa 40–55 (Lebram, *VT* 15 [1965] 234–37). Verses 46–48 may seem to confuse the testimony of vv 1–30 that Babylonian wisdom is worthless and that Daniel is nothing except by God's power (Ehrlich, *Traum,* 103), but we are invited to sense no conflict between this insistence and Nebuchadnezzar's instinct to honor Daniel as God's representative, as the prophetic sage par excellence (Müller, VTSup 22 [1972] 275–77).

Daniel's revealtion had referred to a future assertion of God's rule. Paradoxically, it actually effects a realization of God's rule even now. Nebuchadnezzar acknowledges that God already rules, "on earth as in heaven," and by giving God's servants authority over the sages and over the Babylonian political affairs he institutes another indirect form of divine rule in Babylon itself, "on earth as in heaven." The fact that there is to be a new future makes it possible to hope for a new present. It does not mean we cease to have any hopes for the present.

The book's implied readers under the fourth regime (or its actual readers later) are invited to join Nebuchadnezzar in acknowledging God's wisdom as revealer and his sovereignty as lord of history, the more convincedly now that they have seen regimes passing as Daniel described, and to look with expectation for the rock breaking off from a crag and destined to dominate the world. Whether they are tested by persecution or by success, such testing is designed to draw them to acknowledge that God is Lord. He *is* lord of history, whether or not at present he seems to be acting as such. History *is* going somewhere, even if that can only be perceived by divine revelation and not read off from events themselves (Schreiner, "Gestalt und Botschaft," 141–49). The vision offers no hint regarding the chronology whereby God's rule will arrive; it does invite its recipients to live as people who expect it as a living reality (Grelot, "Histoire," 105).

The world rulers are under God's control, and when he chooses he can make them acknowledge it. The shape of human history is under his control, and the coming of God's rule is certain. People in exposed positions such as Daniel's prove God's wisdom before gentile masters; how much more can ordinary people in the context of their ordinary pressures. The sovereignty of God has been concealed from Nebuchadnezzar, relied on by Daniel, revealed via Daniel, and recognized by Nebuchadnezzar.

God Vindicates His Power When Three Jews Choose Burning Rather Than Apostasy (3:1–30)

Bibliography

Alexander, J. B. "New Light on the Fiery Furnace." *JBL* 69 (1950) 375–76. **Astour, M. C.** "Greek Names in the Semitic World and Semitic Names in the Greek World." *JNES* 23 (1964) 193–201. **Auscher, D.** "Les relations entre la Grèce et la Palestine avant la conquête d'Alexandre." *VT* 17 (1967) 8–30. **Cook, S. A.** "The Articles of Dress in Dan. iii, 21." *J Philology* 26 (1898–99) 306–13. **Coxon, P. W.** *TGUOS* 25 (1973–74) 24–40.———. "Daniel iii 17: A Linguistic and Theological Problem." *VT* 26 (1976) 400–409. **Delcor, M.** "Un cas de traduction 'targoumique' de la LXX." *Textus* 7 (1969) 30–35. **Eichhorn, D. E.** "Sanhedrin 93a and the Third Chapter of Daniel." *Central Conference of American Rabbis Journal* 16, 2 (1969) 24–25. **Finesinger, S. B.** "Musical Instruments in OT." *HUCA* 3 (1926) 21–75. **Gevaryahu, H. M. Y.** "עיונים בספר דניאל." *BetM* 7, 4 [16] (1963) 139–46. **Grelot, P.** "L'orchestre de Daniel iii, 5, 7, 10, 15." *VT* 29 (1979) 23–38. **Haag, E.** "Die drei Männer im Feuer nach Dan 3, 1–30." *TTZ* 96 (1987) 21–50. **Kuhl, C.** *Die drei Männer im Feuer.* BZAW 55 (1930). **Margoliouth, D. S.** "The Greek Words in Daniel." *Exp* 12 (1900–1901) 237–38. **Mitchell, T. C., and Joyce, R.** "The Musical Instruments in Nebuchadrezzar's Orchestra." In D. J. Wiseman et al., *Notes.*, 19–27. **Nyberg, H. S.** "Ein iranisches Wort im Buche Daniel." *Le monde orientale* 25 (1931) 178–204. **Paul, S. M.** "Dan 3:29." *JNES* 42 (1983) 291–94. **Peters, J. P.** "The Three Children in the Fiery Furnace." Sec. 2 of "Notes on the Old Testament." *JBL* 15 (1896) 109–11. **Polin, C. C. J.** *Music of the Ancient Near East.* New York: Vantage, 1954. **Sanders, B. G.** "The Burning Fiery Furnace." *Theology* 58 (1955) 340–45. **Shea, W. H.** "Daniel 3: Extra-biblical Texts and the Convocation on the Plain of Dura." *AUSS* 20 (1982) 29–52. **Wegner, M.** "Das Nabuchodonosor-Bild." In *Pietas,* FS B. Kötting, ed. E. Dassmann and K. S. Frank. Münster: Aschendorf, 1980. 528–38. **Werner, E.** "Musical Instruments." *IDB* 3:469–76. **Wharton, J. A.** "Daniel 3:16–18." *Int* 39 (1985) 170–76. **Yamauchi, E. M.** "Greek Words." In *Perspectives,* ed. J. B. Payne, 170–200. ———. "Daniel and Contacts between the Aegean and the Near East before Alexander." *EvQ* 53 (1981) 37–47.

Translation

1 [a]*King Nebuchadnezzar made a gold statue, sixty cubits high and six cubits wide, and set it up in the vale of Dura in the province of Babylon.* 2 *King Nebuchadnez-zar then sent word for the assembling of the* [a]*satraps, governors, and commissioners,*[a] *the* [b]*counselors,*[c] *treasurers,*[d] *judges, officers,*[b] *and all the provincial officials, to come to the dedication of the statute which King Nebuchadnezzar had set up.* 3 [a]*They assembled, the satraps, governors, and commissioners, the counselors, treasurers, judges, officers, and all the provincial officials, for the dedication of the statue which King Nebuchadnezzar had set up, and stood in front of the statue* [b]*which Nebuchadnezzar had set up.*[b] 4 *The herald*[a] *proclaimed in a loud voice: "Peoples, nations, and languages: you are bidden* 5 *at the set moment, when you hear the sound of the horn,*[a] *the pipe,*[b] *the cithara,*[c] *the trigon,*[d] *the psaltery,*[e] *the ensemble*[f] *with every kind of music, to* [g]*bow prostrate*[g] *before the gold statue which King*

Nebuchadnezzar has set up. 6 Anyone who does not bow prostrate will be thrown straightaway inside[a] a red-hot blazing furnace." 7 So the very moment the peoples all heard the sound of the horn, the pipe, the cithara, the trigon, the psaltery, [a]with every kind of music, the people of all races, nations, and languages would bow prostrate[b] before the gold statue which King Nebuchadnezzar had set up.

8 [a]That very moment some Chaldeans came forward and denounced[b] the Jews. 9 They addressed [a]King Nebuchadnezzar, "Long live the king! 10 Your majesty, you gave notice that everyone who heard the sound of the horn, the pipe, the cithara, the trigon, the psaltery, and the ensemble with every kind of music, was to bow prostrate before the gold statue, 11 and that anyone who did not bow prostrate would be thrown inside a red-hot blazing furnace. 12 There are some Jews whom you appointed over the affairs of the province of Babylon, Shadrach, Meshach, and Abed-nego. These people have not taken any notice of you, your majesty. They have not honored your gods[a] or bowed down to the gold statue which you have set up."

13 Nebuchadnezzar, in a furious rage, commanded Shadrach, Meshach, and Abed-nego to be brought in. These men were brought in before the king. 14 Nebuchadnezzar addressed them, "Shadrach, Meshach, and Abed-nego, do you really[a] not honor my gods or bow down to the gold statue which I have set up? 15 If you are indeed[a] now ready to fall prostrate before the statue I have made, at the set moment when you hear the sound of the horn, the pipe, the cithara, the trigon, the psaltery, and the ensemble with every kind of music . . . . But if you do not bow down, you will be thrown straightaway inside a red-hot blazing furnace. Then who ever[b] is the god who[c] could rescue you from my power?"[d] 16 Shadrach, Meshach, and Abed-nego replied to King Nebuchadnezzar,[a] "We do not need[b] to make any [c]response regarding this.[c] 17 If[a] our God, whom we honor, exists,[b] he is able to rescue us from the red-hot blazing furnace, and he will rescue us from your power, your majesty. 18 Even if he should not,[a] your majesty may be assured that we are not going to honor your gods or bow down to the gold statue which you have set up.

19 Nebuchadnezzar filled with rage, and the expression on his face toward Shadrach, Meshach, and Abed-nego changed. He declared that the furnace was to be heated seven [a] times higher than it was usually[b] heated. 20 He told [a]the strongest men in his army[a] to tie up Shadrach, Meshach, and Abed-nego for throwing[b] inside the red-hot blazing furnace. 21 These men were tied up in their trousers,[a] their pattishin,[b] their headwear and clothes, and thrown inside the red-hot blazing furnace. 22 Now as a result of the king's strict order about the furnace being heated very high, the flames from the fire killed those men who took Shadrach, Meshach, and Abed-nego up.

23 [a]So these three men, Shadrach, Meshach, and Abed-nego, fell inside the red-hot blazing furnace, tied up.[b] 24 Then King Nebuchadnezzar, [a]startled, stood up in alarm[a] and exclaimed to his courtiers,[b] "Was it not three men that we threw into the midst of the fire, tied up?" They answered the king, "Yes it was, your majesty." 25 He declared, "There, I can see four men, free, walking about[a] in the midst of the fire. It has no effect on them. And the fourth one looks like a divine being."[b]

26 Nebuchadnezzar went toward the door of the red-hot, blazing furnace and exclaimed, "Shadrach, Meshach, and Abed-nego, servants of God Most High, come out, come here." Out came Shadrach, Meshach, and Abed-nego from the midst of the fire. 27 The satraps, governors and commissioners, and the royal courtiers,[a]

gathered round to see[b] *these men: the fire had had no power over their bodies, the hair on their heads was not singed, their trousers were unaffected, and the smell of the fire had not come onto them.*

28*Nebuchadnezzar declared, "Blessed be*[a] *the God of Shadrach, Meshach, and*
Abed-nego: he has sent his aide and rescued his servants who entrusted themselves
to him. They defied[b] *the word of the king and gave up their bodies*[c] *rather than*
honor or bow down before any god but their God. 29*I hereby give notice that*
anyone of any people, nation, or language that says anything remiss[a] *about the*
God of Shadrach, Meshach, and Abed-nego will be torn limb from limb, and his
house turned into rubble, because there exists no other God who can deliver in this
way."[b] 30*Then the king promoted Shadrach, Meshach, and Abed-nego in the prov-*
ince of Babylon.[a]

Notes

1.a. On OG's date, see on 1:1.

2.a-a. The *and* separates אחשדרפניא (OP), סגניא, and פחותא (both Akk.) from the other officials, who are apparently less senior. As they mix OP and Akk., they hardly belong to a single ranking structure (e.g., as ministers of satrapies, of provinces, and of smaller areas). Rather the list adds to Persian *satrap* two more familiar Semitic terms known from various contexts in the OT (including 2:48). Both can denote area- or city-governors or officials more generally, and they need not be distinguished too specifically from *satrap* or from each other here.

2.b-b. OP terms of more specific, though sometimes uncertain, meaning.

2.c. אדרגזריא: perhaps equivalent figures to the 'king's eyes' (and ears) known from Gk and Aram. texts, officials in the imperial administration whose task was to keep king informed on affairs in the empire (A. L. Oppenheim, "'The eyes of the Lord,'" *JAOS* 88 [1968] 178; J. M. Balcer, "The Athenian Episkopos and the Achaemenid 'King's Eye,'" *American J Philology* 98 [1977] 256–57; cf. Xenophon, *Cyr.* 8.2.10–12).

2.d. גדבריא = גזבריא (or does it refer to the royal hairdressers? So I. Gershevitch, *SCO* 2:202).

3.a. באדין "then" is used as a connecting particle here and elsewhere in chap. 3; I have left it untranslated.

3.b-b. G omits, simplifying repetitive MT.

4.a. כרוזא, cf. Gk *κῆρυξ*, OP *xrausa: κῆρυξ* may be of oriental origin.

5.a. קרנא, ram's horn (cf. שופר), more a heraldic than a musical instrument.

5.b. משרוקיתא: שרק "hiss" (onomatopoeic?) suggests a whsitle or shepherd's pipe (cf. Judg 5:16).

5.c. קיθרוס corresponds to *κίσαρις*; it is unclear whether it is originally a Gk or Sem. word, and whether it refers to an instrument more like a lyre or more like a zither.

5.d. סבכא, a Sem. word to denote an instrument of Asian origin, a triangular harp with four or more strings, played for entertainment (Atheneus 4.175de; Livy 39.6.8; Macrobius, *Saturnalia* [Bibliotheca Teubneriana] 3.14.7).

5.e. פסנתרין corresponds to *ψαλτηρίον* (√*ψάλλω* "pluck"), another triangular oriental stringed instrument, with a sounding board, played for entertainment (Livy, Macrobius [see n. 5.d]; mentioned earlier in Aristotle, *Problemata* 919b).

5.f. סומפניה corresponds to *συμφωνία*. It can denote ensemble playing, here indicating the instruments playing together after each plays individually, in accordance with common practice. Later it can refer to a particular instrument, perhaps double-flute, drums, or bagpipes. When Antiochus Epiphanes revels to the *συμφωνία* (Polybius 26.1.4), it could have either meaning. Its omission in v 7 (whether original or not) is more natural if it is taken to refer to playing together; it would be less dispensable if it referred to a specific instrument.

5.g-g. תפלון ותסגדון "fall and bow down": see n. 2:46.a.

6.a. לגוא, perhaps "into the very middle of."

7.a. Some MT, Th, and Vg mss add וסומפניא "and the ensemble" (cf. NAB, NEB); it is more likely assimilation to vv 5, 10, 15 than original here.

7.b. Taking the ptpls סגדין . . . נפלין to have impf meaning, though BA ptpls often have aorist meaning, and the context could refer to one occasion. See BL 81n.

8.a. Omitting כל קבל דנה "therefore" with Th, Syr (OG links it to v 7); it makes poor sense and looks like dittog from v 7, where it is also followed by בה זמנא "the moment that/then."

8.b. אכלו קרצ יהון די "ate pieces of," an Akk. expression for "accusing" (*CAD* A, 1:255–56).

9.a. Normally people speak "before" (קדם) not "to" (ל) the king (cf. 2:10, 27). The story may imply discourtesy on the accusers' part (cf. vv 16, 24; 6:7, 16 [6, 15])(Charles).

12.a. As elsewhere, it is unclear whether אלהיך is s or pl; Q אלהך conforms the spelling to a different morphological convention. OG τῷ εἰδώλῳ σου takes as s, and specifically takes the statue as a god/idol.

14.a. צדא (/יצד); cf. Torrey, *JAOS* 43 (1923) 231–32. it need not be equated with or emended to אזדא (BDB) or tr "deliberately" (cf. BH צדיה).

15.a. איתיכון retains an emphatic sense.

15.b. מן הוא (BDB 1100b).

15.c. Reading דִּי, not דֵּי "sufficient" (BDB 191)—against L.

15.d. MT יְדָי "my hands"; some mss, Th יְדִי "my hand"; v 17 has s ידך "your hand."

16.a. Repunctuating with BHS against MT למלכא נבוכדנצר ("to the king: "Nebuchadnezzar . . .' "), which is implausibly discourteous.

16.b. Read חָשְׁחִין with some mss, not חַשְׁחִין "needed," against L (השחין in the BHS fascicle is a misprint). "We have no difficulty . . ." (Ehrlich) is attractive, but difficult to justify. "We do not mind/care . . ." (cf. RVmg, Ps-Saadia) presupposes that חשח = חוש/חשש.

16.c-c. על דנה פתגם; cf. Ezra 5:11, 17; *TTH* 208. EVV "in this matter" assumes דנה qualifies פתגם (cf. G. but not Syr); this would require פתגמא (emph).

17.a הן does not mean "behold" (RSVmg) in BA.

17.b. Cf. NEB; איתי thus, uninflected, usually means "is, exists" (cf. esp. v 29). RSV "If it be so [i.e., if the king does so], our God is able . . ."; cf. Ezra 5:17, but the phrase is abrupt, and the punctuation destroys the parallel with v 15, which v 17 takes up. "If our God . . . is able . . ." (cf. JB) links איתי with יכל, but the separating of copula and ptpl is unparalleled in BA. Further, it is unlikely that the men would be pictured as questioning God's power, wheeas the question whether such a God exists has already been raised (v 15), and v 17 takes this up; cf. v 29. Discussion in Coxon, *VT* 26 (1976) 400–409; Joubert, 56–58.

18.a. והן לא, i.e., "even if he does not rescue us" (not "even if such a God does not exist"). The conditional cl follows on from that in v 17, rather than paralleling it.

19.a. A proverbial hyberbole (cf. Prov 26:16, 25).

19.b. חזה "was seen," hence "was seemly," hence "was customary." Cf. BL 82c.

20.a-a. גברין גברי חיל די בחילה, "men mighty of strength who were in his army"; for this as superlative (JPS, NEB), cf. גבור ב in Ps 112:2 (NEB), Prov 30:30 (BDB 150a). Variants of the same roots are used for "men" and "mighty," then for "strength" and "army," so that the effect is almost "the most forceful he-men in his forces." גבר itself suggests "man as strong" (BDB 150).

20.b. The second inf למרמא is dependent on the first לכפתה "to tie up"; cf. BL 85a. EVV "and to throw them" requires ו before the vb (haplog?).

21.a. See Lacocque. Less plausibly סרבליהון is taken to refer to cloaks (Cook, *J Philology* 26 (1898–99) 306–13; BDB; *DTT*) or headwear (Nyberg, *Le monde orientale* 25 (1931) 178–87).

21.b. פטישיהון is the most puzzling of the four words in the list. *DTT* suggests "trousers," but Gk πέτασος means "headwear." Possibly at least one of the words is an explanatory gl on an unfamiliar expression (see Nyberg, *Le monde orientale* 25 (1931); I have thus transliterated this word which may have been strange to the original hearers.

23.a. The v reads better as a resumptive lead-in to a new paragraph than as (otiose) repetition at the end of the previous paragraph (against MT).

23.b. G adds the confessors' song of praise here.

24.a-a. תוה וקם בהתבהלה suggests fear, not mere amazement (BDB): cf. n. 2:25.a.

24.b. הדברוהי, cf. 3:27; 4:33 [36]; 6:8 [7]. The term is not used in a consistent way, we cannot see how those it denotes relate to the groups listed in v 2. In v 27 it may summarize the second, subordinate group of officials in that list.

25.a. On the vocalization of מהלכין, see Eitan.

25.b. בר אלהין. "The Son of God" (AV) would require emph אלהיא, or better emph s אלהא. Further, in BA pl אלהין does not elsewhere have s meaning like BH אלהים (Ginsberg, *Handbook* i, 2:17; BL 87f).

27.a. See n. 24.b.

27.b See BL 107h.

28.a. בריך is pe'al (contrast 2:20), perhaps implying "blessed is . . ." (cf. E. Bickerman, "Bénédiction et prière," *RB* 69 [1962] 527 = Bickerman, *Studies*, 316–17).

28.b. So EVV for שנא (lit., "change"); BDB "frustrate."

28.c. NEB "to the fire" adds לנורא with G (v 95) (cf. 1 Cor 13:3).

29.a. While שלה might be a misspelling of שאלה ("thing," 4:14), this would be a weak word here—hence perhaps Q שלו ("remissness," 6:5). Perhaps K is שָׁלָה "insult, blasphemy" (NEB; Akk. *sillatu*, BHS; and cf. BH סלה, JA סלא).

29.b. כדנה: "like this [god]" (Bentzen) is grammatically possible, but would be unusual.

30.a. MT correctly marks a section division here (cf. EVV). The medieval chapter divisions locate it three verses later.

Form / Structure / Setting

Form

For necessary background, see chap. 1 *Form.* With chap. 6, Dan 3 can be seen as a tale of court conflict concerning three men who have been promoted in the administration. A royal edict gives their rivals the opportunity to attack them for treason. They are found guilty, but are then vindicated and further promoted. Concerning as it does a religious and not merely a political offense, it can also be seen as a confessor legend telling of heroes of faith who defy a royal edict, despite the sanction of execution, because obeying it would mean contravening a fundamental aspect of their religious commitment. The sceptical king examines them and gives them a final opportunity to obey, but this only provides them with an opportunity to make their confession before the king himself, despite the reiterated threat of death. The penalty is duly exacted.

Matters do not turn out as the king expected, because the story also has features of an aretalogy. The confessors' peril is underlined by repeated motifs such as the king's personal initiative regarding the statue (vv 1, 2, 3, 5, 7, 12, 14, 15, 18) and the ceremony (vv 2, 4–5, 10–11, 12, 15), his wrath (vv 13, 19), the red-hot blazing furnace (vv 6, 11, 15, 17, 20, 21, 23, 26), heated extraordinarily high (vv 19, 22), and the men's being tied up, by particularly strong soldiers (vv 20, 21, 23). The theological necessity of some act of God is underlined by the overt blasphemy (v 15b) that makes explicit the statue's own significance, and the actual possibility of such an act of God is raised by the confession of v 17. The act itself comes at the last moment; the event is announced first by the king's reaction (v 24). It constitutes an extraordinarily complete preserving of the men (vv 25–27) by clearly supernatural means (vv 25, 28), whose results are also witnessed by the ministers of state (vv 25–27). Blasphemy is replaced by blessing, confrontation by recognition, opposition and persecution by tolerance and protection (vv 28–29).

The story combines factual allusions and traditional motifs. For its general oriental court folktale motifs, see Kuhl, *Feuer.* The place-name Dura, colossal gold-plated statues or monuments, dedication ceremonies, lists of state officials, the use of a variety of musical instruments, brick furnaces, and execution by burning are all known from the Babylonian or Persian periods. They might indicate that the story has factual reference, or that the storyteller is giving local color to his fiction. Jer 29:21–23 tells of the burning of two patriotic prophets by Nebuchadnezzar, and Peters (*JBL* 15 [1896] 109–11) sees Dan 3 as a legend based on that event. With Dan 6, the other court conflict tale/confessor legend, the story as a whole is closer to oral models than are other stories in Daniel. This is reflected in the extensive use of repetition (Kuhl, *Feuer,* 21): "the satraps, governors, and commissioners . . .," "the [gold] statue which King Nebuchadnezzar had set up," "people of all races, nations, and languages," "the moment you hear the sound of the horn, the pipe . . . ," "fall prostrate," "Shadrach, Meshach, and Abed-nego," "[thrown inside the] red-hot blazing furnace"; the ten occurrences of גברין "men" are also noticeable. OG removes much of the repetition. Several of the repetitions convey a humorous, mocking impression for the modern Western reader, and thus heighten a sense of satire about the story, but it is doubtful if they had this significance for the author and his readers (cf. the repetitions as a stylistic feature in Gen 1). In two or three other instances, words or phrases recur with different meanings: the king gives notice (v 10), the men take no notice (v 12), the king gives notice in the opposite direction (v 29) (each time שׂם טעם). Nebuchadnezzar's attitude changes (v 19), the men's appearance is not changed (v 27), they change the king's word (v 29) (see Coxon, *JSOT* 35 [1986] 95–121).

Dan 3 can also be seen as a midrash, the story taking as its text Isa 43:1–3 (cf. Ps 27:2; 66:10–12); cf. Isa 48:10; 50:11. Haag (*TTZ* 96 [1987] 21–50) sees Isa 43 as suggesting key aspects to the original form of the story, which was then reworked in the Antiochene period and in other contexts. Its polemic against idolatry gives concrete form to the sarcastic attacks on idolatry in Isa 40:18–20; 41:6–7; 44:9–20; 46:1–7 (cf. Jer 10); סגד "bow down" occurs in the OT only in Isa 44:15–19; 46:6; Dan 3 (10 times), also 2:46 (see Heaton; Gammie, *VT* 31 [1981] 288). OT promises about Yahweh's heavenly aids protecting his people (Ps 34:8 [7]; 91:11) become concrete reality here.

Structure

After the opening statement setting the scene (v 1), the story begins (vv 2–7) with a paragraph involving Nebuchadnezzar/his herald and the state officers summoned for the ceremony; that paragraph hints at the difficulty that becomes explicit in the second paragraph (vv 8–12). This involves Nebuchadnezzar and the accusers and is dominated by the words of the latter. The third (vv 13–18) comprises a confrontation between Nebuchadnezzar and the three men, which brings the confessor legend to its climax. The plot thus far is very simple and is dominated by dialogue (Kuhl [*Feuer,* 18] speaks of its "naive storytelling" technique). Verses 19–29 are more complex. They interweave dialogue and action, bring several actors onto the stage at once, and describe feelings as well as words and deeds (vv 19, 24). The straightforward narrating of words and events is also varied by the suspenseful device of recording the king's response to what happens before relating the event itself; indeed, the main description of the event is given via Nebuchadnezzar's words (vv 24–25), as is the main theological response to its significance (vv 23–29). Finally, v 30 rounds off the court-tale aspect to the story.

As a whole, the story relates how the men are put on the spot, denounced, interrogated, executed, delivered, and promoted. The arrogant king is humbled, the faithful Jews are exalted. Put diagrammatically:

The king commands all to bow to the statue → Jews sentenced
The king commands all to bow to God Most High ← Jews saved
(adapted from Joubert, CO)

Setting

The pressure to assimilation and the mortal price that may be paid for faithfulness suggest a setting in the dispersion, though one can see that the challenge to resist pagan pressure, if necessary to the death, would be very relevant in the Antiochene crisis in Jerusalem. Three of the terms for musical instruments are of Greek origin, which points toward to a setting in the Greek period, though it does not require it, given the evidence for Greek influence in Asia in the Persian era (e.g., Auscher, *VT* 17 [1967] 8–30; Coxon, *TGUOS* 25 [1973–74] 24–40). Shea (*AUSS* 20 [1982] 29–52] connects the event with a ceremonial convocation to pledge loyalty to Nebuchadnezzar referred to in Jer 51:59–64, von Soden (*ZAW* 53 [1935] 85–86) with Nabonidus's introduction of the Sin cult in Babylon.

Dan 3 comprises a sharpened version of Dan 1. The difficulty the three men are put into follows from 2:49, though Nebuchadnezzar's own behavior and his sceptical question (v 15) do not follow on from this experience in chap. 2 and from his confession (2:47). The stories are separate, and they deal in types and cartoons rather than rounded characterization; there is no character development in them, as if they were a modern novel (against Wallace). The final order of the book perhaps implies that building a real statue arose from seeing the visionary statue of chap. 2 (Hippolytus 2.15) and sought to consolidate the empire that the dream threatened.

Comment

1 The setting up of statues is a familiar feature of the Babylonian, Persian, and Greek empires (Montgomery). The various standards for the cubit average just under .5m; this statue stands higher than most, though not than the Rhodes Colossus (70 cubits). Perhaps it included a pedestal such as are said to have been located at one of the various Babylonian sites called Dura/Duru/Dur (Akk. "fortification") (Young; *ANET* 306, 308). This would account for the statue's odd proportions; cf. also inscribed stelas with figures at the top (Saggs, *Babylon,* plate 21b), though a stela is really a מצבה not a צלם (Keil). To reduce the statue to something normal (cf. JB) is, however, to miss the point that the statue is extraordinary and monumental, even grotesque. "Gold" may imply gold plating rather than solid gold (Isa 40:19), though Herodotus (1.183) describes a Bel statue made of 800 talents (22 tons) of gold).

The statue may have represented Nebuchadnezzar himself. The Assyrian kings set up such statues as symbols of their dominion, and Hellenistic monarchs were deified. If Nebuchadnezzar had been insisting that he himself be worshiped, however, one would have expected some overt critique of this (cf. Isa 14:13–21; also Judith's treatment of Holofernes, who seeks this on Nebuchadnezzar's behalf, Jdt 3:8). The association of bowing down before the statue with serving Nebuchadnezzar's god(s) (vv 12, 14) suggests a statue of a divinity, presumably Bel. On such divine images, see Oppenheim, *Mesopotamia,* 183–89. But the text's failure to clarify what the statue represented may reflect the fact that it is more concerned with the challenge it issued to the three Jews, and the fact that god, king, and nation are closely interwoven and support each other (cf. the army commander's combining of pragmatic and religious arguments—the latter themselves mutually contradictory—in 2 Kgs 18–19). Even if this was Nebuchadnezzar's statue, falling prostate before it would imply acknowledgement of his god, as Nebuchadnezzar's falling prostate before Daniel (2:46—the same words) implied acknowledgment of Daniel's God.

2–7 As in many cultures, music draws attention to state and religious processions and ceremonials (v 5). The band probably comprises two wind and three string instruments (see *Notes*). None are used in Israelite worship; most are foreign terms for instruments used in secular contexts. They thus imply a double judgment on the alien, pagan nature of the ceremony Nebuchadnezzar is inaugurating. Commentators usually assume that the furnace (v 6) was metal and beehive-shaped with an opening on the top into which the men were thrown, and a door at the side through which the inside could be seen. Baldwin envisages a tunnel-shaped brick furnace (cf. *LAB* 6.15–18). The burning of criminals is referred to occasionally throughout the Babylonian, Persian, and Greek periods (Jer 29:22; Herodotus 1.86; 4.69; 2 Macc 7; 13:4–8; for Persia, see Bickerman, 89, noting that the Persians would not punish by fire because of its sacredness, so that this should be seen rather as trial by fire: cf. Sanders, *Theology* 58 [1955] 340–45). Alexander quotes an Old Babylonian text that refers to throwing someone into a furnace as a punishment for an offense (*JBL* 69 [1950] 375–76), though there the punishment seems to be designed to fit the crime.

8–12 The *Chaldeans* of v 8 may be people of Babylonian race (as in 1:4) who are hostile to the three Jews on ethnic grounds (cf. Haman in Esther); or they may be Chaldean sages (as in chap. 2) suffering from professional jealousy (cf. chap. 6). Their accusation (v 12) relates to the three men's office, which explains their presence at the ceremony and, perhaps, Daniel's absence (cf. 2:49). The three who were merely *youths* in chap. 1 and merely Daniel's *friends* in chap. 2 are here full-grown *men* (גברין) of importance in their own right.

13–18 For the king's rage, see on 2:12. The arrogance of the king's challenge and the confessors' reply should not be exaggerated. The king's question has special emphasis, being an addition to the form of words used when the command and its sanction have appeared before (Joubert, 55). Yet Nebuchadnezzar may not be seen as purposely slighting God. His scepticism compares with that of the sages in 2:11, and he is not condemned for blasphemy;

indeed he is granted a revelation, to which he duly responds (vv 24–29). He is not a mirror image of the small horn of 7:24–25. In the confessor's reply (vv 16–18), the lack of formal address to the king corresponds to the form of exchanges in chaps. 1–2; their directness also parallels Daniel's elsewhere (though the formal greeting appears in 6:22) and expresses a positive commitment to God more than a contempt for the king. The *this* to which they need make no response is perhaps not the command of v 15a but the theological assertion at the end of v 15 (S. T. Byington, "Hebrew Marginalia iii," *JBL* 64 [1945] 353). (According to Herodotus 1.86–87, Cyrus burned Croesus wondering if some god would save him, and Croesus was saved by a rainstorm in response to his prayer to Apollo.)

With "our God, whom we honor" (v 17), cf. the characterization in vv 28, 29 and the contrast with vv 12, 14. Chap. 3 avoids using the name Yahweh by utilizing these phrases. The three speak as if their God's existence is an open question (see n. 17.b), and thus as if their rescue is an open question. But the allowance is only made "for the sake of argument"; it is the point which Nebuchadnezzar has implicitly questioned (v 15) and which events will have to establish. For themselves, the story assumes, the three have no doubt that he can and will rescue them: v 17 makes this explicit—there is no questioning of God's power or will separate from the questioning of his existence. If his existence is accepted, it is the existence of one who can and will rescue. The confessors' implied confidence of rescue thus parallels Daniel's confidence in 1:12–13; 2:16. Philologically, והן לא could indicate "if he cannot [rescue]" or "if he does not [exist]"; the three would then be genuinely contemplating the possibility that their God lacks existence or power, yet boldly resolving to continue to be loyal to him. But this magnificent idea is impossibly modern. The three are again only granting the theoretical possibility that God will not intervene, and assuring the reader, for whom God will indeed probably not do so, that this would make no difference to their stance.

19–22 The executioners are not even allowed time to strip the prisoners (v 21; contrast Ps 22:19 [18]; Mark 15:24; *m. Sanhedrin* 6:3), which eventually heightens the miracle (v 27). Tormentors are often described as experiencing the torment they had planned (6:25; Esther; *LAB* 6.15–18); but the fate of these *executioners* in the fierce fire once more underlines the confessors' hopeless situation.

23–30 Apparently Nebuchadnezzar alone sees the "divine being" (v 25; cf. theophanies in 2 Kgs 6:17; Acts 9:17). בר אלהין might for Nebuchadnezzar suggest an actual god. Similarly God's aide (מלאך, EVV "angel," v 28; cf. 6:23 [22]) might signify in effect God himself; cf. Yahweh's מלאך, e.g., Exod 3:2. Isa 43:1–3, indeed, has promised God's own presence when Israel walks through the fire. Nevertheless to Jews בר אלהין would indicate a subordinate heavenly being. Cf. the supernatural watchman (עיר וקדיש) of 4:10, 14, 20 [13, 17, 23], and the humanlike heavenly interpreters and leaders of chaps. 7–12. In such a context God's מלאך, too, will denote a nondivine heavenly being.

The title *God Most High* (v 26) is another expression at home on the lips of either a foreigner (3:32; 4:14, 31 [4:2, 17, 34]; Gen 14:18–20; Num 24:16; Isa 14:14) or a Jew (Dan 4:21–29 [24–32]; 5:18, 21; 7:18–27; Gen 14:22;

Deut 32:8; Psalms), though its nuances for each would again differ. To both it suggests a God of universal authority, but of otherwise undefined personal qualities. For a pagan, it would denote only the highest among many gods, but as an epithet of El it was accepted in early OT times and applied to Yahweh, so that for a Jew it has monotheistic (or mono-Yahwistic) implications. Like terms such as *Lord of heaven,* this term of ultimately pagan origin becomes popular after the exile as a substitute for "Yahweh"; unlike the former it continues to increase in popularity over later centuries (cf. 2:18 *Comment;* Eichrodt, *Theologie* 1:88 [ET 181–82]).

Explanation

1–7 This Nebuchadnezzar is one whom God allowed to devastate and pillage the temple in Jerusalem (cf. OG's date), which David had enriched with 100,000 talents of gold; he is one who has been characterized in chap. 2 as the gold head of a multi-metaled statue. He now constructs an immense gold statue of his own. It was to be the most impressive statue that dispersion Jews would ever see, to be dedicated in the presence of as impressive a gathering of state dignitaries as they would ever witness, representing as many nations as they could ever envisage, at a ceremony heralded by as cosmopolitan an ensemble as they would ever hear. So much we might have little grounds for complaint at, unless it sounds like a worrying reversal of the scattering from Babel in Gen 11 (P. W. Coxon, "The Great Tree of Daniel 4," in *A Word in Season,* FS W. McKane, ed. J. D. Martin and P. R. Davies (JSOTSup 42 [1986] 92). The herald's summons comes to its climax, however, with the sanction applied to nonparticipation in the ceremony, a personal holocaust for anyone who refuses to take part. The image now assumes more sinister significance regarding the destiny of any nonconformist, and regarding the thinking of the king himself.

When Nebuchadnezzar summoned, people assembled, and when his band played, people fell on their faces. Jews, of course, could not take part. For most, the problem would not arise; ordinary people did not have to. But the story presupposes contexts where some Jews attain positions of responsibility in the state, and have to face the question of where lie the limits to their acceptance of its authority. There were contexts when bowing before foreign idols was not condemned (2 Kgs 5:18–19). Jews had not minded worshiping idols when they were in Palestine—there were no Jewish martyrs then—Nebuchadnezzar might have reminded them, and Moses himself had said they would do so in exile (Deut 4:27–28) (*Lev. Rabbah* 33:6; cf. Bickerman, 87–88). An impressive ceremony of this kind, supported by the sanction attached to neglecting it, embodies the double pressure of the pagan state, its attractiveness and its unscrupulousness (Porteous). Yet the story simply assumes that Jews had no difficulty in perceiving that they could not take part. It does not even directly state the fact.

8–12 The problem arises from another dispersion experience, the jealousy of members of the host nation at Jewish success. Some of these draw the king's attention to the Jews' indifference to his favor, their flouting of his word, their rejection of his gods, and their disregard for his statute. The story never makes explicit what the statue represented. It could have been Nebuchadnezzar's god or the king himself. The Chaldeans' attack, and Nebuchadnezzar's reaction, suggests that they saw the Jews' stance as involving both disloyalty (as if it were the king's statue) and impiety (as if it were a god's). Whatever the nature of the statue, it held religion and state together. The institution that claims absolute authority is inclined also to claim the sanctions of religion. Empires can have feet of clay and can fall apart, so it is as well to use all means to reinforce their strength and unity (Wallace). God is acknowledged not because he is God, but because this helps to undergird the state. Herr Baldur von Schirach declared in 1936, "One cannot be a good German and at the same time deny God, but an arousal of faith in the eternal German is at the same time an arousal of faith in the eternal God. If we act as true Germans we act according to the laws of God. Whoever serves Adolf Hitler, the Führer, serves Germany, and whoever serves Germany serves God" (*The Times* [London], 29 July 1936; cf. Lang, 42–43). Five years later in an essay, "The Gods of the Nations and God," Martin Buber observed how every nation is inclined to make an idol of its own inner spirit; Israel's calling was to erect a throne to God rather than to itself, and "that is why every nation is bound to desire to get rid of us at the time it is in the act of setting itself up as the absolute" (*Werke* [Munich: Kösel, 1964] 2:1072 = *Israel and the World* [New York: Schocken, 1948] 200; quoted by Wink, *Unmasking*, 95). The reality of the holocaust that followed prevents us from regarding chapters such as Dan 3 as children's stories.

13–18 Nebuchadnezzar's reaction of rage parallels the fury he expressed to the Chaldean sages in 2:12. There is no carry-over from the recognition reached in 2:46–49. The personal nature of his reaction suggests that the statue embodies not only a religious and a national commitment but a personal one. Nebuchadnezzar's own standing was tied up with the statue. He is offended at the affront, not just at their blasphemy or their rebellion. His expectation is, "You shall have no other god but me" (Baldwin). The point becomes explicit when he asks rhetorically whether any *god* could rescue the confessors from *his* power. The challenge recalls those of Sennacherib's field-commander in 2 Kgs 18:33–35; 19:10–13. There, as in the story of the seven martyrs in 2 Macc 7 and here, such expressions of human confidence and skepticism unwittingly function chiefly to provide opportunity for giving testimony in word or event to the reality and power of the God who is slighted.

The confessors begin by declining to respond. There can be various reasons for refusing to reply to attacks and accusations (Ps 38:14–17 [13–16]; Isa 53:7; Mark 14:60–61; 15:4–5; Luke 23:9; 1 Pet 2:22–23). The confessors do so in order to leave events to testify to the sole worth-ship of their God, though they allow themselves two remarks that need to be made before the event. The first is their expression of conviction regarding what God is going to do (v 17). The confessors know a God who makes Nebuchadnezzar's gold-plated statue look tawdry (Frost, *Apocalyptic*, 209). Formally, the existence of their God is expressed hypothetically; but neither they nor the reader actually regard his existence as uncertain. Given that he exists, he is able to rescue (that follows logically), and he *will* rescue (that is a bold, unevidenced wager parallel to those of 1:12–13; 2:14–16). This expectation needs to be expressed before the event, like any prophecy, so that the event can be seen to be the vindication of it, of those who express it, and of the one in whom they hope.

The second remark is in superficial tension with the first, for it speaks of the possibility of not being rescued. Their wager affirms that this will not be the confessors' experience. But it often has been the experience of believers, and for their sake the three heroes make clear that even in that situation they would still maintain their commitment to God. The implicit question being asked of them is the Adversary's question about Job, does he only honor God because of the blessings God gives him? God may be trusted to protect us, but our honoring him is not conditional upon his preserving us from every blazing furnace, so that if he should not do so, we are free to abandon him and try some other god (Kennedy). Death is preferable to apostasy. We regard no other god but God, no matter what happens. We obey God, not human beings (Acts 4:19–20; 5:29). Such a confession means that human potentates are defeated whether their victims escape the flames (as they will here) or whether they do not (as in 2 Macc 7). Their testing takes place in the flames themselves, if these are ever lit, though it has already taken place when the flames have been threatened.

In the dispersion this testing takes place both metaphorically and literally. The exile itself is a white-hot crucible that tests by threatening to consume (see Ps 66:10–12). For many Jews who are not threatened with a literal furnace, the latter gives concrete form to the image of walking through fire. Life in exile brings a potential threat to the distinctiveness of Jews (chap. 1), to their very life (chap. 2), and also to their fundamental faithfulness to God. Its challenge is to a bold trust and obedience that gives Caesar what is his, but reserves what is God's for God. The confession of the three is the more remarkable because it is made without reference to the prospect of resurrection. It thus contrasts with those made in 2 Macc 7 and expected in Matt 10:24–33 (cf. also Dan 12). If they are to be martyred, the confessors envisage no vindication or resurrection. Their confession is made starkly for God's sake.

19–25 While the story reaches one climax with this confession, Nebuchadnezzar's fury sets it on the way to another. He is enraged at the rights of God being at any point exalted over his own, and determines to seal the confessors' fate more securely and speedily, though the possibility of his moves being counterproductive is already advertised: his fury is beginning to rebound (v 22). Nevertheless the confessors fall to their doom (v 23). Suddenly, however, Nebuchadnezzar sees a sign that he cannot ignore, as he could the deaths of his best soldiers. The king who thought that no god could save the confessors from his power is the one who now perceives God's intervention (Joubert, 59). The three have not been delivered *from* the fire, but they are delivered *in* the fire (cf. Rom 8:37) (Philip). The life of blessing and success that is their destiny is reached, not by way of costless and risk-free triumph but by the way of the cross. They are free, looking as if they are enjoying a walk in the garden (Jephet).

It is *four* unbound (v 25) who contrast with three bound. The deliverance comes about through the presence of a fourth person in their midst. The divine aide who camps round those who honor God and extricates them from peril (Ps 34:8 [7]) enters the fire himself to neutralize its capacity for harm by the presence of his superior energy. God's promise "I will be with you" characteristically belongs to contexts of affliction and pressure (Exod 3:12; Isa 7:14; 43:1–3; Matt 28:20; see also Ps 23:4–5). The experience of God's being with his people not only follows on their commitment to him, rather than preceding it; it comes only in the furnace, not in being preserved from it (Kennedy).

26–30 The kiln apparently has a door at ground level as well as the opening at the top through which the confessors were thrown. At Nebuchadnezzar's command they emerge through this door. The courtiers who had looked on at their trial are there; so are the leading figures among the dignitaries who had gathered for the statue's dedication. Once more they are assembled as representatives of the peoples of the world as a whole, now not to bow before a statue and the king and empire it supports, but to witness how God himself may act when people bow before him alone. As chap. 2 shows that there *is* a God who can reveal the mysteries of heaven, so chap. 3 shows that there *is* a God who can intervene in individual and national life, discrediting human pretensions and the monuments that embody them. The statue is now forgotten; both God and human beings have relativized the claim to universal significance made in respect of it (v 28) (Joubert). God has quenched Nebuchadnezzar's flames; so has the faith of those Nebuchadnezzar subjected to them (Heb 11:34), the act of consecration whereby they gave up their bodies for God's sake (Rom 12:2) (Lang).

Nebuchadnezzar's acknowledgment of God brings the story to its second climax. In outward expression of this acknowledgment the king makes Judaism a recognized religion with rights to toleration and resepct. Its theological justification (v 29b) might point to much more, and make this seem anticlimactic, but the act does close off one road that could take dispersion Jews to the furnace (namely, when clashes with the state arise from their religion's not being recognized). The prospering of the confessors in provincial affairs brings a final climax. The power of their God and the power of their commitment to him also brings them political power (Joubert, 62).

A narrative that combines features of court-tale, legend, aretalogy, and midrash does not invite us to treat it as historiography. Yet its picture of a God who rescues from certain death hardly emerges from pure hope-against-hope. Judeo-Christian faith and hope claimed to be based on what God had done, not merely on itself, as if faith were its own miracle. It is *a priori* likely that some *experience* of God's deliverance underlies this *story* of God's deliverance. It might be the experience of God's delivering individuals in some extraordinary way; it might be the experience of his preserving people in the metaphorical fire of exile itself. Whether or not the story was inspired by the real, but metaphorical, fire of exile, it could be applied to that experience. God had promised that he would deliver, and the story gives believers who walk that fire a narrative embodiment of his keeping this promise. Yet it more specifically speaks to the individual experience of actual persecution. Dan 12 (or 2 Macc 7, or Matt 5:11–12) envisages reversal, resurrection, vindication, and reward after death. Dan 3 reminds us that the first fruits of that are sometimes experienced now (Philip). From a position after Christ, we can say that final resurrection is certain because it has begun in Christ himself. Experiences such as the one that underlies Dan 3 also evidence that God was always the God of resurrection. To put it the other way, if final resurrection is certain and its reality has already been at work in Christ, why should it not also be known from time to time in other contexts before and after Christ? Not that the all-powerful God's intervening in the confessors' extremity implies he can be expected to do so for all believers under pressure. Confessors often become martyrs, and their conviction that God can and will rescue from death has to be referred to that resurrection which Dan 12 envisages. But when believers face some white-hot furnace they may be encouraged to be faithful to him confident that their God is Lord of death and that he will demonstrate that he is. The power of paganism offers no ultimate threat. When situations are utterly hopeless, they can trust him to vindicate their commitment and his power by rescuing them one way or the other.

Nebuchadnezzar Testifies to Kingship and Sanity Threatened, Lost, and Restored (*3:31–4:34* [*4:1–37*])

Bibliography

Alonso Díaz, J. "La conversión de Nabucodonosor en bestia." *CB* 20 (1963) 67–74. **Ball, C. J.** "Daniel and Babylon." *Exp* viii, 19 (1920) 235–40. **Bucheim, J. G.** *Dissertatio de μεταμορφώσει regis Nabuchodonosoris.* = *TTP* 876–82. **Coxon, P. W.** "The Great Tree of Daniel 4." In *A Word in Season,* FS W. McKane, ed. J. D. Martin and P. R. Davies. JSOTSup 42 (1986) 91–111. **Cross, F. M.** "Fragments of the Prayer of Nabonidus." *IEJ* 34 (1984) 260–64. **Di Lella, A. A.** "Daniel 4:7–14: Poetic Analysis and Biblical Background." In *Mélanges bibliques et orientaux,* FS H. Cazelles, ed. A. Caquot and M. Delcor. AOAT 212 (1981) 247–58. **Ehrlich, E. L.** *Der Traum im Alten Testament.* BZAW 73 (1953) 113–22. **Freedman, D. M.** "The Prayer of Nabonidus." *BASOR* 145 (1957) 31–32. **Gadd, C. J.** "The Harran Inscriptions of Nabonidus." *AnSt* 8 (1958) 35–92. ———. "The Kingdom of Nabu-na'id in Arabia." In *Akten des vierundzwanzigsten internationale Orientalischen-Kongresses München,* ed. H. Franke. DMG, 1959. 132–34. **García, F.** "4Q Or Nab: nueva síntesis." *Sefarad* 40 (1980) 5–25. **Gowan, D. E.** *When Man Becomes God: Humanism and Hybris in the Old Testament.* PTMS 6 (1975). **Grelot, P.** "Rudolph Meyer, *Das Gebet des Nabonid . . .*" *RevQ* 4 (1963–64) 114–21. ———. "La prière de Nabonide." *RevQ* 9 (1977–78) 483–95. ———. "La Septante de Daniel iv et son substrat sémitique." *RB* 81 (1974) 5–23. **Haag, E.** "Der Traum des Nebukadnezzar in Dan 4." *TTZ* 88 (1979) 194–220. **Mertens, A.** 34–42. **Meyer, R.** *Das Gebet des Nabonid.* Berlin: Akademie, 1962. ———. "Das Qumranfragment 'Gebet des Nabonid.'" *TLZ* 85 (1960) 831–34. **Milik, J. T.** "'Prière de Nabonide' et autres écrits d'un cycle de Daniel." *RB* 63 (1956) 407–15. **Nober, P.** "*Y^{e}baʿon* (Dn 4, 33)." *VD* 38 (1960) 35–37. **Oppenheim, A. L.** *Transactions of the American Philosophical Society* 46 (1956) 179–373. **Rabinowitz, J. J.** "A Legal Formula . . . in the Book of Daniel (4.14 etc.)." *Bib* 36 (1955) 74–77. **Resch, A.** *Der Traum im Heilsplan Gottes.* Freiburg: Herder, 1964. 123–26. **Röllig, W.** "Nabonid und Tēmā." *Compte Rendu de l'Onzième Rencontre Assyriologique Internationale.* Leiden: Nederlands Instituut voor het Nabije Oosten, 1964. 21–32. ———. "Erwägungen zu neuen Stelen König Nabonids." *ZA* 56 (1964) 218–60. **Shea, W.** *AUSS* 23 (1985) 193–202. **Vogt, E.** "Precatio regis Nabonid in pia narratione Iudaica (4Q)." *Bib* 37 (1956) 532–34. **Woude, A. S. van der.** "Bemerkungen zum Gebet des Nabonid." In *Qumrân: sa piété, sa théologie et son milieu,* ed. M. Delcor. BETL 46 (1978) 121–29.

Translation

31 *King Nebuchadnezzar to all peoples, nations, and languages who live in all*
the earth. [a]*Peace and prosperity be yours.*[a] 32 *I want to tell of the wondrous signs*
that God Most High has done for me.

33 *How great are his signs,*
how mighty his wonders!
His kingship lasts through the ages,
his rule through all generations!

1 *I, Nebuchadnezzar, was successful*[a] *and thriving,*[b] *at home in my palace.* 2 *I*
had a dream which disturbed[a] *me. The images*[b] *in the vision*[c] *that came into my*

head[d] *as I lay in bed alarmed me.* 3*So I issued an order that all the sages in Babylon should be brought before me so that they could tell me the interpretation of the dream.* 4[a]*The diviners, the chanters, the Chaldeans, and the exorcists*[a] *came, and I recounted the dream before them, but they could not tell me its interpretation.*
5*Then finally*[a] *Daniel, who is named Belteshazzar after my god,*[b] *came before me. The spirit of holy deity*[c] *is in him. I recounted the dream before him:* 6*"Belteshazzar, head of the diviners, I myself know that the spirit of holy deity is in you and that no mystery*[a] *defeats you. Consider*[b] *the dream I have had, and tell me its interpretation.*
7[a]*The vision that came into my head as I lay in bed:*[a] *I was looking and*
there before me was a tree
at the center of the earth,
of great height.
8*The tree grew*[a] *in stature and might,*
its height reached[b] *to the heavens;*
[c]*it could be seen from*[c] *the ends of the earth.*
9*It had lovely foliage,*
much fruit,
food for everyone.[a]
Beneath it the animals of the wild sheltered,
in its branches the birds of the heavens dwelt;
from it all living beings got food for themselves.

10*"I saw in the vision that came into my head as I lay in bed: there before me was a watchman,*[a] *a holy being,*[b] *descending from heaven.* 11*He proclaimed in a loud voice,*
'Fell the tree, cut off its branches,
strip off its foliage, scatter its fruit.
The animals must flee from beneath it,
the birds from its branches;
12*yet leave* [a]*its deep root*[a] *in the earth.*
With a ring of iron and bronze round him,[b]
with[c] *the grass in the wild,*
he is to be watered with the dew from the heavens
and share[d] *in the plants*[e] *of the earth, with the animals.*
13[a]*His human mind is to become deranged*[a]
and an animal's mind is to be given to him.
Seven periods[b] *are to pass by for him.*
14*The decision is decreed by watchmen,*
the intent[a] *is determined by*[b] *holy beings:*
with the object that human beings may come to acknowledge that the Most High rules over the kingship of men. He can give it to anyone he wishes and set over it the most ordinary of men.'

15*"That is the dream which I, King Nebuchadnezzar, had. You, Belteshazzar, tell me the interpretation, because all the sages in my kingdom are unable to explain the interpretation to me, but you can do so, because the spirit of holy deity is in you."* 16*Daniel, whose name was Belteshazzar, was overcome for a moment. His thoughts alarmed him. The king declared, "Belteshazzar, the dream and the interpretation are not to alarm you." Belteshazzar replied, "My lord, the dream should*[a] *apply to your opponents and its interpretation to your foes.* 17 *The tree you saw which grew in stature and might—its top reached to the heavens, and it could be seen from the ends of the earth;* 18 *it had lovely foliage, much fruit, and food for everyone; beneath it the animals of the wild dwelt, and in its branches the birds of the heavens nested;* 19 *you, your majesty, are the one who has grown in stature and might. Your stature has grown until it reaches the heavens and your rule until it reaches the end of the earth.* 20 *Your majesty saw a watchman, a holy being, descend from heaven and say, 'Fell the tree and destroy it; yet leave its deep root in the earth. With a ring of iron and bronze round him, with the grass in the wild, he is to be watered with the dew from the heavens and share with the animals of the wild, until seven periods pass by for him.'* 21 *This is the interpretation, your majesty. It is the decision of the Most High which has befallen*[a] *my lord the king.* 22 *You are going to be led away from human society; your home will be among the animals of the wild. You will be fed plants like an ox and be watered with dew from the heavens, and seven periods will pass by for you until you acknowledge that the Most High rules over human kingship, and that he can give it to anyone he wishes.* 23 *But in that the deep root of the tree was to be left, your kingship will be* [a]*restored to you, from the time*[a] *you acknowledge that heaven rules.* 24 *But,*[a] *your majesty, be pleased to accept my counsel: break with*[b] *your sins*[c] *by doing justice,*[d] *break with*[b] *your errors by showing favor to the needy, in case there might be* [e]*a prolonging of your success."*[e]

25 *All this befell King Nebuchadnezzar.* 26 *At the end of twelve months, he was walking on the roof of the royal palace in Babylon.* 27 *The king declared, "How great Babylon is! And I myself built it as a royal seat, by my sovereign might and for my kingly honor."* 28 *The words were still on the king's lips when a voice came down from the heavens, "These words are for you, King Nebuchadnezzar. Kingship has passed from you.* 29 *You are going to be led away from human society; your home will be among the animals of the wild. You will be fed plants like an ox, and seven periods will pass by for you until you acknowledge that the Most High rules over human kingship, and that he can give it to anyone he wishes."* 30 *That very moment the words came true for Nebuchadnezzar. He was led away from human society, he ate what grows from the earth like an ox, and his body was watered with dew from the heavens, until his hair had grown long* [a]*like an eagle and his nails like a bird.*[a]

31 *But when the time was over, I, Nebuchadnezzar, looked*[a] *to heaven. As my sanity returned,*[b] *I blessed the Most High and praised and honored the One who lives for ever.*

His rule lasts through the ages,
his kingship through all generations.
32 *All the inhabitants of the earth are to be counted*[a] *as nothing.*[b]
He does as he wishes
with the forces of heaven and the inhabitants of earth.
There is no one who can restrain his hand
or say to him, "What have you done?"

33 *When that same hour my sanity returned, and as for*[a] *my royal honor, my glory*[b] *and my splendor returned to me, my courtiers and nobles sought audience*[c] *with me.* [d]*So I was restored to my kingship,*[d] *and yet more greatness was added to me.*

[34]*Now I, Nebuchadnezzar, praise and exalt and honor the King of heaven. All his deeds are true and his ways just; those who walk*[a] *in pride he can put down.*

Notes

3:31.a-a. שלמכון ישגא "may your peace/prosperity become great." A standard greeting (cf. 6:26).

4:1.a. Paralleled by רענן "thriving" שלה suggests "prosperous" rather than "relaxed" (EVV).

1.b. רענן (see D. W. Thomas, "Some Observations on the Hebrew word רַעֲנָן," *HW* 387–97); used of persons only here and Ps 92:15 [14] in a similar context, though see also the similes in Ps 52:10 [8]; 37:35.

2.a. וידחלנני, like many other vbs in chap. 4, is impf. I have followed BL 78mpq in assuming that these are past continuous or occur in circumstantial cls. But Dan may be using the impf as a simple aorist-type tense, perhaps in imitation of BH's alternation of pf and impf.

2.b. הרהרין; "fantasies" (NEB) is a later meaning, and only in the sense of sexual fantasies.

2.c. On pl חזוי see n. 2:1.a.

2.d. See n. 2:28.c.

4.a-a. On these terms see on 2:2.

5.a. עד אחרין: probably abstract pl of אחר "after" (Montgomery).

5.b. See n. 1:7.b-b. Nebuchadnezzar may imply that "Belteshazzar" is an abbreviated form of a theophoric name; it omits the actual divine name. But it is odd to use the shortened form when the allusion is to what is omitted. More likely the name's interpretation, like many in the OT, is based on assonance rather than etymology (cf. Driver).

5.c. אלהין קדישין. On a pagan's lips, the pl would usually mean "holy gods": cf. 5:11; Eshmunʿazar's inscription (*ANET* 662); Vg. Nebuchadnezzar's pagan faith has just been referred to, and expressions such as this are not used of the true God elsewhere in Dan (see 2:47; 3:32; 4:31; BL 87f). Nevertheless, a Jew writing or reading the phrase could take it to mean "the holy God"; cf. Th; Josh 24:19; the implicit allusion to Gen 41:38. In Akk. the equivalent pl is used for a single deity (Montgomery). See also n. 3:25.b.

6.a. רז (see on 2:18) here denotes a specific problem, not the great mystery of God's plan for all history.

6.b. Reading חזי for חזוי with RSV. MT has Nebuchadnezzar asking Daniel to tell him dream as well as interpretation as in chap. 2 (cf. RV), but this is not what happens, and חזוי חלמי is an odd phrase. Müller (*UF* 1 [1969] 86) takes the ו of ופשרא as epexegetic. See n. 6:29.a.

7.a-a. Perhaps a gl from v 10; the standard phrase stands or falls as a whole, and G, Syr apparently had it (though G omits part, Syr moves part to v 6).

8.a. רבה, perhaps "had grown"; but the visions in Dan characteristically portray happenings rather than static scenes, and Nebuchadnezzar probably sees the tree growing.

8.b. See n. 2.a.

8.c-c. וחזותה ל "and its appearance to": cf. the phrase in 7:20 (n. 7:20.b).

9.a. MT by its maqqeph links לכלא בה "for all [who live] in it" (cf. Keil); more likely בה links with מזון "food . . . in it" (cf. Syr, EVV).

10.a. עיר, perhaps "protector" (see R. Murray, "The Origin of Aramaic *ʿîr*, Angel," *Or* 53 [1984] 303–17 and refs), though this nuance does not esp. fit the context. Perhaps rather cf. BH ציר "envoy" (A. van Selms, "The Expression 'the Holy One of Israel,'" *Von Kanaan bis Kerala* [FS J. P. M. van der Ploeg, ed. W. C. Delsman et al.; AOAT 211 (1982)] 265).

10.b. קדישין are heavenly beings subordinate to God (van Selms [see n. 10.a]) (cf. Ps 89:6–8 [5–7]). The term does not suggest 'holy' in the moral sense but belonging to the supernatural realm. The ו is explicative (n. 6:29.a).

12.a-a. עקר שרשוהי "the stump of its roots." The two words have similar meaning (OG, Syr omit the first); the combination conveys emphasis and/or suggests the superlative (cf. GKC 133i).

12.b. See *Comment.* The vision's reference to a man becomes clearer during the course of v 12; lacking a neuter gender, Hebrew can retain a semblance of ambiguity because it has to use the m throughout vv 7–13 to refer to the tree.

12.c. Emendations are proposed by Torrey (*TConnAAS* 15 [1909] 269–70) and by NEB, but the phrase's repetition in v 20 perhaps argues for MT.

12.d. The noun חלק could refer to his portion of food (cf. Deut 10:8) or to the lot in life allocated to him by God (cf. Isa 17:14); the latter is more common, but the former fits the context well.

12.e. עשב. "Grass" (EVV) is probably too narrow: Nebuchadnezzar's diet need not be that bovine.

13.a-a. JB "let his heart turn from mankind"; but the mind (לבב) "being changed" is an expression for mental disorder (BDB 1040a).

13.b. Not "years" (OG, GNB); this resolves the allusiveness of עדן, which denotes a set definite if unspecified period of time (עדון refers to a woman's monthly "period" [*DTT*]; cf. vv 20, 22, 29; 7:25; also מועד in 11:29; 12:7. Dan *could* have used שנה (cf., e.g., 1:5; 6:1; 7:1; 11:6; also Gen 41:25) and does not; the period denoted may be a year, but this is not the meaning of עדן or מועד themselves (though the Akk. equivalent has this meaning in the Harran inscription [Gadd, *AnSt* 8 (1958) 88], as does Gk χρόνος [Ginsberg, 1–2]): Theodoret makes 7 "seasons" 3½ years, assuming a two-season year; Hippolytus refers to the view that they denote 1¾ years, 7 seasons of three months.

14.a. On שאלתא, see Montgomery; also R. Gordis, "Studies in Hebrew Roots of Contrasted Meanings," *JQR* 27 (1936) 45 = Gordis, *The Word and the Book* (New York: Ktav, 1976) 197.

14.b. מאמר "[by] the determination of": ב is understood from the parallel half-line (GKC 119hh) (Lacocque); some mss provide ב.

16.a. It is not quite clear whether this is a real wish ("may the dream . . .") or only a hypothetical one ("if only the dream . . ."): see v 24 *Comment.*

21.a. מטא is used for "reach"/"befall" in vv 21, 25 as vv 8, 19 (Coxon, *JSOT* 35 [1986] 112).

23.a-a. לך קימה מן די "will be arising/standing/enduring for you from when. . . ." Not "will be kept for you until . . ." (JB).

24.a. See n. 2:6.a.

24.b. פרק "break" can mean "untie" and thus "release"/"redeem"; but the obj is then the thing to be released, not the bond (cf. Ps 136:24; Lam 5:8), so that "redeem your sins . . ." (G λύτρωσαι, cf. NEB, JBmg, GNBmg) is impossible.

24.c. Taking חטיך as pl (cf. BDB).

24.d. צדקה includes seeing to a fair distribution of resources, and it came to mean "charity." NEB takes this as the specific meaning here (cf. G ἐλεημοσύνη); the privatizing of justice into charity is already instanced in, e.g., Tob 12:9; 14:11. But if Nebuchadnezzar is addressed as *king,* the older/broader meaning is more appropriate.

24.e-e. ארכה לשלותך; RVmg "a healing of thine error" (cf. Syr, Th, Vg for the second noun) implies the pointing אֲרֻכָה לְשָׁלוּתָךְ (cf. BDB 74a, 1115b); but שלוה is surely picked up from v 1.

30.a-a. כצפרין . . . כנשרין; NEB "like a goat . . . like an eagle" presupposes כְּצְפָרִין . . . כנשרין.

31.a. "Lifted my eyes" is a literalistic tr of עיני נטלת, which indicates not so much the direction the eyes take as the deliberateness involved in activating them (S. C. Reif, "A Root to Look Up," *Congress Volume: Salamanca 1983* [ed. J. A. Emerton; VTSup 36 (1985)] 230–44, esp. 239). The first idea would be appropriate here, but the second is even more so: see *Comment.*

31.b. On the impf, see BL 78mq; Joüon, *Bib* 22 (1941) 21–24.

32.a. See BL 82c.

32.b. כלה: for the spelling, cf. Deut 3:11; many mss have the more usual spelling כלא. For the use, cf. *GBA* 87.

33.a. ל: see GKC 143e; BDB 514b; F. Nötscher, "Zum emphatischen Lamed," *VT* 3 (1953) 372–80 (esp. 377). GNB apparently takes as emphatic ל. The usual meaning of ל fits less well.

33.b. הדרי; Th (ἦλθον) presupposes הדרת or, more likely, takes as 1 s vb הדר (see *DTT*), "I returned (to the honor of my kingship)." But the form is EA, and MT seems to be taking up the phrasing from v 27.

33.c. יבעון "make request," part of honoring him as king again; virtually "acclaim" (Nober, *VD* 38 [1960] 35–37). These courtiers and nobles are those who had been exercising authority in the king's place. I have taken the vb as a "genuine" impf, the preceding ones in v 33 being subordinate to it (cf. n. 31.b): but such an understanding may be reckoned forced, and the apparent use here of the "impf" as a narrative tense is the starting point for Rosén's reconsideration of the use of tenses in Dan Aram. (*JSS* 6 [1961] 183–203).

33.d-d. ועל מלכותי התקנת "and to my kingship it was restored": variant readings combined? Cf. BHS.

34.a. מהלכין: see n. 3:25.a.

Form / Structure / Setting

Form

See chaps. 1 and 2 *Form*. Elements of court contest tale, legend, and aretalogy reappear here, but they are less pominent than in chap. 2. The king's consultation of the sages is briefer, more formalized, and to us conveys a less cartoon-like impression; there is no reference to Daniel being rewarded or promoted. The chapter's dominant formal features are those of a dream report, with introduction, dream, interpretation, and fulfillment (Oppenheim, "Dreams," 187). The prominence of the fulfillment motif further distinguishes chap. 4 from chap. 2, as does the story's ending with the restoration of Nebuchadnezzar rather than the exaltation of Daniel. The first-person form maintained through much of the chapter is natural to a dream report (examples in Oppenheim, "Dreams") and to the confessional praise with which it begins (see also Nabonidus's testimonies, *ANET* 308–11; 562–63; also 4QPrNab). It also resembles "pseudo-autobiographies" (Grayson, *Texts,* 7) such as the Cuthean legend of Naram-Sin (O. R. Gurney, "The Cuthaean Legend of Naram-Sin," *AnSt* 5 [1955] 93–113) and the second-century Seleucid autobiographical account of Djoser, about a period of seven lean years (*ANET* 31–32). The alternating with third person narrative (4:16–30 [19–33]) is dramatically appropriate and parallels that in Ezra-Nehemiah and Tobit; it hardly gives grounds for identifying two versions or recensions of the chapter (Montgomery). Thus whereas chaps. 2, 3, and 6 are narratives that close with proclamation, chap. 4 is a proclamation that incorporates a narrative; and whereas Daniel has considerable prominence in chap. 2, here he is a role rather than a personality, Nebuchadnezzar having more of the focus.

The pericope begins, however, as a royal encyclical (cf. Ezra 1:1–4). Its opening identification of writer and addressee, and greeting, is a regular feature of Aramaic and other letters (J. A. Fitzmyer, "[Some Notes on] Aramaic Epistolography," *JBL* 93 [1974] 201–25 = Fitzmyer, *Aramaean,* 183–204 = *Semeia* 22 [ed. J. L. White; 1981] 25–57; see also W. G. Doty, "The Classification of Epistolory Literature," *CBQ* 31 [1969] 183–99; P. S. Alexander, "Remarks on Aramaic Epistolography in the Persian Period," *JSS* 23 [1978] 155–70). The Naram-Sin legend also combines an autobiographical account of humbling and advance to meekness with an encyclical (Bickerman, 98–99). The form of a royal proclamation gives the content a special degree of authority, which is used to testify to a higher authority than the human king (cf. Ezra 1 [Barr]); the dream report is bracketed with praise of God that has both confessional features (3:32; 4:31a, 34a [4:2, 34a, 37a]) and hymnic features (3:33; 4:31b-32, 34b [4:3, 34b-35, 37b]). Each is appropriate to the context, though the formal ambiguity that results from their combination also reflects the origin of the verses in a literary rather than a liturgical setting (see further chap. 2 *Form* on 2:20–23). The appearance of praise of God after the beginning of a letter is paralleled in NT epistles. The poetic passage thus fulfills an important didactic function in the chapter (Towner, *CBQ* 31 [1969] 317). The confessional opening and closing of the pericope help to unify diverse formal features into a distinctive, intricately wrought whole, and to give the whole the cast of a testimony to God's intervening, being ignored, chastising, and restoring, which parallels the dynamic of confessional psalms (thanksgivings) (e.g., Ps 30).

Throughout, midrashic features interweave. The basic story of the threatening royal dream interpreted by no one but an exiled Jew again parallels Gen 41; the king's description of the interpreter, as one in whom is the spirit of holy deity, is a correspondence of detail. Job 33 parallels the motif of God's speaking through a dream to warn a man of the judgment coming upon his pride, then drawing him through illness to prayer, repentance, restoration, and testimony. Nebuchadnezzar's sovereignty over all peoples, and God's capacity to give earthly power to anyone he wishes (4:14, 22, 29 [17, 25, 32]), again recall Jer 27:5–7. The theme of God's lordship over kings also parallels Job 12:12–24; 36:5–14; Isa 40:17, which reflect psalmic traditions, as do Nebuchadnezzar's confessions of this lordship (cf. Ps 145, especially v 13): Nebuchadnezzar has all but "crowned all the songs and praises of David" (*b. Sanhedrin* 92b)—under Daniel's tutelege, commentators assume.

The central motif, the tree, appears widely in myth (see *Comment*), but the description of the tree and its felling, and the motif of the humbling of a proud monarch, seem dependent on passages such as Ezek 17 (the Judean king as a tree planted, uprooted, replanted, fruitful, and protective [cf. Lam 4:20]; see especially vv 23:24); 19:10–14 (Jerusalem as a vine, flourishing, strong, and impressive, but uprooted); 28 (the prince of Tyre pretending to deity and to a wisdom greater than Daniel's, but humiliated; the king of Tyre in his splendor in Eden, God's garden, but humiliated for his violence, injustice, and pride); 31 (the Egyptian king as a tree, lofty, flourishing, impressive, protective, but felled for his wickedness; see especially vv 5–6, 12–13); Isa 14:4–23 (the king of Babylon fallen for his pretense to deity and his affliction of men; Wilkie [*JTS* 2 (1951) 36–44] sees Nabonidus behind both Isa 14 and Dan 4); Ps 92 (praise of the Most High for his great works, which the brutish man cannot recognize; the wicked only flourish in the short term, the just flourish like strong trees [see n. 4:1.a]); cf. also Isa 10:5–11:10; Deut 17:14–20. Tree fables (Judg 9:8–15; 2 Kgs 14:9; cf. 1 Kgs 5:13 [4:33]) are a wisdom feature; the theme of the humbling of the proud monarch also recalls aphorisms in the wisdom tradition (Prov 16:5–7, 12) (Gammie, *VT* 31 [1981] 284). See also Coxon, "Tree"; Di Lella (AOAT 212 [1981] 256–58) emphasizes links with Gen 1–3; 11.

The account of the king's chastisement/madness/illness/exile and restoration has several parallels outside the OT. (a) The Greek writer Megasthenes (c. 300 B.C.) writes of Nebuchadnezzar announcing from his palace roof under some god's inspiration the coming fall of Babylon to "a Persian mule," who Nebuchadnezzar wishes might rather take himself off to some animal-like existence (see Eusebius, *Praep. Ev.* 9.41.6). (b) A fragmentary cuneiform text apparently refers to some mental disorder on Nebuchadnezzar's part, and perhaps to his neglecting and leaving Babylon (Grayson, *Texts,* 87–92; cf. Hasel, *AUSS* 19 [1981] 41–42). (c) Josephus refers to an illness of which Nebuchadnezzar died (*C. Ap.* 1.20 [1.146]). (d) "The Babylonian Job" (*Ludlul bēl nēmeqi,* "I Will Praise the Lord of Wisdom," *ANET* 596–600) testifies to chastisement by God, illness, humiliation, seeking interpretation of a terrifying dream, being thrown over like a tree, being put outside, eating grass, losing understanding, being like an ox, being rained on by Marduk, nails being marred, hair growing, and being fettered, and then to a restoration for which he praises the god (Ball, *Exp* viii, 10 [1920] 235–40). (e) In a number of inscriptions, especially from Harran, Nabonidus testifies to praying before Marduk for a long and successful reign and receiving the deity's promise that these would be granted, and to being led by a dream to spend ten years away from Babylon in Tema in Arabia, but then to return to Babylon. Other inscriptions refer in the third person to his years away from Babylon and (with hostility) to his being punished for his "mad" neglect of Babylon's deities (*ANET* 305–16, 560–63; Gadd, *AnSt* 8 [1958] 35–92; Röllig, *ZA* 56 [1964] 218–60). Nabonidus is the only known Babylonian dreamer (Oppenheim, "Dreams," 186). (f) The Qumran "Prayer of Nabonidus" comprises Nabonidus's testimony to his being afflicted by God for seven years in Tema by a physical illness. He prayed to his gods for healing, but received it only after a Jewish exorcist (גזר) exhorted him to honor the true God (see *Bibliography*). On Nabonidus, see Saggs, *Babylon,* 145–52; Oppenheim, *Mesopotamia,* 152–53.

Scholars have held a wide variety of views on the relationship between these various documents and the traditions they represent (Mertens, 37–40). Whether or not we can reach any confident conclusions about the historical questions, study of comparative materials may help us to perceive characteristic and distinctive features of the text that concerns us; for example, Bickerman sees the oracle which lies behind Dan 4 as giving the real divine response to Nabonidus, in contrast to that in the Harran inscriptions.

Structure

Apart from Nebuchadnezzar's introduction, the pericope opens and closes with his praise of God Most High; the whole chapter is in direct speech except for 4:16, 25–27a, 28a, 30 [19, 28–30a, 31a, 33]. The opening announces where the narrative must lead, and the question then is how it can reach this "unlikely" conclusion. Once the first person testimony begins, it uses suspenseful devices similar to those in chap. 2: the affect of the dream on Nebuchadnezzar is announced before its content, the sages are unable to interpret it, the effect of its message on Daniel is announced before its content, and the dream itself is recounted once again before its interpretation is given, the positive aspects of the dream thus standing in contrast to the solemnity of the message it brings. The tree theme is not developed in a sustained way; it is subordinate to the message, and the interpretation enters into the presentation of the dream itself as early as vv 12–13 [15–16]. Nevertheless the first overt climaxes come in the brief interpretative announcements in vv 19a and 22–23 [22a and 25–26], then in the unpresaged admonition/invitation of v 24 [27].

The structure might be presented as

31 introduction to encyclical
32 introduction to opening confession
33 hymnic confession
1–15 report of dream (first person)
1–2 dream's occurrence
3–6 quest for an interpreter (court contest)
7–14 content of dream
7–9 the tree in the dream
10–14 the watchman's intervention in the dream
15 request to Daniel
16–24 interpretation of dream (third person)
16 introductory wish
17–23 interpretation
17–19 interpretation of the tree
20–23 interpretation of the watchman's message
24 closing admonition
25–30 report of fulfillment (third person)
31–33 introduction to closing confession
34 hymnic confession

The chapter begins with stock phrases and expressions familiar from other stories of this kind and from elsewhere in the OT (3:31–33; 4:2–7a [4:1–3, 5–10a]). 3:33 [4:3], however, which is poetical in form (it manifests meter and parallelism) introduces roots that will be of key significance for the story: רב and תקף "great," "mighty" (4:8, 17, 19, 27, 33 [11, 20, 22, 30, 36]), מלך and שלט "kingship," "rule" (4:14, 22, 23, 29, 31 [17, 25, 26, 32, 34]). The poetical form of 3:33 [4:3] reappears in part of 4:31–34 [34–37], its actual phrasing being reworked in part in 4:31b [34b]. 4:31–34 [34–37] also takes up the terms of 4:27 [30] and make clear that the antithesis between divine and human kingship is not to be sharply drawn, nor does the humbling of human kingship necessarily mean dethronement rather than chastisement. Here, too, stock phrases accumulate, yet they become the vehicle of vivid testimony.

Nebuchadnezzar's account of his dream introduces a further key pair of terms, the antithesis שמין—ארע. Both terms are ambivalent. ארע can mean "earth" in the sense of "world," and thus suggest the extent of Nebuchadnezzar's rule (3:31; 4:7, 8, 17, 19 [4:1, 10, 11, 20, 22]), though also its ultimate insignificance compared with God, before whom the whole earth is nothing (4:32, 32 [35, 35]). It can also mean "ground," and thus more directly suggest the extent of Nebuchadnezzar's humiliation (4:12, 12, 20, 29, 30 [15, 15, 23, 32, 33]). שמין means "heaven" (4:8, 9, 10, 12, 17, 18, 19, 20, 20, 22, 23, 28, 30, 31, 32, 34 [11, 12, 15, 20, 21, 22, 23, 23, 25, 26, 31, 33, 34, 35, 37]) both in the physical sense of the sky and in the metaphysical sense of God's dwelling; the passage makes use of the fact that the former is a symbol of the latter, lets one meaning hint at the other, and sometimes leaves it unclear which is referred to. No other chapter of the OT uses שמים/שמין as often, or uses the word as a periphrasis for God (4:23 [26]) or refers to God as king of heaven (4:34 [37]), bringing together the two fields of terms we have noted in the chapter. (Nor does any other chapter of the OT use as often the related title *Most High:* 3:32; 4:14, 21, 22, 29, 31 [4:2, 17, 24, 25, 32, 34].) In their various senses שמין and ארעא can both confront and associate with each other, setting up both links and tensions within the passage.

The accounts of Nebuchadnezzar's dream, its interpretation, and its fulfillment introduce a more sustained lyrical strain to the main body of the chapter. Nebuchadnezzar's description of his own situation in 4:1 [4], the only non-stock element in the material that precedes the dream, anticipates both the theme of the "thriving" tree that is first described in 4:7b-9 [10b–12] and also the content of Daniel's exhortation regarding a prolonging of Nebuchadnezzar's success in 4:24 [27]. The second part of the dream uses the lyricism to solemn, foreboding effect. Its implicit significance is made explicit in more prosaic and direct theological terms and parenesis (4:14b, 24 [17b, 27]). Opinion varies as to how far to present the dream material as lyrical prose or as loose verse; I have followed BHS. Di Lella (AOAT 212 [1981] 252–55) offers a detailed analysis of the literary devices in the verse. The chapter is as repetitive as others, yet sustains interest by the use of variation, drama, and suspense. It is the repetition of literary technique, rather than the more artless repetition of folk-tale.

On OG's distinctive version, see Introduction.

Setting

4QPrNab shows that material such as this could be of interest in Greco-Roman Palestine, and that it could function as an attack on Hellenistic kingship ideology (Meyer, *Gebet,* 111–12). Yet there are no specific pointers to this context. Parallels with the proud Antiochus Epiphanes (cf. 11:37), who was lampooned as Epimanes (Madman) and who acknowledged God on his deathbed according to 2 Macc 9, are too broad to suggest that Nebuchadnezzar directly mirrors Antiochus. The latter's character and story are very different (Keil, 140–42), and Daniel has different hopes of him (11:40–45). There are no concrete indications than Dan 4 was composed in Greco-Roman Palestine; the eastern dispersion is the more natural context. Hall and Haag (*Erretung*) offer reconstructions of a several-stage evolution that they believe the text went through, one stage coming in the Antiochene period, but their reconstructions vary and their evidence is circumstantial and sometimes questionable: for example, alternating between first and third person is not evidence of redactional work in an autobiographical narrative (Berger, *ANRW* ii 25, 2 [1984] 1274).

At first sight 3:31–33 [4:1–3] carries on from 3:29 (hence the medieval chapter division), and the book's arrangement perhaps trades on this apparent link. It soon becomes clear, however, that actually 3:31 [4:1] begins a new pericope (hence Luther's chapter division; EVV follow). The three friends have disappeared, and henceforth the book entirely focuses on Daniel as its hero. Behind chap. 3, Dan 4 links with the earlier dream chapter, Dan 2. Daniel's appearance last among the sages (4:5 [8]) need not be in tension with 2:48; he is not said to be summoned after the others, only (dramatically) to arrive last (Jeffery). There is no development in Nebuchadnezzar's character through chaps. 1–4; they do not provide Nebuchadnezzar's spiritual biography (cf. chap. 3 *Setting;* against Philip). Dan 4 has more direct links, indeed, with chap. 5, where Belshazzar will pay a more conclusive penalty for a more explicit blasphemy accompanied by a refusal to learn from Nebuchadnezzar's experience.

Comment

3:31–33 [4:1–3] Chap. 4 is centrally concerned with the kingship of Nebuchadnezzar and the kingship or rule of the Most High [God] or of [the King/Lord of] Heaven (cf. 4:14, 15, 19, 21, 22, 23, 27, 28, 29, 31, 33, 34 [4:17, 18, 22, 24, 25, 26, 30, 31, 32, 34, 36, 37]; 5:18–23). Nebuchadnezzar does not stand for ordinary humanity being judged for ordinary human pride. Nor does the pericope stress the fact that he is a Gentile, Daniel a Jew, or picture Nebuchadnezzar turning from paganism to faith in the God of Israel—though medieval Jewish commentators refer the story to Nebuchadnezzar's being in charge of *Israel* (v 9 [12]), to his oppression of *them* (v 24 [27]), and to his empire's destruction as the means of the *exiles* being able to escape his rule (v 11 [14]).

4:1–7a [4–10a] Troubled by his dream, Nebuchadnezzar recognizes Daniel as one in whom God's spirit dwells (v 5 [8]). In the OT the presence of God's spirit often implies the activity of God in his dynamic power, giving life and freedom to his people and to the world; the effect of this on human beings is to make them behave in remarkable ways and perform extraordinary deeds. A person who receives out-of-the-ordinary insights or revelations does so by the work of the divine spirit (Gen 41:38; Num 24:2; 2 Sam 23:2; 2 Chr 15:1; 20:14; 24:20). Remarkable words are assumed to suggest the breath of God himself. Whether or not they reflect an ecstatic experience (see Job 32:8, 18; contrast 15:2!), v 5 [8] does not here imply the view that all words of insight by definition indicate the activity of God's spirit. It is referring to knowledge of an extraordinary and inexplicable kind: such insight reflects the spirit of prophecy (Ps-Saadia). This conviction has already been expressed without using the actual word *spirit,* in 2:11. The use of this word reinforces the suggestion of a real presence of God that contrasts with the spurious presence that the statue of chap. 3 claimed to bring. Daniel's references to the human spirit on its own are negative: it is disturbed by divine revelations (2:1, 3; 7:15), insensitive to divine prompting (5:20). Daniel himself only comes to be someone of extraordinary spirit (5:12; 6:4 [5]) through the activity of the divine spirit (4:5, 6, 15 [8, 9, 18]; 5:11, 14) (D. Lys, *Ruach* [Paris: PUF, 1962] 252–55).

7b-9 [10b-12] The portrayal of the tree here has an immediate background in specific OT texts, but a more general background elsewhere in the OT and in other religions (see *Form*). A lofty, pre-eminent, verdant, protective, fruitful, long-lived tree is a common symbol for the living, transcendent, life-giving, sustaining Cosmos or Reality or Deity itself. A sacred tree at the center of the earth symbolically links earth and heaven; a tree of life grows in God's garden; world history can be symbolized as a tree. (See G. van der Leeuw, *Religion in Essence and Manifestation* [London: Allan and Unwin, 1938; tr. by J. E. Turner from *Phänomenologie der Religion* (Tübingen: Mohr, 1933)] chap. 5.3; M. Eliade, *Patterns in Comparative Religion* [London: Sheed and

Ward, 1958; tr. by R. Sheed from *Traité d'histoire des religions* (Paris: Payot, 1949)] chap. 8.) The image can be applied to humanity in general (Ps 1) or to one's own nation—Babylon (S. Langdon, *Building Inscriptions of the Neo-Babylonian Empire* [Paris: Leroux, 1905] no. 19), Israel (Isa 4:2; 5:1–7). It is a natural symbol for the king, who mediates God's life, provision, and protection to his people; he is treelike to them (Isa 11:1; 53:2; Herodotus 1.108; 7.19). (See I. Engnell, *Studies in Divine Kingship* [Uppsala: Almqvist, 1943 = Oxford: Blackwell, 1967] 25–30; G. Widengren, *The King and the Tree of Life in Ancient Near Eastern Religion* [Uppsala: Lundequist, 1951] 42–58.)

The symbol is reworked in Dan 4, as metaphor rather than myth. The obvious interpretation of it is to refer it to the royal dynasty, which will be cut down (the present king will be removed) but will survive as a stump with the potential for renewed growth (a new king will arise) (Ps-Saadia, Bickerman); cf. Isa 6:13; 11:1; also Job 14:7–9, which notes that what can be true of a tree cannot be true of an individual man. Daniel applies the dream, however, to Nebuchadnezzar personally. On the king's authority over the animal creation (v 9 [12]), see on 2:37–45.

10–15 [13–18] "Supernatural watchmen" is one of a number of expressions for heavenly beings in Daniel; for others see 3:28; 7:16; 10:13. These terms utilize the arrangements of a human court to picture God's management of the affairs of heaven and earth. An earthly king had watchmen, for instance, who were the eyes and ears whereby he controlled and provided for his realm (see n. 3:2.c). The heavenly king governs his realm by similar means, members of the Council of Yahweh (1 Kgs 22:19–22; Job 1–2; Ps 89:6–8 [5–7]; Jer 23:18) who act as his eyes (2 Chr 16:9; Zech 4:10; cf. 1:9), keeping him informed on the affairs of his realm and seeing that his will is put into effect throughout it. For "watchmen" in particular, perhaps cf. Isa 62:6. An earthly king's agents, of course, might rebel, and so might God's; "watchmen" became a term for such rebels (*1 Enoch* 1.5; 10.9, 15; 12.4; 13.10; contrast 12.2, 3); cf. the "gods" in Ps 82.

Supernatural figures such as these also feature in Canaanite, Babylonian, and Persian religion (cf. Murray [n. 10.a], not least his allusion to the Babylonian personified night watches who, watchful and never sleeping, are responsible for destinies on earth [*CAD* E:326]). Nebuchadnezzar might then be using a pagan expression, which Daniel later "corrects" (v 21 [24]) ("watchman" is a description of God himself in Ps 121:3–4; as קדוש "holy/supernatural" often is). Yet Daniel refers elsewhere to God's heavenly agents without implying that they rival God himself, and the rest of Nebuchadnezzar's statement (v 14b [17b]) seems "orthodox" enough (see also v 32 [35] and *Explanation*). Nor need one infer that this way of picturing God acting is alien to that which generally appears in the OT (against Eichrodt, *Theologie* 2:105 [ET 199]). It does emphasize the *means* of God's governing the world and not his direct agency, but this need not imply that God is remote and inaccessible. The Isaiah who emphasizes God's transcendence (Isa 6:1) also assumes God's direct involvement in Israelite and international affairs; the Gospels and Acts that stress God's presence with humanity in Christ and in the Spirit also portray the involvement of angels in the story of the Christ event and the beginnings of the church.

The proclamation's addressees are not specified (cf. Isa 40:1), the plurals (v 11 [14]) being impersonal and syntactically, though not rhetorically, equivalent to passives (cf. vv 12–13 [15–16]; Luke 12:20). The point is the certainty that God's destructive purpose will be fulfilled. Their message describes someone being reduced to animal-like existence; restraint by a metal ring is more likely part of that description—Jerome compares it with the chaining of madmen—than an aspect of tree culture, whether designed to keep the tree from disintegrating altogether or to keep it from branching anew. It also suggests a reversal of the treatment Nebuchadnezzar had given Israel (Jer 28:14; 39:7; 52:11; cf. Deut 28:48; also Jer 1:18; Mic 4:13; Ps 107:16). To live in the open, tethered, living off natural vegetation, exposed to the elements, is natural and not unpleasant for animals, but alien for human beings.

Talk of God's being able to do as he wishes (יצבא, v 14 [17]) or acting according to his wish (מצביה, v 32 [35]) reflects the formulae of legal transactions (J. J. Rabinowitz, *Bib* 36 [1955] 74–77; A. Hurvitz, "The History of a Legal Formula," *VT* 32 [1982] 257–67 and references) and is thus another aspect of the portrayal of God's way of acting in the light of that of the human king.

16–24 [19–27] Daniel's interpretation of the dream presupposes Babylon's position as *the* world power of the day, as has 2:37–38; and the acknowledgment Daniel speaks of has, in effect, already been made in 2:47 in response to the revelation there.

In isolation, "heaven" (v 23 [26]) might denote the supernatural watchmen (v 14 [17]). After the assertions about the rule of the Most High in vv 21–22 [24–25], however, more likely it is a surrogate for God himself. The two ideas ("God as king" and "heaven") are brought together at the climax of the pericope (4:34 [37] [Plöger]). As a surrogate, it is unique in the OT; cf. 1 Macc 3:18–19; 4:10; 2 Macc 7:11; *m. ʾAbot* 1:3, 11; 2:12; 4:4, 11, 12; Matt 21:25; Luke 15:18; John 3:27; and the phrase "rule of heaven" in Matthew (see F. Vattioni, "Aspetti del culto del signore dei cieli," *Augustinianum* 12 [1972] 479–515, esp. 498; 13 [1973] 37–73, esp. 48). More significant than these later parallels, however, is the utilization of the term שמין throughout chap. 4 (see *Structure*). Nebuchadnezzar is like a tree reaching from earth to heaven (4:8, 17, 19 [11, 20, 22]) and protecting the birds, which themselves defy the separation between earth and heaven (4:9, 18 [12, 21]); yet he is subject to judgment from heaven (4:10, 20, 28 [13, 23, 31]). The heaven to which he reached will supply his humble needs as it supplies those of the rest of creation (4:12, 20, 22, 30 [15, 22, 25, 33]; 5:21). In the end he will need to look to heaven as the real source of help, rather than pretending to be self-sufficient, to acknowledge that heaven rules, and as a king on earth to worship the King of heaven who rules in heaven as on earth (4:23, 31, 32, 34 [26, 34, 35, 37]; cf. "Lord of heaven," 5:23).

25–30 [28–33] The sense of achievement that Nebuchadnezzar here expresses is severely understated compared with that expressed in his successive building inscriptions in Babylon, which occupy 126 pages of text and translation in Langdon's edition of them (excerpts in Driver, xxiv–xxv). The palace from which he surveyed Babylon was one of the citadels on the north side of the city. It had large courts, reception rooms, throne room, residences, and the famous hanging gardens, a vaulted, terraced structure with an elaborate water supply for its trees and plants, apparently built by Nebuchadnezzar for his Median queen. From the palace he would see in the distance the city's 27km outer double wall, which he had built. His palace stood just inside the double wall of the inner city, which was punctuated by eight gates and encircled an area 3km by 1km, with the Euphrates running through it. The palace adjoined a processional avenue that Nebuchadnezzar had paved with limestone and decorated with lion figures, emblematic of Ishtar; this avenue entered the city through the Ishtar Gate, which he had decorated with dragons and bulls (emblems of Marduk and Bel). It continued south through the city to the most important sacred precincts, to whose beautifying and development Nebuchadnezzar had contributed, the ziggurat crowned by a temple of Marduk where the god's statue resided. In Marduk's temple there were also shrines to other gods, and in the city elsewhere temples of other Babylonian gods, restored or beautified by Nebuchadnezzar. (See R. Koldewey, *Das wieder erstehende Babylon* [Leipzig: Hinrichs, 1913] = *The Excavations at Babylon* [tr. A. S. Johns; London: Macmillan, 1914]; A. Parrot, *Babylone et l'Ancien Testament* [Neuchatel: Delachaux, 1956] = *Babylon and the Old Testament* [tr. B. E. Hooke; London/New York: SCM/Philosophical Library, 1958]; S. Langdon, *Inscriptions* [see on vv 7b-9]; *IBD;* for other ancient testimony to his achievements both as soldier and as builder, quotations in Josephus, *Ant.* 10.11.1 [10.219–28]; *C. Ap.* 1.19 [128–41]; and for the motif of the proud king risking divine judgment, Herodotus 7.10.)

The *bat-qol* (Ps-Saadia), the voice from heaven with nothing to be seen (v 28 [31]), is a common Semitic and biblical motif (Isa 9:7 [8]; *T. Levi* 18.6; Syriac Ahiqar 1.6; Mark 1:11; 9:7). Nebuchadnezzar's subsequent behavior (vv 29–30 [32–33]) may resemble the symptoms of lycanthropy, a psychotic or depressive delusion (Baldwin), though it need not do so—anyone's hair and nails will grow long in the wild, and anyway the pericope itself is more concerned with its theological than its medical significance.

31–34 [34–37] Looking to heaven (v 31 [34]) suggests seeking God's aid (Ps 25:15; 121:1–2; 123:1–2; 141:8) (Young) and thus implicitly recognizing God's kingship. It opens the way to restoration, which is portrayed in v 33 [36] along the lines of the allegory of the Davidic dynasty's restoration in Ezek 17:22–24. It is characteristic of tales of danger/humiliation and restoration that the subject's last state is higher than his first (cf. Daniel himself elsewhere in Dan 1–6, also Job). The restoration of Nebuchadnezzar's sanity and his resuming an ordinary human life is introductory to the restoration of his power: the story is about his power, nor merely about what happens to him as a human being. Similarly Nebuchadnezzar is portrayed as moving, not from the worship of Marduk to that of Yahweh (contrast 2 Macc 9:17), but from acknowledging his own kingship alone to acknowledging the kingship of God (v 34 [37]). "King of heaven" is another expression unique in the OT (though cf. 1 Esd 4:46, 58; Tob 13:7, 11; for similar expressions, Dan 5:23; Jer 7:18; 44:17–19). Here its significance is to bring together at the climax of the chapter its two key motifs, kingship and heaven.

Explanation

3:31–33 [4:1–3] A man of authority speaks to us: the great Nebuchadnezzar, lord of a worldwide empire, sends word round this empire, and his subjects wonder what further demand or obligation is to be placed on them. The content of his message confounds their expectations. The communication ceases to be an encyclical and becomes a testimony such as we read in the Psalms, the testimony of a man whom God has marvelously rescued from some calamity, who now makes public confession of the wonders God has performed for him and offers the praise that recognizes how his power extends beyond this one moment to the whole of history. Earthly might acknowledges the power of God; one who rules for a while as king acknowledges one whose kingship is unconstrained by time. His testimony subverts any tendency to be overimpressed by the significance of human government, as happened within the Near Eastern royal ideologies, as chap. 3 subverts any tendency to be overimpressed by the significance of human religion (Bentzen). The chapter concerns the question, who is king?—but by its form, it gives us the answer before we begin. Elsewhere OT narrative, psalmody, and prophecy speak of nations and kings once acknowledging God, challenged to acknowledge him, and destined to acknowledge him. Nebuchadnezzar actually makes this acknowledgment, in the present, in the history of this age. Whereas often it does not look as if God rules in history, occasional yet momentous events whose memory Scripture preserves give the grounds and the periodic reinforcement for the conviction that he does in fact rule. That is the conviction of faith which the author of Daniel affirms for himself and his readers as he puts it on the lips of the great Nebuchadnezzar.

4:1–6 [4–9] When a confessional psalm (e.g., Ps 30) begins as this pericope has (3:31–33 [4:1–3]), it invites us to pay close attention to the testimony which follows and which takes us over the way its unlikely result came about. As happens in such a psalm, Nebuchadnezzar now begins at the beginning. His confession goes further than that in chap. 2, and his testimony takes us further back than chap. 2 did when recounting his earlier dream. It begins from the secure, successful circumstances of his life before his dream came to trouble him. The very description of things going so well makes us wonder whether catastrophe is imminent, especially as God is omitted from what he says (Deut 8:11–14; Ps 30:6–7 [7–8]; Luke 12:19). The thriving state of Nebuchadnezzar's monarchy, at the head of its mighty empire, is to be reflected in the flourishing tree of his dream, symbolic of the great cosmic provider and of his royal earthly embodiment; but the broken tree of the dream will reflect the dreamer's actually fragile position—and perhaps his subconscious sense of that—which even a dream that hardly required much interpretation (Hippolytus) could nevertheless not enable to become a conscious awareness.

Among those invited to interpret the dream, Daniel arrives last. The other sages' failure heightens the challenge to and our expectations of one who already has a special status deriving from a special divine gift. The Nebuchadnezzar of chap. 2 had been told by the sages that conundrums beyond human insight could not be solved, because the gods' home is not among mortal men; Daniel had then proved to him that the God of heaven could solve them (2:11, 28). Here the king expresses convictions about the presence of God in Daniel, and about his consequent ability to solve conundrums, which the story will vindicate. His insights do not reflect merely human capacities; they come from divine revelation regarding what would otherwise remain mystery. The OT does not assume that the meaning of historical events (such as the dream portrays in symbol) can be read off from them. Neither the unbelieving world, nor the believing community, is at fault for finding history enigmatic. The significance of events may only be perceived on occasions such as this when God chooses to reveal it through some person he endows with prophetic gifts.

7–14 [10–17] Humanity finds ways of reassuring itself that the life and resources of the cosmos are secure. The myth of all-providing science has recently offered that reassurance in our history; the myth of the cosmic tree offered it to the ancient Near Eastern world. Nebuchadnezzar's fearful dream warns of the wasting of this resource, from the very quarter it sought to reach. It is not, after all, a secure locus or source of achievement and transcendence, of life, security, and provision. (It will eventually be a very different tree, one which more effectively links earth and heaven and displays itself—or rather displays the one it bears—before earth and heaven; a tree which, moreover, also has to become a tree of shame—but not for its own shortcomings—before it can be a tree of glory. That tree will offer life, security, and provision in fuller senses—though the fuller sense must not exclude the physical senses which are this vision's concern, and which are God's own concern.) The visionary tree is not totally destroyed; God's judgment characteristically has a "yet" (v 12 [15]) contained within it. But like the survival of a (mere) remnant in OT prophecy, the way in which its remains survive serves to underline the wasting it experiences. From the center of the earth it had reached toward heaven; now it is confined to the earth, fed from the earth, and all it knows of heaven is the rain. It had provided for the animals; now it is provided for in the midst of them. Its abasement will last for a long, but unspecified, period of time, though one determined, not one to last forever.

As happened in chap. 2, the dream-vision is now in the midst of taking a bizarre twist. The tree is being treated like an animal. The animal turns out to be a human being deprived of his senses. The life and resources of the cosmos, then, had been embodied in a person. This, too, is a familiar Near Eastern and OT theme; a nation's king embodies, guarantees, and sustains its life and destiny. For all the repudiation of monarchy in the modern world, the hopes and expectations attached to presidents, prime ministers, and heads of state evidence the same instinct. The OT warns against it (see Jotham's parable, Judg 9:6–15, especially v 15) and often portrays the judgment of kings. It is dangerous to embody too much in one person. Hence severe theological questions are raised by the traditional shaping of ministry (one church, one minister), as well as by the papacy, and by any situation in which monarch, president, prime minister, or party secretary becomes the equivalent to the government, the embodiment of all power—in his or her own thinking or in the people's. Only God is the One in whom all things hold together. Other so-called embodiments of some whole are idols who will disappoint, fail, and fall. So here a royal figure is taken from being the lord of all and source of life for all to being the least of all, unable even to sustain his own life. (The real tree of life will indeed bear such a man.)

The tree's downfall is ordained and announced by supernatural watchmen who make decisions and implement them on behalf of God Most High. Heavenly figures involved in such ways in God's governing of the world appear from time to time throughout Scripture. Their activity indicates the reality of God's involvement in the world to protect his people and to punish evil, yet also indirectly suggests his own exaltedness and transcendent authority, which is implemented, like that of the imperial authority, by means of his subordinate representatives. They belong to heaven, are themselves supernatural beings, and thus bring the word of God. They descend from heaven and speak in the hearing of an earthly king, and thus implement the will of God on earth. Daniel's watchmen well illustrate Barth's thesis that the true ministry of angels is that of witnesses to God's work and word, to the God who alone rules (*Dogmatik* iii, 3:537–41 [ET 460–63]; #51 on the rule of heaven and the ambassadors of God is relevant to Dan 4).

The object of the event they announce removes any possibility that they might be rivals of God himself. It is that people may acknowledge that the Most High rules. This is perhaps a tautology; of course the Most High rules. But it might be possible to understand that rule as holding in the world above and in the world to come but not in this present world. The watchman declares that God rules here and now. Scripture often affirms that God rules *through* human kingship; the calling of political authorities is to be the means of realizing God's provision, justice, and discipline in the world (hence Rom 13:1). Thus God works through the successive kings of the Middle Eastern empires (Isa 10:5; 13:3–6; 45:1). It also affirms that God rules *over* human kingship, for the pride or the failure of political authorities may require that they themselves be disciplined (hence Mark 12:17; and see Isa 10:5–19). His power to overrule them is demonstrated by his ability to deprive the mighty of their authority and to give it to nobodies—like Nabonidus, who broke the power of Nebuchadnezzar's dynasty and whose person is probably part of the background to this chapter. That ability, too, belongs not merely to past history (Ps 78:70–71) or to the moment when God's ultimate purpose is fulfilled (Luke 1:52) but to present events, to current experience. To affirm that heaven rules (as v 23 [26] later does) is to affirm that history is not limited to what seems humanly possible: heaven "is where God is enthroned and thus is the source of the transformative possibilities that God presents to every actual entity. . . . To paraphrase Whitehead, 'Heaven' is the 'home of the possibles' " (Wink, *Naming,* 119).

The first reason the pericope gives for the felling of the tree is that it will show that God rules. Its cause here is not Nebuchadnezzar's pride; it is not for reasons to do with Nebuchadnezzar at all. The watchman is concerned about whether people in general have the right attitude to human governments; the author no doubt has in mind the unbelieving world of his day, and his fellow believers insofar as they are tempted to adopt that world's way of thinking. The felling of the tree proves who is king. The tree speaks of a human authority that has its place (cf. v 33 [36]) but has to be kept in its place. Human power is helpless outside of the permissive will of the divine power.

15–16 [18–19] Dramatically, the inability of Nebuchadnezzar and his sages to understand the dream heightens the suspense and prepares the way for Daniel to do so; though we have noted that the dream's meaning is actually rather obvious—its interpretation requires little more than Nathan's "You are the man" (2 Sam 12:7). An inability to state it reflects an understandable fear on the part of ministers of state as well as king. Messengers who bring bad news sometimes pay for it as if they were responsible for it, and the king reassures Daniel that he is not to fear for his own fate. Daniel's fear, however, is for Nebuchadnezzar. His desire that the dream portrays the fate of the king's enemies rather than that of Nebuchadnezzar himself again builds up the tension, though it implies a positive concern for the king. Daniel encourages us here to long for God to have compassion on world rulers, specifically the wicked ones, and he encourages the world to assume that judgment is never inevitable. If we bait the tyrants and dare them do their worst, they may. Daniel invites us to care about people in power, even people who abuse power, to appeal to their humanness not their sinfulness, and to treat them as people given a responsibility by God and people who may respond to an appeal to right and wrong (Aukerman, *Valley*, 99; cf. Wink, *Naming*, 115–16).

17–24 [20–27] Nebuchadnezzar's Babylon had been the contemporary embodiment of that recurrent ambition of nations to be the one that, God-like, rules and provides for the whole world. But "reaching up to heaven" can suggest a rebellious arrogance on Babylon's part, which Heaven itself must judge (Gen 11:4; Isa 14:13). Only a tree that stands for God's own rule will ultimately be allowed to grow so high and broad that the birds of the heavens shelter in its branches (Mark 4:30–32); in the OT every Nebuchadnezzar has a watchman by his side (Lüthi), one who implements not merely the will of subordinate heavenly powers but that of the Most High himself (v 21 [24]). The action he heralds is designed to bring Nebuchadnezzar himself to acknowledge the Most High (contrast v 14 [17]). Nebuchadnezzar would, no doubt, have acknowledged that the Most High ruled (indeed, see 2:47); but earthly rulers find it difficult to make this more than a formal acknowledgment that does not compromise their sense that they themselves are in control. Andrew Melville reminded James VI, when he was asserting his rights, that Scotland had another King "of whose kingdom King James is neither Lord nor Head, but subject" (Kennedy). Nebuchadnezzar was affirmed in chap. 2, was confronted over religious questions in chap. 3, and is now confronted over his fulfillment of his kingship. At least it is a comfort that even God's judgment has as its object not merely destruction but recognition (cf. the Psalms, e.g., Ps 83 with its surprising ending). Nebuchadnezzar is promised that he can be king from the point he acknowledges that actually he is not, because God is.

Indeed, announcements of judgment have as their object that this recognition may be given without the judgment's having to draw it forth. The prophet is not one who is looking forward with enthusiasm to seeing the guilty get their come-uppance. The wish that disaster be averted was real. "Even now the axe is laid to the root of the trees" (Matt 3:10). John the Baptist and Jesus, like prophets such as Amos, Isaiah, Jeremiah, Ezekiel, and Jonah, along with Daniel utter such warnings in order that what is announced can be averted (Jerome).

The action required is to do justice and to take action on behalf of the needy (v 24 [27]). In the OT these are closely associated governmental obligations (Isa 11:4; Jer 22:15–16; Ps 72:2); in building inscription 12 (see vv 26–27 *Comment*) Nebuchadnezzar claims to be a just king, meek and humble. Such a royal ideal is suggested by the imagery of provision and protection in his dream-vision, but it is omitted in Daniel's description of what Nebuchadnezzar has actually achieved (v 19 [22]). A great national empire such as Nebuchadnezzar's is the political equivalent to the Indian god Vishnu, who was supposed to be the Preserver of human life but whose huge image was traditionally carried in processions on a giant wheeled throne that crushed anything that got in its path: the juggernaut that is supposed to be preserver and provider easily becomes crusher and destroyer, totalitarian and absolute in its demands (Aukerman, *Valley,* 50–51). Even pagan kings are called to be the means of God's caring kingship being implemented (Joubert); this king who has so far failed to do so must take action now if he is not to fall as a result. At least in his case, sin consists in injustice and unconcern. Such sins are like a yoke weighing down on his neck and needing to be broken off if he is to be free of their bondage (cf. *DTT* on פרק; free to take on another yoke, but an easier one [Matt 11:28–30]). Daniel assumes that a regime that puts justice first will itself prosper.

25–30 [28–33] Nineveh received no explicit invitation to repent, yet Nineveh and its king knew that contrition, fasting, prayer, and reform were the appropriate responses to Jonah's warning of judgment. The king of Babylon, however, apparently continues to enjoy the life of a successful monarch, the life he describes at the beginning of his story (v 1[4]); the warning he has received elicits no response. His sense of achievement over his building projects in Babylon is quite justified, yet precisely this—it seems—leads to his downfall. Perhaps his concern with his own kingship hindered him from seriously acknowledging God's (cf. v 22 [25]), though again there is no explicit reference to pride on Nebuchadnezzar's part (contrast Isa 14; Ezek 28; Acts 12:22–23). Perhaps the attention he gave to building projects should have been given to a concern for the needy (cf. v 24 [27]) (Rashi), or perhaps the sense of achievement at these has usurped the place of a desire for a sense of his achievements in the area of justice (cf. Jehoiakim, Jer 22:13–19). Human kingship is called to reflect that of the God who works through it, and to reflect his priorities. Yet further, perhaps anything or anyone that becomes great threatens by that very fact—even in the absence of pride—to rival the greatness of God himself (for "great Babylon," cf. Rev 18:2). God characteristically shames the wise and strong by means of the apparently weak and foolish (1 Cor 1:27) (Rupert). Whenever human beings rejoice in success and achievement, they may be about to experience the imminent action of God to remind them and the world of their place as mere creatures before his, the only true majesty. Absolute human power and achievement are only relative in relation to God's power. Being rich in earthly possessions and achievements must not take the place of being rich toward God (Luke 12:16–21).

Nebuchadnezzar's banishment from human society into the wild is his personal and royal experience of that banishment experienced by the OT's first human beings (that, too, a story about a quasi-royal figure, and involving a tree of life). "The words were still on the king's lips" balances "on the day that you eat of it . . ." (cf. Acts 12:23 "immediately . . ."). A particular word or act, arguably no worse than many others, becomes the occasion of a devastating declaration of judgment. The original act of defiance meant banishment for all humanity; yet Adam and Eve's fellow human beings often earn banishment from the alternative gardens they create for themselves. The desire to be like God led to humanity's losing even its authority over the animals; yet the members of that humanity are sometimes transformed into beasts when they have sought to be like God (cf. also Ps 49:13, 21 [12, 20] [Theodoret]). Insanity can take the form of religious delusion, but in Nebuchadnezzar's case it was irreligious delusion that brought insanity. The achievement and the splendor suddenly seem very insignificant. Perhaps one should say that the true insanity belongs to the Nebuchadnezzar who has earlier been talking as if he were the eternal king and God did not exist. His outward madness is the external expression of a delusion he has already been the tragic victim of. Only a madman thinks he is a king or an emperor (Pascal): politics is the house rules of a lunatic asylum. But those rules are important, because they make the madness as little harmful as possible.

31–34 [34–37] Nebuchadnezzar had looked over Babylon with a justifiable pride. Now the determined period of his chastisement is over and he looks to God in recognition and need. As God demonstrated his power and his faithfulness to his word in bringing judgment on Nebuchadnezzar, so he does once again in bringing the time of Nebuchadnezzar's humiliation to an end. The reason for the timing of Nebuchadnezzar's restoration lies in the will of God. We are not told that the king repented first; it would be difficult for a man in his condition to do so. We are told rather that God's handling of him was effective. As they were destined to do (vv 22, 29 [25, 32]), dethronement and restoration have brought the earthly king to praise and confession before the Most High as the one whose kingship is never set aside. It is the praise and confession that the angel's witness is designed to inspire (Barth, *Dogmatik* iii, 3:538–39 [ET 461–62]). The events follow a significant sequence. The time comes to an end; so the king turns to God for mercy; so God restores him to his full humanness; so he opens his mouth in fervent praise and worship. Nebuchadnezzar makes the confession to which Isaiah of the exile invites his contemporaries in Babylon (Isa 40:12–26) (Theodoret). His own rule can be suspended or terminated; God's never is. His own power can be cast aside as a mere feebleness; *a fortiori* the power or opinion of other human beings counts for nothing. Supernatural watchmen scurry to implement his will; the forces of heaven, too, are under his unquestioned command (see further Dan 10–12). The possibility of rebellion is hardly envisaged (contrast Isa 24:21). If Nebuchadnezzar makes such a confession, readers of Dan 4 who are likely to be impressed by earthly powers, and perhaps by heavenly ones, may be encouraged to live by that confession themselves. Occasions such as the exodus or the return from exile (or the emptying of the tomb) demonstrate that kinglike authority of God and make it possible to continue to believe in it between times.

The confession of God as King might seem to leave no place for human government (cf. Judg 8:23; 1 Sam 8:4–7; 12:12). Rather, the chapter continues to assume that if God's kingship is acknowledged, human kingship can then find its place. Even the majesty and the glory of human kingship are affirmed, in the context of that confession which is the fruit of personal abasement. It really is "the context": the confession appears on both sides of the reference to his own glory, acting like a metaphorical watchman in relation to that dangerous self-description. Rule on earth as well as the rule of heaven come to belong to the one who becomes poor in spirit (cf. Matt 5:3) (Theodoret). The king's sin has been characterized both as pride and as injustice or unconcern. His testimony finally brings the two together. God is the embodiment of faithfulness and justice and the demolition of pride.

Nebuchadnezzar is an example—a warning of how not to be led astray by power and achievement, a model of how to respond to chastisement and humiliation. He is even more a promise, that earthly authorities are in the hand of God, not merely for their judgment, but for his glory.

Belshazzar Fails to Learn from His Father's Experience and Is Put Down (5:1–6:1 [5:1–31])

Bibliography

Alfrink, B. "Der letzte König von Babylon." *Bib* 9 (1928) 187–208. ———. "Darius Medus." *Bib* 9 (1928) 316–40. **Alt, A.** "Zur Menetekel-Inschrift." *VT* 4 (1954) 303–5. **Auchincloss, W. S.** "Darius the Median." *BSac* 66 (1909) 536–38. **Bauer, H.** "Menetekel." *Vierter deutscher Münzforschertag zu Halle.* 1925. 27–30. **Boutflower, C.** "The Historical Value of Daniel v and vi." *JTS* 17 (1915–16) 43–60. ———. " 'Belshazzar the King' (Dan. v. 1)." *ExpT* 36 (1924–25) 526–27. **Bulman, J. M.** "The Identification of Darius the Mede." *WTJ* 35 (1972–73) 247–67. **Cerceau, J.-A. du.** *Balthasar.* Rotomagi: Lallemant, 1695. **Clay, A. T.** "Gobryas." *JAOS* 41 (1921) 466–67. **Clerice, J. de.** *Dissertatio de epulo Belschasar.* Wittenberg: Haken, 1662. = *TTP* 883–86. **Clermont-Ganneau, C.** "Mané, thécel, pharès et le festin de Balthasar." *JA* viii, 8 (1886) 36–67. = Clermont-Ganneau, *Recueil d'archéologie orientale.* Paris: Leroux, 1888. 1:136–59. = "Mene, Tekel, Peres, and the Feast of Belshazzar" (tr. R. W. Rogers). *Hebraica* 3 (1887) 87–102. **Couroyer, B.** "*Lḥn:* chantre?" *VT* 5 (1955) 83–88. **Coxon, P. W.** "A Philological Note on אשתיו Dan 5 3f." *ZAW* 89 (1977) 275–76. **Dougherty, R. P.** *Nabonidus and Belshazzar.* New Haven/London: Yale UP/Milford, 1929. ———. "Ancient Teimâ and Babylonia." *JAOS* 41 (1921) 458–59. ———. "Nabonidus in Arabia." *JAOS* 42 (1922) 305–16. **Eissfeldt, O.** "Die Menetekel-Inschrift und ihre Deutung." *ZAW* 63 (1951) 105–14. = Eissfeldt, *Kleine Schriften.* Tübingen: Mohr, 1966. 3:210–17. **Emerton, J. A.** "The Participles in Daniel v.12." *ZAW* 72 (1960) 262–63. **Galling, K.** "H. H. Rowley, *Darius the Mede* . . ." *ZDMG* 95 (1941) 148–50. ———. "Die 62 Jahre des Meders Darius in Dan 6 1." *ZAW* 66 (1954) 152. **Genouillac, H. de.** "Nabonide." *RA* 22 (1925) 71–83. **Gibson, M. D.** "Belshazzar's Feast." *ExpT* 23 (1911–12) 181. **Grelot, P.** "Le chapitre v de *Daniel* dans la Septante." *Sem* 24 (1974) 45–66. ———. "L'écriture sur le mur (Daniel 5)." In *Mélanges bibliques et orientaux,* FS M. Delcor, ed. A. Caquot et al. AOAT 215 (1985). 199–207. **Gruenthaner, M. J.** "The Last King of Babylon." *CBQ* 11 (1949) 406–27. **Guglielmo, A. de.** "Dan. 5:25." *CBQ* 11 (1949) 202–6. **Halévy, J.** "Balthasar et Darius le Mède." *RevSém* 2 (1894) 186–91. **Hoffmann, G.** "Mene, mene tekel upharsin." *ZA* 2 (1887) 45–48. **Horner, J.** *Daniel, Darius the Median, Cyrus the Great.* Pittsburgh: Horner, 1901. **Koch, K.** "Dareios, der Meder." In *The Word of the Lord Shall Go Forth,* FS D. N. Freedman, ed. C. L. Meyers and M. O'Connor. Winona Lake: Eisenbrauns, 1983. 287–99. **König, E.** "Mené, mené, teḳél upharsin." *NKZ* 12 (1901) 949–57. **König, F. W.** "Naboned und Kuraš." *AfO* 7 (1931–32) 178–82. **Kraeling, E. G.** "The Handwriting on the Wall." *JBL* 63 (1944) 11–18. **Krappe, A. H.** "La vision de Balthassar." *RHR* 98 (1928) 78–86. **Lambert, W. G.** "Nabonidus in Arabia." *Proceedings of the Fifth Seminar for Arabian Studies.* London: Seminar for Arabian Studies, 1972. 53–64. **Linder, J.** "Der König Belšaṣṣar nach dem Buche Daniel und den babylonischen keilinschriftlichen Berichten." *ZKT* 53 (1929) 173–202. **Liptzin, S.** "Belshazzar's Folly." *Dor leDor* 7 (1978–79) 119–26. Repr. in Liptzin, *Biblical Themes in World Literature.* Hoboken, NJ: Ktav, 1985. **Lister, J. M.** " 'Mene, mene, tekel, upharsin.' " *ExpT* 11 (1899–1900) 234. **Nöldeke, T.** "Mene tekel upharsin." *ZA* 1 (1886) 414–18. **Peters, J. P.** "Mene, mene, tekel, upharsin." Sec. 4 of "Notes on the Old Testament." *JBL* 15 (1896) 114–17. **Pinches, T. G.** "Fresh Light on the Book of Daniel." *ExpT* 26 (1914–15) 297–99. **Prince, J. D.** *Mene Mene Tekel Upharsin.* Diss., Johns Hopkins,

1893. **Robinson, A. C.** "Darius the Median." *JTVI* 54 (1922) 1–30. **Rowley, H. H.** 9–60. ———. "The Belshazzar of Daniel and of History." *Exp* ix, 2 (1924) 182–95, 255–72. ———. "The Historicity of the Fifth Chapter of Daniel." *JTS* 32 (1931) 12–31. **Shea, W. H.** "An Unrecognized Vassal King of Babylon in the Early Achaemenid Period." *AUSS* 9 (1971) 51–57, 99–128; 10 (1972) 88–117, 147–78. ———. "Nabonidus, Belshazzar, and the Book of Daniel." *AUSS* 20 (1982) 133–49. ———. "Darius the Mede." *AUSS* 20 (1982) 229–47. ———. *AUSS* 23 (1985) 277–95. **Smith, S.** *Babylonian Historical Texts Relating to the Capture and Downfall of Babylon.* London: Methuen, 1924. **Sparks, H. F. D.** "On the Origin of Darius the Mede." *JTS* 47 (1946) 41–46. **Steyl, C.** "Mĕne mĕne tĕqel ufarsîn." *Nederduitse Gereformeerde Teologiese Tydskrif* 18 (1977) 199–205. **Whitcomb, J. H.** *Darius the Mede.* Grand Rapids: Eerdmans, 1959. **Wilson, R. D.** 1:96–263. ———. "Darius the Mede." *PTR* 20 (1922) 177–211. **Wiseman, D. J.**, et al. *Notes.* 9–16. **Zimmermann, F.** "The Writing on the Wall." *JQR* 55 (1964–65) 201–7.

Translation

1 *King Belshazzar*[a] *gave a banquet for his thousand nobles,*[b] *and he was drinking*
wine [c]*in the company of*[c] *these thousand.* 2 [a]*When he tasted*[a] *the wine, Belshazzar*
gave orders to bring the gold and silver vessels which his father Nebuchadnezzar
had taken from the sanctuary in Jerusalem, so that the king and his nobles, his
consorts, and his mistresses[b] *could drink from them.* 3 *The gold*[a] *vessels which had*
been taken from [b]*the sanctuary in the house of God*[b] *in Jerusalem were brought*
in, and the king and his nobles, his consorts, and his mistresses did drink[c] *from*
them. 4 *As they drank the wine, they praised the gods of gold and silver, of bronze,*
iron, wood, and stone. 5 *That very moment the fingers of a human hand appeared*[a]
and wrote on the plaster of the wall of the royal palace, over against the candelabra.
The king could see the actual[b] *hand as it wrote.* 6 *The king's*[a] *face turned pale*[b]
and his mind was filled with alarm. [c]*His body went weak*[c] *and his knees knocked*
against each other. 7 *The king called in a loud voice for the chanters,*[a] *the Chaldeans,*
and the exorcists to be fetched, and proclaimed to the Babylonian sages, "Anyone
who can read out this inscription and explain its interpretation shall wear the
purple, with the gold chain[b] *round his neck, and rule as a Deputy*[c] *in the kingdom.*
8 [a]*All the royal*[b] *sages came in,*[a] *but they could not read out the inscription or tell*
the king the interpretation. 9 *King Belshazzar grew very*[a] *alarmed and his face*
turned very[a] *pale; his nobles were put in turmoil.*

10 *Because of the debate between the king and his courtiers,* [a]*the queen herself*[a]
came into the banqueting hall. The queen declared, "Long live the king! There is
no need for you to be alarmed or for your face to turn pale. 11 *There is a man in*
your kingdom who has the spirit of holy deity in him. In your father's time he was
found to have insight and ability,[a] *and a wisdom like the wisdom of the gods.*
King Nebuchadnezzar, your father, made him head of the [b]*diviners, chanters, Chalde-*
ans, and exorcists[b]*—your father as king.*[c] 12 *Since this Daniel, whom the king*
named Belteshazzar, was found to have a remarkable spirit, knowledge, and ability,
[a]*interpreting dreams, explaining puzzles, and resolving enigmas,* [a]*Daniel should*
be summoned now, and he will explain the interpretation."

13 *Daniel was brought before the king. The king addressed Daniel: "So you are*
Daniel, one of the Judean exiles whom my father as king brought from Judah? 14 *I*
have heard tell of you, that the spirit of deity[a] *is in you. You have been found to*

have insight and ability and remarkable wisdom. 15 *The sages (the chanters) have just been brought before me to read out this inscription and tell me its interpretation, but they were unable to explain the interpretation of the thing.* 16 *But I myself*[a] *have heard tell of you, that you can give interpretations and resolve enigmas. Now, if you can read out the inscription and tell me its interpretation, you shall wear the purple, with the gold chain round your neck, and rule as a Deputy in the kingdom."*

17 *Daniel made reply before the king, "You may keep your gifts, or give your rewards*[a] *to some other man. Nevertheless, I will read out the inscription for your majesty and tell him the interpretation.* 18 *Your majesty,*[a] *God Most High gave* [b]*royal authority and glorious splendor*[b] *to your father Nebuchadnezzar.* 19 *Because of the authority that had been given him, people of all races, nations, and languages stood in fear and trembling before him. He would kill whom he wished and spare whom he wished, elevate whom he wished and humble whom he wished.* 20 *But when his attitude became elevated and his spirit arrogant, so that he behaved presumptuously, he was deposed from his royal throne, and honor*[a] *was taken away from him.* 21 *He was led away from human society, his mind became*[a] *like an animal's, and he lived with the wild asses.*[b] *He was fed plants like an ox and his body was watered with the dew from the heavens, until he came to acknowledge that God Most High rules over human kingship and sets over it whomever he wishes.* 22 *As his son*[a] *you, Belshazzar, have not humbled your attitude because*[b] *you knew all this,* 23 *but have elevated yourself above the Lord of heaven. The vessels from his house have been brought before you, and you and your nobles, your consorts, and your mistresses have drunk wine from them. You have praised the gods of* [a]*silver and gold,*[a] *of bronze, iron, wood, and stone, which cannot see or hear or know, and not glorified the God* [b]*who has your lifebreath and your whole destiny in his hand.*[b] 24 *That is why from his presence a hand was sent and this inscription written.* 25 *This is the inscription that was written: '*[a]*Counted at a mina,*[a] *a shekel,*[b] *and two halves.*[c]*'* 26 *This is the interpretation of the words. 'A* mina*' means 'God* counted out *the days of your kingship and handed it over.'*[a] 27 *'A* shekel*' means 'You have been* weighed *on the scales and found deficient.'* 28 *'A* half*' means 'Your kingship has been* broken in half *and given to Media and* Persia*.'"* 29 *Then Belshazzar gave order to clothe*[a] *Daniel in the purple, with the gold chain round his neck, and a proclamation was issued concerning him, that he would rule as a Deputy in the kingdom.* 30 *That very night Belshazzar*[a] *the Chaldean king was killed,* 1 *and Darius the Mede acquired*[a] *the kingship as*[b] *a man of sixty-two years.*

Notes

1.a. בלשאצר; Bēl-šar-uṣur, "Bel protect the king." One might have expected in BA בלשראצר (cf. Nergal-sharezer, Jer 39:3) (Plöger). בלאשצר (5:30; 7:1; 8:1) is more anomalous: see n. 30.a.

1.b. Taking the whole phrase לרברבנוהי אלף as determinate. Cf. Th, JPS, BL 95k, against EVV, Ehrlich "1000 of his nobles." Cf. 7:24, "the ten horns," not "ten of the horns."

1.c-c. Cf. JB; for the king to dine with them was an exceptional event. But לקבל may suggest "before them," i.e., sitting at high table facing them (making a display of himself?).

2.a-a. בטעם, perhaps implying "under the influence of" (cf. NEB and the story in Esth 1:10).

2.b. שגלתה ולחנתה: Akk. terms for the most senior of the king's wives (lit. "she of the palace," though S. Feigin ["Word Studies," *AJSL* 43 (1926–27) 47] doubts this understanding and argues for "lady of the harem" more generally) and for a woman in a senior position in the royal household, an official in the harem (*CAD* E:61–62; A/1:294; I. M. Diakonoff, "Some Remarks on I 568," *ArOr* 47 [1979] 40). There is a disparaging tone about the use of the two words, esp. in the pl, and about the combination of the two. These women contrast unfavorably with מלכתא "the queen" who appears in v 10, since the two terms here do not denote people who exercise actual authority; and cf. the two classes of women of the palace and harem in 1 Kgs 11:3; Cant 6:8 (B. Landsberger, "Akkadische-hebräische Wortgleichungen," *HW* 198–204; Oppenheim, *Mesopotamia,* 104). JB "singing women" for לחנתה connects the word with one used at Elephantine (cf. J. Reider, "The Brooklyn Museum Aramaic Papyri," *JQR* 44 [1953–54] 339; Couroyer, *VT* 5 [1955] 86; C. C. Torrey, "More Elephantine Papyri," *JNES* 13 [1954] 150–51, appealing to an Arabic root; cf. BDB for an Arabic cognate).

3.a. Presumably the silver ones are assumed to be included (cf. v 2); Th, Vg, EVV make this explicit.

3.b-b. For the distinction betwen the היכל and the wider complex of temple buildings as a whole, cf. 1 Kgs 6:3. But the expression is pleonastic and perhaps די בית אלהא is a gloss on היכל to make it clear that the latter does not refer to the palace, as it does in 4:26 [29] (Plöger). Vg omits it; Syr, Th omit בית.

3.c. אשתיו (also v 4). The prosthetic א is a mark of eastern imperial Aram., not of late Aram. (Coxon, *ZAW* 89 [1977] 275–76).

5.a. Q נפקה (f vb); K has m vb with f subj. Cf. n. 7:8.b; n. 7:20.a.

5.b. פס usually refers to the palm—which would be hardly visible during writing, even to someone below it (Bentzen)—but essentially it denotes the hand itself as opposed to the lower arm and hand, effectively referring here to the back of the hand or knuckles (NEB, Plöger, comparing Gen 37:3). It thus suggests *merely* a hand (unconnected to an arm) (cf. Hartman). The hand writes on the wall above the high table, illuminated by the candelabra (cf. GNB).

6.a. מלכא in emphatic position at the beginning of the cl, as a hanging nom.

6.b. שנוהי: the suffix is an anomalous indirect obj (BL 75d, GKC 117x; and see Cohen, *Afroasiatic Linguistics* 2, 1 [1975] 21) equivalent to עלוהי in v 9: but see n. 9.a.

6.c-c. קטרי חרצה משתרין, "his hip joints went loose," i.e., he lost the strength to stand.

7.a. 4QDan[a], OG (Pace, 34) have an extra group חרטמיא.

7.b. המונכא (Q המניכא), a Persian word perhaps denoting a collar on the garment rather than a chain; cf. the רבד of Gen 41:42 (and vv 41–42 for the passage as a whole). Cf. Hittite *mannin(n)i* (so H. Kronasser, *SCO* 3:61–66). But Gk *μανιάκης* denotes a bracelet (cf. W. Belardi, *SCO* 1:189–211).

7.c. תלתי has the word for "third" lying behind it; it might connect with the three overseers of 6:3 [2] (cf. OG), or suggest that Daniel would be third in rank within the kingdom (after Nabonidus and Belshazzar? or after Belshazzar and the Queen? cf. EVV). But perhaps, like BH שליש, it has lost its numerical meaning altogether. In form, it may combine Aram. תליתי and the Akk.-influenced תלתא of vv 16, 29 (see *GBA* 69, 71; Torrey, *JAOS* 43 [1923] 232).

8.a-a. The phrase is resumptive after v 7b, to lead into the statement of the sages' incomprehension; it is rather wooden to propose emendation because v 7b suggests the sages are already in the hall (against BHS).

8.b. מלכא is odd; some mss have the more usual בבל, BHS notes the proposal מלכותא.

9.a. שגיא and עלוהי suggest that the king's alarm is understandably increased by the sages' inability to explain the inscription.

10.a. מלכתא is in emphatic position at the beginning of the sentence.

11.a. נהירו ושכלתנו, perhaps hendiadys, "brilliant insight" (Hartman).

11.b-b. See on 2:2.

11.c. מלכא אבוך, perhaps a variant for מלכא נבכדנצר אבוך "King Nebuchadnezzar, your father" (Ehrlich); Th, Syr lack it. But it is the reference to Nebuchadnezzar's elevating Daniel which Belshazzar omits when he recapitulates the Queen's words (vv 13–16) (Plöger); perhaps the words are repeated for emphasis here.

12.a-a. A parenthesis after the abs שכלתנו "ability." מפשר "interpreting" and משרא "resolving" need to be understood as verbal nouns, like אחוית "explaining"; this may not involve emending them, if the ptpl can denote the action as such, without focusing on an agent: so Emerton, *ZAW* 72 (1960) 262–63, noting that Syr, Th do not support emendation. For משרא קטרין (lit., "untying knots") NEB has "unbinding spells"; this meaning fits the Babylonian context well, but it is not clear that the phrase would have been understood thus, and the literary context (v 16) implies that Daniel's interpretative activity will instance the ability referred to here.

14.a. RSV assumes קדישין "holy" has been lost (cf. v 11); it is present in some mss, Syr. But such variation where phrases recur is common in Dan. Keil thinks the omission is significant on the lips of Belshazzar.

16.a. אנה is emphatic (contrasting with v 14, after v 15).

17.a. נבזביתך: the form is odd (*GBA* 62) and may be a corruption of נבזבת ביתך "the gift of your house," cf. Th, Syr (Kallarakkal, 84–85).

18.a. אנתה מלכא "you, your majesty . . .": the hanging nom makes clear that what follows relates to him (Zoeckler).

18.b-b. Taking מלכותא ורבותא ויקרא והדרה "kingship, greatness, honor, and splendor" as a double hendiadys (Hartman).

20.a. ויקרה lacks a suffix; Lucian, Syr, Vg are translating acc. to the sense.

21.a. K שוי peil, Q and some mss שויו pael (3 pl impersonal).

21.b. ערדיא; a few mss read עדריא "flocks/herds," perhaps to harmonize with what follows, "eating plants like an ox."

22.a. NIVmg "descendant" or "successor" are possible renderings of ברה; see on v 2.

22.b. כל קבל די. EVV "although" would be unparalleled; the usual "because" is quite possible if the clause is linked with the vb rather than with the negative (Keil).

23.a-a. JB follows one ms, Th, Syr is reversing these to the more usual order.

23.b-b. Linking לה with what follows rather than with what precedes, with Th (cf. BHS) against MT accents (cf. RV). "Your destiny": ארחתך, "your ways."

25.a-a. מנא מנא. The lack of one מנא in G (OG in its introduction to chap. 5; Josephus, *Ant.* 10.11.3 [10.243–44], does not quote the inscription itself) more likely reflects haplog/assimilation of the inscription to the threefold interpretation than dittog in the MT. On differences between omen text and interpretation, see n. 2:34.a. Cf. rather Syr's suggestion of a play on words, *menê menâ* (according to Montgomery). The first מנא is pass ptpl, the second a noun (Prince); with this use of the vb, cf. 2 Kgs 12:11 [10] (Eissfeldt, *ZAW* 63 [1951] 109).

25.b. תקל. A homonym means "fall" (*DTT*), an appropriate idea in the context (König, *NKZ* 12 [1901] 956). Zimmermann (*JQR* 55 (1964–65] 201–7) tr "the Persian trap is set" on the basis of the related noun.

25.c. פרסין. Again, the s פרס implied by G (Josephus, *Ant.* 10.11.3 [10.243–44], is once more hardly relevant) more likely reflects assimilation to the interpretation (v 28) than MT expansion, since the pl occurs only in v 25. I have taken פרסין as dual in meaning (cf. עדנין, 7:25; and see *Comment* on 6:1 [5:31]), but it could indicate "some halves" (Nöldeke, *ZA* 1 [1886] 415–16).

26.a. השלמה, EVV "brought to an end"; but שלם ha suggests rather God's original entrusting of the kingship to Belshazzar (Ezra 7:19; *DTT*), and this also gives a better sequence and more dramatic effect.

29.a. See BL 106e.

30.a. At the point of his death, the anomalous spelling בלאשצר might suggest "Bel [in] the fire of an adversary" (Poole on 7:1).

6:1.a. קבל need imply neither "took [by force]" (though "grab" was apparently a favorite vb of Darius I [Cook, *Persian Empire,* 66]) nor "received [from God or Cyrus]": it may simply indicate that he succeeded Belshazzar (Young).

1.b. כ denoting time at which; EVV "about" is unnecessary (*GBA* 78; GKC 118s-x).

Form / Structure / Setting

Form

See chap. 1 *Form.* Elements of court-contest tale, legend, and midrash again interweave. The story's background is a royal banquet in the palace; it concerns king, queen, and courtiers. Once more a king receives an alarming omen, of evidently portentous significance and requiring interpretation. His sages are impotent, but finally the hero (now an old, forgotten adviser) arrives, interprets the omen, and is rewarded. The queen's reassurances and the king's response to the oracle (vv 10, 29), both out of keeping with its contents, are court-contest tale motifs. The writing on the wall has been seen as a folk-tale motif (Gunkel, *Märchen,* 142 [ET 153]), though there are no very close independent parallels (see Krappe, *RHR* 98 [1928] 78–86; Baumgartner, *TR* 11 [1939] 134–35).

As in chaps. 1–4, the court-tale is utilized in a religious setting; the story becomes a prophetic legend. The omen is provoked by an act of idolatrous sacrilege in a context of Bacchanalian excess. It is of manifestly supernatural origin and elicits the response appropriate to an announcement of divine judgment. The story's Jewish hero is able to interpret it because the spirit of holy deity is in him. The story closes with the confirming of his word by events that take place that very night; in contrast to chaps. 2 and 4, there is no acknowledgment of God by the hearer. The opening rebuke regarding the hearer's wrong attitude to the prophet (v 17) (?) is also at home in such stories. The message itself includes no "messenger formula" ("thus says Yahweh"), but its form otherwise recalls the indictments of the prophets (C. Westermann, *Grundformen prophetischer Rede* [Munich: Kaiser, 1960] = *Basic Forms of Prophetic Speech* [tr. H. C. White; Philadelphia/London: Westminster/Lutterworth, 1967]; K. Koch, *Was ist Formgeschichte?* [Neukirchen: Neukirchener, 1964, rev. ed. 1967] = *The Growth of the Biblical Tradition* [tr. S. M. Cupitt; London: Black, 1969] chaps. 15–18). It especially resembles ones in the Deuteronomistic History (1 Sam 2:27–36; 15:17–26; 2 Sam 12:7–12); one may suspect that like these it constitutes the narrator's idea as to what an appropriate prophetic word in this context would have been (cf. R. R. Wilson, "Form-Critical Investigation of the Prophetic Literature," *Society of Biblical Literature 1973 Seminar Papers* [ed. G. MacRae; Cambridge, MA: SBL, 1973] 117). It is literary prophecy. After the repudiation of the offered reward, it includes a developed reminder of the history behind the present situation (vv 18–21), which provides the background and grounds for a reproof (vv 22–23). There follows an introduction to the announcement of judgment (vv 24–25a, 26a), then the announcement itself (25b, 26b–28). The last is fairly brief; the heart of the message lies in the preceding indictment (vv 18–23), in the background to the omen rather than in the omen itself (Plöger). It utilizes paronomasia, in the manner of a prophet (Jer 1:11–12; Amos 8:1–2) (see *Structure*), though it follows the pesher form, stating and interpreting the omen element by element. The utilization of the pesher form compares with chap. 2; in contrast, the importance of the "prophetic" indictment of the king distinguishes chaps. 4 and 5, with their focus on events in the kings' own day—Bentzen compares it with the "Jewish mission preaching" in Jonah—from chap. 2, where the message relates more to the readers' time than to the king's. Chap. 5 resembles chap. 2, however, in containing no overt invitation to repentance on the part of the king.

The story has one or two midrashic aspects. The attack on idolatry, the scorning of the sages, and the contrasting portrayal of a God able to declare his intentions and fulfill them, recalls Isa 41:21–29; 44:6–28; 46:1–7, with their focus on the fall of Babylon (Gammie, *VT* 31 [1981] 287–89, also comparing Job 34:16–30; 36:5–14; cf. further the idol polemic of Deut 4:28; Ps 115; 135:15–18). Belshazzar's distraught response to the omen, and the fall of his dynasty to a Median king on a night of revelry, recall other prophecies of Babylon's fall (Isa 21:1–10; also 13:17–19; 14:3–23; Jer 51, especially v 57). The attack on idolatry resembles 4QPrNab, too, where Nabonidus acknowledges his mistaken worship of "gods of silver and gold, [bronze, iron,] wood, stone and clay." The story utilizes ultimately historical traditions about Belshazzar and his regency in Babylon and about the Persian conquest(s) of Babylon, and reflects the local color of Babylonian palace life, including folk tradition about the Queen Mother (cf. Herodotus 1.185–87). The omen itself may be a secular riddle (Ginsberg).

The narrative reveals little of the distinctive personalities of the characters in the story; most of it concerns Belshazzar, yet from it we learn little of Belshazzar himself as an individual. He fulfills a role, acting and being acted on, but in himself a cipher. Even the anxious fear attributed to him is a motif characteristic of such stories. His personal reaction to Daniel's message is unrecorded because it is irrelevant. In the case of the queen, too, we learn only what relates to the dramatic function she fulfills in commending Daniel and incriminating Belshazzar. She is only a voice. The speeches by the queen, Belshazzar, and Daniel are the means of more overt description of the characters' personalities and qualities. The former two repeat and thus emphasize those personal gifts of Daniel which are relevant to the story. The queen's speech also offers preliminary hints of Belshazzar's shortcomings, which Daniel's speech develops.

The distinctive and original element in the chapter is the actual omen and its interpretation (vv 25–28), around which a narrative context has been constructed, using remembered historical facts such as the regency of Belshazzar, the forms of court-conflict tale and prophetic legend, the technique of midrash, and some of the characteristic structural, verbal, and theological features that appear elsewhere in the Daniel stories (see *Setting*). This adds to the omen's impact, giving concrete expression to the king's deserving of punishment, the helplessness of Babylonian wisdom, and the contrasting insight found in the Jewish sage by the gift of God.

Structure

Contrasting with chap. 4, chap. 5 returns to the simple sequential narrative construction of chap. 3 (Plöger). It also resembles chap. 2 in that much of its freight is carried by the speech of Daniel that dominates the latter part of the chapter. Narrative, however, provides the chapter's framework. Verses 1–9 give the introductory setting for the speeches, describing the circumstances and the act of sacrilege itself (vv 1–4), the appearing of the omen and the king's response (vv 5–7), then the failure of his initial attempt to discover its meaning and the consequent deepening and broadening of his dismay (vv 8–9). Tension develops steadily through this narrative introduction (which compares with 2:1–13): the Bacchanalian context already bodes ill, the act of sacrilege makes us look for some heavenly response, the omen's contents are unrevealed but its effect on the king increases our concern regarding them, and the sages' failure to read the omen deepens this concern.

The bulk of the chapter consists of speeches, in a brief narrative setting. The queen appears; she functions as a means of introducing the hero, announcing in anticipation the abilities he is shortly to be challenged to demonstrate, and introducing the theme of the king's looking back from his reign to his father's (vv 10–12; cf. Arioch's role in 2:14–25). Daniel appears, to be addressed by the king (vv 13–16; cf. 2:26). There may be an irony about the king's opening words, where his description of Daniel goes beyond anything the queen has told him, to facts from a past that Belshazzar has not taken account of in his act of sacrilege and in his neglecting to turn to Daniel earlier. Much of the king's subsequent speech merely recapitulates what we have already been told, so that the effect of the two speeches is to promise resolution of the tension established by the narrative opening, but to heighten it in the short term by slowing the pace of the story. Daniel's prophetic indictment (vv 17–28) carries much of the burden of the chapter's message (cf. his speech in 2:27–45), but continues this effect. Finally, the narrative framework of the chapter as a whole reappears (5:29–6:1 [5:29–31]) and the tension is resolved. The truth of Daniel's interpretation is acknowledged, and confirmed by events. The reference to Darius in 6:1 [5:31] looks more like part of the closure of chap. 5 (so EVV), denoting how power passes from the Chaldeans to a Median, than the introduction to chap. 6, which relates a specific incident in Darius's reign (against MT and medieval convention, which begin a new chapter after 5:30).

There are several instances of paronomasia. שרא and קטרין appear together in vv 6, 12, and 16, to denote the weakening of joints (Belshazzar's problem) and the solving of enigmas (Daniel's solution). Nebuchadnezzar was free to kill, elevate, and humble when he wished (קטל, רום, שפל, צבה, v 19); Belshazzar elevated himself as Nebuchadnezzar had done instead of humbling himself, and learns that God enthrones whom he wishes (vv 19–23) when he himself is killed (v 30) (Joubert notes the juxtaposition of קטל with תקל ["shekel/weigh," vv 25, 27]). These come to a climax with the actual omen and its interpretation, which utilize the different significance of מנא, תקל, and פרס as nouns and as verbs and add further additional plays on מנא (repeating the word in different senses) and פרסין (linked also to פרס, "Persia").

Differences between OG and MT are stranger in chap. 5 than in any other chapter (Ashley, 243): OG has a long introduction and a number of omissions, and interestingly the name Artaxerxes or Xerxes (mss vary) instead of Darius in 6:1 [5:31]. As with chap. 4, Grelot argues that OG was translated from a second-century Hebrew version of the Aramaic original (*Sem* 24 [1974] 45–66).

Setting

Of the kings in Daniel, Belshazzar might with most plausibility be viewed as a cipher for the sacrilegious Antiochus Epiphanes (see 1 Macc 1:20–64; also Heliodorus in 2 Macc 3); the careers of Antiochus III and his son (cf. 11:10–19, 21–45) correspond to those of Nebuchadnezzar and his son, and the pattern of father and son in chaps. 4–5 may lie behind that in chap. 11. Thus Davies regards chap. 5 as the youngest of the stories; yet Müller (*UF* 1 [1969] 86) sees chaps. 4 and 5 as the oldest stories in content. There is no specific indication that chaps. 4–5 were themselves written in the light of the experience of Antiochus. The parallels are general; sacrilege and idolatry were not a distinctively second-century phenomenon. For the latter, cf. 4QPrNab, while Antiochus only plunders the temple; he does not misuse vessels in a religious connection. The words for "gold chain" and "proclaim" (המונכא, כרז) appear in Greek (μανιάκης, κηρύσσω), but the former is of Persian origin and even the latter, if not a loan-word in Greek, is likely an early borrowing (Montgomery). Once again the dispersion and as likely the Persian as the Greek period is the story's natural historical setting. As with other chapters, scholars have argued that chap. 5 as we know it came into existence by a process of redaction during different periods, though opinions vary as to the nature of this process (contrast, e.g., Hall; Haag, *Erretung;* Schreiner, "'. . . wird der Gott des Himmels ein Reich errichten, das in Ewigkeit nicht untergeht' (Dan 2, 44): Gestalt und Botschaft apokalyptischens Redens von Gott—am Beispiel von Daniel 2," in *"Ich will euer Gott werden": Beispiele biblische Redens von Gott* (ed. H. Merklein and E. Zenger; SBS 100 (1981)] 132).

As for its literary setting, the story has a close relationship with chap. 4. Its picture of a sacrilegious king who finds no mercy compares and contrasts with the earlier picture of an overbearing king who did find mercy (Plöger). It also has points of contact with chaps. 1 and 2. Like chap. 2 as well as chap. 4, the narrative tells of a buoyant king disturbed by an omen; he summons his sages to interpret it (his promise of rewards parallels chap. 2), but they fail, and only then does Daniel appear on the scene. We have noted that the queen's role parallels Arioch's in chap. 2 and recalls 1:7, 17, 20; 2:48; and 4:5–6 [8–9]. The king's speech refers back to 1:3; 2:25; and 4:6; and thus, behind the queen's words, to 1:17, 20. Daniel's speech refers back to God's dealings with Nebuchadnezzar in chap. 4 (and behind that to 2:21, 37). The sacrilege with the vessels, to which Daniel refers, recalls 1:2. As in 4:28, 30 [31, 33], judgment is declared instantly and implemented instantly (5:5, 30). The announcement of the consequent change of king leads into chap. 6.

Comment

1–4 The last actual Chaldean king, Nabonidus, "entrusted the kingship" in 539 B.C. to his son Bēl-šar-uṣur during his ten-year absence from Babylon, returning as the threat from Cyrus grew. Belshazzar thus fulfilled the functions of kingship, though he was not called king nor did he play the king's part in the New Year Festival (see the "Nabonidus Lampoon," *ANET* 313; the Harran stelae, *ANET* 560–63; other material in Dougherty, *Nabonidus*). Probably this latter reflects more the religious conflict between the Marduk priesthood and Nabonidus's regime than Belshazzar's not technically being king (Lambert, "Nabonidus," 59–61). If Dan 5 relates to the occasion when control in Babylon passed from a Chaldean king to a Median (5:30–6:1 [5:30–31]), this occasion must be the fall of Babylon to the forces of Cyrus. We have various other accounts of this event.

(a) According to the Cyrus Cylinder, "without any battle [Marduk] enabled [Cyrus] to enter his city Babylon, sparing Babylon any calamity. He delivered into his hands Nabonidus, the king who did not worship him. . . . When I [Cyrus] entered Babylon as a friend, I set up the seat of government in the royal palace amidst jubilation and rejoicing. . . . My numerous troops walked around in Babylon in peace . . ." (see *ANET* 315–16; *DOTT* 92–95).

(b) According to the Babylonian Chronicle, in the last year of Nabonidus's reign the New Year Festival was properly observed and the gods of other cities were brought into Babylon. "In the month of Teshrit, while Cyrus was attacking the Babylonian army at Opis on the Tigris, the people of Babylonia revolted, but he [Nabonidus] slew some of the people. On the fourteenth day, Sippar was taken without a battle. Nabonidus fled. On the sixteenth day [12 October] Ugbaru, the governor of Gutium, and the troops of Cyrus entered Babylon without battle. Afterwards Nabonidus was arrested when he returned to Babylon." Religious ceremonies were not interrupted. "On the third of Marcheswan [29 October], Cyrus entered Babylon and they waved branches before him. Peace settled on the city and Cyrus proclaimed peace to Babylon. Gubaru, his governor, appointed local governors in Babylon. . . On the night of the eleventh of Marcheswan [6 November] Ugbaru died. On the . . .th the . . . of the king died. . . ." (See *ANET* 306; *DOTT* 81–83; Grayson, *Chronicles,* 7; according to one reading [cf. Driver], the king's son was killed.)

(c) According to Berossus, "when Nabonidus perceived [Cyrus] was coming to attack him, he met him with his forces, and, joining battle with him, was beaten, fled with a few of his troops, and was shut up within the city Borsippus. Thereupon Cyrus took Babylon, and gave order that the outer walls of the city should be demolished, because the city had proved very troublesome to him, and cost him a great deal of pains to take it." When he went to besiege Borsippus, Nabonidus surrendered, and was exiled to Carmania. (See Josephus, *C. Ap.* 1.151–53 [1.20].)

(d) According to Herodotus (1.190–91), Cyrus brought his siege of Babylon to a successful conclusion by temporarily diverting the course of the Euphrates (the city's western defense) during a nocturnal festival.

(e) Xenophon has a similar story; he adds that the Persians killed the Babylonian king, a riotous, indulgent, cruel, and godless young man. (See *Cyr.* 4–7 on the fall of Babylon.)

Of these sources, the Cyrus Cylinder and the Babylonian Chronicle are closest to the events, but they have their own slant (Cook [*Persian Empire,* 12] calls the former "a propaganda exercise"). We can accept their account of Babylon's falling to Persian troops without a battle in Nabonidus's absence, Cyrus himself entering the city some days later. Herodotus's account of the Persian forces gaining access to the city by temporarily diverting the Euphrates is entirely plausible (though see Cook, *Persian Empire,* 31). The picture of the city feasting when it was about to fall looks like a popular tale. In form and content, Dan 5 has more in common with the two Greek historians than with the Near Eastern sources, all being "traditional developments of the popular memory of the fall of Babylon" (Montgomery, 72).

It is possible that Belshazzar's feast took place after he had held out in a fortified place when the city had been taken, and that he was killed there as a result of a night assault (Driver, xxxi: but see Rowley, *JTS* 32 [1931] 26–

30). It is perhaps more likely that Belshazzar was commander of the Babylonian forces at Opis, and was not in Babylon when the city fell (Rowley, *Exp* ix, 2 [1924] 258–62). However that may be, in Dan 5 there is no suggestion that the empire is about to fall. There is no hint that Belshazzar is holding a bizarre final banquet, aware that the enemy is at the gates; indeed, the portent he receives and his reaction to it presuppose that, like Nebuchadnezzar in chap. 4, he has no present reason for anxiety, while the message conveyed by the portent has its force removed if we presuppose that "the writing was on the wall" already. There is no suggestion that Belshazzar was playing games in promoting Daniel to the position of Deputy. The chapter describes an unexpected coup, not a surprise attack or the climax of a siege (Keil); it portrays God's punishment of one man for his sin, rather than his judgment on an empire.

Although the king would normally dine privately, banquets were a regular enough occurrence (cf. Esth 1). Custom varied regarding whether women were invited (contrast Esth 1 with 1 Esd 1; see Montgomery); their presence here is perhaps part of the exoticness of the story. There is no indication that this was a religious festival (so Xenophon), though it may have been; if people had reason to be aware that the empire was about to fall, then the matter is omitted for dramatic reasons. Like the dedication festival in chap. 3, the banquet is simply the background to the story, and the occasion of the revelry and excess that lead to sacrilege and idolatry. The suggestion that it was a festival to celebrate Belshazzar's taking the throne on the defeat of Nabonidus by Cyrus (Shea, *AUSS* 20 [1982] 142) seems bizarre.

Belshazzar's actual father (v 2) was Nabonidus, who had come to the throne through a coup and did not belong to the royal line. There are two kinds of approach to the description of Belshazzar as Nebuchadnezzar's son. One is to look for some sense in which Belshazzar could appropriately be described as Nebuchadnezzar's son: as his successor, or as his descendant—supposing that Nabonidus had married into Nebuchadnezzar's line (NIVmg). There is, admittedly, no other evidence of this, which would be surprising, and such an indirect relationship perhaps hardly justifies the story's emphasis on the father-son relationship and on the obligations it placed on Belshazzar. The other approach is to recognize that Belshazzar was not Nebuchadnezzar's son, and to look for some other factor that could have led to his being described thus. If the story in chap. 4 really concerns Nabonidus, for instance, Belshazzar *is* his son. Alternatively, the motif may connect with the violent death of Nebuchadnezzar's actual son and successor Evil-merodach, with whom Belshazzar was identified by many commentators (e.g., Keil) before his identity and position became clear from cuneiform texts. Or Daniel may reflect the same understanding as Herodotus (1.188), who makes Nabonidus the son of Nebuchadnezzar (he actually calls both Labynetos) by Nitocris (cf. Megasthenes [Eusebius, *Praep.* 9.41.6]). The two chief points in neo-Babylonian history are the empire's rise under Nebuchadnezzar and its fall under Nabonidus/Belshazzar, so that "Nebuchadnezzar the father of Belshazzar" summarizes and reflects the general historical facts of the period (Prince, *Mene,* 11).

5–9 On the palace, see on 1:3–4; 4:26–27 [29–30]. It included a plastered throne room 52m by 17m (though one thousand guests there would find themselves crowded). Although we are only told of the king's reaction to the portent (v 6), this need not suggest that only he saw it. The story does imply that something actually happened, not that the king in his drunkenness placed a supranatural construction on something natural (Prince, *Mene,* 12; contrast Gibson, *ExpT* 23 [1911–12] 181; Baldwin). There is nothing humorous about the description of Belshazzar's reaction to the portent. It is a deadly serious comprehensive description of the physical manifestations of terror (Towner), the appropriate response to the prospect of divine judgment (Isa 21:3; 45:1 [both the fall of Babylon!]; Ezek 21:6–7; Nah 2:10; Ps 69:24 [23]). To wear purple and a gold chain, and to be given a position of authority close to that of the king himself (v 7), are typical expressions of honor from a king (Gen 41:42–43; Esth 8:15; 10:3; 1 Esd 3:6–7; 1 Macc 10:20; 14:43).

It is not specified what made the words unreadable as well as unintelligible (v 8). There is no suggestion that they were in code or written in an odd way (against *b. Sanhedrin* 22a). Perhaps they were difficult because of their use of ideograms or their peculiar cuneiform (the story might reflect the existence of OP cuneiform, used less than Akkadian or Aramaic but favored—and invented?—by Darius I: see Frye, *Heritage,* 74–75). Weights could be abbreviated, as in English, and perhaps the inscription consisted in a series of abbreviations that were not immediately recognizable as such (Alt, *VT* 4 [1954] 303–5). But most straightforwardly the story envisages them written as unpointed consonants: being able to read out unpointed text is partly dependent on actually understanding it, and Daniel later reads the words out one way and interprets them another.

10–16 "Queen" (מלכתא) suggests not a mere consort (see v 2) but a political figure, presumably the queen mother, often a significant political figure in an ancient court. In the OT, cf. 1 Kgs 15:13; 2 Kgs 11:1–3; 24:12; Jer 13:18; as "senior counsellor to king and people," she could "provide a stabilizing, moderating influence in the political system" and "could circumscribe royal power to some extent and could represent the interests of people or court before the king" (N.-E. A. Andreasen, "The Role of the Queen Mother in Israelite Society," *CBQ* 45 [1983] 191, 194; for Babylon, cf. Oppenheim, *Mesopotamia,* 104; for Persia, see Montgomery). The queen mother could take the initiative in coming into the king's presence, unlike his consort (Esth 4:11). The Queen's identity is uncertain. Nabonidus's mother, Adadguppi, apparently lived through Nebuchadnezzar's reign, and would thus have been in a position to address Belshazzar as the Queen does here, were it not for the fact that she died in 547 B.C. (see *ANET* 306, 560–62). Herodotus (1.185–88) talks at some length of the role in Babylon of Queen Nitocris, who he says was Nebuchadnezzar's wife. The difficulty with this statement is that Nitocris was actively anti-Median, whereas Nebuchadnezzar was pro-Median and had a Median wife (see 4:26–27 [29–30] *Comment*) (Rowley, *Exp* ix, 2 [1924] 193–95).

The skills attributed to Daniel (vv 11–12) relate directly to the interpretation of a portent (Ashley, 147–54). "Insight" (נהירו) suggests illumination from God, the source of light (2:22). "Ability" (שכלתנו) indicates that Daniel not only possesses intellect or talent; he knows how to use it, by God's gift (according to 1:17). "Wisdom" (חכמה) denotes in Daniel the supernatural intuition of an interpreter of dreams or omens, that wisdom which also belongs supremely to God (2:20) and which as his gift makes Daniel outstanding among sages (1:17; 2:21, 23). "Knowledge" (מנדע) likewise denotes the God-given supernatural knowledge of an interpreter (1:17; 2:21). The reference to "the spirit of holy deity"/"a remarkable spirit" (see on 4:5 [8]) underlines the implication that Daniel's extraordinary ability comes from God. The out-working of his gifts develops these points. Regarding "interpreting" (by magical means or by supernatural revelation) (פשר), see n. 2:4.c on the cognate noun. "Dreams" were the specific area of Daniel's expertise in chap. 4, to which chap. 5 refers back, while an enigmatic puzzle is the specific concern of chap. 5 itself (Plöger). "Puzzles" (אחידן) are, with dreams and visions, one of the somewhat opaque forms that supernatural revelation can take (cf. Num 12:6–8; Sir 39:1–4) (see Müller, *VT* 20 [1970] 465–89). The Hebrew equivalent also refers to "allegory" (Ezek 17:2) and other expressions of verbal play and expertise. "Enigmas" (קטרין, literally "knots") are involved and knotty mysteries, such as the writing on the wall, which require extraordinary insight to unravel. The question why Daniel has not been summoned before if he is so gifted has been explained historically (Daniel must now be eighty-five), psychologically (Belshazzar knows the kind of message he will get from him), and rhetorically (the successful interpreter appears after the others have failed).

17–24 Why does Daniel go through the motions of refusing rewards that he has accepted before (2:48) and will accept later (v 29)? Plöger suggests he is inviting Belshazzar to wait till he has heard the message before he decides whether he wants to reward the messenger, but the abruptness of Daniel's words (there is no salutation) suggests that they are more confrontational than this (cf. 2:27, and contrast 4:19, at equivalent points in earlier chapters). More likely he is sidestepping any pressure to modify the portent's message, pressure that derives from the assumption that financial considerations determine the content of a seer's message (see Num 22:18 and Num 22–24 generally; Amos 7:12; Mic 3:5, 11) (Lacocque). There is no danger of that once the hard message has been given (v 29) (though contrast 2 Kgs 5:16); and as refusal at this point indicates his independence, acceptance later will enable his eminence to be revealed (Anderson). There may also be the suggestion that Daniel hereby dissociates himself from sin of the corrupt regime he is sent to indict (cf. 1 Kgs 13:7–9).

Nebuchadnezzar's "spirit" (v 20) contrasts with Daniel's, as Nebuchadnezzar's wife describes it (v 12); see on 4:5 [8]. The "destiny" of a person (v 23) is the "way" (ארח), the course of life that someone follows, which is seen as plotted and controlled by God—without implying that it is predetermined in such a way as to make human decision-making illusory. (Cf. Job 8:13; Prov 3:6; 4:18; also דרך in, e.g., Job 22:28; 24:23; Ps 18:33 [32]; 37:5, 7, 23; 146:9; Prov 20:24; Isa 40:27; Jer 10:23.) The idea is prominent in wisdom writings; the idea of God's holding a person's breath (נשמה or רוח) also appears there (e.g., Job 12:10; 34:14–15; cf. Gen 2:7; Ps 104:29).

25–28 Each word in the inscription has several possible meanings (*DTT*); like a dream, the portent has a surface meaning and one or more allegorical meanings. On the surface, מנא, תקל, and פרס refer to three weights, a mina

(500 or 600g), a shekel (10g), and a half (so since Clermont-Ganneau, *JA* viii, 8 [1886] 36–67]. Elsewhere a "half" is a half-mina, though this seems to be determined by the context, and the context here suggests a half-shekel, פרס then being equivalent to Heb. בקע (Eissfeldt, *ZAW* 63 [1951] 111–12; *IBD* 1635). The inscription thus represents something like a merchant's shout ("Reckoned at a mina, a shekel, and [two] halves!"), or his documentary record of this evaluation (cf. J. P. Brown, "Proverb-Book, Gold-Economy, Alphabet," *JBL* 100 [1981] 187; Eissfeldt, *ZAW* 63 [1951] 109–111). Daniel has to explain what this puzzling phrase really refers to. The only point implicit in the statement is that the shekel suggests something very lightweight compared with whatever is symbolized by a mina. Whatever is symbolized by the half is even less significant than the former (if it is a half-shekel) or more so (if it is a half-mina).

It may be that allegorically the oracle originally referred to Babylonian kings: e.g., Nebuchadnezzar, Nabonidus, Belshazzar (Freedman); Nebuchadnezzar, Evil-Merodach, Belshazzar (Ginsberg); Nabonidus, Belshazzar, Darius and Cyrus (Hoffman); Nabonidus, Belshazzar, Median and Persian kings generally (Prince); Babylonian, Median, Persian kings (Haller). Further possibilities emerge if the first מנא is taken as part of the sequence, making a series of four: Neriglissar, Evil-Merodach, Labashi-Marduk, Nabonidus/Belshazzar (Kraeling); Babylonian, Median, Persian, and Greek kings generally (Lacocque) (see *Bibliography* for references). Whether or not the oracle started off as an allegory of this kind, what is explicit is that Daniel turns the merchant's record into a message about history by playing on each of the three words, utilizing the meaning of the verbal root that underlies each noun. This wordplay approach to interpretation was applied to Scripture in 1QpHab (L. H. Silberman, *RevQ* 3 [1961–62], esp. 333). Daniel uses it to make the statement refer to Belshazzar's being appointed, evaluated, and punished.

מנא is used in the everyday sense of "count," but can also suggest "to appoint" or "to destine" (cf. the god Destiny, מני: see Isa 65:11–12); for the idea of "numbering one's days" as applied to the individual, see Ps 90:12. Weighing (תקל) a person's moral value is an uncommon image (see Job 31:6; Ps 62:10 [9]); more often the OT speaks of measuring it (תכן; see BDB). "Half" (פרס) receives a double interpretation; the noun פרס[ין] suggests first the verb פרס "broken in half," then another noun פרס *Persia.* Median and Persian kings will receive the kingship in 6:1, 29 [5:31; 6:28]. Daniel need not mean that the empire will be divided between the two rather than that Belshazzar's dynasty will be broken and his authority will pass to others. The terms "Median" and "Persian" are often not distinguished (Cook, *Persian Empire,* 42–43).

5:29–30; 6:1 [5:29–31] Except for Xenophon's account of the Persians killing the unnamed Babylonian king (see on v 1), we have no independent record of Belshazzar's death, or of what happened to him when Babylon fell.

No Median Darius (*dārayavahuš,* a Persian name [*OP* 189]) is otherwise known. Critical scholarship has regarded him as an imaginary construct built up from various separate historical and scriptural elements. Cyrus's Persian empire did replace a Median empire, in areas north of Babylonia; Cyrus himself did not immediately assume the title "King of Babylon," but ruled through a vassal-king; Belshazzar's successor as lord of the Babylonian empire (i.e., Cyrus) *was* about sixty-two and may have been part-Median himself; Babylon *was* captured and ruled by a Darius who appointed satraps (6:2 [1] and who was related to Xerxes (9:1—but see *Comment*) (i.e., Darius Hystaspis, Cambyses's successor, Xerxes's father) (see Rowley). The prophets speak of a Median conquest of Babylon (Isa 13:17; 21:2; Jer 51:11, 28) and of a Darius as king when Jerusalem is being restored after the exile (Hag 1:1, 15; 2:10; Zech 1:1, 7; 7:1) (Sparks, *JTS* 47 [1946] 41–46). "Median" might be an archaizing description of the Achaemenids (see A. Caquot, "Les quatre bêtes et le 'Fils d'homme' (*Daniel* 7)," *Sem* 17 [1967] 45).

Those who are inclined to take Daniel as historical point out that known history once contained no reference to Belshazzar (Young). Darius might have been a throne-name for some ruler known to us by another name (cf. Frye, *Heritage,* 97 on the name Darius). Among the identifications proposed for this ruler are Cyrus the Persian himself (Wiseman); Cyrus's son Cambyses, who at some time was titular King of Babylon (Boutflower); the last Median king Astyages (Alfrink); his son Cyaxares II, referred to only by Xenophon (*Cyr.* 1–8) (Keil); Cyrus's general Gobryas (Gubaru/Ugbaru, OP Gaubaruwa) who captured Babylon for the Persians, ruled there on Cyrus's behalf for a period, and as governor of Gutium could be thought of as a Mede (Koch; Shea); and—on the hypothesis that this Gobryas/Ugbaru died very soon after the fall of Babylon (so one understanding of the Babylonian Chronicle)—Cyrus's governor in Babylon, another Gubaru (Whitcomb) (see *Bibliography* for references).

The significance of Darius the Mede for Daniel is first that he represents the beginning of the fulfillment of Belshazzar's portent regarding the destiny of Belshazzar's empire (5:28; 6:29 [28] will bring a second stage). In the perspective of the stories as a whole, he is the third of the four rulers of Babylon envisaged by Nebuchadnezzar's dream (see on chap. 2). Read in the light of subsequent visions, he will become the embodiment of the second of Daniel's four empires (Koch, "Dareios").

The precision of "sixty-two" makes it unlikely that Daniel is merely indicating that Darius was rather old and therefore reigned only a short time. Sixty-two years takes us back to the beginning of the exile, so the reference might suggest that the seeds of the downfall of Nebuchadnezzar's dynasty were sown even then (Ashley, cf. Ps-Saadia, Rashi). More likely sixty-two derives from the omen. If the mina in the latter is the 600g mina comprising 60 shekels (not the more usual Palestinian 500g mina comprising 50 shekels), then a mina, a shekel and (two) halves (of a shekel) come to 62 shekels (Lister, Galling [see *Bibliography*]). The years attributed to Darius "sum up" another aspect of the omen's meaning: he is the actual person who brings its fulfillment upon Belshazzar.

Explanation

1–4 Belshazzar's story begins like Nebuchadnezzar's, with a flourishing monarchy in royal majesty. But Nebuchadnezzar's success had an ambiguity about it: the description of things going so well—God being unmentioned—

already hinted that catastrophe might be imminent. There is a similar ambiguity about the story of Belshazzar's state banquet. A banquet is a sign of honor appropriate to a king (1 Kgs 3:15), but the temperate streak in Jewish thinking is reserved about such occasions. They can bode ill. Things tend to go wrong at royal banquets (Gen 40:20–22; Esth 1; Mark 6:21–28). A further contrast with the previous chapter likewise bodes ill. The story of Nebuchadnezzar's humiliation was prefaced by a testimony that revealed that all turned out well in the end. Belshazzar's story has no such preface. It begins with a scene that can be read as one of ostentation, decadence, carousing, coarseness, wantonness, and self-indulgence, a scene that might have been designed to illustrate the wisdom literature's warnings about power, sex, and drink (e.g., Prov 23:29–35 [Wallace]).

From self-indulgence issued sacrilege and blasphemy; what was wrong with the banquet was not the thing itself but where it led. It is in Belshazzar's attitude to God and to his position before God that Daniel in due course explicitly locates Belshazzar's sin (vv 22–23). We are not told why Belshazzar sent for these particular vessels. Perhaps they are assumed to be the most valuable he possessed; theologically, the OT would reckon they certainly were. To a pagan, drinking the customary libations with the vessels might mitigate the suggestion of sacrilege involved in utilizing temple vessels at a palace banquet. Like saying grace, it set the celebration in the context of faith; it signified that people knew they were having their celebration before God. But the fact that these vessels sacred to one who hates idolatry are used for libations to idols actually compounds the offense. The exile might be thought to have established the power of Babylon's gods over the God of Israel; therefore the exile produces all the stronger affirmations of God's sole authority and power and of the powerlessness of idols (Isa 40–41; 44). To offer libations to them is to slight the deity of God. The story is one of the many that indicate that the Bible comes from a multi-faith context; Daniel's approach to multi-faith questions is one of the ones that reflection on these questions has to take into account (though not the only one).

Belshazzar's "father" had captured the vessels and had learned to honor the God to whom they belonged, as has just been pointed out (4:34 [37]); Belshazzar remembers the one fact, but not the other. Belshazzar's actual father, Nabonidus, had likewise learned to repent of his attachment to gods of gold, silver, brass, iron, wood, and stone (4QPrNab). The presence of the temple vessels in Babylon is a reminder of something significant that had happened in recent political history, but asserting the authority of Babylon and its gods over the exiles and their God succeeds in provoking the exiles' God to send Belshazzar a portent that only an exile can interpret for him. It will prove that the God who is treated as powerless has power, and it will expose the gods who are manifestly powerless for what they are (cf. Ps 115:1–8 and, in the context of Babylonian exile, Isa 40:12–31; 41:1–7; 44:6–20). It was a mad gesture, and the story perhaps hints that it would only have taken place under the influence of alcohol (v 2).

5–9 To the reader, it is clear enough that there must be some divine response to the enormity that has been described. It comes instantly, like the judgment on Nebuchadnezzar (4:28 [31]), and that on Herod in Acts

12:23, to make clear that this *is* its significance. Jephet saw Belshazzar as deliberately disdaining the God of Israel, whose prophecy that Babylonian rule would end after seventy years had not come true. Whether or not he recognizes it, Belshazzar and in him the whole Babylonian empire has issued a challenge that God must accept. There thus follows an item that did not appear on the program for the evening, yet one that had been wished into being by Belshazzar's act itself; his worship of lifeless gods provokes a hidden theophany in the form of a living hand, that hand which wrote at Sinai (Exod 31:18) but which now inscribes a more sinister message (Lüthi, Lacocque). Although it seems to be assumed that everyone could *see* the inscription, its message will concern Belshazzar himself more than the people he represents, and it may be that the hand, which appeared for the sake of one man, was visible to him alone. Initially it is he who is devastated by a portent that replaces the sense of confidence and security by shaking and terror. Its content is not yet stated, but its implications are clear.

As in chap. 2, the king now gives a double task to his multiform sages. They must declare what the portent actually said, then declare what it meant or referred to—and, no doubt, what measure could be taken to evade its fulfillment. Whoever can do this will receive a share in the king's royal prestige and power in Babylon. Of course none can—not "of course" for Belshazzar, but "of course" for the hearer, who is familiar with this feature of previous chapters. Motifs in the stories recur to drive key points home more forcefully (Anderson): alien wisdom really is helpless when God intervenes to speak and act. The king's alarm is deepened and extends to the nobles at his banquet.

10–12 It is from within his own court that a witness to the God of the exiles comes to Belshazzar. This motif, too, is paralleled in chaps. 1 and 2: the power of God at work among the exiles is clear enough for the king's aides and family to see it, even if the king himself cannot. The queen's description of Daniel is yet more laudatory than those in previous chapters. The extraordinary insight required to interpret dreams and portents comes through being subject to supernatural influence, and Daniel has proved himself someone to whose mind God has access. The Bible sometimes envisages the spirit of God working through the human spirit by means of the ordinary analytic functioning of the human mind, but more characteristically associates the spirit of God with the receiving of extraordinary insights that one might associate more with intuition, creative imagination, or second sight. It assumes that such inspiration is not an everyday event, but does occur periodically, then being testimony to the very activity of God through a particular person. It is capable of being described both theologically and anthropologically, as divine inspiration or as intuitive imagination, as a matter of the spirit of God being present (v 11) or as a matter of having a remarkable spirit (v 12).

13–16 Belshazzar's words to Daniel refer back beyond Nebuchadnezzar's recognition of him to Nebuchadnezzar's having brought him from Judah in the first place. The mighty Babylonian kings acknowledge a Judean exile as the one in whom the supreme God is active and in whom supreme wisdom is found.

17–24 Daniel responds to the king like a prophet, not a mere sage, with the same tone he had used to Nebuchadnezzar in chap. 4. Financial dependence on the listeners threatens constraints upon a speaker; Daniel refuses to allow any prospect of rewards to influence the nature of his message. He is characteristically confident that he can read and interpret the inscription, and direct in his confronting of the king, like Nathan before David, or Jonah at Nineveh. As in these cases, it is through a prophetic figure that God exercises his kingship, manifesting before the human king that actually God is king. As in those cases, the prophet issues no demand for repentance and offers no prospect of averting the disaster. David and the people of Nineveh did repent, and found mitigation or cancellation of the threatened punishment, and one may presume that this path is open to Belshazzar. It will not be taken, and Daniel's words already hint at this, as does the absence of the invitation to repentance that Daniel had extended to Nebuchadnezzar (4:24 [27]). Belshazzar has shown that he was unwilling to learn from his father's experience. He is unlikely, therefore, to respond to the preaching of his father's counselor (cf. the argument of Heb 6:4–8).

Daniel begins by recalling the powerful position occupied by Nebuchadnezzar, though he does this in such a way as to underline the ambiguity of that position. Nebuchadnezzar possessed royal authority and glorious splendor: the terms correspond particularly closely to the description of God himself in 1 Chr 29:11; cf. Dan 4:33 [36]; 2:37 *Explanation.* Within his realm he had a power of life and death, of ennoblement and disgrace, which is also quasi-divine (cf. Deut 32:39; 1 Sam 2:6–7; Ps 75:8 [7]; also Dan 2:21; 4:14 [17]). In reminding Belshazzar of Nebuchadnezzar's experience, however, Daniel begins by drawing attention to the derivative nature of Nebuchadnezzar's authority. The chapter had begun from what Nebuchadnezzar took (v 2); no doubt that would be how Belshazzar had spoken. Daniel invites him to think in terms of what Nebuchadnezzar was given, by one whose own royal authority and glorious splendor are *a fortiori* greater. All human authority and power is an echo and a servant of that divine authority and power from which it derives and on which it depends (Lacocque). Further, to attribute to Nebuchadnezzar a quasi-divine power over the people within his realm is to draw attention to the temptation with which people in power live. There is a link and a contrast between Nebuchadnezzar's great power and his great fall. It was his area of strength that became his area of vulnerability; his power became his weakness. His power then had to become actual weakness before it could be restored.

"You knew, you ignored, you exalted yourself, you desecrated, you committed idolatry, you disregarded." Daniel emphasizes Belshazzar's responsibility for his attitudes and actions; he is the subject of a series of strong verbs in vv 22–23. Belshazzar's willful blindness makes him brazenly proud, just like his father (the same words are used), in the very presence of the one who is actually Lord of heaven—the phrase comes only here; both elements in it suggest the almightiness of the one Belshazzar disdains. It makes him sacrilegiously contemptuous of the sacred possessions of this God, who entrusted them to his father; the vessels that should have reminded him of God who *gave* them into Nebuchadnezzar's power (1:2) become means of his self-indulgence. It makes him grotesquely idolatrous in worshiping senseless objects and ignoring the God who has actual power over his personal destiny; he fails to take God himself seriously, like his father—but with less excuse, because his father's story has made clear to him that God has this power. Historically, Belshazzar perhaps fell because he could not handle a political crisis; but more profoundly, as Daniel sees it, he fell because of his irresponsibility before God (Joubert).

25–28 Daniel recognizes that on the surface the inscription records the assessment of something in terms of monetary weights: "counted at a mina, a shekel, and halves." The three nouns also reflect three verbal roots (as, in English, "pound" and "halve" can be verbs as well as nouns). Under the surface of the inscription Daniel sees in these verbs a message for Belshazzar. They hint at three moments in God's dealings with him as king, the past moment when he appointed him, the present moment when he is evaluating his performance, and the coming moment when he breaks off his dynasty because of its failure. All three are past from the perspective of the prophecy; like many OT prophecies, it speaks of coming events as already actual, on the basis of God's decision that they should take place. Belshazzar's sin has exceeded Nebuchadnezzar's, and so will his fall, not merely to banishment in humiliation, but to death and the end of his dynasty, without finding repentance (Joubert).

At first sight, to say that Belshazzar's days were numbered from the beginning of his reign suggests that the nature of his reign and the coming of judgment upon it were irreversibly predestined. If Daniel says that Belshazzar's reign has been evaluated and found deficient, however, he implies that Belshazzar has not been an automaton; he is responsible for the way he has exercised his sovereign authority. Perhaps Daniel indicates that the "counting out" of Belshazzar's reign had a provisional nature, establishing how long he *could* reign; in the event, his reign is to end earlier than it should. Or perhaps Daniel presupposes the alternative perspective that God's being able to foresee the nature of Belshazzar's reign also enables him to predetermine its length, without implying that Belshazzar's responsibility is reduced or his judgment imposed independently of his character and actions. "All is foreseen, but freedom of choice is given" (*m. ʾAbot* 3:16; cf. Russell, *Apocalyptic,* 232). God's sovereignty and human responsibility are both factors in history. Both are real.

God's judgment also at first sight involves his acting in sovereign independence of ordinary processes of cause and effect rather than through them. A historical study of the course of events, however, would likely be able to describe them in terms of ordinary processes of cause and effect; God's purpose needs to be seen at work behind the ordinary process of cause and effect that the historian seeks to trace (the emphasis of K. Koch, "Gibt es ein Vergeltungsdogma im Alten Testament?" *ZTK* 52 [1955] 1–42 = *Um das Prinzip der Vergeltung in Religion und Recht des Alten Testaments* [ed. K. Koch; Darmstadt: Wissenschaftliche, 1972] 130–80 = "Is There a Doctrine of Retribution in the Old Testament?" [tr. T. H. Trapp], *Theodicy in the Old Testament* [ed. J. L. Crenshaw; IRT 4 (1983)] 57–87).

Another insight on history that Belshazzar's story suggests is that revolutionary violence is an important factor through which God works in history, but what it brings in is not the final rule of God but the rule of Darius the Mede to replace that of Belshazzar the Chaldean (Collins, FOTL 70). The story recognizes that the fall of Belshazzar is a major historical turning-point, which it sees as coming about because the Chaldeans failed to recognize the God of the Judean exiles, whose agents they had unwittingly been. The worldly empire has had its opportunity, and missed it. But elsewhere in the OT, the fall of Babylon is not merely the end of an era, but one realization of the Day of Yahweh. Daniel is interested in that Day, though he does not use this term, but he does not see the fall of Babylon in this light; it is just the moment when power passes from one dynasty to another. The story warns against overestimating the significance of history and politics. Yet it also indicates that when God casts off one ruler for his arrogance, he does not thereby dissociate himself from all world events and exercise of power (Atzerodt, *CW* 10 [1934] 246).

5:29–6:1 [5:29–31] If chap. 5 were centrally concerned with the story of Belshazzar's personal relationship with God, as the modern reader may be inclined to assume, Belshazzar's response to Daniel's words would appear bizarre. It might seem to suggest that Belshazzar refuses to accept an implicit invitation to repentance, or perhaps on the contrary accepts God's judgment upon him and therefore accepts the death coming to him (Lacocque). But the story offers no negative comment on Belshazzar's response. It omits reference to his inner relationship with God (contrast Josephus, *Ant.* 10.10.4 [10.204]) because its concerns focus on the public vindication of Daniel and of his God. Belshazzar's response parallels that of Nebuchadnezzar in 2:46–48, where similar considerations obtain. Belshazzar explicitly acknowledges Daniel and not his God; but the story itself comes to a climax with the fulfillment of prophecy, not with the exaltation of Daniel.

Belshazzar's story does show that in the case of every person there is a sense in which "the limitation of human life" by birth and death is "a trace of the divine world-governance" (Barth, *Dogmatik* iii, 3:267 [ET 235]). In the case of a Belshazzar, the fulfillment of Daniel's prophecy comes with that common Near Eastern phenomenon, a coup d'état involving the assassination of the one who has ruled until this moment—the process whereby Belshazzar's actual father, Nabonidus, came to power. The historical and human factors that brought this revolution, and the means by which it was effected, are again ignored. Belshazzar *was killed,* by whom we are not told (in effect by God?). Only the sovereign purpose of God in the event is of interest. When people act with violence, the story encourages us to believe that God can effect his purpose through them, and that we can trust him to fulfill his just purpose in events one way or another. Worldly empires are demonstrated to be subject to the God of the Judean exiles. The impression encouraged by Belshazzar at the beginning of the story, that Nebuchadnezzar was lord of history and the God of Jerusalem was powerless, is controverted by the way the story ends. He brings calamity to the conquerors he once used (cf. Isa 10; Jer 25) (Barr). Worldly power is real, but it is subservient to the will of God (Joubert).

As the portent came while Belshazzar was yet committing his act of idolatry, the end comes that very night, to make explicit the sovereign power of Daniel's

God and the authority of his sage. "In a single night the brilliant revel is changed, first into terror and bewilderment, and then into disaster and death" (Driver); compare the warnings of Amos 6; Matt 24:38–39 (Rupert). The moment when God says "You fool" (Luke 12:20) is one all have to fear, but a moment leaders especially have to fear. They may seem the embodiment of order, destiny, power, and divinity. Yet death comes to them, too, an incontrovertible proof of their pretension to power and significance (see Aukerman's comments on the implications of J. F. Kennedy's death, *Valley,* 119; and Gammie's on the Shah's fabulous banquet at Persepolis in 1971 that opened a decade in which the Shah lost first his empire and then his life).

Both chap. 4 and chap. 5 tell of a portent and a personal calamity, but one is a story with a happy ending, the other ends unhappily. One is comedy, the other tragedy. One reveals the divine mercy, the other the divine judgment. Even in the heathen world can be perceived God's election of some to a positive place in his purpose, of others to a negative one (Rom 9:13–14). In everyday events and in political affairs some find life, others find death. Human responsibility is real, and every experience tests by eliciting a response that either draws people toward God and his blessing, or draws in the opposite direction. Behind the whole is the purpose of God, whose wisdom and sovereign acts are deep and mysterious (Rom 9:33), but ultimately trustworthy (Wallace). Ps 2 talks about God laughing when nations and governments assert themselves against him and his purpose. He knows they always end up falling into the pit they dug. Hearing God's laughter is important for the Belshazzars of the world; it is a way God may get through to them (see Aukerman, *Valley,* 102–8). It is important for their subjects, who can afford to sit lighter to them than they sometimes realize, and may be able to stand up to them better when they do realize it.

God Vindicates His Power When Daniel Chooses the Lion Pit rather than Apostasy (6:2–29 [1–28])

Bibliography

Bentzen, A. "Daniel 6." In *Festschrift Alfred Bertholet*, ed. W. Baumgartner et al. Tübingen: Mohr, 1950. 58–64. **Boutflower, C.** "The Historical Value of Daniel v and vi." *JTS* 17 (1915–16) 43–60. **Cassin, E.** "Daniel dans la 'fosse' aux lions." *RHR* 139 (1951) 129–61. **Derrett, J. D. M.** "Daniel and Salvation-History." *Downside Review* 100 (1982) 62–67. = Derrett, *Studies in the New Testament*. Leiden: Brill, 1986. 4:132–38. **Levinger, J.** "דניאל בגוב האריות." *BetM* 22,3 [70] (1977) 329–33, 394–95. **Mayer, R.** "Iranischer Beitrag zu Problemen des Daniel- und Esther-Buches." In *Lex tua veritas,* FS H. Junker, ed. H. Gross and F. Mussner. Trier: Paulinus, 1961. 127–35. **Montgomery, J. A.** "The 'Two Youths' in the LXX to Dan. 6." *JAOS* 41 (1921) 316–17. **Paul, S.** "Dan 6, 8." *Bib* 65 (1984) 106–10. **Schmidt, N.** "Daniel and Androcles." *JAOS* 46 (1926) 1–7. **Shea, W. H.** "A Further Note on Daniel 6." *AUSS* 21 (1983) 169–71. **Whitcomb, J. H.** *Darius the Mede.* Grand Rapids: Eerdmans, 1959. **Wilson, R. D.** "Darius the Mede." *PTR* 20 (1922) 177–211.

Translation

2 *Darius decided to put satraps over his realm, 120 to be spread through the*
whole realm, 3 *and to put above them three heads,*[a] *Daniel being one of them, to*
whom these satraps would be accountable, so that the king would not be troubled.[b]
4 *This man Daniel distinguished himself above the other heads and satraps because*
of his remarkable spirit, and the king was minded[a] *to put him over the whole*
realm. 5 [a]*The heads and satraps looked for grounds for indicting Daniel in connection*
with the affairs of the realm, but they could not find grounds for indictment for
corruption, because he was trustworthy. So no negligence or corruption was found
in him. 6 *These men said, "We shall not find any grounds for indicting this Daniel*
unless we find[a] *them against him in connection with the law*[b] *of his God."* 7 *These*
heads and satraps mustered[a] *to see the king, and said to him, "Long live King*
Darius! 8 *All the heads of the realm, the governors, the satraps, the advisers, and*
the commissioners, are of the opinion that the king[a] *should issue a statute and*
enforce an injunction that for thirty days anyone who petitions any god or man
except you, your majesty, will be thrown into a lion pit. 9 *Now, your majesty, issue*
this injunction and sign[a] *the written regulation, so that as a law of the Medes*
and Persians, which shall not pass away, it can in no way[b] *be changed."*
10 *Accordingly, King Darius signed the written injunction.*

11 *But Daniel, when he learned that the document had been signed, went home,*
where he had a room on the top of the house with windows facing toward Jerusalem.
Three times a day he would kneel[a] *in prayer and thanksgiving before his God*
because[b] *he had been doing so previously.* 12 *These men mustered and found Daniel*
in petitionary prayer before his God. 13 *They approached the king and spoke before*
him [a]*about the royal injunction:*[a] *"Did you not sign an injunction that for thirty*
days anyone who petitioned any god or man except you, your majesty, would be

thrown into a lion pit?" The king replied, "Yes, that decision stands absolute as a
law of the Medes and Persians, which shall not pass away." [14] *They declared before*
the king, "Daniel, one of the Judean exiles, has not taken any notice of you or of
the injunction you signed, your majesty. Three times a day he makes his petition."
[15] *When the king heard of this, he was very displeased.*[a] *He applied his mind to*
delivering Daniel, and worked on rescuing him until sundown.[b] [16] *These men mus-*
tered to see the king and said to the king, "Your majesty must recognize that it is
a law of the Medes and Persians that any statutory injunction which the king
issues cannot be changed."

[17] *The king gave orders to fetch Daniel and throw him into the lion pit.*[a] *The*
king declared to Daniel, "Your God, whom you honor so consistently, he must[b]
deliver you." [18] *A rock was brought and put over the mouth of the pit, and the*
king sealed it with his signet and with those[a] *of his nobles, so that what was intended*[b]
for Daniel might not be changed. [19] *The king went off to his palace and spent the*
night without food;[a] *nothing*[b] *was brought into his presence. But sleep eluded*
him. [20] [a]*When morning came*[a] *the king got up*[b] [a]*at sunrise*[a] *and went back agitatedly*[c]
to the lion pit. [21] *On approaching the pit he called to Daniel in an anguished*
voice. The king spoke out to Daniel, "Daniel, servant of the living God, could
your God, whom you honor so consistently, deliver you from the lions?" [22] *Daniel*
spoke to[a] *the king, "Long live the king!* [23] *My God sent his aide and shut the*
lions' mouths, and they have not injured me, because [a]*I was found innocent*[a]
before him—as also before you, your majesty, I have done nothing injurious." [24] *The*
king was very glad and ordered Daniel to be lifted out of the pit. So Daniel was
lifted out of the pit, and no injury was found on him, because he had trusted[a] *in*
his God. [25] *The king gave orders to fetch*[a] *those men who had attacked Daniel*
and throw them into the lion pit, they, their children, and their wives. They had
not reached the floor of the pit when[b] *the lions were on top of them and had* [c]*torn*
their bodies to pieces.[c]

[26] [a]*King Darius wrote: "to the people of all races, nations, and languages who*
live in all the world.[b] *Peace and prosperity be yours!* [27] *I am giving notice that in*
all the[a] *realm over which I am king, people are to tremble with fear before the*
God of Daniel.

He is the living God;
he endures through the ages.
His realm will suffer no injury;
his rule will persist to the end.
[28] *He delivers and rescues;*
he performs signs and wonders
in heaven and on earth.
He delivered Daniel from the power of the lions."

[29] *So this Daniel flourished during the reign of Darius and*[a] *during the reign of*
Cyrus the Persian.

Notes

3.a. סרכין (OP); apparently not a technical term.

3.b. EVV generally refer נזק to a financial, military, or political burden, but Akk. *nazāqu* suggests "troubled/worried" (*CAD;* H. L. Ginsberg, "Lexicographical Notes," *HW* 81); cf. Th ἐνοχλῆται; JPS. So also Ezra 4:13, 15, 22; Esth 7:4.

4.a. עשית is pass (cf. Ehrlich "was inclined").

5.a. It is not clear how the cls in v 5 fit together; EVV vary. Th lacks the last sentence.

6.a. Pf vb in an exceptive clause (cf. GKC 163c).

6.b. דת comes to be used to signify "religion," viewed as the keeping of a God-given rule of life (*DTT;* cf. NEB, GNB). But the parallelism with the law of the state (vv 9, 13, 16) suggests this is not the meaning here. R. Rendtorff ("Esra und das 'Gesetz,'" *ZAW* 96 [1984] 166–69] questions whether דת is ever a synonym of תורה.

7.a. רגש (cf. vv 12, 16) has troubled translators since the ancient versions (cf. BHS). Montgomery notes that it occurs in parallelism with סוד "counsel/council" in Ps 55:15 [14]; 64:3 [2] (also with הגה "growl/murmur" in Ps 2:1), and tr "acted in harmony." But סוד also appears alongside המה "growl/bustle" in Ps 83:3–4 [2–3] (cf. המה in 46:4, 7; סוד in Jer 6:11; 15:17); cf. BDB "came thronging" for רגש. The objection that thronging is inappropriate to court etiquette (vv 7 and 16) and to catching a man unawares (v 12) misses the point that Daniel's accusers do act in a peremptory way (vv 8, ?13, 16; also v 7, cf. v 16, where they speak *to* the king, not *before* him as court etiquette generally requires), and that Daniel's commitment to his faith was open enough not to require espionage. The vb suggests a group acting by agreement but with the bustle that a crowd inevitably makes. Or might it be that a different meaning is required in v 12 from vv 7 and 16? The author of Daniel likes homonyms/paronomasia.

8.a. Taking מלכא as the subj of the vb, with MT accents; Th, however, links it with the preceding noun, "about the issuing of a royal statute," or —if the passage suggests a peremptory attitude on the part of the group (cf. n. 7.a)—about issuing a royal statute.

9.a. Or perhaps תרשם denotes "put your seal to."

9.b. לא rather than אין with the inf is emphatic (*TTH* 202).

11.a. הוא probably needs repointing הֲוָא (NAB, BL 81q); BHS (with some mss הֲוָה).

11.b. EVV "as" (cf. BL 109n); but BA nowhere else uses כל קבל די in the weakened sense (cf. Bevan).

13.a-a. Cf. JPS; not "about the injunction: 'Your majesty . . .'" (EVV), which would require emph אסרא, not the abs constr אסר (Hartman). G, Syr take מלכא as vocative, but they omit על אסר (cf. BHS, JB). This may be a gl, and omitting it reduces the jerkiness of v 13a, though one need not do so merely to make the conspirators' speech begin in a less peremptory way (cf. n. 7.a).

15.a. BA/BH באש more naturally means "displeased" (cf. also BH רעע, e.g., Jonah 4:1 [BDB]) than "distressed" (EVV, cf. 1QapGen 21.7).

15.b. "High noon" is etymologically possible and would make good sense, leaving time for the events in vv 16–19 to take place in the afternoon (Mayer, "Iranischer Beitrag," 128–29); but מעלי שמשא regularly means "sunset" (*DTT*).

17.a. See BL 106e.

17.b. Hartman, noting, however, that ישיזבנך must be parsed as impf, not juss (RSV), otherwise the נ would be elided: *GBA* 108, 175. NEB takes the vb as future, but this ill fits Darius's agitation in vv 15, 19–21, and some modal sense (could/might?) is appropriate—cf. 3:15.

18.a. עֲזָקַת; but many mss, Th point as s עִזְקַת (cf. JB).

18.b. צבו seems to keep its original meaning "purpose" (cf. BDB).

19.a. Not "fasting" in a religious sense, for which the word is צום not טות.

19.b. דחון (Eastern Q דהון) is a puzzle. Ps-Saadia understands it to mean "girls," perhaps relating it to לחנה (cf. 5:2) (Marti emends it to לחנן). This meaning has been supported by connecting the word with the root דחה "push (down)" which in Arabic eventually produces a noun meaning "woman" (hence NEB?). Ha הנעל suggests a personal obj (Plöger). But this tertiary sense of דחה in Arabic is not otherwise known in Aram. or Heb. (Bevan). Ibn Ezra takes it in another sense derived from דחה, "music" (cf. RV), but this is also forced (Driver), though it is said that at night 300 concubines were available to watch over the king with music and song by lamplight (see Cook, *Persian Empire,* 136): either of these meanings fits that picture. Related words denote revelry, feasting, and feast-tables (*DTT*). Th, Syr understand it to mean food; the cl thus expands on "spent the night without food." The Elamite root *dahyu* might suggest "servant" (cf. I. Gershevitch, *SCO* 2:180); OP *dahyav* "land" could suggest "countrymen" or "vassals" (cf. Mayer, "Iranischer Beitrag," 129–30).

20.a-a. Perhaps one of these expressions is a gl, though the second, בנגהא, is slightly more specific than the first, בשפרפרא.

20.b. יקום is impf, perhaps as following באדין (cf. BH usage after אז) (Montgomery); but the perf is used elsewhere, and more likely the impf is used to throw emphasis on the main vb אזל (BL 78q).

20.c. Not merely "in haste" (RSV): see n. 2:25.a.

22.a. Not "with," as if suggesting a conversation; the word for "with" is used for speaking "to" in Syriac (Bevan).

23.a-a. Lit., "innocence was found for me": זכו comes to mean "deserve" and thus "blessing/ success" (*DTT*, cf. NEBmg).

24.a. הימן: practically "had stood firm in his confidence" (cf. H. Wildberger, "Glauben," *HW* 372–86, repr. in Wildberger, *Jahwe und seine Volk* [TBü 66 (1979)]; *TWAT* אמן).

25.a. See BL 106e.

25.b. עד די: see BL 79i.

25.c-c. Hartman's tr of כל גרמיהון הדקו "smashed all their bones." Cf. the use of both גרם and עצם in BH (see BDB). But NEB "crunched them up, bones and all" highlights the piquant spirit of this story.

26.a. It is not quite clear where to locate the beginning of Darius's words here. Bentzen treats the whole as part of Darius's letter, except for the editorial באדין . . . כתב ([then] . . . wrote); the phraseology of v 26a is identical with that of the opening of the letter in 3:31 [4:1].

26.b. Wilson (*PTR* 20 [1922] 190) and Whitcomb (*Darius*, 38–39) tr ארעא "land" and refer it to Babylonia, over which a ruler of Babylon under Cyrus could be reckoned to rule (see *Comment*); cf. 3:31 [4:1].

27.a. בכל; JB "in every," but it is perhaps less likely that Darius is represented as drawing attention to the various parts of his empire.

29.a. NIVmg "that is" takes the ו as explicative. For other examples, see 1:3; 4:10 [13]; 7:1; 8:10, 24; 11:38 (and notes) (see S. Erlandsson, "Några exempel på waw explicativum," *SEA* 41–42 [1976–77] 69–76; D. W. Baker, "Further Examples of the *waw explicativum*," *VT* 30 [1970] 129–36). See *Comment*.

Form / Structure / Setting

Form

See chaps. 1 and 3 *Form*. Like Dan 3, chap. 6 is a tale of court conflict and intrigue; more specifically, the story of the fall and rehabilitation of a minister of state, a common folkloric plot (A. H. Krappe, "Is the Story of Aḥikar the Wise of Indian Origin?" *AJSL* 61 [1941] 280–84; Barton, "Aḥiḳar"; Collins, *Vision*, 49–54). A certain man has achieved prominence in the imperial administration and favor with the king. The other ministers of state plot to engineer his downfall by getting the king to issue a statute which he will not obey, but which carries a capital sentence. They watch for his disobedience, report it to the king, and insist that the death penalty be exacted. He survives, however, and his accusers and their families are killed instead. The motifs of the story are larger than life: the thronging plotters, the implausible statute, the inexorable law, the extraordinary escape, the monumental requital. But the tale reflects a desire to teach as well as a desire to entertain; it has a wisdom perspective (Joubert). Its characters, like ones in Esther and Ahiqar, "exemplify the traditional wisdom-triangle: the powerful, but witless dupe—the righteous wise—the conniving schemer" (S. Talmon, " 'Wisdom' in the Book of Esther," *VT* 13 [1963] 441; cf. Rosenthal, *ZAW* 15 [1895] 278–84; 17 [1897] 125–28). Jealous conspirators attack a man of uprightness and insight; they are clever enough to fool a stupid king but in the end pay the penalty for their own wicked folly, while the wise man triumphs (Prov 6:12–19; 14:30, 32, 35; 24:16; 29:12).

The hero is not only a man of wisdom and uprightness, but a man of a remarkable spirit (a God-given spirit: cf. 5:11–12), of faithfulness to God in life and in prayer, and of trust in God in danger. His persecutors see where his vulnerability lies: he believes in obeying God rather than human beings when these two obligations are made to conflict. For his insistence he will pay with his life. The court tale is thus also a confessor legend (though there is no confrontation between confessor and king or accusers). His fate is (literally) sealed; there is no escape. Even the king cannot rescue him. Yet the king is open to the possibility that God may do so; he spends the night anxiously wondering what Daniel's fate will be, and prepares us for Daniel's own testimony to God's miraculous and complete deliverance of him, which turns the legend into an aretalogy. The wonder of his deliverance is underlined by the contrasting fate of his persecutors. The king enjoins his whole empire to recognize Daniel's wonder-working God.

Darius's injunction takes the form of a royal encyclical, beginning precisely like that at 3:31–33 [4:1–3] (see chap. 4 *Form*); the content is also similar. Like that example, however, the form is tailored to the context, and is thus dovetailed into the narrative (see n. 6:26.a). The form and content soon become those of hymnic and confessional praise (6:27b–28a; 28b [26b–27a; 27b]), again a form here utilized in a literary context and designed to bring the narrative itself to a climax, so that the confession relates to what God has done to a third party, not to the speaker himself. Earlier in the chapter, Collins (FOTL) also finds the forms of petition, accusation, and petitionary prayer (vv 7–9, 13–14, 17 [6–8, 12–13, 16]).

The chapter may have midrashic aspects. As a wisdom tale, it illustrates aphorisms from Proverbs (see above). As a story about descent into a pit and about being threatened by lions, it illustrates experiences described in these symbolic terms in Ps 22:14, 22 [13, 21]; 57:5–7 [4–6]; 91:10–13 (cf. later 1QH 5.1–19). Other OT passages about lions (e.g., Ezek 19) seem less relevant. Bentzen (*Festschrift Bertholet,* 58–64) suggests a link between Dan 6 and mythical accounts of a hero/god's descent to and escape from Sheol, but more likely this link is via the reuse of this motif in the Psalms. The same applies to Gunkel's seeing a folk-tale motif in the lions' refusal to eat Daniel (Gunkel, *Märchen,* 33 [ET 53]).

Like chap. 3, the story combines factual allusions and traditional motifs. Its historical background corresponds to aspects of the circumstances of the Babylonian period (lions kept in captivity, Jewish faith under pressure) and the Greek period (divinization of the Ptolemaic and Seleucid kings, cf. Jdt 3:8), but it predominantly suggests the Persian period (the bureaucratic organization of the empire to avoid loss to the king [cf. Ezra 4:13–14], satrapies, the possibility of Jews' being in responsible positions in the empire [cf. Nehemiah], the strict law of the Persians; the Babylonian name Belteshazzar is no longer used). The story contains a number of historical difficulties. Satraps are most familiar as the governors of between twenty and thirty provinces into which the empire was organized by Darius I. The three "heads" (n. 3.a) are an otherwise unknown office. The content of the injunction, the treatment of Daniel and his accusers, and the requirement that the whole world worship Daniel's God correspond ill with what we otherwise know of the liberal early Persian period. The keeping of lions in a bottle-shaped pit is otherwise unknown, and it is difficult to envisage a pit big enough to contain the five hundred or more people apparently envisaged by v 25 [24]. In general the grounds for rehabilitating Darius as a historical figure probably make him viceroy of Babylon (see on 6:1 [5:31]), whereas in this story he has the autocratic power and instinct of a later Persian emperor such as Darius I. These difficulties are not insuperable, but combined with the use of narrative forms that are associated more with fiction than fact they suggest that the chapter does not present itself to the hearer as actual history. Not that it need not have its ultimate origin in some amazing deliverance; it is perhaps implausible that such stories were created out of nothing. On the other hand, some of the apparently factual allusions noted above may only give color to the fiction. The injunction is thus a means of lampooning the pagan powers and their religious pretension, which also makes it possible to represent a dispersion Jew under pressure to abandon his characteristic religious practice and to portray the faithfulness and vindication of God that were testified to in Israel's history, no doubt experienced in personal ways in the exile, and believed in even when current experience did not witness to them.

Structure

The story follows a straightforward narrative sequence ([ב]אדין) ["then," omitted in translation; cf. BH ו] occurs 16 times), though its structure can be expressed chiastically:

2–4 [1–3] introduction: Daniel's success
  5–11 [4–10] Darius signs an injunction but Daniel takes his stand.
    12–16 [11–15] Daniel's colleagues plan his death.
      17–19 [16–18] Darius hopes for his deliverance.
      20–24 [19–23] Darius witnesses his deliverance.
    25 [24] Daniel's colleagues meet with their death.
  26–28 [25–27] Darius signs a decree and takes his stand.
29 [28] conclusion: Daniel's success

Introduction and conclusion in simple narrative locate the story's starting point in Daniel's life, which is also its finishing point, though the intention declared in v 4 is not resumed—which reflects the fact that this is merely background. Verses 5–11 have his colleagues getting Darius to sign the injunction that sets up the point of tension for the drama; vv 26–28 have Darius signing the decree that brings the drama to its climax. In both sections narrative is the framework for speech, though speech of very different kinds: that in vv 5–11 is entirely the scheming words of the plotters, that in vv 26–28 begins as the formal speech of a royal decree, then turns abruptly into the lyric parallelism of a psalm. Verses 12–16 and 25 are narrative, with dialogue in vv 12–16; death in a lion pit is first envisaged, then experienced, by the plotters. The middle two sections of the story concern Darius and Daniel.

The focus is first on Darius's final words to Daniel, with their ambiguity, and then on his sleepless night, with its ambiguity: we are told nothing of Daniel's words or feelings. With Darius we return to the tomb to discover what has happened; with Darius, we learn from Daniel's words the answer to the question about Daniel's fate when for the only time he speaks—there is no direct description of the event.

The story offers three quite different studies in characterization. Daniel's colleagues appear as simply (in both senses of the word) plotters. Most of the speech in the story is theirs, and they condemn themselves out of their own mouths; every word they speak, as well as every move they make, concerns intrigue, manipulation, treachery, duplicity, and scheming. They have the arrogant boldness of a crowd bolstered by each other into bravado and folly. To "muster" (רגש) is their distinctive style (vv 7, 12, 16 [6, 11, 15]). They care nothing for truth, for the state, for the king, for religion, for law. Everything is subordinate to their desire to get rid of Daniel. Together they plot, but together they die. For most of the story, Daniel is silent. He is described adjectivally in passing (vv 4, 5 [3, 4]), then in a telling verse of narrative (v 11 [10]), whose witness is summarized by the king himself (vv 17, 21 [16, 20]). The story is silent about Daniel's experience and feelings as he approaches the lion pit, reserving his words for the climax in v 23 [22]; and even here his words concern God's act and his own innocence rather than his faith or his feelings. The king is caught between the conspirators and the confessor. He is the unspeaking victim of manipulation, opening his mouth only to confirm that he is the conspirators' victim (v 13 [12]). In relation to Daniel, however, he is the mouthpiece of unqualified recognition but ambiguous hope, renouncing indulgence and losing sleep, hurrying back to the execution scene in anxious agitation, rejoicing to lift Daniel to life and quick to send his assailants to their death, and finally fervent in his confession of Daniel's God.

Some points in the story are underlined by the words used. The story concerns obedience to God's law or to state law (דת, vv 6, 9 [5, 8]). Daniel has done nothing injurious, he suffers no injury, and this shows that God's realm will never suffer injury (חבל, vv 23, 23, 27 [22, 22, 26]). The satraps are to take notice of Daniel, they accuse Daniel of taking no notice of the king, the king gives notice that all peoples are to revere Daniel's God (טעם, vv 3, 14, 27 [2, 13, 26]). The king is very displeased, then very glad (באש and its antonym טאב, vv 15, 24 [14, 23]). The king goes off to the palace and comes back next morning (אזל, vv 19, 20 [18, 19], cf. 2:17, 24). The conspirators can find nothing against Daniel until they find him praying, but he is found innocent before God and found unharmed by the lions (שכח, vv 5, 5, 6, 6, 12, 23, 24 [4, 4, 5, 5, 11, 22, 23]). The conspirators go in a crowd to see the king, to catch Daniel, and to tell the king he must impose execution (רגש, vv 7, 12, 16 [6, 11, 15]). The chapter does not repeat phrases such as the lists of officers and instruments in the companion narrative, chap. 3. It does repeat key words (King, Daniel, realm, seek/petition, lion, pit), and includes a set of instances of hendiadys (vv 5, 5, 8, 9, 10, 11, 12, 16; cf. הא־בשפרפרא . . . בנג "when morning came . . . at sunrise," v 20).

OG again represents a quite different form of the chapter.

Setting

The story contains no specific pointers toward the Maccabean period; neither the motivation and aims of Daniel's enemies, nor the harshness of Darius's edict, nor his concern for Daniel suggest it. Observance of the sabbath law and of Jewish feasts were proscribed in the second century B.C.; private prayer was not. Darius's insistence that petitions be made to him alone does not correspond specifically to the irreligious actions of Antiochus described in 11:36–39; in a dispersion context, private prayer of the kind described here is of great importance. The story might belong to any time in the Persian or Greek period. As with previous chapters, scholars have formulated varying hypotheses regarding earlier forms of the story and stages by which it reached the form that we know.

The chapter takes up from chap. 5, illustrating how Daniel continues to function during the reigns of the Median and Persian kings who succeed Belshazzar (5:28; cf. 6:1, 2, 29 [5:31; 6:1, 28]). Bringing the stories in Dan 1–6 to a close, it offers a final example of the varying behavior of pagan kings, of the varied testing of God's man, and of the wonderful deeds of his God. Daniel's deliverance from death prefaces the promise of deliverance after death at the end of the vision sequence (chap. 12), and Darius's confession recapitulates the affirmations that bring earlier stories to a climax (2:44; 3:28; 3:33 [4:3]; 4:31 [34]) (Towner).

The story has a special relationship with chap. 3, which in a parallel way combines features of court conflict tale, confessor legend, aretalogy, and midrash, and holds together factual allusions, traditional motifs, and historical implausibilities. Both chapters are tales of two decrees. Both involve introduction, accusation, sentence, deliverance, and confession. Many words recur: אכל קרציהון "attack," טעם "notice," שלו "negligence," שיזב "deliver," צלח "flourish," בהתבהלה "in agitation," שלט "overpower." In both, Judean exiles who have reached positions of authority in the empire are put in a position where a royal edict requires them to abandon a fundamental outward concrete expression of their Jewish faith. In both, jealous colleagues gather to indict them for their stand, accuse them of slighting the king's authority, and insist that he implement the unpleasant capital sanction required by the edict. In both, the king does so, ensuring that there is no way that they can escape. In both, there is ambiguous talk of the possibility that God may deliver, then description of the king rising in agitation to perceive that he has done so, as the Psalms promise he does in the context of such experiences, because of the confessors' trust in him; he has sent one of his heavenly servants into the place of execution, so that the confessors are quite unharmed. In both, the king orders them to be released and others die in their place. In both, the king declares that all peoples are to recognize the unique power of their God, and the story closes by noting how they continue to flourish. The stories are bracketed together in Heb 11:33–34.

Yet chap. 6 by no means simply repeats chap. 3. The setting is Persian, not Babylonian; Darius's edict results from his being manipulated, not from his own initiative; Daniel's accusers are other officials, not other sages; Daniel's loyalty to the state is emphasized; Daniel's area of testing is private prayer, not public religion; it concerns what is forbidden, not what is required; his danger comes from the lion pit, not the furnace; Darius is concerned for Daniel, not enraged; he accepts Daniel's religious practice, instead of seeking to persuade him; he allows for the possibility of God's delivering Daniel, rather than excluding this; Daniel himself makes no statement of his faith; Darius learns of what happens from Daniel, rather than witnessing it; he orders the punishment of Daniel's attackers; he requires empire-wide worship of Daniel's God, rather than mere tolerance of the Jews' religion. Thus some motifs are heightened, some appear in varied form, some are reduced.

Similarities and differences enable us to perceive aspects of the stories' respective significance. Recurring features may suggest recurring experiences, pressures, challenges, insights, and promises. As well as reflecting the diverse forms these may take, distinctive features may highlight important themes: the exiles are to be willing both to maintain their "no" to public practices that are incompatible with their commitment to God, and to maintain their "yes" to private practices that are essential to their commitment to God.

Comment

2–3 [1–2] Appointing satraps was apparently an aspect of Darius's organization of the realm at the beginning of his reign. The number of satraps (120) compares with the 127 provinces in the time of Xerxes (485–465 B.C.) mentioned in Esth 1:1; 1 Esd 3:2 (to which OG assimilates Dan 6:2 [1]). It contrasts with the 20 to 29 satraps/provinces by which the Persian empire was organized from the time of Xerxes' predecessor Darius I (522–485 B.C.) (so Herodotus 3.89, Darius's inscriptions, and the inscription on his tomb). In this strict sense the satraps were the king's viceroys in each of the provinces, responsible for security and for the collecting of tribute; the term means "protector of the realm." If Dan 6:2 [1] reflects a historical act by a ruler of Babylon early in the Persian period, then, "satrap" must refer to provincial officials in a looser sense, perhaps to government officials generally. When control of Babylon passed to Cyrus's governor Gobryas, most officials in the administration retained the posts they had held under the Chaldeans. "Satrap" is used by Xenophon to refer to officials appointed by Cyrus and to other rulers who were not satraps in the strict sense (e.g., *Cyr.* 8.11; *Hellenica* 3.1.10–12). It has already been used in Dan 3:2 with reference to the Babylonian period. The form of the word (אחשדרפניא) is closer to Median *kšatrapan* than OP *kšaśapawan*, which might suggest that it, with the office it denoted, was familiar in Aramaic before the Persian period (cf. Cook, *Persian Empire*, 242; more generally 77–85, 167–82, etc.).

There is no known parallel to the three "heads," though cf. 1 Esd 3:9; Dan 5:7; also the seven counselors/princes of, e.g., Ezra 7:14; Esth 1:14; Herodotus 3.71, 76, 83–84; Cook sees them as judges rather than ministers (*Persian Empire*, 144–45, 167–70). As checks on the satraps, Darius I appointed two other officials in each province, a commandant and a civil servant, who reported to the king (Herodotus 3.128); he also had personal advisers at court (Cook, *Persian Empire,* 71).

4–10 [3–9] Daniel's "remarkable spirit" is assumed to be of supernatural origin (see on 4:5 [8]). An injunction of the kind proposed (v 8 [7]) is otherwise unknown. In Persia the king was not regarded as divine in the Egyptian sense, though in court ceremonial people did obeisance before him as one would to a god, and the general idea that the king is a manifestation or representative of deity and a key mediator with deity appears in Persian writings, as in Mesopotamian and Hellenistic ones—and, in a sense, Israelite (see G. Widengren, "The Sacral Kingship of Iran," *The Sacral Kingship* [Numen Sup 4 (Leiden: Brill, 1959)] 242–57; Frye, *Heritage,* 95–97). Darius's injunction satirizes the link that many of Israel's pagan overlords claimed between their monarchy and the godhead, as do Isa 14:13–14; 36–37 that claimed by Babylon and Assyria, and as Isa 40–55 lampoons Babylonian idols, taking their implications to their ridiculous logical conclusion.

"Pit" (גב, v 8 [7]) is an ordinary word for an underground cistern, used for water storage or as a prison. For keeping lions there, see Oppenheim, *Mesopotamia,* 46; Keil; 2:38 *Comment.* Hunting continued to be a royal pastime in the Persian period (Cook, *Persian Empire,* 142; for lions, 249 and plate 33). Access to the pit was by the top, into which people would be lowered and from which they would be lifted out (v 24 [23]; cf. Jer 38:6–13). There is no need to suppose that the pit would have a door in the side, like the furnace of chap. 3. For the Persian kings' power of life and death, and their "almost exquisitely horrible" forms of execution, see Cook, *Persian Empire,* 132, 142. The satire continues with the appeal to the permanence of Medo-Persian law (v 9 [8]), on which cf. Esth 1:19; 8:8; on Darius I as a law-giver, see the varying estimates in Olmstead, *Persian Empire,* 119–34; Frye, *Heritage,* 104–6; Cook, *Persian Empire,* 72–73. The law of the state was designed to be proof against evasion or subversion by the king's subordinates; here Darius will be portrayed as being unable to evade it himself. For the motif, cf. the story of Darius III unable to undo the sentence of death on a man who turned out to be innocent (Diodorus 17.30; or is he unable to undo the actual execution?). (See Cook, *Persian Empire,* 132; he also speaks of the venality, corruption, and treachery of the court.)

11–16 [10–15] Daniel's practice of prayer is unusual not only for its bravery. We have no other reference to praying three times a day (Ps 55:18 [17] is surely no more a guide to anyone's regular practice than is the "seven times" of Ps 119:164) until *m. Ber.* 4:1; *Didache* 8. The times of morning and evening offerings were regular hours for prayer (1 Chr 23:30, cf. Exod 29:38–39; also twice-daily prayer in 1QS 10.1–3), especially the latter (Ps 141:2; Dan 9:21; Ezra 9:5; Jdt 9:1; Acts 3:1; 10:3, 30). Standing is the regular posture for prayer (1 Chr 23:30; Neh 9; Matt 6:5; Mark 11:25; Luke 18:11, 13). Kneeling, which implies prostration, indicates a marked self-lowering in circumstances of particular solemnity or need (1 Kings 8:54; Ezra 9:5; Luke 22:41; Acts 7:60; 9:40; 20:36; 21:5). "Before his God" also suggests a meekness in the presence of authority: it is the term used for addressing the king (e.g., 2:9, 10, 11), though at the same time it indicates the actuality of standing in a real person's presence. Having an attic that could be used for a private meeting, for guests, or for prayer, would also be unusual, and the luxury is perhaps a sign of Daniel's status (Judg 3:20; 2 Kgs 1:2; 4:8–11; Jer 22:14; Luke 22:12; Acts 1:13; 9:37, 39; 20:8); ordinary people would have a makeshift shelter on the roof itself for these purposes (1 Sam 9:25; 1 Kgs 17:19; Jdt 8:5; Acts 10:9). Facing the land, the city, and the temple during prayer is emphasized throughout Solomon's prayer in 1 Kgs 8 but is referred to rarely elsewhere (Ps 5:8 [7] [in the temple court!]; 1 Esd 4:58; cf. Tob 3:11). In expressions such as בעא ומתחנן "praying and petitioning," the first verb is a general one for (formal, liturgical) prayer, the second specifies the kind of prayer; here "petitioning" (התחנן) suggests casting oneself on someone's grace (חן) and pleading (see n. 9:3.b).

17–25 [16–24] Kings and others commonly authenticated documents by a signet or other seal (v 18 [17]; 1 Kgs 21:8; Esth 3:12; 8:8, 10; cf. Oppenheim, *Mesopotamia,* 281–82; Olmstead, *Persian Empire,* 177–78). Apparently here cord or cloth was fastened across the rock with clay, which was then impressed with the seals (Herodotus 1.195) (Jeffery).

There is no suggestion in vv 22–24 [21–23] that Daniel is exercising lordship over the animal creation in accordance with the purpose envisaged in Gen 1 and that promised in Isa 11:6–9; 65:25. Nor is there any suggestion that the animals had more sense than their master (cf. Num 22:26–33; 1 Sam 6:12) or lacked spirit (like some Ignatius speaks of, *Romans* 5). It is God's act that the story relates, not Daniel's or the lions'. We are told nothing of what actually happened in the lion pit. There is a contrast between the restraint of Daniel's story and the extravagance of (e.g.) the second century A.D. *Acts of Paul and Thecla* 8–9 (see E. Hennecke, *New Testament Apocrypha* vol. 2 [London/Philadelphia: Lutterworth/Westminster, 1965 (ET ed. by R. McL. Wilson from *Neutestamentlichen Apokryphen* 2, ed. W. Schneemelcher; 3rd ed., Tübingen: Mohr, 1964)] 322–90).

The story has implied that all the heads and satraps associated themselves with the attack on Daniel, so all 122 (plus wives and children) are apparently killed (v 25 [24]). This raises logistical problems, among others. OG executes only the two heads, a characteristic simplification of the story, while Young says the plot was the work of only a few men, but the story rather emphasizes that everyone was against Daniel (see vv 2–8 [1–7]) and here emphasizes how great was the miracle of Daniel's preservation by noting the subsequent capacity of the lions.

26–29 [25–28] It might be possible to make these affirmations without being "converted" and abandoning the acknowledgment of heathen gods (so Keil), but this is to miss the point of Darius's confession at the end of the story. The confession goes far beyond that at the end of chap. 3 in acknowledging the living, enduring, secure and active power of Daniel's God (cf. 3:31–33; 4:31–34 [4:1–3, 34–37]).

Explanation

2–10 [1–9] A state requires an administration if it is to hold together and if its various parts are to be obliged to contribute to the expenses of government; the administration needs internal checks if it is to be protected from the very fissiparous and dishonest tendencies it is designed to safeguard against. Positions within the administration give people the opportunity to reveal their capacity for even higher responsibility. They also give those who reveal this capacity the opportunity to incur the sullen opposition of those who do not. If these malcontents then want to put the others down, suggesting that they are unfaithful or disloyal in their work is a way to do that. It is the more incumbent on them to be blameless in their work. One slip gives a hostage to fortune. It is noteworthy that Daniel has nothing to fear from his colleagues' close probing of how he executes his office. Why they decide to subvert Daniel's position is only vaguely explained. There is a hint of professional jealousy and/or resentment at their being unable to use their office to indulge their own rapacity. There is behind that a hint of what we would now call anti-Semitism, developed in v 14 [13]. There is behind that the mysterious, perverse antagonism toward what is good that people sometimes manifest (Wallace). These are phenomena already illustrated in the Joseph story, and they will subsequently find mature expression in the cross and in the holocaust.

Daniel's colleagues cannot catch him out, until they perceive that his vulnerability lies in his commitment to God. Daniel's distinction derives from his remarkable spirit, and that reflects God's involvement in his life and in the shaping of the person he was (5:11–12). At one level there is nothing intrinsically religious about Daniel's colleagues' hostility; it is simply that religion is of key significance to Daniel, and therefore constitutes his weak point. At another level the possibility of conflict over Daniel's religious commitment is inherent in his position as a minister of state, for the state characteristically assumes it has quasi-divine significance. One can see this in the Marxist state and its opposition to religion, which invites people to accept a higher commitment than that to the state; it can be as real if more subtle in the "Christian" democracy. One can see it in the ancient monarchies' inclination to claim varying forms of sacral significance. Jealousy, resentment, anti-Semitism, and the mystery of human hostility to the good plot to utilize, as their means of putting Daniel out of the way, the state's inclination to deify itself and the believer's obligation to confess no god but God. The law of Daniel's God (v 6 [5]) and the law of the Medes and Persians (v 9 [8]) are deliberately brought into conflict. God's law makes an absolute demand. So does the king's law, for he contributes to the state's stability and to the authority of his own position by insisting on the irrevocability of his injunctions: once his decision is declared, it cannot be undone. Such firmness adds strength to good decisions, but compounds the weakness of poor ones.

Darius's civil servants' words and actions imply that their calculating cynicism cares nothing for state, God, or truth themselves. Whether they are conscious of this or not, their mad edict (Calvin) contemns and blasphemes God more boldly and dangerously than Belshazzar's libations did. The godless arrogance of the Assyrian king's field-commander and that of the Babylonian king himself (2 Kgs 18–19; Isa 14:13–14; cf. Jdt 3:8; 6:2) reappear in the next of the Middle East's succession of empires. It does not really know what is in its own interests: fancy stopping people praying, when the prayer of the saints is designed to release God's peace and blessing in the world (Hippolytus).

How much of all this Darius himself perceived, the story leaves open. Perhaps he is the victim of his own vanity (Anderson), or perhaps he colludes with his ministers because he realizes the advantages to the state of its having quasi-divine authority, or perhaps he is initially unaware of being manipulated as a puppet by his civil servants in a way which denies the divinity they overtly attribute to him (Lacocque). All three possibilities become actual in politics at one time or another.

11 [10] Circumstantial evidence suggests that living in dispersion put pressure on distinctive Jewish practices such as observance of the sabbath, adherence to the food laws, and the rite of circumcision. In Daniel, the specific emphasis is on a public disavowal of idolatry (chap. 3) and sacrilege (chap. 5), and a private commitment to purity (chap. 1) and prayer (2:17–23; 6:11 [10]; 9:3–20) (Lacocque). Individual prayer is also prominent in other post-exilic writings such as Chronicles-Ezra-Nehemiah and the Psalter, which no doubt reflects the prayer life of post-exilic Judaism, even if individual psalms are of earlier date. Thus Daniel's response to the prohibition on prayer is to continue praying. There is no fuss or rush about his stand, such as characterizes every action of his assailants. Nor is he a man who has lost his true human freedom. He retains that, while neither civil servants nor king behave as free men. He cannot hide the fact that he prays. When prayer is fashionable, it is time to pray in secret (Matt 6:5–6), but when prayer is under pressure, to pray in secret is to give the appearance of fearing the king more than God: one must "render to Caesar . . ." (Matt 22:21; cf. Acts 4:18–20; 5:29) (Hippolytus). In fact, Daniel's "seemingly innocuous act" was "more . . . revolutionary than outright rebellion would have been. Rebellion simply acknowledges the absoluteness and ultimacy of the emperor's power, and attempts to seize it. Prayer denies that ultimacy altogether by acknowledging a higher power" (Wink, *Naming,* 110–11).

Daniel's prayer follows his customary practice, but it is a practice that marks him out. People did not commonly have a special prayer room facing Jerusalem, or pray as frequently as Daniel, or adopt the prostrate posture he adopted. Daniel is presumably set forward as a model to which, in at least some of these respects, other people might aspire. They too belong to another city (despite Jer 29) and need outward ways of demonstrating that they live as strangers among the Chaldeans, whether they feel secure or insecure there (Calvin). (The NT points to an application of this principle to the Christian community: see, e.g., Phil 3:20; Heb 13:14.)

"Prayer and thanksgiving" suggests two major aspects of praying (cf. Phil 4:6). Daniel's prayer may include intercession for the state in which he lives in exile (Jer 29); but the context also suggests prayer for Israel herself in exile (cf. Dan 9) and prayer on his own behalf in his situation of need (cf. Dan 2:17–23). The psalmist who prays three times a day (Ps 55:18 [17]) does so because of the urgency of his personal need. He interweaves plea with testimony to his conviction that God hears and answers: and it is presumably this characteristic confession of the Psalms that is indicated by the "thanksgiving" with which Daniel's prayer is accompanied (cf. 2:17–23). Daniel is confident that the living God knows his situation and his peril and that he has already determined how he will preserve him through it.

12–16 [11–15] So Daniel is caught petitioning God when he is only allowed to petition the king, and is duly denounced. The accusation includes reference to Daniel's Jewish origin (cf. 3:12 in a similar context, though also 2:25; 5:13). The other ministers may imply that as a foreigner he cannot really be trusted, or that as an exile his maintaining his alien religious practices is a political act, an act of rebellion; but the hint of anti-Semitism may be stronger here than it was in vv 4–6.

The king is displeased: perhaps with Daniel, for ignoring his injunction; perhaps with the ministers, for engineering his downfall; perhaps with himself, for being manipulated by them into becoming the victim of his own power and authority; perhaps with the situation in general into which he is now cornered (cf. Herod, Mark 6:26). But the law is the law is the law. If the king accepts it, he has to accept unacceptable constraints and unfairness when the law is an ass; if he suspends it, he risks the collapse of the social order, and ultimately of the state itself (Towner).

17–24 [16–23] There are significant parallels and contrasts between the words that take Daniel's three friends to the furnace (3:15–18) and those that take Daniel to the lion pit. There the king asked, "Who ever is the god who could deliver you from my power?" Here the king declares, "Your God, whom you honor so consistently, he must deliver you" (compare his acknowledgment of "the living God" in v 21 [20]). There the king's challenge requires a response and draws forth a magnificent confession from the three men. Here the king has said all that needs to be said, and it is his confession that resounds in our ears until Daniel testifies to God's saving power the next day (v 23 [22]). It is Darius who comes into focus at this point in the story, not Daniel. Yet both confessions manifest ambiguities. Even if it is right that the friends themselves believe that their God can and will rescue them (in 3:17–18), they nevertheless have to grant that only events will demonstrate whether this is actually so. Darius, in turn, uses a form of the verb that leaves open whether God must, will, may, or can rescue Daniel (see n. 6:17.b). Like other ambiguities in Daniel, the unclarity over whether Darius offers a challenge to God, or a statement of faith, or a wistful hope, functions to invite the hearer to decide what he or she would mean in a situation of this kind.

Daniel's fate is sealed. It will neither be possible for his friends to feed the lions or to engineer his survival in some other way, nor for his enemies to kill him if the lions do not (Rashi). There is also a deeper matter at issue than the conflict between Daniel's foes and his friends. The king has spoken of the possibility of *God's* delivering Daniel, and the sealing will make it necessary for God to prove himself in an extraordinary way if he is to act at all. "In testing Daniel, the king knows . . . that he is testing God" (Lacocque).

Darius is unable to eat, relax, or sleep as he awaits the outcome of the action forced on him. Perhaps he is even praying against the effectiveness of his action (Plöger) or expressing his penitence for his foolish injunction (Delcor); perhaps we are to recall the Babylonian custom whereby a prisoner who was tortured but survived overnight was then pardoned (Lacocque). When daylight comes, he returns to the lion pit in turmoil and trepidation instead of in the stately dignity and composure of a monarch. By addressing

Daniel to ask whether he has survived the ordeal, he builds up our expectation that actually he has. By enquiring whether the "living God" has been able to preserve Daniel, he speaks of that God in terms that contain the seeds of the answer to his question. This rich OT title for God suggests not merely that God is alive rather than dead, but that he is active and powerful, awesome and almighty, involved in bringing judgment and blessing. It is appealed to when human beings are inclined to slight him or to doubt him in situations of pressure and weakness (Deut 5:26; Josh 3:10; 1 Sam 17:26; 2 Kgs 19:4; Jer 10:10; 23:36; Hos 2:1 [1:10]; Ps 42:3 [2]; 84:3 [2]; oaths are taken "by the living God"—i.e., at the risk of his intervening in case of default!). Darius's confession of "the living God" thus also builds up our expectation regarding what we are about to discover.

Daniel's calm and polite reply, observing courtly protocol, underlines by contrast the king's anxiety and agitation. At the same time his "Long live the king" strikingly affirms Darius's kingship. It is the first time the phrase has occurred on the lips of Daniel or his friends (cf. Neh 2:3). If to be the living God implies activity and power, to be the living king implies having a share in God's life and power (cf. P. A. H. de Boer, " 'Vive le roi!' " *VT* 5 [1955] 225–31). Daniel's prayer that Darius may do so both honors and relativizes Darius's kingship by the interweaving of references to the living God with those to the living king (vv 7, 21, 22, 27 [6, 20, 21, 26]), as have his earlier affirmations of Nebuchadnezzar's kingship as God-given (2:37; 5:18).

As Daniel's friends were not preserved from the furnace, so Daniel has not been preserved from the lion pit; as the divine aide entered the furnace to stand with Daniel's friends, so God has sent his aide into the pit to stand with Daniel; as Daniel's friends were preserved in the furnace, so is Daniel in the lion pit. The first generation of Christian believers had similar experiences. They refused to obey human beings rather than God and found themselves in prison: but the Lord's aide opened the prison doors and released them (Acts 4:18–20; 5:19–20; 12:1–10; 16:19–26). So "what happens when a state executes those who are praying for it?" It is "demonstrating the emperor's powerlessness to impose his will even by death. The final sanction had been publicly robbed of its power. Even as the lions lapped the blood of the saints, Caesar was stripped of his arms and led captive in Christ's triumphal procession. His authority was shown to be only penultimate after all" (Wink, *Naming*, 111).

The message of Dan 6 is hardly that the innocent, believing confessor can always expect to be saved from martyrdom. Though the promise of Ps 91:10–13 generalizes the experience of Daniel, the psalmist and the author of Daniel knew that life is often not like that. The promise may more often hold in a metaphorical sense (cf. Ps 22:14, 22 [13, 21]; 124:6; Rom 8:36–37; 2 Tim 4:17); the reader is no doubt entitled to rejoice in the story's implicit promise of such divine protection. God does grant a victory of life over death, of innocence over guilt, of justice over enmity, of hope over fear. He who loses his life *will* save it. In Daniel's day, in that of the early Christians, and in our own, it is often the case that the lions who are set upon the children of God do devour them. They experience not only the pit (and are rescued from death) but the Pit itself. The story affirms that occasional experiences of divine intervention are more important than regular experiences of divine nonintervention. That invites us to a more God-centered perspective: the fulfilling of God's purpose, whether by my deliverance or by my death, is what matters, not the fulfilling of what is most comfortable to me (cf. Phil 1:12–20). The story does recognize, however, that our deliverance does matter to us. We are not expected to manifest a heroism that cares nothing for our own destiny. The Book of Daniel sets the individual's experience of attack by wild beasts and being thrown into the pit into a wider and at first more threatening context, but one which is then comforting. In Dan 7, a lionlike animal will be the first to typify the gentile world-powers, more threatening now than they were pictured in chap. 2, but destined for defeat. Dan 12 then encourages us to look to deliverance after death if not before it, and Christ's resurrection is the proof that such a deliverance is not fanciful hope (thus Phil 1:21–26 continues Paul's reflection). Daniel's deliverance from the pit in this age anticipates and promises a more general deliverance from the Pit into a new age; there, too, God's aide comes to deliver those who have obeyed God rather than Caesar, so that they may yet look in triumph on their attackers and testify to the power of the living God (Hippolytus). But the story does also witness to the experience of the powers of the age to come operating now (Philip). Even if its form invites us not to take it as a straightforward narrative of historical events, its logic requires that some concrete experience of God acting in marvelous ways in this age underlies it, and its implication is that we may occasionally look for such experiences in this age.

Daniel's adversaries have attempted to make it impossible for him to remain innocent before God *and* loyal to the state, but they have failed. He has obeyed God rather than the human king, but has done no injury to the state. He has not been guilty of rebellion or treachery. By putting loyalty to God above loyalty to the state he has been loyal to the truth and thus more loyal to the state than those who make of it more than it is—and certainly than those who use it to serve their own ends, as his adversaries have. It is appropriate for the king to be glad that his attempt at execution has failed.

Darius's state of mind has been in focus for some while. We have not been told what Daniel was feeling. Lest we had not assumed it, however, we are assured that Daniel's ability to shut the lions' mouths derived from his standing firm in his trust in God (Heb 11:33). Admittedly he himself preferred to speak of *God* shutting their mouths; and we should not even assume that God is limited to delivering those who are innocent and trusting (cf. Towner). That would be to fall into an error akin to that of Job's friends.

25 [24] That Daniel's adversaries should be executed in his place is in keeping with Deut 19:16–21; Prov 19:5, 9; 21:28; Esth 7:10. It is more broadly in keeping with the prophetic promise that as Israel is saved, her oppressors will be turned upon themselves and annihilated (Isa 41:11–12; 49:25–26). That their families should suffer with them is in keeping with Num 16:27–33; Josh 7:24–25; Esth 9:25; Isa 13:15–16; though it contrasts with Deut 24:16; 2 Kgs 14:6. Perhaps the story implies no moral judgment on the event beyond the implication that "life is like that (so watch it)." It very well illustrates maxims in Proverbs (see especially 26:27; 28:10; cf. Ps 7:16 [15]; 9:16 [15]; 57:7 [6]). Perhaps at this point we need again to recall that this is not a straightforward piece of history; at this point it is a dramatized warning and promise of God's judgment on wickedness (which recognizes that for good and for ill the fate of children is tied up with that of their parents). Josephus has Daniel's accusers saying that the lions fail to eat Daniel because they have been fed; the lions' appetite for them then proves that Daniel's escape *was* a miracle (*Ant.* 10.11.6 [10.262]).

26–29 [25–28] From the beginning, Darius has been more sympathetic to Daniel and his faith than Nebuchadnezzar had been in relation to Daniel's friends; at the end, he acknowledges Daniel's God more fully. Through his entire empire, Daniel's God is not merely to be tolerated but to be worshiped with reverence and awe. The other side to the vision of later prophecy comes true (Isa 42:1–12; 49:1–7; Zech 2:11 [15]; 8:20–23); Daniel has himself functioned as a light to enlighten the Gentiles (Gammie). Heathen powers suffer if they oppose God and his servants, but they have the opportunity to find God through his servants instead. Nations were created by God (cf. Gen 10, at the end of the creation story), they rebelled against him as the individual men and women did (Gen 11), but they are destined to worship (Rev 15:4; 21:26; 22:26); the worship called for here is an anticipation of that which will come at the End (in the meantime, admittedly, rebellion will more often characterize them) (Wink, *Naming*, 97–99).

The pagan king thus brings the story to its climax as he expresses the wonder to which every hearer is invited as he or she enters into Daniel's story. Perhaps Darius's decree is as foolish as his earlier injunction and his order to kill Daniel's adversaries: compulsion or violence cannot be effective on God's behalf any more than in opposition to him (Kennedy). But this highlights the symbolic significance of each of these elements in the story. They witness to the fact that pagan powers do put believers under pressure, but that these powers are destined to be defeated, and ultimately to bow before the name that is above every name (Isa 45:23; Phil 2:10–11). The chapter is the story of two decrees (Anderson): Darius revokes his irrevocable decree and replaces it by another. It is not merely a story about a miraculous escape from martyrdom, but about all human claims to immutability yielding to God's abiding law and will (there is simply no contest between the two) and about the miracle of the king himself acknowledging that (Towner). As with Nebuchadnezzar's, the form of an encyclical presupposes and expresses Darius's own authority, but its use thus actually underlines the higher authority of the one to whom it bears witness. The world powers testify to the sovereign authority of God, which they have witnessed at work. Once more the familiar affirmations of Israel's hymns issue from unexpected lips and express a new message. In a similar way, the "impossible" legal requirement that people tremble with fear before Daniel's God gains part of its significance from the fact that its author is the person before whom people have earlier trembled with fear (5:19). Something similar happens when Darius testifies to God as the living God who endures for ever. Daniel has just greeted him with that standard wish "Long live the king" (literally, "May the king live forever"): the courtly homage is relativized by the royal confession itself. To be living is to be active and powerful: the living God is enthroned as King forever (Ps 10:16; 29:10), and he can therefore also be his people's savior.

Even if the divine victory that the chapter portrays will only be consistently demonstrated in the age to come, the story actually portrays God demonstrating his power in this age, and on this basis Darius acknowledges a power that persists through the ages.

So Daniel, far from being put out of the way, is established in a position that he retains through Darius's reign and into the next. As dynasties pass (Babylonian, Median, Persian), the Jewish presence persists and grows in importance. Darius's earlier plan to give Daniel a special position is more than fulfilled. It is possible for the faithful Jew not only to survive but to triumph.

The story as a whole has a series of motifs parallel to Ps 2. Heathen rulers have mustered and devised their plot, but God has acted on behalf of his servant, giving him the power to have them torn to pieces, to rule over their realm, and to compel them to serve God with trembling fear. They are to heed the decree of which his servant speaks, to learn a wisdom they do not yet possess, and to put their trust where he puts his. The first Christians saw this psalm recapitulated in the story of Jesus (Acts 4:26–28), and they might also have seen Daniel's experience recapitulated there (so Derrett, "Daniel"; for the comparison, see Aphrahat, *Demonstration* 21.18 [NPNF ii 13:399]). He, too, is the victim of conspiracy and betrayal from people whose position is threatened by him and who seek occasion to manipulate higher authorities into executing him, professing that they have no king but Caesar. They, too, will eventually pay for their hostility, along with their children. He, too, is arrested at his customary place of prayer. These higher authorities, too, find no fault in him and labor to free him, but are reminded that the law forbids it. He, too, has to rely on God to deliver him as his tomb is sealed. Indeed, he actually dies, and injury can be found on him after he comes back from the dead: more extraordinary is it, then, that very early, at sunrise, he, too, is discovered to be alive after all.

God Most High Reveals the World's Destiny to Daniel (7:1–28)

Bibliography

Abbott, E. A. *"The Son of Man."* Cambridge: CUP, 1910. **Altpeter, G.** *Textlinguistische Exegese alttestamentlicher Literatur.* Bern: Lang, 1978. **Aspinwall, W.** *An Explication and Application of the Seventh Chapter of Daniel. . . .* London: Livewell Chapman, 1654. **Baeck, L.** "Der 'Menschensohn.'" *MGWJ* 81 (1937) 12–24. = Baeck, *Aus drei Jahrtausenden.* Berlin: Schocken, 1938. 313–24. = Baeck, *Judaism and Christianity.* Tr. W. Kaufmann. New York: Leo Baeck Institute, 1958. 23–38. **Balz, H. R.** *Methodische Probleme der neutestamentlichen Christologie.* WMANT 25 (1967) 48–112. **Barrett, C. K.** "The Background of Mark 10:45." In *New Testament Essays,* FS T. W. Manson, ed. A. J. B. Higgins. Manchester: Manchester UP, 1959. 1–18. **Beasley-Murray, G. R.** *Jesus and the Kingdom of God.* Grand Rapids/Exeter: Eerdmans/Paternoster, 1986. ———. "The Interpretation of Daniel 7." *CBQ* 45 (1983) 44–58. **Beek, M. A.** "Zeit, Zeiten und eine halbe Zeit." In *Studia biblica et semitica,* FS T. C. Vriezen, ed. W. C. van Unnik and A. S. van der Woude. Wageningen: Veenman, 1966. 19–24. **Bentzen, A.** *Messias—Moses redivivus—Menschensohn.* ATANT 17 (1948). = *King and Messiah.* London: Lutterworth, 1955; 2nd ed., Oxford: Blackwell, 1970. ———. "King Ideology—'Urmensch'—'Troonbestijgingsfeest.'" *ST* 3 (1949) 143–57. **Bietenhard, H.** "'Der Menschensohn,'" *ANRW* ii 25, 1 (1982) 265–350. **Black, M.** "The 'Son of Man' in the Old Biblical Literature." *ExpT* 60 (1948–49) 11–15. ———. "Die Apotheose Israels: Eine neue Interpretation des danielischen 'Menschensohns'" (tr. A. Berz). In *Jesus und der Menschensohn,* FS A. Vögtle, ed. R. Pesch and R. Schnackenburg. Freiburg: Herder, 1975. 92–99. ———. "The 'Parables' of Enoch (1 En 37–71) and the 'Son of Man.'" *ExpT* 88 (1976–77) 5–8. ———. "The Throne-Theophany Prophetic Commission and the 'Son of Man.'" In *Jews, Greeks, and Christians,* FS W. D. Davies, ed. R. G. Hamerton-Kelly and R. Scroggs. SJLA 21 (1976) 57–73. **Borsch, F. H.** *The Son of Man in Myth and History.* London: SCM, 1967. **Bousset, W.** *Die Religion des Judentums.* Berlin: Reuther, 1903. 2nd ed., 1906. 3rd ed., Tübingen: Mohr, 1926. **Bowker, J.** "The Son of Man." *JTS* 28 (1977) 19–48. **Bowman, J.** "The Background of the Term 'Son of Man.'" *ExpT* 59 (1947–48) 283–88. **Brekelmans, C. H. W.** "The Saints of the Most High and Their Kingdom." *OTS* 14 (1965) 305–29. **Bruce, F. F.** "The Background to the Son of Man Sayings." In *Christ the Lord,* FS D. Guthrie, ed. H. H. Rowdon. Leicester/Downers Grove, IL: IVP, 1982. 50–70. **Buchanan, G. W.** "The Son of Man in Daniel and Enoch." *To the Hebrews.* AB 36 (1972) 42–48. **Buzy, D.** *RB* 27 [n.s. 15] (1918) 403–31. **Campbell, J. Y.** "The Origin and Meaning of the Term 'Son of Man.'" *JTS* 48 (1947) 145–55. **Caquot, A.** "Sur les quatre bêtes de *Daniel* vii." *Sem* 5 (1955) 5–13. ———. "Les quatre bêtes et le 'Fils d'homme' (*Daniel* 7)." *Sem* 17 (1967) 37–71. **Caragounis, C. C.** *The Son of Man.* WUNT 38 (1986). ———. "The Interpretation of the Ten Kings of Daniel 7." *ETL* 63 (1987) 106–12. **Carpzov, J. B.** *De Filio Hominis ad antiquum dierum delato.* Leipzig: Hahn, 1679. = *TTP* 887–901. **Casey, [P.] M.** *Son of Man.* London: SPCK, 1979. ———. "The Use of the Term 'Son of Man' in the Similitudes of Enoch." *JSJ* 7 (1976) 11–29. ———. "The Corporate Interpretation of 'One Like a Son of Man' (Dan. vii 13) at the Time of Jesus." *NovT* 18 (1976) 167–80. **Caspari, W.** "Die Gottesgestalt in Daniel." *NKZ* 36 (1925) 175–99. **Cheyne, T. K.** *Bible Problems and the New Material for Their Solution.* London/New York: Williams and Norgate/Putnam, 1904. 213–35. **Collins, J. J.** "The Son of Man and the Saints of the Most High in the Book of Daniel." *JBL* 93 (1974) 50–66. Cf. Collins, *Vision,*

123–52. **Colpe, C.** "ὁ υἱὸς τοῦ ἀνθρώπου." *TWNT* 8 (1969) 403–81. = *TDNT* 8 (1972) 400–477. ———. "Der Begriff 'Menschensohn.'" *Kairos* 11 (1969) 241–63; 12 (1970) 81–112; 13 (1971) 1–17; 14 (1972) 241–57. ———. "Neue Untersuchungen zum Menschensohn-Problem." *TRev* 77 (1981) 353–72. ———. "Kearns, Rollin: Vorfragen zur Christologie. I . . ." *TRev* 77 (1981) 373–78. **Coppens, J.** *Le Fils d'homme vétéro- et intertestamentaire.* Ed. J. Lust. La relève apocalyptique du messianisme royal 2. BETL 61 (1983). ———. "Le messianisme sapiential et les origines littéraires du Fils de l'homme danielique." In *Wisdom in Israel and in the Ancient Near East,* FS H. H. Rowley, ed. M. Noth and D. W. Thomas. VTSup 3 (1955) 33–41. ———. "Le Fils d'homme danielique et les relectures de Dan., vii, 13." *ETL* 37 (1961) 5–51. = Coppens and L. Dequeker, *Le Fils de l'homme et les Saints du Très-Haut en Daniel, vii.* ALBO iii, 23 (1961). 55–101. ———. "Le chapitre vii de Daniel." *ETL* 39 (1963) 87–94. = *MB* 28 (ALBO iv, 8 [1963]) 87–94. ———. "Les Saints du Très-Haut sont-ils à identifier avec les milices célestes?" *ETL* 39 (1963) 94–100. = *MB* 28 [see above] 94–100. ———. "L'origine du symbole du 'Fils d'homme,'" *ETL* 39 (1963) 100–104. = *MB* 28 [see above] 100–104. ———. "Le Serviteur de Yahvé et le Fils d'homme danielique sont-ils des figures messianiques?" *ETL* 39 (1963) 104–14. = *MB* 28 [see above] 104–14. ———. "Les saints dans le Psautier." *ETL* 39 (1963) 485–500. = *Fils d'homme,* 78–93. ———. "Le Fils d'homme danielique, vizir céleste?" *ETL* 40 (1964) 72–80. = *MB* 33 (ALBO iv, 12 [1964]) 72–80. ———. "Les origines du symbole du Fils d'homme en Dan., vii." *ETL* 44 (1968) 497–502. = *MB* 50 (ALBO iv, 46 [1968] 497–502. ———. "Un nouvel essai d'interpréter Dan., vii." *ETL* 45 (1969) 122–25. = *MB* 51 (ALBO iv, 48 [1969]) 122–25. ———. "La vision danielique du Fils d'homme." *VT* 19 (1969) 171–82. ———. "Daniel vii, un rituel d'intronisation?" *ETL* 46 (1970) 112–16. = *MB* 57 (ALBO v, 3 [1970]) 112–16. ———. "La vision du Très-Haut en Dan., vii et Hén. éthiop. xiv." *ETL* 53 (1977) 187–89. = *MB* 85 (ALBO v, 26 [1977]) 187–89. ———. "L'interprétation collective du Fils d'homme danielique." *ETL* 53 (1977) 189–91. = *MB* 86 (ALBO v, 26 [1977]) 189–91. ———. "Le chapitre vii de Daniel." *ETL* 54 (1978) 301–22. = *Fils d'homme,* 28–49. ———. "Dan., vii, 1–18—note additionnelle." *ETL* 55 (1979) 384. ———. "Le dossier non biblique de l'expression araméenne *br ʾnš.*" *ETL* 56 (1980) 122–24. = *Fils d'homme,* 108–11. **Creed, J. M.** "The Heavenly Man." *JTS* 26 (1925) 113–36. **Dalman, G. H.** *Die Worte Jesu.* Leipzig: Hinrichs, 1898. 191–219. = *The Words of Jesus,* tr. D. M. Kay. Edinburgh/New York: Clark/Scribner's, 1902. 234–67. **Day, J.** *God's Conflict with the Dragon and the Sea.* Cambridge/New York: CUP, 1985. **Deissler, A.** "Der 'Menschensohn' und 'das Volk der Heiligen des Höchsten' in Dan 7." In *Jesus und der Menschensohn,* FS A. Vögtle, ed. R. Pesch and R. Schnackenburg. Freiburg: Herder, 1975. 81–91. **Delcor, M.** "Les sources du chapitre vii de Daniel." *VT* 18 (1968) 290–312 = Delcor, *Etudes,* 154–76. **Dequeker, L.** "Daniel vii et les Saints du Très-Haut." *ETL* 36 (1960) 353–92. = ALBO iii, 23 [see Coppens], 15–54. ———. "Les Qedôšîm du Ps. lxxxix à la lumière des croyances sémitiques." *ETL* 39 (1963) 469–84. ———. "The 'Saints of the Most High' in Qumran and Daniel." *OTS* 18 (1973) 108–87. **[Ps-] Dexter, F. L.** [? = J. R. de la Higuera] "In prophetiam Danielis de quatuor animalibus." 1610. Repr. in *PL* 31 (1846) 573–92. **Dhanis, E.** "De filio hominis in Vetere Testamento et in Judaismo." *Gregorianum* 45 (1964) 5–59. **Di Lella, A. A.** "The One in Human Likeness and the Holy Ones of the Most High in Daniel 7." *CBQ* 39 (1977) 1–19. = Hartman, 85–102. **Dodd, C. H.** *According to the Scriptures.* London: Nisbet, 1952/New York: Scribner's, 1953. **Donahue, J. R.** "Recent Studies on the Origin of 'Son of Man' in the Gospels." *CBQ* 48 (1986) 484–98. **Dumbrell, W. J.** "Daniel 7 and the Function of Old Testament Apocalyptic." *Reformed Theological Review* 34 (1975) 16–23. **Emerton, J. A.** "The Origin of the Son of Man Imagery." *JTS* 9 (1958) 225–42. = *The Communication of the Gospel in New Testament Times.* SPCK Theological Collections. London: SPCK, 1961. 35–56. **Engnell,**

I. "E. Sjöberg, *Der Menschensohn im äthiopischen Henochbuch. . . .*" *BO* 8 (1951) 187–92. ———. "Die Urmenschvorstellung und das Alte Testament." *SEA* 22–23 (1957–58) 265–89. ———. "Människosonen." In *Svenskt Bibliskt Uppslagsverk,* ed. I. Engnell. 2nd ed., Stockholm: Nordiska, 1962. 2:229–32. = "The Son of Man" (tr. J. T. Willis), Engnell, *A Rigid Scrutiny.* Nashville: Vanderbilt UP, 1969. 237–41. = *Critical Essays on the Old Testament.* London: SPCK, 1970. 237–41. **Ferch, A. J.** *The Son of Man in Daniel 7.* Berrien Springs, MI: Andrews UP, 1983. Incorporating material from *JBL* 99 (1980) 75–86. **Feuillet, A.** "Le Fils de l'homme de Daniel et la tradition biblique." *RB* 60 (1953) 170–202, 321–46. = Feuillet, *Etudes d'exégèse et de théologie biblique: Ancien Testament.* Paris: Gabalda, 1975. 435–93. **Fiebig, P.** *Der Menschensohn.* Tübingen: Mohr, 1901. **Fitzmyer, J. A.** "The New Testament Title 'Son of Man' Philologically Considered." *Aramaean,* 143–60. ———. "Another View of the 'Son of Man' Debate." *JSNT* 4 (1979) 58–65. **Frank, R. M.** "The Description of the 'Bear' in Dn 7,5." *CBQ* 21 (1959) 505–7. **Gall, A. G. von.** *βασιλεία τοῦ θεοῦ.* Heidelberg: Winter, 1926. **Gaster, M.** "The Son of Man and the Theophany in Daniel, ch. vii." *The Search* 1 (1931) 15–30. **Gaston, L.** "The Son of Man." *No Stone on Another.* NovTSup 23 (1970) 370–409. **Gelston, A.** "A Sidelight on the 'Son of Man.'" *SJT* 22 (1969) 189–96. **Gerlemann, G.** *Der Menschensohn.* Leiden: Brill, 1983. **Gese, H.** "Der Messias." *Zur biblischen Theologie.* Munich: Kaiser, 1977. 128–51. = "The Messiah." *Essays on Biblical Theology,* tr. K. Crim. Minneapolis: Augsburg, 1981. 141–66. ———. "Die Weisheit, der Menschensohn und die Ursprünge der Christologie." *SEA* 44 (1979) 77–114. = "Wisdom, Son of Man, and the Origins of Christology" (tr. U. Mauser). *HBT* 3 (1981) 23–57. **Ginsberg, H. L.** "'King of Kings' and 'Lord of Kingdoms.'" *AJSL* 57 (1940) 71–74. **Glasson, T. F.** *The Second Advent.* London: Epworth, 1943; 3rd ed., 1963. ———. "The Son of Man Imagery." *NTS* 23 (1976–77) 82–90. **Goldingay, J.** "'Holy Ones on High' in Daniel 7:18." *JBL* 107 (1988) 495–97. **Graham, E. A.** "The Heavenly Man." *Church Quarterly Review* 113 [226] (1931–32) 224–39. **Gray, J.** *The Biblical Doctrine of the Reign of God.* Edinburgh: T.&T. Clark, 1979. **Grelot, P.** "Daniel vii, 9–10 et le livre d'Hénoch." *Sem* 28 (1978) 59–83. **Gressmann, H.** *Der Messias.* FRLANT 26 (1929) 343–414. ———. *Der Ursprung der israelitisch-jüdischen Eschatologie.* FRLANT 6 (1905). 334–49. **Gross, H.** "Der Messias im Alten Testament." *TTZ* 71 (1962) 154–70. **Gunkel, H.** *Schöpfung und Chaos in Urzeit und Endzeit.* Göttingen: Vandenhoeck, 1895. 323–35. **Haller, M.** "Das Alter von Daniel 7." *TSK* 93 (1920–21) 83–87. **Hanhart, K.** "The Four Beasts of Daniel's Vision in the Night in the Light of Rev. 13.2." *NTS* 27 (1980–81) 576–83. **Hanhart, R.** "Die Heiligen des Höchsten." *HW* 90–101. **Hardt, H. von der.** *Danielis quatuor animalia. . . .* Helmstadt: Literis Hammianis, [?1710]. **Hasel, G. F.** "The First and Third Years of Belshazzar (Dan 7:1; 8:1)." *AUSS* 15 (1977) 153–68. ———. "The Identity of 'the Saints of the Most High' in Daniel 7." *Bib* 56 (1975) 173–92. **Haupt, P.** "The Son of Man." *The Monist* 29 (1919) 125–33. ———. "Hidalgo and filius hominis." *JBL* 40 (1921) 167–70. **Hertlein, E.** *Die Menschensohnfrage im letzten Stadium.* Berlin: Kohlhammer, 1911. ———. "Die Wolken des 'Menschensohns' (Dan 7 13)." *ZAW* 37 (1917–18) 134–36. **Herzfeld, E.** *Zoroaster and His World.* 2 vols. Princeton: Princeton UP, 1947. **Higgins, A. J. B.** "Son of Man-*Forschung* since 'The Teaching of Jesus.'" In *New Testament Essays,* FS T. W. Manson, ed. A. J. B. Higgins. Manchester: Manchester UP, 1959. 119–35. **Hill, D.** "'Son of Man' in Psalm 80 v. 17." *NovT* 15 (1973) 261–69. **Hommel, F.** "The Apocalyptic Origin of the Expression 'Son of Man.'" *ExpT* 11 (1899–1900) 341–45. **Hooker, M. D.** *The Son of Man in Mark.* London: SPCK, 1967. **Horbury, W.** "The Messianic Associations of 'the Son of Man.'" *JTS* 36 (1985) 34–55. **Kearns, R.** *Vorfragen zur Christologie.* 3 vols. Tübingen: Mohr, 1978, 1980, 1982. **Kim, S.** *"The 'Son of Man'" as the Son of God.* WUNT 30. Tübingen: Mohr, 1983/Grand Rapids: Eerdmans, 1985. **Kobelski, P. J.** *Melchizedek and Melchirešaʿ.* CBQ MS 10 (1981). **Koep, L.** *Das himmlische Buch im Antike und Christen-*

tum. Bonn: Hanstein, 1952. **König, E.** "Der Menschensohn im Danielbuche." *NKZ* 16 (1905) 904–28. **Kraeling, C. H.** *Anthropos and Son of Man.* New York: Columbia UP, 1927. **Kraeling, E. G. H.** "Some Babylonian and Iranian Mythology in the Seventh Chapter of Daniel." *OrSt* 228–32. **Kristensen, W. B.** "De term 'Zoon des Menschen.'" *Theologisch Tijdschrift* 45 (1911) 1–38. **Kruse, H.** "Compositio Libri Danielis et idea Filii Hominis." *VD* 37 (1959) 147–61, 193–211. **Kvanvig, H. S.** "Struktur und Geschichte in Dan 7, 1–14." *ST* 32 (1978) 95–117. ———. "An Akkadian Vision as Background for Dan 7." *ST* 35 (1981) 85–89. ———. "Henoch und der Menschensohn." *ST* 38 (1984) 101–33. **Lacocque, A.** "The Vision of the Eagle in 4 Esdras, a Rereading of Daniel 7 in the First Century C.E." *SBLSP* 20 (1981) 237–58. **Lamberigts, S.** "Le sens de qdwšym dans les textes de Qumrân." *ETL* 46 (1970) 24–39. = ALBO v, 1 (1970). **Lust, J.** "Daniel 7, 13 and the Septuagint." *ETL* 54 (1978) 62–69. **Luther, M.** "Heerpredigt wider den Türken." 1529. *WA* 30, 2:149–97. **Maddox, R.** "The Quest for Valid Methods in 'Son of Man' Research." *ABR* 19 (1971) 36–51. **Manson, T. W.** "The Son of Man in Daniel, Enoch, and the Gospels." *BJRL* 32 (1949–50) 171–93. = Manson, *Studies in the Gospels and Epistles.* Manchester: Manchester UP, 1962. 123–45. **Marlow, R.** "The *Son of Man* in Recent Journal Literature." *CBQ* 28 (1966) 20–30. **Marsch, E.** *Biblische Prophetie und chronographische Dichtung: Stoff- und Wirkungsgeschichte der Vision des Propheten Daniel nach Dan. vii.* Berlin: Schmidt, 1972. **Marshall, I. H.** "The Son of Man in Contemporary Debate." *EvQ* 42 (1970) 67–87. **Moloney, F. J.** "The End of the Son of Man?" *Downside Review* 98 (1980) 280–90. **More, J.** *A Trumpet Sounded: or, The Great Mystery of the Two Little Horns Unfolded. . . .* [London], 1654. **Morenz, S.** "Das Tier mit den Hörnern." *ZAW* 63 (1951) 151–54. = Morenz, *Religion und Geschichte des alten Ägypten.* Cologne: Böhlau, 1975. 429–32. **Morgenstern, J.** "The 'Son of Man' of Daniel 7 13f." *JBL* 80 (1961) 65–77. ———. "Jesus as the 'Son of Man.'" *Some Significant Antecedents of Christianity* SPB 10 (1966) 61–80. **Mosca, P. G.** "Ugarit and Daniel 7." *Bib* 67 (1986) 496–517. **Moule, C. F. D.** "From Defendant to Judge—and Deliverer." *Bulletin of the Studiorum Novi Testamenti Societas* 3 (1952) 40–53. = Moule, *The Phenomenon of the New Testament.* SBT ii, 1 (1967) 82–99. ———. "Neglected Features in the Problem of 'the Son of Man.'" In *Neues Testament und Kirche,* FS R. Schnackenburg, ed. J. Gnilka. Freiburg: Herder, 1974. 413–28. = Moule, *Essays in New Testament Interpretation.* Cambridge/New York: CUP, 1982. 75–90. **Mowinckel, S.** *He That Cometh.* Nashville: Abingdon, 1955/Oxford: Blackwell, 1956. Tr. G. W. Anderson from *Han son kommer.* Copenhagen: Gad, 1951. ———. "Urmensch und 'Königsideologie.'" *ST* 2 (1948) 71–89. **Muilenburg, J.** "The Son of Man in Daniel and the Ethiopic Apocalypse of Enoch." *JBL* 79 (1960) 197–209. **Müller, K.** "Beobachtungen zur Entwicklung der Menschensohnvorstellung in den Bilderreden des Henoch und im Buche Daniel." In *Wegzeichen,* FS H. M. Biedermann, ed. E. C. Suttner and C. Patock. Das östliche Christentum 25. Würzburg: Augustinus, 1971. 253–61. ———. "Menschensohn und Messias." *BZ* 16 (1972) 161–87; 17 (1973) 52–66. ———. "Der Menschensohn im Danielzyklus." In *Jesus und der Menschensohn,* FS A. Vögtle, ed. R. Pesch and R. Schnackenburg. Freiburg: Herder, 1975. **Müller, U. B.** *Messias und Menschensohn in jüdischen Apokalypsen und in der Offenbarung des Johannes.* Gütersloh: Mohn, 1972. **Niditch, S.** *Vision,* 177–215. **Noth, M.** *TSK* 98–99 (1926) 143–63. = Noth, *Studien* 2:11–28. ———. "Die Heiligen des Höchsten." In *Interpretationes ad Vetus Testamentum pertinentes,* FS S. Mowinckel, *Norsk teologisk tidsskrift* 56 (1955) 146–61. = Noth, *Studien,* 274–90. = "The Holy Ones of the Most High." *Laws,* 215–28. **Orrieux, L.-M.** "Le problème du Fils de l'Homme dans la littérature apocalyptique." *LumVie* 12 [62] (1963) 9–31. **Owen, J.** "Concerning the kingdom of Christ, and the power of the civil magistrate about the things of the worship of God." 1652. = *The Works of John Owen.* Repr. London: Banner of Truth, 1967. 7:365–95. **Perrin, N.** "The Son of Man in Ancient Judaism and Primitive Christianity." *BR* 11 (1966) 17–

28. Cf. Perrin, *Rediscovering the Teaching of Jesus.* London/New York: SCM/Harper, 1967. 164–99. ———. "The Interpretation of a Biblical Symbol." *JR* 55 (1975) 348–70. Cf. Perrin, *Kingdom,* 15–88. **Porter, P. A.** *Metaphors and Monsters: A Literary-Critical Study of Daniel 7 and 8.* ConB OT Series 20 (1983). **Poythress, V. S.** "The Holy Ones of the Most High in Daniel vii." *VT* 26 (1976) 208–13. **Procksch, O.** "Die Berufungsvision Hesekiels." In *Beiträge zur alttestamentlichen Wissenschaft,* FS K. Budde, ed. K. Marti. BZAW 34 (1920). 141–49. ———. "Christus im Alten Testament." *NKZ* 44 (1933) 57–83. **Proudman, C. L. J.** "Remarks on the 'Son of Man.'" *CJT* 12 (1966) 128–31. **Raabe, P. R.** "Daniel 7." *Hebrew Annual Review* 9 (1985) 267–75. **Rhodes, A. B.** "The Kingdoms of Men and the Kingdom of God." *Int* 15 (1961) 411–30. **Rimbach, J. A.** "Bears or Bees? Sefire I A 31 and Daniel 7." *JBL* 97 (1978) 565–66. **Rost, L.** "Zur Deutung des Menschensohnes in Daniel 7." In *Gott und die Götter,* FS E. Fascher, ed. G. Delling. Berlin: Evangelische, 1958. 41–43. = Rost, *Studien zum Alten Testament.* BWANT 101 (1974) 72–75. **Rowe, R. D.** "Is Daniel's 'Son of Man' Messianic?" In *Christ the Lord,* FS D. Guthrie, ed. H. H. Rowdon. Leicester/Downers Grove, IL: IVP, 1982. 71–96. **Roxas, A. de.** *Commentarii in Apocalypsin, et in cap. iv. Zachariae, et vii. Danielis.* Seville: Diaz, 1732. 526–42. **Sahlin, H.** "Wie wurde ursprünglich die Benennung 'Der Menschensohn' verstanden?" *ST* 37 (1983) 147–79. **Schaberg, J.** "Daniel 7, 12 and the New Testament Passion-Resurrection Predictions." *NTS* 31 (1985) 208–22. **Scheifler, J. R.** "El hijo del hombre en Daniel." *Estudios Eclesiásticos* 34 (1960) 789–804. **Schmid, H.** "Daniel, der Menschensohn." *Judaica* 27 (1971) 192–220. **Schmidt, N.** "The 'Son of Man' in the Book of Daniel." *JBL* 19 (1900) 22–28. **Schweizer, E.** "The Son of Man Again." *NTS* 9 (1962–63) 256–61. **Scott, R. B. Y.** "Behold, He Cometh with Clouds." *NTS* 5 (1958–59) 127–32. **Shea, W. H.** "The neo-Babylonian Historical Setting for Daniel 7." *AUSS* 24 (1986) 31–36. **Sjöberg, E.** "בן אדם und בר אנש im Hebräischen und Aramäischen." *AcOr* 21 (1950–53) 57–65, 91–107. **Smith, M. S.** "The 'Son of Man' in Ugaritic." *CBQ* 45 (1983) 59–60. **Sokoloff, M.** "'*ʿămar nĕqēʾ*, 'Lamb's Wool' (Dan 7:9)." *JBL* 95 (1976) 277–79. **Staub, U.** "Das Tier mit den Hörnern." *FZPT* 25 (1978) 351–97. **Stott, W.** "'Son of Man'—a Title of Abasement." *ExpT* 83 (1971–72) 278–81. **Süring, M. L.** "The Horn-motifs of the Bible and the Ancient Near East." *AUSS* 22 (1984) 31–36. **Theisohn, J.** *Der auserwählte Richter.* SUNT 12 (1975). **Tillman, F.** "Der Menschensohn." In *Biblische Studien,* ed. O. Bardenhewer, xii, 1. Freiburg: Herder, 1907. **Towner, W. S.** "Were the English Puritans 'the Saints of the Most High'?" *Int* 37 (1983) 46–63. **Tuckett, C.** "Recent Work on the Son of Man." *Scripture Bulletin* 12 (1981) 14–18. **Vermes, G.** *Jesus the Jew.* London: Collins, 1973/New York: Macmillan, 1974. 160–91. ———. "The Use of בר נש/בר נשא in Jewish Aramaic." In M. Black, *An Aramaic Approach to the Gospels and Acts.* 3rd ed. Oxford: Clarendon, 1967. 310–20. = Vermes, *Post-Biblical Jewish Studies.* SJLA 8 (1975) 147–65. ———. "The Present State of the 'Son of Man' Debate." *JJS* 29 (1978) 123–34. = [abbreviated] *JSNT* 1 (1978) 19–32. = Vermes, *Jesus and the World of Judaism.* London: SCM, 1983/Philadelphia: Fortress, 1984. 89–99. **Völter, D.** "Der Menschensohn in Dan 7, 13." *ZNW* 3 (1902) 173–74. **Wagner, M.** "Der Menschensohn." *NKZ* 36 (1925) 245–78. **Walker, W. O.** "Daniel 7:13–14." *Int* 39 (1985) 176–81. **Walvoord, J. F.** *BSac* 124 (1967) 99–105. **Waterman, L.** "A Gloss on Darius the Mede in Daniel 7 5" *JBL* 65 (1946) 59–61. **Weimar, P.** "Daniel 7. Eine Textanalyse." In *Jesus und der Menschensohn,* FS A. Vögtle, ed. R. Pesch and R. Schnackenburg. Freiburg: Herder, 1975. 11–36. **Wifall, W.** "Son of Man—a Pre-Davidic Social Class?" *CBQ* 37 (1975) 331–40. ———. "David—Prototype of Israel's Future?" *BTB* 4 (1974) 94–107. **Wilson, F. M.** "The Son of Man in Jewish Apocalyptic Literature." *Studia biblica et theologica* 8 (1978) 28–52. **Wittstruck, T.** "The Influence of Treaty Curse Imagery on the Beast Imagery of Daniel 7." *JBL* 97 (1978) 100–102. **Young, E. J.** *Daniel's Vision of the Son of Man.* London: Tyndale, 1958. Repr.

in *The Law and the Prophets*, FS O. T. Allis, ed. J. H. Skilton. [Nutley, NJ]: PRPC, 1974. 425–51. **Zevit, Z.** "The Structure and Individual Elements of Daniel 7." *ZAW* 80 (1968) 385–96.

On the four kingdoms, see also chap. 2 *Bibliography.*

Translation

1 *In the first year of Belshazzar,*[a] *king of Babylon, Daniel had a dream,* [b]*a*
vision which came into his head as he lay in bed.[b] *He wrote the dream down.*
[c]*The beginning of the account:*[c] 2 *Daniel related,*[a] *"I watched in my vision during*[b]
the night, and there before me were the four winds of the heavens stirring up[c] *the*
Great Sea, 3 *and four huge animals coming up out of the sea, each differing from*
the others. 4 *The first was like a lion, but it had the wings of an eagle.*[a] *I watched*
as its wings were plucked off; it was raised[b] *from the ground* [c]*and lifted up*[d] *on*
[e]*two feet*[e] *like a man, and a man's mind was given to it.*[c] 5 *Then there before me*
was a second animal, a different[a] *one. It resembled a bear, but it was lifted up*[b]
on one side.[c] [d]*It had three ribs*[e] *in its mouth, between its teeth. It was told, "Get*
up, eat lots of meat."[d] 6 *After that I watched and there before me was another*[a]
like a leopard, but it had four bird's wings on its back.[b] *The animal also had four*
heads, and authority was given to it. 7 *After that, as I watched in the vision during*
the night, there before me was a fourth animal, fearful and terrifying,[a] *extraordinarily*
strong and with big iron teeth,[b] *eating and crushing and trampling underfoot*
what was left: it behaved differently[c] *from all the animals before it. It also had ten*
horns. 8 *As I looked at the horns, there before me another, small horn came up*[a]
among them, and three of the first horns were uprooted[b] *before it. And there in*
this horn were eyes[c] *like a man's and a mouth* [d]*making great statements.*[d]

9 *I watched*
as thrones were [a]*set in place*[a]
and one advanced in years[b] *took his seat.*
His clothing was [c]*like white snow,*[c]
the hair on his head like lamb's[d] *wool.*
His throne was flashes of flame,
his rings[e] *a blazing flame.*
10 *A stream of flame was surging forth,*
issuing from his presence.
Thousand upon thousand ministered to him,
myriad upon myriad stood in attendance on him.
The court sat and books were opened.

11 [a]*I watched then from the time when I heard the sound*[a] *of the great statements*
which the horn was making, watched as the animal was killed and its body destroyed;
it was put [b]*into fire for burning.*[b] 12 *The rest of the animals had*[a] *their authority*
taken away, but they were[a] *given an extension*[b] *to their lives for a set period of*
time.

13 *As I watched in the vision by night, there before me*
among[a] *the clouds of the heavens*
one in human likeness[b] *was coming.*
He went to[c] *the one advanced in years*
and was presented before him.

14 *To him was given glorious kingly authority*
so that people of all races, nations, and languages would honor[a] *him;*
his authority would last for ever and not pass away,
and his kingship would not be destroyed.

15 *I, Daniel,*[a] [b]*was disturbed in spirit*[b] *at this. The visions that came into my*
head alarmed me. 16 *I approached one of those who stood in attendance to ask*[a]
him the true meaning of all this, and he told me he would explain[a] *to me the*
interpretation of the matter.
17 *'These huge animals of which there were four: four kings*[a] *will arise from the*
world, 18 *but holy ones on high*[a] *will acquire the kingship. They will take hold of*
the kingship for ever, until the very end.' 19 *Then I wanted to know the true meaning*
of the fourth animal which differed from all the others, being extraordinarily fearful,
with its iron teeth and bronze claws, eating, crushing, and trampling underfoot
what was left; 20 *and of the ten horns on its head and the other one which came*
up and three fell[a] *before it, that horn which had eyes and a mouth making great*
statements and which looked bigger[b] *than its companions.* 21 *I watched*[a] *while that*
horn was making war on holy beings and overcoming them, 22 *as the one advanced*
in years came and judgment was given[a] *for*[b] *holy ones on high, when the time*
came for holy ones to take hold of the kingship.

23 *He said, 'The fourth animal:*
there will be a fourth kingship in the world.
It will differ from[a] *all the other kingships.*
It will consume the whole world,
trample it down and crush it.

24 *The ten horns:*
from that[a] *kingship ten kings will arise,*
but another will arise after them.
He will differ from the ones before him.
He will lay low three kings.

25 *He will make statements hostile to the Most High*
and oppress[a] *holy ones on high.*
He will try to change [b]*times set by decree*[b]
and they[c] *will be given into his control*
for a period, periods,[d] *and half a period.*

26 *But the court will sit and his authority will be taken away,*
to be completely and permanently destroyed.

27 *The mighty kingly authority*
of the kingships under the whole heavens
will have been given[a] *to a holy people*[b] *on high.*
Its kingship will be one that stands for ever;
every authority will honor and show obedience to it.' "

28 *That is the end of the account. "I, Daniel, was very alarmed in my thinking*
and my face turned pale, but I kept this matter in my own mind."[a]

Notes

1.a. On the spelling, see n. 5:30.a.

1.b-b. *Waw* explicative (see n. 6:29.a). The double description of the dream vision is characteristic of Dan style (Plöger deletes the whole phrase); cf. esp. 4:2 [5]. Hartman adds the vb יבהלנה (alarmed him; cf. NAB), comparing 4:2, 19 [5, 22]; 7:15; but in those verses the refs to the visionary being disturbed by his dream are also repeated, whereas there are no such refs at all in 7:1. Dramatically, Daniel's response is reserved for v 15. On pl חזוי "visions" see n. 2:1.a.

1.c-c. ראש מלין and the phrase in v 28a seem to open and close Daniel's account of the dream (cf. JB). Thus the phrase here cannot mean "a summary of matters" (cf. OG). The אמר "he said" which follows may be a gl (G lacks), perhaps presupposing the alternative meaning of ראש מלין (cf. RV); or perhaps its redundancy relates to problems in v 2 (see n. 2.a). Th omits the whole phrase but has the subscription in v 28.

2.a. NEB omits ואמר and ענה and follows Th (cf. OG); but the Aram. flavor of this phrase may suggest it is original (Montgomery).

2.b. Perh. "through": cf the עם in 3:33 [4:3]; 4:31 [34]; Ps 72:5.

2.c. BDB 1127 takes מגיחן as intrans (cf. RV); more likely it is trans (cf. instances of the qal in BH) and ל is the sign of the obj, as often in BA (for "upon" על would be more natural).

4.a. Perh. "vulture" (Driver), but see BDB 676–77.

4.b. See Rowley, *VT* 5 (1955) 274–76, against Ginsberg; also *DTT*.

4.c-c. Ginsberg moves this cl to v 5 to follow ולשטר חד הקמת "it had lifted up one side." Cf. n. 5.d-d.

4.d. The form הֳקִימַת is surprising (cf. *GBA* 140) and may be a mixed form, the first vowel suggesting ho, the י suggesting haphel (?impersonal), so that the tr is the same. It corresponds to the Arabic equivalent to hophal (BL 28s), but would be the only such form in Dan (Ginsberg, 2–3: he emends).

4.e-e. "Wings" גַּפִּין was pointed as pl, רַגְלַיִן "feet" as dual (also שִׁנַּיִן "teeth" [!—the reference being to two jaws] and קַרְנַיִן "horns" [!—because they usually come in pairs] in v 7). In later Aram. and Syriac the dual disappears, and this has probably affected MT pointing in Dan; some MT plurals will thus have been originally dual.

5.a. JB (cf. the BH usage, BDB 29). If אחרי simply means "another," either it or תנינה "second" looks redundant; G, Syr have equivalents to only one of the two words. Perh. MT conflates (Charles).

5.b. Ben Chayyim's ed. (cf. BDB) points הֲקֵמַת (ha); but this involves taking לשטר חד "on one side" as direct obj, whereas ל can hardly be obj marker since the noun is abs. L's הֳקֵמַת is apparently another mixed form (cf. n. 4.d.): ho is easier, since here the vb cannot be impersonal. Cf. G ἐστάθη; but Syr has *qmt* (peal), Vg *stetit*. As in v 4, the vb must be taken in an aorist (or plupf) sense—it does not mean "it was in a state of having been lifted up" (see BL 83b).

5.c. שטר; RVmg "dominion" presupposes the alternative but inferior reading שטר (cf. BH משטר); cf. Waterman, *JBL* 65 (1946) 59–61. It is doubtful if שטר can mean "end" (suggesting the bear lifting itself up on its hind legs; GNB, Hartman).

5.d-d. Ginsberg moves to v 4 (cf. n. 4.c-c); but if this "improves" the picture, that does not make it original. The similarity between Ginsberg's text and Rev 13:1 (Hartman) is not so marked that Rev must presuppose Ginsberg's text; the similarity reflects the fact that both are more naturalistic than Dan 7:4–5 MT (Coppens, *Fils d'homme*, 29–30).

5.e. עלעין; JPS "fangs" follows Vg *ordines* "rows [of teeth]," Ps-Saadia and Arabic usage (though cf. BH מתלעות); see Frank, *CBQ* 21 (1959) 505–7. But would עלעין have been understood here as "fangs," given the usual meaning "ribs" in Aram. (cf. BH צלע)?

6.a. Perh. add חיוה "animal" (Kallarakkal, 72, following G, Syr).

6.b. Perh. Q גבה is s and means "back," K גביה pl and means "sides" (cf. JB). But Q regularly spells pl suffixes defectively (cf. גפה/גפיה "its wings" in v 4, שנה/שניה "its teeth" in v 5); thus גבה could also mean "sides."

7.a. RV "powerful" follows a dubious Arabic etymology for the reading אמתני instead of אימתני (for which cf. BH אים) (Montgomery).

7.b. Dual: see n. 4.e-e.

7.c. משניה (pa: cf. Montgomery). Form and meaning are the same whether parsed act or pass (*GBA* 67; *DTT* 1605–6).

8.a. סָלְקַת seems to be a mixed form, a cross between pf סִלְקַת (read by some mss) and ptpl סָלְקָה. Ptpl appears in v 3 and might have been expected after אלו "there before me," but pf vb comes in v 20 and the following vb is also pf; an original pf might have been influenced by the ptpl in v 3.

8.b. אתעקרו: see n. 5:5.a.

8.c. עינין, pl not dual, which might denote that the horn had many eyes (cf. Ezekiel's chariot wheels); but see n. 4.e-e.

8.d-d. ממלל רברבן (cf. v 20) is not unequivocally negative, the explication being kept for v 21 for dramatic effect (against OG, Charles, Niditch [*Vision*, 180–82] who add an explicative phrase here).

9.a-a. RVmg "cast down" follows the more common meaning of רמא (cf. Ps-Saadia); but ref to the casting down of the animals' thrones is out of place here. See BDB for the meaning "set."

9.b. Lit., "days." The phrase is a fairly straightforward one for someone of great age; cf. the use of עתק "advance" in Job 21:7 and of בא בימים "gone [on] in days" in Gen 24:1. Cf. the descriptions of God in Ps 9:8 [7]; 29:10; 90:2; also Sir 25:4.

9.c-c. כתלג חור; following MT accents and OG (contrast EVV "white as snow" [cf. Th]; next half-line כעמר נקא MT, G "clean as wool"). Cf. also the final two half-lines of v 9, which lack כ "like/as" but are similar in structure.

9.d. Taking נקא as from נקי/נקא ii (*DTT*) with Sokoloff, *JBL* 95 (1976) 277–79; "clean" (נקי/נקא i) (EVV) would be a Hebraism (though cf. *1 Enoch* 106.2; Rev 1:14; and Hebraisms are not out of place in Dan 7). See also n. 9.c-c.

9.e. גלגלוהי: EVV "its wheels," but in descriptions of God's fiery throne the motif of the sun has a natural place (cf. *1 Enoch* 14.8–22) and I take this to be the ref here (cf. Grelot, *Sem* 28 [1978] 80–81; Kearns, *Vorfragen* 3:179–81).

11.a-a. חזה הוית באדין מן קל raises three problems. (i) חזה הוית "I was watching" is repeated later in v 11; G lacks the repetition, but not Vg, and cf. the resumptive repetition in 9:1–2 (Driver notes also Lev 17:5; Judg 11:31; Zech 8:23). (ii) Elsewhere in BA באדין "then" always appears at the beginning of a sentence—though cf. 1QapGen 22.2 (Casey). (iii) מן could mean "from" (cf. JB, GNB) or "because of" (NEB, RSV). Now מן אדין "from that time" occurs once in BA, in Ezra 5:16; it does not come at the beginning of the sentence, and it is followed by עד "until." Apparently באדין מן here, followed by עד (here translated "as") has a similar meaning; cf. Montgomery's comparison with BH מאז. The cl as a whole is thus unusual, but the text need not be questioned. Syr omits v 11a (homoioarkton?): see Kallarakkal, 52–53.

11.b-b. ליקדת אשא: "the burning of fire," not, strictly, "burning fire." Cf. Isa 64:10 [9] אש לשרפת.

12.a. The first vb (NIV) or the second (Calvin) or both (Plöger) have been taken to be plupf, but this involves reading back from the interpretative vision or from the assumed historical reference.

12.b. ארכה: perh. "limit" (Tg. Gen 6:3).

13.a. Cf. Th; Mark 14:62; Rev 1:7. עם could mean "in," as in v 2 (cf. Mark 13:26; Luke 21:27). OG, Matt 24:30; 26:64 have "on": Yahweh can be spoken of as "in" or "on" the clouds, so this hardly proves an original על—translations anyway vary in their rendering of prepositions and are poor grounds for emendation (see Scott, *NTS* 5 [1958–59] 128).

13.b. כבר אנש "[one] like a son of man." The BH equivalent בן אדם appears in poetic passages in parallelism with some other word for "man" (e.g., Ps 80:18 [17]; Job 16:21), but most commonly in Ezek to suggest mere man (e.g., 2:1, cf. Dan 8:17). In later Aram. בר אנש is a more prosaic term for "a man," an alternative to אנש (v 4), though in a poetic context such as this it might add solemnity (Sjöberg, *AcOr* 21 [1951] 105). It might originally have meant "a son of somebody," i.e., a significant person (Haupt, *JBL* 40 [1921] 167–70); cf. Kearns's connecting it with a different Sem. word for a vassal landowner, later provided with a false etymology (*Vorfragen*, Teil 1). Gerlemann's proposal (*Menschensohn*, 1–13) that בר here means not "son of" but "set apart from [humanity]" seems implausibly imaginative.

13.c. OG apparently has ὡς "as" not ἕως (cf. Rahlfs; Ziegler emends). It thus identifies the human figure and the one advanced in years. Lust thinks this reflects an old, pre-MT, Heb. text (*ETL* 54 [1978] 62–69), but this makes poor sense of vv 9–14 as a whole. More likely it reflects OG midrash (F. F. Bruce, "The Oldest Greek Version of Daniel," *OTS* 20 [1977] 25–26], perhaps subsequent to the main translation since OG elsewhere does not suggest that the human figure is divine (Pace, 257–60).

14.a. Elsewhere BA פלח refers only to revering God, but outside the OT it denotes service more generally (KB, *DTT*).

15.a. The seer mentions himself as he comes to himself (Montgomery): cf. 7:28; 8:15, 27. Lit., "My spirit was disturbed, I, Daniel . . .": the pronoun referring back to the suffix is emphatic.

15.b-b. אתכרית רוחי . . . בגוא נדנה "my spirit was disturbed in the midst of the sheath." נִדְנֶה should probably be repointed נְדָנָה (Brockington); cf. the form of the phrase in 1QapGen 2.10. That occurrence makes other proposed emendations (cf. BHS) less plausible.

16.a. Taking impf אבעא and יהודענני as not merely temporally consecutive in relation to the preceding vbs, but as indicating purpose and indirect speech respectively.

17.a. מלכין; the kings stand for their kingdoms (cf. NIV; 2:38; 7:23; 8:20–22). There is hardly need to emend the text to make the point explicit (against BHS, NEB, following G).

18.a. Cf. Calvin, Lacocque; GKC 124q for the use of a second pl when the expression as a whole is pl (and indeterminate [Ginsberg, 71]); against the usual view that עליונין is pl of majesty (see Goldingay, *JBL* 107 [1988] 495–97). "Holy ones of the Most High" would be קדישי עליון (CD 20.8); cf. the use of s עליא for "the Most High" in v 25. The Hebraism only occurs in this phrase (cf. vv 22, 25, 27); it may be a distinctive expression used among those the book is written for.

20.a. נפלו: see n. 5:5.a.

20.b. חזוה רב "its appearance [was] greater": cf. expressions in 4:8, 17 [11, 20].

21.a. חזה הוית; JB "I had watched" reflects the fact that this detail might have been expected to come earlier (hence some scholars see vv 21–22 as later expansion). But it is a standard phrase which must surely have its standard meaning.

22.a. יְהִב: BHS reports a variant reading יְהַב "he gave," reflected in G, Syr, Vg.

22.b. ל; not "to" (G, RV). The holy ones, whether angels or the people of God, do elsewhere share in judgment with God (cf. the allusion in Rev 20:4), but here the judgment is given on their behalf rather than exercised by them. God is judge (vv 9–14). Ewald suggested that two words had been omitted and that the text should read . . . ודינא יתב ושלטנא יהב "the court sat [cf. v 10] and authority was given [cf. v 27] . . ."; cf. BHS).

23.a. תשנא; Th ὑπερέξει "excel" as if from a different vb שנא (see J. A. Emerton, "The Meaning of *šēnā'* in Psalm cxxvii 2," *VT* 24 [1974] 25–30); but in the context of a number of usages of שנא "change" in Dan 7 (see esp. v 7), תשנא here can hardly be connected with a different vb.

24.a. See BL 74a.

25.a. בלא (lit., "wear out"), cf. BH בלה in 1 Chr 17:9. There is thus no need to posit another בלא related to an Arabic vb "offend" (against Noth, *Studien*, 286 [ET 224–25]).

25.b-b. זמנין ודת "times and law" taken as hendiadys, a frequent device in chap. 7. On דת, see n. 6:6.b.

25.c. Presumably the times (so G), not the holy ones: the former is the antecedent and this makes entire sense (see *Comment*).

25.d. עדנין should presumably here be taken as dual (see n. 4.e-e).

27.a. יהיבת; cf. Bevan for the future pf, comparing נעשתה "will have been achieved" in 11:36.

27.b. Taking the constr chain as exegetical throughout ("a people consisting in holy ones who are on high") rather than possessive throughout ("a people that belongs to holy ones who belong to the Most High"): see *Comment*.

28.a. בלבי probably suggests "to myself" (JB); this is the implication of the equivalent expression in *T. Levi* 6.2; 8.19 (and Luke 2:19?).

Form / Structure / Setting

Form

See also chap. 2 *Form*. Dan 7 is the report of a dream or nocturnal vision. Characteristic expressions are verbs for "watch" (חזה, שכל), followed by temporal expressions such as עד די (lit., "until") or באדין מן "from the time when" or by the particle ואלו/וארו "and there before me" and the preposition כ "like." The opening half recounts a symbolic dream, set in a standard brief narrative context recording the date at the beginning and the visionary's troubled response at the end (vv 1, 15). It relates first a description of an allegorical animal vision, introduced by a fragment of myth (vv 2–8, partly recapitulated and expanded in vv 19–21; the interpretation [v 17] will make explicit that it offers an allegorical periodization of history). It goes on to a judgment scene (vv 9–14), which itself incorporates descriptions of one seated on a divine throne (vv 9–10) and of the appearing of a second heavenly figure (vv 13–14) (see Black on the "throne-theophany" form). The significance of vv 9–10, 13–14 is emphasized and their effect heightened by their being expressed in a rhythmic, elevated style, with instances of the parallelism characteristic of Semitic poetry, and instances of simile and metaphor. The pattern of vv 8–11 (presentation of wrongdoing, judgment scene, implementation of punishment) suggests that of the secular/prophetic lawsuit (Niditch, *Vision*, 202).

The second half reports the interpretation of the symbolic dream. A standard brief narrative context reports the subject's seeking the interpretation (v 16) and his reaction to it (v 28). The initial interpretation is brief (vv 17–18) and in response to the subject's supplementary request (vv 19–22) later verses add a more detailed explanation of part of the symbolism (vv 23–27). Rhythm and parallelism reappear here at a further key point in the chapter, though with less consistency and with less heightened effect than in vv 9–10, 13–14 (because of the more prosaic subject-matter?), so that some interpreters print them as prose. Niditch (*Vision*, 189–93) points out that rhythm, parallelism, and other rhetorical devices also appear elsewhere in Dan 7; a division between poetic prose and actual poetry is hard to make. The interpretation of the symbolic dream takes place within the context of the dream itself. This thus compares more closely with the nocturnal visions in Zech 1–6 and in 2 Esd 11–13—though in the latter the interpreter is God himself—and with the vision in Dan 8, than with those in Dan 2; 4, where a human interpreter explains the dream after it is over, and where the story in which the dream report is set has a significance in its own right far exceeding that of the mere narrative framework of chap. 7: here the dream is everything. The interpretation takes the form of political oracles (vv 17, 23–25) that lead into eschatological oracles (vv 18, 26–27). The combination of forms parallels that in the "Animal Apocalypse," *1 Enoch* 85–90, which addresses the Maccabean crisis (see Porter, *Metaphors*, 43–60). Such parallels suggest that the political oracles are quasi-prophecies, not actual ones (see further chaps. 10–12 *Form*). The self-presentation formula "I, Daniel" supports this view; it is characteristically a formula of self-presentation by someone who cannot be seen or who speaks through someone else (e.g., a prophet, a messenger, or a medium). The chapter as a whole is thus often assumed to be a literary creation, not the report of an actual dream (Murdock, *Int* 21 [1967] 181–82), but this need not follow (Gaston, NovTSup 23 [1970] 377–78).

The dream involves myth, symbol, allegory, scriptural allusion, and revelation concerning things above and things future. It both reveals and conceals, by the interpretation (e.g., v 25b) as well as by the symbolic dream. The response it twice attributes to Daniel (vv 15, 28) is the response these seek to evoke in the reader.

Dan 7 uses symbolism in varied ways. Its symbols have been viewed as a code: lion = Babylon, leopard = Persia or Greece, small horn = Antiochus or some other historical or future person. . . . Such identities can be substituted for their ciphers without losing anything except a slight air of mystery, which might have enabled the author to escape the attention of the authorities. This is an oversimple view. The symbols are not a random allegorical code speaking of realities that could just as adequately be referred to directly; they contribute to the text's meaning. Thus when vv 17–27 add a God-given interpretation to the God-given revelation in vv 2–14, some of the symbolism remains (e.g., v 26), and even where symbols are in some way interpreted by other terms, the "explanatory" term may still not be a straightforward one (e.g., "holy ones"). Allusiveness remains.

Part of the symbols' significance is that they function like similes. The entities described have features of the symbol. Thus a horn suggests strength; or the interrelationships of the symbols may be significant: for example, the movement between the animal and the human. Beyond that, individual symbols belong to systems and thus call to mind "numerous ideas, images, sentiments, values and stereotypes" which are (selectively) projected on the entity symbolized (Porter, *Metaphors,* 5, following M. Black; Porter further suggests that the "root metaphor" of the shepherd underlies Dan 7 and 8 as a whole—though shepherds are never actually mentioned). In P. Ricoeur's terminology, they are symbols, not merely signs; in P. Wheelwright's terminology, they are tensive symbols, not steno-symbols (see Perrin, *Kingdom,* 29–31). As symbol and not merely metaphor, the figures in Dan 7 come from public usage. They are not an individual poet's new minting. They thus bring with them the resonances and the hallowing of tradition, the more so where they come from the community's sacred scriptures. It is yet more so in the case of mythic symbols that make it possible to refer to transcendent realities.

Influences and traditions that may underlie the dream.

(a) *Earlier chapters of Daniel.* The motif of the symbolic dream itself goes back to Dan 2 and 4; the four kings/regimes motif takes up that of chap. 2. The description of the first animal parallels that of Nebuchadnezzar in chap. 4; those of the third and fourth animal parallel those of the corresponding regimes in chap. 2. Since the lion represents Babylon, the lion's being the most "human" of the creatures corresponds to the Babylonian king's position as world ruler in chaps. 2, 4, and 5, while the power given to the humanlike figure in relation to power the animals had exercised is that ascribed to the Babylonian king over the animals in 2:37–38; cf. 5:18–19 (Porter, *Metaphors,* 111–12). For particular phrases, see 2:1 (v 1, the date formula); 2:28; 4:2 [5] (v 1); 5:19 (v 14, people of all nations, races, and languages); 2:44; 3:33 [4:3]; 4:31 [34]; 6:26 [27] (vv 14, 26–27, the lasting reign); 2:1; 4:2, 16 [5, 19]; 5:6, 9, 10 (vv 15–16, 28); 2:9, 21 (v 25, times set by decree); 4:13, 20, 22 [16, 23, 25] (v 25, 3½ periods).

(b) *Other parts of the OT.* Animals feature throughout the OT in metaphor, simile, and allegory, to portray God, Israel, leaders or nobles, and other nations. Dan 7's particular sequence recalls Hos 13:7–8 and Jer 5:6. The former likens Yahweh to a lion, a leopard, a bear, a lion (though see BHS), and finally "the creature of the wild"—unidentified, as in Dan 7. Jer 5:6 warns Judah of ravaging by a lion, a wolf (זאב, Aram. דב; "bear" in Dan 7:5 is דב, suggesting a play on words to *Gen. Rabbah* 99 [see *DTT*]), and a leopard. The characterization of Babylon as lion-eagle recalls Jer 49:19–22, though lion-eagle-man also parallels three of the creatures supporting God's throne in Ezek 1:10. More systematic animal allegories appear especially in Ezek 17; 19; 29; 32. The lion and the horn are common metaphors for violent and aggressive strength, exercised by Yahweh, by Israel, or by their enemies: Dan 7 sees the gentile predators attacking God's flock in the light of psalms that lament such attacks, and sees the promise of final deliverance from them that features in psalms and prophets as about to be fulfilled. The portrayal of the nations as hybrids, which transgress nature's laws and threaten nature's harmony, and as predators who are as such unclean, has part of its background in the Torah's categorization of the animal world and its concern with preserving distinctions between species. (See Porter, *Metaphors,* 63–86, 95–118, 121; Massyngberde Ford, *JSJ* 10 [1979] 204–6.)

The broadest OT parallels to Dan 7 lie in Ps 2 with it's account of nations and kings striving in rebellion against Yahweh and his anointed, then of Yahweh calmly rebuking them and affirming the king's destiny to crush them and/or rule over them (cf. Ps 110). Behind such psalms with their theology of kingship is an understanding of the king as one who represents the people as a whole, embodies their destiny, yet also mediates God's rule to them (Heaton). Dan 7 has more general parallels with other psalms that describe the nations attacking Israel, their kings flaunting their power, their being apparently certain of victory but then being defeated as God appears to overthrow them (e.g., Ps 48); also with psalms calling for judgment on oppressors depicted as lions and horned animals (e.g., Ps 22; 75; 74, which has in common with Dan 7 reference to a חיה "animal," the devastation of the sanctuary, blasphemy, and other motifs). Some of these psalms reassert affirmations of God's victory over such chaos powers represented by the sea or the sea monster, which God destroys (e.g., Ps 9; 29; 46; 93), or recall such affirmations in contexts like that of Dan 7 when the oppression of enemies made them questionable (e.g., Pss 74; 89). If such psalms reflect a festal celebration of Yahweh's kingship and of the king's triumph, then this festival lies further behind Daniel's vision. Nearer to his day and his purpose, however, is the reappropriating of such motifs in Israelite prophecy, sometimes explicitly addressing particular contexts where the chaotic sea (/monster) is historicized, sometimes more consciously eschatological (e.g., Isa 17:12–14; 27:1; 29; 51:9–10; Ezek 29:3; 38–39; Joel 4 [3]; Zech 12–14; cf. also Job 26:12–13; 40:25–41:26 [41:1–34]; the rare verb גוח/גיח ["stir up," v 2] appears in related contexts in Ezek 32:2; Job 38:8; 40:23). Like some of these prophets, Dan 7 functions as an answer to the appeal in such lament psalms for deliverance and vindication (Porteous). The mythic pattern of God's victory in conflict with the powers of disorder, which had been used to interpret Israel's experience at the exodus and in the exile, is appropriated once again in the context of an equivalent experience of order collapsing (Collins, *VT* 25 [1975] 596–600). (See Bentzen, *Messias,* 71–74 [ET 73–75]; Engnell, *BO* 8 [1951] 191–92; *SEA* 22–23 [1957–58] 288.)

The vision of God enthroned especially parallels Ezek 1: the stormy wind, the cloud, the four animal-like creatures with four faces and four wings emerging from them alongside the wheels with rims full of eyes, a mighty sound (see also Deut 33:2; 1 Kgs 22:19; Isa 6; Jer 49:38; Ps 50; and for the background to the books that are opened, see *Comment*).

The phrase used to denote the humanlike figure in v 13, בר אנש (BH

בן אדם) is familiar from various OT contexts. Most commonly, it simply denotes a human being, especially as the term by which God addresses Ezekiel. In Ps 8 it suggests humanity as both weak and unimpressive—a common connotation—yet endowed with glory, honor, and authority in relation to the animal creation (cf. Gen 1:27–28 and Gen 1–3 as a whole, though the term itself does not appear). In Ps 80 it appears in the context of a description of Yahweh's people as a vine ravaged by wild beasts; it refers to Israel in general or to the king in particular (cf. Ps 146:3), who may be seen as the embodiment of humanity (as also in Mic 5?). (On this theme, see Bentzen, *Messias,* 37–42 [ET 39–44]; Wifall, *BTB* 4 [1974] 103–7.) God himself is described as humanlike (דמות כמראה אדם) in Ezek 1:26; the manlike person in Ezek 8:2 (דמות כמראה איש [see BHK]), however, may be a separate heavenly figure (see Zimmerli, *Ezechiel* in loc.; on this as possible background to the humanlike figure, see Procksch, BZAW 34:141–49; Feuillet, *RB* 60 [1953] 170–202, 321–46 [adding as background the hypostatized Wisdom of Prov 8]; Black, "Theophany," 60; cf. Balz, *Probleme,* 80–89). The clouds that accompany the humanlike figure's epiphany recall OT descriptions of God's own coming (see BDB ענן). The nations' acknowledgment of the humanlike figure and the holy ones corresponds to their acknowledgment of Israel in Isa 49:23; 60.

Dan 7 has clear links outside the actual OT with *1 Enoch.* The animal allegory in chaps. 85–90 also features predators symbolizing rulers or kingdoms, an animal transformed into a man, animals with horns of extraordinary size, a throne set up for God to sit in judgment as books are opened before him, and animals being destroyed by fire. In chap. 14, Enoch is carried by winds and clouds into heaven, where he sees a throne from which flaming fire issues and on which God sits in a gown whiter than snow, surrounded by myriad upon myriad of attendants. There are also parallels in chaps. 46–48 and 71 with the throne scene and the humanlike figure in Dan 7. There is disagreement over whether different parallels suggest Dan 7 is dependent on 1 Enoch (e.g., Grelot, *Sem* 28 [1978] 59–83; Kvanvig, *ST* 38 [1984] 101–33; Müller, *Wegzeichen,* 253–61; Rowland, *Heaven,* 255–58) or vice versa (e.g., Emerton, *JTS* 9 [1958] 226; Casey, *JSJ* 7 [1976] 20–22), or whether both are dependent on other sources (e.g., Coppens, *ETL* 53 [1971] 187–89; Müller, *BZ* 16 [1972] 175–79).

(c) *Other Near Eastern religions.* The existence of this wide and detailed Jewish background to Dan 7, near home for author and audience, makes appeal to foreign influence inappropriate where the material has Jewish parallels. Nevertheless, over the past century, scholars have studied parallels between Dan 7 and material from Egypt, Iran, Babylon, and Canaan. Egyptian influence has been seen in the parallels between the relationship of Atum and Re with that of the one advanced in years and the humanlike figure in Dan 7, and in the portrait of Antiochus as foe of godly order (Gressmann, *Menschensohn,* 403–9; Lebram, *VT* 25 [1975] 743–50) but the evidence is hardly compelling. Nor is Morgenstern's hypothesis of the influence of an equivalent Tyrian myth (*JBL* 80 [1961] 65–77)—which even he later abandoned (*Antecedents*). Nor is the more common belief that there is a connection between Daniel's humanlike figure and Iranian figures who are the embodiment of humanity, who form one root of Near Eastern kingship ideology and thus relate to OT ideas of humanity noted above (systematic exposition in Borsch, *Son of Man,* 55–106). Daniel's allusive reference to a humanlike figure hardly justifies or requires such connections to be made, and neither do parallels such as the stream of fire; it is in any case a problem that the Persian material itself is difficult to date, and parallels are rarely specific to Persia. The fourfold historical scheme (see chap. 2 *Form*) is the most plausible instance of Iranian influence on Dan 7. (See survey in Hultgård, *ANRW* ii 19, 1:515–36.)

Parallels between the Babylonian Adapa myth and the humanlike figure (see *ANET* 102; Gunkel, *Schöpfung,* 148; Hommel, *ExpT* 11 [1899–1900] 341–45) are again less compelling, as are the incidental parallels between Dan 7 and an Akkadian dream-vision about hybrid beings (*ANET* 109–10; Kvanvig, *ST* 35 [1981] 85–89). But when the Babylonian myth *Enuma Elish* tells of rebellious monsters born from the primordial ocean, of the destruction of the sea monster, the embodiment of disorder, who is burst by the winds, and of the elevation of its destroyer as king and lord of heaven and earth (see *ANET* 60–72, 501–3; Gunkel, *Schöpfung,* 323–35; Kraeling, *OrSt* 228–31), it is harder to see the links with Dan 7 as coincidental. They are themselves paralleled, however, in the equivalent Ugaritic combat myth *Baal,* which has more links with Dan 7 and is likely the less indirect background to it. Here, similarly, Sea tries to usurp the place of Baal, the son of the highest god, the venerable, gray-headed, and gray-bearded El. One of his titles, *'b snm,* might mean "father of years" and correspond to עתיק יומין "one advanced in days" (but see the careful discussion in Kearns, *Vorfragen* 2:173–74). Before the assembly of the holy ones, Baal, rider on the clouds, is declared destined for an eternal kingship, and he duly kills Sea—later characterized as Leviathan, the seven-headed dragon. In due course El agrees to a temple being built as a palace for Baal, where he takes his seat as king over the earth. He is then overcome by Death, but Death is eventually defeated. In the OT, Yahweh effectively combines the positions of El and Baal, except in Dan 7, where the humanlike figure takes Baal's position. In recapitulating this old ritual pattern, Dan 7 may then have its own links with these ancient myths, via learned circles in Judaism rather than because they lived on in the temple cult. (See *ANET* 129–42; *CML;* Eissfeldt, *Baal Zaphon,* 25–30; Emerton, *JTS* 9 [1958] 225–42; Rost, *Studien,* 72–75; Colpe, *TWNT;* Hanson, *Dawn,* 292–324, 369–401, for parallels in Zech; Kearns, *Vorfragen* 2:83–194; Collins, *Vision,* 95–106; Day, *Conflict;* critique in Casey, *Son of Man,* 34–38; Coppens, *ETL* 44 [1968] 497–502; Ferch, *Son of Man,* 54–77; Mosca, *Bib* 67 [1986] 496–517).

(d) *Other aspects of Near Eastern life.* The animals in Dan 7 have often been likened to Babylonian engravings, sculptures, and reliefs or to the sphinxes (see, e.g., *ANEP* 644–53; *IBD* 58–61), but the parallels are not very close. The same applies to warnings in treaties of attacks by animals (Wittstruck, *JBL* 97 [1978] 100–102; but see Rimbach, *JBL* 97 [1978] 565–66); though in any case these will surely have influenced Daniel only via passages such as Hos 13:7–8 (D. R. Hillers, *Treaty Curses and the Old Testament Prophets* [BibOr 16 (1964)] 56). Parallels with the animals in the zodiac (Caquot, *Sem* 5 [1955] 5–13) are also imprecise (Coppens, *ETL* 45 [1969] 124–25; Day, *Conflict,* 154–55).

Mesopotamian divination offers more promising background to vv 4–6.

It had a particular interest in anomalous human and animal births that might offer portents of the future of individuals or the state. The series *Šumma izbu* (see on 1:3–5; also Porter, *Metaphors,* 15–29) includes sheep born with some resemblance to a wolf, a lion, a fox, a tiger, or a human being, and animals with deformations such as a raised shoulder, lungs in its mouth, extra horns, multiple heads, or displaced eyes. These portend events such as a royal death, an enemy attack, conflicts among rulers or a king enjoying a long and peaceful reign. Not all details in the omens are interpreted, and not all details in the interpretations connect with specific aspects of the omen. Also interesting is the custom of describing a king as having characteristics of various animals (cf. *ANET* 585–86; cf. Porter, *Metaphors,* 84–85). In the Hellenistic period, on his coins Alexander wears a headpiece much like an elephant head, Antiochus III uses the elephant as a state emblem, and Hellenistic monarchs generally are often pictured as possessing horns, a common Semitic symbol for power: all this may lie behind the figure of the fourth animal (Morenz, *ZAW* 63 [1951] 151–54; Staub, *FZPT* 25 [1978] 351–97). It is possible to link characteristics of individual creatures to those of empires they represent: for instance, the Medes might be seen as fierce and destructive (v 5; cf. Isa 13:17–18)—though it is not clear that they were more so than others! Or the four nations may be explained on the basis of second-century political geography as Egypt, Parthia, Syria, and Rome (Hanhart, *NTS* 27 [1980–81] 576–83).

(e) *Conclusions.* Tracing the development of ideas and motifs that appear in a text does not in itself explain their significance there, but in principle it can add to our historical insight on the development of Israelite faith and thought, enable us to perceive more of the meaning and resonances that ideas and motifs had for author and audience, and explain tensions or other apparent problems in the text. Thus it is illuminating to imagine the author of Dan 7 combining the combat myth as adopted in the OT but also as known in the learned tradition with the four-regimes scheme and the form of the dream from chap. 2, and developing these in the light of second-century experience into a powerful portrayal of Antiochus as the doomed embodiment of chaos (e.g., Beasley-Murray, *CBQ* 45 [1983] 44–58). But we must acknowledge that such pictures are hypothetical. It remains difficult to evaluate the significance of parallels for tracing the tradition-history behind Dan 7. At some points the evidence is such as not to prove a direct link, but this does not mean there was not one. In other cases, the parallels are close enough to make a direct link seem likely, but coincidence is not impossible. Even where historical links are real, it is difficult to know how far the author was aware of the material's original meaning or was influenced by it: we must beware of reading into Daniel too much of what went before or what came after (Heaton). Even when he was aware of his material's background, the picture as a whole is not one he received from existent sources; it is creative, imaginative, and original (cf. Plöger). Further, the significance of motifs in Dan 7 is their significance in this context, which may even contradict the significance they brought to it. It may be that the chief value of investigating the background to the chapter is to see what is different about Dan 7 itself; this process may enable us to perceive important aspects of the chapter even if the hypotheses that lead to these perceptions turn out to be mistaken.

Thus, in *Enuma Elish,* the winds restrain the sea and its monsters; here they churn it up and generate the sea-monsters. In Ezek 1 the animals support God's throne and serve his kingship; here they serve themselves and are judged (Rowe, *Christ the Lord,* 84–85). In Ps 2 the one enthroned is an actual king, whose people are unmentioned; here the bestowing of God's rule is projected onto the future, and the one on whom it is bestowed explicitly represents a people. Thus the dethronement of evil belongs not to the Beginning or to ever-repeated events in history but to the End (Plöger). Nevertheless, the sea and the animals stand here not for otherworldly cosmic or cosmogonic chaos forces but for historical ones; yet the animals stand not for forces ruling through all history as in *1 Enoch,* but only for the rulers of the post-exilic period. Whereas Marduk fought and killed the beasts, as does the humanlike figure in 2 Esdras, here there is no battle—all is determined by the word of God (Gressmann, *Messias,* 346; cf. Gen 1 in relation to earlier myths). The humanlike figure has no explicit connection with creation, nor does he undergo suffering, or enter into conflict with the senior figure, or die, as Baal is commonly held to have done. Whatever temple background the chapter has, and despite the presence of the temple theme in *Enuma Elish,* it is striking that it makes no mention of the temple.

Structure

- 1–2a introduction
  - 1a narrative preface
  - 1b commencing formula
  - 2a narrative opening
- 2b–14 vision report
  - 2b–3 four creatures appear
    - 4–6 the first three creatures
      - 7 the fourth creature with its ten horns
        - 8 a small horn on the fourth
          - 9–10 a throne scene
        - 11a the small horn
      - 11b the fourth creature
    - 12 the first three creatures
  - 13–14 a manlike figure appears
- 15 visionary's response
- 16–18 initial interpretation
  - 16 visionary's request for interpretation
  - 17–18 framework for interpretation
    - 17 the beasts are kings
    - 18 the new kingship
- 19–20 request for further interpretation
  - 19 the fourth creature
  - 20 the horns
- 21–22 further vision report
  - 21 the small horn's behavior
  - 22a the judgment
  - 22b the new kingship

23–27 detailed interpretation
  23 the fourth kingship's behavior
  24–25 the new king's behavior
  26 his judgment
  27 the new kingship
28 conclusion
  28a closing formula
  28b the visionary's response

For the chiastic structure of the vision report, I have combined insights from Ferch (*Son of Man,* 136–37) and Kvanvig (*ST* 32 [1978] 101–2). The larger chiasm Ferch (142) finds in Dan 7 as a whole (cf. Raabe, "Daniel 7," 267–68) seems more forced.

At a number of points, aspects of the vision are introduced by formulae:

v 2: חזה הוית בחזו יעם ליליא וארו . . . "as I watched in my vision during the night,
2 there before me . . ."
v 4b: חזה הוית עד די . . . "I watched as . . ." (cf. vv 9, 21–22; also 2:34)
v 5: וארו . . . "then there before me . . ." (cf. v 8b)
v 6: באתר דנה חזה הוית וארו . . . "after that I watched and there before me . . ."
v 7: באתר דנה חזה הוית בחזוי ליליא וארו . . . "after that, as I watched in the vision by night, there before me . . ."
v 8: משתכל הוית . . . ואלו . . . "as I looked . . . there before me . . ."
v 11: חזה הוית באדין . . . חזה הוית עד די . . . "I watched then . . . I watched as . . ."
v 13: חזה הוית בחזוי ליליא וארו . . . "as I watched in the vision by night, there before me . . ."

The formulae comprise stock phrases, though used in varying combinations; further variants appear in 2:31 (= 4:7 [10]); 4:10 [13]; and in Hebrew 8:3, 5, 15. The phrases that end with the conjunctive expression עד די "as" are naturally followed by a verbal clause; they introduce an event. Those that end with the particles ארו/אלו "there before me" are generally followed by a noun clause; they introduce a new scene. Partial exceptions are in vv 8 and 13, where the particles introduce new scenes; but these involve events, expressed in verbal clauses (cf. the mixture of verbal and noun clauses in a comparable context after והנה "there before me" in Joseph's dream report, Gen 37:6–9). The formulae are used to introduce each element in the vision report in vv 2b–14 (and 21–22) as we have analyzed it, except that vv 4 and 12, both relating to the first three creatures, lack formulae, while a formula appears in v 4b. Some of the variation in formulae is of rhetorical significance. The vision report appropriately opens with a long formula, and the fourth creature is advertised to be of special significance by a particularly long and resumptive formula (v 7). The same effect is achieved for the small horn by the use of a different and stronger verb and a different particle, which is repeated (v 8). As the judgment presaged by vv 9–10 is awaited, v 11 uses a complex repetitive/resumptive version of the formula to heighten suspense. The final climax of the vision is marked by a further long and resumptive formula (v 13).

In contrast, the variation in the use of formulae in vv 2–6 seems to be stylistic. Here and elsewhere the vision builds drama and impact through a variety of other devices. The description of the first three creatures is heightened by the use of simile and concrete characterization. To us it is allusive and mysterious, and it may well have been so from the beginning. The relatively less colorful description of the third creature is counterbalanced by the use of one of the longer formulae to introduce it. The centerpiece and the final climax of the symbolic vision are marked by the use of poetic parallelism and rhythm, repetition, assonance, and hendiadys (vv 9–10, 13–14; see especially the close parallelism in vv 9b, 9c, 10b, 10c, 14b). Considered in isolation, vv 9–10 at least might be seen as actual poetry (so Niditch, *Vision*), but in the context of Dan 7 as a whole with its movement into and out of a more rhythmic and poetic prosody, it seems more appropriate to see these verses as representing one end of a spectrum of more poetic and more prosaic language. In vv 13–14, the creatures coming from the sea are balanced by the human figure coming with the clouds of heaven; the two correspond to the characteristic OT and ancient Near Eastern antithesis between (chaos) waters/kings and heaven/Yahweh's anointed. The gifts of humanness and authority (vv 4, 6) reach mature though transformed expression in the humanness and authority of the heavenly figure.

After this high point, the account of Daniel's reaction and his request for interpretation increases suspense and focuses attention on what follows. This effect is furthered first by the provision of the merest framework of interpretation, silent on the details that most concern people in the second century (vv 17–18), then by the request for more interpretation, which itself unexpectedly provides further information on the symbolic vision itself (the bronze claws, v 19; the small horn's larger appearance, v 20), then by a further actual vision report adding more such information (vv 21–22). The final section of the interpretative vision, vv 23–27, which brings another climax with its most detailed and explicit portrayal of Antiochus and of the kingship of the holy ones, draws attention to its significance by using language elaborately rather than economically, employing strings of terms of synonymous or overlapping meaning, and partly rhyming verbs (v 23), nouns (v 27), and purpose clauses (v 26), and building up a rhythm by sequences of clauses of parallel imagery, syntax, or language (vv 25a, 27b) (Niditch, *Vision,* 189–92).

The vision's contents and meaning are in fact repeated four times, in vv 2–14 (symbolic vision), 17–18 (framework of interpretation), 19–22 (further symbolic vision material), and 23–27 (interpretation of that detail). Synoptically, they comprise the following elements:

A	four animals/kings	2b–3	17		
	lion-eagle-man	4			
	bear	5			
	four-headed winged leopard	6			
	monster	7ab		19	23
B	ten horns/kings	7c		20a	24a
C	small horn/another king	8 (11a)		20–21	24–25
D	divine judgment	9–10		22a	26a

E	fourth animal destroyed	11b			
F	small horn punished				26
G	first three animals deposed	12			
H	human figure appears	13			
I	new kingship of holy ones	14	18	22b	27

Despite the repetition, there is no interpretative comment on the first three animals, and no representation in the symbolic vision of the horn's punishment. There is more symbolism than interpretation and more interpretation than symbolism; each stands on its own as a revelation. At the same time, the repetition and the elaboration show what the chapter regards as important, namely, the suffering and triumph of the holy ones (Casey, *JTS* 37 [1986] 480–81): the four-empire scheme is there because of its traditional importance, and it is omitted in chap. 8.

A major tradition of scholarship, mainly European, has taken the view that the elements in the above pattern have accumulated through a more or less complex process of growth: among important figures representing variant forms of this tradition are Hölscher, Noth, Haller, Ginsberg, Dequeker, Coppens, Weimar, K. Müller, Kearns, and Kvanvig. While they work out this approach in different ways, two tendencies characterize their work. One is to date material later the further right one moves across these columns: most, if not all, of the interpretation material is regarded as later than most of the vision material. The tendency is also (though less consistently) to date material later the further one moves down the columns, because dating follows the material's historical reference. Thus A (vv 2b–7ab, at least) can be fourth century or earlier (cf. Kruse). BE (vv 7c, 11b) can be pre-Antiochene, and BE or ABE then handles the question of how long the fourth kingship will last. Verses 9–10, 13 (?14) may also belong to one of these stages, giving a more transcendent explanation of the expected act of judgment. C and the rest of the material in D, F, and I reflect the Antiochene crisis and may represent several stages in its development: e.g., vv 8, 11a its beginnings (c. 168 B.C.); vv 21–22, increasing pressures and hopes (c. 166 B.C.); vv 25–27, the depths of oppression and urgent need. Expressions used in the introduction and conclusion (vv 1–2a, 28) and within the vision (e.g., vv 4b, 14, 25) parallel expressions used in chaps. 1–6 and 8–12 (cf. *Form*), and this might suggest the further possibility of recensional work on the chapter designed to link it with this broader context (e.g., Weimar, "Daniel 7," 15–25; Hölscher, *TSK* 92 [1919] 120–21). Scholars in this tradition ground their argument for the separate origin of different parts of the material on a number of literary, linguistic, and material features such as the varied introductory formulae and verbal forms, the movement into and out of more poetic form, and the chapter's general lack of straightforwardness and its repetitions.

An alternative tradition of approach (e.g., Rowley, Collins, Casey, Ferch) maintains the chapter's unity, except perhaps for seeing vv 21–22 as an addition from later in the Antiochene period. We have noted how the chapter's stylistic and rhetorical features with their variations and unevennesses can be understood as contributing to a coherent whole. The view that repetition, unevenness, variation, and clumsiness of expression are likely to reflect the work of more than one hand is unargued. Even where it does not function rhetorically, variation in expression may reflect either random variation or variation for literary effect on the part of one hand. It is paralleled in other texts. There is no presumption that unevenness or jerkiness indicates the work of more than one hand; a single author may construct his work in an awkward way or modify his presentation by means of an afterthought as he proceeds. In the history of forms, the simple often develop from the complex, and in the history of the text, emendations are usually designed to remove unevenness rather than to create it. So the simplified versions of a passage such as Dan 7 which source- and redaction-critics have offered are as likely to be secondary editions as to be primary ones.

Setting

Dan 7 presents itself as a dream experienced by Daniel c. 550 B.C., the beginning of the co-regency of Nabonidus and Belshazzar. In the light of its formal characteristics noted above, it is more likely a quasi-predictive vision deriving from the period on which it focuses and to which it is especially relevant (that of the king symbolized by the small horn) than an actual predictive vision from the sixth century. It thus presupposes actions by Antiochus IV against Jerusalem such as 1 Macc 1:29–40 describes, but it does not refer to the introduction of offensive forms of worship in the temple (contrast 8:13; 9:27; 11:31), and implies that Jewish deliverance is still future. Its date is thus mid-167 B.C.

The vision's implicit social setting is quite different from that of earlier parts of the book. It emerges not from a minority community in a foreign country tempted to surrender faith and commitment in order to survive and succeed, but from people religiously affronted, threatened, and oppressed in their own land. Unlike groups who were open to some cooperation with Hellenistic culture and religion, the Danielic group was a sect in the sense of a "self-distinguishing protest movement" (Wilson, *Magic,* 12)—though protesting against Antiochus in particular, not against Hellenism as such. Such movements may take a variety of attitudes to what is required in the light of the institutions they confront: a change in human hearts; a revolutionary, transforming act of God; withdrawal from the world (cf. Qumran); a new way of looking at the world; miraculous experiences; effort to reform the way the world works; revolutionary action to establish a new order (typology adapted from Wilson, *Magic,* 18–30). The last is the response adopted wholeheartedly by the Maccabees; Daniel's stance is closer to the supernaturalist/transformationist response (Reid, 162–63).

It is one that looks to the somewhat distant past and to the hoped-for future as the contexts of meaningful revelation and experienced deliverance and political power. These are not present realities, as they are portrayed to have been in the stories. We do not know what connection there was between the circles in which Dan 7 emerged and the circles that had generated the stories some time earlier. There is no specific reason to suppose that the connection is other than a literary one.

The vision's setting in the Book of Daniel makes it the book's central hinge. In language, it belongs with the preceding chapters, while structurally it rounds off a chiasm begun in chap. 2:

2 A vision of four kingdoms and their end (Nebuchadnezzar)
3 Faithfulness and a miraculous rescue (the three friends)
4 Judgment presaged and experienced (Nebuchadnezzar)
5 Judgment presaged and experienced (Belshazzar)
6 Faithfulness and a miraculous rescue (Daniel)
7 A vision of four kingdoms and their end (Daniel)

(see Lenglet, "Structure"; Weimar, "Daniel 7," 33–34).

Like chap. 2, chap. 7 relates a symbolic dream that is interpreted as referring to four diverse regimes. The first is particularly impressive, the second is less so, the third has parallels to the first, being endowed with special authority. Most attention is given to the violent fourth regime. It has an ironlike strength (פרזל) and crushing power (דקק), though it suffers from division and conflict. It is destined to be destroyed from heaven; its power will be taken over by a regime instituted by God himself and destined to last forever.

The chapters differ in that Dan 2 relates a dream of the foreign king (when the Babylonian empire is at its height) whose interest focuses on the regimes themselves, while Dan 7 relates a dream of the Judean sage (when the Babylonian empire is declining) which is specifically interested in the suffering of his people and in their destiny to share God's rule. In Dan 2 Daniel is actively involved as interpreter, providing his God-given wisdom; in Dan 7 he is a mere passive recipient of revelation, needing to be given his symbolic dream's interpretation. Dan 2 sees the fourth regime as weak, but not as wicked, its destruction being an act of judgment; whereas Dan 2 implicitly stresses God's power in replacing the regimes by his own, Dan 7 at this point implicitly stresses God's justice. The imagery of Dan 2 is simpler and relatively stately, that of Dan 7 more complex and fantastic. The outward impressiveness of the humanlike statue contrasts with the dangerous yet merely animalic sequence of creatures; the unimpressive rock that destroys the statue contrasts with the stately figure whose word brings the creatures' judgment and the humanlike being whose rule replaces theirs.

In part the features that distinguish Dan 7 from Dan 2 reflect the portrayal of empires in the intervening chapters (Plöger). Dan 2 offered world rulers a vision of their position as a God-given calling. Dan 3–6 has portrayed them inclined to make themselves into God; they are thus also inclined to put mortal pressure on those who are committed to God (chaps. 3; 6), but are themselves on the way to catastrophe (chaps. 4; 5). These motifs are taken up and taken further in chap. 7. The tension between the human and the bestial that appeared in chaps. 4 and 6 becomes a key motif: bestiality is now turned on God himself (Barr), but he puts an end to the reign of the beast and gives authority to a humanlike figure (Lacocque). As the real statue of chap. 3 follows on the dream statue of chap. 2, the dream animals of chap. 7 follow on the real animals of chap. 6. As people of all races, nations, and languages were called to bow before the statue (3:4; cf. 5:19), so now they honor the human figure of Daniel's vision (7:14). Once Nebuchadnezzar testified to God's lasting power (3:33; 4:31; cf. 6:27 [4:3, 34; cf. 6:26]); now Daniel's human figure has this power (7:14). Once Nebuchadnezzar's humiliation was limited to seven periods of time (4:13 [16]); now the humiliation of the heavenly ones will be limited to 3½ such periods (7:25). Once God demonstrated in history that as ruler in the earthly realm he could give royal authority to the most ordinary of human beings (4:14 [17]); now he gives it to a humanlike being at the end of the story of earthly kingdoms (7:13–14). Once Darius took hold of power (6:1 [5:31]); now the heavenly ones do so (7:18). Once Darius acknowledged that God's rule would persist until the end (עד סופא) (6:27 [26]); now the king symbolized by the small horn has his authority destroyed permanently (עד סופא) (7:26). Dan 2–6 have affirmed that God controlled times and epochs, his decree being victorious over the decrees of kings (2:9, 13, 15, 21; 6:6, 9, 13, 16 [5, 8, 12, 15]); now a king who thinks to control times set by decree will lose all power (7:25–26). Chaps. 3–6 indicate why the sequence of earthly regimes is destined to be brought to an end in the way chap. 2 describes. Chap. 7 combines the thrust of the preceding chapters as a whole, and puts them in a new perspective. Their theme of the history of the kingdoms and their appointed time and destiny is brought to its climax—though they still stand, and set before second-century readers implicit challenges and promises regarding their own lives (Towner). They are not just called to a passive, secret waiting for the End, but to an active, courageous, expectant, faithful, direct self-application.

As the hinge of the Book of Daniel as a whole, chap. 7 also opens the way to the following chapters. Its opening verse begins a new chronological sequence, which then runs through the visions, as an earlier chronological sequence ran through chaps. 1–6. Its closing verse opens the way to further material, which will elaborate on the sometimes allusive contents of chap. 7. This series of Daniel's further first-person visions will in different ways focus more sharply on the crisis that the fourth creature and its small horn bring to the people of God and their shrine. Chap. 7 with its continuing concern for God's reign provides the broad context for their narrower focus; they provide further interpretation and detail in regard to its allusiveness and broad brush strokes.

Comment

1 Historically, Belshazzar's first year will have been the first year of the regency he exercised in Babylon during the ten years Nabonidus spent in Tema (see Nabonidus's Harran stelae, *ANET* 562–63; cf. chap. 4 *Form*). This period probably began in 550/549 B.C., the year of Cyrus's decisive victory over Astyages, king of Media (Hasel, *AUSS* 15 [1977] 153–68). Babylonian documents were not dated by Belshazzar's reign but by Nabonidus's, but Belshazzar had had the kingship in Babylon entrusted to him and it is natural enough for a Jewish story to be dated by his years. Although it is suggestive to note that the visions in chaps. 7 and 8 come from the beginning of the ten-year regency that ends with the portent of chap 5, the structure of the book emphasizes rather the links between chap. 5 and the other narratives, chaps. 7 and 8 and the other visions.

For the writing down of prophecies, see 8:26; 12:4, 9; Isa 8:1, 16; 30:8; Jer 30:2; 36:2; 51:60; Ezek 43:11; Hab 2:2; *1 Enoch* 33.3–4; *T. Moses* 1.16; 2 Esd 14:42; Rev 1:11, 19; 21:5. This made a prophecy more solid, concrete, and certain of fulfillment; indeed, putting something into writing initiated its fulfillment. It also made prophecy, prophet, and God open to vindication: the written word was fixed and could be tested by events. A related conviction, which could even survive apparent disconfirmation by events, was the belief of a prophet and his associates that a particular prophecy was a word from God and therefore needed to be preserved to allow it to continue to speak.

With quasi-predictions, reference to writing also helps to establish the authority of a document. What was occasional for prophets, and incidental to fulfilling their characteristically oral ministry, was intrinsic to quasi-predictions. Writing is a necessary medium whereby a message can reach the audience whom it concerns, when it either was delivered or spoke as if it was delivered some centuries earlier. The "esoteric" aspect to visionary writings stems from this same aspect of their origin: see on 8:26.

The fact that the vision happens by night does not in itself make it something terrifying, a nightmare: visions often happen at night (cf. the revelation in 2:19).

2–3 Talk of four winds, heaving sea, and huge animals calls to mind mythic material from Babylon and Canaan reflected in earlier parts of the OT (see *Form*). These motifs suggest supernatural forces: the winds, the power of God effecting his will (cf. Gen 1:2); the sea, the dense concentration of energy that threatens to disrupt and overwhelm order; the animals, the embodiment of that threatening energy in particular beings (cf. Rev 13:1–7; 17:8). *Four* winds and *four* creatures suggest the world-encompassing totality of divine power and disorderly energy (cf. the fourfold stream of Gen 2:10). Yet four winds can more prosaically denote the winds that come from the four points of the compass (8:8; 11:4; cf. Zech 2:10 [6]; 6:5; 2 Esd 13:5, a passage related to Dan 7). Further, "the Great Sea" elsewhere always denotes the Mediterranean; it is a standard title for it (see BDB 410; for Aram., 1QapGen 21.16). To refer to the mythic Sea, the more general term "the sea" is used (e.g., Isa 5:30; 27:1; Jer 51:42; Ps 74:13; 89:10 [9]; Job 3:8 [see BHS; NEB; NIVmg]; 26:12; Rev 21:1), or "the [Great] Deep" (תהום [רבה]) (e.g., Gen 7:11; Isa 51:10; Amos 7:4). Again, the text does not describe the animals as four similar embodiments of one hostile basic substance; they are explicitly varied.

Daniel's vision is thus of winds from all directions turning the Mediterranean into a tumult. The animals correspond to the four metals of chap. 2, which the author of Dan 7 (at least) takes to denote four earthly empires; it was a recognized convention to symbolize nations by creatures from the animal world. The point becomes explicit in v 17, which understands the sea and its animals to denote the world and four of its kings. As with the winds, however, *four* suggests totality. Daniel is concerned with a particular segment of history, not history as a whole. But he is concerned with that segment as a whole, with the totality of earthly forces that over this period dominate the people of God (cf. the four horns/smiths of Zech 2:1, 4 [1:18, 21]). Each of the points of the compass spawns an animal. So mythic motifs lie behind the vision rather than on its surface, but their resonances carry through, adding depth and force to statements about history that are the text's direct concern (as in Isa 17:12–13; 51:10). A world-transcending or world-encompassing scheme is adapted to communicate a perspective not on the cosmos as a whole, nor even on history as a whole, but on the particular segment of history that directly concerns Daniel and his readers.

4–8 The four creatures emerge from the ocean consecutively, not concurrently, though this in itself hardly excludes the possibility of understanding the kings they represent as contemporaries, the consecutiveness being merely a feature of the presentation, nor the possibility of associating one creature with each point of the compass.

On the animals, see *IBD* 58–61. Each is fierce and dangerous. They are also ominous in a narrower sense. The first three, at least, are anomalous creatures, resembling one kind of animal but also having the features of another or being deformed in some other way. In Babylonian lore such actual or theoretical anomalies were believed to portend specific historical events (Porter, *Metaphors,* 15–29). In OT law, such hybrids implied a contravention of the prohibition on mating members of different species, behind which lay the emphasis on species being created "after their kind" (Gen 1). In Hellenistic Palestine, hybrid creatures on charms and amulets symbolize demonic forces (Goodenough, *Symbols,* vol. 1; cf. Massyngberde Ford, *JSJ* 10 [1979] 209). While it is possible to link characteristics of each of the creatures with features of the kingdoms they may represent, the text itself does not make such connections. It would make little difference to the vision's meaning if bear and leopard exchanged positions in the vision or if the third creature were likened to a wolf rather than a leopard.

The features of a lion (v 4) to which the OT appeals are ferocity, strength, destructiveness, courage, rapacity, and fearsomeness; it can be used as a simile or metaphor for any nation or individual with such characteristics, and in particular to suggest kingship (see *TWAT*). The eagle's key characteristics are speed and rapacity (Hab 1:8; Lam 4:19). The bird referred to is perhaps strictly the large and majestic, high-flying and swooping griffon vulture (see A. Alon, *The Natural History of the Land of the Bible* [London/New York: Hamlyn/Doubleday, 1969] 220–21). Lion and eagle appear together to characterize Saul and Jonathan in 2 Sam 1:23, the unnamed northern foe in Jer 4:7, 13, and Nebuchadnezzar in particular in Jer 49:19, 22, but neither has a distinctive association with Babylon or with Nebuchadnezzar, though winged lions in relief decorated the Processional Way in Babylon (Saggs, *Babylon,* 479–80; plate 53). Lions and eagles are the leading animals and birds symbolizing the nations in *1 Enoch* 89–90. They thus appropriately symbolize the first king, whoever is actually referred to (cf. the gold in chap. 2).

In isolation, what happens to the lion-eagle might be read negatively: it is reduced from being able to soar above the earth to experiencing the limitations of mere humanity. The removal of the eagle's wings, reducing the creature to a mere four-legged animal, could be an act of judgment paralleling the one Nebuchadnezzar experienced in chap. 4. There, however, coming to share the appearance of an eagle is itself an act of judgment; it accompanies coming to share the life of an animal as part of Nebuchadnezzar's being deprived of his humanity before he has his human sanity restored. More likely, then, to have one's feathered wings removed, to be stood on one's feet like a human being, and to be given a human mind, are all blessings, not deprivations. Caquot (*VT* 23 [1973] 114) takes them as reflecting a positive assessment of the succession of the destroyer Nebuchadnezzar by Nabonidus: Babylonian rule is humanized. The lion-eagle become humanlike even anticipates or foreshadows the judgment of the beasts and the bestowal of their authority on the humanlike figure of v 13 (Kvanvig, *ST* 32 [1978] 103; Porter, *Metaphors,* 112). The positive description of the lion-eagle corresponds with those of the bear (which is encouraged to eat) and the leopard (which is given authority). The first of the creatures is the most human—not necessarily in the sense that it actually behaves in a more human way, but in the sense that God appoints it to a humanlike position of honor, authority, responsibility, and caring for the world (cf. 2:38; 4:17–19 [20–22]). It is given a role in the world with a significance like that of a *symbolic* human figure—that is, a celestial being (cf. Noah's becoming a man to build the ark—i.e., to undertake an angelic task—in *1 Enoch* 89 [Porter, *Metaphors,* 53]).

5 The second, bearlike, creature is introduced with the briefest of formulae (וארו, "and lo!"). This could point toward a close association with the first creature; but there is no other indication of close association, so it is best taken as a mere stylistic variation.

Its size and strength make it a source of fear to human beings second only to the lion (1 Sam 17:34–37; Amos 5:19; Prov 28:15; before the lion in Lam 3:10; see also 2 Sam 17:8; Isa 11:7; Hos 13:8; Prov 17:2; and for a vivid instance of its dangerousness, 2 Kgs 2:24). While the bear would be a fit simile for any king or empire, nothing specific associates it with any particular king or empire.

Both text and grammar (see *Notes*) and meaning and reference in v 5 are problematic. The description of the bear as lifted up on one side is often taken to indicate that it was rearing up on its back legs or had one paw raised ready to strike or was half-crouching ready to spring, though this is not clearly expressed; perhaps more likely the phrase refers to a physical anomaly (cf. the parallels in *Šumma izbu* 14.10–11 [Porter, *Metaphors,* 17]). But the language is allusive. Torrey relates the description to the remoteness of Media, the presumed referent of the bear (*JAOS* 66 [1946] 11–12), while Plöger links the bear's clumsiness with the Medes' lack of historical achievements in the sixth century. It is less hazardous to explain details in the vision from within Daniel: thus the one side (or ruler: see n. 5.c) could be Darius, the sole Median mentioned in the book (Waterman, *JBL* 65 [1946] 59–61; Hartman). Lebram (*VT* 20 [1979] 517–18) sees it as suggesting that the bear is half-human.

The bear's three עלעין are traditionally taken to be ribs (cf. Amos 3:12 [legs]), but it is odd to picture a bear with such a mouthful being told to eat lots of meat (it would be more plausible if the bear were told to eat up and then take some more). More likely this, too, describes an anomaly: the עלעין are growing in the bear's mouth. *Šumma izbu* 17.16 is a near parallel (lungs in the mouth; Porter, *Metaphors,* 17). The allusion to ribs located in the bear's mouth would then follow on from the description of the bear's being distorted on one side. The three ribs could be Babylonian kings (e.g., Nebuchadnezzar, Evil-Merodach, and Belshazzar) or earlier empires (so Hippolytus) or conquered cities (so Ibn Ezra) or conquered peoples (Young) or conquered kings (so *Cant. Rabbah* 3:3, *Esth. Rabbah* 3), plausibly the three subordinate kings of Jer 51:27 (Gurney). Or the three עלעין might rather be tusks or fangs, identified by Torrey (*JAOS* 66 [1946] 12) as Cyaxares I, Darius the Mede, and Cyaxares II (Xerxes). To take the עלעין as fangs leads well into the exhortation that follows; but see n. 5.e.

6 The leopard appears with the lion and other animals as a fearsome predator (Isa 11:6; Jer 5:6; Hos 13:7; Cant 4:8). Its distinctive features are its spots (Jer 13:23) and its speed (Hab 1:8). The Persians and the Greeks had speedy armies (Isa 41:3; Dan 8:5), but the text does not specify such an allusion. The four wings and four heads indicate that the creature is not a real or ordinary leopard but a heraldic figure, or more likely an anomaly; as a winged predator, it resembles the first creature. While four wings or heads could denote the four Persian kings of 11:2 or the fourfold Greek empire of 8:8; 11:4, four is a frequent indicator of totality or universal activity and extension (cf. Ezek 1:5–6), and the point here may simply be that the leopard can see and move quickly in any direction.

7 The fourth animal is described without being named, like many of the anomalies in *Šumma izbu* (Porter, *Metaphors,* 28). It has none of the dragon- or serpent-like attributes of Leviathan (the distinction between the dragon and the fourfold hybrid is still preserved in Rev 13:1–4). If it represents Greece (see v 17 *Comment*), then circumstantial factors suggest it is an elephant. The battle elephant was brought west by the Greeks and the elephant came to be a particular symbol for Alexander and for Antiochus III (see *Form*). Antiochus IV's use of elephants was well known (e.g., 1 Macc 1:17; 3:34; cf. 6:28–47). The reason for its not being named is hardly to conceal the vision's message from the authorities (against Staub, *FZPT* 25 [1978] 351–97; Hanhart, *NTS* 27 [1980–81] 577): it would hardly have done that. Nor is it because this would have made it difficult to introduce the ten horns (against Coppens, *ETL* 55 [1979] 384): the vision readily ascribes anomalous features to named animals. In not naming the animal, Dan 7 follows Hos 13:5–6, where the fourth animal is also unnamed (Day, *Conflict,* 156–57); and not naming it is part of the difference in representation from that of the first three. They have been described, in terms of their form and appearance and of what happens to them, reported by means of passive verbs—so that the emphasis has been on what God does to them, says to them, and gives them. The fourth animal's form and appearance are not described, the effect being to give it a touch of mystery and to suggest that it is even less a mere earthly creature than its lionlike, bearlike, and leopardlike predecessors. It is characterized by means of active verbs, so that the emphasis is on its own deeds. The way is thus prepared for the action of God that directly confronts the self-initiated action of the fourth creature.

The bear's one side and three ribs and the leopard's four wings and four heads are capped by the fourth creature's ten horns. While there was a violent and destructive aspect to Alexander's own achievements, the portrayal here no doubt reflects the oppressiveness of subsequent Hellenistic rulers. Horns suggest strength for defense or attack; they are a symbol for a king, who needs to have strength for defense or attack (cf. v 24). Ten is a standard round number, here suggesting fullness (Brongers [see on 1:12]; *TWNT*). While the number might also have been suggested by the toes of Nebuchadnezzar's dream statue (2:41–42), there being ten of them is not mentioned there. As likely is a connection with the ten generations/kings mentioned in other apocalypses in connection with four empires (e.g., *Sib.Or.* 4: see Flusser, *IOS* 2 [1972] 162–65; J. J. Collins, *OTP* 1:381–89).

8 "Ten horns," then, might not signify an actual number. But there is less ground for taking "three horns" nonliterally. They "were uprooted before it": the implication is not yet that the small horn itself uprooted the three; indeed, the passive suggests the action of God (as in vv 4, 5, 6), who clears the way for the small horn by removing three others.

Like the first animal, the fourth animal's small horn has an appearance that suggests it is more than a mere animal. It has human features, which point toward the right and responsibility to rule over God's creation (see v 4 *Comment*). Reference to the look of the eyes can suggest people's desires, their generosity or meanness, or their awareness (see BDB 744). The most suggestive parallels are passages that assume that the look of the eyes reveals a person's self-estimate, the pride and arrogance (or humility) located in the inner person (in the "heart"): see Isa 2:11; 5:15; Ps 18:28 [27]; 101:5; 131:1; Job 22:29; Prov 21:4; 30:13, 17. People's talk also reveals the pride and arrogance (or the humility) located in the inner person (1 Sam 2:3; Ezek 35:1; Obad 12; Ps 17:10). Pride and arrogance tend to be accompanied by deceit and flattery: so in Ps 12:4–5 [3–4], where the phrase מדברת גדלות "making great statements" occurs (cf. Ps 31:19 [18]). An arrogant look and a lying tongue head the list of Yahweh's seven hates in Prov 6:16–19. More significantly, arrogance of look and word characterized the king of Assyria (Isa 10:12–13), who had raised his voice and eyes against the Holy One of Israel (Isa 37:23), and who is also Daniel's model for the northern king in 11:36–45. The small horn is not actually said to be arrogant in look and word, however, but only to look like a man and to speak impressively. The wickedness of the looks and words here referred to will become explicit only in v 25 (cf. 8:23; 11:36; 1 Macc 1:24; Rev 13:5–6).

9–10 A number of descriptions of God on his throne of fire surrounded by numerous attendants locate the scene in heaven: see 1 Kgs 22:19–22; ?Isa 6; ?Ezek 1; Ps 82; *1 Enoch* 14.18–22; 40.1; 60.1–2; 71; 91.15–16; Rev 4–5. Where it is specifically a matter of God judging, however, the scene is normally on earth: see Jer 49:38; Joel 4 [3]:1–2, 12; Zech 14:1–5; Ps 50; 96:10–13; *1 Enoch* 1.3–9; 25.3; 90.20–27. In Dan 7, there is no reason to suppose that the scene on earth that Daniel has been watching (vv 2–8) has changed. Indeed, the opening phrase of v 9 implies a continuity of perspective: Daniel continues to look in the direction he had been looking. That the scene takes place on earth is presupposed by v 22 (the one advanced in years *came;* Beasley-Murray, *CBQ* 45 [1983] 49).

"Thrones" (כרסון) is plural; an interesting parallel is Ps 122:5. There the plural may include seats for other members of the royal family associated with the king in judgment; but the OT's few actual descriptions of the king giving judgment do not picture him as accompanied when doing so (e.g., 2 Sam 14; 15:2–6; 1 Kgs 3), and the word כסא is nowhere else used in the plural (except with a plural subject in Isa 14:9; Ezek 26:16). Perhaps, then, the plural in Ps 122:5 is for emphasis (see *GKC* 124def): it suggests the exalted, glorious throne of David. Daniel's vision, too, may have actually included a number of thrones, as a Near Eastern myth might portray a number of gods seated in counsel to make decisions about future events (e.g., *Enuma Elish* 1.33–34, 151–57; 2.126–27; 3.8–10 [*ANET* 61–64]). But if so, they are now apparently merely part of the furniture of the scene. God's heavenly attendants do not occupy them; they stand (v 10). Perhaps, then, the plural here, too, is for emphasis (cf. Kearns, *Vorfragen* 3:178, suggesting "a huge throne"). When the court sits (v 10) it is only the one advanced in years who occupies the throne(s). All the focus is on him in vv 9–10.

The creatures were visually animals, but they stood for kings and their domains, and this significance was allowed to exercise a retroactive influence on their portrayal as animals (e.g., vv 4b, 8). Similarly, the one advanced in years is visually a human being, but he stands for God; this significance, too, exercises a retroactive influence on the portrayal in the vision. Picturing him as an old man suggests someone august, venerable and respected, judicious and wise. There is perhaps an allusion to the notion of God's existing from eternity (Isa 41:4; Ps 90:2; 93:2; 102:25–28 [24–27]; Job 36:26). White clothing (and hair) could suggest purity (cf. 11:35; 12:10; Isa 1:18; Ps 51:9 [7]), but in the context, with its description of the flaming throne, more likely חור has its more basic meaning of brightness and luminosity, thus nobility and splendor (cf. the related description in *1 Enoch* 14.20; the use of חור in connection with royal clothing in Esth 1:6; 8:15; also Dan 10:5–6; Ps 104:1–2; 2 Esd 2:39–40; Matt 28:3; Mark 9:3) (see A. Brenner, *Colour Terms in the Old Testament* [JSOTSup 21 (1982)] 90, 93, 133).

There is an ambiguity about the OT's frequent association of fire with God (on which see *TWAT* אש; Eichrodt, *Theologie* 2:1–4 [ET 16–20]). Fire can be an entirely positive image, associated with light, protection, and guidance. More commonly, however, it suggests something transcendent and absolute, awesome and dangerous, mysterious and destructive. God's appearing is often described in imagery derived from a violent storm, whose lightning flashes with the fire of heaven: so the Sinai story (Exod 19:16–18; 20:18; 24:17; Deut 4:36), so more generally in the apprehension of nature (Ps 104:4; 148:8). God's splendor can also naturally be expressed by the fiery brightness of the sun: so the visions of Ezekiel (1:4, 13, 27; 8:2; 10:2, 6, 7) and *1 Enoch* (14.8–22); cf. also Dan 10:5–6. This will have been encouraged by the fact that the sensation of dazzling light or fire is one of the most frequent aspects of visionary experience (Eichrodt, *Theologie* 2:3 [ET 18]). The destructiveness of fire also makes it a natural symbol of judgment (Deut 4:24; Ps 18:9–14

[8–13]; 21:10 [9]; 50:3; 97:3). "The unapproachable holiness and terrifying power" of God made Israel see "as the appropriate symbol and speaking likeness of the divine nature that element distinguished above all others for the suddenness of its outbreaks and for the mockery which it makes of all human defences" (Eichrodt, *Theologie* 2:2 [ET 18]).

The thousands and myriads of courtiers attend upon the one advanced in years (cf. Deut 33:2; 1 Kgs 22:19; Ps 68:18 [17]; *1 Enoch* 1.9); it is not they who are to be judged (against Jeffery). They are God's heavenly army, though their military role is not in focus here.

The notion of books being consulted again has its background in the life of the royal court, which necessarily kept records of events and decisions (Ezra 4:15; Esth 6:1). This feature of court practice was naturally included when the royal court image was used to picture the workings of heaven (see Koep, *Buch,* 1–39). God's books sometimes record God's purposes regarding the final issues of history or regarding particular segments of history (cf. the sealed books of 8:26; 9:24; 10:21; 12:4, 9). Sometimes they record his expectations of human conduct and his intentions regarding the judgment of humanity in the light of how far they fulfill these expectations, or fail to do so (e.g., *1 Enoch* 81; 93.1–3; 103.2; *Jub.* 5.12–19; 16.9; 23.32). Any of these might be relevant in the present context. The idea of books that list the people who belong to God (12:1) or that record people's deeds and afflictions seems less relevant here: the people whose names would be in God's book have not yet come into focus in the vision, while the deeds that are to be judged are those before our eyes in the vision, not ones recorded in books. The scene is not a "great assize" when judgment is passed on all human beings individually (against Murdock, *Int* 21 [1967] 167–87).

11–12 Execution by burning was a familiar idea (Gen 38:24; Lev 20:14; 21:9; Josh 7:15, 25) and a common way of speaking of divine punishment (e.g., Isa 30:33; Ezek 28:18; 38:22; Ps 11:6). Other passages that speak of victory over the sea/dragon (e.g., Isa 27:1; 51:9–10) are using different imagery to speak of the same judgment as is executed here. The destructive fire seems not to be identified with the theophanic flame of vv 9–10: the words are different, the stress there being on brightness. More important is a more detailed judgment scene in *1 Enoch* 90.20–27, of parallel significance to Dan 7. It describes wicked stars, shepherds, and sheep being thrown into a fiery abyss. As with the books of v 10, a motif in Daniel is thus worked out in more detail in other apocalypses; we must see the allusion against this background, but not read the detail of other apocalypses into this brief allusion. Nor can we infer a doctrine of hell from it.

The vision in chap. 2 pictures the whole statue being destroyed at once. Here, similarly, all four creatures lose authority together, though v 12b adds a nuance to the picture. The data have been interpreted historically, of Babylonia, Media, and Persia keeping their identity within succeeding empires down to the Greek period, or being expected to regain independence on the dissolution of the Greek empire (Rowley, 123–24; Ginsberg [6–11] relates this to specific decades within the Greek period). But this is probably to allegorize. More likely, the vision is making a theological point, taken up in vv 14 and 27: the kingdoms submit to God and his people either in receiving judgment or in doing honor. Heaton suggests that the three are allowed to survive in order to serve the people of God, in accordance with the promises in Isa 14:1–2; 49:22–23; 60:12. This is in keeping with vv 26–27, though the point is not explicit here.

13–14 The lengthy formula that opens v 13 advertises that we are by no means yet through the awesome scenes the vision report relates. The formula resembles those in vv 2 and 7, which introduced the four animals and then the fourth in particular; the scene we are about to witness balances both (Kvanvig, *ST* 32 [1978] 101–2).

The vision is located on earth; but the phrase "among the clouds of the heavens" (עם ענני שמיא) draws our attention away from earth. Scott (*NTS* 5 [1958–59] 129–31) takes this phrase as qualifying "there before me" (וארו) and thus denoting the location of the whole scene described in vv 13–14 (cf. that in Ezek 1). He notes that וארו is elsewhere followed directly by its predicate (cf. vv 2, 5, 6, 7). On his own interpretation, however, v 13 is still unique, in following וארו with this qualifying phrase, which is not a predicate and hangs in the air. It is easier to understand "among the clouds of the heavens" as relating only to the coming of the one in human likeness, and as being brought to the front of its clause, despite its thereby separating וארו from its predicate, for the reason just stated: it thereby draws our attention away from the earth where it has been for verses 2–12 (Ferch, *Son of Man;* Casey, *Son of Man*). The court is seated on earth (vv 9–10), and "among the clouds of the heavens" denotes the position of the figure about to be described as it moves toward that court. The description then compares with the coming of God to earth in, e.g., Isa 19:1; Ps 18:10–13 [9–12] (cf. L. Sabourin, "The Biblical Cloud," *BTB* 4 [1974] 304, following J. Luzerraga, *Las tradiciones de la nube en la biblia y en el judaismo* [AnBib 54 (1973)]). Independently of their context in Dan 7, vv 13–14 might describe an ascent from earth to heaven, as in *1 Enoch* 14; 4 Ezra 13, or a movement within heaven, in which the whole scene is then set, as in the Baal myth; but in their context in Dan 7, they more likely describe a movement from heaven to earth.

The figure who comes is "one in human likeness." The literal translation of the phrase בר אנש is "a human being" (cf. BH בן אדם "a human being," בן עולה "a wicked person," BA יד אנש "a human hand," etc.). "Son of man" is a literalistic Semitism.

בר אנש and בן אדם are always anarthrous in the OT: the term "*the* human being" (*the* son-of-man) does not occur. It does come to be a title for some individual in *1 Enoch* 37–71, 4 Ezra 13, the NT, and rabbinic writings, but these documents use the motif in varying ways; even here it is doubtful whether we should think in terms of a "Son of man concept" in Judaism. Still less is there evidence that in the second century B.C. the phrase is used as a title or alludes to a well-known concept. Nor is there indication of this in Dan 7:13–14, any more than is the case with expressions such as "a lion"—or "a man"—in v 4, "a leopard" in v 6, or even "one advanced in years" in v 9. In each case the terms are anarthrous; contrast "the Great Sea" in v 2, "the Most High" in v 25.

בר אנש is qualified by כ "like": hence "one in human likeness," or more literally "one like a human being." The phrase "like a human being" formally compares with the earlier phrases "like a lion," "resembling a bear," and "like a leopard" (vv 4, 5, 6). Each of those phrases, however, was followed by a clause that qualified the description and explained how the creatures were "like" but not identical with these animals. In the case of the "one like a human being" there is no such qualification, unless it lies in the preceding phrase "among the clouds of the heavens." The expression rather parallels the varied, though more complex, כ phrases in 8:15; 10:16, 18. Like the figures who appear there, the one here entirely resembles a human being; it is not partly animal, like the cherubs in Ezek 1 (Mowinckel, *He That Cometh,* 352; against Kraeling, *Anthropos,* 142–44). The כ adds mystery to the description, in a way appropriate to a vision (cf. Volz, *Eschatologie,* 11–12; Gressmann, *Ursprung,* 342). In Dan 7, the four creatures together, the fourth creature, and the one advanced in years are described without כ; there is comparable variation within Ezek 1, and it would be hazardous to infer that this was more than a matter of stylistic flexibility. It is not that the creatures and the one advanced in years exist, in a sense in which the human being does not, though it might be that a pointer was needed to the fact that the "human being" is not actually human (Coppens, *ETL* 37 [1961] 12).

What are the implications of describing the figure as humanlike? Earlier verses in Dan 7 have used the motif of being human over against being animal to denote being in a position of authority. It is this that was granted to the first animal and grasped for by the small horn (vv 4, 8). This connotation seems to continue in vv 13–14. If there is a link with extrabiblical connotations of the term, it is that in some contexts both בר אנש and בן אדם can be lofty terms to mean a "Somebody" (Herzfeld, *Zoroaster,* 835–40; Caquot, *Sem* 17 [1967] 68; Wifall, *CBQ* 37 [1975] 331–40).

In other contexts "a humanlike figure" could suggest the frailty of *mere* humanity (e.g., Ps 144:3–4; 146:3): a feeble human standing over against the horned beast! A British tradition of approach to Dan 7, chiefly among NT scholars, associates this with the motif of the affliction of the supernatural beings in vv 21–22, 25: the humanlike figure thus stands for the frail, afflicted, but faithful element within Israel, to be vindicated and given lasting kingly power (so, e.g., Moule, *Essays,* 77, 79). This understanding is unlikely, given the contextual indications in Dan 7 that "humanity" suggests being put into a position of authority under God. Nor is there ground within Dan 7 for linking the humanlike figure with primal humanity concepts known from elsewhere (see *Form*). בר אנש may—perhaps subconsciously—reflect the בן אדם of Ps 8:5–7 [4–6]; 80:18 [17]; Job 25:6, texts which overlap theologically with Dan 7:13–14; but again, the evidence is not compelling. Describing the figure as humanlike does not in itself indicate that a figure representing Humanity is here appearing to be enthroned as king of the universe.

The humanlike figure comes in order to be invested as king (v 14). The sovereignty he is given is like God's own (cf. 3:33 [4:3]; 6:27 [26]), the rule the first symbolic dream spoke of (2:44–45). He is given the power Nebuchadnezzar once exercised (2:37; 5:19; cf. 6:26 [25]). In serving him, people indirectly serve God, like the foreigners pictured as serving Israel in Isa 60:7, 10; 61:6 (Feuillet, *Etudes,* 454).

He is, then, a symbol for some entity given authority by God. But whom does he stand for? What is the referent of the symbol? The symbolic vision does not make that explicit. This arises partly from the nature of such a vision. It is the interpretative vision that reveals the referents of the symbols. Part of the point about a symbolic vision is to engage its recipients in such a way that they are drawn into the significances and value judgments it attaches to the referents while being discouraged from overtly focusing on what the referents are—and thus perhaps resisting the vision's message. Indeed, to be mainly concerned when we are studying the symbolic vision with identifying the referent of the symbols is to miss the point of the vision.

The interpretative vision, however, also seems less than completely clear even on those elements in the vision that it professes to explain. While it might be that the vision's interpretation was clear to author and original audience but unclear to us out of their context, its allusiveness makes it at least as likely that an element of mystery is built into the vision (cf. vv 15–16, 28). While the beasts clearly enough portray the rise and fall of worldly kingdoms, what would replace them is less transparent; the beasts are closer to being steno-symbols, while the judgment scene and the humanlike figure are more tensive symbols. They affirm that the worldly kingdoms will be replaced by God's kingdom; they do not make explicit how. With the four creatures, their historical reference is primary, though they are then portrayed theologically. With the judgment scene and the humanlike figure, their meta-historical or theological reference is primary; they represent ultimate events and realities which will come, but which are not yet present, and therefore cannot be described straightforwardly like the kingdoms the beasts represent (see Niditch, *Vision,* 209–15; against [Hartman and] Di Lella, 93). It is of a piece with this that Daniel's requests for interpretation, and the content of the interpretation he receives, relate more to the most important of the symbols with historical reference, which hardly requires actual explanation, than to the humanlike figure, which remains enigmatic.

Nevertheless, a wide range of suggestions has been offered regarding the figure's identity. The expression "a human being" can, of course, denote a person such as Ezekiel or Daniel. Like Ezekiel, Daniel is addressed as בן אדם in 8:17, and in *1 Enoch* the visionary is identified by an equivalent to this phrase. Dan 1 has described Daniel, with the three other young men, in royal terms. Yet this is hardly enough to make it natural to read 7:13–14 as referring to Daniel (against Schmid, *Judaica* 27 [1971] 192–220).

As the animals stand for gentile kings who also represent their peoples, the humanlike figure could refer to a leader of Israel who at the same time represents Israel as a whole, as in some other OT passages (see *Form*). On the basis of Deut 32:1–4, the humanlike figure has been identified as a promise that Moses will return to redeem Israel; but the pointers are too scanty (against Gaster, *Search* 1 [1931] 15–30). It has been seen as a symbol for the Maccabean leaders on the way to the Davidic throne: cf. the association of God's kingship and those who are committed to him (חסידים) in Pss 145; 149 (cf. 1 Macc 2:42) (G. Klein, "Daniel," 239). More specifically, it has been identified as the actual leader of Israel whose rule followed that of Antiochus, Judas Maccabeus; the vision thus marks God's approval of the Maccabean victory. This view presupposes that Daniel was written after the temple restoration; and in any case, there are no specific pointers to

Judas, while in general the book's sympathies within loyal Judaism are usually thought to be more with the nonviolent strand that was looking for God to act than with the violent resistance of the Maccabees (cf. 11:34?) (against Haupt, *Monist* 29 [1919] 130; Sahlin, "Antiochus"; Buchanan, *Hebrews*, 42–48).

Tradition, both Christian and Jewish, has commonly understood the humanlike figure to be the hoped-for future king of Israel who would fulfill the hopes of a Davidic redeemer expressed in OT prophecy (the "messiah"). One of the thrones mentioned in v 9 might then be meant for him, so that the scene parallels Ps 110:1; cf. 80:18 [17] (Rowe, *Christ the Lord*, 95–96; cf. Mowinckel, *He That Cometh*, 352). Daniel does later refer to an anointed leader (משיח נגיד, 9:25, cf. 26), though the expression does not seem there to denote a "messiah" (see *Comment*). Seeing the humanlike figure as the fulfillment of Israel's hopes of a coming king does draw attention to links between Dan 7 and Dan 1–6. Dan 7 is concerned with God's reign in the world, not with God's temple in Jerusalem—as chaps. 8–9 are. Whether or not the human figure is royal, he is not priestly (against Lacocque, who identifies him as the true high priest to hold civil, military, and religious authority in place of the Antiochene Jason).

For the anointed one to be a heavenly figure would be a novel idea; by definition, the anointed one is an earthly descendant of David. The visionary portrayal of him coming with the clouds of the heavens might simply signify that he comes by God's initiative and as his gift, without suggesting that he is in himself other than human. Moses enters the theophanic cloud in Exod 24:18, while Ps 2, after all, describes the anointed king as begotten by God and installed by God, without implying he is other than human. Nevertheless, if the humanlike figure is the anointed, the anointed as Daniel pictures him now has a very transcendent dimension. If the idea of the anointed moves between a God pole and a human pole, this humanlike figure is at the former (Gross, *TTZ* 71 [1962] 167–69).

The grounds for identifying the humanlike figure as the Davidic anointed are circumstantial ones. There are no direct pointers to this in the text, though as the one whom God commissions to exercise his kingly authority, the humanlike figure fulfills the role of the anointed one, whether or not he is actually an earthly Davidide.

The implied identification of the humanlike figure with the holy ones on high (v 18) has led to the alternative proposal that the humanlike figure denotes not the Davidic ruler in particular but the Israelite people as a whole; it, too, could be portrayed as coming among the clouds to suggest its coming by God's initiative. The humanlike figure is then a symbolic abstraction (Barrett [*Essays*, 17] compares John Bull as a symbol of the English people). Some OT references to a human figure (בן אדם) may refer either to Israel or to the Israelite king: Ps 80 thus pictures the nations behaving like animals and prays for God to support and restore the human figure at God's right hand (Hooker, *Son of Man*, 19). In Dan 7, if the humanlike figure balances the creatures, it would not be surprising if, like them, it could have both individual and corporate reference. Since a body can be focused in or symbolized by its head, there is no need for appeal to the notion of corporate personality (against Coppens, *ETL* 37 [1961] 17; in criticism of this notion, see, e.g., J. W. Rogerson, "The Hebrew Conception of Corporate Personality," *JTS* 21 [1970] 1–16 = *Anthropological Approaches to the Old Testament* [ed. B. Lang; IRT 8 (1985)] 43–59).

The interpretative vision will in due course indicate that the holy ones on high with whom the humanlike figure is associated are afflicted (v 21); this affliction is in turn associated in some way with the oppression of conservative Jews by Antiochus Epiphanes. As we have noted above, it has been inferred that the humanlike figure is himself by implication a suffering figure. The inference is logical and may have been drawn in the NT, partly through the association of the Son of Man with the servant of Isa 52:13–53:12, but it is not drawn in Dan 7 itself. In the symbolic vision, the four creatures do not attack the humanlike figure, and the logic that makes them do so is the logic of allegory. The picture is of conflict and victory rather than affliction and suffering (Bruce, *Christ the Lord,* 58; Casey, *Son of Man*). The verses describe the appearing, presentation, and investiture of someone notable and imposing, not the exaltation of a previously lowly figure.

To describe the figure as humanlike is to indicate a contrast between it and the four animals. It is not necessarily to indicate that the actual figure is human, or that its extra-visionary referent is human. Indeed, in isolation from the context, v 13a would most naturally denote God himself. He characteristically appears with the clouds of the heavens (Baal's entourage in myths); he characteristically appears humanlike (cf. Ezek 1:26). Thus Feuillet took the human figure as a hypostatized manifestation of God, like the figure of Wisdom in Prov 8 (*Etudes,* 435–93); Procksch saw the human figure in Daniel as taking up the portrayal of God as manlike in Ezek 1: it is a hypostatized image of God, embodying his lordship ("Berufungsvision," 148–49; *NKZ* 44 [1933] 80–81); while Caragounis (*Son of Man*) described the figure as a heavenly being with honors and powers normally predicated of God. Black, too, sees the one in human likeness as standing for a divine figure, though he understands the divine figure to suggest the deification of Israel at the End (*Menschensohn,* 92–99; *Jews, Greeks, and Christians,* 60–62). It is a long step, however, from a belief in a renewed, celestial Israel such as the interpretative vision may envisage, to the deification of Israel. And with any of these approaches, since the one advanced in years stands for God, it is difficult to attribute the same significance to this second figure.

The scene's pointers toward the unlikely conclusion that it envisages two divine beings reflect its background in mythic material concerning the installation of a junior god by a senior god (Day, *Conflict,* 162). Now the OT often pictures a heaven of the same hierarchy as such material, but with the place of lesser gods being taken by the one God's heavenly but nondivine aides. In subsequent visions in Daniel, humanlike figures are regularly celestial beings (8:15–16; 9:21; 10:5 [?], 16, 18; 12:6–7). Human beings over against animals in apocalypses such as *1 Enoch* 89–90, too, suggest supernatural beings over against human beings. To speak of a scheme of symbolism in the apocalypses, whereby God is represented by light, fire, and cloud [!], angels by stars or men, the righteous by clean animals, the wicked by unclean animals and predators, demons by hybrids (Massyngberde Ford, *JSJ* 10 [1979] 204), is to overschematize the presentation (cf. Hooker, *Son of Man,* 15), but the parallels are suggestive, and add to hints that the humanlike figure has a celestial rather than a human referent. Admittedly celestial beings other than God do not appear in or on the clouds of the heavens elsewhere in the OT. Only God comes on the clouds (Isa 19:1; Ps 104:3); but it may then be significant that the humanlike figure comes with/among them, not on them. The cloud comes to collect Moses in Josephus, *Ant.* 4.4.48 [4.326] (cf. *b. Yoma* 4a; *Pes Rabbah* 20:4), to collect Jesus in Acts 1:9, to collect Christians in 1 Thess 4:17, and to carry Israel in targums to Exod 19:4 (Vermes, *Jesus,* 170, 186).

So perhaps the humanlike figure is a celestial being, one who represents Israel in heaven (Völter, *ZNW* 3 [1902] 173–74). The fact that celestial beings appear elsewhere in the vision as attendants and interpreters (vv 10, 16) hardly excludes the possibility that in v 13 one has a more substantial role. Chaps. 8–12 portray celestial beings fulfilling various roles, and offer several concrete possibilities regarding the identification of the humanlike figure in chap. 7. It might be identified with the further unnamed awesome and mysterious man dressed in linen of 10:5–12:13, who is also described in quasi-divine terms, linking him with Michael and the Metatron of *1 Enoch* (cf. Coppens, *ETL* 40 [1964] 72–80; F. Stier, *Gott und sein Engel im Alten Testament* [Münster: Aschendorf, 1934] 96–104). This, however, seems to explain one enigma by another. A less opaque possibility is Gabriel, but he is supremely the heavenly interpreter (8:16–26; 9:21–27). If he appears in chap. 7, it is as the one who fulfills this role in vv 16–23 (Day, *Conflict,* 171–72, against Zevit, *VT* 28 [1978] 488–92; see on 9:21). K. Müller (*Menschensohn,* 47–48) compares the "coming" (אתה) of the humanlike figure with that of the heavenly watchman in 4:10–14 [13–17], though again the significance of the two comings—in the form of the chapters as we know them—is rather different.

The function the humanlike figure fulfills is closer to that of Michael in 10:13, 21; 12:1. Michael is one of the supreme celestial leaders who is especially identified with Israel and is committed to standing by them and standing firm on their behalf against celestial leaders identified with other peoples (cf. Stier [see above]). The authority he exercises in heaven parallels that bestowed on the humanlike figure in 7:14, who appears at a similar moment (when evil power overreaches itself and God's final intervention comes) to the one when Michael appears in chap. 12 (see Schmidt, *JBL* 19 [1900] 26–27; Collins, *Vision,* 123–52; Sahlin, *ST* 37 [1983] 147–50). The Qumran War Scroll (1QM 17.5–8) promises the overthrow of the prince of the wicked kingdom as the kingdom of Michael is exalted in the midst of the gods, and the realm of Israel in the midst of all flesh (U. B. Müller, *Messias,* 7–8). Admittedly the humanlike figure is not a combatant here, as Michael is in chaps. 10–12 (Caquot, *Sem* 17 [1967] 59–60). This may only reflect the fact that the scene takes place on earth; the battles Michael fights take place in heaven. That the same celestial person could have different roles in different contexts, as Michael would be envisaged as doing, is indicated by the portrait of Melchizedek in 11Q*Melchizedek* (see, e.g., M. de Jonge and A. S. van der Woude, "11Q Melchizedek and the New Testament," *NTS* 12 [1965–66] 302–6).

If the figure is Michael, or Gabriel, or any other specific individual, it is odd that he appears only here and not in vv 18, 22, and 27. Further, K. Müller's suggestion that in an earlier form v 13 named a particular celestial being (*Menschensohn,* 49) highlights the fact that the being is unnamed in chap. 7 as we know it. The figure (like the interpreter of v 16) is actually unidentified; this is a facet of the chapter which interpretation has to preserve. Later chapters must not be read back into this one (against Collins, *Vision,* 123–52). Chap. 7 invites us to focus on the humanlike figure's role rather than its identity. Indeed, it has been argued that the humanlike figure's failure to appear in the interpretative section of the vision indicates that it is not a particularly important feature of the chapter (Porteous).

15–16 Although the response of troubled perplexity is one to which the chapter genuinely invites its audience, accounts of a symbolic vision regularly involve, as well as the visionary himself, another being who explains his vision. This was so with chap. 2, where Nebuchadnezzar's response on waking after his symbolic dream was described in terms similar to the ones used here of Daniel. The giving of a mysterious vision which combines ominous and encouraging features yet which is not of wholly patent meaning creates a suspense that is heightened by the separation of symbolic vision and explanation. Alarm and encouragement are invited, but the basis for them is withheld. It will come with the more force when revealed.

Chap. 7 resumes the pattern of symbolic visions elsewhere in the OT, where the interpretation was given within the vision. For pre-exilic prophets, God was the interpreter (Amos 7–8; Jer 1). In Ezek 40–48; Zech 1–6 God again appeared, but angels played the major interpretative role. In Dan 7, Daniel instinctively turns to one of the celestial attendants in his symbolic vision (probably identified as Gabriel in 8:16). In Dan 8–12, interpretative revelations are given on heavenly initiative. The source of the interpretation guarantees that it comes from heaven, not from mere human insight.

17 The initial interpretation of the vision in vv 17–18 is brief. It both puts a focus on the central fact of a heavenly kingdom to succeed the earthly ones, and increases suspense as by its omissions it draws attention to aspects of the symbolic vision that remain at the moment unexplained. The Great Sea in the symbolic vision stands for the world (the Mediterranean is the sea in "the middle of the world"—though the term is not used in this sense in ancient times). The idea that the forces of disorder symbolized by crashing waters are embodied in the turbulent history of the nations perhaps underlies Isa 17:12–13; Jer 46:7–8, and the interpretation of the Great Sea here.

The four kings stand for their kingdoms (cf. v 23); cf. the alternating of reference to both in 2:37–45, also the understanding of the animals in 8:20–22 as referring to the two lines of kings as wholes, while the buck's large horn denotes one individual king. As is the case there, the identity of the kingdoms is at most only partly explained. They could possibly be the four powers that divided Alexander's empire among them (so Gressmann, *Messias,* 344, 366; J. Bright, *The Kingdom of God* [Pierce and Washabough, 1953; repr. Nashville: Abingdon, 1981] 184; cf. also Wittstruck, *JBL* 97 [1978] 101–2). That the animals emerge from the sea one by one need not in itself rule out the kingdoms' being concurrent, as the ten horns of v 7 seem to appear together, yet to represent consecutive kings; this is simply a feature of the visionary presentation to Daniel (see the comment below on the fact that all four are pictured as future). The fourfold Greek empire appears in connection with the four winds of the heavens (cf. v 2) in 8:8; 11:4. They could alternatively, however, be taken as four second-century powers looked at from an eastern Mediterranean perspective (cf. v 2), Egypt in the south, the Parthians in the east, Rome in the west, and Syria in the north (K. Hanhart, *NTS* 27 [1980–81] 576–83). But the major obstacle to these theories is that they involve taking chap. 7 in isolation not only from Dan 1–6 but also from Dan 8–12. The four-empire scheme of chap. 7 need not be identical to that of chap. 2 (against Montgomery; Hartman), but it does link with it. Chap. 2 explicitly refers to a sequence of kings beginning with Nebuchadnezzar, and the portrayal of the first animal in 7:4 takes up that of Nebuchadnezzar. Similarly, there may be differences of detail between chaps. 8–12 and chap. 7, but these visions again link with each other, and each of those in chaps. 8–12 begins in Daniel's own time and offers a perspective on history from the Babylonian/early Persian period to the Antiochene period. The interpreter speaks as if Babylon as much as the succeeding empires is still future. The effect is to distance even the (implied) sixth-century reader from the sixth-century context: we stand back from the total history of the kingdoms and survey it as a whole.

I have suggested that if we are to attempt to identify the four regimes in chap. 2 at all, they are those of the four kings who appear in Dan 1–6, Nebuchadnezzar, Belshazzar, Darius, and Cyrus. Nothing specific points to this being the right understanding of chap. 7; indeed, chap. 7 offers no specific indications of the empires' identity. The chapter itself would permit the fourth empire to be Rome, as traditional Jewish and Christian interpretation held (cf. recently Gruenwald, *ANRW* ii 19, 1:90). But we have just noted that succeeding visions suggest that the four kingdoms span the period from Daniel's own lifetime to the Greek period. This would make one expect the fourth kingdom in chap. 7 to be Greece, which fits the chapter just as well. Greece is the general concern of the subsequent visions; in particular, there is a match between the portrait of the small horn in v 8 (cf. vv 20–21, 24–25) and that in 8:9–14, 23–25, which unequivocally denotes Antiochus IV Epiphanes (175–163 B.C.). In chap. 7 the small horn seeks to behave in an impressive and humanlike way, comes to look bigger than the others, makes war on holy beings and prevails over them, makes statements hostile to God himself, and plans to change times set by decree, which are given into his control for a time limited to "three and a half periods" until his authority is taken away by God's judgment. In chap. 8 the small horn grows in several directions, attacks the celestial army and overthrows some of it, grows within reach of the army commander, attacks the sanctuary itself and is given control of the daily offerings, for a time limited to 2,300 evenings and mornings, until it is broken by supernatural power. The interpretation further emphasizes the king's trickery, power, and destructiveness. The features of the two portraits are essentially similar: the small horn's size and strength, its partially successful attack on the holy/celestial beings, its interference with God's own realm, and the assurance that its power has a limit set to it.

The different images and details complement each other. In chap. 8 the small horn emerges after the appearance of *four* earlier horns (8:8; contrast the ten here): in other words, it is put in connection with a group of four kings, not a group of ten. In chap. 8 it grows *from* one of the four existent horns, without harming any of them or increasing their number, whereas in chap. 7 it grows as an additional horn among the ten, three of which are uprooted; this follows directly from the fact that chap. 7 focuses on the king's relationship to other kings in his line, whereas chap. 8 focuses on the king's relationship to the four "parent" post-Alexander kingdoms. The differences between the two chapters do not mean that at any point the portraits of the small horn are incompatible. They *could* denote different kings, but—juxtaposed in the same book—this is not the natural understanding.

The small horn in chap. 8 is Antiochus Epiphanes. The parallels just considered suggest that he is also the last king referred to in chap. 7; within the OT period, he alone fits the portrait in v 8. Further, in 8:17 Daniel is told that his vision of Antiochus as the small horn relates to the time of the end; the Greek empire is evidently viewed as the last. A similar perspective emerges in Dan 10–12. He could hardly be told that if he had already received a vision that looked beyond the Greek period to another historical era (Bevan, 66). His being the small horn that appears after the others and displaces some of then (see on v 24) refers to the fact that he was not in line for the throne, being a younger son of Antiochus III (cf. 11:21).

The oldest allusion to Dan 7, in *Sib. Or.* 3.388–400, presupposes this same understanding. It may be that the main oracle there originally referred to Alexander (J. J. Collins, *OTP* 1:359), but vv 396–400 at least allude to Antiochus IV, in terms that correspond to Dan 7:7–8 (ten horns and an extra horn). The lines presumably come from the second century B.C., perhaps c. 140 (Casey, *Son of Man,* 119). Their understanding of Dan 7 is also presupposed by 2 Esd 12:10–12 (see below). It reappears in Porphyry (A.D. 233–304), the fourth-century Syrian writers Aphrahat and Ephrem and later writings representing the "Syrian tradition" (Casey, *Son of Man,* 51–70). *Sib. Or.* 4 also assumes a four-empire scheme culminating with the Greeks, but adds Rome to the sequence, without actually bringing it into the scheme as a fifth empire (Flusser, "Empires"; Collins, OTP 1:381–89). Dionysius of Halicarnassus (first century B.C.) treats Rome as the fifth in the traditional scheme, following Assyria, Media, Persia, and Greece. Rome also features in Daniel as a power rising in the west in the second century (11:30). In the context of contemporary expectation that Rome was destined to be the fifth empire (cf. Appian, *Wars* 8.19 [132]), Daniel may be covertly denying it such a status. It gives Rome no place in the scheme of empires. From NT times Rome came to be incorporated into the scheme of empires, as the fourth and climactic power in the sequence (cf. Casey, *Son of Man,* 71–73). The small horn was then assumed to be Vespasian (so, recently, Hertlein, *Menschensohnfrage,* who dated Daniel in the first century A.D.) or, more commonly, Titus. That the Roman interpretation is a novel one unknown to Daniel himself is explicit in 2 Esd 12:10–12 (c. A.D. 90). Here God explains a vision that "Ezra" has seen: "the eagle you saw rising from the sea represents the fourth kingdom in the vision seen by your brother Daniel. But he was not given the interpretation which I am now giving you or have given you . . ." (God goes on to describe the Romans).

It is as certain an exegetical judgment as most that the contextual meaning of Dan 7 is that the first empire is Nebuchadnezzar's Babylon, the fourth is Greece. There is less certainty about the identity of the second and third kingdoms. Porphyry understood them as Medo-Persia and Alexander's Greek empire, the fourth creature then representing the Seleucid kingdom in particular (so also, e.g., Lagrange, *RB* 1 [1904] 494–520; Buzy, *RB* 27 [n.s. 15] [1918] 403–31). But Dan 7 sees the fourth empire as stronger and more violent than the third: this is not the estimate of the Seleucids in relation to Alexander generally suggested by historians or that indicated by 8:22; 11:3–4 (Keil). Further, Dan 8 seems to see the Seleucid monarchy as part of the Greek empire (Gruenthaner, *CBQ* 8 [1946] 210). The "Syrian tradition" generally takes the intermediate empires to be Media and Persia, in line with the traditional scheme noted above (so also nearly all critical scholars). Admittedly these are treated as the two parts of one empire in chap. 8 (cf. the references to the [one] law of the Medo-Persian empire in 6:9, 13, 16 [8, 12, 15]; and the prophecy that Belshazzar's kingdom will be given to the Medes and Persians in 5:28). On the other hand, earlier chapters have portrayed the Babylonian empire giving way to rule by a Mede and then by a Persian (5:31; 6:29 [28]; cf. 9:1; 10:1), and historically Cyrus's Persian empire possessed an authority that Darius's Median rule did not (cf. 7:5–6). Van Hoonacker (*ExpT* 13 [1901–2] 420–23) suggests that the second and third kingdoms are, as in chap. 2, the two regimes that the stories have majored on after Nebuchadnezzar, Belshazzar and Darius. The description of the second creature with its voracious appetite then takes up the banquet theme of chap. 5. The description of the third as being given domain follows that of the worldwide authority attributed to Darius in chap. 6.

There is little evidence to go on in identifying the second and third kingdoms, and each interpretation gives a slightly artificial result. This reflects two facts. First, Daniel is not really interested in the second and third kingdoms, and perhaps had no opinion regarding their identity. Second, the four-empire scheme as a whole is more important than the identification of its parts. Dan 7 is applying a well-known scheme to a period that has to begin with the exile and end with the Antiochene crisis. As is the case with Paul's horticultural analogy in Rom 11 (grafting branches out of a tree and then grafting them back in), utilizing the four-empire scheme involves squeezing historical and theological material into a pre-existent mold that was not designed for it; we should not therefore allegorize the details. The phenomenon recurs with the 490–year scheme of Dan 9.

18 The interpreter goes on to identify those who, when the regular sequence of kingdoms has run its course, will "take over the kingship" (קבל מלכותא)—the ordinary term for succeeding to the throne (cf. 6:1 [5:31]). They will take over the same kingship that these preceding regimes held. There is only one kingship, and this kingship which succeeds other kingships is presumably, like them, a rule exercised in the world, as in earlier chapters. Yet it is a rule derived from heaven. As much has been implied by the earlier symbolism of the humanlike figure coming among the clouds of the heavens, but it is now explicit in the description of those who exercise this rule, קדישי עליונין ("holy ones on high": see n. 18.a).

Who are they? The phrase appears only in Dan 7:18, 22, 25, 28, though a near-equivalent in Hebrew, קדושי עליון "holy ones of the Most High" occurs in CD 20.8. קדוש (EVV "holiness") is not essentially a moral term; it denotes the distinctive, absolute, transcendence of deity. By extension, the term applies to other supernatural beings, to earthly entities associated with deity such as shrines and their personnel, and to Israel as the people distinctively set apart by God. The status of being קדוש "holy" implies being called to be קדוש in the way one lives; thus within Israel there would be people who in this sense were קדושים and others who were not. BA קדישין, then, could denote supernatural beings, or Israel as a whole, or people within Israel who were faithful to God, or a sacral group within Israel such as the priesthood.

In the OT, קדושים most commonly denotes heavenly beings. This is clearest in Ps 89:6, 8 [5, 7]; Job 5:1; 15:15; see also Deut 33:2–3; Hos 12:1; Zech 14:5; Ps 16:3; Prov 9:10; 30:3. The usage is also common in extra-canonical writings (e.g., Sir 42:17; Wis 10:10; *Jub.* 17.11; *T. Levi* 3.3; *1 Enoch* 12.2; 14.23; 1QapGen 2.1; 1QM 15.14). In the OT, only in Ps 34:10 [9] does the noun קדושים clearly refer to human beings (though cf. the adjective in Lev 19:2; Num 16:3). In extra-canonical writings this usage is more common (e.g., Tob 12:15; 1 Macc 1:46; *T. Levi* 18.11, 14; *T. Iss.* 5.4; *1 Enoch* 93.6 [OTP has a misprint here]; 1QM 3.4–5; 10.10). The term can denote Israelites in general, the righteous on earth, or believers kept safe after death. Brekelmans (*OTS* 14 [1965] 305–29) lists references fully, though he includes many from *1 Enoch* 37–82 whose date is likely to be significantly later than Daniel.

A large number of passages in the OT and in extra-canonical writings are of uncertain reference. Some of this ambiguity may reflect a close association between the earthly people of God and his servants in heaven. A suggestive passage is 1QM 12.8–9: "You, O God, are awesome in your kingly glory, and the congregation of your holy ones is among us for eternal help. We despise kings, we mock and scorn the warriors, for a holy one, the Lord, the glorious King is with us, a people of [עַם: but should it be pointed עִם, 'with'?] holy warriors, and an army of angels is among our levy. The Mighty Warrior is in our congregation and the army of his spirits is with our infantry and horsemen."

General Jewish usage would thus permit a reference either to supernatural or to earthly beings in Dan 7. Whoever the holy ones are, the notion of their receiving permanent royal authority on earth is a new one in the OT, though not without antecedents. Prophets envisage the world bowing down to Israel (e.g., Isa 14:2; 60:12), and this idea reappears in extra-canonical writings (cf. 1QM 1.5; 12.14–16 = 19.7–8). Wis 3:8 speaks of the righteous ruling over nations after their death (cf. 5:6; 6:20–21). Supernatural beings rule individual nations according to Deut 32:8 (cf. Ps 82), while 1QM 17.6–8 refers to the princely authority exercised by Michael, though this is an authority in the heavenly realm.

Within Daniel itself, קדוש/קדיש regularly denotes heavenly beings (seven times in chaps. 4–5, also 8:13; 8:24 corresponds to the use of the expression in chap. 7 [especially v 27] and its interpretation will follow from that). Conversely, the book has so far made no allusion to Israel and its destiny. Dan 2:34, 44–45 envisages a kingdom set up by God; Israel is not referred to. And if the author wished to refer to the "saints," Israel or the faithful within Israel, he has available the term חסיד (*ḥasid*), familiar from the OT (Ps 30:5 [4]; 31:24 [23]) and in use in the second century (cf. 1 Macc 2:42; 7:13), or other expressions used in chaps. 10–12. On the other hand, references given above indicate that several documents (e.g., *1 Enoch*, 1QM) use terms such as קדישין to refer both to heavenly and to earthly beings, in different contexts. The use of קדושים to denote heavenly beings elsewhere in Daniel cannot be reckoned to determine its meaning in chap. 7 (עם קדש in 12:7 presumably denotes an earthly people).

Similar considerations arise when we move on to consider the word that qualifies קדישין, עליונין ("[on] high"; see n. 18.a). עליון "high" refers to Israel (as עם קדש, "a holy people") in comparison with other nations in Deut 26:19; cf. 28:1; to the human ruler in Ps 89:28 [27], cf. perhaps בני עליון "sons of the Most High" in Ps 82:6; and to the temple in 1 Kgs 9:8. Plural עליונים, however, commonly denotes heavenly beings in MH (so *DTT*: e.g., *Lev. Rabbah* 9).

The compound expression could grammatically mean "the most holy ones among those on high" and thus designate a particular category of heavenly beings (cf. *1 Enoch* 14.23), but it need not be understood thus, and Daniel gives no indication elsewhere of thinking in terms of various groups of heavenly beings. Nor is there specific reason to understand the phrase to denote Israel or the faithful within Israel transformed into heavenly beings after death and joining other supernatural beings, in rest in heaven or in ruling on earth, as in *1 Enoch* 90.38 and later apocalypses (cf. *1 Enoch* 39; *T. Dan* 5.11–12) (against Charles).

The conclusion we reach regarding the "holy ones on high" is similar to our conclusion regarding the humanlike figure that this expression explains: the phrase is allusive, though marginally more likely to denote celestial beings than earthly ones (with Procksch, Noth, Dequeker, Coppens, Collins; against Brekelmans, Hanhart, Deissler, Hasel, Poythress, Casey [see *Bibliography*]). Again, however, we need a caveat: whereas v 17 explicitly indicates that the four creatures stand for four kings, v 18 does not actually say that the humanlike figure stands for the holy ones on high (Young, *Son of Man,* 9; Ferch [*Son of Man,* 175–80] stresses the differences between the humanlike figure and the holy ones). Further, as we have seen, the dichotomy between earthly and supernatural may be a false one. Collins (*Vision,* 123–52) notes that in 1QM celestial beings and glorified Israelites mingle and suggests that קדישין in Dan 7 can thus embrace both (cf. Lamberigts, *ETL* 46 [1970] 34–39; see Mertens, 145–65). Poythress objects (*VT* 26 [1976] 208–13) that the double reference is rarer than either of the individual references and has the advantage of neither, and Beasley-Murray (*CBQ* 45 [1983] 54–55) suggests that if the heirs of God's kingdom are to be a body that includes both celestial beings and faithful Israel, this ought to be said somewhere clearly. But the trouble with Dan 7 is that it does not say *anything* unequivocally about the identity of the holy ones: that is why there is a scholarly argument over the expression. As is the case with the humanlike figure, Dan 7 is too allusive to enable us to decide with certainty whether the holy ones are celestial beings, earthly beings, or both.

The effect of this, however, is at least to make it clear that the vision does not imply that a supernatural people quite separate from Israel is to rule the world—though that might not be as irrelevant as [Hartman/] Di Lella assumes: it is an intelligible answer to questions about theodicy raised by the Antiochene crisis. But neither does the vision simply promise that the earthly Israel to which visionary and audience belong is to rule the world: that is to underplay the supernatural overtones of "holy ones on high." If v 18 refers to Israel at all, it is Israel as a supernatural people. The vision hardly suggests a purely this-worldly, historical victory of a purely this-worldly, historical Israel over its purely this-worldly, historical enemies. Its hope is based on the fact that the attacks of Antiochus have as their object more than a merely earthly people. God's own people, purpose, and authority are involved. He will see that a more-than-earthly victory is achieved in a situation where there can be no earthly hope. But the vision leaves unclear whether the holy ones who are destined to rule are Israel's celestial protagonists, or their protagonists mingling among Israel, or Israelites who are dead but glorified, or living Israelites viewed as having supernatural significance now. Perhaps the visionary did not know.

Subsequent verses ask for and receive clarification on aspects of the outline interpretation in vv 17–18, but it is more v 17 than v 18 that is elaborated. In focusing our attention on the clarification of v 18, we divert from the vision's own agenda.

19–22 The recapitulated description of the fourth beast in vv 19–20 adds that it had bronze claws, like the Babylonian *sirussu* creature, and that the small horn eventually looked bigger than its companions. A more significant elaboration of vv 9–14 in vv 21–22 is signaled by the return to the report of a symbolic vision, with the resumptive חזה הוית "I watched." The wickedness of the small horn becomes explicit. Noth (*Studien,* 286–90 [ET 225–28]) did not attempt to sustain here his celestial interpretation of "holy ones," as he thought the small horn could not be being said to be attacking and overcoming celestial beings, though this is actually in keeping with 8:10–12, 24 (cf. earlier Isa 14:12–15). The war imagery, not least in relation to celestial beings, is developed further in chaps. 10–12.

23–25 The further interpretation in vv 23–27 again largely repeats motifs from vv 7–14, 17–18, and 19–22. We cannot with certainty identify the ten kings arising from the fourth kingship, or the three who are overthrown. On the assumption that the chapter is fundamentally a unity (see *Structure*), the ten must be predecessors of the king symbolized by the small horn, and the three must be among the ten, not additional to the ten (cf. vv 7–8, 20). These assumptions exclude a number of theories. Ten might well be a round number that should not be pressed; three looks a more precise figure. The one responsible for overthrowing them seems to be Antiochus (see on v 17). We cannot press the symbolism of vv 7–8 to indicate that the ten kings must be contemporaries, on the basis that the small horn appears among the ten horns, as if they had grown simultaneously, any more than we can press the symbolism of chap. 2 to indicate that its four empires were contemporary, on the basis that the four metals appear simultaneously.

Various rulers might be seen as "uprooted" (v 8), "fallen" (v 20), and "laid low" before Antiochus IV, including a number of foreign rulers (see, e.g., Porphyry, Ginsberg, Goldstein [*1 Maccabees,* 42], Buchanan [*Hebrews,* 42–48]), but v 8 seems to point to people who can be seen as Antiochus's predecessors. Among these, the following have been suggested:

(a) His father, Antiochus III (223–187 B.C.), met a violent end (Dan 11:19), and Antiochus IV may have been thought to have been in some way responsible for this. He was in Rome at the time.

(b) Antiochus IV's elder brother and predecessor, Seleucus IV (187–175 B.C.), was murdered by his prime minister, Heliodorus. There is no evidence that Antiochus was behind this (he was now in Athens), though he may have been or may have been thought to have been; certainly Seleucus's murder opened the way to the throne for Antiochus.

(c) Seleucus IV's eldest son Demetrius I (who later ruled 162–150 B.C.) was displaced by Antiochus in 175. He was in Rome as a hostage, having replaced his uncle Antiochus there.

(d) Seleucus's younger son Antiochus was proclaimed king and acted as co-regent with Antiochus IV for five years but was eventually killed, allegedly at Antiochus's instigation (see Sachs and Wiseman, *Iraq* 16 [1954] 208).

(e) Heliodorus had aspirations to the kingship and apparently hoped to rule the empire via the young Antiochus as puppet king; he was displaced by Antiochus IV.

(f) Ptolemy VI, ruler of Egypt 181–146 B.C., was Antiochus IV's uncle and had some claim to the Seleucid throne. Antiochus might be seen as having displaced him; in addition, Antiochus later invaded Egypt, defeated and captured him, and caused him temporarily to lose his throne to Ptolemy VII.

It is impossible to be confident which of these vv 8 and 24 point to. Seleucus IV, Demetrius, and the young Antiochus may seem most likely: Antiochus III's death is very distant to be relevant, Heliodorus was neither heir nor actual king, Ptolemy VI was not permanently displaced from his throne in Egypt nor certainly displaced from the Seleucid throne, to which he had less claim than Antiochus IV. But we do not know what precise information about events earlier in the century would have been available to an audience in the 160s B.C. and thus how they could have been expected to understand the allusion.

As for the ten kings, by Antiochus IV's time many more than ten kings had arisen within the kingdoms into which Alexander's empire had fragmented (see chap. 11 *Comment*). Which ten might v 24 denote?

(a) Dan 11 refers altogether to twelve Seleucid and Ptolemaic kings who are there treated as relevant to the history of Palestine. This would be near enough to ten as a round number, but only two of the twelve (Seleucus IV and Ptolemy VI) could in any sense be described as overthrown by Antiochus.
(b) It is possible to compile alternative lists of ten Seleucid and Ptolemaic kings who were relevant to the history of Palestine as rulers or would-be rulers there, and to include three overthrown by Antiochus, but it is impossible to know whether any one of these corresponds with the one envisaged by Dan 7.
(c) Five Ptolemies and two Seleucids had actually ruled Palestine, from 323 B.C. to 200 and after 200 B.C. respectively. The list includes Antiochus III and Seleucus IV. It becomes precisely ten by the addition of (e.g.) Demetrius, the young Antiochus, and Ptolemy VI or Heliodorus; or by adding Alexander at the beginning and (e.g.) Demetrius and the young Antiochus at the end.
(d) *Sib. Or.* 3.388–400 assumes that the ten are the Seleucid line, *the* most powerful continuing embodiment of a Greek empire in the second century (Rowley, 103–5), and this continues to be the most popular scholarly view. Again, Antiochus then had seven Seleucid predecessors, including Antiochus III and Seleucus IV, so that the list becomes ten by one of the devices just listed under (c), or by adding Alexander I *and* Alexander II at the beginning and (e.g.) the young Antiochus or Demetrius at the end.

Antiochus's distinctiveness (v 24) presumably lies in what is symbolized by the eyes and mouth of the small horn (vv 8, 20), which the end of v 24 and v 25 go on to interpret. The eyes apparently suggest the covetousness and arrogance that issue in Antiochus's forcing his way to the throne and then in his attacks on the holy ones, while the great statements that come from his mouth now explicitly constitute expressions of enmity to God himself (see further on 8:10–12; 11:30–39). The times set by decree (זמנין ודת) that Antiochus will attempt to change are often understood to indicate an attempt to replace the 364-day solar calendar by a 360-day lunar calendar. Questions of calendar were certainly of great importance in various circles in this period (see, e.g., J. C. VanderKam, "The Origin, Character, and Early History of the 364-Day Calendar," *CBQ* 41 [1979] 411; "2 Maccabees 6, 7a and Calendrical Change in Jerusalem," *JSJ* 12 [1981] 55–60; see further on 12:11–12). But more detailed accounts of Antiochus's interfering with Jewish religious affairs (Dan 8:11–14; 11:31–38; 1 Macc 1–4; 2 Macc 4–6) do not refer explicitly to a change of calendar, and it is strange if conversely Dan 7 should single out this sole feature of Antiochus's religious policy. More likely, then, "changing the times" has the same significance as in 2:21 (cf. also 2:9): it denotes the taking of decisions regarding how human history unfolds and in particular how one regime follows another. These are fixed by decree—God's, not a human being's (cf. the use of the word in 2:9, 13, 15) (Barr). In forcing his way to the throne and bulldozing his way through history, Antiochus has defied the shaping of history otherwise laid out.

The question implicitly raised at the end of v 25 is "How long will this be allowed to go on?" (cf. the question "How long . . . ?" in the Psalms) (Beek, *Studia biblica,* 19–20). The answer comes in the last words of the verse: Antiochus will be allowed to control events for a period, periods, and half a period. This has commonly been taken as a cryptic way of saying 3½ years (GNB). The time from the desecration of the temple on 15 Kislev in the 145th year of the Seleucids, 167 B.C. (1 Macc 1:54) to its rededication on 25 Kislev in the 148th year, 164 B.C. (1 Macc 4:52) was three years and ten days. The time of oppression is closer to 3½ years if it is reckoned to begin with events earlier in the 145th year (see 1 Macc 1:20, 29–53) or if its end is reckoned to involve Antiochus's death, which took place in the 149th year (see 1 Macc 6:16). But such observations rest on a mistaken premise. "A period, periods, and half a period" is not a cryptic way of saying 3½ years, whatever the significance of later time references in 8:14; 9:27; 12:7, 11, 12. "Period" (עדן) is not simply a substitute for "year" (שנה) (G has καιρός, not ἔτος). A period could be a year long, but need not be (see v 12, also n. 4:13.b). Nor is "a period, periods, and half a period" simply a convoluted way of saying 3½ periods. It suggests a time that threatens to extend itself longer: one period, then a double period, then a quadruple period . . . but the anticipated sequence suddenly breaks off, so that the seven periods (in effect an eternity) that were threatened are unexpectedly halved (Keil). The king symbolized by the small horn has his time allotted; it is not without end. He himself is under control. The period he rules is a long one, but it is brought to a sudden termination. This way of speaking carried no implications whatsoever for the chronological length of time that will correspond to these periods.

If the earlier part of v 25 alludes to the reign of Antiochus more generally rather than to events after 168 B.C. in particular, the periods referred to here as likely began with his appropriation of the throne in 175 B.C., his encouragement of the Hellenistic reforms of Jason, his appointee as high priest, or his first desecration of the temple in 169 B.C. (1 Macc 1:10–28). Both the rededication of the temple and Antiochus's death a few months later would be seen as partial fulfillments of what is promised at the end of the time in vv 26–27.

26 The death and destruction of the fourth creature (v 11) is effected through the utter destruction of the authority of the king symbolized by the creature's small horn.

27 Earlier references to a humanlike figure (v 13) and to holy ones in some way symbolized or represented by it (vv 18, 21, 22, 25) permit and perhaps point to the conclusion that the holy ones are in some way celestial yet are closely associated with earthly Israel. The same conclusion emerges from this last allusion. Noth suggested that the holy people on high was the celestial army, pointing to a use of עם "people" to refer to a celestial army in 1QH 3.21 (*Studien,* 280, 284–85 [ET 219–20, 223–24]), but most editors understand there עִם "with" not עַם "people" (see, e.g., Brekelmans, *OTS* 14 [1965] 321). Similar uncertainty obtains with regard to 1QM 12.8. Even there, if עם means "people," the construct may be possessive rather than epexegetical. And if that allusion fails, there is no passage in the OT or in the Qumran literature that uses עם to refer to celestial beings. In Dan 12:1, 7 Israel is described as "your [i.e., Daniel's] people" and as "the holy people" (cf. 8:24, though the reference there is less clear); cf. the description of Israel in 1QM 10.10 as עם קדושי ברית "the people of the holy ones of the covenant." The holy people stands on earth; the earthly ones shine in heaven (12:1, 3, 7) (Hanhart, *HW* 99–101). Grammatically, the phrase could mean "a people of holy ones on high" (n. 27.b) and be taken to refer to Israel as the people associated with the celestial beings. As Michael can be described as Israel's lord (10:21), so Israel could be described as the supernatural beings' people (Collins, *Vision,* 143). But such an allusive, sudden reference in the last verses of the chapter would be odd; it is more likely that all three varied expressions in vv 18, 21, 22, 25, 27 have the same significance.

In considering vv 13–14, we noted that the description of the humanlike figure permitted the possibility that it stood for the hoped-for king, but did not point toward this. Whether "(the people of) the holy ones on high" refers to earthly or celestial beings or both, nothing in vv 17–27 suggests an individual "messianic" figure. There is "messianic" and non-"messianic" eschatology in the OT, and Dan 7 invites us to read it as an instance of the latter.

28 For the closing formula, cf. Jer 51:64; Qoh 12:13. The interpretative vision has not resolved the anxieties provoked by the symbolic vision (v 15); it leaves Daniel still concerned to discover what it meant. The report of that encourages the reader to reflection and to read on in the chapters that follow. The chapter's ending on this note of perplexity encourages us as we find ourselves in some perplexity over key aspects of it. If we thought we had a clear and certain understanding of it, that would be a sign that we had misunderstood it.

Explanation

1 We are surprised to find ourselves back in the reign of Belshazzar, indeed at its beginning. That is to return to a point from which we can get a broader perspective on the disturbing tale of the abominations of Belshazzar in his last year, the apparent ousting of Daniel himself from the court circle, the portent that speaks of Belshazzar's Babylonian regime yielding not to an Israelite kingdom but to a Medo-Persian one, and the realization of that in the feeble but dangerous person of Darius. Chap. 7 offers a retrospective context for understanding those strange events, as chap. 2 offers a prospective one for the reign of Nebuchadnezzar.

A perspective on history set in the reign of Belshazzar and following on the stories in chaps. 3–6 might be expected to have a more somber tone and to offer a gloomier picture of the world powers than the one suggested by chap. 2 at the beginning of Nebuchadnezzar's reign. If the year when Belshazzar became regent was about 550 B.C., this was also the year that Cyrus, king of Anshan, took over the Median empire and signaled the chain of events that would lead historically to Belshazzar's death and Babylon's fall. For Judean exiles that should be good news; so it is in the oracles in Isa 40–48, which relate to those years. Daniel's vision shares a perspective more like that of the Book of Ezekiel, whose dates refer to slightly earlier years in the sixth century, but whose prospect includes a further crisis beyond the restoration of the Jews to their land (see Ezek 38–39). History will continue to be like a troubled sea.

Daniel's notional audience continues to be Jews living in the early years of the Persian empire, but the message for them now comes not from the recent past, Daniel's experiences at court, but from the broad span of the future. For the book's implied audience in the second century B.C., the message no longer comes simply from the distant past, but from a past that anticipated their present, and from their own actual future. It speaks not only of survival despite pressure but of deliverance from pressure; not only of life in history but of life at the end of history; not only of God's past interventions but of his one final intervention; not only of past rebukes of human power but of a final numbering of its days.

Whence comes such a perspective on the significance of the nations and the relationship of international politics to the rule of God? Overtly, it reflects the imaginative intuition and insight of a visionary: Daniel has a dream. But we are no doubt intended to infer that his dream is God-given. His insight is received by revelation. This is explicit with regard to the explanation of the dream.

But how does imagination operate, how is revelation mediated? The content of the dream hints that it is via earlier scriptures, the acts of God they reflect, and the kind of experiences previous chapters have described. That is the clearer when we look at the dream in its second-century B.C. context, which implies that the dream is in part the fruit of reflection on empirical events from the exile to the second century B.C. This history has become a means of revelation cast in the form of prophecy. Empire after empire has risen and fallen. If Antiochus rises higher, that will mean he falls harder.

History did not *have* to be read that way. The second-century B.C. crisis was an unprecedented one, and imagination and faith had to undertake a quantum leap in order to express what the vision declares. History becomes revelatory when it is viewed in the light of the tradition of what God has said and done in the past, and in the light of the word he is speaking now, both suggestive of God's promise about history which hope is invited to grasp despite the extent to which it contrasts with present experience (Moltmann, *Hoffnung*, 92–95 [ET 102–6]). It looks in the face the dark realities of history since the exile and the even darker realities of the second century B.C., but insists on also gazing steadily at how the future must be, given who God is. In this sense, the vision's perspective is the gift of revelation received by faith, which accepts the risk of its being the fruit of fantasy received in wishful thinking (Walker, *Int* 39 [1985] 180). The outrages of the present make it morally necessary for there to be judgment and reversal in the future: otherwise all that people have believed about God and humanity's relationship to him is shattered. A crisis deepens faith in the power of God rather than destroying it.

For the first time in the book, a vision is written down. Earlier OT prophecies were put into writing as a stage in implementing them and, when they were disbelieved, as an evidence that they had been given before the events of which they spoke, and thus were indeed words from God (see Isa 8:1, 16; 30:8; Jer 36; Hab 2:2). In an apocalypse the first of these motivations may still apply, but another takes the prominence. The literary and historical context of Dan 5–7 and 550–537 B.C. are only one level of the chapter's reference, and (it will turn out) not the most significant. It has most to say concerning events centuries ahead to a people yet unborn. In the literary form of a quasi-prophecy, writing it down is the necessary link between the "prophet" and his actual audience.

Theologically, narrating history as if it were prophecy affirms that the events that unfold have been within the control and purview of God. Beyond that device, the chapter achieves much of its effect by its use of symbolism (see *Form*). Even the later sections that "explain" the opening part of the vision still use symbols in order to do so. In general, these symbols make possible a way of speaking that communicates without removing all allusiveness; the chapter is the most allusive of the book, and our explanation of it must preserve that feature rather than resolving it by reference to other chapters. Referring to historical realities by means of ciphers hints that there is something not quite straightforward, something mysterious about them. Representing them by means of metaphor and simile points indirectly to aspects of their inner meaning and transcendent significance, without quite making these overt. Describing them by means of such figures of speech, which are already familiar from tradition and which interrelate within tradition, not least that sacred tradition embodied in Israel's scriptures, brings to them resonances and power that newly minted simile and metaphor do not have. Portraying them by means of ancient mythical motifs that identify them as contemporary embodiments of primordial forces expresses and adds to their horrific aspect, yet also conveys the sense that they represent nothing novel or immune from judgment. The use of mythic motifs also makes it possible to speak of realities that by their very nature could not be spoken of in any other, more straightforward way.

2–3, 17 Daniel's vision invites us to stand with him near the shore of the Mediterranean at a spot such as the promontory at Joppa where the waters always crash onto the Rock of Andromeda. A well-known voyage from this port ended in Yahweh's hurling a great wind into the sea, causing a mighty tempest, and eventually bringing about an encounter with a bizarre monster (Jonah 1). In Daniel's vision, not merely one wind but gales from every direction whirlwind over the water and arouse it into a turbulent swell.

In themselves, wind, sea, and animals need not imply anything supernatural or alarming. But the collocation of supernatural winds, agitated sea, and huge animals suggests that the vision relates more than an ordinary storm in the Mediterranean. The sea stands for the world, the interpreter will tell us; the huge animals represent the grimness of history. The first three, at least, are not explicitly evil, though they are grotesque, fierce, dangerous, and frightening. Further, the cosmic storm recalls motifs from myth. These are already taken up in Gen 1:1–2. The story of the Beginning spoke first of God's creative activity, then of the existence of formless waste, then of a supernatural wind/breath/spirit sweeping over it preparatory to God's uttering his life-giving word. The Red Sea story, too, had long ago demonstrated that the operating of God's wind/breath/spirit on the sea had been known in Israel's history as well as at the creation (Exod 15:10; cf. 14:21). In Job 40–41, Yahweh affirms that he controls the heaving and thrashing of those huge creatures that symbolize forces of chaos asserting themselves against order and meaning.

Daniel's vision combines the cosmic perspective of Gen 1, the broad perspective on human history and experience of Job, and the Israelite perspective of Exod 14–15: the totality of the winds of heaven generates the totality of the events of history in which Israel's own story unfolds. Here the powers of chaos are not natural forces but historical forces. The taming of the powers of chaos has not yet taken place, either at the Beginning, or at the exodus, or ever-repeatedly in history. We are already prepared for a vision of wider significance than that of chap. 2, yet it is the Mediterranean which the cosmic gale stirs up and from which the animals emerge onto the shore. Like the prophets Daniel believes that God is Lord of historical events and can achieve his own purpose through them. Like them he recognizes that the process of history is nevertheless an unsavory, unnatural, dark, and unreassuring one, despite God's being Lord of it—in a sense, the more so because of that. If Dan 7 takes up such motifs from myths, the assumption that one God rules in heaven and on earth carries with it the implication that even the upheavals of history somehow derive from him, not from a clash of wills in heaven that mirrors the clash of wills on earth. To put it another way, God's creative work on the formless Deep does not mean he has exorcised from it all potential forces of disorder. Within history there continue to emerge entities that embody that disorder, yet Daniel assumes they are called forth by God himself. Perhaps we may even say that behind the fourfold wind we may see the Holy Spirit acting "to bring forth those forms and frames of rule which he will make use of" (Owen, *Works* 7:369). It is on this basis that lament psalms can utter their characteristic "How long?" (e.g., 74:10; 80:5 [4]), to which Daniel's visions are, in effect, an answer.

The use of animal symbols already suggests that it is the history of nations that unfolds before us; specifically the animals signify the kings who rule the nations (v 17). Israelite tribes were symbolized by animals such as the ox, the lion, and the wolf (Gen 49; Deut 33); modern nations are symbolized by the eagle, the bear, the bull, the springbok, and modern tribal societies use the same symbolism (Gammie). None of this implies there is anything "bestial" about the nations' character or behavior, though as the vision unfolds it will picture something higher than the animal as the nations' destiny, aspiration, and successor (vv 4, 8, 13).

If the animals stand for the totality of the nations, their origin both in the initiative of heaven and in the turmoil of the Deep suggests something of their ambiguity. It is they that embody the disorder of the formless Deep, its energy uncontrolled by any desire to serve God or humanity. Evil is not a unity. Yet they are called into being by God himself. Earlier chapters have made clear that they stand under the sign of Rom 13; chap. 7 adds that they also stand under the sign of Rev 13. The ambiguity is also that of Gen 10–11. Modern nations symbolized by animals, such as the ones listed above, also stand under both these signs, as do international entities such as the European Community, the United Nations, and the World Council of Churches.

4–8, 19–21, 23–25 First emerges a lion: king of animals, symbol of strength, courage, ferocity, destructiveness, rapacity, and fearsomeness. It has the wings of an eagle or vulture, king of birds, large and majestic, high-flying and deep-swooping, symbol of speed and rapacity. The first animal represents a large, powerful, and expansionist nation, a mortal threat to smaller peoples. We are reminded of the power and authority given to the first of the four regimes in chap. 2, that of Nebuchadnezzar. The respective distinguishing characteristics of an animal and a bird are to walk on four feet and to fly. Extraordinarily, the lion-eagle is relieved of both these characteristics: its wings are removed and it is set on two feet. It is enabled to behave and think like a human being. That reminds us of Nebuchadnezzar's restoration in chap. 4, and it underlines the present vision's affirmation of the nation symbolized by the first animal. Where animals symbolize nations, human beings often symbolize heavenly beings. This nation occupies a godlike position of honor, responsibility, and caring for the world, as humanity itself does in Gen 1–2 (cf. Dan 2:38; 4:17–19 [20–22]). Nations have their origin in dark forces, aggressive impulses, and defensive fears, but they can sometimes become means of heaven's will being effected.

The second animal to emerge onto the shore is a bear, a huge, ungainly, strong, and fearsome creature, not normally a predator, but here encouraged to indulge its appetite. The greedy expansionism of nations can evidently have a place within the purpose of God. Its distinctive characteristics may link with features of a specific people, but they are rather allusive.

The third animal is another fearsome predator whose natural speed is enhanced by an unnatural capacity to see and swoop in any direction. God gives a powerful, energetic nation a wide-reaching dominion.

Then something new is heralded. The fourth animal to come from the sea is the one of most pressing importance. It is the most explicitly fearsome of the four and the most explicitly destructive. It is likened to no species and retains a touch of mystery over its identity, though it seems in fact to be an elephant, a fit symbol for the Greek empire as a whole or for the Seleucids in particular. The line of animals as a whole represents the empires of the Middle East from Nebuchadnezzar to the Seleucids, the totality of powers that dominated the history of the Jews from the end of the Jewish monarchy in 587 to its revival in the second century B.C. It is this sequence of world empires that Daniel's vision affirms to have been summoned up from the primeval and formless depths by the activity of heaven itself, so that it manifests something of the purpose of God for responsible government of his world, but something of the instinct of humanity for self-aggrandizement and destructiveness.

The last of these four empires is the most destructive and—we will soon discover—the most arrogant and godless, but this does not in itself imply that all history is degenerating rather than progressing. The animals represent history as a whole as it was experienced by Jews up to the second century B.C. It had been consistently threatening, but now becomes for a while consumingly so. The artistic or intellectual achievements of Greek civilization do not feature in the vision's portrayal of the fourth animal. It is distinguished from its predecessors chiefly by being more bellicose. There is perhaps a reflection here of Palestine's experience of being fought over by rival Greek empires during two centuries (cf. chap. 11).

Like the first three, the fourth animal has an anomalous feature, ten horns, suggesting a comprehensive totality of royal strength. The horns symbolize Hellenistic kings, though we cannot refer them with certainty to ten specific kings; perhaps the author did not have ten specific kings in mind. Likewise a number of historical persons could be more or less plausibly identified as the three displaced kings. The small horn that emerges among the ten, however, we can identify as Antiochus IV, the Seleucid king who precipitated the greatest crisis in the history of the Jews between the fall of Jerusalem in 587 B.C. and the events of the first century A.D. As with the Greek empire in general, much could be said about the positive stature of Antiochus IV, but it is irrelevent to the religious perspective of Dan 7. Antiochus sought to bring order to Palestine, but it met resistance as a pseudo-order. Because it was the only order he was prepared to envisage, it had to be imposed by force. Pseudo-order soon exposed itself as a masked embodiment of chaos, not a bulwark against chaos. The principalities and powers in theory undergird and protect human life, but in reality easily threaten it (Aukerman, *Valley*, 76–77). It is only with the fourth empire that this surfaces, but what does then surface is the inner nature of all the empires, because it reflects their origin in the chaos of the primeval Deep.

Like the first animal, the small horn on the fourth animal has certain human features. It looks and speaks like a human being. If the animal symbolizes the human and the human the supernatural, Antiochus sees himself as having the power of a heavenly being, and speaks accordingly. But he is not given such a position by God, as the first three animals were given their different commissions. It gradually becomes apparent that Antiochus is someone of arrogant look and tongue whose person and activity constitute a challenge to heaven itself, like the challenge of the Babylonian king in Isa 14:12–15.

The first three animals were clearly under control. The fourth decides for itself what to do. It was brought into being by God, but it is overreaching itself. Instead of playing the part that God's purpose had designed for him (the times set by decree), the eleventh king grasps the rudder of history for himself. And he is able to take charge of the process of history. So it goes on for a time, and for a longer time, and for yet more time . . . but the promise is that a limit is set to this. It will not go on for ever. Antiochus thinks he controls history, but there is a stronger hand on its rudder.

It is possible to make out a plausible case for identifying Rome as the fourth animal (see *Comment*); whether one finds later identifications (the Turks,

Islam, the church, the pope, Nazism, communism, capitalism, the European Community, the United States) more or less plausible will depend on one's political and ecclesiastical commitments as much as anything else. The very use of symbolism in the vision encourages its reapplication to later embodiments of the same dark forces as Antiochus, initially Rome (cf. 2 Esd 12; Rev 13; cf. K. Koch, "Vom profetischen zum apocalyptischen Visionsbericht," in *Apocalypticism,* ed. D. Hellholm, 439). Even in his interpretation of the vision Daniel does not name its historical referents, and thus he permits its reapplication to subsequent situations where there is a reappearance of the pattern seen in the events of the second century B.C., a pattern itself known from earlier situations and here being reworked. The process of such reapplication of Daniel's animal images to later empires reflects the fact that international history continues to be a process in which "one ethnic group, then another, becomes through rampaging expansion a monstrous coherence of power and peoples" (Aukerman, *Valley,* 79).

Another tradition of interpretation identifies the small horn with Antichrist. Antiochus could, indeed, be seen as a kind of antimessiah, a royal figure who realizes the opposite of the messianic ideal, a negative to which the humanlike figure of vv 13–14 is the corresponding positive, one who aspires to the authority of heaven itself. But he is not a mere anticipation of something still to come. He is actual, unpleasant reality in the life of the people of God. It is his reality that makes it possible for later generations to take him as a model for their own portrayal of evil.

9–12, 26 The four animals have appeared and their characteristics have emerged. The first three are worryingly fearsome, but their instincts are such that God could use (cf. the description of God himself in Hos 13:7–8). With the fourth, assertiveness against God and his glory is becoming overt. It is a moment when a nation threatens to make itself God, and when it least seems that God is in control. But this is the moment when God himself acts. In Ezek 1, the animals support God's throne; in Dan 7 the fourth, at least, has sought to subvert it, and is now judged before it (cf. Rowe, *Christ the Lord,* 84–85). The very act of portraying Antiochus's attack on God as a reenactment of the primordial battle offers an understanding of the earthly events involved, and a promise that matters will again turn out all right. The stories of Nebuchadnezzar and Belshazzar have illustrated God's judging activity within the course of the history of the nations. Here a final judgment is to be executed, not upon the deeds of individuals but upon the life of an empire. History has been allowed to unfold enough. It is time for action from heaven finally to terminate the pretension of this human power. The victory of cosmos over chaos that creation stories associate with the Beginning is here both brought into history and associated with the End (Moltmann, *Hoffnung,* 123–24 [ET 137]). The world itself has to be understood not merely in the light of the story of its Beginning but in the light of the story of its End, for only then is the story of its Beginning actually completed.

There is a sense in which the whole of history can be forseen by God, as is presupposed by the vision's predictive form, and even predetermined by God, since the animals emerge from the sea at heaven's prompting. Yet the bulk of history proceeds in a way that reveals no particular pattern or meaning, and no salvation history. The nations are "themselves," however, not automatons; and God's judgment is a response to actual actions by the king symbolized by the small horn. (Daniel thus suggests insights belonging to various theologies of history distinguished by Towner.) Thus even while Antiochus is mouthing his arrogance (vv 8, 11 either side of vv 9–10), a court is being calmly set up, and a judge is serenely taking his seat. "God then began to seat himself, as he had previously appeared to be passive, and not to exercise justice in the world. For when things are disturbed and mingled with much darkness, who can say, 'God reigns'? God seems to be shut up in heaven, when things are discomposed and turbulent upon earth. On the other hand, he is said to ascend his tribunal when he assumes to himself the office of a judge, and openly demonstrates that he is neither asleep nor absent, although he has hid from human perception" (Calvin). The affirmations that God reigns and judges (e.g., Ps 93; 96–99) become reality—though still in vision.

The judge, then, is not one who is merely *granted* human (= heavenly) features or who aspires to them: indeed, he not merely *is* human (= heavenly), but possesses the dignity, grandeur, and honor of an elder, bright and splendid in his appearance. The heavenliness, indeed divinity, symbolized by his venerable humanity is suggested by the fire that issues from his transcendent, awesome presence, representing also the dangerous power he embodies when he acts to implement his judgment. As in any king's court, he is served and honored by countless courtiers, his counselors and executives; and as in any king's court, he has available written records of the regime's policy decisions, his purposes with regard to the final issues of history, including the punishment of evil and the implementing of his rule on earth, his plans regarding specific segments of history such as the permitting but the delimiting of particular periods of oppression, and his expectations regarding how humanity is to conduct itself and how he will judge the fulfillment or otherwise of his expectations.

The visionary has stood in suspense awaiting the judgment that the small horn's arrogance must incur. The actual court's coming to a verdict is implicit, not stated: we move straight from the horn's words to the creature's execution. "The loquacity of the little horn has been judged by the mute language of the heavenly books" (Ferch, *Son of Man,* 153). Who kills the creature is also unstated; the passive verb again implies it is God or his agent. The vision offers no mandate for the belief that God commissions human beings to act to destroy the old order and bring in the new, as many seventeenth-century revolutionaries believed (Towner, *Int* 37 [1983] 46–63).

Although the vision looks at the history of the empires as a whole, they rule successively, receiving and surrendering authority one by one. For the first three, a time comes within God's purpose when they cease to exercise authority, but the animals that represent them are not killed. They live on in retirement ready to join in honoring the new kingship of which we shall shortly read. Again, the ambiguity of human empires is implied. Not all are condemned: there is an exercise of power that is relatively responsible. Yet all are subject to constraint: no empire lasts. The alternative destinies of these nations correspond to those in Isa 40–55, which sometimes describes them as receiving enlightenment, sometimes as experiencing destruction. Nations either submit to God and his purpose in the way they govern their affairs and relate to his people, and in the way they acknowledge his new kingdom; or they assert themselves against him and his purpose in the way they govern their affairs and relate to his people, and experience his asserting himself over them in judgment.

13–14, 18, 22, 27 After the death of one animal and the dismissal of the others, the vision reaches another climax. A further humanlike figure appears, his heavenly nature underlined by his coming with the clouds of heaven. He is presented before the enthroned judge and given the authority taken from the animals—a much greater and more lasting authority. They appeared as a result of a heavenly initiative, and are within heaven's purview and control, but they emerged from the sea, which suggests their disorderly, threatening nature. The humanlike figure who answers to them comes unequivocally from heaven, and as a human figure is also implicitly destined to exercise authority over animals (Gen 1; cf. Jer 27:6; Dan 2:38; 4:17–19 [20–22]). In contrast to the eagle-lion become human, it is inherently humanlike. In contrast to the leopard, the authority it is given is lasting, royal, and glorious. In contrast to the small horn, its humanlikeness is genuine, not contrived, and its heavenly glory is given, not seized.

Of the figure's identity, beyond its heavenly origin, the vision initially offers no indication. The point about it is the good news its coming implies. History neither continues as the distressing tale of terror at best, blasphemy at worst, nor does it simply break off in judgment and cataclysm. The pretense to heavenly authority yields to the reality of heavenly authority. The grasping of the king symbolized by the small horn has paved the way for an endowment of supernatural power to be exercised on earth and recognized on earth. Ruling God's world on God's behalf, the humanlike figure fulfills the role once given to humanity as a whole at creation (Gen 1–2) and later bestowed on the king of Israel in particular (e.g., Ps 2). The realization of God's creation ideal comes not through the world's becoming more human but through God's gift of this humanlike person. There is no doubt a biblical imperative to us to make the world more human, but it is not expressed here. Nations and governments are inclined to see themselves as the embodiments of order, but the best they can really do is restrain disorder. They act as lawgivers or policemen, but easily end up running a police-state. The real order is not that of the earthly kingdoms but that which comes from heaven (Koch, *HZ* 193 [1961] 24). People of all races, nations, and languages had acknowledged Nebuchadnezzar (5:19), and he had acknowledged that God alone possessed lasting authority (3:33; 4:31 [4:3, 34]; these motifs also come in Darius's story, 6:26–27 [25–26]). Now people of all races, nations, and languages acknowledge that this authority is given to the humanlike figure who takes the place of Nebuchadnezzar and succeeding empires.

In time we learn that the humanlike figure stands for holy ones on high; they receive his kingship. If the holy ones are Israelites, the vision's significance for its readers is clear. It promises the great reversal that scatters the proud and dethrones princes, that gives aid to Israel and exalts the lowly. That may, however, have a worrying aspect for us. There is little evidence that Israelites or Christians make less oppressive rulers than Babylonians or Greeks.

(I write in a week of harsh Israeli suppression of resistance to their occupation of Gaza, but Christian nations have too long a history of oppression for them to act superior with regard to such events.) It is characteristic of the chosen people to take on the characteristics of the world. The reapplication of Daniel's picture of the fourth animal to post-Constantinian Rome or to the modern Christian democracies of Europe or America is a quite plausible one. The humanlike figure can become merely another animal. The point cannot be safeguarded by declaring that the vision depends on the emergence of a faithful group within Israel who can be trusted with the kingship; the chapter offers no reason of this kind for the kingdom being given to the holy ones. It contains no exhortation to faithfulness, no exhortation to any form of resistance to Antiochus, and no hint that acts on earth bring about the kingdom. It is not concerned with the conflict between the faithful and the state but with the development of the kingdoms and their appointed time (Koch, *HZ* 193 [1961] 12), and with the promise that Antiochus does not have the last word; God will see to that. The violence is his; the unquestioned sovereignty will then be theirs. Even the humanlike figure takes no active role in the drama. He does not fight, like Marduk, or like the messiah; he is simply invested. He receives without acting or striving. The vision does not picture Humanity coming to save humanity (Feuillet, *RB* 60 [1953] 177). Likewise the holy ones do not fight—at least, not successfully. It is their *defeat* that brings their attacker's downfall. One is reminded of God's disarming principalities and powers through Christ's being crucified (Col 2:15).

If the chapter implies a safeguard regarding the worry that human recipients of the new sovereignty will likely only turn it into a fifth empire, it is the fact that the humanlike figure comes from heaven. The ones who fulfill this vision will be those who come from God, who can be perceived to share God's priorities. Perhaps they have not yet been born.

But it is not clear that the holy ones who receive the sovereignty are earthly figures. They may well be celestial beings. So what would be the significance for the audience of the information that celestial beings will be given a kingdom? The second-century B.C. crisis brought not only physical suffering but a crisis of faith. Though there is no talk of the humanlike figure's having been under attack, the small horn is said to have attacked and overcome the holy ones. Antiochus has threatened, assailed, and even overcome heaven itself (chap. 8 will take these ideas further). Israel is not alone in being threatened, assailed, and even overcome by atheistic arrogance. Heaven itself is part of that creation which is included in the suffering of the last days (Moltmann, *Hoffnung*, 124 [ET 137]). This brings consolation to those on earth who suffer, not least because it compounds the necessity for the small horn's judgment. It also further explains the reason for the first three animals' being treated differently. Not all nations and kings actively oppose the glory of God and the concerns of heaven. The realm of heaven has been despised and attacked, but it will have the final word. The holy ones do not destroy the fourth animal, but their suffering is the cause of its destruction.

The cosmic significance thus attached to Antiochus becomes especially illuminating in the nuclear age. Humanity now has the power to destroy itself and the world in which it lives. There is something utterly unprecedented about this situation, and something theologically quite novel. God has allowed humanity to discover how to bring to an end the story he began (cf. Garrison, *Darkness;* J. Schell, *The Fate of the Earth* [London: Pan, 1982]). The prospect is "apocalyptic," and it is in an apocalypse such as Dan 7 that we may find the scriptural resources for formulating what faith and hope may mean in such a context (Hanson, *HBT* 7, 2 [1985] 10–14; Bauckham, *SJT* 38 [1985] 583–601). What is extravagance in Daniel's visions is now reality. Precisely in its extravagance, then, Daniel's vision helps us. It imagines the unimaginable. It looks in the face the possibility of human power and arrogance toppling the rule of heaven over the world. It affirms that the powers of heaven may be assailed and hurt, but that God will still reserve the last word.

It might be tempting to infer that human efforts for peace are therefore unnecessary; bringing about world peace is God's business. We may again recall that Dan 7 makes no suggestions regarding the human conduct that is appropriate in the Antiochene crisis. It is God's act that counts. Yet the Daniel whose visions we are considering is the man of political commitment and religious faithfulness portrayed in chaps. 1–6; his is no privatized faith. And the inference that human efforts are unnecessary if peace must be God's achievement parallels the inference that righteousness is unnecessary if our relationship with God must be his gift (Rom 6:1). Paul's response to this inference is not to qualify his affirmation that everything depends on grace; it is to recall the objector to the fact that righteousness is an end, not a means. Similarly we seek peace because that is the God-like thing to do, not because he is necessarily dependent on our doing so. But as we do so, he may likely choose to bring about his peace utilizing our peace-seeking.

What happens when we consider the humanlike figure in the light of the coming of Christ? The actual title "the Son of Man" is a literalistic rendering of the phrase in v 13, though such links between OT and NT are more formal than substantial. Yet Christ is indeed the one who was to come in human likeness from heaven, and the one still to come in human likeness on the clouds of heaven to receive a kingdom and to accept the honor of all nations. The rule of God on earth *is* implemented through one who is himself from heaven. Along with figures such as the prophet and priest, the angel is one of Jesus' role models: he fulfills a place analogous to each of these (Sahlin, *ST* 37 [1983] 173–74). In the view of theologians such as John and Paul, he is so heavenly that he must share God's own divinity: the similarity of judge and humanlike figure becomes a similarity of Father and Son (cf. Procksch, *NKZ* 44 [1983] 81–83). Thus the Christ event initiates the reign of God on earth that Dan 7 promises. It brings that unveiling of the mystery of God's plan for the world (Eph 3:1–12) which is spoken of here as the opening of the books (v 10).

According to *b. Sanhedrin* 98a, if the Jews deserve it the messiah will come "with the clouds of heaven," if not he will come "lowly and riding upon an ass." Jesus himself spoke of the Son of Man coming "not to be served but to serve" (Mark 10:45), and there may be here a similar deliberate contrast with Dan 7:13–14 (Barrett, *Essays,* 8–9; cf. P. Stuhlmacher, "Existenzstellvertretung für die Vielen," *Werden und Wirken des Alten Testaments* [FS C. Westermann, ed. R. Albertz et al.; Göttingen/Neukirchen: Vandenhoeck/Neukirchener,

1980] 419–20). Talk of the holy ones' being oppressed, however, could easily be transferred to the humanlike figure himself, even though our text does not make the transfer; and when Jesus goes on to speak of the Son of Man's calling to give his life as a ransom for many, the suffering of the holy ones may have been one of the motifs in his mind. (Jesus' proclamation of the kingdom's coming [Mark 1:15] also reflects Daniel's description of the holy ones' receiving the kingdom [C. H. Dodd, *Scriptures,* 69].) He is to be the one to whom every knee bows, but only after accepting the form of a servant and the humiliation of the cross (Phil 2:5–11). The one who stands in the midst of the throne and of the four animals is a lamb bearing the marks of slaughter (Rev 5:6).

The power of the Seleucid monarchy was not broken in the 160s B.C.; nor was the power of Rome broken in the century of Christ's coming. Our longing for God's kingdom continues to be frustrated, though we do see evil's power circumscribed and at such moments rebuked, and those experiences buttress our conviction that we *will* see God's dominion endure and triumph. Further, the affliction and the glory of Christ are not just consecutive. The affliction manifests a peculiar form of glory; the glory has the marks of the cross about it. Perhaps the same is true for the holy ones: not just affliction (v 21) then glory (v 22), but a rule exercised in a strange, crosslike way. Avravanel was right that the reign of the holy ones is to be exercised on earth, but Calvin was right that the nature of that reign has to be understood in the light of the cross.

15–16, 28 When the symbolic vision comes to an end, and even after it has been "explained," and even in the light of the coming of Christ, the response that the vision invites is alarm and openness. It does not encourage us to assume that we have yet reached understanding. When God acts, it is commonly in ways other than his people anticipate. Jesus' birth, ministry, and death were not what people expected of God's redeemer. Daniel himself does not seem to know what the giving of kingship to a holy people on high will look like. Like Jacob confronted by Joseph's dream (Gen 37:11), Daniel is mystified and confused, but hopeful and open to surprise. He is determined not to discount the dream and not to miss anything, so he is going to keep thinking about it and looking for further revelation (W. Brueggemann, *Genesis* [Atlanta: Knox, 1982] 303).

Gabriel Explains Daniel's Vision of the Breaking of the Greek Empire (8:1–27)

Bibliography

Allen, S. *AUSS* 4 (1966) 105–6. **Cumont, F.** "La plus ancienne géographie astrologique." *Klio* 9 (1909) 263–73. **Finkelstein, J. J.** 'Mesopotamia.' *JNES* 21 (1962) 73–92. **[Graves, R. H.]** *Daniel's Great Period of "Two Thousand and Three Hundred Days."*. . . London: Nisbet, 1854. **Hasel, G. F.** "The First and Third Years of Belshazzar (Dan 7:1; 8:1)." *AUSS* 15 (1977) 153–68. **Hasslberger, B.** *Hoffnung in der Bedrängnis: Eine formkritische Untersuchung zu Daniel 8 und 10–12.* St Ottilien: Eos, 1977. **Köbert, R.** "Eine alte Erklärung von 'palmoni' (Dan. 8, 13)." *Bib* 35 (1954) 270–72. **Koch, K.** "Vom profetischen zum apokalyptischen Visionsbericht." In *Apocalypticism,* ed. D. Hellholm, 413–46. **Krauss, S.** "Some Remarks on Daniel 8. 5ff." *HUCA* 15 (1940) 305–11. **Miller, P. D.** "Animal Names as Designations in Ugaritic and Hebrew." *UF* 2 (1970) 177–86. **Moore, G. F.** "Daniel viii.9–14." *JBL* 15 (1896) 193–97. **Nestle, E.** "Zu Daniel." *ZAW* 4 (1884) 247–48. **Niditch, S.** *Vision.* 215–33. **Porter, P. A.** *Metaphors and Monsters: A Literary-Critical Study of Daniel 7 and 8.* ConB OT Series 20 (1983). **Schedl, C.** "Mystische Arithmetik oder geschichtliche Zahlen?" *BZ* 8 (1964) 101–5. **Schwantes, S. J.** "*'Ereb bōqer* of Dan 8:14 Re-examined." *AUSS* 16 (1978) 375–85. **Vaucher, A.-F.** "Daniel 8:14 en occident jusqu'au Cardinal Nicolas de Cusa." *AUSS* 1 (1963) 139–51. **Waterman, L.** "A Note on Daniel 8 2." *JBL* 66 (1947) 319–20.

Translation

[1]*In the third year of the reign of King Belshazzar,*[a] *a vision appeared to me,*
Daniel, [b]*following on*[b] *the one which had appeared*[c] *to me earlier,*[d] [2]*and* [a]*I looked*
at the vision.[a] [a]*As I looked*[a] *I was in Susa, the fortress-city*[b] *in the province of*
Elam. [a]*I looked at the vision,*[a] *and I was at* [c]*Ulay Gate.*[c] [3]*I looked attentively,*[a]
and there before me was a[b] *ram standing in front of the gate. It had* [c]*two horns.*
Both horns were long,[c] *but one was longer than the other, though the longer one*
came up later.[d] [4]*I watched the ram charging west*[a] *and north and south; no animal*
could stand[b] *against it, and there was no one who could rescue things from its*
power. [c]*Acting as it pleased, it did great things.*[c] [5]*As I myself was looking on,*[a]
there before me was [b]*a male goat*[b] *coming from the west over the face of the whole*
earth, without[c] *touching the ground. The goat had* [d]*a conspicuous horn*[d] *between*
its eyes. [6]*It came toward the ram with the two horns which I had seen standing in*
front of the gate and ran at it in mighty fury. [7][a]*I saw it close in on the ram and*
rage at it, attack the ram, and smash its two horns.[a] *The ram had no strength to*
stand against it. It threw it to the ground and trampled on it; no one could rescue
the ram from its power. [8]*The male goat* [a]*grew very great.*[a] [b]*Then just as it had*
become so strong[b] *the big horn broke; but* [c]*four came up in its place toward the*
four winds of the heavens. [9]*Out of* [a]*one of them a*[b] *small*[c] *horn came up.*[a] *It*
[d]*grew abundantly*[d] *southward and eastward* [e]*and toward the fairest.*[e] [10]*It grew*[a]
within reach of the heavenly army and threw to earth some of that army ([b]*some of*

the stars) and trampled on them. [11]*He grew*[a] *within reach of the leader of the army;* [b]*by him the daily offering was removed and* [c]*his sacred place*[c] [d]*and an army*[d] *were overthrown.*[b] [12a]*It will be set over the daily offering in an act of rebellion*[a] *and* [b]*will throw truth to the ground. It will succeed in whatever it does.*[b]

[13]*Then I heard one*[a] *holy one speaking, and another holy one saying*[b] *to the individual who had spoken,*[c] *"How long will the vision last—the daily offering*[d] *and the desolating*[e] *rebellion, the surrendering*[f] *of both*[g] *a sacred place and an army*[h] *to be trampled down?"* [14]*He said to me,*[a] *"For 2,300 evenings and mornings. Then a sacred place* [b]*will emerge in the right."*[b]

[15a]*As I, Daniel, was watching the vision and seeking some understanding of it,*[a] *there standing in front of me was someone of man*[b]*-like appearance,* [16]*and I heard a human voice* [a]*amidst Ulay*[a] *which called out, "Gabriel, explain the revelation to this man."* [17]*He came near the place where I stood. When he came, I was overwhelmed*[a] *and fell down on my face. He said to me, "You must understand, mortal man, that*[b] *the vision relates to the time of the end."* [18]*While he was speaking to me, I fell into a trance*[a] *as I lay face down on the ground, but he touched me and stood me up in my place.* [19]*He said, "I am here to tell you what is going to happen as* [a]*wrath draws to a close,*[a] *because* [b]*at a set moment an end will come.*[b]
[20]*The ram you saw, which had two horns, is*[a] *the kings*[b] *of Media and Persia.*
[21]*The buck (the he-goat)*[a] *is the king*[b] *of Greece,*[c] *and the big horn between its eyes is the first king.*[b] [22]*The one which broke and the four which arose*[a] *in its place: four* [b]*kingdoms will arise*[b] *from its midst,*[c] *but without its strength.*

[23a]*As their kingship draws to a close,*[a]
when the rebels[b] *reach full measure,*[c]
a fierce-looking king will arise,
expert at enigmas.[d]
[24]*His strength will be mighty* [a]*(but without its strength).*[a]
[b]*He will cause astounding devastation,*[b]
and succeed in whatever he does.
He will devastate mighty ones,
[c]*a people of holy ones,*[c] [25a]*with his skill.*[a]
He will succeed in deceit by his power,
[b]*by his courage*[b] *he will do great things.*
With ease[c] *he will devastate many.*
He will stand against a leader supreme;
then he will break without being touched.
[26]*The revelation of evening and morning which has been related is reliable. But you are to close up the vision, for it relates to distant days."*

[27]*I, Daniel,* [a]*fell ill*[a] *for some days, then I got up and dealt with the king's business. But I was overcome by the revelation and* [b]*I could not understand it.*[b]

Notes

1.a. On the spelling, see n. 5:30.a.

1.b-b. אחרי hardly denotes merely the redundant observation that this vision came *after* the earlier one (so EVV) but that it was different yet related to it in form and content (cf. Ehrlich).

1.c. הנראה is pointed as pf, but see GKC 138k.

1.d. Etymologically חלל suggests "[at the] beginning," but in usage בתחלה can mean simply "previously," like בראשונה (with which it appears in Gen 13:3–4; Isa 1:26), and this makes better sense here. It would be odd to refer to the immediately preceding chap. as "at the beginning" (against Zevit, *VT* 28 [1978] 489). Cf. 9:21.

2.a-a. ראה ב = "to look at" (see BDB). Of the three expressions for looking at [the visions], OG omits the third, Th the first two, Syr the second. Both OG, through its paraphrase, and Th give the impression that Daniel was physically in Susa (so JPS; cf. Josephus, *Ant.* 10.11.7 [10.269]), while MT's cumbersome repetitions are perhaps intended to underline that Susa was only the setting of the vision (Plöger).

2.b. הבירה is in apposition to שושן "Susa" and thus does not refer to a fortress within Susa (against BDB), but denotes Susa as a fortress-city (cf. Neh 1:1; Esth 1:2, etc.).

2.c-c. JB. אובל (MT) occurs here only in the OT. EVV "canal/river" identifies it with יובל, but the variation is odd, as would be the expression "before the river" (vv 3, 6). OG πύλη, Syr *'bwl* suggests it rather derives from Akk. *abullu* "city-gate"; cf. MH/Aram. אבול[א] (*DTT*). אבל (as in vv 3, 6) is perh. then original here; it may have been confused by association with אולי or with יובל. Waterman (*JBL* 66 [1947] 320) objects that אבל אולי should mean the (main) gate of (the city of) Ulay: but see Ginsberg, 84. Th transliterates. For אולי "Ulay," OG has Ωλαμ (or variants); Th omits. But perh. א[ו]בל is a gl, so that Daniel is at the bank of the Ulay. In Heb., אולי "perhaps" is an expression of hope or fear, reflecting an acceptance of the uncertainty of what God may do (e.g., Gen 16:2): an appropriate feeling in the context (Lacocque), but the passage gives no hint of the play on words.

3.a. ואשא עיני ואראה "I lifted my eyes and looked": see n. 4:31.a. A common phrase not distinctive of visions (Hasslberger, *Hoffnung*).

3.b. והנה איל אחד as Gen 22:13 (?—see BHS), but this does not seem significant. On אחד = "a," see GKC 125b; Charles "a single." 4QDan[a] lacks אחד, 4QDan[b] has איל אחד גדול (Pace, 19).

3.c-c. קרנים והקרנים גבהות: NAB omits והקרנים as dittog following G; 4QDan[a] and [b] add an extra קרנים (Pace, 19).

3.d. NEB "behind," but this is a rarer meaning of באחרנה, and if the phrase were intended to indicate that the two horns were one behind each other rather than alongside each other as usual, one might have expected this point to come earlier in the sentence. OG connects באחרנה with the next sentence, but it always comes after the phrase it qualifies and thus regularly appears at the end of a sentence.

4.a. 4QDan[a] adds ומזרח ("and east"; Pace, 19); OG has the order east, north, west, south. The Persians did extend their territory eastward, but for MT Persia itself is perhaps eastward enough for anything further to be ignored.

4.b. יעמדו: on dislike of the 3rd pl f, see GKC 145pu.

4.c-c. ועשה . . . והגדיל: frequentative *waw* consecs only loosely related to preceding cls (GKC 112dd). הגדיל (cf. vv 8, 11, 25) is an inwardly trans or declarative hi ("manifest greatness"; cf. GKC 53def). More abstract trs ("grew great"/"magnified itself," EVV) are less likely in this context: see vv 8–11 and n. 8.a-a.

5.a. מבין: hardly an Aramaism (against Hartman); see BDB 106.

5.b-b. צפיר העזים. BHS deletes the ה to make the phrase more regularly indeterminate ("a he-goat of she-goats"); but this is too easy a simplifying of an anomalous reading. For indeterminate constr followed by a determinate abs, see GKC 127e. Jeffrey "a buck of the goats," i.e., the proud leader of the herd; but n.b. other idiomatic phrases שעיר עזים, גדי עזים, etc. (BDB 777). Better take the whole phrase as determinate, denoting "the he-goat (who is already in a sense well known and is about to be described)" (see GKC 126qr; cf. Marti).

5.c. ואין has come virtually to mean ולא here and in v 27; see J. Carmignac, "L'emploi de la négation אין dans la Bible et à Qumrân," *RevQ* 8 (1972–75) 410–11. Shortening of ואיננו by haplog could explain one occurrence, but not two.

5.d-d. קרן חזות "a horn of visibility." חזות is missing from G but not from Vg; OG suggests אחת "one," but the unusualness of חזות suggests it is original, and a word indicating the notable size of the horn seems to be needed (cf. v 8). מראה in 2 Sam 23:21 is comparable, but there are also textual problems there.

7.a-a. Perhaps וראיתיו is *waw* consec and the meaning thus past impf; but more likely this is simple *waw*, instancing the dissolution of *waw* consec. The three following *waw* consecs plus impf, however, may continue the participial construction begun by מגיע "close in" (cf. GKC 116x).

8.a-a. הגדיל עד מאד. The vb which occurred first in v 4 reappears in each of vv 8–11, the forms of expression working toward a climax: simple הגדיל ("he did great things," v 4); הגדיל עד מאד ("he grew very great," v 8); ותגדל יתר ("it grew abundantly," v 9), cf. Isa 56:12; ותגדל עד צבא השמים ("it grew within reach of the heavenly army," v 10); הגדיל ועד שר הצבא ("he grew within reach of the leader of the army," v 11). The more abstract tr "grew great" is appropriate here (contrast v 4). Vv 8, 11 use hi, vv 9, 10 qal; the difference is purely stylistic, גדל being one of a number of vbs which can be used in both qal and hi with similar meanings (cf. רשע "be wicked," 9:5, 15; חזק "be strong," 11:5, 7; צלח "be successful," 11:27, 36). Trs such as "grew arrogant" (GNB), "made a show of its strength" (NEB) are not justified (perhaps not even for hit התגדל in 11:36, 37). The value judgments emerge from the context in which the vb is set; though it is noteworthy that even then the prep עד is preferred to the more pejorative על (contrast Ezek 35:13). See further n. 25.b-b.

8.b-b. וכעצמו is the better attested and more difficult reading than ובעצמו (C and others). כ can be temporal, expressing an exact point of time (virtually "as soon as"; cf. 10:9, 19; 11:4), though NEB takes it concessively (cf. *HS* 262, 258, 505).

8.c. MT includes חזות "visibility" here as in v 5, but it is more difficult grammatically (since it precedes "four"), textually (Th omits it; OG *ἕτερα* suggests it read it as אחרות [cf. NAB], but this, too, should follow the numeral, and OG seems to be simplifying the text as in v 5), and contextually (since the four were not notable, as the one was; cf. v 22; 11:4); it looks like an intrusion from v 5 (Ehrlich). Hartman sees an Aramaizing pass ptpl חזיות.

9.a-a. . . . [f] קרן אחת [m] יצא [m] מהם [f] האחת: on the genders see GKC 135o, 145o.

9.b. Taking אחת as an Aramaism; NEB "one" takes it in the Heb. sense.

9.c. מצעירה, apparently "[a horn] from smallness." BDB does not note this occurrence of the noun, but the real problem is the prep. Perh. repoint to the hypothetical noun מְצָעָרָה (Hartman) or מַצְעִירָה (Brockington) ("[a horn of] smallness" = "a small horn") or emend to אחרת צעירה ("another small [horn]," cf. 7:8), which might have become assimilated to אחת מהם in the preceding line (Bevan).

9.d-d. See n. 8.a-a.

9.e-e. Syr omits ואל הצבי "and to the [embodiment of] beauty," which may be a gl, but there is no reason to assume that ארץ הצבי ("the land of beauty," 11:16, 41) is the original expression and הצבי an abbreviation (against BHS); see *Comment.*

10.a. See n. 8.a-a.

10.b. Explicative *waw* (see n. 6:29.a); the phrase it introduces may be a gl.

11.a. See n. 8.a-a.

11.b-b. The vbs of v 11b may be read as pass (הורם Q, וְהֻשְׁלַךְ cf. G) or as act (הרים K, וְהִשְׁלִךְ suggested by Syr, Vg); ממנו means "by him" (BDB 580a) or "from him" correspondingly. The evidence is closely balanced, the meaning similar. Goldstein ("Persecution," in *Proc Sixth WCJS* [1977] 1:142–43) connects וממנו with what precedes and tr "and beyond him" (cf. Gen 48:19). The singular vb can have a pl subj, as required if וצבא is linked with v 11 (see n. 11.d-d); see GKC 145o.

11.c-c. מכון מקדשו comes only here, but cf. such compounds as מכון שבתו ("the place of his dwelling," e.g., Ps 33:14); מכון כסאו ("the place of his throne," e.g., Ps 97:2).

11.d-d. Taking וצבא, the first word of v 12, with v 11: so G (cf. BHS). Cf. n. 12.a-a. Sanctuary and army are linked in v 13.

12.a-a. The most plausible tr of MT וצבא תנתן על התמיד בפשע is "thus an army will be set over the daily offering in an act of rebellion." נתן על regularly means "set over" (BDB 680) and the two words can hardly be interpreted independently (against, e.g., NIV). צבא must surely still mean "army," not change meaning to "warfare" (Driver) or "hard service" (Plöger). It is odd that תנתן is impf, but see *Comment.* It is also difficult that צבא has to be f (it may be so in Isa 40:2, though see Bevan) and to have a different referent from vv 10, 11, 14. These difficulties make one suspect MT. Syr, Vg follow MT, but G suggests linking וצבא to v 11 (n. 11.d-d), which is an improvement, though v 12 now begins even more abruptly. Other suggested emendations are not compelling. Most difficulties stem from the relationship of v 12a to its context; perhaps it is an explanatory gl.

12.b-b. The tense of ותשלך (simple *waw* plus juss), ועשתה and והצליחה (both *waw* plus pf) is puzzling; so is that of תנתן (impf) in v 12a. EVV tr תנתן and ותשלך as past, but they are hardly impf in meaning, and this really presupposes emendation to *waw* consec or pf (cf. BHS); cf. G's aorists. For RSV's "was cast down" for ותשלך, see BHS. I take the whole v to have future reference, ותשלך being a final or consec cl. (GKC 109c suggests juss is used for rhythmic reasons.)

13.a. EVV take אחד as equivalent to indef art, but this would require it to follow the word it qualifies, as in v 3 (GKC 125b). Further, אחד . . . אחד is idiomatic for "one . . . another" (cf. Amos 4:7; see BDB, GKC 125b). This is also a difficulty for Lacocque's suggestion that the same "holy one" is referred to both times. See further n. 13.c.

13.b. Taking ויאמר as another *waw* consec following a ptpl (cf. n. 7.a-a).

13.c. Lacocque takes פלמוני המדבר to refer to Daniel himself, but has to tr אמר (usually "said") as "asked" to make this work. More likely Daniel's vision follows the pattern of Zech 1:7–17, where the seer overhears heavenly figures speaking to one another.

13.d. NEB adds מורם, ptpl from רום ("overthrown"—cf. v 11), on the basis of OG.

13.e. שמם is usually taken as poel ptpl without a preformative (BDB), but this is hardly justified by appeal to GKC 52s (puals without מ [which may be qal passives] and piels without מ of vbs beginning with מ). Elsewhere in the OT (incl. 9:18, 26, 27) שמם is a quite regular qal ptpl, usually meaning "desolated"—which fits the state of the temple through Antiochus's action (Hammer). In MH/Aram., forms of שמם can suggest "be demented"; this meaning could suggest a splendid allusion to the derision of Antiochus Epiphanes, "[God] Manifest," as Epimanes, "Madman" (Rowley, *ZAW* 50 [1932] 264–65). Such polysemy may be present, but the basic idea is more likely to be that the rebellion will *bring* desolation (cf. 9:26–27): i.e., the ptpl is act in meaning. This is in any case the natural way to take the qal ptpl in 9:27 "the desolater." Cf. also Ezek 36:3 MT, defended by Zimmerli, *Ezechiel* in loc. The poel, too, can have either trans or intrans/pass meaning. Presumably the qal form is chosen to correspond consonantly to שמ[י]ם (see *Comment*), which also explains the omission of the art. In this connection, there may be further polysemy in the vb's capacity to suggest "appalling" (cf. v 27, also 4:16 [19]), though the basic idea is still likely to be "desolating" given the stress on desolation (using שמם) in 9:18, 26 in the context of the use of this vb in 9:27, and on devastation (שחת) in the present context (vv 24, 25); cf. G's ἐρημώσεως and the use of ἐρημόω in 1 Macc 1:39; 4:38.

13.f. תת: the tr of v 13b follows MT, but MT is odd, and one might have expected that a form of נתן appearing here would refer to the setting up of the pagan altar. Thus NEB moves it before הפשע שמם, BHS emends to נִתַּן. Jephet interprets it absolutely, "the giving/setting," a further specific reference back to the wording of v 12.

13.g. GKC 154a, n. 1.

13.h. NEB emends צבא to צבי "fairest."

14.a. אלי; Vrs, EVV have "to him," but they may be conforming the text to what they expect, rather than reflecting an original אליו. For the seer's involvement in his vision, cf. Zech 3:5 (where again G removes it). Or has MT understood פלמוני ("individual," v 13) to refer to Daniel himself, as Lacocque does (n. 13.c)?

14.b-b. Cf. NEB for this tr of צדק ni, which occurs only here; but it differs little from a pass "be put right/justified/vindicated" (cf. BDB), which would presumably be a divine pass (Porter, *Metaphors*, 60). Vrs, RV "be cleansed" suggests taking נצדק as an Aramaism. Zimmermann (*JBL* 57 [1938] 261–62) suggests that it represents Aram. זכי "be cleansed/justified"; the translator then used צדק as if it had both meanings. But if the author were translating, or even thinking in Aram., why did he not use Heb. זכה with its meaning "be cleansed"? (BH זכה also shows the close relationship between "be clean" and "be justified.") Ginsberg, 41–42, 79–80, says Aram. זכי can only mean "be justified" and posits a confusion with דכי "be clean"; but see *DTT* on זכי.

15.a-a. Taking the *waw* consec (. . . ואבקשה, "and seeking . . .") as continuing the infinitival cl (. . . בראתי, "while I was having [seeing] . . ."); cf. GKC 114r. So JB. MT apparently takes the second as the main cl—so NEB, RSV, the latter translating the two clauses as plupf and aorist, not as both impfs; the effect is more prosaic.

15.b. גבר (*geber*): cf. the name גבריאל (Gabriel, "man of God") in v 16.

16.a-a. בין אולי is an odd phrase, since like English "between" בין is not used with a s noun; the only clear exception is Num 17:2 where it must mean "amidst" (in Isa 44:4 and Jer 48:45 the text is dubious on other grounds). The phrase is usually taken elliptically, "between [the banks of] the Ulay," and 12:6–7 may presuppose that understanding, though it uses על "above," not בין. ἀνὰ μέσον τοῦ Οὐβαλ (Th) may give a better interpretation—not that we need necessarily read אובל for אולי (against Hartman), but that the reference is to the Ulay Gate, amidst which the heavenly being stood. J. J. Finkelstein (*JNES* 21 [1962] 88–90) notes that the Akk. counterpart of בין, *bīri(t)*, can also be a noun meaning "middle ground" or "interval," and sees בין אולי as an Akkadianism designating a peninsula between two streams.

17.a. EVV "terrified": but בעת commonly means "overwhelm" without in itself specifying the cause. The context often indicates something other than fear (e.g., 1 Sam 16:14–15) and fear is not indicated here. BDB tr "be terrified" also in 1 Chr 21:30; Esth 7:6 (but see NEB); and for pi "terrify" only Job 7:14 (even there it may be unnecessary); likewise with the nouns בעתה ,בעותים.

17.b. "Because" (Montgomery; cf. v 19b, and see n. 19.b-b., also 11:27, 35) is less natural after הבן here.

18.a. Ginsberg takes נרדם as a mistranslation of Aram. דמך, which he says means both "lie" and "sleep," but *DTT* suggests that דמך means "lie asleep," not simply "lie down."

19.a-a. באחרית הזעם "at the end of the wrath" in the sense of "during the latter part of . . ." (NIV), not "at [or after] the actual termination of . . ."; see on 2:28.

19.b-b. Cf. Hasslberger, *Hoffnung;* Young. MT accents, G, most EVV take as constr "it will be for the time of the end," parallel to עת קץ in v 17. But that cl has החזון as subj; this cl would lack an equivalent (supplied by Th[AB], cf. BHS). Ginsberg repoints to assimilate to 11:27, but there the phrase as a whole is different. Calvin assimilates the tr of v 17 to that accepted here for v 19.

20.a. There being no Heb. equivalent to "is," vv 20–21 simply set visionary feature and interpretation alongside each other (cf. v 22).

20.b. "King(s)" need not be changed to "kingdom(s)" in vv 20–21 (against Hartman, cf. NEB); Dan elsewhere uses the former for the latter (and n.b. the m suff in v 23a [Hasslberger, *Hoffnung*]).

21.a. הצפיר השעיר, the Aram. and then the Heb. word for "he-goat" instead of the idiomatic expression used earlier (see n. 5.b-b). EVV may be right to take השעיר as an adj., "hairy." G, NEB assimilate to vv 5, 8; more likely הצפיר alone is original and השעיר an explanatory gl (Charles).

21.b. See n. 20.b.

21.c. יון, the regular BH word for Greece, reflecting the fact that Ionia made the earliest contacts eastward.

22.a. Once again the *waw* consec continues the ptpl construction (see n. 7.a-a. and cf. n. 15.a-a.; GKC 116wx).

22.b-b. מלכיות . . . יעמדנה. Perh. both are mixed forms, combining מלכים . . . יעמדו ("kings will arise"; Vrs) and מלכות . . . תעמדנה ("kingdoms will arise"; EVV), though מלכיות is a MH form (Montgomery) and יעמדנה could be an Aramaism (Ginsberg, 56, cf. GKC 47k), so perhaps the forms are original here.

22.c. מגוי (Ginsberg, 56; cf. גו in 3:6 etc.) rather than מגוי ("from a nation"; MT). מגויו "from his nation," following G, is too easy. Eitan suggests "from the world," comparing גוי in 12:1.

23.a-a. See n. 19.a-a.

23.b. BHS repoints הַפְּשָׁעִים ("sins"; so JB): cf. G, perh. an assimilation to פשע in, e.g., 8:12, 13; 9:24. The use of the s distinguishes these passages which refer to "rebellion" rather than "rebels."

23.c. Or "come to an end" (cf. n. 9:24.e-e).

23.d. There is no need to take חידות here (alone) to mean sayings intended to deceive (against EVV; see *Comment*), though this motif does come in v 25.

24.a-a. ולא בכחו, as in v 22, and the meaning is likely the same (against Syr, RV, JB), reaffirming that this king's strength, too, does not bear comparing with his great predecessor's. But G omits, and such a qualifying of the description of Antiochus's power is unexpected here as vv 23–25 build up the suspense. A gl from v 22, either accidental or introducing a negative evaluation of Antiochus.

24.b-b. נפלאות ישחית ("he will destroy [with] wonders"; see GKC 100d, 118mp). 11:36 has ידבר נפלאות "he will speak in an astounding way" and Hartman assimilates 8:24 to it. Bevan similarly emends ישחית to ישיח or ישחח "he will utter"; but such a meaning of שיח is not clearly instanced and this seems an implausible way to achieve an unnecessary end.

24.c-c. Explicative *waw* (n. 6:29.a); the phrase may be a gl (Bentzen) or be misplaced from v 25 (BHS)—see n. 25.a-a.

25.a-a. Cf. Hasslberger, *Hoffnung*. Montgomery takes as casus pendens, but examples and cross-refs in *TTH* 123; GKC 143 include none that are so abrupt (Qoh 5:6 comes nearest). OG presupposes קדשים after ועל (Graetz), dropped by haplog (cf. end of v 24).

25.b-b. Taking בלבבו "in/by his heart/mind" as parallel to בידו "in/by his hand" in the previous line. For לבב "courage" cf. 11:25, similarly linked with כח "power." "In his mind [he will grow great]" (EVV) is difficult to parallel, and see further n. 4.c-c., n. 8.a-a. on the vb; here, too, there is no need to understand it as suggesting pretension, for the king really does "do great things."

25.c. EVV generally refer בשלוה here and in 11:21, 24 to the (apparent) security of those who are attacked, unawares. It more naturally refers to the attacker himself: cf. Th, Vg; Syr (which lacks it at 11:24); OG (but in 11:21, 24 ἐξάπινα: if בשלוה means "suddenly" it is an Aramaism—so Hartman also at 8:25); also JB at 11:21, 24.

27.a-a. נהייתי ונחליתי "I fell [?] and was ill"; for the first vb BDB "I came to an end" is very dubious. OG omits; Ehrlich suggests dittog. Rather see n. 2:1.c.

27.b-b. Vrs, NEB tr ואין מבין "and no one could understand/explain it"; but אין has already been used as virtually equivalent to לא "not" in a similar cl in v 5 where the subj of the previous cl has to be the subj of the ואין cl. This is also the natural understanding here.

Form / Structure / Setting

Form

The chapter is the report of a symbolic vision. It uses the term חזון six times (vv 1, 2, 2, 13, 15, 26); also expressions for "appear"/"see"/"look" (vv 1, 1, 2, 2, 2, 3, 3, 4, 5, 6, 7, 15, 20), the preposition כ "like," the demonstrative particle הנה ("there before me," vv 3, 5, 15, 19), and terms such as רדם "fall into a trance" characteristic of vision reports. The root חזה appears also as חזות ("conspicuous," v 5, recurring in v 8 MT [see n. 8.c]). The symbolic nature of the vision is indirectly noted by the use of terms for "(cause to) understand," vv 15, 16, 17, 19, 23. The chapter also uses מראה to denote not only appearance (v 15) but (verbal) revelation (vv 16, 26, 27); the auditory aspect to the vision is of great importance (cf. שמע "hear," vv 13, 16). Its broad contours follow those of chap. 7 and earlier visions: it includes a narrative introduction giving the date and geographical setting, which helps to establish the actuality of the vision. There follows the symbolic vision itself. After that one expects a description of the seer's response and puzzlement (cf. 7:15). In chap. 8 this is syntactically incorporated into the initiative from heaven that brings the vision's interpretation to the seer (vv 15–19). This elaborate section takes the form of the description of an epiphany (cf. Ezek 8; also the more elaborate equivalent in Dan 10). This establishes the heavenly authority of the explanation that follows in the next major section, an interpretative vision explaining the symbolic vision. It opens with the characteristic noun clauses of an interpretation, but changes to verbal clauses as it moves to providing information about events that were not precisely represented in the vision. The climactic importance of these verses is emphasized by the use of rhythm and occasional parallelism. Finally there is a conclusion to the vision as a whole and a narrative closure (v 27) corresponding to 2:46; 7:28; also Ezek 3:15. The symbolic vision and the portrait of the fierce-looking king parallel texts such as the Animal Apocalypse in *1 Enoch* and the dynastic prophecies, and presumably chap. 8 is for the most part a quasi-prophecy (see chap. 2 *Form,* chaps. 10–12 *Form*). The "I, Daniel" formula appears at the three appropriate key points here (vv 1, 15, 27; see chap. 7 *Form*).

Although Daniel links this vision with the one in chap. 7 (v 1), the dreams of Nebuchadnezzar (chaps. 2; 4) and Daniel (chap. 7) are now over; chaps. 8–12 are not dreams. The characteristic terms to denote a dream-vision (see 7:1, 2, 7, 13) do not appear here; OG's addition of *τοῦ ἐνυπνίου μου* ("of my dream," v 2) highlights this. Daniel is awake for the symbolic vision, though he is put into a deep sleep for a short time in v 18 (cf. 10:9–11). This motif, like the dream form elsewhere, deepens the sense of transcendent mystery about the experience being described, and thus the authority of the revelation that issues from it. Like a dream, such trancelike sleep cannot be humanly generated: it indicates supernatural involvement (Niditch, *Vision,* 224).

On the use of symbols, see first Dan 7 *Form.* Like those in chap. 7, these symbols are not merely a code of random ciphers. They indicate that the entity described possesses qualities belonging to the symbol (e.g., a horn suggests strength); they call to mind a body of ideas, images, and values attaching to them in their interrelationships, which are (selectively) projected onto the entity symbolized—thus the king "breaks" (v 25), a term which literally applies rather to the horn that symbolizes him. But the symbolism of chap. 8 involves less of the mythic or poetic than that of chap. 7; it refers less to events or realities beyond present experience. It is also less cryptic, unless the aspects of 7:4–7 that are cryptic to us were not so to the original audience. Conversely, chap. 8 contains more literal description of the small horn's deeds, which makes the symbolism more transparent (in theory: in practice, the literal description is now cryptic to us in a way it, too, may not once have been). To oversimplify, chap. 7 is myth, chap. 8 is allegory (Hölscher, *TSK* 22 [1919] 129). The symbolic vision in chap. 7 comes to a climax with this transition to myth, while chap. 8 comes to a climax with a date. Chap. 7 is an impressionist painting open to several interpretations, chap. 8 a political cartoon with the names of the characters incorporated to make sure the reader understands it. As exercises in theology and communication, the two visions thus complement each other. Chap. 7 is deep, allusive, imaginative; chap. 8 is sober, explicit, concrete. Thus the identification of the empires and kings in chap. 8 is all but universally agreed, whereas the identification of those in chap. 7 leaves more room for dispute. Chap. 8 interprets chap. 7 for us (it is a sort of midrash on chap. 7 [L. Dequeker, *OTS* 18 (1973) 109]); chap. 7 reminds us that the historical realities chap. 8 names are but one set of historical referents of its symbols. It implies a broader horizon.

While chap. 8 thus follows the general form of chap. 7, it is also influenced by earlier scriptures (see Porter, *Metaphors,* 61–120). According to Niditch (*Vision,* 232), Dan 8 is modeled on earlier visions to add to its credibility and pedigree; but its inclination to scriptural allusion counterbalances its less profound use of symbolism. The depth and resonance suggested by mythic allusion or tensive symbol in chap. 7 is suggested by scriptural allusion in chap. 8. Even the mythic allusions in vv 10–11 have already been taken up into scripture in Isa 14.

Aspects of Daniel's description of his experience in vv 1–2 and of the epiphany in vv 15–18 correspond to aspects of Ezekiel's: the provision of date and geographical setting (vv 1–2; cf. Ezek 1:1–3); the visionary journey to the scene of what is to be revealed (v 2; cf. Ezek 8:3); the location by a river (? vv 2, 3, 6; cf. Ezek 1:1–3—Ezekiel's physical, not his visionary location); the one of manlike appearance (v 15; cf. Ezek 8:2 [see BHS]); the form of address, "mortal man" (בן אדם, v 17; cf. Ezek 2:1; 8:5; etc.); the setting upright of one who falls on his face to the ground (vv 17–18; Ezek 1:28–2:2; 3:23–24). But Daniel's vision report is not in content a call narrative, like Ezek 1–3; as a vision of the desecration of the sanctuary and the desolating rebellion (vv 11–12), in substance, though not in forms of expression, it corresponds rather to Ezek 8.

The celestial dialogue that introduces the interpretative part of the vision (vv 13–19) also reflects Zechariah's visions. The first of these (Zech 1:7–17) features dialogue between humanlike figures, including a supernatural messenger who explains the vision to Zechariah. Yahweh's aide asks "how long" (עד מתי) beyond the seventy years of which Jeremiah spoke Yahweh is to be wrathful (זעם) toward Jerusalem and Judah, and is reassured that the moment of restoration and vindication is coming (cf. Dan 8:13, 14, 19; 9:2; the isolated parallel with the "How long" of Isa 6:11 is likely coincidental [against Nicol, *VT* 29 (1979) 504]; and the talk of "wrath" in Isa 10 is background to Dan 9 and 11 but not specifically to Dan 8). In Zechariah's second vision (2:1–4 [1:18–21]), four horns have scattered Judah, Israel, and Jerusalem; these horns of the nations will be knocked down (cf. Dan 8:24–25). The third vision (2:5–8 [1–4]) features another dialogue involving both celestial beings and Zechariah himself; it uses the very rare term הלז "this man," which also appears in Dan 8:16. These links with Zechariah hint that like chap. 9, but more implicitly, Dan 8 belongs with that postexilic tradition that sees the Jews' position long after the sixth century B.C. as still an experience of exile. Visions analogous to Zechariah's are related to an End centuries after the prophet's time by allusion in vv 17, 19 to Habakkuk's comment that חזון למועד ויפח לקץ ("the vision relates to the appointed time and pants [?] for the end"; Hab 2:3); compare the systematic application of Habakkuk to such an End in 1QpHab.

A key theological assessment of Antiochus is given by taking up the myth of a subordinate celestial being seeking to usurp the place of God himself. This myth was applied to a historical figure, the king of Babylon, in Isa 14 (kings are described as goats [עתודים] in Isa 14:9). It is here reapplied (though Yarbro Collins notes that the myth appears in a form closest to Dan 8 in Nonnos's *Dionysiaca* 1.163–64, 180–81, fifth century A.D.; *Myth,* 76–83; cf. Niditch, *Vision,* 229). The mythic language of Isa 14 is given precision by the more literal language of the laments in Isa 59:1–15; 63:7–64:11 [12]. Here already truth has fallen in the public squares and cannot be found (59:14–15; cf. Dan 8:12), and God's sanctuary is trampled down by Israel's adversaries (63:15, 18; cf. Dan 8:11, 13). In the context of these parallels, that between the three occurrences of פשע in Isa 59:12, 13 and the two in Dan 8:12, 13 may not be coincidental; nor may that between the description of Jerusalem as a desolation (שממה) in Isa 64:9 [10] and mention of the desolating rebellion (הפשע שמם) in Dan 8:13. Isa 63:9 also pictures Israel looked after by Yahweh's personal aide, whose position may be analogous to that of the leader of the army in Dan 8:11. Earlier, Isa 52:14; 53:12 provides terms (שחת, עצומים, רבים) that appear in Dan 8:24–25 (Brownlee, *BASOR* 132 [1953] 13).

The quasi-predictive animal allegories of Daniel and *1 Enoch* take up a tradition that goes back to Gen 49 via Ezekiel's nature allegories (e.g., Ezek 15; 17; 19; also 39:18). *1 Enoch* 90 illustrates the motif of a horn growing, fighting, and breaking in a way parallel to Dan 8. The vision of ram and goat also has varied extrabiblical background. These two animals are the signs under which Persia and Syria appear in the zodiac (Cumont, *Klio* 9 [1909] 265). Indeed, there is nothing distinctively Jewish about the portrait of the ram and goat (vv 3–8a). It could have existed already and been taken into the vision as a whole (Hasslberger, *Hoffnung,* 401–2). The horns have a varied background in Babylonian omen-literature, as well as in OT and wider Semitic symbolism (cf. Dan 7 *Form*). Stylized aspects of the description of Antiochus's tyranny (vv 23–25) have a background in Greek writers (Niditch, *Vision,* 220–30); Lebram (*VT* 25 [1975] 739–43) connects the characterization of Antiochus as the clever transgressor due for his comeuppance with the link between wisdom and pride already made in Isa 10:13; Ezek 28:2–5 (the king of Tyre compared with Daniel!). On the background of the 2,300 days, see *Comment.*

It has been assumed that the mythic and poetic aspects to chap. 7 suggest that it reflects a "real" visionary experience, while the more concrete aspects to chap. 8 suggest that it is a more consciously contrived elaboration or expansion of part of chap. 7. Both these assumptions can be questioned.

Structure

- 1–2a Introduction: date and place
- 2b–14 Symbolic vision (beginning ויהי בראתי)
  - 2b the seer's circumstances
  - 3–4 ram
    - its appearance 3
    - its activity 4
  - 5–12 goat
    - its arrival 5
    - its activity 6–7
    - its increase 8a
    - its shattering and new growth 8b
  - its small horn
    - its arrival 9
    - its activity 10–12
      - in relation to the heavenly army 10
      - in relation to the army leader 11
      - in relation to the sanctuary 12
  - 13–14 the limit set to the visionary events
    - one holy one asks 13
    - another holy one explains 14
- 15–26 Interpretative vision (beginning ויהי בראתי)
  - 15–19 epiphany of interpreter
    - 15a the seer's circumstances
    - 15b the interpreter appears
    - 16 the interpreter commissioned

17a the interpreter approaches
17b the interpreter speaks
18 the seer's response
19 the interpreter's introduction to the message
20–26 message of interpreter
20 the ram interpreted
21 the goat interpreted
22 the shattering and new growth interpreted
23–25 the fierce-looking king
23 his rise
24–25a his success
25b his fall
26 concluding affirmation and instruction
27 Conclusion: the visionary's response

Like chap. 7, chap. 8 uses introductory formulae to mark significant transition points. Thus vv 3 and 5 have long visionary formulae to introduce the ram and the goat; in v 8b the resumptive reference to the goat's strength fulfills a similar function (Koch, *Apocalypticism,* 418). The symbolic vision builds up to v 12, as the same elements recur in the portrait of ram, goat, and small horn: each appears, acts aggressively, enjoys success, but then falls. The sections of the symbolic vision characteristically open with noun clauses—an unusual number of these appear here—then change to verbal clauses. The effect is to draw attention to ongoing, enduring situations, then to punctiliar, changing events. The symbolic vision comes to its climax with a string of verbal clauses in vv 11–12 (Koch, *Apocalypticism,* 417–18). The symbolic vision encourages us to view the small horn's career in the light of patterns in earlier secular history (the story of the ram and the goat), the visions of Zechariah, and the myth of the rebellion against the authority of heaven; in each of these the assertive powers get their comeuppance. The portrait of the small horn, however, stops short of this final element. The symbolic vision thus terminates at a surprising point and leaves us in suspense. Here there is no visionary presentation of judgment, restoration, or reign of God, and there will be no direct promise of it till the very end of the interpretative vision (v 25b). While vv 13–14 do not directly resolve the tension set by vv 8b–12, they bring the symbolic vision to a further climax with their transition from portraying animals to portraying celestial beings. The latter's conversation indicates that the small horn is under control, though it does not reveal what will actually happen to it. That is left for the climactic line of the vision in v 25. Our anticipation of that is heightened by the fact that something of the sort is presupposed without being announced in vv 13–14. Here, however, another concern surfaces, the question of how long the crisis is to last. This concern is highlighted by its coming at the climax of the vision and by the transition from vision to audition and from an earthly scene to a dialogue between supernatural beings (Collins, FOTL 88).

The symbolic vision comes to an end with a celestial conversation; the interpretative vision opens with a celestial conversation. While the symbolic vision gives nearly twice as much space to the ram and the goat as it gives to the small horn, the interpretative vision gives less space to the kings of Medo-Persia and Greece than to the final, fierce-looking king. As usual, some aspects of the symbolic vision are not explicitly interpreted, while some aspects of the interpretative vision have no antecedent in the symbolic vision. Formally, vv 20–25 do interpret vv 3–12 by identifying the chief referents of the symbolic vision, but they only tell the audience what they could work out and will have worked out for themselves; the symbols for the various nations are of transparent significance. In a sense it was the symbolic vision that was interpretative: it was designed to suggest the significance of the history the audience knew. The kingdoms named in vv 20–21 have been portrayed so as to show that they embody more than they themselves are, trans-historical, supernatural realities. What vv 23–25 do is not explain ciphers from earlier verses but complement one set of enigmatic sayings with another set. Thus in vv 20–25 a portrait in terms of animals and astrological motifs is complemented by a portrait of a human-superhuman aggressor who still, however, remains incognito (Koch, *Apocalypticism,* 436). In the manner of chap. 7, chap. 8 marks the importance of vv 23–25 as the vision's climax by a transition to a rhythmic prosody with some parallelism. The importance of this climax is heightened by the expansion on the contents of the original vision that it offers, especially by the unheralded conclusion in the last line of v 25. The arrangement of the cola contributes to the sense of working to a climax. Verse 23 comprises two balancing bicola (a-a^1, b-b^1). Verse 24 comprises two bicola arranged chiastically (a-b-b^1-a^1); omitting the bracketed phrase as a gloss improves the prosody, but is not actually necessary. In OG, at least (see n. 25.a-a), v 25 begins with two further bicola arranged chiastically (a-b-b^1-a^1), then a further bicolon (taking up ועל and יד from the first) carries the deeds of the previous four to an even greater height of enormity, and finally resolves the tension by declaring the divine response.

A number of expressions recur through the chapter: גדל "become great," vv 4, 8, 9, 10, 11, 25 (see n. 4.c-c., n. 8.a-a); עמד "stand"/"arise"/"place," vv 3, 4, 7, 15, 17, 18, 18, 22, 22, 23, 25; שלך "throw down," vv 7, 11, 12; רמס "trample," vv 7, 10, 13; יד "hand"/"power," vv 4, 7, 25 (the first two with מציל "rescue"); כח "strength," vv 6, 7, 22, 24, 24; עצם "might," vv 8, 24, 24; cf. the use of עשה "act" in vv 4, 12, 24. These repetitions help to bind together the symbolic vision, the angelic epiphany, and the interpretative vision. They have a cumulative effect in establishing the tone of what is being described as it repeats itself through the story of the Medo-Persian empire, Alexander and his successors, and Antiochus.

The atmosphere of thrusting aggression conveyed by these terms is furthered by a series of expressions suggesting directions of movement. The ram charges west, north, and south (v 4). The goat comes from the west over the whole earth (v 5). Its four horns grow toward the four points of the compass (v 8). The small horn grows south, east, and toward Palestine (v 9). This aggressive movement then moves onto a different plane, to reach to the celestial army and the commander of that army (vv 10, 11). Alongside the references here to השמים ("heaven/the heavens," vv 8, 10) appear a number of references to [ה]ארץ ("the earth/ground," vv 5, 5, 7, 10, 12, 18): both are capable of referring both to the this-worldly plane and to movement between earth and heaven. Spatial allusions in the chapter actually begin with the book's most elaborate determining of Daniel's own—visionary—location, Elam/Susa/the Ulay (v 2). The spatial references are complemented by a series of temporal references. These, too, begin with Daniel's visionary time (v 1), but they cluster at the transition from the symbolic vision to the interpretative vision (vv 13–19). A holy one asks עד מתי "how long" the crisis is to last and another sets its term. Gabriel tells Daniel that the vision relates to the time of the end and that an end will come at an appointed time; the events will happen באחרית הזעם "as wrath draws to a close," and Antiochus will arise באחרית מלכותם ("as their kingship draws to a close," v 23). In v 26 Gabriel finally brings these two temporal motifs together, describing the burden of the revelation in terms of how long the crisis is to last, and declaring that it relates to ימים רבים "distant days." The narrative even includes a related temporal expression (ימים, "some days") in its conclusion (v 27), as it had begun with a chronological note (v 1). The effect of these various characteristics of the chapter is to combine a strong sense of aggressive horizontal movement, aggressive movement between earth and heaven, and temporal constraint.

There is some redundancy within vv 15–19; perhaps v 19 is in a narrower sense an introduction to vv 20–25, v 26 then being a corresponding conclusion to the interpretation (Plöger). Scholars who trace a recensional history behind chap. 7 find a parallel one behind chap. 8 (see Ginsberg, 29–38, developing Noth, *TSK* 98–99 [1926] 160–61): e.g., vv 13–14, 16–17, 26a, 27b may be attributed to the author of Dan 9, who is especially concerned with the timing of the crisis. In addition, vv 18–19 may be attributed to the author of Dan 10–12, with which they share a distinctive use of נרדם ("fell into a deep sleep," 8:18; 10:9) and a less supra-historical way of talking about the End than that of v 17 (compare 10:14; 11:27, 25 with v 19).

Setting

If the vision is for the most part a quasi-prophecy, its historical setting lies just after the fulfillment of its portrait of the wicked acts of the small horn/fierce-looking king and before the reversal promised in vv 14b, 25b. The point of suspense at which v 12 stops is the point of suspense at which the vision's audience lives. This suggests some time between the desecration of the sanctuary in December 167 B.C. and its restoration in December 164. The specific deeds of Antiochus referred to perhaps presuppose a slightly later period than that to which chap. 7 belongs. The vision comes from conservative rather than reformist groups within the Jewish community. Its concern with the violation of the sanctuary hardly need point to a priestly circle; many others would be concerned about the sanctuary, and the sanctuary is by no means the chapter's exclusive focus (see vv 23–25). Neither need the expectation that the fierce-looking king will break without being touched suggest that the vision had its background in an antimilitarist group within the hasidim. The poor Hebrew and the syntactical differences may point to a different author from chap. 7 (Niditch, *Vision,* 226).

In its literary setting, v 1 makes a double link with chap. 7: the date is just after and the vision explicitly follows on that earlier one. The date also links the vision of Antiochus's sacrilege specifically with the reign of the sacrilegious Belshazzar of whom we read in chap. 5. The chapter supplements the vision of oppression and judgment contained in chap. 7. It reaffirms the promise of chap. 7, perhaps in the light of a worsening situation. Repetition in itself also functions to strengthen the main impression conveyed by the previous vision (see Dan 6 *Setting*). Similar to chap. 7 in length, the chapter also divides into halves that resemble the corresponding halves of chap. 7 in length and structure.

	Symbolic vision		*Interpretative vision*	
	Chap. 7	Chap. 8	Chap. 7	Chap. 8
Introduction	1	1–2	16	15–19
Summary	2–3		17–18	
Babylon	4	(1)		
Media	5	(2) 3–4		20
Persia	6	3–4		20
Greece: Alexander	7a	5–8	19, 23	21
His successors	7b	8b	20a, 24a	22–23a
Antiochus	8	9–12	20b–22, 24b–25	23b–25a
God's judgment	9–12		26	.25b
God's purpose restored	13–14	13–14	27	
Conclusion	15	(15)	28	26–27

The comparison highlights chap. 8's lack of any overall scheme for the period from the exile to Antiochus. It concentrates more exclusively on the Greek period, giving particular attention in the symbolic vision to Alexander and slightly more attention to his successors. Its more concrete portrayal of Antiochus's actions also conveys a deeper sense of appallment at what is envisaged, and the seer's reaction to the epiphany is one of shock unparalleled in chap. 7. It lacks the divine judgment scene but includes the heavenly dialogue that opens the interpretative vision. The actual nature of God's judgment and the positive fulfillment of his purpose is quite differently conceived in 7:9–14, 26–27 and 8:13–14, 25b; in particular, the focus on the kingdom in previous chapters is supplemented by an interest in the temple here.

With chap. 8, Hebrew resumes. A clear rhetorical function was fulfilled by the transition from Hebrew to Aramaic at 2:4a; it is not quite so clear that a rhetorical function is fulfilled by the return to Hebrew, as is also the case with the equivalent transition in Ezra, though it may take place because chaps. 8–12 focus more on specifically Jewish concerns. They are mostly written in idiosyncratic Hebrew, less consistent in its use of *waw* consecutive and its word order, using pronouns in a distinctive way, and often lacking the simplicity characteristic of classical Hebrew prose (*TTH* 196); these characteristics are more marked than they were in chap. 1, which might suggest different authorship (Charles, xlvii, 1–2). Some can be seen as influenced by Aramaic and as resulting from translation from Aramaic (Zimmermann, *Books;* Ginsberg; Hartman lists the Aramaisms). The Hebrew must at least have been written by someone who was as much at home in Aramaic; though some of the oddities Zimmermann explains by the translation theory presuppose that he was both a poor Hebraist and a poor Aramaist!

Chap. 8 is the last of the book's symbolic visions; the succeeding revelations are more verbal than visual and still cryptic but not symbolic. The explanation of the symbolic vision in chap. 8 actually explains little, and this prepares the way for the following vision(s). Verse 8:27b thus leads into chaps. 9 and 10–12, which offer further reaffirmation and more explanation of the vision's fundamental perspective. The chapter's connection with the exile (its setting in the reign of the sacrilegious Belshazzar) links with the focus on the question—how long is this exile to last?—that concerns chap. 9. Its epiphany and detailed quasi-prophecies are paralleled on a larger scale by those of chaps. 10–12.

Comment

1–2 The date links back with chap. 7; it might indicate that in reality two years have passed since that vision (Lacocque). The third year of Belshazzar was probably 548/547 B.C. (Hasel, *AUSS* 15 [1977] 153–68; see 7:1 *Comment*).

Elam lies between Babylon and Persia, and corresponds to modern Khuzistan, north of the Persian Gulf (see *IBD* 432–34). In 548/547 B.C. it probably still belonged to Babylon, but in any case the chapter presupposes the status and circumstances of Susa in the period to which the vision refers. It had been destroyed by Asshurbanipal; Darius I rebuilt it as a fortified city, beginning in 521 B.C. Elam was then a province of the Persian empire, and Susa was in Jewish thinking *the* seat of the Persian empire (Neh 1:1; Esth 1:2). It was subsequently within the Seleucid empire; Antiochus III was killed there in 187 B.C. (On Susa, see Cook, *Persian Empire,* 73–74, 145, 158–66; Olmstead, *History,* 163–71.) The ruins of Susa lie near the River Karun, but the names and the locations of the watercourses in the area seem to have changed over the centuries (*IBD* 1496, 1609). Ulay is an ancient name for a waterway near Susa. The vision is located at a gate opening toward a waterway, in the tradition of Ezekiel's vision by the Kebar canal (cf. 10:4; 12:5–7; *1 Enoch* 13.7–8; also Pharaoh's dream set at a river, Gen 41); it presupposes a visionary journey such as Ezekiel also experienced (see *Form*), which has taken the subject far from his bodily setting.

3–4 Within the OT and elsewhere, leaders are often symbolized by animals such as the ram and the goat (see *Form*). These two, which are singled out in Ezek 34:17, are both clean animals; contrast the unclean hybrids—and fierce predators—that represent nations in Dan 7 and in *1 Enoch* 89–90 (Massyngberde Ford, *JSJ* 10 [1979] 205–8). So these animals are less fearful or objectionable symbols of authority and power. The ram might be readily identifiable as a symbol for Persia. In the zodiac, Persia was under Aries, the ram. The name Ulay (אולי) is reminiscent of the word for ram (איל) (Ps-Saadia). According to Ammianus Marcellinus (fourth century A.D.) 10.1, on the march Persian kings carried a gold ram's head. The two horns on the single ram then suggest Media and Persia, here recognized to be one yet distinguishable. Persia entered the world stage later than Media but ultimately played a more major part. Verse 4 more likely described Medo-Persia's initial triumphs under Cyrus in Asia Minor and Babylon than later victories over Egypt (Cambyses), Scythia and Greece (Darius), and Athens itself

(Xerxes), since Daniel suggests the order "west and north and south." Cyrus's victories to the east are omitted: from a Palestinian perspective he *is* the ruler of the east (Isa 41:2).

There is nothing inherently wrong about "doing great things" (הגדיל); but the expression is only used in an unequivocally good sense of God (1 Sam 12:24; Ps 126:2, 3); of human beings it tends to suggest arrogance (Jer 48:26; Joel 2:20; Zeph 2:10; Ps 35:26; Ps 55:13 [12]), or at least achievement at someone else's expense (Zeph 2:8; Lam 1:9)—here achievement that presages calamity. The expression has the foreboding ambiguity of the mouth speaking great things in 7:8, 20.

5–8 The opening resumptive phrase heralds a new development. The goat is a less frequent symbol for leadership than the ram (see Isa 14:9; Zech 10:3), but goats are fierce creatures, more powerful than sheep (cf. Jer 50:8). The imperial leadership more powerful than that of Persia will be Alexander's. The goat might inherently suggest the post-Alexandrian Greek empire of the Seleucids, because as the zodiac placed Persia under the ram, so it placed Syria under the horned goat, Capricorn. The goat is also the symbol of the god Amurru. The notion of the unicorn (cf. the *sirussu*) may derive from the profile reliefs that merge two horns as one (Montgomery). The description of Alexander's flying advance recalls that of Cyrus in Isa 41:3 and the winged leopard of Dan 7:6 (cf. 1 Macc 1:1–4). Over a period of four years between 334 and 331 B.C. Alexander quite demolished the Persian empire and established an empire of his own extending from Europe to India. On the breakup of his empire, see 11:4 *Comment.*

9 The small horn growing from the Seleucid line is Antiochus IV, an insignificant person compared with Alexander, the youngest of several brothers who had no right to the throne, a hostage in Rome through much of his earlier life, and a king who would treat Judea ignobly—even if from a broader historical perspective he was an impressive ruler. On his expeditions and deeds, see 11:21–45 *Comment.*

"The fairest" (הצבי) is a term for the land of Israel, the land flowing with milk and honey, in Ezek 20:6, 15, of which the allusion here may be a reminiscence. The word is used in phrases denoting both the land, in 11:16, 41; Jer 3:19; *1 Enoch* 89.40, and the hill of Zion in particular, in 11:45 (cf. 1 Macc 2:12; also of the city of Babylon in Isa 13:19). Both references are appropriate here. Cf. parallel expressions נחלת צבי "fair possession," ארץ חמדה "lovely land," Jer 3:19; Zech 7:14; Ps 106:24; ארץ חפץ "delightful land," Mal 3:12; and descriptions of Zion as יפה נוף "beautiful in loftiness," Ps 48:3 [2]; מכלל יפי "totality of beauty," Ps 50:2; cf. Lam 2:15; also Ezek 27:3, of Tyre.

10–11 In the interpretation of the small horn's attack on the heavenly army (צבא השמים) similar issues arise to those raised by chap. 7. References to the earthly sanctuary in vv 11–12 could suggest that the heavenly army is the Jewish people, or the priesthood in particular, viewed as of heavenly significance because of their relationship with the God of heaven. They are the Lord's armies (Exod 7:4; cf. 6:26; 12:17, 51; Num 33:1); they are his heavenly children (2 Macc 7:34). It is they who are attacked by Antiochus (1 Macc 1:29–38). Yet the people attacked include "some of the stars," which rather points to the heavenly army being a supernatural body. Elsewhere "the heavenly army" denotes the actual stars in the heavens (Isa 34:4; cf. Gen 2:1; Ps 33:6), and more commonly the stars as personalized objects of worship (Deut 4:19; Jer 8:2; Zeph 1:5). The stars in the heavens are Yahweh's servants (Judg 5:20). Dan 12:3, however, promises that the faithful are destined to shine like the stars. The notion of attacking the stars, which goes back to Isa 14:13, is applied retrospectively to Antiochus in 2 Macc 9:10; and from 169 B.C. Antiochus's coins picture his head surmounted with a star, and he entitles himself King Antiochus God Manifest (Βασιλευς Αντιοχος Θεος Επιφανης). Perhaps it is the case, then, that an attack on the Jerusalem temple, the people of Israel, and the priesthood is presupposed to be implicitly an attack on the God worshiped there and on his supernatural associates who identify with Israel (so 4Q Serek šîrôt, the Angelic Liturgy: cf. J. Strugnell, "The Angelic Liturgy at Qumrân," *Congress Volume: Oxford 1959* [VTSup 7 (1960)] 318–45). But the manner of expression is allusive, as in chap. 7.

The fall of some of the heavenly army/stars has a very different significance from that in *1 Enoch* 6; 86. The idea of their being thrown down and trampled on presupposes that the small horn is now being portrayed by synecdoche in terms appropriate to earthly leaders also symbolized by animals (cf. v 7; also 7:7, 19, 23). The same portrayal continues in vv 11–13 as the sanctuary and the truth are overthrown, and sanctuary and army are given over to be trampled down. Army, sanctuary, and truth are all portrayed as victims of the goat's charging and butting (Porter, *Metaphors,* 57, 65–66, 89–95). The king himself, too, becomes momentarily visible in v 11a ("He grew . . .").

The identity of the army leader is also disputed. In 1:7–11, 18; 11:5, שר denotes a foreign official; in 9:6, 8, an Israelite leader; in 10:13, 20, 21; 12:1, heavenly beings. In 1 Chr 24:5; 2 Chr 36:14; Ezra 8:24, 29; 10:5, it denotes leaders among the priesthood. But it is significant that שר הצבא is a standard term for an army leader (e.g., Gen 21:22; 1 Sam 12:9), and the compound expression needs to be understood in the light of the reference to "the army" in v 10. The one denoted by the term is the leader of Israel or of Israel's celestial equivalents (not, surely, the sun as commander of the heavenly host—against Goldstein, *Proc Sixth WCJS,* 142–43). So who is this leader?

The high priest could be seen as Israel's leader, and the high priest Onias III had been murdered in 171. Admittedly this antedated the events of v 10, and Antiochus is not elsewhere blamed for Onias's murder (2 Macc 4:34; Dan 9:26; though see 11:22). Perhaps, then, the reference is more generally to Antiochus's usurping the authority of the priesthood over the religious life of the Jerusalem temple. Behind such an arrogation of power, however, is an attack on heaven itself. In Josh 5:13–15 the leader of Yahweh's army is a celestial being, and the leader of the army here might thus be Michael, though the description of his authority goes beyond that of Michael elsewhere: he is only one of the prominent leaders (10:13), having a special relationship with Israel parallel to that of other leaders with Persia or Greece (10:21; 12:1). More likely it is God himself, who is presumably the "leader supreme" (שר שרים) of v 25, the one who is יהוה צבאות ("Yahweh of armies," EVV "the LORD of hosts"). The term cannot be a personification of the holy ones (a plausible view of the humanlike figure in 7:13), since he is distinguished from the rest of the army; nor does an attack on Israel thus constitute an attack on God, so that anti-Semitism is deicide (against Lacocque). It is an attack on the Jerusalem sanctuary that constitutes an attack on God. Although Antiochus hardly made himself an object of worship, his self-designation as Epiphanes could be taken to imply something approaching such arrogance, and theologically his assuming authority over the affairs of the temple involved assuming an authority that belonged to God alone (cf. 11:36–37 and *Comment*).

The expression התמיד (the daily offering, lit. "the [offering of] continuity"; 8:11–13; 11:31; 12:11) is a regular term in MH for the whole offering sacrificed every morning and evening (עלת [ה]תמיד): see Exod 29:38–42; Num 28–29; Ezek 46:1–15; Ezra 3:5; Neh 10:34 [33]. Other passages speak of the daily grain offering (מנחת התמיד, Num 4:16; Neh 10:34 [33]; cf. Lev 6:13 [20]), the daily incense offering (קטרת תמיד, Exod 30:8), and the daily (Presence) bread (לחם התמיד, Num 4:7; cf. 2 Chr 2:3 [4]). 1 Macc 1:45 records the suspension of whole offerings, sacrifice, and libation. While התמיד refers primarily to the morning and evening whole offering (cf. v 14), it can thus also hint at a wider range of observances; it may here suggest the religious practices of the temple in general, which were suspended by Antiochus. The temple was not literally overthrown or destroyed in 167 B.C., in the manner of 587 B.C. and A.D. 70, though it was robbed of its valuables, emptied of its worshipers, and defiled by the accoutrements of an alien cult (1 Macc 1:20–24, 39–40; 3:45; cf. 4:43–48). Its overthrowing consists in its being prevented from functioning as a place of worship of the true God.

12 Antiochus and his army now become even more transparent in MT (but see n. 12.a-a) (cf. v 21 in chap. 7). The seer entirely abandons the visionary way of speaking proper to one who has been watching an event, which he thus describes in the past, and adopts the future tense proper to an interpretative vision. On the army set over the sacrificial system of the temple, see 11:31 *Comment.* If the army of vv 10–11 is an earthly people as well as its heavenly equivalent, however, the same may be true of this hostile army: cf. Isa 24:21 and the allusions to the individual celestial leaders of Persia and Greece in Dan 10:13, 20.

In isolation, the rebellion (פשע) the seer speaks of could be that of the compromised priesthood or the people generally, seen as bringing about Yahweh's punishment. But the Jews have been portrayed as sinned against rather than sinning, and Daniel seems positive in his attitude to the postexilic temple in principle (contrast *1 Enoch* 89.73); Daniel envisages the vindication of the temple, not a new temple (cf. R. Hamerton-Kelly, "The Temple and the Origins of Jewish Apocalyptic," *VT* 20 [1970] 1–15). Further, in v 13 "rebellion" refers to Antiochus's sacrilege. Thus this is also likely to be the reference in v 12 (cf. v 23). The truth (אמת) that is thrown to the ground is likely to denote concretely the Torah, whose authority over the religious life of Judaism is abrogated by Antiochus's acts; Torah scrolls were destroyed by his forces (1 Macc 1:56). On Antiochus's "success," cf. 2 Macc 6:6.

13–14 Presumably the holy ones are discussing the vision's meaning. The seer only catches the end of their conversation; cf. the allusive nature of the vision/audition in Zech 1:7–17. While they may be assumed to be members of the heavenly/earthly army who are themselves discomfited by Antiochus's actions, perhaps their "how long" (cf. 12:6) stems simply from their concern for afflicted Jews, as in Zech 1:7–17 (which underlies Dan 8). The "how long" connects with that vision, but behind it with this question—rather, plea—as it is expressed in lament psalms, not least concerning the devastation of the land and the defiling of the sanctuary (Ps 74:9–10; 79:5; 80:5 [4]; 89:47 [46]; cf. 6:4 [3]; 13:2 [1]; 90:13; 94:3; also Isa 6:11; Jer 12:4; 2 Esd 6:59). The cry of the holy ones takes up the cry of afflicted Israel. A number of these passages presuppose or permit a context in the exile, of which subsequent afflictions such as those of the Antiochene period are seen as a continuance (cf. chap. 9 and the exilic setting of Daniel generally); and the response they look for—at least as such psalms would be understood in the late OT period—is that final turning to his people and restoring of them which Dan 8 speaks of as "the time of the end" (v 17) (Porter, *Metaphors*, 63–65, referring to Childs, *Introduction*, 517–18; J. Becker, *Israel deutet seine Psalmen* [SBS 18 (1966)] 41–68).

"Desolating rebellion" (הפשע שמם), like "desolating abomination" ([ה]שקוצים] [מ]שמם], 9:27; 11:31; 12:11), apparently parodies the name of the god בעל שמים (*Baʿal Šamem*, "Lord of heaven") (Nestle, *ZAW* 4 [1884] 248; Eissfeldt, *ZAW* 57 [1939] 24). "Rebellion" or "abomination" replaces "Baal," indicating a theological evaluation of the religious innovations (cf. v 12). "Desolating" replaces "heaven," using similar letters, and indicating the effect these innovations have had on Jerusalem and its sanctuary (cf. vv 24–25; 9:26; 1 Macc 1:39; 3:45; 4:38). The phrase is apparently a technical term of recent creation, not yet having a fixed form (Hasslberger, *Hoffnung*, 343). In an earlier period, "Lord of heaven" was a foreign epithet for the highest God, but one which Jews could utilize as entirely appropriate for the true God (see 2:18 *Comment*). The title is now, however, one the Seleucids especially use. Its Greek equivalent is Ζεὺς Ὀλύμπιος (Olympian Zeus): see, e.g., Josephus's quotation from the Phoenician historian Dius in *C. Ap.* 1.17 [*C. Ap.* 113]. This is the title 2 Macc 6:2 gives the god to whom Antiochus dedicated the Jerusalem temple. According to 1 Macc 1:54, the abomination was erected on the altar of sacrifice, and this has usually suggested it was an image of Zeus (and of Antiochus, according to Porphyry). 1 Macc 1:59, however, speaks of there being a (pagan) altar erected on the altar of sacrifice (cf. Josephus, *Ant.* 12.5.4 [12.253]). This implies rather that the setting up of the abomination consists in the rebuilding of the altar for it to serve a different cult (as in Judg 6:25–26): Antiochus had it turned into an old-fashioned high place (Bickermann, *God*, 67–72; Goldstein's suggestion [e.g., *I Maccabees*, 146–47] that the abomination constituted meteorites fixed to the altar as objects to be worshiped seems implausible).

On the daily offering, the trampling down of sanctuary and army, and Daniel's attitude to the temple, see on vv 10–12. The charging of the ram and its own eventual overthrow and trampling down were events no one could resist and from which there was no rescue (vv 4, 7). The trampling down of the sanctuary, however, does have a term set to it. The forensic metaphor of judgment being given for the holy ones on high (7:22) reappears as the vision promises that the sanctuary will "emerge in the right" (נצדק, "be vindicated": see n. 14.b-b, and cf. 1 Macc 2:29).

The 2,300 evenings and mornings before this takes place is usually taken to denote 2,300 occasions when an evening or a morning whole offering was not sacrificed—that is, 1,150 days. The period from the erection of the pagan altar in the temple to the rededication of the sanctuary was three years and ten days (1 Macc 1:54; 4:52–53), and no doubt orthodox rites had been suspended a little before the first of these dates. The number 1,150 has thus commonly been understood as simply denoting, by guess or by revelation or by hindsight, the actual chronological period during which no regular sacrifices were offered, and as being at least approximately correct. (For more precise—but speculative—interpretations, see Schedl, *BZ* 8 [1964] 102–3; Burgmann, *ZAW* 86 [1974] 544–45.) But why should 2,300 evenings and mornings be taken to denote 1,150 days? An evening and morning make one day (Gen 1:5–31; the order of evening and morning there explains that here). The morning and evening whole offering was seen as one unit rather than as two independent ones which could then naturally be counted separately (Schwantes, *AUSS* 16 [1978] 375–80, noting especially Ezra 3:3–5). As G indicates, the natural way to understand the phrase is as denoting 2,300 days (so Thiering, *NovT* 23 [1981] 49, though her calendrical explanation is also questionable: see on 12:11–12).

If it were necessary to relate 2,300 days to an actual period of approximately this chronological length, it might still begin with the cessation of sacrifice in late 167 and go on to the prospect of complete victory over the Seleucid power and release of the temple area from foreign overlordship or the threat of it. This might be reckoned to have come about in 160 with the victory described in 1 Macc 7, though this was soon followed by the death of Judas Maccabaeus and the triumph of the Hellenizing party (1 Macc 9) (Burgmann, *ZAW* 86 [1974] 544–45). If the 1,150 days is not far from the 3½ years that might be indicated by 9:27 (cf. 7:25) then 2,300 days would be not far from the 7 years of 9:27, which would stretch from the removal of the high priest Onias III in 171 to the rededication of the sanctuary in 164 (Keil); though the events referred to in v 13 perhaps have a closer connection with those of 167 than those of 171.

The periods of time in chapters on either side (7:25; 9:24–27) have symbolic significance, however, and it is appropriate to look for a significance for this one beyond the purely chronological—whether or not it is a coincidence (in each case) that the periods are approximately correct chronologically. Now the figure twenty-three occurs in *1 Enoch* 90.5. Of the seventy shepherds who have oversight of the Jews during the gentile domination, twenty-three have this responsibility for the early Hellenistic period. By implication, another group of twenty-three are responsible during the Persian period (so Porter, *Metaphors*, 44). The first sixty-nine of the seventy weeks of years from the exile to Antiochus (Dan 9:24–27) might also be seen as three times twenty-three. The 2,300 days may, then, suggest a fixed "significant" period, which might or might not denote a chronological period in the region of six or seven years.

15–19 That the one of humanlike appearance is a celestial being is here overt (contrast 7:13, even if this is to be inferred there; cf. 3:25, 28; 10:16, 18). His appearance is that of a גבר. In origin גבר is a rather macho word for a male (Judg 5:30), but it comes to denote a man who is strong in and because of his relationship to God (e.g., Jer 17:5–8), and in the Qumran literature one especially chosen by God (see H. Kosmala, *Hebräer-Essener-Christen* [SPB 1 (1959)] 208–39; "The Term *geber* in the OT and in the Scrolls," *Congress Volume: Rome 1968* [VTSup 17 (1969)] 159–69; *TWAT*). גבריאל "man of God" is thus an appropriate name for God's celestial servant, and גבר is an appropriate term by which to refer to him, both for its sound (*geber*) and for its meaning. Although Gabriel is the first named angel within one of the books that came to be included in the Hebrew canon, he is only one of a number who already appear in older parts of *1 Enoch.* He features with Michael, Raphael, and other leading holy ones in *1 Enoch* 9–10; 20; cf. also 1QM 9.15–16. Familiarity with such figures is presupposed here, though Gabriel's role in Dan 8 and 9—and Michael's in Dan 10–12—does not particularly link with the descriptions in *1 Enoch,* and the place of these figures is reduced compared with some such approximately contemporary writings. Further, the names of Michael and Gabriel and the other leading holy ones are parallel in form to that of Daniel—or rather, vice versa. Daniel's name hints at a kinship between him and the angels (Daniel is the name of an angel in *1 Enoch* 6.7) and the possibility of a link between the seer and the heavenly world. The voice that commissions Gabriel (v 16) is described as a human one (קול אדם); that recalls the description of God's own appearance when he speaks in Ezek 1:26. To bring the vision to a climax, then, there appears not merely an anonymous celestial being but a specific, named one, who belongs to the number of the well-known leading holy ones; and God himself not only appears, as in 7:9–10, but speaks (Plöger). The supernatural conversation refers to both a vision (חזון) and a revelation (מראה). Each word relates to a verb for seeing and thus suggests a visual disclosure. In v 26, however, and presumably then in v 27, the latter refers to the verbal message about the 2,300 evenings and mornings; the same will apply in v 16, the revelation being that in vv 13–14. The term refers to a verbal message in 9:23; but see further n. 10:1.f.

Gabriel is a "man of God" and is himself addressed by a "human" voice, that is, the voice of God. He addresses Daniel as "mortal man" (בן אדם, traditionally "son of man"), using God's characteristic form of address to Ezekiel (e.g., 2:1, 3). It suggests both solemnly and encouragingly the awesomeness and the honor of an ordinary human being hearing this man of God address him (Keil). Falling on the face is a traditional courtly way of expressing a recognition of the king's majesty, the most extreme possible form of personal obeisance (2 Sam 9:6; 14:4; 25:23). It is naturally also an expression of a similar recognition of God's majesty, especially in a cultic context (Lev 9:24; 1 Kgs 18:39; 2 Chr 7:3). That context of the expression is the background to Ezekiel's characteristic falling on his face in self-effacing obeisance (e.g., 1:28). This is in turn the immediate background to Dan 8:17. Here, however, the object of the seer's recognition is God's heavenly representative, as in Josh 5:14 (a passage noted in connection with v 11) and Tob 12:6 (involving Gabriel's associate Raphael). Falling into a trance (נרדם) has different connotations. It is not an everyday or cultic word; it denotes a coma-like state of deep sleep brought about by supernatural agency, especially in connection with visionary experiences (Gen 2:21; 15:12; 1 Sam 26:12; Job 4:13; 33:15; cf. *T. Levi* 2.5; ironically, Isa 29:10; Jonah 1:5–6; Prov 10:5; 29:10; ?Judg 4:21). נרדם recurs in 10:9; see further the seer's description of his experience in 10:7–19 and the *Comment.* The touching of the seer also recurs there. Isaiah and Jeremiah refer to God touching their lips in the course of a vision (Isa 6:7; Jer 1:9; cf. Dan 10:16), but the only antecedent for touching to awaken, to reassure, and to strengthen is Elijah in 1 Kgs 19:5, 7. The more general background is again Ezek 1:28–2:2, where God takes hold of the prophet and sets him on his feet.

The terms "time" (עת), "end" (קץ), "closing part [of the wrath]" (אחרית [הזעם]), and "set moment" (מועד) appear in vv 17, 19; cf. the further expressions "closing part [of their kingship]" ([מלכותם] אחרית, v 23) and "distant days" (ימים רבים, v 26). Like their English equivalents, all are everyday words. None inherently refers to the absolute End, and only their contexts tell us whether the expressions in the various combinations refer to the end of a particular period of time or to the End of Time. The notion of a period characterized by wrath is one of the aspects of Dan 8 that reflects Zech 1, where the exile is a period of wrath (1:12). The context there indicates that reference to wrath does not denote that God is punishing Israel for their sin: although their sin was the original cause of the exile, the ongoing period of wrath is one in which they are continuing to be treated harshly rather than compassionately because of the hostility of their enemies rather than because of their own sin. In a parallel way 1 Macc 1:64 speaks of Antiochus's persecution as the coming of very great wrath on Israel (cf. 2 Kgs 3:27). There, too, Israel's transgressions contributed to what happened (1:11–15, 43, 52–53), but 1 Maccabees hardly implies that Antiochus's persecution is simply God's punishment of Israel's sin. Neither in Dan 8 is it likely that the seer views Israel's experience as God's punishment for their sin (against, e.g., Steck, "Weltgeschehen," 71). Dan 11:30 may even mean that it is not *God's* wrath that is (solely) in mind (cf. Collins, FOTL 95).

Both the seventy years of exile, which Dan 9 sees as extending to the Antiochene period, and the Antiochene period in particular are periods of wrath in the sense of oppression and suffering. The time of wrath referred to in 8:19 might be either of these, but the link with Zech 1 and the fact that the vision begins with the Persian era suggest that the whole period from the exile to Antiochus is the period of wrath denoted here. There is a striking contrast between this retrospective view of the postexilic period and the prospect Zech 1, like exilic prophecy earlier, set before its audience. The postexilic period has not been the time of God's comfort but the time of God's absence (de Vries, *Achievement,* 342). The "closing part" of this period is thus also the "closing part" of the four kingships (v 23), namely the time of Antiochus (on אחרית, see on 2:28). The "end" of v 19 is then the actual termination of this period of wrath. קצת/קץ "end" and אחרית "latter part" appear in similar phrases (see, e.g., 2:28 and 4:31 [34]) and sometimes in the same context (cf. 12:8–9). קץ differs from אחרית in being an essentially punctiliar word: קצץ means "cut off," קצה "extremity" or "edge."

The time that v 19 describes as an "end" it also describes as "a set moment" (מועד). יעד means "to appoint or assign," and the noun denotes a set time, place, or meeting (cf. 11:29; 12:7). It is the notion of designating rather than that of time which is essential to מועד. So קץ "end" and מועד "set moment" refer to the same time, but קץ denotes its character as punctiliar in relation to what leads up to it, while מועד denotes its character as designated by God. קץ relates to the horizontal, chronological plane, מועד to the vertical, meta-historical plane.

"The time of the end" (עת קץ, v 17) is a more allusive expression. The "end" must still be the punctiliar moment of the termination of the Antiochene persecution and the vindication of the sanctuary, but this more absolute expression hints that v 17 sees this as *the* End; at least it implies that the end of the Antiochene oppression (v 19) is also the end of the era (אחרית יומיא), the closing scene of the history of Israel and the nations (2:28), and the moment of a final judgment (עד סופא, 7:26). It is open to the further explication of what the End will involve, to be offered in chap. 12; yet the context here (v 14b) also includes a more down-to-earth understanding of what the End will mean for Israel than the one that appears in chap. 12. In 11:35, 40; 12:4, 9, "the time of the end" is the period leading up to the End, the period in which the audience of these visions themselves live. This also fits 8:17–19: the phrase denotes the final act of that historical drama which will come to its actual end with Antiochus's fall and the sanctuary's restoration (cf. Wilch, *Time,* 111–14). But Daniel is not thinking of "the absolute eschatological 'End,' " of "the final and absolute End for all events" when "human history comes to a close" (against Wilch; contrast Jones, 178–219). If anything, further human history on earth is *presupposed* by talk of the restoration of the sanctuary, as it was by talk of a new kingdom in 2:44; 7:14, 18, 27. The End in Daniel is not so different from the Day of Yahweh in the prophets. קץ is, of course, one of the expressions Daniel derives from the prophets: see Hab 2:3; also Amos 8:2; Ezek 7:1–7; cf. Lam 4:18. The seer's use of Hab 2:3 may be compared and contrasted with that in 1QpHab, where it is interpreted to mean that "the last time will lengthen, far beyond anything the prophets said: for the mysteries of God are awesome" (7.5–8: here קץ means "time," as often in the Qumran literature). 1QpHab is directly commenting on Hab, though its interpretation alters the text's meaning more explicitly than the less direct allusion in Dan 8:19 does; 1QpHab's use of Hab 2:3 corresponds more to the reinterpretation of Jer 25 in Dan 9.

Chronologically, then, "the time of the end" denotes a similar period to "the latter part of the wrath." The former, however, looks at this period—in which the seer actually lives—from the perspective of where it is leading, the latter from the perspective of what has led to it. "Distant days" (v 26) and "the closing part of their kingship" (v 23), will both also refer to approximately the same period. The former looks at it purely chronologically in relation to the period of the exile. The latter looks at it chronologically in relation to the history of the empires, but perhaps also hints that that violent story will come to some sort of cataclysmic end.

The comparative significance of these various terms may be seen diagrammatically:

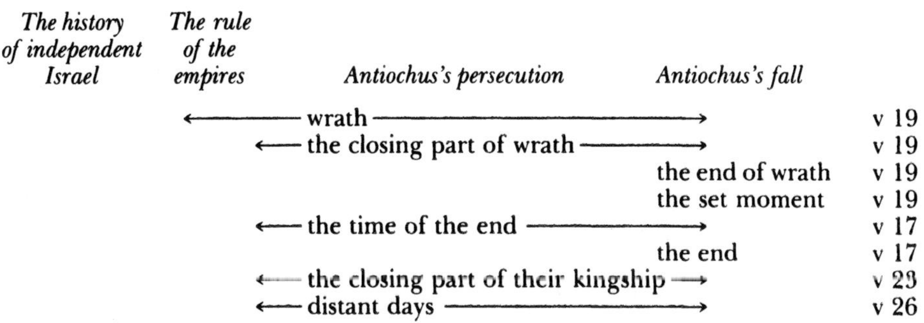

20–25 The identification of the political entities denoted by the animals and horns is hardly made to unveil something that was otherwise obscure; it was obvious enough who vv 3–12 referred to.

On "the closing period of their kingship" (v 23) see on vv 15–19. פשעים "rebels" denotes the breaking of obligations to another party. In international relationships the verb thus denotes rebellion (2 Kgs 1:1; 3:5, 7); in interpersonal relationships it suggests an offense (cf. EVV "transgression"). Either significance is appropriate in relationships with God. There were certainly Israelite rebels who could be seen as opening the way for Antiochus (1 Macc 1:11–15, 34, 41–52), but Dan 7–12 elsewhere makes little if any mention of these, and the rebellion of vv 12–13 was that of the small horn. Likely here, then, the rebels are Gentiles. Further, the notion of rebels or rebellions reaching full measure applies better to Gentiles: see Gen 15:16; Wis 19:1–4; but especially, with reference to the Antiochene period, 2 Macc 6:13–16. This passage most explicitly states the difference the notion presupposes between God's treatment of Jews and Gentiles. God is forbearing with the sin of Gentiles, but that involves allowing their sin to reach an extreme form that necessitates radical punishment. He chastises Jews without waiting for their sins to reach full measure, so that they are drawn back to him and not finally forsaken. His forbearance with Gentiles in the time of Abraham (Gen 15:16), the exodus (Wis 19:1–4), and Antiochus (2 Macc 6:13–16) gives them the opportunity to repent of their sin, but serves his purpose to bring deliverance and blessing to Jews through a judgment justified by Gentiles' failure to repent.

Two key aspects of Daniel's portrait of Antiochus are summarized in v 23b and expanded in vv 24 and 25 (Keil), his ruthless boldness and his artful cleverness. These are not merely randomly observed aspects of a particular person's character. Nor does the seer imply that Antiochus only *looks* fierce and compensates for lack of real strength by trickery. Used for evil ends, Antiochus's two characteristics are both key elements in the standard portrayal of a tyrant (Niditch, *Vision,* 230–31). They are thus not so much descriptions of Antiochus's personal character as elements in a stylized characterization of him as a wicked king (see also *Form*). More neutrally, they are key attributes of any king. Even if Antiochus cannot be compared with Alexander (but see n. 24.a-a), he is quite strong enough to do just as he wishes with Judea. The "ease" with which he achieves his ends is another part of the standard characterization (cf. Ezek 38–39; Lebram, *VT* 25 [1975] 739–43) rather than having specific historical reference, and his expertise with the enigmatic (חידות, "riddles") is also a necessary attribute for a king, as is reflected in the portrayal of Solomon in comparison with the Queen of Sheba and King Hiram of Tyre (1 Kgs 10; Josephus, *Ant.* 8.5.3 [8.141–49]) (H. P. Müller, "Der Begriff 'Rätsel' im Alten Testament," *VT* 20 [1970] 477–79). Perhaps there is a pejorative implication about this expression: it might suggest that Antiochus can interpret heavenly secrets as a result of forcing his way into the heavenly realm (Barr). For Antiochus's deceitfulness, see 11:21, 23, 24, 27, 32. It is illustrated in 1 Macc 1:29–30; see also his manipulation of the high-priesthood, 2 Macc 4:7–29.

Throughout these verses, the objects of his violence and trickery are probably the people of God. While "mighty" (עצומים) would be a natural term for foreign enemies (cf. 11:25), this reference is less relevant in the context: cf. the focus on Jews in 1 Macc 1:24–32; 2 Macc 5:11–14 and the עם עצום of Ps 35:18. Before God, the people of Judea are mighty ones, so Antiochus's contempt for them augurs ill for him. Probably the following phrase makes this explicit (see n. 24.c-c): the mighty are a people of holy ones. The holy ones who are the object of his attacks are further described as רבים ("many," v 25). רבים parallels עצומים "mighty" in Isa 53:12; it seems that all these terms are the self-descriptions of the conservative Jews. The "many" becomes a frequent term in Daniel's visions and a technical term for the faithful community in 1QS 6.20–23 (Lacocque). The term suggests that the objects of Antiochus's attacks are earthly beings; קדשים and עצומים might be used of either earthly or heavenly beings.

The leader supreme (שר שרים, "leader of leaders") against whom Antiochus sets himself must be God himself (see v 11 *Comment*). Antiochus's setting himself against God will bring his rebellion to its ultimate point, but thus to that point where God intervenes. He breaks: once again the term appropriate to the horns in the symbolic vision enters the interpretative vision. Antiochus's breaking by no human hand recalls 2:34, 45 (cf. 11:40–45). It might suggest that the seer did not believe in the Maccabeans' violent resistance to Antiochus, but it *need* not do so. The combination of human activity and divine judgment appears at the climax of the Animal Apocalypse, *1 Enoch* 90. It is the *fact* of Antiochus's fall, not the means, that the vision emphasizes (Hasslberger, *Hoffnung,* 82–83). 1 Maccabees and 2 Maccabees agree that Antiochus died in the course of a not-wholly-successful campaign in Persia. His death took place in November/December 164 B.C. (Sachs and Wiseman, "King List").

26–27 Ezekiel's contemporaries dismissed at least one of his visions on the grounds that it related to distant days (12:27). Ezekiel knew that God does not speak about distant days: his promises and his warnings relate to the future that is coming upon the prophet's hearers. The apparent exception here (cf. 10:4) proves the rule, because the real date of the seer's vision is in the 160s B.C. and it concerns events that are present and imminent, not distant, for seer and audience. Closing up (סתם) the vision because of its relevance to that far future context might denote merely keeping it safe until the day when it is needed. The verb more naturally suggests, however, keeping it secret until that day. It appears alongside the verb "to seal" (חתם) in 12:4, 9. For a second-century B.C. audience, this "explains" why the vision has not been heard of before. At the same time, the motif gives parabolic expression to the conviction that the revelation the seer was bringing to his contemporaries really came from God. Its very emergence was a sign that the End, the breaking off of oppression and the fulfillment of God's purpose of his people, was near (see Russell, *Apocalyptic,* 107–14, with references to other apocalypses).

Explanation

Suppose we imagine Daniel reflecting on his own vision. . . .

1–2 My second vision took my first further, and it, too, seemed to be set in the reign of the sacrilegious Belshazzar. Belshazzar's acts foreshadowed events of our own day—but his fall foreshadowed the judgment we looked forward to, too. There can be comfort in the lessons of history. In one sense it was not as awesome a vision as the previous one, but I knew it was one that I, and other people, needed to pay careful attention to. Its very geographical setting made clear that it did not relate to the period of the exile but to later circumstances.

3–12 It began with animals again, animals that symbolized national powers full of aggressive strength. Picturing them that way did not imply any great critique of nations: nations are like that. Force and violence are of the essence of their lives. It is how they come into existence and how they stay in existence. My vision offered no further hint regarding the origin of that violence. It did not suggest that supernatural powers, heavenly or demonic, lay behind the activity of the nations. It assumed that they have to be taken seriously in themselves.

New to this vision was the picture of two of these powers in conflict with each other. Neither was particularly good or bad, nor was it the case that one was God's agent and the other opposing God (Plöger). There was no hint of an antimessiah in the vision. Events were proceeding in a way that did not manifestly involve God at all. He was either absent from this history or way behind the scenes. The origins of human power did not come into focus. What the vision revealed was their destiny—that is, their fall. Horns, and the human strength they symbolize, are strong yet also strangely vulnerable (Lüthi). Each mighty, even apparently unassailable human power is in due course broken by another—sometimes at the height of its achievement, as if the effort involved in that achievement proves too much. God can view the process with distanced disdain, if he chooses: the nations will resolve their own destiny (Ps 33:10–17). History, then, has its patterns, but they are not imposed on it so as to shape it in a way unrelated to the intrinsic significance of events. The patterns are ones that emerge from the consistencies inherent in human nature, in the world, and in God himself. The arrogance of power works itself out as the aggrandizing growth of one kingdom arouses the envy of another, which challenges and defeats the one that had grown excessively powerful. My vision was designed to help people cope with a life-threatening crisis by building up faith and hope. It sought to build up faith by making the present more intelligible, revealing how it linked logically to the past and took further a shaping of events that could be perceived in the past and thus showed how history was "less out of control and so somewhat less terrifying" (Newsom, "Past," 43; also 48). It built up hope by using that same patterning as a basis for future projection: "if God made x end in y, he will surely make X end in Y."

When a nation reaches beyond violence toward other nations like itself to violence toward the people of God and the worship of God, that seems a terrible further transgression, but it is also the event that makes its fall inevitable. The events that overtook us in the 160s were not merely acts of cruel oppression like others. Behind the earthly place of worship, the earthly people, and the earthly priesthood stood supernatural realities: the being of God himself who was worshiped there, a purpose of God to have a witness to himself in the world, a reminder that human power is subject to limits. Attacks on Israel are not the same as attacks on other peoples. Anti-Semitism has an extra dimension. The kind of acts we had witnessed made God subservient to politics, and that is not merely politics' sin but its downfall. When they happen, they are a strange kind of encouragement. It is difficult for their victims to view it this way until they can see what is at stake in events like that.

13–14 There was a further encouragement in the awareness that these events were matters of scandal and concern not only on earth but in heaven. Of course we ourselves were groaning "how long?" to ourselves and to God, like the psalmists. But in my vision that groan was shared by others (cf. the "how long?" of the martyrs in Rev 6:10).

The central feature in the act of deliverance would be not the destruction of an enemy but the fate of a sanctuary. That was reflected in the way the holy one set a term to the offensive events: they would last for a period conceived in terms of how long daily sacrifices would be suspended. The climax would come with the vindication of the sanctuary, which would be for the world as significant an event as the granting of a worldwide lordship in my first vision (cf. Isa 2:2–4; Koch, *HZ* 193 [1961] 25).

The figure itself should not be misinterpreted. Its first significance was to promise that there *would* be an end, and then that this end was not too far off. But it looked like a symbolic number, and I am not sure it had a literal reference—though I cannot deny that it is interesting that the time from Onias's death to the restoration was about that period.

15–19 I do not believe all that was merely a comforting human reassurance for people that everything was going to be all right. It was ultimately God-given. I am not claiming to have heard God speaking to me. I know I am a mere human being. I *am* claiming that my message reflects God's word and suggests a heavenly perspective on events. Nor is it a message about events of mere passing significance. The attacks of earthly powers on the people of God, the worship of God, and the name of God raise ultimate questions, not mere transient ones (Plöger). We had seen a fearful intensifying of human despite of God and that had to lead to an "End." It is suggestive that those should have been the words. I was not actually saying that *the* End was imminent. But there *was* something ultimate about that outbreak of sin, and thus something ultimate about its punishment. I was not implying that there was something demonic about all history (I did not mention the demonic at all, in fact), only that there was something distinctively godless about the history we had to live through. It was like being on the receiving end of someone's intense anger. I do not mean we thought God was angry with us (I actually said "wrath," not "God's wrath"; Heaton). There have been times when he was, and I am not against that way of speaking, emerging as it does from our relationship with a deeply personal God. But there are times when calamity strikes and it is as if someone has struck out at you in anger when there seems no reason why someone should, and that is how it was for us—as if Antiochus was the rod of God's anger the way Sennacherib had once been. I might have described it as Antiochus's anger (cf. 11:30). Not that I mean to ascribe feelings to him—it may have all been very calculated—but he was the actual author of the calamity that came to us.

20–26 To a greater degree than was the case with my previous vision, the symbols were fairly transparent. The interpretative part mostly made explicit things that were not very mysterious, though they thus still reinforced the point, yet left the picture with a touch of mystery and allusiveness. There were several reasons for that. One was that I am not sure I was clear about it all myself. Another was that the vision *did* concern ultimate realities, and one cannot reduce these to down-to-earth prosaic terms without losing something. A further ramification of this is that the significance of those symbols transcended the events we were involved in. People who have said my visions were about the pope or Antichrist are wrong in the sense that they were designed by God to speak as his word to the Antiochene period in terms that meant something then. But keeping the metaphor even in the interpretative sections of the vision retained the hint of ultimate realities that were embodied for us in one particular historical situation. Those ultimate issues have surfaced on other occasions, and I cannot say that people who lived in such circumstances did wrong to find themselves in my visions, even if I might prefer to speak of that process as one of reapplication or appropriation rather than as exegesis (Koch, *Apocalypticism,* 439).

The idea of rebels reaching full measure is another motif that is solemn, but simultaneously reassuring because it suggests that an act of judgment must follow upon full measure being reached. That comes about in a mysterious way. It is not merely the fruit of historical forces, like the passing of power from one empire to another at earlier stages. Even if the historical forces that bring the downfall of evil can be traced, there is something supernatural about it. People and events had a transcendent significance. Antiochus *is* a Satanic figure, an embodiment of demonic pretension, but my vision did not suggest that separate from Antiochus there was an independently existent supernatural being using Antiochus, or foreshadowed by Antiochus. It did not point us toward a mythic understanding of the battle of the godless against God ("spiritual warfare"). Antiochus was not literally fighting angels; rather, that was the significance of his attack on people and sanctuary. The visible realities such as the Jewish people and the Jerusalem temple had a transcendent significance that Antiochus denied. When believers are hurt, heaven is hurt. At this point, whatever might have seemed to be the case earlier in the vision, it was clear that heaven and earth are not two disconnected, discontinuous worlds. Each underlies the other. Heaven cannot but be involved with earth, earth with heaven (Lacocque).

The motif of rebels reaching full measure is taken up and applied to the Jewish people itself in Matt 23:32; 1 Thess 2:16 in the light of their refusal to acknowledge Jesus; presumably its openness to being reapplied in that way means it can be reapplied again to the Church if the Church turns its back on God's way (cf. Rom 11:17–22). As well as being "a call to faith, not a call to arms," a challenge to loyalty under persecution (Reid, 184, 188), my vision was thus a call to humility and repentance on the part of people not under persecution.

27 Awareness of where history is going puts you into a complicated position (Lüthi). Of course it gives you confidence where you might otherwise have been overcome by worry: you know that a supernatural hand has already broken all power of evil and that the risks you have to live with can be lived with. But you may also be awed and troubled, by having been put in touch with heavenly realities, by the knowledge of what the future may bring to you and to other people. And at the same time you have to get on with the job of living.

Daniel Prays for the End of His People's Exile and His Prayer Is Heard (9:1–27)

Bibliography

Anderson, R. *The Coming Prince.* London: Hodder, 1881; 13th ed., London: Pickering, [1939]. ———. *Unfulfilled Prophecy and "The Hope of the Church."* London: Prophecy Investigation Society, [1917]; 2nd ed., London: Thynne/Nisbet, 1917. **Baltzer, K.** *Das Bundesformular.* WMANT 4 (1964; rev. ed., 1964). = *The Covenant Formulary.* Tr. D. E. Green. Philadelphia/Oxford: Fortress/Blackwell, 1971. **Baumgarten, J. M.** "The Heavenly Tribunal and the Personification of Ṣedeq in Jewish Apocalyptic." *ANRW* ii 19, 1 (1979) 219–39. **Bayer, E.** *Danielstudien.* 1–106. **Bebber, J. van.** "Zur Berechnung der 70 Wochen Daniels." *BZ* 4 (1960) 119–41. **Beckwith, R. T.** "The Significance of the Calendar for Interpreting Essene Chronology and Eschatology." *RevQ* 10 (1979–81) 167–202. ———. "Daniel 9 and the Date of Messiah's Coming in Essene, Hellenistic, Pharisaic, Zealot, and Early Christian Computation." *RevQ* 10 (1979–81) 521–42. **Blayney, B.** *A Dissertation by Way of Inquiry into the True Import and Application of the Vision related Dan. ix. ver. 20. to the end. . . .* Oxford: Clarendon, 1775. **Bosanquet, J. W.** *Chronology of the Times of Daniel, Ezra, and Nehemiah. . . .* London: Longman's, 1848. ———. *Messiah the Prince. . . .* London: Longmans, 1866; 2nd ed. 1869. **[Bosanquet, J. W.]** *Daniel's Prophecy of the Seventy Weeks.* London: Rivington, 1836. **Bowker, J. W.** "Intercession in the Qur'an and the Jewish Tradition." *JSS* 11 (1966) 69–82. **Buis, P.** "Notification de jugement et confession nationale." *BZ* 11 (1967) 193–205. **Bullinger, E. W.** *Number in Scripture.* London: Eyre, 1894; 6th ed., London: Lamp, 1952. **Burrows, E.** *The Gospel of the Infancy and Other Biblical Essays.* London: Burns and Oates, 1940. **Cooper, D. L.** *The 70 Weeks of Daniel.* Los Angeles: Biblical Research Society, 1941. **Cornill, C. H.** "Die siebzig Jahrwochen Daniels." *Theologische Studien und Skizzen aus Ostpreussen* 2 (1889) 1–32. **Day, J.** *God's Conflict with the Dragon and the Sea.* Cambridge/New York: CUP, 1985. **Déaut, R. le.** "Aspects de l'intercession dans le Judaïsme ancien." *JSJ* 1 (1970) 35–57. **DeVries, S. J.** "Excursus on the Reversal of Saving History in Daniel 9." *Achievements.* 340–43. **Doukhan, J.** "The Seventy Weeks of Daniel 9." *AUSS* 17 (1979) 1–22. **Driver, G. R.** "Numbers." **Eusebius of Caesarea.** Εὐαγγελικῆς ἀποδείξεως δέκα λόγοι. c. 318. = *PG* 22 (1857) 13–794. = *The Proof of the Gospel.* Tr. W. J. Ferrar. 2 vols. London/New York: SPCK/ Macmillan, 1920. **Fraidl, F.** *Die Exegese der siebzig Wochen Daniels in der alten und mittleren Zeit.* Graz: Leuschner, 1883. **Frischmuthus, J.** *Evidens demonstratio Messiam secundum computum Danielis pridem apparuisse.* = *TTP* 902–37. **Gerhardt, O.** "Wann sollte der Messias kommen?" *Forschung und Forschritte* 11 (1935) 8–9. **Gilbert, M.** "La prière de Daniel." *RTL* 3 (1972) 284–310. **Gowan, D. E.** "The Exile in Jewish Apocalyptic." In *Scripture in History and Theology,* FS J. C. Rylaarsdam, ed. A. L. Merrill and T. W. Overholt. PTMS 17 (1977) 205–23. **Grabbe, L. L.** "Chronography in Hellenistic Jewish Historiography." *SBLSP* 17 (1979) 43–68. **Grelot, P.** "Soixante-dix semaines d'années." *Bib* 50 (1969) 169–86. **Gruenthaner, M. J.** "The Seventy Weeks." *CBQ* 1 (1939) 44–54. **Gunkel, H.** *Einleitung in die Psalmen.* Göttingen: Vandenhoeck, 1933. **Harvey, J.** *Le plaidoyer prophétique contre Israël après la rupture de l'alliance.* Bruges/Montreal: Desclée/ Bellarmin, 1967. **Heard, W. J.** "The Maccabean Martyrs' Contribution to Holy War." *EvQ* 58 (1986) 291–318. **Hengstenberg, E. W.** *Christologie des Alten Testaments.* 3 vols. Berlin: Oehmigke, 1829–35; 2nd ed., 1854–57. = *Christology of the Old Testament.* Tr. T. Mayer and J. Martin. 4 vols. 2nd ed., London: Rivington, 1856–58. **Hoehner,**

H. W. "Daniel's Seventy Weeks and New Testament Chronology." *BSac* 132 (1975) 47–65. **Jepsen, A.** "Gnade und Barmherzigkeit im Alten Testament." *KD* 7 (1961) 261–71. **Jones, B. W.** "The Prayer in Daniel ix." *VT* 18 (1968) 488–93. **Kline, M. G.** "The Covenant of the Seventieth Week." In *The Law and the Prophets,* FS O. T. Allis, ed. J. H. Skilton. [Nutley, NJ]: PRPC, 1974. 452–69. **Knibb, M. A.** "The Exile in the Literature of the Intertestamental Period." *HeyJ* 17 (1976) 253–72. **Knowles, L. E.** "The Interpretation of the Seventy Weeks of Daniel in the Early Fathers." *WTJ* 7 (1945) 136–60. **Koch, K.** "Die mysteriösen Zahlen der judäischen Könige und die apokalyptischen Jahrwochen." *VT* 28 (1978) 433–41. **König, E.** "Die siebzig Jahrwochen in Dan. 9, 24–27." *NKZ* 11 (1900) 1003–13. ———. "Die chronologisch-christologische Hauptstelle im Danielbuche." *NKZ* 15 (1904) 974–87. **Lacocque, A.** "The Liturgical Prayer in Daniel 9." *HUCA* 47 (1976) 119–42. **Lagrange, M. J.** "La prophétie des soixante-dix semaines de Daniel." *RB* 39 (1930) 179–98. **Lambert, G.** "Une exégèse arithmétique du chapitre ix de Daniel." *NRT* 74 (1952) 409–17. **Laurentin, R.** *Structure et théologie de Luc i-ii.* Paris: Gabalda, 1957. 45–63. **Lebram, J. C. H.** "Apokalyptiek als keerpunt in het joodse denken." *NedTT* 30 (1976) 271–81. **Lipiński, E.** *La liturgie pénitentielle dans la Bible.* LD 52 (1969). **McComiskey, T. E.** "The Seventy 'Weeks' of Daniel against the Background of Ancient Near Eastern Literature." *WTJ* 47 (1985) 18–45. **Montgomery, J. A.** "A Survival of the Tetragrammaton in Daniel." *JBL* 40 (1921) 86. **Moore, C. A.** "Toward the Dating of the Book of Baruch." *CBQ* 36 (1974) 312–20. **Nestle, E.** "Zu Daniel." *ZAW* 4 (1884) 247–48. **Newman, R. C.** "Daniel's Seventy Weeks and the Old Testament Sabbath-Year Cycle." *JETS* 16 (1973) 229–34. **Nolland, J.** "*Sib. Or.* iii. 265–94, an Early Maccabean Messianic Oracle." *JTS* 30 (1979) 158–66. **Payne, J. B.** "The Goal of Daniel's Seventy Weeks." *JETS* 21 (1978) 97–115. ———. "The Goal of Daniel's Seventy Weeks." *Presbyterion* 4 (1978) 33–38. **Plöger, O.** " 'Siebzig Jahre.' " In *Festschrift Friedrich Baumgärtel,* ed. J. Herrmann. Erlangen: Universitätsbund, 1959. 124–30. = Plöger, *Aus der Spätzeit des Alten Testament.* Göttingen: Vandenhoeck, 1970. 67–73. **Quervain, A. de.** *Busse: Eine Auslegung von Daniel 9,4–19.* TExH 45 (1936). **Rad, G. von.** "Gerichtsdoxologie." In *Schalom,* FS A. Jepsen, ed. K.-H. Bernhardt. Stuttgart: Calwer, 1971. 28–37. = von Rad, *Gesammelte Studien zum Alten Testament.* TBü 48 (1973) 2:245–54. **Sawyer, J. F. A.** "Types of Prayer in the Old Testament." *Semitics* 7 (1980) 131–43. **Scholl, Dr.** *Commentatio exegetica de septuaginta hebdomadibus Danielis.* Frankfurt: Andreae, 1829. **Shea, W. H.** "Poetic Relations of the Time Periods in Dan 9:25." *AUSS* 18 (1980) 59–63. **Sostmannus, A.** *Commentarius . . . de LXX. hebdomadibus. . . .* London: Boutestein, 1710. **Steck, O. H.** *Israel und das gewaltsame Geschick der Propheten.* WMANT 23 (1967) 110–37. **Steudel, J. C. F.** *Disquisitio in locum Dan. ix, 24–27.* Tübingen: Ludovici, 1833. ———. *Quid de recentioribus quibusdam loci Dan. ix, 24–27. interpretationibus judicandum sit. . . .* Tübingen: Ludovici, 1835. **Stonard, J.** *A Dissertation on the Seventy Weeks of Daniel the Prophet.* London: Rivington, 1825. **Torrey, C. C.** "The Messiah Son of Ephraim." *JBL* 66 (1947) 253–77. **Towner, W. S.** *USQR* 26 (1970–71) 203–14. **Wacholder, B. Z.** "Chronomessianism." *HUCA* 46 (1975) 201–18. = Wacholder, *Essays on Jewish Chronology and Chronography.* New York: Ktav, 1976. 240–57. **Walvoord, J. F.** "Is the Seventieth Week of Daniel Future?" *BSac* 101 (1944) 30–49. **Wambacq, B. N.** "Les Prières de Baruch (1,15–2,19) et de Daniel (9,5–19)." *Bib* 40 (1959) 463–75. **Wieseler, C.** *Die 70 Wochen und die 63 Jahrwochen des Propheten Daniel.* Göttingen: Vandenhoeck, 1839.

Translation

[1] *In the first year of Darius, son of Ahashweros,*[a] *a Median by birth, who* [b]*was made king*[b] *over the realm of the Babylonians—*[2] *in the first year of his reign, I*

(Daniel) noted[a] in the scriptures the number of years [b](the word of Yahweh which came to the prophet Jeremiah)[b] to be completed for the ruins of Jerusalem, seventy years. 3 So I turned to the Lord[a] God to [b]make prayers of supplication[b] with fasting, sackcloth, and ashes; 4 I prayed a prayer of confession[a] to Yahweh my God: "O[b] Lord, the great and awesome God who keeps his covenantal commitment[c] with people who love him and keep his commands, 5 we have failed [a]and gone astray, we have done wrong and rebelled,[a] [b]we have turned our backs[b] [c]on your authoritative commands[c] 6 and not listened to your servants the prophets who spoke [a]as your representatives[a] [b]to our kings, our leaders, and our fathers, and to all the people of the country.[b] 7 Right belongs to you, Lord, while [a]a look of shame[a] attaches to us this day,[b] to the people of Judah and the citizens of Jerusalem, and to all Israel near and far away in all the countries where you have driven them because of the trespasses they have committed against you. 8 Yahweh, a look of shame attaches to us, our kings, [a]our leaders, and our fathers, in that we have failed you; 9 [a]a deep compassion which keeps pardoning[a] belongs to the Lord our God. Because[b] we have rebelled against him 10 and have not listened to the voice of Yahweh our God by living according to his instructions[a] which he set before us by means of his servants the prophets, 11 and all Israel has overstepped your instruction and turned[a] their backs to avoid listening to your voice, [b]the solemn curse[b] written in the instruction of Moses the servant of God has overwhelmed us. Because we have failed him,[c] 12 he has kept his words[a] which he uttered against us and against [b]those who acted as our leaders[b] [c]by bringing[c] great trouble upon us, [d]in that[d] nothing has happened in all the world such as happened to Jerusalem, 13 just as it is written in the instruction of Moses, [a]all this trouble—it has come[b] upon us. [c]We have not sought mercy from[c] Yahweh our God by turning from our waywardness and [d]giving heed to[d] your faithfulness,[e] 14 and Yahweh has kept this trouble ready and brought it upon us. Yes,[a] Yahweh our God [b]has been right[b] in all the things that he has done, and we have not listened to his voice.

15 But now, Lord our God, who brought your people out of the land of Egypt by strength of hand and earned renown for yourself this day: we have failed, we have done wrong. 16 Lord, in keeping with all your [a]right deeds,[a] O may your burning fury turn away from your city, Jerusalem, your sacred mountain; for because of our failures and our ancestors' wayward acts, Jerusalem and your people have become objects of scorn to everyone around us. 17 But now, our God, listen to your servant's prayers of supplication, and smile upon your desolate sanctuary, for [a]my Lord's sake.[a] 18 My God, give ear and listen,[a] open[b] your eyes and look at our desolate state in the city which bears your name,[c] for it is not on the basis of our right deeds that we are laying down our supplications before you, but rather on the basis of your great compassion. 19 Lord, listen. Lord, pardon. Lord, hear and act, do not delay, for your own sake, my God, because your city and your people bear your name."

20 [a]I was still speaking, confessing in prayer[b] my failure[c] and the failure[c] of my people Israel and laying down my supplication before Yahweh my God concerning the sacred mountain of my God, 21 still speaking in prayer, when Gabriel, [a]the being[a] I had seen in the vision I had previously,[b] [c]when I was tired and weary,[c] approached[d] me at[e] the time of the evening offering. 22 [a]He explained to me:[a] "Daniel, I came forth[b] specifically[c] [d]to give you clear insight.[d] 23 When you began your supplications a word came forth,[a] and I have come to declare it,[b] for you are [c]held in high regard.[c] [d]So heed the word and give heed to the revelation.[d]

24 *Seventy sevens*[a] *have been assigned*[b]
for[c] *your people and for*[c] *your sacred city,*
to end[d] *the rebellion,*
[e]*to do away with*[e] *failures,*[f]
to wipe away[g] *waywardness,*
to bring in lasting vindication,[h]
to seal [i]*a prophet's vision,*[i]
to anoint [j]*a most sacred place.*[j]
25 *You must understand and perceive,*
from the coming forth of a word to [a]*build a restored*[a] *Jerusalem*
to an anointed, a leader, there will be [b]*seven sevens.*
For sixty-two sevens[b] [c]*it will be restored and rebuilt,*[c]
square[d] *and moat.*[e]
[f]*But in the pressure of the times*[f]
26 [a]*(that is, after the sixty-two sevens)*[a]
an anointed will be cut off[b]
[c]*and will have neither the city nor the sanctuary.*[c]
A leader to come[d] *will devastate*[e] *a people,*[f]
and its end[g] *will come with the flood.*
Until the end of[h] *battle* [i]*desolations are determined.*[i]
27 *A covenant will prevail*[a] *for the multitude*[b] *for one seven;*
[c]*in the middle of the seven*[c] *sacrifice and offering will cease,*[d]
and [e]*upon a wing*[e] *will be a desolating abomination:*[f]
until [g]*a conclusion which has been decreed*[g]
overwhelms a desolate one.[h]"

Notes

1.a. אחשורוש, cf., e.g., Esth 1:1, 2; Aram. חשיארש corresponds better to Persian *Ḳšayāršā.*

1.b-b. הָמְלַךְ, the only instance of the ho in BH; BHS compares קבל מלכותא (taken as "received the kingship") in 6:1. G, Syr have act vb "he reigned" (cf. JB), perh. indicating הָמְלַךְ understood in an "inwardly trans" sense (cf. GKC 53def for other vbs; PS 277 for this vb in Syriac). An Aramaism (Lacocque)?

2.a. Qal בינתי (instead of בנתי) is a shortened hi in form (see GKC 73a). For the meaning ("consider" is better than "understand": that is part of Daniel's problem!), see BDB; it need not be an Aramaism (against Hartman).

2.b-b. The wording of the parenthesis, אשר היה דבר יהוה אל ירמיה הנביא, follows that of passages such as Jer 14:1, where אשר "which" is defined by the subsequent noun דבר (see BDB 82b); it is not acc of respect (as EVV) (cf. Charles, comparing Deut 5:5).

3.a. In chap. 9 God is referred to as יהוה "Yahweh," אדני "Lord," and אלהים "God." OG uses *δέσποτα* ("Master," only in the voc), *κύριος* "Lord," and *θεός* "God." In vv 3, 15, 16, 17, and 19a (twice), where L has אדני, some mss have יהוה. Q אדני may have replaced יהוה in the text sometimes, though the substitution of יהוה for אדני is also explicable (e.g., in v 3, assimilating to v 2). In vv 15, 16, and 17 OG has *δέσποτα*, but not in v 3 (though this might simply be because the term there needs to be acc), nor in v 19a; OG also has *δέσποτα* where MT has יהוה in v 8. OG's use of *δέσποτα* must be utilized with caution as evidence for an original יהוה, however, since *δέσποτα* also appears as an equivalent of אלהינו ("our God," v 17) and אלהי ("my God," v 19b).

3.b-b. לבקש תפלה ותחנונים. "To seek prayer . . ." gives an odd sense. "To inquire with prayer . . ." gives good sense, but when בקש means seeking a word from God, it needs an obj (2 Sam 21:1; Ezek 7:26; Amos 8:12); so also the similar use of דרש. Rather the lit. meaning is "to ask a prayer . . . ," i.e., to utter one: an Aramaism—cf. the use of בעה in 6:8 [7] (Zimmermann, *JBL* 57 [1938] 263). Appeal to Akk. *baqašu* [G. R. Driver, acc. Porteous] seems forced and unnecessary. The first noun is a general one for (formal, liturgical) prayer, the second specifies the kind of prayer. Cf. vv 17, 18, 23; also for the compound expression 1 Kgs 8:30, 33, 45, 49; Dan 6:12 [11] for an Aram. equivalent with vbs. See Sawyer, *Semitics* 7 (1980) 131–43.

4.a. ואתפללה . . . ואתודה "I prayed and confessed": again the first word is a general one for (formal, liturgical) prayer, the second specifies the kind of prayer. See n. 3.b-b.

4.b. "O" in EVV before a voc rarely has a BH equivalent, as here (contrast vv 7, 8, 15, 16, 17, 18, 19): אנא is "a strong part[icle] of entreaty" (BDB). But cf. the enclitic נא (v 16).

4.c. הברית והחסד "the covenant and the commitment."

5.a-a. The three vbs are pf + simple *waw*, the events being coordinate not consecutive (*TTH* 131–33). Q omits ו "and" from והרשענו "[and] we have done wrong," assimilating to 1 Kgs 8:47; G omit this "and" and the previous one for stylistic reasons.

5.b-b. וסור, inf abs continuing the series of finite vbs; cf. GKC 113z (cf. v 11).

5.c-c. ממצותך וממשפטיך "from your commands and from your decisions."

6.a-a. בשמך "in your name."

6.b-b. The terms are in descending order of status, אבות thus referring to heads of local social/kinship groups (not here "ancestors," as JB, GNB) and עם הארץ to ordinary people; cf. Jer 1:18 (Jeffery).

7.a-a. בשת הפנים "shame of face."

7.b. כיום הזה regularly means "today," "this very day," not "as at this day" (EVV); see, e.g., Jer 44:6, 22, 23. Cf. *HS* 262.

8.a. ולשרינו "and our leaders" acc. Oriental mss (so BHK), G, Syr.

9.a-a. הרחמים והסלחות, both pl, perhaps suggesting "acts of."

9.b. It is hard to instance כי meaning "although" (NEB), though "when" comes near that (cf. BDB 473b). See A. Aejmelaeus, "Function and Interpretation of כי in Biblical Hebrew," *JBL* 105 (1986) 193–209, esp. 207; contrast T. C. Vriezen, "Einige Notizen zur Übersetzung des Bindesworts *kī*," in *Von Ugarit nach Qumran* (FS O. Eissfeldt, ed. J. Hempel et al.; BZAW 77 [1958]) 272; A. Schoors, "The Particle כי," *OTS* 21 (1981) 272–73. But the כי clause is an odd follow-up to v 9a, and more likely begins a new sentence (Joubert, 162–63).

10.a. OG, Vg have s, but the less usual pl is surely original.

11.a. Cf. n. 5.b-b.

11.b-b. האלה והשבעה "the curse and the oath."

11.c. Some mss correct לו "him" to לך "you." But the prayer keeps moving between 2nd and 3rd person (as psalms do); God has been referred to in the 3rd person three words previously, and the 3rd person ref is presupposed by the opening of v 12. This cl is prob the beginning of that sentence (Wambacq, *Bib* 40 [1959] 469).

12.a. Q has s, perhaps rightly (Plöger).

12.b-b. שפטינו אשר שפטונו "our judges who judged us": the noun can denote leaders other than *the* "judges" (BDB).

12.c-c. להביא, perhaps "that he would bring" (JB).

12.d-d. אשר; Bevan "so that." For both, cf. BDB 83b.

13.a. את כל הרעה perhaps resumes רעה גדלה "great trouble" (v 12)—hence the obj marker (so Behrmann, Marti). It is doubtful if את simply emphasizes the noun, which is then actually the subject of באה (see *EWS* 148–54 against GKC 117m; P. P. Saydon, "Meanings and Uses of the Particle את," and J. Macdonald, "The Particle את in Classical Hebrew," *VT* 14 [1964] 192–210; 264–75). The phrase may be the quasi-obj of the pass כתוב "is written" (Bevan; cf. GKC 117k, 121c); or the construction may simply break down (so in different ways Montgomery; J. Blau, "Zum angeblichen Gebrauch von את vor dem Nominativ," *VT* 4 [1954] 9).

13.b. באה accented on the first syllable and thus taken as pf. Some mss הבאה (ptpl, "which came").

13.c-c. ולא חלינו את פני "and we have not sweetened the face of": a different חלה from חלה "be sick": cf. BDB. EVV continue from the previous cl, implying that v 13b denotes a failure to seek God after his punishment fell. But this is an unlikely understanding of either the exile or the postexilic period, and more likely v 13b again reviews Israel's history more broadly; if the ref should be tied down more specifically, it would be to the preexilic period (cf. v 9b and the last cl of v 11).

13.d-d. השכיל ב might mean "gaining insight in/by means of": cf. v 25.

13.e. אמת suggested "true religion" in 8:12, "reliability" in 8:26, but this more common OT meaning (cf. NEB "[remembered] that thou art true to thy word") fits well here.

14.a. EVV "for": we should perh. attribute even to apparently asseverative כי some connective function (Aejmelaeus [see n. 9.b] 205), but this כי introduces a closing cl which balances v 7 (see *Structure*) and the connection is with vv 9b-14a as a whole, not just with v 14a.

14.b-b. The context has to determine the time ref of a noun cl (a verbless cl) in Heb., and a past ref seems appropriate here.

16.a-a. Taking צדקתך as literal pl (BDB 842b, cf. Syr) rather than pl of amplification ("true justice," see GKC 124e; cf. G).

17.a-a. למען אדני, an odd expression (esp. in a 2nd person context), but apparently original, since Th ("for your sake, Lord"), OG ("for your servants' sake, Lord"), and Syr ("for your name's sake, Lord") all offer different "improvements" on MT.

18.a. וּשֲׁמָע: the composite shewa emphasizes the vocal character of the shewa after ו (GKC 10g).

18.b. K reads פקחה as a lengthened form of the imper (cf. v 19); cf. Q פקח. But the ה might be an abbreviation for יהוה; the cl's structure then parallels its predecessor and the pair parallel 2 Kgs 19:16 (Lacocque).

18.c. אשר נקרא שמך עליה "over which your name has been proclaimed."

20.a. On the circumstantial cl, see *TTH* 169; GKC 116u.

20.b. On ומתפלל ומתודה "praying and confessing," see n. 4.a.

20.c. Vrs presuppose pl pointing each time.

21.a-a. G "behold the man . . ." perhaps presuppose reading והא האיש (Montgomery); for הא see BDB 210b, 1089b. "The man Gabriel" is odd, even in the light of 8:15; Ehrlich compares Exod 11:3 and suggests translating "the lord Gabriel."

21.b. See n. 8:1.d.

21.c-c. Grammatically, מעף ביעף "wearied with weariness" could apply to Daniel or Gabriel, but the word order implies the former (Keil), and also suggests referring it to the faint of 8:17–18 rather than to the result of this time of prayer and fasting. Vrs, EVV, however, connect the phrase with Gabriel's flight (cf. JBmg "lit. 'flying in flight [touched me]' "). This presupposes that יעף "be weary" has a homonym meaning "fly," a by-form of עוף (Brockington emends to מעפף עף, forms of עוף itself), and implies that angels, like seraphs/cherubs, have wings to fly with. V 21 itself makes explicit, however, that Dan (like other parts of the OT) presupposes that angels are human in form, and can be distinguished from seraphs (Isa 6) and the figures of hybrid appearance in Ezek 1. See esp. Gen 28:12 (angels moving between heaven and earth by ladder); even 1 Chr 21:16 does not say that the angel has wings to fly with.

21.d. נגע can mean "touched" (so Th, cf. 8:18; 10:16), but "reached" (so OG, Syr, cf. 8:7; 12:12) probably fits better here. For the ptpl referring to a punctiliar event in a double ptpl construction, see GKC 116u.

21.e. כ indicating time at which, not to be tr "about" (against NIV) (cf. *HS* 262); the variants ל and ב make this explicit.

22.a-a. ויבן וידבר עמי ויאמר "he explained and spoke with me and said." NAB emends to ויבינני . . . "he made me understand," comparing Th, Vg—but they may only be tr ad sensum; הבין can be used absolutely (BDB). RSV, JB emend to ויבא, comparing OG, Syr—but they are more likely resolving some typical Danielic fulsomeness.

22.b. יצאתי "come forth," as in vv 23, 25 with respect to the message "issuing," suggests a supernatural commission more specifically than the בוא of the similar passage Josh 5:13–15 (cf. 2 Sam 14:15).

22.c. עתה hardly has a specifically temporal reference ("now") in such contexts; it rather draws attention to the "moment-ousness" of the occasion; cf. Josh 5:14 (Ehrlich).

22.d-d. להשכילך בינה "to instruct you [in] insight"; the noun is adv acc.

23.a. יצא, as in v 22 to refer to Gabriel himself.

23.b. Heb. lacks "it"; direct and indirect obj can be omitted after הגיד (BDB 616b). לך ("to you"; 2 mss, cf. G, Syr) is presumably an addition. The following cl (כי חמודות אתה) might be obj of הגיד ("that you are held in high regard") (cf. UBS).

23.c-c. חמודות, intensive pl (see GKC 124e). The term is usually preceded by a constr noun, and איש might be added here as in 10:11, 19 (cf. Th), but grammatically the noun in the predicate of a noun cl is quite regular (GKC 141c, *TTH* 189).

23.d-d. ובין בדבר והבן במראה, a double hendiadys, "give careful heed to the revelatory word."

24.a. שבעים; שבוע is the regular BH word for "week," but literally it means a heptad (a period or group of seven of something); as well as meaning seven days, it can thus mean seven years in *Jub.* and in MH (*DTT*). Its pl outside Dan (9:24–27; 10:1–2) is שבועות; שבועים may be an Aramaism (Hartman).

24.b. The s נחתך implies "there has been determined/God has determined seventy sevens" (GKC 121ab), or perhaps "[a period of] seventy sevens has been determined" (cf. GKC 145h, 124ab).

24.c. Montgomery tr על "against," but the context points rather to the frequent meaning "concerning" (cf. BDB 754b; also in BA, BDB 1106a).

24.d. K probably implies לְכַלֵּא from כלא "restrain," leading into לחתם "seal" in the next phrase (see n. 24.e-e) (RVmg). The vbs through v 24a then develop, but not in a very plausible way. More likely with Q they are synonyms, and לכלא comes from כלה not כלא (cf. BDB 476b, 478a; GKC 75aa, rr; G συντελεσθῆναι; cf. Q and many mss לכלה). כלה can mean "complete" or "eliminate": cf. 9:27; 11:16, 36; 12:7. "Eliminate" better fits the general context here (Bevan, contrast Plöger).

24.e-e. Reading ולהתם (from תמם) with Q, many mss, cf. OG, Syr, Vg, NEB. L ולחתם K "to seal" (cf. Th, JB) perhaps follows on from לְכַלֵּא (n. 24.d); after לְכַלֵּא it might imply sealing up as complete (Bentzen), but this is also rather allusive, and it is more likely than לחתם here is assimilated to לחתם in v 24b than that the word is used twice and with different meanings.

24.f. Following K חַטָּאוֹת (cf. G, Syr); Q and many mss חַטָּאת "failure." The s looks like assimilation to s פשע (Bevan). Perhaps the three expressions for sin ("the rebellion," "failures," "waywardness") deliberately vary (article with s, anarthrous pl, anarthrous s).

24.g. כפר; in Arabic *kpr* can mean "to cover," but the Heb. meaning links rather with Akk. *kaparu/kuppuru* "cleanse": *CAD;* B. A. Levine, *In the Presence of the Lord* (SJLA 5 [1974]) 56–66, 123–27; against BDB.

24.h. MT punctuation divides v 24 after צדק עלמים "lasting vindication," but more likely we should divide the inf cls between the three negatives (all two-word cls) and the three positives (all three-word); cf. BHS.

24.i-i. חזון ונביא "vision and prophet."

24.j-j. קדש קדשים "a sacredness of sacrednesses." There is no word for "place," but the phrase always refers to locations or objects (the tabernacle or temple, esp. its inmost room, also its altars, vessels, incense, sacrifices, etc.—see Driver). Vg (cf. JBmg) takes it to refer to a person, but it never does so elsewhere in the OT, except for one possible understanding of 1 Chr 23:13 (see RVmg). *A fortiori* the reference cannot be to *the* Anointed One, the "Messiah" (cf. Syr *mšyḥ'*). G's literal ἅγιον ἁγίων could be read either way, but OG hardly presupposes a messianic interpretation, since it even lacks the verb "anoint" (its εὐφρᾶναι "rejoice" apparently misreads למשח as לשמח [Montgomery]).

25.a-a. להשיב ולבנות "to restore and to build." "To rebuild" (cf. Vg; RSV) would require emending להשיב to לשוב (BHS), since שוב is always in the qal when it is used in coordination with another vb to indicate repeating an act (GKC 120d). Bevan repoints לְהֹשִׁיב "to populate," but this would be a unique sense of ישב hi.

25.b-b. שבעים שבעה ושבעים ששים ושנים. NIV "seven 'sevens,' and sixty-two 'sevens' " (cf. G, Syr) suggests that the appearance of "an anointed, a prince" comes after sixty-nine "sevens," but MT's division of the verse (which this ignores) seems more natural. In support of the NIV understanding, Young questions whether Heb. syntax allows שבעים ששים ושנים to be acc of duration; but see GKC 118k. Shea (*AUSS* 18 [1980] 59–63) argues for it on poetic grounds, but not compellingly. But do the vbs imply that the process of restoration and rebuilding continues over the sixty-two years (so Hengstenberg, *Christologie*)? If so, that would be odd, and NIV could then be right. MT might be antimessianic (Beckwith, *RevQ* 10 [1979–81] 522).

25.c-c. Qal תשוב "be restored" could here stand in coordination with נבנתה "be built" and the phrase as a whole mean simply "be built again" (cf. GKC 120e on the construction). The usage in v 25a suggests rather that תשוב is quasi-pass of השיב, as נבנתה is pass of בנות. For this usage of שוב in qal cf. 1 Kgs 13:6. Bevan (cf. n. 25.a-a) repoints תֵּשֵׁב.

25.d. רחוב; a "broad open place" (cf. root רחב), not "street" (NEB), though hardly the temple court specifically (against A. van Selms, "The Origin of the Name Tyropoeon in Jerusalem," *ZAW* 91 [1979] 173); this would need to be made explicit, as in Ezra 10:9.

25.e. חרוץ; the root means "cut," the adj "sharp." In Akk. *ḫarīṣu* denotes a ditch (cf. NEB "conduit") or a moat, associated with a rampart (cf. Th τεῖχος, JB). Van Selms (see n. 25.d) plausibly takes חרוץ to refer to the Tyropoeon Valley here and in Joel 4:14 (the Tyropoeon was once more of a ravine, like the Kidron).

25.f-f. Linking ובצוק העתים with v 26, with NEB (though n.b. it is "the trouble of the times" not "the times of the trouble"; contrast 12:1). The ו "but" looks like the beginning of a new sentence or cl. Syr *lšwlm zbn'* suggests ובקץ העתים "but at the end of the times," which would also naturally link with v 26 (Bevan); cf. OG *καὶ κατὰ συντέλειαν καιρῶν* (in v 27) (influenced by Syr?). Yet Syr looks like the substitution of a more familiar expression for a less familiar one. Van Selms (see n. 25.d) ingeniously suggests that the phrase means "mound [cf. BDB on בצק, בצקת] (and) bends [cf. BDB on עות]," the last four words of v 25 thus referring to Jerusalem's east (temple court), west (Tyropoeon), north (the more elevated hill), and south (the valleys below the city). If MT is right, v 25b as a whole refers to the two features of postexilic history that could be known from the OT, the rebuilding of the city and the pressure of Israel's hostile neighbors (Hartman).

26.a-a. Perhaps a gl (Plöger).

26.b. כרת ni: "disappear" (Plöger).

26.c-c. Ozanne, *JTS* 16 (1965) 446–47; MT punctuation of ואין לו והעיר והקדש makes the first phrase very cryptic (cf. Vrs, EVV). For ו . . . ו = "both . . . and," see GKC 154a; cf. 8:13.

26.d. הבא; for indeterminate noun followed by determinate ptpl, see GKC 126w. נגיד "prince" is perhaps implicitly determinate (cf. *TTH* 209). On OG *καὶ ἥξει*, see n. 26.g.

26.e. ישחית, cf. 8:24–25; also 11:17, though there it could refer to moral/religious rather than to physical damage. If we read עִם (see n. 26.f), it will then be understood as an intensive hi, "will act corruptly" (cf. GKC 53dg)—or follow one ms יְשָׁחֵת "will be corrupted/destroyed" (cf. Syr *tthbl*).

26.f. עַם—One ms עִם "with" (cf. Th, Syr, also OG, Vg which conflate readings); but this looks like an attempt to make easier sense of an apparently difficult MT, and/or a reinterpretation of it based on the conviction that "a prince to come" is the same as the "prince" of v 25.

26.g. In 11:45 קצו refers to the end the prince comes to, but this meaning would require a very sudden change in the meaning of קץ in the next cl. More likely קץ denotes the end he brings, or the people's end (JPS). שטף (vb and noun) more often denotes the flood of calamity brought by an oppressor (11:10, 22, 22, 26, 40). OG [*καὶ ἥξει*] *ἡ συντέλεια* (cf. n. 26.d), "[and] the end [will come]," substitutes a more familiar for a less usual expression.

26.h. So MT, Th, Syr; Aq, Sym "Until the end there will be . . ." (cf. EVV). קץ is used in a nontechnical sense in 11:6, 13.

26.i-i. נחרצת שממות "a decree of desolation," נחרצת being ni ptpl f s constr, שממות qal ptpl f pl abs.

27.a. הגביר; Vrs, EVV tr "confirm" or the like (cf. 1QH 8.35) and ברית "covenant" as obj, but one might then have expected the subj to be indicated more clearly. "Prevail" (cf. OG) fits well with other occurrences of הגביר, Ps 12:5; 1QH 2.24; for m vb with f subj, see GKC 145c (cf. Bentzen, Plöger).

27.b. הרבים "the many" is becoming a commonplace term for the main body of the (faithful) community (11:33, 39; 12:3; Esth 4:3; 1QS 6.20–23); thus hardly "the mighty" (NEB), cf. Isa 53:12. The ל is equivalent to a dative of disadvantage, "against" (cf. Charles). Anarthrous רבים retains the commonplace meaning "many" (against Wiklander, *SEA* 39 [1974] 59–73).

27.c-c. חצי could denote duration of time ("for half of," so RV, strongly Keil; cf. GKC 118k), but point of time reads better (so G, NIV, strongly Doukhan, *AUSS* 17 [1979] 13; cf. GKC 118i). While one would expect ב "in" before חצי, cf. the absolute use of חצות in Ps 119:62; Job 34:20.

27.d. Cf. G, Vg. MT ישבית (EVV "cause to cease") could have this meaning (cf. GKC 53def); it hardly needs repointing.

27.e-e. ועל כנף: the noun repointed as abs, see n. 27.f. Perh. emend to בעל כנף, "lord of wing" i.e., "winged one" (cf. בעל הקרנים, "horned one," 8:6, 20), a title of the Syrian god of heaven, who is then the subject of ישבית "cause to cease."

27.f. MT שקוצים, pl, preceded by כנף: hence RV "upon the wing of abominations" (also NEB "in the train of these abominations"—but this meaning for כנף is difficult). But שקוצים משמם looks like one of the phrases for the desolating rebellion/abomination (see 8:13; 11:31; 12:11). The pl is odd, but G also has a pl expression, *βδέλυγμα τῶν ἐρημώσεων*: see *Comment.*

27.g-g. Hendiadys (Bentzen). כלה "destruction" denotes putting an end to something; it can hardly mean merely "in the end" (NEB). Cf. n. 24.d.

27.h. In 8:13, 12:11, שמם has trans meaning, but there it is preferred to משמם for paronomasia. Here in 9:27 משמם has been used for the trans and שמם for "desolate" in vv 18, 26, following general OT usage. Intrans is thus also more likely here. Cf. AV.

Form / Structure / Setting

Form

The framework of chap. 9 is a report of an angelically mediated revelation to a seer, like those of a Near Eastern oracular dream (Collins; see *ANET* 606). It thus opens (vv 1–3) with a note of the historical and personal context, though it lacks any corresponding closure after v 27 (contrast 7:28; 8:27); indeed, the revelation itself comes to an abrupt end (contrast 8:26; 12:5–13). The revelation (vv 24–27) has the form of a quasi-prophecy (see chap. 2 *Form* and chaps. 10–12 *Form*), with vv 24, 27b probably being actual prophecy. As will the final revelation in chaps. 10–12, it speaks allusively, but not symbolically, in the manner of the symbolic visions in chaps. 7 and 8, though its allusiveness is not unlike that of the interpretative visions in 7:17–18, 23–27; 8:22–25. Indeed, the revelation can be compared with these two interpretative visions; chap. 9 contains no equivalent to the symbolic vision, the latter's role being played by a passage of scripture.

Beginning as it does, not with a dream or vision but with the text of scripture, chap. 9 comes nearer than any other passage in Daniel to being expository midrash, midrash which explicitly concerns itself with issues raised by a specific biblical passage, while still concerned—like all midrash—with questions that arise from the context in which scripture is being read. In taking the passage as a prophecy of events in the audience's day, the hermeneutic of Dan 9 corresponds to that which appears in pesharim such as 1QpHab, but the chapter does not use the term פשר, nor is the revelation in the pesher form (see chap. 2 *Form*). The angelic revelation offers illumination from the text which emerges from setting it in the context of other passages of scripture, as is often the case with midrashic study.

The passage's "text" is Jer 25:8–14 (cf. 29:10), which refers to the completing of seventy years of punishment for Judah's sin. Jeremiah's "seventy years" was earlier taken up in Zech 1:12 (cf. 7:5; see E. Lipiński, "Recherches sur le Livre de Zacharie," *VT* 20 [1970] 35–42). There could be various ways of calculating the actual length of the desolation envisaged by Jeremiah. It could be dated from Judah's submission to Babylon in 605 B.C., from the invasion of 597, or from that of 587; it could be dated to Babylon's fall in 539, or to the completion of the temple rebuilding in 517 B.C. Clearly seventy actual years could thus be reckoned to have passed by Zechariah's time. This might encourage people to take as a precise calculation a figure that did not have this significance for Jeremiah. 2 Chr 36:20–23 nuances Zechariah's prophecy by understanding the seventy years in the light of Lev 25:1–7; 26:31–35, 43. The period of ruin and desolation comprises seventy years during which the land is uncultivated, to make up for the approximately 490 sabbathless years of the monarchic period. The "Epistle of Jeremiah," perhaps written soon after Alexander and taking Jer 29 as its jumping-off point, turns the seventy years into seven generations—280 years, according to the OT way of reckoning? (C. A. Moore, *Daniel, Esther, and Jeremiah: The Additions* [AB 44 (1977)] 334–35).

Dan 9 dates itself in the period Zech 1 and 2 Chr 36 refer to, but it presupposes a time of "desolation" (national subservience to foreign powers coming to a climax with the oppression of Antiochus) that has lasted a comparable period to that of the monarchy. How could this be? Considering Jer 25:11/29:10 in the light of Lev 26:18, 21, 24, 28 as well as 25:1–7; 26:31–35, 43 provides the answer: the seventy sabbath years that were due have been exacted sevenfold.

This way of using 70 and 490 in structuring history appears elsewhere in writings of the Persian and Greek periods. From the flood to the End is seventy generations (*1 Enoch* 10.12) or seventy weeks (4Q180 1.9); *1 Enoch* 91.1–17; 93.1–10 divides history into seven followed by three weeks. Seventy shepherds pasture Israel from the Assyrian captivity to the End (*1 Enoch* 89–90); it is probably this period which is covered by the seventy weeks of *T. Levi* 16.1; 17.1. From the exodus to the building of the temple was 480 years or twelve generations (1 Kgs 6:1), and there are hints that the patriarchal, monarchic, and postexilic periods could also be reckoned at 480 years each; but there are other hints of an understanding of biblical history as involving 490-year sequences (cf. Bullinger, *Number*, 5–6), and 11QMelch envisages a period of ten jubilees, thus 490 years, up to the final judgment. Some of these documents may be later than and dependent on Daniel, but not all of them; they represent a way of thinking that Daniel takes up rather than one it initiates. (See Cornill, *Studien*, 7–9, 14–18; Milik, *Enoch*, 248–59; Koch, *VT* 28 [1978] 433–41; Thiering, *NovT* 23 [1981] 43–45; J. A. Fitzmyer, "Further Light on Melchizedek from Qumran Cave 11," *JBL* 86 [1967] 25–41 = Fitzmyer, *Essays*, 245–67.) (Lev 25:8–17 also describes the jubilee year, and 490 years is seen as ten jubilees in 11QMelch; cf. the structuring of history by jubilees in *Jubilees*. But the seven sevens of Dan 9:25 are insufficient to indicate that Dan 9 reflects jubilee thinking, given that it does not describe the 490 years in these terms.) The last part of Lev 26 is more encouragingly relevant. Years of desolation and ruin do not mean that Yahweh has ratified Israel's breaking of the covenant (vv 15, 44); if they acknowledge their waywardness and the appropriateness of their punishment, he will remember the covenant (vv 40–42).

The angelic revelation in Dan 9 presupposes reading Jer 25:11/29:10 in the light of other passages as well as Lev 25–26. The נגיד "prince" who is משיח "anointed" recalls the oracle on the king of Tyre in Ezek 28 (see vv 2, 14), which shares other motifs with Dan 9:24–27, such as ruin and desolation (שחת, שמם, vv 8, 17, 19), God's sacred mountain (vv 14, 16), and the profaning of sanctuaries by failure and waywardness (vv 16, 18) (Doukhan, *AUSS* 17 [1979] 16). Isa 10:22–23 declares that שוטף צדקה: . . . כי כלה ונחרצה ("justice is in full flood. Yes, an end which has been decreed [is the Lord . . . bringing about . . .]"). Each word recurs in Dan 9:24–27; the second phrase appears in the identical form in v 27, apparently indicating that the consummation which is now effected is that of which Isaiah spoke. The allusive

הגביר ("[?]prevail": see n. 27.a) might also have its background in the אל גבור "God the champion" of Isa 10:21 (Kline, *Law and Prophets,* 466–67). Brownlee (*BASOR* 132 [1953] 13–14) suggests links between Dan 9 and Isa 52:13–53:12. The most plausible are in 52:14: שמם, רבים, שחת (1QIsa[a] משח!).

Within the framework of the angelic revelation Dan 9 is dominated by a long communal prayer of confession (vv 4–19), comparable to other postexilic prayers in Ezra 9:6–15; Neh 1:5–11; 9:5–38; Bar 1:15–3:8; 1QS 1.22–2.1; 4Q Words of the Luminaries (and less so to Isa 59:12–15; 64:4–11 [5–12]; Jer 14:7–9, 19–22; Pss 51; 106; Prayer of Manasseh) (Harvey, *Plaidoyer;* earlier Gunkel, *Einleitung,* 117–39). Each of these prayers is distinctive, however, in relation to its context (see H. G. M. Williamson, *Ezra, Nehemiah* [WBC, 1985] in loc).

Thus the prayer begins with an ascription of praise to God (v 4), a motif which recurs in the body of the prayer (e.g., vv 7a, 9a, 15). The recognition that right is on Yahweh's side is of key importance to this element of the prayer, which can be described as an act of praise at the justice of the judgment of God (von Rad, "Gerichtsdoxologie"). The main part of the prayer is thus an acknowledgment of wrongdoing (vv 5–14). It takes the form of a statement in general terms of what people have done and failed to do (vv 5–6, 9b–11a, 11b, 13b, 14b), of God's acts in response (especially vv 11b, 12–13a, 14), and a contrasting of the consequent moral positions of God and people (especially vv 7–8a). It incorporates some description of the afflicted state of those for whom Daniel prays, material corresponding to the lament in a psalm of lament. This second section of the prayer is the longest, yet it does not express its main aim. The prayer is not just an acknowledgment of wrongdoing and acceptance of responsibility for it, like Josh 7:20–21; 2 Sam 12:13a, and the Deuteronomistic History as a whole. The acknowledgment of being in the wrong is designed to open the way to a plea for mercy, as in Judg 10:15; 1 Sam 15:24–25; Ps 106 (J. Hoftijzer, "David and the Tekoite Woman," *VT* 20 [1970] 425–27); contrast—among the communal prayers of confession—Ezra 9. Thus the third element in the prayer's form is a plea for God to turn back to his people in forgiveness and restoration (vv 15–19). The transition to the plea is marked by the emphatic particle ועתה "but now." This is repeated in v 17: for the repetition, cf. 2 Sam 7; 1 Kgs 8—it expresses an outburst of emotion contained throughout the confession; it is both a conjunction and an interjection (A. Laurentin, *"We ʿattah—Kai nun," Bib* 45 [1964] 190–97). The plea is dominated by motive clauses and phrases that indicate the reasons why God should forgive and restore (vv 15a, 16a [two phrases], 16b, 17b, 18a, 18b, 19b).

The prayer's alternating between "we/our" and "I/my," and between "you" and "he" in speaking of God, reflects the features of the corporate prayer of the Psalter. While the "we" is appropriate to a prayer that concerns Israel's sin, the "I" puts Daniel in the position of intercessors such as Moses and Jeremiah (Gilbert, *RTL* 3 [1972] 303–4). It may take up the picture of Dan[i]el as a just man who might be the means of the deliverance of others (Ezek 14:12–20; cf. Jer 15:1). The prayer's language has the characteristic repetition of liturgical style. It assembles series of near-synonyms (vv 4b, 5a, 15b, 18a;

also instances treated as hendiadys, vv 4b, 5b, 9a, 11b), similar phrases (v 4b), parallel clauses (vv 5b–6, 9b–10, 11, 13b), and whole sentences of similar meaning (vv 7 and 8–9a; vv 9b–11, 11b–13a, and 13b–14). Similar effect is achieved by chains of related expressions (e.g., vv 6b, 7b, 8a). The pathos and effectiveness of the climax to the plea in v 19a depends on the repetition of imperative phrases calling on God, as well as on their novel brevity.

The prayer's repetitiveness also reflects that of the Deuteronomistic covenant tradition to which the prose prayers of confession belong (cf. Harvey, *Plaidoyer;* Buis, *BZ* 11 [1967] 193–205; Kline, *Law and Prophets,* 454–58; Baltzer, *Bundesformular*). In terms of that tradition, the prayer is an acknowledgment of the covenant God (vv 4, 7a, 14b, 15a), of the breaking of the covenant through Israel's failure to keep covenantal commitment (vv 5–6, 7b, 8, 9b–11, 15b), and of the appropriateness of God's treatment of Israel in the framework of the covenant (vv 11b–14). It appeals to the graciousness that lay behind God's covenantal commitment (vv 9a, 16a, 18b) and implicitly to the possibility of forgiveness and restoration announced in the covenant for people who repent of their covenantal failure. Among Deuteronomistic motifs in the prayer are terms such as חסד, תורה, אהב, שוב, and היום ("commitment," "teaching," "love," "[re]turn," and "today"), the significance attached to Moses, kings, and prophets as scribes, hearers, and preachers of Yahweh's instruction (i.e., Deuteronomy itself) (vv 6, 8, 10, 11, 13), the phrase "as it is written," the idea of the curse, the references to Yahweh's name (vv 18, 19), the actual use of the name, and the stress on shame and scorn (vv 7, 8, 16: בשת and חרפה do not come in Deuteronomy itself, but for the idea, see, e.g., 22:13–21; 24:10–11; 25:3, 9; 27:16). Both Leviticus and Deuteronomy envisage the relationship between Yahweh and Israel being fundamentally disturbed by Israel's faithlessness and disobedience, yet see Yahweh's response in punishing Israel as stopping short of finally terminating the covenant. If those in exile acknowledge their wrongdoing and the justice of Yahweh's punishment of them, he will remember his covenant with them (Lev 26:39–45); if they return to Yahweh, he will restore them (Deut 30:1–10; cf. 1 Kgs 8:46–53; Jer 29:10–14). Dan 9:4–19 perhaps expresses the repentant confession that these passages look for (so Lacocque, *HUCA* 47 [1976] 122–24; Fishbane, *Interpretation,* 488–89; against Towner, *USQR* 26 [1970–71] 203–14: but Towner is right that there is a conventional element in the confession—Dan 9 is not simply a transition to "retribution theology").

This response is also offered in the other communal prayers of confession. Practically every phrase in vv 4–20 can be paralleled in Ezra 9; Neh 1; 9, or in the traditions that underlie these four prayers: the Deuteronomistic prose of Deuteronomy, 1 Kgs 8, and Jeremiah, or the more cultically oriented traditions of Leviticus, Chronicles, and the Psalter (lists in A. Szörényi, *Psalmen und Kult im Alten Testament* [Budapest: St Stefans Gesellschaft, 1961] 105–9; also Montgomery, Lacocque). The prayer was hardly composed with any of these texts before the writer, but it was composed by someone who knew this tradition well, probably both from study and from worship, and who instinctively but also consciously prayed in ways stimulated and hallowed by it. The prayer has a closer relationship with that in Baruch. As with parallels with *1 Enoch* in chap. 7, a case can be argued for dependence either way or for mutual dependence on a third source, in this case some already existent liturgical prayer (discussion in Moore, *CBQ* 36 [1974] 312–17).

The communal prayer of confession is a postexilic phenomenon. Likely it develops from the preexilic community lament, but lament and protest with their characteristic "Why?" have disappeared now that the Deuteronomistic covenant theology offers an intelligible understanding of contemporary experience of adversity to which the appropriate response is rather confession of God's justice and of human failure (Westermann, "Struktur und Geschichte der Klage im Alten Testament," *ZAW* 66 [1954] 48–49, 74–75 [ET in *Praise,* 171–72, 206]).

Structure

- 1–2 narrative introduction to the revelation
  - 1 date
  - 2 occasion
- 3–4a narrative introduction to the prayer of confession
- 4b–19 prayer of confession
  - 4b ascription of praise
  - 5–14 acknowledgment of wrongdoing
    - 5–6 Israel's disobedience
    - 7–9a God in the right, Israel's shame
      - 7a God in the right
      - 7b Israel's shame because of wrongdoing
      - 8 Israel's shame because of wrongdoing
      - 9a God's mercy
    - 9b–11 Israel's rebellion and Yahweh's punishment
    - 11b–13a Israel's failure and Yahweh's bringing trouble
    - 13b–14a Israel's recalcitrance and Yahweh's deliberate response
    - 14b God in the right, Israel's disobedience
  - 15–19 plea for mercy
    - 15 resumptive acknowledgment of wrongdoing
    - 16–19 fourfold plea for God's mercy, each with motivation
- 20–27 revelation
  - 20–22a narrative introduction resumed
    - 20–21a occasion
    - 21b angelic epiphany
    - 22a introduction to angelic speech
  - 22b–27 angelic speech
    - 22b–23 introduction
    - 24–27 revelation
      - 24 summary: what will be achieved by the end of 70 sevens
      - 25–27 detailed outline of the 70 sevens
        - 25a the first 7 sevens
        - 25b the next 62 sevens
        - 26–27 the 70th seven
          - 26 initial events and final events
          - 27 the week as a whole and final events

The narrative opening (vv 1–2) provides the date necessary to a vision or revelation (see chap. 2 *Form*) and indicates the circumstances that led to the prayer of confession. The introduction to the prayer (vv 3–4a) discloses that it will be a prayer of supplication and confession, both by the acts that accompany it and by the titles it is given. In the prayer, then, Daniel is seeking the fulfillment of the prophecy referred to in the narrative opening, by offering the response that opens up the possibility of its fulfillment. As the passage of scripture fulfills the role of the symbolic vision in chaps. 7 and 8, the prayer takes the structural place occupied by the symbolic vision there.

There are links between the revelation and the preceding prayer. The revelation concerns "your people and your sacred city" (cf. v 20). It promises that rebellion, failure, and waywardness will be dealt with: the prayer also began here (v 5, cf. vv 7, 8, 9, 11, 13, 15, 16, 20—though in the prayer the idea of rebellion is expressed by terms other than פשע). Its concern with justice corresponds to a feature of the prayer (vv 5 [רשע, the antonym], 7, 14, 16, 18—though never צדק itself). The rebuilding and restoring of the desolate city and sanctuary correspond to motifs in the prayer (vv 17, 18); both speak of God's judgment overwhelming (vv 11, 27). The covenant's prevailing (see n. 27.a) recalls the covenant-keeping God of the prayer (v 4). The introduction to the revelation promises insight, lack of which the prayer had confessed (see n. 13.d-d) (Jones, *VT* 18 [1968] 491; Doukhan, *AUSS* 17 [1979] 8–9). The revelation does not take up other motifs: God's angry fury, his solemn curse, his compassionate forgiveness, and his name borne by those who belong to him; the trouble, shame, abuse, and dispersion inflicted on city and people. Conversely, the prayer makes no reference to the anointed prince or the prophetic vision; the prayer's concern with prophecy has a different focus, and this motif in the revelation goes back to v 2. The comparisons and contrasts between prayer and revelation open up two readings of the latter. It can be understood in the light of the prayer at each point, so that it is Israel's wrongdoing which necessitates the prolonging of the years of devastation, but which can now be dealt with in response to the (second-century B.C.) prayer, or it can be understood semi-independently, the wrongdoing then being that of Israel's oppressors.

As happens with words of revelation in other chapters, vv 24–27 are written in rhythmic language, with some of the symmetry and balancing of parallelism (especially in v 24) and with the terseness and allusiveness of poetry, though they are better seen as elevated prose than strictly as verse (against Shea, *AUSS* 18 [1980] 59–63). The allusiveness of the revelation, with the lack of articles, is also that characteristic of "sibylline" quasi-prophecies (Delcor). After its opening in v 24, the bidding in v 25 suggests another new beginning there (see *Comment*).

The introduction and the revelation are in comparable Hebrew to that of chaps. 8 and 10–12, characterized by jerkiness, Aramaisms, and complex resumptive sentences (vv 1–2, 20–21). In contrast, the prayer is composed in good literary Hebrew, without Aramaisms. Further, the prayer can be removed from its context without disturbing the latter's coherence; indeed, the omission of the prayer along with vv 4a, 20 improves the flow of the chapter as a whole. Because the prayer stands out from its context in its language, its use of the name Yahweh, its overtly Palestinian perspective, and its emphasis on the sin of Israel as a cause of their troubles, a number of scholars have followed von Gall in seeing the prayer as a later addition to chap. 9, like those in chap. 3 (3:24–90 G).

Some of the considerations that have led to this conclusion are questionable. It is not the case that vv 1–3 make one expect a prayer for illumination rather than a prayer of confession; Daniel in the sixth century B.C. had no reason to be puzzled by the prophecy, and the observances of v 3 are appropriate to penitence. It is not the case that there are no links between prayer and revelation (see above). Variations in expression between vv 20 and 21a do not imply a change of author, nor is the repetitiveness of vv 3, 4a and 20, 21a uncharacteristic of Danielic prose. The fact that a prayer of this kind appears in the place occupied in chaps. 7 and 8 by a symbolic vision does not argue against its originality. Nor do the features noted in the previous paragraph point strongly to its being a later addition. The possibility of removing it is not evidence of its being secondary; its distinctive language reflects its nature and background as a quasi-liturgical prayer; the same is true of its distinctive use of the name Yahweh, which is paralleled in Neh 1:4–11 in relation to its context, and by the way that other names for God concentrate in specific chapters in Daniel (Bayer, 49); its Palestinian perspective *is* the author's perspective, and here he simply omits to conceal it; the revelation's not needing the prayer to lead into it reflects the conviction that God's sending Gabriel was independent of the prayer—it issued from his prior plan.

Some of the arguments for the prayer's originality are also weak. While the chapter would be short without it, it would not be a torso: its structure would more closely correspond to that which appears on a much larger scale in chaps. 10–12 (see chaps. 10–12 *Structure*). Nor is it the case that a prayer of confession *must* meet with an oracle of response, such as a lament looks for (against Lipiński, *Liturgie,* 83–106). The difficulty of the hypothesis that the prayer is a later addition to the chapter lies in the close links between prayer and context, noted above.

These links are not as marked as those in Ezra 9; Neh 1; 9. Those prayers cannot have existed independently of their context, though their specificity to their setting varies (it is most marked in Ezra 9). It is possible that the prayer already existed and was taken over by the author of chap. 9, but this is not a compelling hypothesis. It is as easy to believe that the author wrote the whole chapter.

Setting

The chapter offers sharply divergent pointers regarding its historical setting. The form of the revelation suggests it is a quasi-prophecy, whose setting would then be Jerusalem between the introduction of new forms of worship in 167 B.C. and their abolition in 164 B.C. (cf. chap. 8). The fact that the End is described by reference to prophecy (v 27), as in 11:40–45, suggests that this is still future for the seer (Heaton). The prayer also suggests a Jerusalem setting (vv 7, 16); its perspective might suggest the period of the exile, and those who have reckoned it independent of its context have dated it as early as 600 B.C., perhaps with second-century B.C. glosses (Lacocque). But its "exilic" perspective is not very different from that of Ezra 9; Neh 1; 9, and—like them—it combines with that perspective allusions to the community's experience in a later day, which here take the form of references to Jerusalem's "desolation," paralleling those in vv 24–27. Writings from the Persian, Greek, and Roman epochs commonly see these periods as a continuation of the exile (Knibb, "Exile"; Gowan, "Exile"). The narrative introduction refers explicitly to a setting in the exilic period and presumably in Babylon, but that is presumably part of the fictional scene-setting for the revelation which aligns the chapter as a whole with the rest of the book.

Collins (*Daniel* [FOTL]) offers a typology of attitudes to the postexilic temple and its worship, a priestly perspective that views these positively (the Chronicler), a sectarian perspective that rejects them (*1 Enoch* 89.73; 93.9; *T. Levi* 16), and the nonpriestly but mainstream perspective of Daniel, which comes between these in attitude. It is doubtful if Dan 9 is actually less positive about the temple than the Chronicler's tradition, at least as represented by Ezra 9; Neh 1; 9, and thus questionable if Dan 9 is necessarily nonpriestly. Unlike Ezra 9; Neh 9, however, it includes neither positive nor negative references to the priesthood (and only positive references to prophets); further, as Collins notes, concern with the temple and its offerings is shared by many outside priestly circles. (Nor need *1 Enoch* 89.73; 93.9, at least, indicate a negative attitude to the postexilic period as a whole; their comments may have second-century B.C. events in mind.) Dan 9 does, however, reflect the views of conservative rather than reformist groups in second-century B.C. Jerusalem.

Reference to praying "before Yahweh" at the time of the evening offering (vv 20, 21) might suggest that the prayer presupposes a temple setting (Gilbert, *RTL* 3 [1972] 288); this is so in Ezra 9; Neh 9, but such features appear in a dispersion setting in Dan 6:11 [10]; Neh 1:4, 6. The study of the Scriptures and the liturgical style of prayer at least as naturally suggest a setting in the synagogue, which encouraged study of the Scriptures and a way of praying that reflects the study of the Scriptures.

As for the chapter's setting in the book, its concern with insight (בינ[ה]) links it with chap. 8 (Doukhan, *AUSS* 17 [1979] 4–6). Chap. 9 begins here (v 2; cf. 8:5), as chap. 8 had ended here, the positive contrasting with the preceding negative. This motif is prominent as the angel appears with his revelation (9:22–23), as it had been at the equivalent point earlier (8:15–17, also 23). The implication might be that Dan 9 was intended to clarify issues raised in chap. 8; it takes up the question of the fate of the temple and seeks light from Scripture on what dream and vision left opaque. In general, however, chap. 9 is not closely linked to chap. 8, as chap. 8 was to chap. 7. Although it takes further the theme of the restoration of desolate Jerusalem and its temple, it does so by means of different forms, structure, and motifs. It shares its emphasis on insight with chap. 1 (vv 4, 17, 20), which also concerns itself with the question of the length of the exile. Koch (*HZ* 193 [1961] 20–21) sees a link between the 70/490 years and the date in 1:1, though he notes that the concern with Israel's history over the postexilic centuries is more explicit in chap. 9, and only there—elsewhere chaps. 7–12 focus more on world history and structure events by the history of world empires. In chap. 9 alone, too, is preexilic history referred to (Gowan, "Exile," 214, referring to E. Janssen, *Das Gottesvolk und seine Geschichte* [Neukirchen: Neukirchener, 1971] 51–52). Chap. 9 relates sacred history, other chapters profane history (Hanhart, *Fourth WCJS Papers* 1:82). The model prayer in chap. 9 is that of the model Israelite in exile who has been portrayed in chaps. 1–6. Is this the kind of prayer the Daniel of chap. 6 is assumed to have prayed, soon after Darius was made king (compare the terms of vv 3–4a with those of 6:11–12 [10–11])?

Bickermann's suggestion that chap. 9 is the center of the book (*Gott,* 26 [ET 16]) overestimates the importance of its stress on sin, which actually is another feature that makes it stand out from its context.

Comment

1 Although Zech 1 links Jeremiah's seventy-years prophecy with the events of 519, which are close to seventy years after the fall of Jerusalem in 587 B.C., the Darius by whose reign chap. 9 is dated must be not Darius I (Porphyry) but the Darius of Median birth introduced in 6:1 [5:31]. His "being made king" of Babylon here may reflect his "acquiring/receiving" the kingship of Babylon there (and see *Setting* above). אחשורוש (Ahashweros) is the regular BH equivalent of OP Khshayarsha, Greek Ξερξης (Xerxes: so OG here; Th transliterates—cf. RV); see Esther; Ezra 4:6. Historically, Darius I was the *father* of Xerxes I; the order of events in Ezra 4 might have suggested that Xerxes (v 6) preceded Darius (v 24). Khshayarsha, like Dārayavaush itself, is probably a throne name, meaning "hero among rulers" (Frye, *Heritage,* 97), and Wiseman infers that it could thus have been borne by an earlier figure such as Darius the Mede's father, though it seems a problem with this suggestion that Khshayarsha is a Persian name. In Esther, G takes אחשורוש to refer to Artaxerxes, while in Tob 14:15, Ασυηρος (Asueros) denotes Uvakhshtra or Cyaxares the Median conqueror of Nineveh in 612 B.C. (Frye, *Heritage,* 72–73). He might be seen as Darius the Mede's predecessor/ancestor/father, and אחשורוש is actually as close a transliteration of Uvakhshtra (Akk. *U-ak-sa-tar*) as it is of Khshayarsha (see W. S. Auchincloss, "Darius the Median," *BSac* 66 [1909] 536–38; Torrey, *JAOS* 66 [1946] 7–8).

2 The resumptive opening phrase may simply arise from grammatical need (Th omits it); yet v 1 is not so very long, and perhaps the phrase suggests that this is the very year in which fulfillment of Jeremiah's promise was due. Jeremiah's seventy-year period of Babylonian rule might be reckoned to begin with Judah's submission to Babylon in 605 B.C. or with the fall of Jerusalem in 597 or 587 B.C.; it might be reckoned to end with the fall of Babylon in 539, the initiation of a Jewish return in 538, or the completion of the rebuilding of the temple in 517 B.C. It is thus possible to argue that Jeremiah was chronologically right. But it is unlikely that he intended the "seventy years" to have a precise chronological reference; nor is there reason to infer that Daniel necessarily understood it this way. "Seventy years" suggests a human lifetime (cf. Isa 23:15; Ps 91:10; also Esarhaddon's inscription, "Seventy years as the period of its desolation he [Marduk] wrote down [in the book of fate]" [D. D. Luckenbill, "The Black Stone of Esarhaddon," *AJSL* 41 (1924–25) 167]).

Presumably the context in which it was noted that Jeremiah's prophecy was (over)due for fulfillment was the corporate study of Scripture that characterizes the synagogue. Although the revelations given in dream and vision elsewhere in Daniel are influenced by Scripture, here alone is Scripture explicitly referred to. "The Scriptures" (הספרים, "the books") suggests the existence of an identifiable collection of authoritative religious writings, though this need not imply a precisely defined and closed "canon." The inclusion of Jeremiah among them suggests that "the Scriptures" denotes at least "the Torah and the Prophets," perhaps a collection not very different from what became the Hebrew Bible—less, of course, Daniel itself (see J. Barton, *Oracles of God* [London/Philadelphia: DLT/Westminster, 1986] 47–48, on the reference to the "prophets" in the near-contemporary Prologue to Sirach). It is often supposed that it was the existence of such a collection of "Scriptures" that necessitated recourse to the "pesher" method of interpretation and to the device of pseudonymity. Both dream or vision and Scripture would be seen as the true loci of revelation concerning present and future that contrasted with the Babylonians' heavenly tablets (Lacocque). It was the God of Israel who really gave such revelations, sometimes hidden in the symbols of dream, vision, and portent, sometimes hidden in the apparently straightforward words of Scripture.

3–23 On the prayer, see *Form* and *Structure* above. Motifs that recur in the prayer are (a) God as its object, (b) his characteristics, (c) his ways of speaking and his means of speaking; (d) Israel as the ones who are addressed and who are prayed for, (e) the response he looks for in them, (f) their actual characteristics, and (g) their needs; also significant are (h) the nature of the prayer, (i) its content, and (j) the response it meets.

(a) The object of prayer is God (אלהים). But this most general word appears only once, in the introduction to the prayer (v 3). Even here it is combined with the title "Lord" (אדני, also vv 4, 7, 9, 15, 19, 19). While Ezekiel frequently uses the title "Lord" with its philological meaning, suggesting God's authority and awesomeness, Daniel's usage does not stress this connotation. Rather it reflects Judaism's developing inclination to use the title "Lord" to avoid uttering God's actual name Yahweh (cf. Q אדני, G κύριος, EVV LORD). Each occurrence of "Lord" in chap. 9 comes at a point where Israelite prayer would more traditionally have used "Yahweh": compare the general preference for אלהים "God" rather than יהוה in Pss 42–79. "Lord," then, is suggestive of reverence before the person of the God of Israel. The name Yahweh itself comes in vv 4, 8, 10, 13, 14, 14, 20; also 2 (and see n. 3.a). Whereas "Lord" generally appears as a vocative, and thus especially in the plea itself, "Yahweh" characteristically appears in third person references, and not at all in the plea. Here only in Daniel does this distinctively Jewish name for God feature; Dan 9 follows earlier prophetic and liturgical usage. The very use of the name constitutes an appeal to the special relationship between Yahweh and the Israel who alone knew the name.

That also lies behind the references and appeals to "our God" (אלהינו, vv 9, 10, 13, 14, 15, 17) and "my God" (אלהי, vv 4, 18, 19, 20, 20). Daniel uses "my God" when referring to his own prayer, at its opening and closing; he uses "our God" in the midst of the prayer when referring to those on whose behalf he prays. Much of Daniel's usage is comparable to the Psalms, where the phrases "Yahweh my God"/"Yahweh our God" are common or "my God"/

"our God" appears in parallel with "Yahweh." Sometimes the context suggests that "my God"/"our God" appeals directly to the special personal relationship indicated by the pronouns (e.g., Pss 22:3, cf. 2 [2, cf. 1]; 38:22 [21]; 48:15 [14]; 71:4; 86:2; 91:2; 94:22; 95:7; 106:47; 118:28). The combination of "my" and "our" in one psalm is rare. Interesting is 94:22–23, where the psalmist appeals to the fact that Yahweh is "our God" as the basis for expecting him to act as "my God." The argument in Dan 9 takes the opposite form: Daniel appeals to "my God" to act as "our God." This way of praying appears in one other prose confession, Ezra 9. A person such as Ezra or Daniel prays as one who has a close relationship with God, one to whom God may be expected to listen. Their prayer to "my God" to act as "our God" is therefore a powerful one. The personal nature of Daniel's appeal on behalf of the people as a whole is clearest in vv 18–20.

At the opening of the prayer, the Lord is reverenced as the great and awesome God (האל הגדול והנורא, v 4). The phrase corresponds to Neh 1:5. "God" is here *ʾel,* the name of the Canaanite high god (e.g., Gen 14:18–24), but often in the OT a common noun for God (cf. Dan 11:36). There is a courage about beginning with a recognition of the majestic aspect to God. It is a threat to those who fail to yield to him, whether foreigners or Israelites (cf. the closely comparable phrases in Deut 7:21; 10:17; Neh 4:8 [14]; 9:32). It is precisely such failure that Daniel will have to go on to acknowledge.

(b) "Great and awesome" is the first of a series of terms to denote God's characteristics; v 4 adds that he is one who keeps his covenantal commitment (הברית והחסד) with his people. As in English, a "covenant" (ברית) is a formal agreement involving two parties, which has been entered into in a solemn and binding fashion. It may be primarily an undertaking by one party to the other, who is only required to receive what the first offers; or it may presuppose that a more powerful party requires certain reciprocal undertakings from a less powerful one in response to benefits promised or given by the former; or it may be a mutual bond between equal parties. For secular instances, see, e.g., Gen 21:22–32; Josh 9:3–20; 1 Sam 11:1; 18:3; 2 Chr 2:3; 15:12. "Covenant" then provides a natural image for describing relationships between God and humanity. The emphasis in such relationships may be on God's commitment (Gen 9:8–17; Lev 26:40–45; Num 25:10–13; Jer 31:31–34; 2 Chr 13:5), or on human beings' commitment to God (Job 31:1; Ezra 10:3; 2 Chr 29:10), or on a reciprocity in the relationship—though hardly, for theological reasons, an equality between the two parties (Exod 19:3–6; Deut 28:69–29:20 [29:1–29]; 2 Kgs 23:1–3; 2 Chr 34:30–32). This last application of the covenant image is characteristic of D, which seems to utilize Israel's knowledge of the equivalent political covenants (i.e., treaties); it is this kind of covenant relationship that is presupposed by Dan 9 (see *Form*).

"Commitment" (חסד) has its background in human relationships more broadly, where it denotes an attitude of kindness or generosity or mercy that expresses itself in acts of this kind and thus initiates or presupposes a relationship of mutual loyalty and faithfulness (Josh 2:12; Judg 1:24; 8:35; 1 Sam 15:6). Appeal to someone's חסד presupposes that he or she has taken on a responsibility and can be expected to fulfill it. Applied to God, it suggests his turning to humanity in his unconditional friendship and magnanimity, thus working toward his divine claim to have fellowship with human beings (Stobe, *VT* 2 [1952] 254). In the OT, the most common application of the idea to the attitude God shows to human beings appears, not surprisingly, in the very context in which it comes here, that of prayer, in the Psalms (e.g., 25:6–10; 36:6–11 [5–10]). חסד is not essentially a "covenant" word (against Glueck, *Ḥesed*), but the human relationships in which חסד is expressed may be described in "covenantal" terms (1 Sam 20:8, 14–16; 1 Kgs 20:31–34), and God's חסד may also be associated with his covenant. This is so in Dan 9:4; it stems from Deuteronomy (see 7:9, 12; cf. 1 Kgs 8:23; Isa 54:10; 55:3; Pss 89:29 [28]; 106:45; Neh 1:5; 9:32).

The prayer's opening allusion to God's keeping his covenant commitment is not an implicit appeal for mercy, but an acknowledgment that Yahweh has kept his side of the covenant and bears no responsibility for its collapse. It offers no direct basis for Daniel's prayer; the latter will have to acknowledge that Israel has not kept its covenantal commitment, and thus has no claim on him. Yet it is necessary that the prayer begins from an acknowledgment of these facts as they are. Further, if Israel's relationship with God began from an unearned commitment on God's part, perhaps it could be reestablished on the same basis? There is a close connection between commitment (חסד) and grace (חן), in human relationships (Gen 19:19; 47:29; Ps 109:12; Esth 2:17), and in God (Exod 34:6 and related texts) (see Sakenfeld, *Hesed,* 137, 237–38).

Reliability, faithfulness, or constancy (אמת, v 13) commonly accompanies commitment (חסד) both in references to God and in references to human conduct (Gen 47:29; Exod 34:6; Josh 2:14; Pss 25:10; 40:11–12 [10–11]; 57:4, 11 [3, 10]; 61:8 [7]; 85:11 [10]; 89:15 [14]; 108:5 [4]; Prov 3:3; 16:6; 20:28; Isa 16:5; Hos 4:1; Zech 7:9). Sometimes the two terms are a hendiadys suggesting a commitment that can be relied on; where they can be distinguished, the former may suggest protective faithfulness, the latter active kindness (see *TWAT* on אמן). For God's faithfulness as our protection, see Pss 25:5; 40:12 [11]; 43:3; 57:4 [3]; 61:8 [7]; 91:4; 96:14 [13]. Yahweh is אל אמת, the God who is by nature reliable and constant (Ps 31:6 [5]). That is revealed in his deeds; they always correspond to his words (Ps 111:7). Thus another of the prose confessions declares that Yahweh has been entirely faithful in his relationship with Israel over the years (Neh 9:33). It is precisely this point that Dan 9:13 echoes: the history of Israel is the story of God's faithfulness to them; his promises have been reliable, his protection has been constant.

A similar point is made when Daniel declares that Yahweh is in the right over against Israel. A prominent motif in the prayer is that any breakdown in relationship between Yahweh and Israel is the responsibility of the latter, not the former. Yahweh is in the right, Israel is in the wrong. Near the beginning and end of his confession Daniel declares that "right" belongs to God and that he is "in the right," in his relationship with Israel (הצדקה, צדיק; vv 7, 14). The second affirmation corresponds closely to ones that appear in prose confessions in Ezra 9:15; Neh 9:33 (cf. also Exod 9:27; 2 Kgs 10:9; Ezek 18:9; Lam 1:18; 2 Chr 12:6). The first corresponds to forms of expression in Gen 15:6; Deut 6:25; 24:13. "Right" is another term from human relationships, but here relationships looked at within a framework of law. In a court contest between God and Israel, Daniel affirms, God would win the case. Right is on his side.

This narrow, forensic connotation of צדיק/צדקה is directly appropriate to vv 7 and 14. In other OT contexts צדק[ה] has a wide range of significance, suggesting God's establishing of order, salvation, and wholeness in his world (Gammie). In v 16, these broader meanings are closer to hand: part of the evidence of God's being in the right is the concern for what is right that has characterized his behavior in relation to Israel. The declaration at the opening of the confession that צדקה attaches to Yahweh, and at the end that he is צדיק, could signify that Yahweh is justified in the punitive action he has taken (compare the use of צדק in Isa 5:16; 10:22). But the prayer goes on to refer to his צדקת ("right deeds," v 16), concrete expressions of צדקה, acts of faithfulness, commitment, mercy, and deliverance: see the context in which צדקה comes in Isa 51:6, 8; 59:16–17; 60:17; Hos 2:21 [19]; Pss 33:5; 36:6–11 [5–10]; 40:11 [10]; 71:2, 15–16, 19, 24; 98:1–13; Prov 21:21. We should hardly confine the reference in vv 7, 14, then, to God's being justified in his punishment of Israel: it denotes more broadly his being in the right in the way he has dealt with Israel. He has been a faithful rock and deliverer in accordance with his word.

The allusion to his right acts recalls Judg 5:11b; 1 Sam 12:7; Isa 45:24; Mic 6:5; Ps 103:6. These right acts are his acts on behalf of Israel attacked or afflicted by oppressors in Egypt, in the wilderness, in the "judges" period, and in the exile. The dynamic aspect to צדקה is brought out by its common association with משפט, which denotes authority and decisiveness (RV "judgements": cf. שפט "judge"). A king's calling is to exercise משפט וצדקה (2 Sam 8:15; 1 Kgs 10:9): to act with authority on behalf of what is right. That is also characteristic of God (Isa 5:16; Pss 33:5; 36:7 [6]). At the beginning of the plea (v 15), Daniel specifically refers to the exodus, Yahweh's paradigm צדקה. God brought Israel out of Egypt by strength of hand and thus established his reputation for doing what is right. It is that reference to the exodus which leads into the generalization about Yahweh's צדקות in the next verse.

The opening allusion to Yahweh's being in the right begins a chiasm in vv 7–9a (see *Structure*) that closes with a balancing allusion to Yahweh's being compassionate and pardoning. There is no tension between these two. In the same way, Yahweh's abandoning anger at Israel's wrongdoing is reckoned to be in keeping with his right deeds, not in conflict with them. צדקה (EVV "justice"/"righteousness") is not a justice that is concerned above all to see wrongdoing punished. It is a concern for what is right that rejoices in being merciful to the weak; and those who suffer as a consequence of sin are still seen as those who suffer and need to be restored.

Like צדקת ("right deeds," v 16), "compassion" and "pardon" (v 9) are both plural, suggesting deep or repeated compassion and pardon—though רחמים is always plural and סל[י]חות is in two of its three occurrences (here and Neh 9:17; the third is Ps 130:4). Compassion and pardon are two outworkings of commitment (חסד, v 4): see Exod 34:6–7; Num 14:18–19; Isa 54:7–10; Hos 2:20–25 [18–23]; Pss 25:6–7; 51:3 [1]; 69:17 [16]; 86:5, 15; Neh 9:17.

רחמים (also v 18) is a feelings word: it denotes a strong emotion. רחם

itself refers to the womb, and a sense that רחמים denotes the strong feelings of love and concern that might be expected within the family on the part of a mother, a father, a husband, or a brother underlies a number of occurrences of this and the related verb (see Gen 43:30; 1 Kgs 3:26; Isa 13:18; 49:13–15; 54:6–8; 63:15–16; Jer 31:20; Hos 1–2; 14:3; Amos 1:11; Ps 103:13; Lam 4:10; P. Trible, *God and the Rhetoric of Sexuality* [Philadelphia: Fortress, 1978] 31–59). רחמים also features in combination with terms such as "commitment," "faithfulness," and "grace" (see Exod 34:6 and related texts; Isa 63:7; Pss 25:6; 40:12 [11]; 51:3 [1]; 77:10 [9]; 145:9; Lam 3:22; and especially the prose confession Neh 9:16–33). In such contexts, with which Dan 9 may be compared, the significance of רחמים as a word that suggests the feelings of a mother or a father is not in the foreground; but the frequency of that usage elsewhere in the OT suggests it would be present in the background.

Although רחמים is thus a feelings word, it does not denote *mere* feelings. It suggests a compassion that instinctively issues in action. רחמים is life-giving (Jepsen, *KD* 7 [1961] 262). The particular outworking of compassion here is pardon, as in some of the passages where the reference to family feelings is overt (Jer 31:20; Hos 1–2; Ps 103:12–13); this is also so in Exod 34:6 and related passages, and others where רחמים appears in combination with terms such as "grace" and "faithfulness" (Pss 25:6; 51:3 [1]), including a number which speak in covenant terms (Deut 4:31; 13:18 [17]; 1 Kgs 8:50; Neh 9). רחמים expresses itself in סלחות (cf. vv 18–19). We have noted that this term for pardon reappears only in the prose confession in Neh 9:17 and in Ps 130:4. The verb סלח (v 19) comes in passages we have had cause to note already as containing many motifs common to Dan 9 (Exod 34:9; 1 Kgs 8:30–50; Pss 25:11; 103:3). The verb and noun are used only of God. They thus contrast with the use of the verb נשא "take away," which can refer to human forgiveness (e.g., Exod 10:17). While סלח may have been used of human beings (e.g., a king), likely it suggests "pardon" (by a superior), whereas נשא suggests "forgiveness" (which may be by an equal).

M. Noth has suggested that in the postexilic period law gained a significance of its own independent of covenant—necessarily, because the covenant had been broken ("Die Gesetze im Pentateuch," *Studien*, 9–141 [first published 1940]; ET 1–107). If so, this is not an understanding reflected here; covenant provides the context for all that follows by way of an understanding of the relationship between God and Israel. There is no hint here that the Judaism represented by Daniel has a legalistic understanding of the relationship between God and his people. That relationship is the "covenantal nomism" that E. P. Sanders describes (*Paul and Palestinian Judaism* [Philadelphia/London: Fortress/SCM, 1977]). The relationship stems from the gracious initiative of God. It then requires the responsive obedience of Israel. Israel's sin breaks the covenant, but not in such a way as inevitably to terminate the relationship. The fact of sin leads to a casting of oneself on mercy.

(c) Yahweh's relationship with Israel involves words as well as deeds. These are first referred to as מצות ("commands," vv 4, 5). They declare the will he expects to be obeyed. They embody his authority—they are משפטים (v 5). The term is another one for commands, but we have noted in (b) that the underlying idea of משפט is the exercise of authority, on behalf of what is right and against what is wrong. משפטים are thus authoritative declarations concerning the kind of behavior that is acceptable and the kind that is not. In the Pentateuch the term has a specific reference to particular enactments, but it also has a more general reference to the authoritative commands that belong to the covenant (Lev 26:15, 43, 46; Deut 26:16–17; 30:16; Ps 147:19–20; 2 Chr 33:8; and, in prose confessions like this one, Neh 1:7; 9:13, 27).

Daniel's favorite general term for God's words is instruction(s) (תורה/ת, vv 10, 11, 11, 13). "Law(s)" (EVV) can give a misleading impression, since תורה can refer to the teaching given by a prophet or a parent. Alongside מצוה and משפט, תורה does denote a set of directives regarding how Israel is to live its life, along with associated warnings regarding the consequence of disobedience. *The* repository of God's instructions is the teaching of Moses, the pentateuchal "law." When "word(s)" are specifically mentioned (דבר[י]ו, v 12), they are not words of instruction nor words of information, but words of warning.

Yahweh's words have two ways of reaching people. His instructions concerning his expectations of them come to them orally through his servants the prophets (vv 6, 10). They speak in his name, as his representatives (v 6); they make his voice audible (v 11). As in Neh 9, prophets appear only in a good light in Dan 9. Heeding their word could have prevented the exile; they did not cause it (Towner). The prophets' oral word is backed up by the word "written in the instruction of Moses" (vv 11, 13), who is also "the servant of God" (v 11). The assumption here is that the prophets teach orally what Moses teaches in writing. Yet the specific reference to Moses' teaching is also not to information or instruction, but to those words of warning. The words that back up the actual teaching emanating from the prophets constitute the solemn oath that Yahweh has now kept (see Deut 29:19–26 [20–27]).

(d) The people to whom prophets spoke were in particular "our kings, our leaders, and our fathers" (vv 6, 8). Whereas in 1 Kgs 8 "the king himself serves the people by interceding for them and teaching them how to do penance," here the kings appear only in a bad light (so also Neh 9:34) (Towner).

"Leader" (שר) is a broad term that gains its specific connotation from its context. It often denotes people in authority under the king (2 Kgs 24:12, 14; Jer 34:21; 1 Chr 22:17; Neh 9:32, 34): they may be ministers of state, royal advisers, army commanders, magistrates, or the king's representatives in a particular city or area. Such a meaning fits the word's appearance after the reference to kings. On the other hand, it precedes the term "fathers," and in the light of that usage might denote the leaders of the tribes and clans that were composed of the fathers' houses. (See N. K. Gottwald, *The Tribes of Yahweh* [Maryknoll, NY: Orbis, 1979/London: SCM, 1980] 257–92, 365; R. de Vaux, *Les institutions de l'Ancien Testament* [Paris: Cerf, 1958] 1:21–22 [ET *Ancient Israel* (tr. J. McHugh; London/New York: DLT/McGraw-Hill, 1961) 7–8].)

"Our fathers" are those who rule in the local community by virtue of an authority associated with their seniority and age; this authority is reinforced by describing their relationship to the community in kinship terms: they have the kind of authority in the community that a father has in the family.

Strictly, then, fathers are those who stand at the head of an (extended) family, a בית אב "father's house"; but the term בית אב can be used to denote the larger social unit of the clan or the even larger one of the tribe (see Num 1; 3; 17). A clan or even a tribe is a large family. "Heads of families" or "fathers" similarly suggests tribal, clan, and family leaders in a broad sense. (See the passages in Gottwald and de Vaux just cited.)

Like "leaders," "fathers" later appears in a different sense, in v 16, where "kings" and "leaders" are not mentioned; "fathers," too, is apparently here a more general term, for *ancestors.* The OT refers to the sin of the founding fathers or forefathers, the patriarchs, but in this context more likely the expression refers to generations previous to that of the speaker—that is, the generations before the exile. It is a common human experience that one generation will pay for the wrongdoing of the previous generation; the exile, in particular, resulted from the actions of earlier generations, as well as those of people actually alive in the sixth century B.C. (Lev 26:39–40; Lam 5:7). This does not mean that a generation may be punished despite being relatively innocent itself: if a generation repents, it finds mercy (see the discussion in Ezek 18; also Jer 31:29–30). It does mean that the effects of wrongdoing accumulate over time, and that the next generation will likely walk the same way as the previous one. Thus OT confessions often acknowledge the wrongdoing of previous generations, as Lev 26:40 requires (2 Kgs 22:13; Jer 3:25; 14:20; also the prose confessions Ezra 9:7; Neh 1:6; 9:2, 16). (See *TWAT* "אב.")

God's message comes directly to such leaders, but it concerns the whole people, the "we/us" with whom Daniel often associates himself: "all the people of the country" (v 6), "all Israel" (v 11), Judah, Jerusalem, and the dispersed Israel far and near (v 7), "your people," "your city," "your sanctuary" (vv 15, 16, 17, 18, 19, 20). The first of these expressions (כל עם הארץ, v 6), follows up the reference to kings, leaders, and fathers, and thus denotes the mass of ordinary members of the people (cf. 2 Kgs 16:15; Jer 1:18; 34:19; 44:21; Ezek 22:25–29; Hag 2:4, for the use of the term with this meaning in similar contexts). Elsewhere in the Persian, Greek, and Roman periods it became a pejorative term, for non-Jewish people in Palestine (e.g., Ezra 9) or for Jews who were unobservant or ignorant of the law, but there is no suggestion of pejorative connotation here (see de Vaux's book just referred to, 1:111–13 [ET 70–72]; also J. H. Charlesworth, *The Old Testament Pseudepigrapha and the New Testament* [Cambridge/New York: CUP, 1985] 20–21, 146–47).

The chapter three times refers to the people to whom God's word came and for whom Daniel prays as "Israel" (vv 7, 11, 20). As the whole people saw Jacob/Israel as their ancestor, the whole people bore his name. When they split into northern and southern kingdoms, the former, being much the larger, assumed continuing use of the name. The Judeans, however, saw themselves as the preserved remnant of that whole people of God, and thus came to apply the name "Israel" to themselves (cf. 1:6). To speak of Israel, then, is to make a significant theological claim for the little community of Judeans who survived the exile, by seeing them as the successors of that whole people with whom Yahweh entered into covenant (vv 11, 20). Chronicles emphasizes how "all Israel" took part in events such as making David and Solomon king, bringing up the ark, and dedicating the temple. The unity of "all Israel" in Dan 9:11, however, is a unity in wrongdoing. Yet, like the Chronicler, Daniel has not abandoned an awareness that "Israel" was designed to be a much bigger entity than "Judah and Jerusalem" (v 7). The latter is the nucleus of Israel, but as such it does not exclude others; it is rather a "representative centre, to which all the children of Israel should be welcomed if they return" (H. G. M. Williamson, *1 and 2 Chronicles* [London/Grand Rapids: Marshall/Eerdmans, 1982] 26, referring to Williamson, *Israel in the Books of Chronicles* [Cambridge: CUP, 1977] 87–140). The exilic and postexilic community represents Israel as a whole: cf. the reference to Ephraim and Manasseh as well as Judah and Benjamin at the head of the list of the postexilic community in 1 Chr 9:3; also the twelvefold leadership of "the men of the people of Israel" in Neh 7:7; and the first of Nehemiah's prose confessions, offered on behalf of "the descendants of Israel" (Neh 1:6).

Daniel's description of them as "my people Israel" (v 20) is striking. When Israel is "my people," the pronoun normally refers to Yahweh. In prayer, they would normally be "your people": so vv 15, 16, 19 (in a similar way, Daniel speaks of "your city" and "your sanctuary" in vv 16, 17, 19). Such an expression indicates the special relationship Yahweh has with Israel, which is fundamental to the basis on which one prays for them. Sometimes, however, Yahweh speaks to their representative in terms of "your people" (Exod 32:7; 34:10; contrast 32:11, 12; 33:13, 16). He is then dissociating himself from them. Here Daniel takes the initiative in identifying himself with the people whom Yahweh has every ground for repudiating. His speaking of them as "my people" links to his addressing Yahweh on their behalf as "my God." It is by their association with him that he commends them to Yahweh. Daniel belongs to that company of persons such as patriarchs, prophets, kings, priests, and heavenly beings whose prayer can be expected to be heard by God. If Ezek 14:14 refers to this same Daniel, rather than to an ancient hero belonging to the epoch of Abraham and Job, there is a certain tension between this view and the warning about the effectiveness of Daniel's prayer for himself alone in Ezek 14:14 (Calvin). He prays as one who is *persona grata* with Yahweh, though the passage does not quite make the explicit assumption that an intercessor's personal merits may "count" on behalf of people for whom he prays (see Bowker, *JSS* 11 [1966] 79–80; le Déaut, *JSJ* 1 [1970] 35–50).

Daniel has a special focus on Judah, Jerusalem, and its sanctuary (vv 7, 16, 17, 18, 19, 20). It was Judah that remained faithful to David and to Zion; it was Judah (and Benjamin) that continued to be the embodiment of the *actual* Israel after the exile (cf. the list in Neh 11). Administratively, Judah was a separate area from that of the old northern kingdom, Samaria; the arrival of the Persians meant it became a province of the Persian empire, ruled by its own provincial governor (see Hag 1:1; Ezra 2:1, 63; Neh 1:3; 5:14–15; 8:9; G. Widengren, *Israelite and Judaean History* [ed. J. H. Hayes and J. M. Miller; OTL (1977)] 510–11). In the Hellenistic period, the Ptolemies treated it as part of the larger major province of Syria and Palestine; within that Judah (Judea) remained a distinguishable unit over against Samaria to the north and Idumea to the south (see Hengel, *Judentum,* 32–105 [ET 1:18–55]).

There are also both theological and political reasons for special mention of the city of Jerusalem in the prayer (vv 7, 16, 18, 19). Yahweh's city, centered on Mount Zion, is the perfection of beauty, the joy of all the earth; it is the place where Yahweh has made himself known in the history and the worship of his people (Pss 48; 50:2). It is the city Yahweh chose as the dwelling place of his name (Neh 1:9, identifying Jerusalem as the place denoted by Deut 12:5). Admittedly, Daniel emphasizes rather that it is the city that *bears* Yahweh's name—that is, the city he owns. Nor does Daniel specifically speak of it as Zion, the name which carries the most theological freight and which thus most often features in the praise and prayer of the Psalms, though he does refer to it as "my God's sacred mountain" (הר קדש אלהי, v 20, cf. v 16), an epithet of Zion (Pss 2:6; 48:2 [1]; 99:9). In any case, the Babylonians' desolation of Jerusalem put a question mark by the theological claims that had been made for Zion (Lam 2:15). The restoration of the city is of key importance for prophets and leaders of the exilic and postexilic community, but even in the time of Nehemiah the city lacks inhabitants and requires a semicompulsory repopulation (Neh 11:2). The prose confessions in Ezra-Nehemiah do not focus on Jerusalem, despite the context of Neh 1 in concern for Jerusalem, and the Jerusalem setting of Ezra 9 and Neh 9. Although itself set in the exile, Dan 9 thus contrasts with these. Politically, the city increased in significance in the Hellenistic period. "As the only 'city' of Judea, Jerusalem completely dominated the country. . . . Judea could now be regarded by outside observers as the territory of what seemed to be the *'polis'* of Jerusalem, although this was not in fact the constitutional position" (Hengel, *Judentum,* 101 [ET 1:53]).

Within the city, Daniel is specifically concerned for the sanctuary. The significance of the sacred mountain (הר קדש) lies in the presence of the sacred place (מקדש) (v 17; cf. 8:11; also the use of קדש itself in 8:13, 14; 9:24 [?], 26). In 587 B.C. and in the 160s B.C. the sanctuary was despoiled and emptied of its thronging worshipers: "[Jerusalem's] sanctuary was laid waste like a wilderness, her feasts were turned into mourning, her sabbaths into reproach, her honor into contempt"; sacrifices were suspended and the building defiled (1 Macc 1:39, 45–47; cf. Lam 1:4, 10; 2:6, 7). The prayer's cultic interest corresponds to that of other material in chaps. 7–12.

(e) The response God looks for from his people is stated first in the initial description of his characteristics: he is faithful to those "who love him and keep his commands" (v 4); the phrase recalls, behind Neh 1:5, Deut 7:9 (also Deut 5:10 = Exod 20:10); the theme of loving God is most common in Deuteronomistic contexts. There, as in Dan 9:4, the context characteristically indicates that this love is not so much an emotion as a moral commitment (see Deut 6:5; 10:12; 11:1; 30:16, 20). This same emphasis features subsequently in Dan 9 in repeated references to listening to/obeying (שמע) God's voice speaking through the prophets (vv 6, 10, 11, 14), which issues in living (הלך, "walk") by his teaching(s) (v 10). These expressions, too, are characteristically Deuteronomistic (e.g., Deut 11:22; 12:28; 13:4–5 [3–4]; 19:9; 28:1–2; 30:2, 8, 10, 16; Josh 22:5). The significance of this is that the response God looks for from his people is the one required by that covenant expounded in Deuteronomy.

If the people give God that response, they will be in the right with him, able to appeal to him on the basis of their צדקת ("right deeds," v 18). That people should be able to do that is presupposed by the specific use of the term in Ezek 3:20; 18:24; 33:18. With the use of different words it is a common theme elsewhere in Israelite prayers. These often protest the innocence of those who pray (e.g., Ps 7:4–5 [3–4]; 44:18–23 [17–22]; Job 31), in the conviction that casting oneself on God depends on one's relationship with him being right.

An element of disobedience on Israel's part is inevitable. Their task then is to turn (שוב) from it and pay attention (שכל) to God's faithfulness (v 13). The idea of turning from wrongdoing—as opposed to (re)turning to God or simply (re)turning/repenting—is characteristic of the prose of Jeremiah and Ezekiel (e.g., Jer 15:7; 18:7–11; 23:14; 25:5; 26:3; 35:15; 36:3, 7; Ezek 3:19; 13:22; 18:21–30; 33:9–19; see also 1 Kgs 8:35; 13:33; 2 Kgs 17:3; Jonah 3:10; Zech 1:4; Neh 9:35; but not Deuteronomy). It is thus an idea especially associated with the exile and with the religious situation in which Daniel's prayer is set. Its assumption is that the wrongdoing of Israel does not in itself actually end their relationship with Yahweh. If they turn from such wrongdoing, the relationship continues.

If there is any specific background to the idea of paying attention (שכל) to God's faithfulness (v 13), it lies in the communal confession of Ps 106, which acknowledges that Israel's ancestors did not pay attention to and learn from Yahweh's wondrous acts in Egypt (v 7; cf. Deut 32:29). As significant is the fact that Daniel uses words from this root more than any other OT book except Proverbs (and Psalms, if one includes the word משכיל). It is a wisdom word; Daniel's concern here is for Israel to be wise in their relationship with God as they reflect on his dealings with them.

That is the way for them to persuade Yahweh to take a warm and favorable attitude toward them (חלה את פני יהוה, v 13). The phrase comes sixteen times in the OT, and like many OT theological expressions has its background in the royal court (cf. Ps 45:13 [12]; Job 11:19; Prov 19:6). It apparently refers to some concrete expression of respect, homage and honor that prepared the way for the making of a request. It does not have to suggest that the superior party is angry, only that the inferior is needy. Such a way of speaking is easily transferred to the theological sphere. It would then naturally connect with the making of offerings to God (1 Sam 13:12; Mal 1:9), though—as here—the offering could belong to the realm of morality and piety, not explicitly that of cult (cf. Ps 119:58). (See K. Seybold, "Reverenz und Gebet," *ZAW* 88 [1976] 2–16; "חלה . . . ," *TWAT* 2:969–71 [ET 4:407–9]; D. R. Ap-Thomas, "Notes on Some Terms Relating to Prayer," *VT* 6 [1956] 239–40; Sawyer, *Semitics* 7 [1980] 136–37.)

(f) The prayer presupposes that such expectations have not been met: most of the terms just surveyed actually appear in Dan 9 in the negative. Israel have not listened, not lived by Yahweh's teachings, not turned from their wrongdoing or paid heed to his faithfulness, not sought his favor, and are not in the right with him.

The term used most often to describe their shortcomings is failure (חטא, vv 5, 8, 11, 15, 16, 20, 20; EVV "sin"). In secular usage the verb suggests missing a target (Judg 20:16) or missing the way (Prov 19:2), though the religious usage of the word in other Semitic languages antedates the OT's, and it may be hazardous to assume that the secular usage is basic to understanding the religious usage (see K. Koch, "חטא . . . ," *TWAT:* according to Koch, חטא fundamentally means "to commit an offence against someone with whom one stands in an institutionalized community relationship" [ET 4:311]). Certainly חטא does not suggest that people have been seeking to live in accordance with God's expectations yet failing to achieve what they were aiming at. Their failure is willful. (See also R. Knierim, *Die Hauptbegriffe für Sünde im Alten Testament* [Gütersloh: Mohn, 1965].)

Daniel's opening confession in v 5 adds to failure four other images. "We have gone astray" (עוה; cf. v 16, עון "waywardness") has a similar background meaning to that of חטא (see KB for the nontheological use of עוה—against BDB, which posits separate roots). "We have done wrong" (הרשיע; also רשענו, v 15) is a forensic expression, the antonym of צדק ("do right," vv 7, 14, 16, 18). It indicates action that puts a person in the wrong in a legal or quasi-legal setting. It is used in connection with the covenant relationship in 11:32. "We have rebelled" (מרד; also v 9) may be a stronger term, and a less technically religious one, than פשע (see v 24). "We have turned our backs" on your commands (סור also v 11) is another Deuteronomistic expression (e.g., Deut 17:11, 17, 20), though it goes back to the very beginning of Israel's covenant relationship with Yahweh (Exod 32:8). Perhaps the verbs build up through v 5 (and v 6a): turning the back and closing the ears is the climactic rejection of Yahweh's word and the crowning insult.

Later verses in the confession introduce two further terms. "Trespass" (מעל, v 7), a common expression for unfaithfulness to Yahweh in worship or life in Ezekiel and Chronicles, suggests encroachment on what is holy, including God's name (by violating an oath) (J. Milgrom, "The Concept of *maʿal* in the Bible and the Ancient Near East," *JAOS* 96 [1976] 236–47; expanded in Milgrom, *Cult and Conscience* [SJLA 18 (1976)] 16–35). "We have overstepped your instruction" (עבר, v 11) indicates a contravention of the enactments of the covenant in a broader sense.

The wrongdoing Daniel confesses characterizes not only the present generation but past generations (v 16) (see the discussion of the "fathers" above). It characterizes the people as a whole, and specifically Israel's secular institutional leadership (v 8); neither priests nor prophets are specifically included. There is a contrast here with the outlook of prophets such as Jeremiah and Ezekiel, who saw the exile as in part issuing from the failure of prophets and priests.

(g) The consequence of being in the wrong in relation to Yahweh is to find oneself overcome by great trouble (vv 12, 13, 14), trouble unprecedented (v 12). The term Daniel uses, רעה, is a most general one, equivalent to English "bad": it covers what is unpleasant or objectionable, what is distressing or calamitous, what is hurtful or injurious, and what is evil or wicked. In the last senses it applies to Israel's conduct before Yahweh, in the earlier senses it applies to the judgment he brings on their conduct (e.g., Jer 36:3, 7, 31; 44:2, 3, 5, 7, 9, 11, 17, 23, 27, 29).

The concrete descriptions of this trouble are twofold. It has meant the desolation of city and sanctuary (שמם, vv 17, 18). The term suggests the wasting of a place: the devastation and ruin of what is built and the consequent emptying of what is inhabited. That a place should be wasted is a standard threat (Lev 26:22, 31–43; Jer 4:27; Amos 7:9); that the land has been wasted is a standard element in the depiction of the exile (Isa 59:8, 19; Ezek 36:34–36; Zech 7:14; Lam 1:4, 13, 16; 5:18; 2 Chr 36:21) and of the Antiochene period (1 Macc 1:38–39; 3:45; 4:38) (see 8:13 *Comment*).

"Trouble" also takes the form of banishment (נדח, v 7) from Judah and Jerusalem to countries near and far away. That phrase is characteristic of Jeremianic prose. There is a pathos about the phrase "all the countries where you have driven them"; it thus features prominently in promises that Yahweh will restore the people even from all these countries (Jer 16:15; 23:3, 8; 29:14; 32:37; 46:27; also Deut 31:1, where this is the context of the exiles coming to their senses).

One of the passages that speaks in such terms of Israel's banishment in the context of threat, Jer 29:18, also refers to this bringing abuse (חרפה) on Judah—not to say taunts and curses; cf. also Jer 24:9; 49:13. Daniel, too, speaks of the way the desolation and emptying of Jerusalem has brought upon it shame and abuse (בשת, חרפה; vv 7, 8, 16). The two terms come together in Isa 54:4; Jer 51:51 to denote the real or imaginary sense of contumely and contempt brought about by the exile (also Isa 30:5; Ps 69:20 [19]). The visible shame to which Daniel refers appears also in Jer 7:19; Ps 44:16; Ezra 9:7; 2 Chr 32:21, while passages such as Ezek 5:14–15; 36:15; Lam 5:1 speak of the abuse brought upon Israel by the exile (cf. also ברעה גדלה ובחרפה "in great trouble and reproach" in Neh 1:3, leading in to Nehemiah's prose confession).

The prayer is prayed as out of the situation of exile. As in other apocalypses, this is not a mere fictional conceit. It was from the exile that many of the problems of second-century B.C. Jews stemmed, and exile was their model experience—as it is in many of the laments in the Psalter, though the content of their prayer is different (see *Form*) (Gowan, "Exile," 219). As the prayer overtly takes up the experience of the sixth century B.C., it covertly takes up that of the second, in which the experience of exile continues.

Thus far, Daniel's description of the people's experience bears comparison with that in 1 Macc 1:39–40; 2:7–12 (Towner): desolation, mourning, dishonor, banishment. Daniel's understanding of its cause, however, differs from that in 1 Maccabees. The cause can be pictured impersonally: in it a solemn, written curse has its effect (v 11). "Curse" (אלה) does not denote an imprecation, but a sanction imposed in the name of legal rights or religio-ethical demands (J. Scharbert, "אלה . . . ," *TWAT*). Such a conditional curse buttresses, for instance, the commitment to fidelity that two parties make to a treaty. By analogy, the treaty/covenant relationship that Yahweh lays upon Israel is protected by a curse, that declared in Deut 29 (see especially vv 18–20 [19–21]), which backs up the promises and warnings of chaps. 27–28. The curse has "overwhelmed" Israel (נתך): the image is of something pouring forth and flowing over, like a torrent of rain or a flooding waterfall (Exod 9:33; Job 3:24). The word is regularly used of God's wrath overwhelming people; and—solemnly—of the smelting of metal in a furnace, a figure of judgment (e.g., Ezek 22:17–22).

To speak of a curse overwhelming Israel is to exclude explanation of their calamity in terms of chance or of the demonic. It is not, however, to exclude an explanation in terms of the magical (cf. Scharbert, *TWAT* [see above]). Thus here immediately the origin of the calamity is described more personally: in it Yahweh is keeping his spoken undertaking (v 12). The personal deliberateness of his deed is underlined by speaking of him as watching over the trouble, keeping it ready; it comes as his carefully considered act (v 14), the determined realization of a predetermined plan. The unusual verb Daniel uses (שקד) again recalls Jeremianic prose (Jer 1:11–12; 31:28; 44:27).

At the same time, his act expresses his burning fury (אף וחמה, v 16). The OT can speak of wrath as an impersonal disaster that comes on people irrespective of what they deserve (e.g., 2 Kgs 3:27; Qoh 5:17), or as disaster that comes on people as retribution for wrongdoing but without the idea of God's personal activity being prominent (e.g., Josh 9:20; cf. Ezra 7:23). In each of the passages just quoted, the noun is קצף. In Daniel the term זעם is used in a similar way (8:19; 11:36; following Isa 10:25; 26:20). But אף and חמה, the OT's two most frequent words for anger, appear much more consistently with a possessive pronoun or noun, or with another indication in the context that they are essentially personal expressions. Feelings are more integral to the aspect of wrath they convey: wrath as it shows in the appearance of the face (and the snort of the nostrils?) (אף); wrath as burning rage (חמה).

(h) The antonyms of anger in the OT are words such as רחמים "compassion" and חסד "commitment" (E. Johnson, "אנף . . . ," *TWAT*). Yet the God of Israel has already been described in the prayer as the God of compassion and commitment. It is on the basis of this that Daniel intercedes with God on Israel's behalf. This involves his turning to God (v 3). In 6:11 [10] Daniel prayed in a room facing Jerusalem, and here turning to the Lord probably has a similar implication (S. Layton, "Biblical Hebrew 'To Set the Face,'" *UF* 17 [1986] 171–72). At the same time, turning (ואתנה את פני, "I set my face") implies a deliberate, purposeful act expressive of determination in the face of a crisis or challenge: cf. 2 Chr 20:3; also Gen 31:21; and 2 Kgs 12:18 [17] with Luke 9:51; contrast Dan 10:15. The deliberateness of Daniel's action is underlined by his describing it as "laying down" supplications before Yahweh (הפיל, "cause them to fall"; v 20). There lies behind the expression the fact that in prayer people cause themselves to fall before God. "Supplications" (תחנונים, vv 3, 20, 23) are prayers in which one casts oneself on grace (חן) and pleads on the basis of that.

Daniel's prayer for Jerusalem's restoration begins as a confession (see also v 20). The verb ידה[הת] means "to acknowledge": it can be used to acknowledge the great things God has done (2:23; 6:11 [10]), or the wrong things we have done. In either case, the form the acknowledgment takes is characteristically pure statement: either the declaration of God's acts (e.g., Ps 40) or the declaration of our acts (as here). In either case, expressions such as "we thank you" or "we are sorry" have less prominence than is the case with our worship. The acknowledgment lies in the statements themselves. (On ידה, see Westermann, *Lob,* 20–24 [ET 25–30].) Further, in the case of acknowledgment of sin, this act also is an acknowledgment of the justice of God—an act of praise at the justice of his judgment (see *Form*).

This turning to God is thus a matter of words, spoken out loud (vv 20, 21). But words spoken out are accompanied by deeds acted out (v 3); that adds to the sense of seriousness and earnestness expressed by the prayer. In the OT, fasting, sackcloth, and ashes are indications of grief and self-abasement in the context of calamity or loss experienced or threatened, or of wrongdoing committed (Isa 58:5; Jonah 3:5–9; Neh 9:1; Esth 4:1–4). Fasting involved abstaining from (regular) food during the day (Judg 20:26; 1 Sam 14:24; 2 Sam 1:12; 3:31–35; 12:15–23; Jer 16:7; Ezek 24:17; fasting for the whole of twenty-four hours is less usual—see Lev 23:32; Esth 4:16). Sackcloth was dark, rough, cheap material worn in contrast to the more presentable smart clothing in which a respectable person would normally wish to appear in public (1 Kgs 20:31–32; 2 Kgs 19:1–2). The reference to ashes denotes the practice of putting ashes (or dust or earth) on the head or head and body, or of lying or sitting in a pile of ashes (Josh 7:6; 1 Sam 4:12; 2 Sam 1:2; 13:19). The background of such practices presumably lies in the way shock, loss, and grief naturally express themselves in a loss of interest over food and one's appearance and in an inner gloominess that expresses itself in gloominess of appearance. Practices such as these give formal, stylized, ritual expression to feelings people have or purport to.

Fasting also features in the context of special meeting with God, or the seeking of a meeting with God or of a revelation from him. Here there is no suggestion of loss or grief; as in such circumstances, however, fasting suggests an abandoning of regular human preoccupations for the sake of concentration on seeking God or being with God (Exod 34:28; 1 Kgs 19:8; 2 Esd 6:31; *2 Apoc. Bar.* 20.5–6; 47.2; Matt 4:1–2; Acts 13:2–3). In the apocalypses, the two contexts or significances of fasting coalesce. The seers behave as people who are grieving and abasing themselves—the background of many apocalypses, notionally or actually, in one or other of the falls of Jerusalem may be relevant here; they are also people who hope for and receive revelations from God after a period of such self-abasement (2 Esd 5:13, 20; 6:35; *2 Apoc. Bar.* 5.7; 9.2; 12.5).

Either of these contexts or significances could be appropriate to Dan 9. Daniel's mourning belongs in the context of his asking God, "When are you going to restore Jerusalem?" Such a question might represent a seer's plea for information regarding God's purpose, or a suppliant's plea for action to implement God's purpose. Reading it in the light of the apocalypses (and of v 22, also 10:2) would suggest the former, but reading it in the light of the OT (and of vv 1–2) would suggest the latter. The two need not be dissociated. Verses 1–2 do not directly portray Daniel as in need of revelation—he understands the revelation and seeks its fulfillment. But the second-century B.C. author and audience is in need of revelation, and its puzzledness also underlies vv 1–2. The expression of grief and self-abasement is both a plea for divine revelation and a plea for divine action.

The prayer of confession, then, is one of the expressions of self-abasement before God appropriate to someone who longs for God to reveal and implement his purpose for his people. Like the prayers of confession at the beginning of some church services, it indicates a sense that sin is always an obstacle between humanity and God, and needs to be confessed and forgiven before we can expect God to speak or act. It does not carry the implication that it is Jewish sin that explains Jewish suffering in the second century B.C. (with Towner, *USQR* 26 [1970–71] 203–41). Further, while such a prayer is a necessary undertaking on the part of someone who seeks for God to speak and act, God's response is not directly a response to this confession—as is suggested by the fact that Gabriel was commissioned at the beginning of the prayer, not after its end.

(i) The content of Daniel's supplication is expressed in vv 16–19, most directly and movingly in v 19, the close and climax of the prayer. It asks first that God may "listen" (שמעה). That note has appeared already in v 17, and in v 18 ("give ear and listen"), while v 19 itself later adds a plea to "hear" (הקשיבה). It is the standard first element in the actual plea in a lament, as Westermann analyzes them (*Lob,* 40, 49, 50 [ET 54, 67, 69]). Such prayer arises out of a context where God seems to have been ignoring his people's plight and their prayer. It pleads first that he give attention.

The other feature of the plea in a lament, as Westermann analyzes it, is the appeal to God to act—to save the petitioner(s), and perhaps to punish their oppressors. Daniel's closing plea asks that God may "pardon" (סלחה; cf. v 9). Perhaps that is the equivalent to the appeal to "punish" that sometimes features in a lament. The unjustly afflicted seek justice; the justly afflicted seek pardon. "The Israel which acknowledges its God's justice even when disaster comes to it can ask for his mercy. Only those who know that they are struck down as guilty before God, only they can appeal to God's mercy" (Plöger).

The same idea lies behind the plea for God's burning fury to turn away from the city (שוב, v 16). Like the use of שוב to refer to turning from wrongdoing (v 13), its use to denote God's wrath turning from people is frequent in Jeremianic prose (Jer 2:35; 18:20; 23:20; 30:24; cf. Isa 12:1; Hos 14:5 [4]; Prov 29:8). It is elsewhere used of other figures like Daniel and Jeremiah who caused God's wrath to turn away (Num 25:11; Ps 106:23; 2 Chr 12:12; 29:10; 30:8) (for turning away human wrath, see Gen 27:44–45; Prov 15:1). The image seems to picture anger as a violent, dynamic force like a fierce wind that would destroy all in its path. It cannot be instantly calmed once generated; it has to spend itself. Someone in its path must bear its force or hope it may veer and dissipate itself harmlessly elsewhere.

To put the point more positively, Daniel asks that God's face may shine on the sanctuary (האר פניך, v 17). He takes up one element in the Aaronic blessing (Num 6:25), which becomes a prayer in Psalms (31:17 [16]; 67:2 [1]; 80:4, 8, 20 [3, 7, 19]; 119:135; cf. 4:7 [6]; 118:27). The metaphor presupposes first that a person's happiness shows in the brightness of his or her face (cf. 1 Sam 14:27, 29); then that this same brightness directed toward other people is an indication of regard and favor (cf. Job 29:24; Prov 16:15). In such passages, the expression is regularly used in association with words such as "save," "bless," and "redeem," the verbs characteristic of a lament's plea for God to act. Thus Daniel, too, in his final plea bids God "act" and not "delay" (עשה אל תאחר). Such an appeal to God not to delay acting closes off the pleas in Pss 40:18 [17]; 70:6 [5]. It recalls the "how long . . . ?" that features in the lament itself (Pss 6:4 [3]; 13:2–3 [1–2]; 74:10; 79:5;

80:4; 89:46; 90:13) and the positive plea not to delay, "hurry" to help us (e.g., 22:20 [19] 38:23 [22]; 40:14 [13]; 70:2, 6 [1, 5]; 71:12).

Each verse in the plea offers some motivation for God to hear, forgive, and act. It would be in keeping with his acts in the past, rescuing his people from oppression in Egypt (vv 15–16) (cf. Isa 63:7–64:12; Jer 32:16–25; Pss 80; 106; and the prose confessions in Neh 9). Daniel appeals to the saving act that led to Yahweh's covenant relationship with Israel and always underlay it—an aspect of the covenant that offered promise for the future rather than merely explaining the trouble of the present. God is urged to open his eyes and look at the desolate state of the people, city, and sanctuary (see [g] above). That is an appeal to his compassion, but also an appeal to his honor. In rescuing people from Egypt, he made a name for himself as a God of compassion who did the right thing by that afflicted people (vv 15, 16, 18). People, city, and sanctuary bear Yahweh's name. Calling something by your name (see n. 18.c) indicates that you own it (2 Sam 12:28; Isa 63:19; 65:1; Amos 9:12). Their being desolate brings discredit on him; for his own sake, he should act (vv 17, 18, 19). "To the degree that he has committed himself to preserving the safety of those things which are named by his name (identified with him, blessed in his name and with his sanction), to that extent the God of Israel has limited and compromised his own freedom to act in the future" (Towner). It is on that note that the prayer closes.

(j) The OT assumes that prayers meet responses. OT narratives picture laments meeting responses (e.g., Josh 7:7–15; 2 Chr 20:1–30), passages within the prophets suggest the same experience (e.g., Jer 3:21–4:2; Hos 14:2–9 [1–8]; cf. the promise of Isa 58:9), and some laments in the Psalter preserve responses (Pss 12; 60). Others show a marked change of mood reflecting an assurance that God has heard and granted the prayer, which is plausibly taken to indicate that a response from a priest or prophet was to be given to the plea part of the lament (Pss 6; 13; 22; 28). The suppliant of course hoped for a positive response, but could not be sure of one (Jer 14:1–15:9; Hos 5:15–6:6) (see Westermann, *Lob,* passim). Here the response comes at the time of the evening offering (v 21), the special hour for prayer (see 6:11 [10] *Comment:* cf. Ezra 9:5, the introduction to Ezra's prose confession). In Dan 9 the note could have special point, for the offerings may not have been regularly made during the exile, and they were certainly suspended by Antiochus (cf. 8:11; 11:31; 1 Macc 1:45). The implication may then be the reassurance that the relationship between God and Israel still holds, notwithstanding the lack of offerings; compare the promise of Ezek 11:16 for the people exiled from the temple. God behaves as though the offerings are still being made. The cosmic temporal order, reflected in the rhythm of the hours of prayer, stands despite the vicissitudes of history (Lebram, "Piety," 187).

The exiles were inclined to think that God was indifferent to his people's cries in their affliction (Isa 40:27; 49:14; cf. 58:3); the point expressed in loving hyperbole in Isa 65:24 (cf. 65:1) here becomes prosaic narrative reality, but its message is similar—not that the actual prayer was unnecessary or unheard, but that God is eager to respond to his servants when they come to him on behalf of his people in need. The picture of God "responding" before Daniel actually prays perhaps also safeguards the sovereignty of God, a concern that underlay some hesitation over the whole idea of intercession in Judaism (le Déaut, *JSJ* 1 [1970] 51–55).

We noted that Daniel's self-abasement ([h] above) may suggest both a plea for divine revelation and a plea for divine action. The response promises action on behalf of those who pray this prayer in the second century B.C., but it takes the overt form of a revelation to the seer set in the sixth. (It offers little revelation to the second-century context, and little good news to the sixth-century context!) The message brings insight and understanding to Daniel (v 22) as one who is "held in high regard" (חמודות, v 23). Like words such as אהב "love," חמד suggests both a feeling and an attitude that expresses itself in being drawn toward the object of love and committing oneself to it (Isa 53:2; Pss 19:11 [10]; 68:17 [16]) (BDB; cf. J. Herrmann, "Das zehnte Gebot," *Sellin-Festschrift* [Leipzig: Hinrichs, 1927] 69–82). Daniel is one to whom God is committed. As we have seen, he has prayed as *persona grata* to Yahweh. This may be partly because of the faithful obedience that the stories have portrayed (Anderson). Yet in the stories Daniel models the faithfulness to which all believers are called, and chap. 9 implicitly promises that all those who show this faithfulness will discover the meaning of history (Koch, *HZ* 193 [1961] 22).

The revelation (v 23) will take the form of an explanation of the passage of scripture from which the chapter started. The *meaning* of the words might be clear; their *reference* was not. Theologically, then, the significance of this passage cannot be discerned by ordinary human study; it can only be received by revelation—like the original prophecy, or like visions such as those received elsewhere by Daniel. To understand the prophecies one needs the same divine inspiration that the prophet himself had received (Gregory Thaumatourgos, *Panegyricus* 179; cf. Bickermann). Yet historically, it emerges from a situational context, in the second century B.C., in the light of which Scripture is studied and enabled to become newly illuminating. It is not exactly that history is revelatory. But history poses the questions about the meaning of Scripture, to which revelation provides the answer.

Daniel's lament thus receives the expected response, though via a heavenly being rather than an earthly one. The image of a message "issuing" (יצא) comes from everyday life, where it is used of the deliberate proclamation of significant words (Num 30:3 [2]; Josh 6:10; Judg 11:36; Jer 44:17), especially by the king (Esth 1:19; 7:8; cf. נפק in Dan 2:13). Thus it is naturally applied to God's declaration of his will and intention (Isa 2:3; 45:23; 48:3; 51:4; 55:11; Ezek 33:30). The word of interpretation issues authoritatively from God himself, as the original word of prophecy had done.

There has been disagreement over which figure in which previous vision is alluded to here. If בתחלה means "previously," it is natural to take the vision to be that of chap. 8, where Gabriel first specifically appears (v 16). If בתחלה means "original," the vision must be that of chap. 7; chap. 9 then identifies the unnamed interpreter (v 16) as Gabriel, who regularly fulfills this role (Day, *Conflict,* 171–72; but on בתחלה, see n. 8:1.d). Zevit (*VT* 28 [1978] 490) implies that this cannot be, on the grounds that the interpreter appears outside the vision in chap. 7; but the interpreter, while outside the symbolic vision, is within the interpretative vision, as Zevit grants Gabriel is in 8:15–18. On either understanding of בתחלה, there is no need or grounds for Zevit's further suggestion that 9:21 identifies the humanlike figure of 7:13 with Gabriel.

24 "Seventy sevens" presumably denotes "seventy times seven *years,*" as the original "seventy" of Jeremiah was explicitly a period of years (v 2). The period suggests that the seventy years of punishment due according to Jer 25:11/29:10 is being exacted sevenfold in accordance with Lev 26 (see *Form*).

Ancient and modern interpreters have commonly taken vv 24–27 as designed to convey firm chronological information, which as such can be tested by chronological facts available to us. It may then be vindicated, for instance, by noting that the period from Jeremiah's prophecy (605 B.C.) to that of Cyrus's accession (556) was 49 years and the period from Jeremiah's prophecy to the death of the high priest Onias III (171) was 434 years so that the sum of these periods is 483 years, the final seven years taking events to the rededication of the temple in 164 (e.g., Behrmann). Or it may be vindicated by noting that according to some computations the period from Nehemiah (445 or 444 B.C.) to Jesus' death at Passover in A.D. 32 or 33 was exactly 483 years, the seventieth seven being postponed (Hoehner, *BSac* 132 [1975] 47–65; Anderson, *Prince,* following Julius Africanus reported in Eusebius; Driver instances other comparable theories). Both these understandings of the seventy sevens may be faulted on the grounds of their arbitrariness. In the case of the first, it is not obvious why two partly concurrent figures should be added together. In the case of the second, it is not obvious why the word about building a restored Jerusalem should be connected with Artaxerxes' commission of Nehemiah to rebuild the walls of Jerusalem; nor why we should accept the basis of the computation, that of a 360-day year; nor why we should separate off the seventieth seven, as the theory requires; nor why we should date Nehemiah's commission in 444 B.C. or Jesus' crucifixion in A.D. 32—the computation requires one or the other, but the usually preferred dates are 445 and A.D. 30 or 33 (see, e.g., *IBD* 278–79; J. Finegan, *Handbook of Biblical Chronology* [Princeton: Princeton UP, 1964] 285–301; according to J. K. Fotheringham, A.D. 32 is "absolutely impossible"! ["The Evidence of Astronomy and Technical Chronology for the Date of the Crucifixion," *JTS* 35 (1934) 160]). Further, it is striking that the NT itself does not refer to the seventy sevens in this connection; Luke 1–2 applies v 24 in a quite different way (see Introduction).

The critical view has usually been that the seventy sevens extend as one sequence from some point in the sixth century to the period of Antiochus Epiphanes. Dan 9 is then an overestimate and Daniel is faulted for its "wrong-headed arithmetical calculations" (Porteous).

A fundamental objection to such attempts either to vindicate or to fault Daniel's figures is that both are mistaken in interpreting the 490 years as offering chronological information. It is not chronology but chronography: a stylized scheme of history used to interpret historical data rather than arising from them, comparable to cosmology, arithmology, and genealogy as these appear in writings such as the OT (Grabbe, "Chronography," 43–44; Young describes it as symbol).

It would be an exaggeration to suggest that writers of the Hellenistic period were neither interested in nor capable of discovering the real chronology of preceding centuries, as Grabbe implies (see Beckwith, *RevQ* 10 [1979–81] 521–42). That in itself suggests that the attempt to interpret as chronology figures that are not amenable to any consistently literal interpretation may be misguided; and a general consideration of OT dates supports the view that a figure such as 490 years is not designed to offer chronological information. Kings frequently offers precise indications regarding how long kings reigned (28 years, 41 years, etc.), and while its figures raise detailed problems, they clearly seek to convey chronological information. In contrast, Judges frequently speaks of periods of forty years of oppression, peace, or some other experience, which do not look as if they are chronological markers of that precise kind. 1 Kings itself tells us that the building of the temple began 480 years (twelve times forty years!) after the exodus (6:1), and this, too, does not have the appearance of a chronological note. When treated as such, it raises difficulties, since other evidence suggests that the exodus happened in the thirteenth century B.C., not the fifteenth. Elsewhere 490 also seems to have been used as a principle for periodizing history. Eventually *Jubilees* structures the whole of history by periods of 490 years (see, e.g., Beckwith, *RevQ* 10 [1979–81] 168–71). Dan 9 is to be related to these ways of speaking. It begins from Jeremiah's "seventy years," which was hardly a chronological calculation but a term denoting a period such as human lifetime that extends beyond the years that the hearers will see; it combines that with the principle of sevenfold punishment from Lev 26. None of this background suggests that either the total period of 490 years or its subdivisions are to be expected necessarily to correspond numerically to chronological periods. Our attempt to link them with such periods is to be made on the basis of exegetical considerations as these arise from the passage, not of actual chronology.

By the time the seventy sevens end, six things are to be achieved for people and sacred city. The concern of v 24 is thus Israel and Jerusalem. It does not have a worldwide perspective; it is not speaking of the end of all history, or of the sin of the whole world. Daniel is returning to "salvation history" from the secular history that dominated chaps. 7–8 and will dominate chaps. 10–12. His moving between these two reflects the fact that both are of God. God is the God of all history, but nature and grace are not simply identified; there are special purposes he is achieving in the history of Israel. God is the God of Israel's history, but nature and grace are not to be sundered; he purposes to reign in all history. (See N. Lash, *Theology on the Way to Emmaus* [London: SCM, 1986] 66–69; cf. K. Rahner, "Weltgeschichte und Heilsgeschichte," *Schriften zur Theologie* 5:115–35 [Einsiedeln: Benziger, 1962] = *Theological Investigations* 5:97–114 [tr. K. H. Kruger; London/Baltimore: DLT/ Helicon, 1966]).

The three negatives in v 24 are near-synonyms: wickedness is characterized as rebellion, failure, and waywardness (פשע, though with the article; חטאת, though plural in K; עון). Daniel's prayer has used such terms to describe Israel's wickedness: see *Comment* on vv 3–23 (f). In speaking of the "wiping away" of waywardness, v 24 uses the key cultic verb כפר. It presupposes that cleansing is God's own act of salvation in history rather than a human cultic act (B. Janowski, *Sühne als Heilsgeschehen* [WMANT 55 (1982)] 115–37).

The oracle might then be a response to Daniel's confession of Israel's sin, promising cleansing and relief from the afflictions that have come as sin's punishment; it would then parallel Isa 40:1–2, but postpone the fulfillment of such promises to the second century B.C. (Anderson; Steck, "Weltgeschehen," 65–75). Yet several considerations point against this view. Daniel has not so far pictured the afflictions of the second century as punishment, and it would need to do so more clearly if this was the implication here; Antiochus is the desolater rather than the rod of Yahweh's anger (Collins, *Daniel* [FOTL] 94–95). The fact that the oracle issues before the prayer (and is to be fulfilled centuries after it) points away from the suggestion that relief from affliction relates directly to the confessional content of the prayer: like Job 38–41, Gabriel's oracle ignores what precedes because it is designed to give a new perspective on issues raised so far (Jones, *VT* 18 [1968] 493). Indeed, Towner (*USQR* 26 [1970–71] 213) sees the prayer as an entirely typical act of postexilic piety whose confession is not to be related to an awareness of a link between particular people's sin and a particular experience of trouble; one might compare the stress on sin in the services of the Church of England *Book of Common Prayer.* There is no direct indication in the oracle that the whole postexilic period is seen as a period of wickedness. Only the last "seven" is specifically characterized by wickedness, wrath, and desolation. The events that vv 24–27 promise emerge from God's sovereign will; they are not a response to Israel's sin or Daniel's confession at all. Further, the expression "the rebellion" recalls 8:12–14, 23 (Charles), where the offending acts of Antiochus have at least part of the focus.

Daniel subsequently makes clear that a distinction between faithfulness to the covenant and wickedness ran within Israel itself (see 11:30–35; 12:10). Dan 9 might presuppose this distinction; the innocent identify with the wicked, and God responds to their prayer (cf. Heard's study of the perspectives of 2 Maccabees and *T. Moses, EvQ* 58 [1986] 293–308). But chap. 9 itself is allusive. Perhaps its allusiveness, to be resolved by later chapters, parallels that of chap. 7 over the identity of the humanlike figure. Perhaps, like other instances of ambiguity in the OT, it functions to set questions before the hearer: to drive us to ask what relationship between calamity, confession, and promise obtains between us and God. But the ambiguity over whether the wrong referred to is Antiochus's or Israel's may indicate that the agency or subject of this wrong is not in focus. It is the objective result in the sacrilege of the sanctuary that is Gabriel's concern.

Three positives correspond to the three negatives. צדק "vindication" recalls the use in the prayer of צדיק/צדקה ("right," vv 7, 14, 16, 18), which denoted the idea that Yahweh was in the right over against Israel. "Bringing in צדק" thus suggests causing right to be acknowledged. But it is also natural to connect this "lasting vindication" with the vindication of the sanctuary in 8:12–14, one facet of the close parallelism between this oracle and the vision in chap. 8. It is less natural to take צדק in a NT sense, to refer to the justification of sinners (against Young), or in the broader OT sense, to refer to salvation (against Delcor, comparing Isa 45:17), or in the Qumran sense, to refer to a personified divine attribute (against Baumgarten, *ANRW* ii 19, 1 [1979] 222–23).

Reference to the sealing of the vision recalls 8:26 (for the verb, cf. Dan

12:4, 9; also 6:18 [17]). Yet it is Jeremiah, not Daniel, whom chap. 9 describes as a prophet (v 2). The phrase has been taken to suggest that prophecy is to be sealed up and thus silent through this period (Keil), but this is a lot to read out of the phrase. Sealing elsewhere suggests authenticating (1 Kgs 21:8), and this fits the present context well: the promise is that Jeremiah's prophecy will be fulfilled and thus confirmed.

The anointing of a most sacred place (קדש קדשים: see n. 24.j-j) again recalls the treading down and vindication of the sacred place (קדש) in 8:13–14. The tent of meeting, the altar, and associated objects had been anointed to consecrate them at the beginning (Exod 30:26–29; 40:9–11; cf. also 29:36–37, where כפר, משח, and קדש קדושים appear together [Doukhan, *AUSS* 17 (1979) 11–12]). They are now anointed to reconsecrate them after their defiling (cf. the account in 1 Macc 4:36–59). There are no specific grounds for seeing a secondary reference to a most sacred people (against Lacocque) or to a most sacred one or "messiah."

A coherent understanding of v 24 emerges, then, if we take it as a restatement of the visionary promises of chap. 8. Like that vision, it looks forward from the time of Daniel himself to the Antiochene crisis, and promises God's deliverance. There is no reason to refer it exegetically to the first or second coming of Christ.

25 The opening of v 25 ("you must understand and perceive") repeats the contents of v 23b ("heed the word," "give heed to the revelation"). This resumptive exhortation marks v 25 as a new beginning. Verses 25–27 subdivide the seventy sevens into 7, 62, and 1; vv 26–27 focus on the last. Chronologically, v 24 describes what will have been achieved by the end of vv 25–27; within vv 25–27, matters are treated in chronological order (against Payne, *JETS* 21 [1978] 97–115; Doukhan, *AUSS* 17 [1979] 12–15).

The coming forth of a word from the mouth of Yahweh has already been referred to in v 23, but v 25 surely refers to a different proclamation: the word v 23 introduces—the whole of vv 24–27—does not focus on the building of a restored Jerusalem. The term is one for a solemn royal proclamation (e.g., Esth 1:19), and thus for the solemn proclamation of Yahweh (e.g., Isa 2:3; 45:23; 48:3; 51:4; 55:11; Ezek 33:30). "From the coming forth of a word to build a restored Jerusalem to an anointed, a leader" lasts seven sevens. While these seven sevens must come at the beginning of the period from the exile to Antiochus, we cannot certainly identify either their beginning or their end. By the proclamation to restore Jerusalem, Gabriel may have meant Jeremiah's prophecy referred to in v 2 (605 B.C. in the case of 25:12; 597 B.C. in the case of 29:10); or his prophecies recorded in connection with the fall of Jerusalem in 587 B.C. (30:18–22; 31:38–40); or Gabriel's own words to Daniel (?539); or the decree of Cyrus in 539 B.C. (Isa 45:1; Ezra 1:1–4; seen as a rebuilding of *city*, not just of *temple*, in 4:12–16); or the decree of Darius in 521 B.C. (Ezra 6:1–12; also seen as a rebuilding of city in anticipation in 4:21); or the decree of Artaxerxes in 458 (Ezra 7:12–26); or the warrant given to Nehemiah in 445 B.C. (Neh 1). "To restore and build" is a rich and suggestive phrase that combines reference to the restoring of the community and the rebuilding of the city (Lacocque). It would be wooden to suggest it could only denote one or another of the events envisaged by these passages. All were part of the restoration of Zion. More prosaically, "square and moat" makes clear that the restoration Gabriel speaks of is a quite material one. The phrase perhaps refers to the internal layout of the city and its external defenses (Hartman).

"An anointed, a leader" (משיח נגיד) could conceivably refer to a non-Israelite ruler: the first term denotes Cyrus in Isa 45:1, the second the ruler of Tyre in Ezek 28:2. But both are more characteristically used of Israelite leaders, and there is something out-of-the-ordinary about the exceptions in Isa 45:1; Ezek 28:2 (see Westermann and Zimmerli in loc). A non-Israelite ruler would more naturally be referred to here as מלך, as commonly in Daniel. In the absence of indication to the contrary, then, "an anointed, a leader," is more likely an Israelite figure. The term could then denote either a prince (e.g., 1 Sam 2:10, 35; 9:16; 10:1) or a (high) priest (e.g., Lev 4:3; 2 Macc 1:10; Jer 20:1; Neh 11:11; cf. Dan 9:26; 11:22). If the seventy sevens commence about the time when the exile begins, and the anointed ruler appears after the first seven sevens, then the term likely refers either to Zerubbabel or Joshua, בני היצהר "sons of oil" according to Zech 4:14. If the punctuation of v 25a in the ancient versions and NIV is right (n. 25.b-b), it is probably the same "anointed" as in v 26, one who appears after seven plus sixty-two sevens.

Some of the periods that might be denoted as seven sevens come near to forty-nine calendar years, but the principles about chronography and chronology suggested above forbid us to infer that the period nearest forty-nine calendar years must be the one referred to. The point about a period of seven sevens is that it constitutes one jubilee. Daniel might, indeed, have described the whole period as ten jubilees, but he does not, and specific jubilee themes do not feature in vv 24–27. Jubilee thinking is not all-important to him (against, e.g., Lacocque; Buchanan, *Hebrews,* 42–43). Similarly Torrey's suggestion that vv 24–27 refer to the expectation of two messiahs known from other Jewish writings (*JBL* 66 [1947] 268–72) seems to build too much on an allusive text.

26 The sixty-two sevens that follow the seven sevens are characterized by or end in that situation of oppression which especially concerns the seer and his audience, the oppression whose termination v 24 promised. "The pressure of the times" (צוק העתים) contrasts with "the stability of your times" (אמונת עתיך) promised in Isa 33:6.

Talk of devastation, battle, and desolation (v 26) reflects the seriousness of the trouble brought to people, city, and temple by the combined force of heathen ruler(s) and usurper priest(s). They are described at length in 1 Macc 1–4 and 2 Macc 4–5, and are reflected in the early Maccabean messianic oracle *Sib. Or.* 3.265–94, which overtly refers to the events of the exilic period, including the destruction of the temple, but covertly refers to the Antiochene crisis (Nolland, *JTS* 30 [1979] 162–63). They are not to be minimized, as they are by writers who seek to dissociate Dan 9:24–27 from the second century B.C. (Hengstenberg, *Christologie;* Baldwin; but also Montgomery, 383). At the same time, one may grant that the terms used to describe these troubles are theologically freighted. The crisis is an anticipatory embodiment of the last great battle, a historical embodiment of the first great battle between the forces of chaos and the forces of order. Porteous compares Ezek 38–39 and 1QM.

Thus after the seven plus sixty-two sevens "an anointed is to be cut off" (יכרת משיח). The description of him as *an* anointed cannot be argued to indicate that he must be the same משיח as the one in v 25 (against Young) or that he *must* be a different one (against Keil). Nouns in Daniel's visions are commonly anarthrous (e.g., a vision, a prophet, a most sacred place [v 24]; a word, an anointed, a leader, a square, a moat [v 25]; an anointed, a leader, a people [v 26]; a covenant, a wing, an abomination, a conclusion, a desolate one [v 27]). The effect is to contribute to that allusiveness appropriate to a vision, which cannot be resolved from within chap. 9 itself. Those who connect the seventieth week with the Antiochene crisis generally identify this "anointed" with the high priest Onias III, who seems to be the one referred to as "a covenant prince" in 11:22. On the accession of Antiochus in 175 B.C., Onias was displaced as high priest by his brother Jason. In 172 B.C. Jason in turn was displaced by Menelaus, brother of another of Onias's opponents; in 171 Menelaus had Onias killed (see 2 Macc 4). Onias's being "cut off" could be his displacement/disappearance, or his death (see BDB 504a). His losing city and sanctuary sounds like a reference to his displacement and withdrawal for safety to Daphne, near Antioch (2 Macc 4:33); but his actual death in 171 B.C. marks the beginning of the seven years of trouble.

Presumably the "leader to come" (נגיד הבא) is also a representative of the high-priestly line, one who follows Onias. The reference will then be to Onias's successor Jason (Bevan), who both corrupted and devastated—the two possible senses of ישחית—the people of Jerusalem (see 2 Macc 4–5). The hostility of Jason's action may well be indicated by the expression "to come" (הבא): the verb is used frequently of an aggressive "coming" in chap. 11 (e.g., v 10, with the term "flood" [שטף] as here; cf. NEB here). "His end" and "the end" are closely related.

27 The covenant prevailing for the body of the Jews for the final seven could refer to the covenant between God and Israel referred to in 9:4; 11:22, 28, 30, 32. The words then denote either the faithfulness of conservative Jews despite the pressure placed on them (cf. 1 Macc 1:62–63), or the faithfulness of God (cf. Lev 26:42 [Phillip]). The verse goes on, however, to describe aspects of the sacrilege of the Antiochene crisis, and this suggests that ברית in v 27a has negative connotations. Charles takes it as an Aramaism for an edict imposed by Antiochus. More likely it refers to the covenant between reformist Jews and Gentiles reported in 1 Macc 1:11. The multitude is presumably still the body of (faithful) Jews (see n. 9:27.b). If so, the idea of the clause is that the covenant made between the reformist Jews and the Greeks will last for seven years, to the hurt of the conservative Jews. 1 Macc 1:11 implicitly associates this covenant with the beginning of Antiochus's reign in 175 B.C., but it is hazardous to infer that the seventieth seven is the period that begins then, so that the events of the actual crisis belong to a further seven (against Lebram, *VT* 20 [1970] 513–15).

Halfway through this final seven the worship prescribed by the Torah will cease and be replaced by a repellent alternative (cf. 1 Macc 1:41–59). Sacrifice and offering covers on the one hand the bloody sacrifices involving the death of an animal, on the other the offering of grain, oil, and wine, and thus the total system of sacrifice and offering. To describe its replacement, Gabriel uses a variant on the term used in 8:13, the desolating rebellion (הפשע שמם). Here the expression is "a desolating abomination" (שקוצים משמם: see n. 27.f). שקץ replaces פשע, perhaps because its numerical value is 490 (Klein, "Daniel," 240), perhaps because of the association of שקץ and שמם in passages such as Jer 4; 7; 44; Ezek 5; 6; 7 (Ford, *Abomination,* 148). It is plural, if we accept MT, perhaps because it substitutes for the quasi-plural noun אלהים "God" (Lacocque). The desolating abomination will appear "on a wing" (כנף). NIV follows G and Vg in taking the "wing" to be the winglike top corner of the temple, the "pinnacle" of Matt 4:5. But the desolating sacrilege lay not on the temple pinnacle, but on the altar within the temple. Now the altar had "winglike" top corners, usually described as horns. Perhaps Gabriel speaks of wings rather than horns because "winged one" (בעל כנף, "lord of wing" or "winged one") is a title of Baal (Delcor; cf. JPS; see n. 27.e).

Devastation will continue to overwhelm desolate Jerusalem until what God has decreed is exhausted. Yet within the gloom are gleams of light. The calamity fulfills the prophecy of Isa 10:22–23: so it is not meaningless. And it is de-termined, not endless. (If שמם really means "desolater," not "desolate one" [see n. 27.h] or if the desolate one is actually Antiochus himself as his end comes, the gleam of light is an explicit beam of light.)

Explanation

1–2 We move on once more to the year in which the Babylonians lost control of Babylon. In previous chapters, beneath the surface many passages from Scripture have contributed to the shaping of those stories and visions which we have been invited to take as clues to understanding the history of the Babylonian, Persian, and Greek periods. But the stories and visions stood in their own right. Their scriptural allusions may often have remained unnoticed. They commended themselves to us on the basis of the experience and insight they embodied. Here, in contrast, insight emerges overtly from the study of Scripture. Babylon is now ruled by a king of Median birth, as Jeremiah had promised (51:28). The punishment that Jer 25:12–14 threatened has begun. The restoration of the exiles that Jer 29:10 associates with that same moment, and the restoration of Jerusalem that prophecies in Isaiah and Ezekiel promise, ought therefore to be imminent.

It is easy enough to imagine an exilic Daniel noting the passages in Jer 25/29 that spoke of a seventy-year exile and wondering about their fulfillment; Zechariah, after all, did so. It is also easy enough to imagine a second-century B.C. "Daniel" doing the same thing; Yahweh never acts without revealing his purpose to his servants, the prophets (Amos 3:7), and the existence of the more-or-less collected prophetic scriptures will have encouraged people to look there for some explanation even of the devastating experiences of the second century B.C. (Koch, *HZ* 193 [1961] 21). But the fact that God has spoken through the prophets does not mean that all the believer does is sit, newspaper in hand, awaiting the outcome. The appropriate response to prophecy is prayer.

3–19 There is a form of prayer that is appropriate to every day, the prayer Daniel prayed in chap. 6. There is a form of prayer that arises in extraordinary situations, the prayer Daniel prays here. Or perhaps both prayers are the same: Dan 9 may have been a way people prayed throughout the postexilic period. A particular prayer may then be prayed every day and with new significance in particular situations—especially when it comes to be newly juxtaposed with Scripture. There is an interplay between the words of Scripture and the words of prayer. Scripture stimulates prayer. Prayer constitutes the appropriate response to Scripture. Prayer naturally reflects Scripture. At the same time, it naturally reflects the traditional liturgical prayer of the believing community. The reality of the individual's experience of life and of God keeps the prayer of the ongoing community alive and real. The tradition of the community's prayer over the centuries gives the individual's prayer its means of expression and its context in the prayer of the whole community of faith. So Daniel prays, and perhaps says, "When you pray, say . . .

'Lord, you are our God. You have committed yourself to us. And you are my God, because in your sovereignty you have chosen to work through me, and through me to reveal your purpose to your people. You have proved your commitment to me, and I come to ask you to do so again in response to my prayer for your people.

'You revealed your name to us, but I hesitate to use it lest I do so wrongly, perhaps falling into overfamiliarity. For you are the great and awesome God, and I am going to have to acknowledge that we have not often treated you as such. Yet no sooner do I recall your greatness and awesomeness than I also find myself affirming your loving compassion. At Sinai and before, you committed yourself to us as your people, in the way that mighty powers like Assyria would commit themselves to the protection of lesser powers. But the great powers were always clear about what they would get out of the relationship. Your commitment to us was more unmotivated; and you have always kept that commitment. When we pray, as we do now, out of desolation and affliction, we know that such desolation and affliction does not stem from *your* failure to keep your commitment. You are the God who is by nature reliable and faithful, true to his word and constant in his protection. If you and we should find ourselves in court, you would win any case that the court considered. You are in the right. There is nothing on your side to cause a breakdown in the relationship between us and you. Part of the evidence of this is that you have always been concerned to do what was right for us, you wanted the best for us. It goes back to the exodus again, when you showed yourself concerned for the rights of a people afflicted by oppressors, and you have been like that in your relationship with us and in your acts on our behalf ever since. In other words, you have been a compassionate God, caring about us with the deep feeling of love that we associate with family life. You make allowances for us, like a king being merciful to his servants when they fail him.

'We know that the basis of our relationship with you is not what we do for you; it is what you have done for us. Yet we know we are called to respond to what you have done for us. You have issued to us commands to be obeyed, authoritative declarations regarding the deeds you approve, directions regarding how we are to live our lives. We have heard all these through your prophets who spoke to us as your representatives, made your voice audible, and we have read the warnings of Moses about the consequences of ignoring them. Although the covenant did not stem from our initiative, we know that it demands our obedience, and that disobedience imperils it.

'Your word came directly to those who have exercised leadership among us over the generations, kings and people who have authority in the community. But it relates to the whole people for whom I am concerned to pray and whom I long to commend to you on the basis of your regarding me with your favor, that people of Judea which has a certain self-awareness as a political entity within the empire that governs it, but which more importantly is the remnant of the people of Israel that you have preserved and to which your covenant commitment still applies. It relates to that city, Jerusalem, which is the focus of Judea politically and religiously—because it is the city that you made your own. It relates to that sanctuary where you are worshiped.

'So your word came to us; and you expected from us a response that was at least as much moral as emotional. You expected us to heed your words and live by them. Your design was that we would then be in the right with you, as you are with us, in a position to cast ourselves on you in need because our relationship with you was right. Not that we would never fail—but when we did, it was our task to turn from wrongdoing, reflecting wisely on your faithfulness in the past and giving you that respect and homage which prepares the way for renewed prayer. What has actually happened is that leaders and people, past and present, have not listened to you or lived by your teachings or turned from our wrongdoings or paid heed to your faithfulness or sought your favor. We are not in the right with you. We have failed, willfully, to live in accordance with your expectations. We have avoided the path you laid before us. We have contravened the enactments of the covenant. We have put ourselves in the wrong in relation to you. We have rebelled against your authority. We have turned our backs on your commands. We have been unfaithful to our relationship with you.

'As the people of God, we accept responsibility for our actions and neglects. We are not fatalistic. Our history has not been out of our control, imposed on us by you. Your dealings with us are not predetermined to unfold in a sequence uninfluenced by human acts. We recognize them as a response to our acts. We know that our own acts affect history as it subsequently unfolds. It is because we are in the wrong in relation to you that we find ourselves overcome by unimagined calamity. City and sanctuary have become wastes: as buildings devastated and ruined, as habitations emptied because their people are banished. We feel the contumely and contempt of people whose wrongdoing has been exposed. It is as if we have been overwhelmed by a curse—the solemn curse written into the covenant as a legal document, designed to protect the relationship between you and us, but inevitably bringing harm to us as the price of being able to be protective in other circumstances. You yourself saw to it that the curse fell. It was your premeditated, carefully considered act. Calculated, but not cold: it expressed the burning fury that accompanies your warm compassion and commitment, both aspects of your being a real person.

'It is because this is the situation of my people that I come to you determined to gain your attention for myself and my prayers, casting myself on your grace, that instinct of yours to show favor when none is deserved. By that grace I have sought to stand firm in my commitment to you, but I also stand firm in my commitment to my people in their waywardness and their affliction, and I dare to ask you to look on them in mercy because of your love for me, because you are my God. I began my confession by acknowledging that you are the awesome yet loving God of Israel. But the goal of my confession was to acknowledge that we are in the wrong in relation to you. You are in the right. I start there; but on the basis of starting there, I believe I can plead with you for mercy upon these who have justly experienced disaster from your hand. I turn aside from concern with food or my appearance: I come in an inner gloominess which expresses itself in a gloominess of appearance. I long for you to reveal and to implement your purpose for your people. You seem to be ignoring our plight and our prayer, as you have the right to do. Lord, listen. You seem to be holding our sin against us, as you have the right to do. Lord, pardon, let your anger dissipate itself somewhere else. You seem to be refusing to give us that blessing you promised through Aaron, as you have the right to do. Lord, look on us with the bright smile of your love. You seem to be intent on doing nothing in our lives. Lord, act. That is what you have done in the past. That is what we need now. That is what will bring you honor.' "

If this is indeed how people prayed in those days, we can see how they came through the storms and stresses of that terrible time (Porteous).

20–23 It is to be expected that prayers meet with answers, and so it is with Daniel. The answer indicates that communication between earth and heaven goes on, even though the sacrificial system may be interrupted. The content of the answer will correspond to the content of the lament, as the prayer has offered the response to God's prophetic word that makes the fulfillment of that word possible. The promise of fulfillment issues when Daniel turns to God, yet it issues before he actually prays his lament, so the story affirms not only the importance of prayer and the place it plays in the outworking of God's purpose (it is in response to prayer that God acts) but also the importance of God's sovereignty (prayer is a means of God's own good will being put into effect). One person's prayer brings about the restoration of the people of God; but it is a matter of releasing that restoration which God already purposed. The dynamics of the interrelationship of prayer and divine act here may be compared with those in Gen 18:17–33.

24–27 Jeremiah had spoken of seventy-years' desolation for Jerusalem, but it was actually to last centuries longer than that. God is free to exact whatever chastisement he chooses. But the message's good news is that it is not chastisement without end. The number 490 is not an arithmetical calculation to be pressed to yield chronological information. It is a figure that puts together two symbolic figures, the seventy years (a lifetime) of Jer 25:11/29:10 and the sevenfold chastisement of Lev 26:28. The result is a doubly symbolic figure extending from the beginning of chastisement in the exile to whenever it is seen as ending. The description of the end in vv 24–27 is allusive. But fortunately we are in a position to move from the known to the unknown. The climax to which chap. 8 looks lies in the crisis in the second century B.C., when God delivered his people and his sanctuary from the combined threat of Antiochus Epiphanes and reformist Judaism. The same crisis is the focus of chaps. 10–12. The natural inference would be that chap. 9 has in mind the same events, and the details of vv 24–27 support that inference.

The period between the two desolations of Jerusalem may naturally be divided into the period of exile itself, which began with a promise of restoration and ended with its fulfillment, and the long postexilic period from the late sixth to early second centuries B.C., the period of Jerusalem rebuilt (v 25). The Antiochene crisis is heralded by the death of one high priest and the wickedness of another (v 26). It brings a period of unholy alliance, the disruption of temple worship, its replacement by an apostate alternative, and a devastation that will continue to overwhelm desolate Jerusalem until what God has decreed is exhausted (v 27). Yet this gloomy prospect is set in the context of a promise that by the end of the seventy sevens God will have purged people and city of evil—Greek evil and Jewish evil alike, perhaps—and vindicated the sanctuary and the prophecy of Jeremiah from which we started (v 24). The fulfillment of God's promise is described in 1 Macc 4:42–61; what Gabriel pictures as a divine work, 1 Maccabees relates as an achievement involving human initiative and activity.

To speak of God determining history over 490 years at first seems to suggest a "radically deistic" view of God's activity; time is now autonomous and unalterable, and even God has to wait upon it (DeVries, *Achievements,* 342). Yet we must recall that such a way of speaking belongs at the end of the 490 years; only retrospectively is God's "control" affirmed. The period itself unfolded in the ordinary way that history does. If Gabriel's quasi-prophecy were actual prophecy, a deistic view might be implied; but it is not. Again, the quasi-prophecy says nothing of God's being positively involved in the historical events of the exilic and postexilic periods, but this is because its real focus lies on the events of the 160s rather than because God was actually believed to be absent.

In Jewish and Christian tradition, Gabriel's promise has been applied to rather later events: the birth of the messiah, Jesus' death and resurrection, the fall of Jerusalem, various subsequent historical events, and the still-future manifesting of the messiah. Exegetically such views are mistaken. The detail of vv 24–27 fits the second-century B.C. crisis and agrees with allusions to this crisis elsewhere in Daniel. The verses do not indicate that they are looking centuries or millennia beyond the period to which chaps. 8 and 10–12 refer. They do not suggest that the cleansing and renewal of which v 24 speaks is the cleansing and renewal of the world: it is the cleansing and renewal of Jerusalem. The passage refers to the Antiochene crisis. Yet its allusiveness justifies reapplication of the passage, as is the case with previous chapters, in the following sense. It does not refer specifically to concrete persons and events in the way of historical narrative such as 1 Maccabees, but refers in terms of symbols to what those persons and events embodied, symbols such as sin, justice, an anointed prince, a flood, an abomination. Concrete events and persons are understood in the light of such symbols, but the symbols transcend them. They are not limited in their reference to these particular concrete realities. They have other embodiments. What these other embodiments are is a matter of theological, not exegetical, judgment—a matter of faith, not of science. But if I am justified in believing that Jesus is God's anointed, and that his birth, ministry, death, resurrection, and appearing are God's ultimate means of revealing himself and achieving his purpose in the world, they are also his means of ultimately achieving what the symbols in vv 24–27 speak of. It is this point that is made in traditional categories by speaking of a typological relationship between the events and people of the Antiochene crisis and deliverance and those of the Christ event and the End we still await.

There is another aspect to the significance of Gabriel's allusiveness. It accompanies an inclination to speak in the words of Scripture reapplied. Daniel is doing with Isaiah what subsequent exegetes do with Daniel. This, too, reflects the fact that the author speaks "with faith rather than knowledge" (Heaton). The period of deepest oppression did last about 3½ years, but that is not the point. This is not prognostication or prediction. It is promise.

It is promise given from the midst of a life and death crisis—life and death for human beings and for Jewish faith. It contains no exhortation to action. It is not concerned to urge people to obedience or resistance, but to offer them hope. Scripture is often content to do that.

A Celestial Figure Reveals to Daniel What Will Happen to His People at the End of the Era (10:1–12:13)

Bibliography

Abel, F.-M. "Antiochus Épiphane." *RB* 50 (1941) 231–41. **Alfrink, B. J.** "L'idée de résurrection d'après Dan xii, 1–2." *Bib* 40 (1959) 355–71. Repr. in Alfrink, *Studia biblica et orientalia.* Rome: 1959. **Allen, L. C.** "Isaiah liii.11 and Its Echoes." *Vox Evangelica* 1 (1962) 24–28. **[Anon.]** *A New Interpretation of Daniel xi.* Liverpool: Barker, [1866]. **Armerding, C.** "Russia and the King of the North." *BSac* 120 (1963) 50–55. ———. "Dan 12, 1–3: Asleep in the Dust." *BSac* 121 (1964) 153–58. **Bampfylde, G.** "The Prince of the Host in the Book of Daniel and the Dead Sea Scrolls." *JSJ* 14 (1983) 129–34. **Barrett, D. S.** "Patterns of Jewish Submission in the Hellenistic-Roman World." *Prudentia* 5 (1973) 99–115. **Barth, K.** *Dogmatik.* Chap. 51. **Bauckham, R. J.** "The Delay of the Parousia." *TynB* 31 (1980) 3–36. **Beckwith, R. T.** "The Earliest Enoch Literature and Its Calendar." *RevQ* 10 (1979–81) 365–403. **Bertholet, A.** "Die Schutzengel Persiens." *OrSt* 34–40. **Bevan, E. R.** *The House of Seleucus.* 2 vols. London: Arnold, 1902. **Birkeland, H.** "The Belief in the Resurrection of the Dead in the Old Testament." *ST* 3 (1949–50) 60–78. **Bonora, A.** "Il linguaggio di risurrezione in *Dan.* 12,1–3." *RivB* 30 (1982) 111–25. **Botterweck, G. J.** "Marginalien zum atl. Auferstehungsglauben." *Wiener Zeitschrift für die Kunde des Morgenlandes* 54 (FS H. Junker, 1957) 1–8. **Brightman, T.** *A Most Comfortable Exposition of the Last and Most Difficult Part of the Prophecie of Daniel.* Tr. anon from Latin (first published in Basel, 1614) 1635. = Brightman, *Workes.* London: Samuel Cartwright, 1644. 891–970. **Bringmann, K.** *Hellenistische Reform und Religionsverfolgung in Judäa.* Göttingen: Vandenhoeck, 1983. **Bunge, J. G.** "Der 'Gott der Festungen' und der 'Liebling der Frauen.' " *JSJ* 4 (1973) 169–82. ———. " 'Theos Epiphanes.' " *Historia* 23 (1974) 57–85. ———. "Die sogenannte Religionsverfolgung Antiochus IV. Epiphanes und die griechischen Städte." *JSJ* 10 (1979) 155–65. **Campbell, J.** *An Exposition of Daniel xii. 5, 6, 7.* Glasgow: privately published, 1817. **Carroll, R. P.** *When Prophecy Failed.* London: SCM, 1979. ———. "Prophecy and Dissonance." *ZAW* 92 (1980) 108–19. **Cavallin, H. C. C.** *Life after Death.* Part 1. ConB NT Series 7:1 (1974). ———. "De visa lärarnas död och uppståndelse." *SEA* 37–38 (1972–73) 47–61. ———. "Leben nach dem Tode im Spätjudentum." *ANRW* ii 19, 1 (1979) 240–345. **Clifford, R. J.** "History and Myth in Daniel 10–12." *BASOR* 220 (1975) 23–26. **Collins, J. J.** *CBQ* 36 (1974) 21–43. Repr. in *Visionaries*, ed. P. D. Hanson, 61–84. **Conrad, D.** "On זְרוֹעַ = 'Forces, Troops, Army' in Biblical Hebrew." *Tel Aviv* 3 (1976) 111–19. **Davies, P. R.** *JJS* 28 (1977) 127–40. **Day, J.** "*Da'at* 'Humiliation.' " *VT* 30 (1980) 97–103. **Del Medico, H. E.** "L'identification des Kittim avec les Romains." *VT* 10 (1960) 448–453. **Dubarle, A.-M.** "Belief in Immortality in the Old Testament and Judaism." (tr. R. Ockenden). *Concilium* 10, 6 (1970) 34–45. **Emerton, J. A.** "A Consideration of Some Alleged Meanings of ידע in Hebrew." *JSS* 15 (1970) 145–80. **Erling, B.** "Ezekiel 38–39 and the Origins of Jewish Apocalyptic." In *Ex orbe religionum*, FS G. Widengren, Leiden: Brill, 1972. 1:104–14. **Festinger, L.,** et al. *When Prophecy Fails.* Minneapolis: U Minnesota, 1956. Repr. New York: Harper, 1964. **Fischer, T.** *Seleukiden und Makkabäer.* Bochum: Brockmeyer, 1980. **Gese, H.** "Der Tod im Alten Testament." In Gese, *Zur biblischen Theologie.* Munich: Kaiser, 1977. 31–54. = Gese, *Essays on Biblical Theology.* Tr. K. Crim. Minneapolis: Augsburg,

1981. 34–59. ———. "Das Geschichtsbild des Danielsbuches und Ägypten." In *Fontes atque pontes,* FS H. Brunner, ed. M. Görg. Wiesbaden: Harrassowitz, 1983. 139–54. **Gibbs, G. L.** *Daniel's Last Vision.* London: Hatchard, 1883. **Ginsberg, H. L.** "The Oldest Interpretation of the Suffering Servant." *VT* 3 (1953) 400–404. **Granot, M.** "ותעמד לגרלך לקץ הימין . . ." *BetM* 21, 2 (1975–76) 217–26, 317. **Greenspoon, L. J.** "The Origin of the Idea of Resurrection." In *Traditions in Transformation,* FS F. M. Cross, ed. B. Halpern and J. D. Levenson. Winona Lake: Eisenbrauns, 1981. 247–321. **Grelot, P.** "La promise de la résurrection et de la vie éternelle, Dn 12 1–3." *Assemblées du Seigneur* 64 (1969) 36–40. = Grelot, *De la mort à la vie éternelle.* LD 67 (1971) 181–86. **Griffiths, J. G.** "Apocalyptic in the Hellenistic Era." In *Apocalypticism,* ed. D. Hellholm, 273–93. **Hanhart, R.** "Die Übersetzungstechnik der Septuaginta als Interpretation (Daniel 11, 29 und die Aegyptenzüge des Antiochus Epiphanes)." In *Mélanges Dominique Barthélemy,* ed. P. Casetti et al. OBO 38. Freiburg/Göttingen: Editions Universitaires/Vandenhoeck, 1981. 136–57. **Hasel, G. F.** "Resurrection in the Theology of Old Testament Apocalyptic." *ZAW* 92 (1980) 267–84. **Hasslberger B.** *Hoffnung in der Bedrängnis: Eine formkritische Untersuchung zu Daniel 8 und 10–12.* St Ottilien: Eos, 1977. 111–374. **Heard, W. J.** "The Maccabean Martyrs' Contribution to Holy War." *EvQ* 58 (1986) 291–318. **Herrmann, W.** "Das Buch des Lebens." *Das Altertum* 20 (1974) 3–10. **Hunt, B.** "A Short Note on Daniel 12:11–12." *Scripture* 9 (1957) 84–85. **Itō, G.** "Old Persian a p^a d^a a n^a." *Orient* 8 (1972) 46–51. **Jaubert, A.** "Fiches de calendrier." In *Qumrân,* ed. M. Delcor. BETL 46 (1978) 305–11. **Jones, B. W.** "Antiochus Epiphanes and the Persecution of the Jews." In *Scripture in Context,* ed. C. D. Evans et al. PTMS 34 (1980). 263–90. **Kaiser, O.,** and **Lohse, E.** *Tod und Leben.* Stuttgart: Kohlhammer, 1977. = *Death and Life.* Tr. J. Steely. Nashville: Abingdon, 1981. **Keil, V.** "Onias III." *ZAW* 97 (1985) 221–33. **Kellermann, U.** "Überwindung des Todesgeschicks in der alttestamentlichen Frömmigkeit." *ZTK* 73 (1976) 259–82. **Kleinknecht, K. T.** Der leidende Gerechtfertigte. Diss., Tübingen, 1981. 75–78. = WUNT 13 (1984). **Kooij, A. van der.** "A Case of Reinterpretation in the Old Greek of Daniel 11." In *Tradition and Re-interpretation in Jewish and Early Christian Literature,* FS J. C. H. Lebram, ed. J. W. van Henten et al. SPB 36 (1986) 72–80. **Kosmala, H.** *"Maśkîl." JANESCU* 5 (1973) 235–41. = Kosmala, *Studies,* 1:149–55. **Kossen, H. B.** "De oorsprong van de Voorstelling der opstanding uit de doden in Dan. 12:2." *NedTT* 10 (1955–56) 296–301. **Lindenberger, J. M.** "Daniel 12:1–4." *Int* 39 (1985) 181–86. **Luther, M.** *Vorrede,* 30–124. **McHardy, W. D.** "The Peshitta Text of Daniel xi. 4." *JTS* 49 (1948) 56–57. **Martin-Achard, R.** *De la mort à la résurrection d'après l'Ancien Testament.* Neuchatel: Delachaux, 1956. = *From Death to Life.* Tr. J. P. Smith. Edinburgh: Oliver and Boyd, 1960. ———. "L'espérance des croyants d'Israël face à la mort selon Esäie 65, 16c–25 et selon Daniel 12, 1–4." *RHPR* 59 (1979) 439–51. = Martin-Achard, *Permanence de l'Ancien Testament.* Geneva: Revue de Théologie et de Philosophie, 1984. 285–97. ———. "Trois remarques sur la résurrection des morts dans l'Ancien Testament." In *Mélanges bibliques et orientaux,* FS H. Cazelles, ed. A Caquot and M. Delcor. AOAT 212 (1981) 301–17. = *Permanence* [see above], 170–84. **Moore, M. S.** "Resurrection and Immortality: Two Motifs Navigating Confluent Streams in the Old Testament (Dan 12,1–4)." *TZ* 39 (1983) 17–34. **Morgenstern, J.** "The King-God among the Western Semites and the Meaning of Epiphanes." *VT* 10 (1960) 138–97. **Myers, T.** *A Translation of the Prophecies of Daniel.* York: Coultas, 1854. **Nickelsburg, G. W. E.** *Resurrection, Immortality, and Eternal Life in Intertestamental Judaism.* HTS 26 (1972). **Nikolainen, A. T.** *Der Auferstehungsglaube in der Bibel und ihrer Umwelt.* 2 vols. Helsinki: Finnish Academy, 1944–46. **Nötscher, F.** *Altorientalischer und alttestamentlicher Auferstehungsglauben.* Würzburg: Becker, 1926; new ed., Darmstadt: Wissenschaftliche, 1970. **Owen, J.** "The Labouring Saint's Dismission to Rest." 1651. = *The Works of John Owen.* Repr. London: Banner of Truth, 1965. 8:341–63. **Paul, S.** "Heavenly Tablets and the Book of Life." *JANESCU* 5 (1973) 345–53. **Pfeiffer, R. H.** "Wisdom and Vision in the Old Testament." *ZAW* 52 (1934) 93–101. **Preuss, H. D.** " 'Auferstehung' in Texten alttestamentlicher Apokalyptik." In *"Linguistische" Theologie,* ed. U. Gerber and E. Güttgemanns. Forum theologicae linguisticae 3. Bonn: Linguistica Biblica, 1972. 101–33. **Rigsby, K. J.** "Zeus Olympius." *Transactions of the American Philological Association* 110 (1980) 233–38. **Rost, L.** "Alttestamentliche Wurzeln der ersten Auferstehung." In *In memoriam Ernst Lohmeyer,* ed. W. Schmauch. Stuttgart: Evangelische, 1951. 67–72. = Rost, *Studien zum Alten Testament.* BWANT 101 (1974) 61–65. **Rowley, H. H.** "The 'Prince of the Covenant' in Daniel xi. 22." *ExpT* 55 (1943–44) 24–27. **Sawyer, J. F. A.** "Hebrew Words for the Resurrection of the Dead." *VT* 23 (1973) 218–34. **Schäfer, P.** "The Hellenistic and Maccabaean Periods" (tr. F. C. Prussner). In *Israelite and Judaean History,* ed. J. H. Hayes and J. M. Miller. OTL, 1977. 539–604. **Schedl, C.** "Mystische Arithmetik oder geschichtliche Zahlen?" *BZ* 8 (1964) 101–5. **Schlatter, A.** "Die B^{e}ne pariṣim bei Daniel: 11, 14." *ZAW* 14 (1894) 145–51. **Schubert, K.** "Die Entwicklung der Auferstehungslehre von der nachexilischen bis zur frührabbinischen Zeit." *BZ* 6 (1962) 177–214. **Shea, W. H.** "Wrestling with the Prince of Persia." *AUSS* 21 (1983) 225–50. **Sparkes, S.** *A Historical Commentary on the Eleventh Chapter of Daniel.* Binghampton, NY: Adams and Lawyer, 1858. **Spronk, B.** *Beatific Afterlife in Ancient Israel and the Ancient Near East.* AOAT 219 (1986). **Stemberger, G.** "Das Problem der Auferstehung im Alten Testament." *Kairos* 14 (1972) 273–90. **Sutcliffe, E. F.** *The Old Testament and the Future Life.* London: Burns Oates, 1946. **Swain, J. W.** "Antiochus Epiphanes and Egypt." *ClassPh* 39 (1944) 73–94. **Szold, B.** "The Eleventh Chapter of the Book of Daniel." In *Semitic Studies,* A. Kohut Memorial, ed. G. A. Kohut. Berlin: Calvary, 1897. 573–600. **Täubler, E.** "Jerusalem 201 to 199 B.C.E.: On the History of a Messianic Movement." *JQR* 37 (1946–47) 1–30, 125–37, 249–63. **Thomas, D. W.** "Note on הדעת in Daniel xii.4." *JTS* 6 (1955) 226. **Thomson, H. C.** "Old Testament Ideas on Life after Death." *TGUOS* 22 (1967–68) 46–55. **Toll, C.** "Die Wurzel prṣ im Hebräischen." *OrSuec* 21 (1972) 73–86. **Torrey, C. C.** " 'Yāwān' and 'Hellas' as Designations of the Seleucid Empire." *JAOS* 25 (1904) 302–11. **Tsafrir, Y.** "The Location of the Seleucid Akra in Jerusalem." *RB* 82 (1975) 501–21. **Wacholder, B. Z.** "The Beginning of the Seleucid Era and the Chronology of the Diadochoi." In *Nourished with Peace,* S. Sandmel Memorial, ed. F. E. Greenspahn et al. Chico, CA: Scholars, 1984. 183–220. **Walbank, F. W.,** et al., ed. *CAH* vii, 1. 2nd ed., 1984. **Williams, S. K.** *Jesus' Death as Saving Event.* Missoula, MT: Scholars, 1975. **Wilson, R. D.** "The Title 'King of Persia' in the Scriptures." *PTR* 15 (1917) 90–145. **Yarbro Collins, A.** "The Political Perspective of the Revelation to John." *JBL* 96 (1977) 241–56.

Translation

10:1 *In the third*[a] *year of Cyrus* [b]*the king of Persia,*[b] *a message was revealed*[c]
to Daniel (who had been named Belteshazzar). The message was reliable and con-
cerned a great war.[d] *He heeded*[e] *the message and gave heed to the vision.*[f]
2 *"During that time I, Daniel, was mourning for* [a]*a period of three weeks.*[a] 3 *I*
ate no rich food, no meat or wine passed my lips, and I did not anoint myself at
all,[a] *until the period of three weeks was completed.* 4 *Then on the twenty-fourth*
day of the first month, when I was by the bank of the Great River, the Tigris,[a] 5 *I*
looked expectantly[a] *and there before me was a man dressed in linen, his waist*
belted with pure[b] *gold,* 6 *his body like topaz,*[a] *his face with the brightness of lightning,*
his eyes like flaming torches, his arms and feet with the gleam of polished brass,
the sound of his words like the sound of thundering.[b] 7 [a]*Now I, Daniel, alone saw*
this sight.[b] *The men who were with me did not see the sight;*[b] *nevertheless, such*
terror came over them that they fled into[c] *hiding.* 8 *So I myself remained alone. I*
looked at this great sight, and no strength remained in me; my vigor[a] *dissolved*

into confusion [b]*and I had no strength left.*[b] 9 [a]*Then I heard the sound of his words.*[a] *When*[b] *I heard the sound of his words,* [c]*I was falling in a trance,*[c] [d]*with my face*[d] *to the ground.* 10 *Then*[a] *a hand touched*[b] *me and shook me*[c] *onto* [d]*my hands and knees.*[d] 11 *He said to me, 'Daniel, a man held in high regard, attend to the words which I am about to speak to you, and stand up in your place, because I have now been sent to you.' As he told me this, I stood up, trembling.* 12 *Then he said to me, 'Do not be afraid, Daniel, because from the first day you set your mind to understand by humbling yourself before your God, your words were heard—I have come because of your words.* 13 *The leader of the kingdom of Persia was opposing me for twenty-one days, but then*[a] *Michael, one of the supreme leaders, came to help me, when* [b]*I was left alone*[b] *there with* [c]*the kings of*[c] *Persia.* 14 *So I have come to explain to you what will happen*[a] *to your people at the end of the era,*[b] *because* [c]*there is yet a vision concerning that era.'*[c]

15 *"While he spoke these words to me, I bowed my face*[a] *to the ground and kept silence.* 16 *Then*[a] [b]*someone of human form*[b] *touched my lips, and I opened my mouth and spoke. I said to the one who stood before me: 'My lord, at this sight turmoil*[c] *has convulsed me, I have no strength left.* 17 *And how can my lord's mere* [a]*servant speak with such as*[a] *my lord? Now,*[b] *I have no strength left in me. There is no breath in me anymore.'* 18 *Again one of human appearance touched me and encouraged me,* 19 *saying 'Do not be afraid, man held in high regard. All will be well with you.*[a] *Take courage, take courage.'*[b] *When*[c] *he spoke to me, I took courage and said 'My lord may speak, for you have encouraged me.'* 20 [a]*Then he said, 'Have you realized*[b] *why I have come to you? But now,*[c] *I must return to fight with the leader of Persia, though when I go,*[d] *then*[e] *the leader of Greece will come.* 21 *Nevertheless, I will tell you what is inscribed in a reliable book.*[a] *No one supports me against these, except Michael, your leader.* 11:1 *And* [a]*in the first year of Darius the Mede,*[a] *I myself took my stand*[b] *to support and strengthen him.* 2 *But now,*[a] *I will tell you a reliable message.*

" '[b]*Three further kings will arise in Persia, and the fourth will be far wealthier than anyone.*[c] *But by the power he obtains by means of his wealth, he will stir up*[d] [e]*everyone in relation to the Greek empire.*[e] 3 *Then a warrior-king will appear who will rule* [a]*a great realm*[a] *and act as he pleases.*[b] 4 *But as soon as*[a] *he arises, his empire will break up and divide*[b] *toward the four winds of the heavens.* [c]*It will not belong to his surviving family nor be a realm such as he ruled,*[c] *because his empire will be uprooted and will belong to others besides these.*

5 *" 'The southern king will then be powerful,* [a]*but one of his officers will himself*[a] *be more powerful than he, and will rule a greater realm than his.*[b] 6 *Then after some years an alliance will be made*[a] *and the daughter of the southern king will go to*[b] *the northern king to establish an agreement. But she will not be able to hold onto* [c]*her power,*[c] *nor will his power*[d] *last out; she will be given up,*[e] *as will those who escorted her*[f] *and the one who fathered her*[g] *and* [h]*sustained her.*[h] *In time*[i] 7 *one of*[a] *the shoots from her roots will arise*[b] *in his place. He will attack the army*[c] *and enter the stronghold of the northern king. He will deal with them as their conqueror;*[d] 8 *their gods with their molten images and their precious silver and gold ware he will also take off to Egypt. Although he*[a] *will then keep away from the northern*[b] *king for some years,* 9 *he will then invade the southern king's empire, but will return to his own country.* 10 *His sons*[a] *will commit themselves to war. They will gather a massive horde which* [b]*will advance and advance and*

sweep through like a flood.[b] Then it will again battle on as far as his stronghold;[c]
11 but the southern king will be provoked to come out to fight with them—with the
northern king.[a] He[b] will raise a large horde, but the horde will be given into his
power. 12 When the horde is carried off,[a] his[b] mind will be elated[c] and he[b] will
put down tens of thousands,[d] but he will not be victorious. 13 The northern king
will return[a] and raise a larger horde than the first. Thus [b]after a period of years[b]
he will advance and advance[c] with a large force and much equipment. 14 During
those times many will rise up against the southern king, but when wild men among[a]
your people assert themselves, in fulfillment of[b] a vision, they will stumble. 15 Then[a]
the northern king will advance, throw up siegeworks,[b] and capture a fortified
city.[c] The southern forces will not be able to withstand. Even their picked troops[d]
[e]will be powerless[e] to withstand. 16 His attacker will thus[a] be able to act as he
pleases and no one will be able to withstand him, and he will take his stand in the
fairest land,[b] with destruction[c] in his power. 17 He will determine[a] to [b]come into
control of his whole empire[b] and will make an agreement[c] with him and give him
a wife[d] in order to destroy it.[e] But it[f] will not succeed; it[f] will not come about for
him. 18 So he will turn[a] his attention to the sea lands[b] and capture many. [c]But a
commander will put an end to his challenge for him,[c] [d]so that he will not be able
to return[d] his challenge to him. 19 So he will turn[a] his attention to the strongholds
in his own land. Be he will stumble and fall, and disappear.

20 " 'There will arise in his place one who will send round an oppressor[a] of[b]
imperial splendor. But in a few days he will break, though not in the heat of
battle.[c]

21 " 'There will arise in his place a despised[a] man who has not been given
royal honor; he will advance with ease and gain power over the empire by means
of empty words. 22 Overwhelming forces[a] will be overwhelmed before him and [b]broken,
and so too a covenant prince.[b] 23 Thus by means of[a] alliances being made with
him he will act deceitfully. He will [b]advance to power[b] with a small group; 24 with
ease[a] with the powerful ones of a province[b] he will go on to act as his fathers and
grandfathers did not. Spoil, booty, and wealth he will scatter among them. He
will also devise plans against fortresses, until a certain time.

25 " 'He will assert[a] his strength and act with determination against[b] the southern
king with a large force, but the southern king will commit himself to war with an
exceedingly large and powerful force, though he will not be able to stand firm,
because plans will be devised against him: 26 people who eat his provisions[a] will
break him. His force will pour away,[b] and many will fall slain. 27 The two kings
themselves, their minds set on trouble, will sit at a common table and speak lies,
but to no avail, because an end will yet await the set time. 28 Then he[a] will return
to his country with great wealth. [b]He will act with determination against a holy
covenant,[b] and then return to his own country.

29 " 'At the set time he will again invade the south, but it will not be like the
first and the second occasion.[a] 30 Ships from the west[a] will attack him, and he will
quail and return; [b]he will take harsh action[b] against a holy covenant and return.[c]
He will pay heed to such as have abandoned a holy covenant, 31 and forces of his
will take their stand and desecrate the sanctuary (the stronghold[a]). They will remove
the daily offering and set up the desolating abomination.[b] 32 Such as have acted
wickedly in relation to a covenant[a] he will turn into apostates[b] by means of empty
words, but a people that acknowledges[c] its God will offer firm resistance.[d] 33 Discerning

ones[a] *within a people will enlighten the multitude,*[b] *though they will stumble*[c] *by*
sword and by fire, [d]*by captivity and by becoming prey, for some time.* 34 *When they*
stumble, they will receive a little help.[a] *But many will join them with empty words,*[b]
35 *and some of the discerning will stumble, to refine, to purify, and to cleanse them,*[a]
[b]*until the time of the end—for it*[b] *will still await*[c] *the set moment.*
36 *" 'The king will act as he pleases and exalt himself and magnify himself over*
any god;[a] *concerning a God of gods*[a] *he will utter awesome statements. And he*
will succeed, until wrath is complete,[b] [c]*for what is determined shall be done.*[c] 37 *Thus*
he will pay no heed to the god of his fathers,[a] *nor to the one women love,*[b] [c]*nor to*
any god[c] *will he pay heed, but will magnify himself over everything.* 38 *In his*
place[a] *he will honor a stronghold god,*[b] [c]*honor a god*[b] *his fathers did not acknowledge,*
with gold and silver, with precious stones and rich gifts. 39 *So he will deal with*[a] *a*
most secure stronghold[b] *by the aid of*[c] *an alien god: those he regards*[d] *he will*
endow with great honor and make them rule over the multitude, and will divide
up[e] *land as payment.*
40 *" 'At the time of the end the southern king will engage in a struggle with*
him. The northern king will storm against him with chariots, cavalry, and many
ships. He will invade other countries, sweep through like a flood,[a] 41 *and invade*
the fairest land. Many of them[a] *will stumble, but while these*[b] *will escape from his*
power, Edom, Moab, and the leaders[c] *of the Ammonites,* 42 *when he lays his hand*
on[a] *other countries,*[b] *Egypt will not go free.* 43 *He will gain control of the gold*
and silver treasures and of all the riches of Egypt, and the Libyans and Sudanese
will fall at his heels.[a] 44 *Then reports from the east and north will alarm him and*
he will set off in great fury to devastate and annihilate[a] *many.* 45 *He will pitch his*
royal headquarters[a] *between the Sea and*[b] *the fairest holy hill. But he will come to*
his end, with no one to help him.

12:1 *At that time there will arise*
Michael the supreme leader,[a]
Michael who stands by[b] *those who belong to your people.*[c]
There will be a time of trouble
such as has not occurred[d]
since they became a nation[e] *until that time.*
But at that time your people will escape,
everyone who can be found written in the Book.
2 *Thus many of those who sleep*[a]
in a land of earth[b] *will wake up,*
[c]*some to lasting*[d] *life,*
others to utter shame,[e] *to lasting*[d] *abhorrence.*
3 *The discerning will shine as bright as the sky,*
those who set the multitude right[a]
will shine like the stars to all eternity.

4 *You, Daniel, are to close up these words and seal the book until the time of the*
end. Many will hurry to and fro,[a] *and suffering*[b] *will increase.'*
5 *"Then I, Daniel, looked, and there before me two other figures were standing,*
one on the river[a] *bank on this side, one on the river*[a] *bank on the other side.*
6 *The man dressed in linen who was* [a]*further upstream*[a] *was asked,*[b] *'How long is*
it to the end[c] *of these awesome events?'* 7 *I listened to the man dressed in linen*
who was further upstream: he raised his right hand and his left to the sky and

swore by the One who lives for ever that it would be for a set period,[a] *two set periods,*[a] *and a half, and that when the shattering*[b] *of the power of the holy people is ended,*[c] *all these things will come to an end.* 8*I listened, but could not understand, and said, 'Sir, what will be the last stage*[a] *of these events?'* 9*He said, 'Go your way, Daniel, because these words will be closed up, sealed until the time of the end.* 10*Many will purify themselves, cleanse themselves, and refine themselves,*[a] *but the wicked will act wickedly; none of the wicked will give heed,*[b] *though the discerning will give heed.*[b] 11*From the time the daily offering is taken away and the desolating abomination is set up will be 1290 days.* 12*Happy the one who waits and reaches the 1335 days.* 13*But you may go your way*[a] *and rest. You will rise*[b] *to your destiny on the final day.' "*

Notes

10:1.a. OG "first" may assimilate to 1:21 or may be an inner Gk corruption (so Pace, 225–227).

1.b-b. In secular usage, this title belongs to the Greek period, but in Ezra it is a regular title for the Persian kings (see Wilson, *PTR* 15 [1917] 90–145).

1.c. נגלה could mean "revealed itself" (cf., e.g., 1 Sam 3:21); but here a reverential pass may be more likely.

1.d. צבא most often means "army"; cf. 8:10–12, though there the phrase צבא השמים "heavenly army" is more explicit. It can refer metaphorically to an appointed time of hard service (Isa 40:2; Job 7:1; 14:14), and might denote the long (גדול) period to elapse before the vision's fulfillment (Rashi) or the toil it demanded of Daniel in order to understand it (NEB, GNB). In Num 4; 8:24, 25 it denotes Yahweh's sacred "army," the Levites, fulfilling their "service." But it can also mean "war," and a reference to the heavenly and earthly conflicts of 10:12–12:4 (cf. JB, NIV) best fits the context, even if Isa 40:2 suggested the word (see *Form, Structure*).

1.e. ובין, perhaps a qal derived from a hi form (Hartman), though hardly itself hi (against GKC 73a). The text may be suspicious (cf. OG, Aq, Syr); for emendations, see, e.g., Hartman, Brockington. The vb and the following cognate noun can denote understanding or attentiveness. Either would be appropriate here, but in 12:10 (which the phrase anticipates: see *Structure*) the context suggests attentiveness; so also 9:23 where two forms of the root appear.

1.f. Def art is required (against NIV). The ref is hardly confined to the vision in chap. 10 (see *Structure*).

2.a-a. שלשה שבעים ימים "three weeks days": see GKC 131d, though "three whole weeks" (cf. EVV) overinterprets (Driver). The idiom may derive here from the Joseph story (Gen 41:1) or may indicate literal weeks of days not of years (contrast chap. 9; Lacocque).

3.a. Hartman explains the odd phrase here as a mistranslation from Aram.

4.a. There is little ground for seeing this as a gl. Elsewhere in the OT "the Great River" is the Euphrates, but it is always specified as such—"the Great River" does not occur unqualified, and the Tigris is not *so* far from Babylon (Hasslberger, *Hoffnung*).

5.a. See n. 4:31.a.

5.b. Uphaz (EVV) is otherwise unknown (except when this phrase recurs in Jer 10:9). Rather אופז is to be connected with פזז ("refine [?]," 1 Kgs 10:18), פז ("pure gold," e.g., Cant 5:11, 15); cf. Ibn Ezra, Ps-Saadia, JPS. The initial א perhaps reflects the variant reading אופיר (Ophir, cf. NEB) (Hartman).

6.a. תרשיש is apparently a yellow topaz or yellow quartz, known in Gk as chrysolite (Aq, Vg, and G elsewhere). Beryl (JB) is green. See *IBD, IDB* "jewels," "Tarshish."

6.b. This basic meaning of המון fits well here (cf. BDB); EVV "crowd" (cf. 11:10–13) is a derived meaning. See G. Gerleman, "Die lärmende Menge: Der Sinn des hebräischen Wortes *hamon*," in *Wort und Geschichte* (FS K. Elliger, ed. H. Gese and H. P. Rüger; AOAT 18 [1974] 71–75.

7.a. Taking וראיתי ("now I saw": *waw* plus pf) as a circumstantial cl rather than merely an Aramaism (against *TTH* 160).

7.b. MT in Dan apparently distinguishes מַרְאָה (also vv 8, 16) from מַרְאֶה ("vision"; 8:16, 26,

27; 9:23; 10:1)—though the nature of the difference is unclear (BDB, Montgomery take מַרְאָה as "vision") and C fuzzes it. See A. Brenner, " 'מַרְאֶה'-ו 'מַרְאָה'," *BetM* 25 (1980) 373–74.

7.c. One would expect ל, not ב; Bevan tr. "in the act of hiding."

8.a. See BDB for this meaning of הוד; the phrase takes up v 7 (Hasslberger, *Hoffnung*).

8.b-b. There are no textual grounds for removing this phrase, even though it repeats the content of "no strength remained in me" and anticipates actual words in v 16.

9.a-a. Omitted by OG, Syr (haplog/to simplify?).

9.b. See n. 8:8.b.

9.c-c. הייתי נרדם, cf. 1:16; see GKC 116r. But it could be a plupf (Bevan) or simply an Aramaism for "I fell . . ." (Zimmermann, *JBL* 57 [1938] 259–61). On רדם see n. 8:18.a.

9.d-d. MT על פני ופני ". . . on my face, with my face. . . ." Th omits the first phrase, OG, Syr the second. The first might be assimilation to 8:18, the second assimilation to 10:15 or dittog, or MT might be conflate.

10.a. הנה, marking this as a sudden experience (Hasslberger, *Hoffnung*).

10.b. נגע most often means "touch," cf. v 16; it can mean "strike," but not "grasp" (cf. BDB).

10.c. ותניעני, cf. JPS. 6QDan להניעני "to shake me." "Set me trembling" (EVV) is too gentle.

10.d-d. ברכי וכפות ידי "my knees and the palms of my hands": Th lacks the second phrase; one ms, OG have רגלי "my feet" for ידי.

13.a. See n. 10.a.

13.b-b. נותרתי is difficult, but Syr, Vg presuppose it and G κατέλιπον looks more like an attempt to interpret than a witness to original הותרתי (against RSV)—which would anyway mean "left him alone," not just "left him" (Driver). The meaning might be "I held out" (NEB) or "I gained the superiority" (Keil, cf. the hi) or "I was left over" (i.e., no longer needed; RVmg).

13.c-c. מלכי: 6QDan (מלכות, "kingdom") and G looks like assimilation to v 13a.

14.a. Following K יִקְרֶה; Q יִקְרָא assimilates to Gen 49:1.

14.b. See on 2:28.

14.c-c. עוד חזון לימים. The word order suggests "yet a vision," not "days yet (to come)," and חזון "vision" has no article; cf. JB against RSV, which assimilates to 8:26 (with G?).

15.a. פני; 6QDan אפי.

16.a. See n. 10.a.

16.b-b. כדמות בני אדם "like the appearance of sons-of-man": the pl is odd but s (one ms, Th, Vg) looks like a simplification of a difficult text. 6QDan כדמות יד אדם ("like the appearance of a human hand"; cf. OG) is perhaps assimilation to v 10—or was the יד lost by assimilation to 8:15; 10:18? MT's difficult י may preserve a variant יד (Montgomery).

16.c. ציר, properly the fearsome and helpless convulsion of childbirth (1 Sam 4:19).

17.a-a. זה . . . זה: cf. BDB 261, 262.

17.b. [מ]עתה (cf. 10:20; 11:2) is not a chronological "now" but an emphatic or adversative one: see E. Jenni, "Zur Verwendung von *ʿattā* 'jetzt' im Alten Testament," *TZ* 28 (1972) 8–10. Jenni queries the text here, but see Ehrlich; cf. *DTT*. The pronoun אני is also emphatic.

19.a. NEB: on this meaning of שלום here (cf. 3:31; 6:26 [4:1; 6:25]) in the context of Daniel's reaction in vv 9–17 see W. Eisenbeis, *Die Wurzel* שלם *im Alten Testament* (BZAW 113 [1969]) 212–15; against Montgomery.

19.b. Some mss חזק ואמץ "take courage and be strong" for חזק וחזק—cf. Vrs, RSV; assimilating to Josh 1:6–9 etc. The ו is unusual when an imper is repeated (Bevan); cf. the greater frequency of ו copulative with repeated nouns in LBH (GKC 123c).

19.c. See n. 8:8.b.

20.a. The train of thought in 10:20–11:2a is difficult, though there are no textual grounds for querying the order of the verses, and commentators vary in how they reconstruct them.

20.b. הידעת (pf) takes up vv 12, 14 (Hasslberger, *Hoffnung*).

20.c. See n. 17.b.

20.d. Or perh. "come forth [from that battle]"—cf. RSV "am through with him," though this reads rather a lot into יוצא (despite 1 Sam 14:41; Qoh 7:18).

20.e. See n. 10.a.

21.a. Not "the," and אמת suggests dynamic reliability rather than merely objective truth. (תכתב in the BHS fascicle is a misprint for בכתב.)

11:1.a-a. The phrase's similarity to introductory dates elsewhere (e.g., 10:1) presumably led to the anomalous chap. division here. EVV remove as a gl and emend v 1 in varying ways.

1.b. עמדי (inf constr, "my standing [was]"). OG εἶπεν, Syr *qm* perhaps suggest עמד (ptpl; Bevan, NAB), a more usual expression than MT (cf. Job 9:27 and GKC 159u), which may have been corrupted by the preceding word המדי ("the Mede") (Hartman). The tr would be unaffected unless other words were changed (see n. 1.a-a).

2.a. See n. 10:17.b.

2.b. See n. 10:10.a.

2.c. Not "any of them" (EVV): מכל is abs (Hasslberger, *Hoffnung*).

2.d. G ἐπαναστήσεται hardly requires יעור (against BHS), since יעיר could mean "act in an aroused manner" (BDB). Cf. the use of [ἀνα]στήσεται in v 3a to tr עמד qal.

2.e-e. הכל את מלכות יון. Hardly "the whole Greek empire" (cf. G, Syr): why then does את follow הכל? Even as an explanatory gl, "the Greek empire" raises problems (see *Comment*). If these can be overcome, more likely הכל "everything" is the subj (Barr; Torrey, *JAOS* 25 [1904] 302–11, adding שר). More likely את denotes a less direct obj. "Against" (EVV, cf. Vg) presupposes את ii = "with" (cf. Aq); cf. Jer 38:5 (Bentzen), also עם following קום and יצב in Ps 94:16 (Bevan). For "toward" (cf. Syr) see examples in S. Izre'el, "אל בעברית המקראית = את," *Shnaton* 3 (1978–79) 204–12, xxii; BDB.

3.a-a. The adverbial understanding of phrases here and in vv 4, 5 is less straightforward.

3.b. Cf. vv 16, 36.

4.a. See n. 8:8.b.

4.b. The shortened impf (jussive) following simple ו would suggest a result cl (Montgomery) were there not so many such forms in chap. 11; rather it is a stylistic preference.

4.c-c. Taking these as noun cls (even though the pronoun is omitted) rather than noun phrases (Bevan, cf. 8:19, 26; GKC 116s, 147). אחרית is broader than "descendants" (cf. Amos 4:2; 9:1) (Keil); OG (cf. BHS) assimilates to 8:22, 24.

5.a-a. Casus pendens at the beginning of a new cl, for emphasis (against MT accents): see *TTH* 123, 125.

5.b. Reading מממשלתו (cf. Luc) for MT's ממשלתו (haplog): see *Comment.*

6.a. Taking יתחברו as impersonal; EVV "they will make an alliance," but see *Comment.*

6.b. בוא אל is an expression for a bride's going to live in her husband's home (Josh 15:18; Judg 12:9; Jeffery).

6.c-c. כוח הזרוע "the power of the arm": OG, JB take הזרוע as subj, but cf. 10:16; and a change of subj for the vb would need to have been made earlier (Hasslberger, *Hoffnung*, 212–13).

6.d. וזרעו. The ו is pleonastic, for emphasis (P. Wernberg-Møller, "Pleonastic *waw* in Classical Hebrew," *JSS* 3 [1958] 324–25). EVV "his posterity" repoints זְרֹעוֹ to זַרְעוֹ with Th. But Dan 11 likes to repeat words—thus זרע twice here; see also n. 6.g. Philologically זר[ו]ע could mean "army" in v 6 like the pl in vv 15, 22, 31 (Conrad, *Tel Aviv* 3 [1976] 111–19), but this does not fit here (see *Comment*).

6.e. For the abs of נתן, cf., e.g., 2 Sam 20:21.

6.f. מביאיה, picking up בוא from v 6a; some mss have s מביאה here.

6.g. EVV "her child" reads הַיַּלְדָּהּ with one ms, Th (Syr, Vg "children"; OG lacks). MT seems to assume that throughout v 6 the reference is to those involved in establishing the marriage—and thus to father rather than to child.

6.h-h. Or "the one who had power over her," her husband (GNB): but see n. 6.g.

6.i. The time phrase makes more sense as the introduction to v 7 (cf. EVV).

7.a. Partitive מן (GKC 119w and n).

7.b. ועמד follows the casus pendens (see n. 6.i; cf. *TTH* 123); there is no need to emend.

7.c. NEB "the defences" repoints הַחַיִל as הַחֵיל.

7.d. ועשה בהם והחזיק "he will deal with them and will prevail."

8.a. Emphatic הוא precedes the vb, suggesting a circumstantial cl (Montgomery).

8.b. חצפון in BHS is a misprint for הצפון.

10.a. בניו Q; K בנו "his son." Historically K is more accurate (see *Comment*). S and pl both appear in v 10, the subj of some vbs being unclear.

10.b-b. ובא בוא ושטף ועבר "will go [with] going and will pour through and will overwhelm." Inf בוא suggests repeated action; some mss (cf. OG, Syr) have בו, but this is idiomatically simpler and fits the context less well.

10.c. מעזה: presumably the southern king's, as he is antecedent in MT; the southern king has actually changed since v 9 from Ptolemy III to Ptolemy IV, but the seer often views the sequences of kings corporately, esp. the southern, who is merely the opponent of the great northern king (Hasslberger, *Hoffnung*). Driver suggests Gaza (ועזה!), though Antiochus may have already occupied that; more likely Raphia (see *Comment*).

11.a. For such defining phrases explaining a pronoun, see GKC 131n.

11.b. Probably the northern king, since he is the antecedent; his army is therefore overcome by the southern king.

12.a. Like chaff carried off by the wind (Delcor, comparing 2:35). "Rises up [for battle]" (cf. Keil) is less likely, since the usage of נשא is more unusual and ההמון "the horde" has to refer to a different army.

12.b. After v 11, presumably the southern king; this leads naturally then into v 13.

12.c. K ירום; Q, C, many mss ורם. M. Dahood ("Hebrew-Ugaritic Lexicography," *Bib* 46 [1965] 323) takes ירום as ptpl from ירם, a by-form of רום.

12.d. רבאות, a mixed form (BHS).

13.a. שב could simply indicate repetition ("will again [raise a horde]"), cf. vv 10a, 29a; but chap.11 often uses שוב for north-south movement (cf. vv 9 [with בוא) as here], 28–30).

13.b-b. לקץ העתים שנים "at the end of the times, years"; cf. the expression in 10:2 and n.

13.c. יבוא בוא; see n. 10.b-b.

14.a. בני פריצי "the sons of the violent of [your people]": see *Comment.*

14.b. להעמיד could denote their aim or simply the result of their action.

15.a. If v 15 refers to further stages in the campaign (see *Comment*); but v 15 could resume from v 13 after a parenthesis in v 14.

15.b. וישפך; 4QDan[a,c] ושפך is more what one would have expected (Pace, 34).

15.c. See *Comment.* Th, Syr take עיר מבצרות as pl (cf. GKC 124r). The standard pl expression is ערים בצרות (e.g., Neh 9:25) or ערי מבצר (e.g., Jer 34:7), and the term here might have been misdivided through the influence of מבצר in vv 24, 39 (cf. Syr?).

15.d. Or perh. "their fortresses" (B. E. Schafer, "מבחר/מבחור = 'Fortress,'" *CBQ* 33 [1971] 395). The suffix on מבחריו apparently has הנגב "the south" as its antecedent (cf. JB).

15.e-e. ואין כח: emphatic ו (Ehrlich).

16.a. See n. 4.b.

16.b. See on 8:9.

16.c. כָלָה, as 9:27. G, Syr understand וְכָלָה as a vb ("and it will be destroyed by his hand"; cf. Jer 16:4); the vb occurs in 12:7. "All of it" (RSV) presupposes repointing to כֻּלֹּה.

17.a. וישם פניו "and he will set his face": see n. 4.b.

17.b-b. לבוא בתקף כל מלכותו: "to come in all his imperial might" (cf. NIV) leads into the rest of v 17 less well.

17.c. See BHS on ישרים; there is no need to emend. The *waw* consec ועשה follows its subj as casus pendens (*TTH* 123).

17.d. ובת הנשים, "the daughter of women."

17.e. The empire: not "to destroy her" (it did not) nor "to corrupt her" (it did, from Antiochus's angle, but this is too subtle).

17.f. Not "she" (against NEB); the phrase follows Isa 7:7 (Hasslberger, *Hoffnung*).

18.a. Reading K וישב not Q וישם ("set," cf. JPS "head for")—assimilation to v 17; see also n. 4.b.

18.b. The term can denote any islands or countries around the Mediterranean.

18.c-c. והשבית קצין חרפתו לו; G, Syr suggest "and he will stop a commander who challenges him" (or ". . . with his challenge to him," cf. Keil); but see *Comment.* קצין is an archaic poetic term for a military leader; a consul *was* both a magistrate and a military commander.

18.d-d. Not "indeed he will return" (cf. RSV); בלתי is a negative. Charles suggests emending בלתי לו to לבלתי ("so that not"; cf. JB), but probably בלתי alone could mean this (cf. the alternatives of למען and יען). The cl then refers to the northern king's inability to deal with the commander's response to his original challenge. Ozanne (*JTS* 16 [1965) 447–48) emends to לבלתי ("by wearing him down"; cf. NEB).

19.a. Reading וישב not וישם with some mss: see n. 18.a.

20.a. נגש usually means "to rule (in a domineering way)"; it can mean to exact (Deut 15:2, 3) (see *Comment*).

20.b. There is no prep; "for" is also possible. Plöger takes as direct obj (cf. RSV, JB), understanding "the splendor of an empire" to be Israel.

20.c. ולא באפים ולא במלחמה "but [some mss, Syr, Vg omit] not in anger and not in battle"; cf. OG. Th, JB, NEB, GNB take אף in an Aram. sense (*DTT*).

21.a. Or "contemptible" (RSV) or "worthless" (cf. GNB); but the next cl suggests נבזה means "despised" (cf. Isa 53:3).

22.a. זרעות השטף "the forces of the flood." NEB repoints to הַשֹּׁטֵף, RSV to הַשֶּׁטֶף.

22.b-b. וישברו וגם נגיד ברית; NEB emends to . . . וישבר גם, making the covenant prince subj. Suggestively, Goldstein makes the covenant prince (then Menelaus) the subj of vv 23–24 (*II Maccabees*, 262): but the transition after v 24 is difficult.

23.a. מן rarely means "after" (NIV) except with temporal expressions such as יום.

23.b-b. ועלה ועצם "come up and grow powerful."

24.a. See n. 8:25.c.; RSV links with v 23, Syr omits.

24.b. משמני מדינה: of various possible trs (cf. EVV) this best fits the context of vv 23–24 (see *Comment*), following on from v 23b (Hasslberger, *Hoffnung*).

25.a. NEB repoints to וְיֵעֹר, "he will be aroused [in]."

25.b. Lit., "his heart will be against" (cf. Hasslberger, *Hoffnung*, and n. 28.b-b).

26.a. ואכלי פת־בגו perhaps belongs to the end of v 25 as the subj of יחשבו ("[people . . .] will devise") (BHS, though there is no need to delete the emphatic ו). On פת־בג see n. 1:5.b.

26.b. ישטוף is clearly qal (cf. vv 10, 40) but can hardly have the usual meaning "overflow" either trans or intrans (against UBS). But שטף can mean "wash away" (trans) (Ezek 16:9), to which this can be taken as an intrans correspondent; there is no need to assimilate to the ni of v 22 (against BHS).

28.a. The northern king. See n. 4.b.

28.b-b. ולבבו על ברית קדש ועשה "and his heart [will be] against a holy covenant, and he will act." I ignore MT punctuation and assume that he takes this action on the way home; the last cl in v 28 is then resumptive.

29.a. With Th against EVV: see Hanhart, "Übersetzungstechnik," 136–57.

30.a. כתים (Kittim), originally a town in Cyprus, then the island as a whole, hence a term for "Cyprus and beyond."

30.b-b. וזעם . . . ועשה "and he will be harsh . . . and will act." Antiochus's harshness is hardly his personal rage at his humiliation in Egypt; the word denotes the harshness of his actions as experienced by his victims rather than his personal feelings. Cf. the noun in v 36; 8:19.

30.c. The balanced arrangement of cls in v 30 (Hasslberger, *Hoffnung*) suggests that ושב belongs with what precedes (against MT).

31.a. Grammatically it is easiest to take מעוז as a description of the sanctuary, but it is an odd word to use of it and historically refers more easily to the citadel near the temple (see *Comment*).

31.b. השקוץ משומם: as in 8:13 (see n. 8:13.e) the ptpl lacks the article but it is here poel, while פשע is replaced by שקוץ.

32.a. מרשיעי ברית (cf. 1QM 1.2): giving the vb its usual meaning in Dan and taking the gen as defining (cf. RV; GKC 116h, 128x). "Such as wrong a covenant" (cf. the use of הכשיל in Mal 2:8) or "such as condemn a covenant" are possible. "Covenant" might virtually mean "covenant people"; but "such among the covenant people who act wickedly" (partitive) is unlikely, as Daniel would hardly make a point of stating that they belong to the covenant people. The phrase denotes the people referred to in v 30b.

32.b. יחניף; חנף suggests keeping the outward form of a faith which one has really abandoned.

32.c. It is perh. significant that ידע appears here in a covenant/treaty context (cf. H. B. Huffmon, "The Treaty Background of Hebrew *yādaʿ*," *BASOR* 181 [1966] 31–37).

32.d. יחזקו ועשו "display strength and act."

33.a. The more common meaning of the hi vb in BH, though ptpl משכיל commonly means "teacher" in QL (Kosmala, *JANESCU* 5 [1973] 240). It is possible to take the phrase to refer to the whole group of those who acknowledge their God (v 32; Delcor), but more naturally it suggests a group within the conservative Jews.

33.b. See n. 9:27.b.

33.c. There is perh. a play on words between "discerning" (*śkl*) and "fall" (*kšl*) (vv, 33, 34, 35) (JB). כשל can mean "be caused to sin" (Jer 18:15; Mal 2:8) but this ill fits the context.

33.d. 6QDan, G have "and."

34.a. Or "strength": see P. D. Miller, "Ugaritic *ǵzr* and Hebrew *ʿzr* ii," *UF* 2 (1970) 171.

34.b. JB refers בחלקלקות to covert support, but this is less likely than covert hostility, as v 21 (and cf. v 32 בחלקות).

35.a. The many potentially insincere adherents of v 34b are a more plausible antecedent for בהם than the discerning of v 35a (Hasslberger, *Hoffnung*).

35.b-b. עד עת קץ כי; NEB reverses the last two words.

35.c. If "it" is the final moment; "last for" if "it" is the persecution.

36.a. [אל[ים may *refer* to subordinate heavenly beings, but it can hardly be *translated* "angel[s]" (against Collins, *Vision,* 135): English "god[s]" in relation to "God" gives just the right impression.

36.b. כלה. Perhaps wrath on the northern king being "full and ready to be expressed" (cf. 1 Sam 25:17) (so JB), or being "fully expressed, poured out" (cf. Ezek 5:13; 2 Chr 36:22), but more likely wrath on Israel being "exhausted, at an end" (cf. Isa 10:25; Dan 8:19). See n. 9:24.d.

36.c-c. כי נחרצה נעשתה: pf of certitude, as following כי and as paralleling the impf after נחרצה in 9:27 (cf. GKC 106n), rather than "when what is determined is done."

37.a. As the standard BH expression for "the God of his fathers," this is more likely s than pl (Bunge, *JSJ* 4 [1973] 170): see *Comment.*

37.b. Grammatically חמדת נשים "the love of women" might be objective gen "love for women," but this does not fit contextually.

37.c-c. 2 mss omit (cf. OG).

38.a. על כנו: the antecedent is "his fathers' god," the one this new god replaces. Hartman "on his stand," but this also involves reordering the words to fit in the context, and the meaning as in vv 7, 20, 21 is more natural.

38.b. Preceded by ל marking the obj (BDB 512). "Stronghold god" is lit. "god of strongholds" (אלה מעזים).

38.c. Taking the ו as explicative (cf. NEB): see n. 6:29.a.

39.a. עשה ל: as with other occurrences of עשה in chap. 11, the vb's meaning is further defined by the following vb(s), with which it forms a compound idea. Cf. also Josh 8:2 for the construction in v 39 (Keil).

39.b. Taking מבצרי as pl of extension/amplification (cf. GKC 124abe), referring to Jerusalem (Lacocque).

39.c. עִם "with." NEB, NAB, JB repoint עַם to provide עשה with an obj, but the resultant expression is dubious, and see n. 39.a.

39.d. אשר הכיר; JPS, JB "the man who regards him," but this changes subj between this and the next vb and changes number between this and the following vb's suffix. Q יכיר is prob. a correction of K הכיר (Bevan).

39.e. וחלק, following its obj as casus pendens (*TTH* 123).

40.a. ושטף ועבר "and pour through and overwhelm."

41.a. רַבּוֹת, apparently referring to the ארצות of v 40. But EVV repoint רִבּוֹת "ten thousands" (so Sym; cf. n. 12.d).

41.b. Taking the cl beginning ואלה as circumstantial.

41.c. ראשית suggests the flower of a people (Pss 78:51; 105:36; Baldwin). Most EVV emend to שארית "remnant"; but cf. Num 24:20; Jer 49:35; Amos 6:1.

42.a. The phrase can indicate plotting rather than actual action (H. Tawill, "Two Notes . . . ," *CBQ* 42 [1980] 36), but the usage is rarer and is not indicated by the context here.

42.b. בָּארצות; some mss בַּארצות.

43.a. במצעדיו: Kopf (*VT* 9 [1959] 272–73) "to his power," on the basis of Arabic.

44.a. ולהחרים, perh. from חרם ii "cut off," not חרם i "forbid, ban" (see BDB): so G. R. Driver, "Hebrew Homonyms," *HW* 56–59.

45.a. אהלי אפדנו "the tents of his pavilion." אפדנו comes from a Pers. word for a colonnaded audience hall; it entered Aram. via late Babylonian (see Itō, *Orient* 8 [1972] 46–51; Wagner, *Aramaismen,* 28). On the magnificent palace complexes at Susa and Persepolis see Olmstead, *History,* 272–87; Cook, *Persian Empire,* 158–63.

45.b. Taking ימים "seas" as pl of extension (cf. GKC 124b) and referring to the Mediterranean (as Judg 5:17; cf. Montgomery). NIV "between the seas, at . . ." is possible, but its ref is unclear.

12:1.a. I.e., one of the supreme heavenly beings (not the sole one), several of whom appear in chaps. 8, 10.

1.b. העמד על; cf. NEB "who stands guard over."

1.c. בני עמך "the sons of your people." There is no reason to limit the phrase's ref to the seer's own group (Collins, *VT* 25 [1975] 603, against Plöger).

1.d. But see n. 2:1.c.

1.e. Grammatically it is easier to take גוי as subj of היות (EVV), but taking it as complement gives a better meaning (Spronk, *Afterlife,* 339).

2.a. "Many who sleep" (which might then mean "all who sleep"—all Jews or all people) would require taking מן as explicative, which is rare (BDB 581), unlikely with רבים (contrast Qoh 3:12; Esth 8:17; 2 Chr 30:18), and not indicated by the context.

2.b. אדמת עפר: not "the dust of the earth," both because of the word order, and because עפר means "soil" (Hartman, cf. BDB) and this tr is more natural in a quasi-geographical expression (Nickelsburg, *Resurrection,* 17). S. Talmon ("Double Readings in the Massoretic Text," *Textus* 1 [1960] 167–68) takes the phrase as a conflation of two readings.

2.c. It is grammatically possible to begin a new cl here: "they will go to lasting life, while others will go to utter shame . . ." (cf. Alfrink, *Bib* 40 [1959] 355–71), though the second אלה lacks an antecedent (Hasslberger, *Hoffnung*). The idea of the wicked being awakened in order to be exposed and condemned seems bizarre, but the idea of this taking place after death without such awakening is little less so, and the problem arises from taking vv 1–2 literalistically. The notion of a double resurrection is not clearly stated elsewhere for two centuries (2 Esd 7:32–44; Rev 20).

2.d. עולם: see on 2:20.

2.e. לחרפות ("to shames"; pl of amplification, GKC 124e); perhaps a gl on the less familiar דראון ("abhorrence," only here and Isa 66:24).

3.a. Or "vindicate," a common meaning of הצדיק in Dan 7–12. "Justify" in the sense of "atone for" (Delcor) is not suggested by the context.

4.a. ישטטו: BHS suggests emending to ישטטו "will fall away." שטט can hardly refer to searching the book (against Delcor).

4.b. EVV "knowledge" fits ill in the context; hence JB's "wickedness," presupposing emending דעת to רעה (cf. OG). Better follow NEB in linking דעת to a ידע ii meaning "be still, submissive" different from ידע "know" (cf. Thomas, *JTS* 6 [1955] 226; Emerton, *JSS* 15 [1970] 150, 177; Day, *VT* 30 [1980] 98–99).

5.a. Not נהר as in 10:4 but יאר, a loan-word from Egyptian, usually referring to the Nile, derived here from the Joseph story (see the several verbal links between 12:5–7 and Gen 41:1; cf. n. 6.a-a).

6.a-a. ממעל למימי היאר "above in relation to the waters of the river"—but this hardly means in the air (against EVV); cf. n. 9:21.c-c., also על in Gen 41:1.

6.b. Taking ויאמר as indef 3rd s (cf. GKC 144d), rather than inferring that one of the figures in v 5 is the subj (NIV, JB); cf. Gen 19:17; 38:28. No need to emend to ואמר (NEB, RSV, cf. OG).

6.c. In QL קץ often means "time," and this meaning is possible here; but "end" fits well (cf. vv 7–9) and corresponds to usage elsewhere in Dan.

7.a. See n. 4:13.b.

7.b. נַפֵּץ: the Heb. is unusual and often emended (NEB נֹפֵץ, JB נֹפֵץ, interchanged with the next word יד), but no one emendation carries conviction. NEB also derives the word from נפץ ii "scatter," not נפץ i "shatter."

7.c. ככלות: "stopped" rather than "brought to completion" (so NIV?); see n. 9:24.d-d.

8.a. אחרית, not קץ "end": cf. Driver.

10.a. יצרפו; C יתצרפו, 4QFlor יצטרפו, both hit.

10.b. "Explain [it]" (Lebram, "Piety," 179) is oversubtle, esp. given the rarity of בין hi used absolutely.

13.a. Omitting לקץ ("until the end"—i.e., your death) with G (but not Vg [Hasslberger, *Hoffnung*]), cf. JB, as dittog from the next line.

13.b. עמד is used as an equivalent to קום in LBH (BDB 764a).

Form / Structure / Setting

Form

See first chap. 2 *Form.* Dan 10–12 is the report of a vision and an audition granted to a human being by a supernatural being. The content of the revelation lies in the audition; the vision prepares for the audition rather than conveying the content of the revelation, like a prophetic vision (Plöger). The content is expressed less allusively and more directly than is the case in any of the other visions. Chaps. 10–12 include mythic motifs but in general communicate more by means of ciphers and less by means of symbols than earlier visions.

The revelatory message concerns present, past, and future, illustrating how apocalypses have a much broader interest than the preoccupation with speculation concerning the future that is often attributed to them (see Rowland, *Heaven*). But the central part of the audition is a regnal prophecy outlining the rise, activities, achievements, and fall of a series of kings who are unnamed but can be identified on the basis of the events referred to. Such prophecies have no parallels elsewhere in the OT, but a number outside it from Mesopotamia, Egypt, and Greece from the late second millennium to the Hellenistic period. *ANET* 606 gives an Assyrian example (cf. *NERT* 118–22):

> . . . A ruler will arise, he will rule for thirteen years.
> There will be an attack of Elam against Akkad, and
> the booty of Akkad will be carried off.
> The temples of the great gods will be destroyed, the defeat of Akkad will be decreed [by the gods].
> There will be confusion, disturbance, and unhappy events in the land, and
> the reign will diminish [in power]; another man, whose name is not mentioned [as a successor] will arise, and
> will seize the throne as king and will put to death his officials . . .

These texts are for the most part not actual prophecy but quasi-prophecy. They combine extensive quasi-prophecy of events before the writer's day with more limited actual prophecy of events still to come. The formulae and the detail compare with Daniel; so does the anti-Hellenistic nature of instances from the later period. On Grayson's interpretation (*Texts,* 13–37), the "Dynastic Prophecy" from the Hellenistic age, which covers the history of the Assyrian, Babylonian, Persian, and Hellenistic empires, ends particularly similarly to Dan 10–12, with an actual prediction of the fall of the Seleucid empire and a rubric regarding keeping the prophecy secret (see also Lambert, *Background,* 9–16; more broadly Hengel, *Judentum,* 337–45 [ET 1:184–89]; Osswald, *ZAW* 75 [1963] 27–44; also Collins, *Apocalypse,* on *Sib. Or.*, especially the oracle on Alexander in 3.388–400, updated to refer to Antiochus).

Like other parts of the OT, Dan 11 must be seen against its ancient Near Eastern background, and this material makes clear that the Danielic visions, too, in their context could only be understood as mostly quasi-prediction. This is a more natural assumption than the view that the author has turned a familiar way of giving quasi-prophecies into a way of giving actual prophecies. Such reuse takes place with some forms, but would require evidence: "the burden of proof must fall on those who wish to argue that Daniel is different from the other examples of the genre" (Collins, *Daniel* [FOTL] 34). The difference in Daniel's theology does not invalidate this (against Baldwin, *TynB* 30 [1979] 92–94); rather these quasi-predictions "are distinctively Jewish, yet are a Jewish form of a widespread contemporary phenomenon" (Fishbane, *Interpretation,* 520).

In her commentary, Baldwin expresses clearly some common hesitations about such a conclusion. It implies that the "revelation" was nothing of the sort (but to conclude that the author knew of the historical events he referred to by the same means as other OT writers knew of historical events they referred to leaves quite open whether his understanding of these events is God-given in the same way theirs can have been). It implies that the preparation for the vision in chap. 10 was also fictional (this does not follow, though even if it were the case, that would not imply that it was merely "local color" from which we were not intended to learn theologically). It means that what the chapter says about the efficacy of prayer or about the heavenly warfare it describes reflects only the writer's subjective ideas (this does not follow; it can be just as God-given as other parts of Scripture). It means assuming that the author speaks parabolically when he gives no indication of that (the opposite is the case: he uses a way of speaking that is characteristic of quasi-prophecy, not of actual prophecy). It means inferring he is wrong in his prediction about how Antiochus died, which implies that he is no more likely to be reliable in his understanding of spiritual issues (this involves assuming that vv 40–45 purport to offer actual prediction, which is questionable: see *Form, Comment, Explanation;* nor does the alleged implication follow).

There is no evidence to tell us how many of the author's contemporaries or how many of those among whom the book soon became popular misunderstood quasi-predictions as actual predictions, or to establish whether the author intended them to do so in order to get his work taken seriously. Jude 14 instances the quoting of a quasi-prediction as if it were actual prediction, and whatever view we take of that may also be appropriate to Daniel. Perhaps *1 Enoch* deceived Jude; we know that a mistaken belief that Paul wrote Hebrews contributed to its inclusion in the NT, and we may believe that the Fathers there did the right thing for (partly) wrong reasons. Or it may be that Jude knew very well that *1 Enoch* was a quasi-prediction but colluded with the document's own convention; the convention is rather widespread for us to imagine all the people being fooled all the time, even if most people except Porphyry later forgot or refused to acknowledge it. Or it may be that the distinction between real prediction by a saint of old and quasi-prediction by a later person "inspired" by him, obvious to us, was less sharp both to the author of *1 Enoch* and to Jude.

Chaps. 10–12 take up motifs from chap. 7: with 7:25 compare the characterization of the northern king in 11:36 and the limit placed on the time of trouble in 12:7. It has more links with chap. 9: with the account of Daniel's preparation for and receiving of his revelation in 9:3, 21–23 compare 10:1–3, 9–11; with the content of the revelation in 9:24–27, compare 11:10, 16, 22, 31, 36 (floodlike destruction, the removal of the anointed/leader, the suspension of regular sacrifices and the desolating abomination, the implementing of what has been determined). Many of these motifs appear also in chap. 8, however, and it is with chap. 8 that chaps. 10–12 have most detailed points of contact. Reminiscences of almost every verse of chap. 8 reappear here (lists in Boutflower, 224–25). Chaps. 10–12 are a reworking of those earlier visions. Hasslberger (*Hoffnung*, 190–91) understands 10:14 to refer to chap. 8 and to indicate that chaps. 10–12 offer an interpretation of that vision in particular.

Dan 10–12, like the previous visions, is also shaped by earlier Scriptures, so that we can describe it as another instance of situational midrash. Clearest influence in chap. 10 is exercised by the accounts of God's appearing in Ezek 1–3; 9–10: the detailed chronological reference, the river setting, the man dressed in linen, each detail of his description (v 6), Daniel's reaction (v 9), the man's response (vv 10–11), the one of human appearance (דמות, v 16). Behind Ezekiel's description of how his vision came is a long tradition concerning the seeking and receiving of oracles, which goes back to Mari (M. Weinfeld, "Patterns in Prophetic Literature," *VT* 27 [1977] 181–82). The address of the supernatural being as "my lord" corresponds to Zech 1:9; 4:4, 5, 13; 6:4; the rhetorical question in v 20 also compares with such questions in Zech 1–6; his touching Daniel corresponds to Jer 1 and Isa 6, though with different significance. For v 14, cf. Gen 49:1.

A number of key words from Dan 11 parallel the warning of Jerusalem's destruction in Ezek 7:19–27. The temple as the fairest (v 16) will be attacked by violators (v 14); people who seek a vision (v 14) will fall over (כשל, v 14) the stumbling block (מכשל) of their iniquity; the sanctuary/strong[hold] will be desecrated by abominations and made a desolation (v 31); people hear reports that alarm them (v 44). More generally, the vision takes up aspects of the Book of Isaiah that may have seemed enigmatic in the light of events; the seer seeks, receives, and relates illumination on what these texts now signify. Thus he begins in 10:1 from Isa 40:1–11, with its key references to conflict/servitude (צבא, v 2), to the reliability of God's message (v 8), and to something being revealed (v 5); and with the vision's setting in the reign of Cyrus, compare Isa 45:1 (Lacocque). In the body of the revelation we can see the influence of earlier passages from Isaiah concerning the Assyrians, upon which Dan 11 is an actualizing commentary in the manner of the Qumran literature (Seeligmann, VTSup 1 [1953] 171). Allusions to armies flooding through the land (vv 10, 22, 26, 40) recall Isa 8:7–8. The characterization of the last northern king (vv 36–37) recalls that of the Assyrians in Isa 10, especially vv 5–6, 12, 15 (cf. 33:10), while the desolations that are determined (v 36) reflect Isa 10:22–23, 25 (cf. 28:22). See also Isa 17:12 (cf. v 10), 30:18 (cf. 12:12); 34:17 (cf. 11:39; 12:13). Phrases from servant passages in Isa 40–55 appear at several points. Clearest are allusions to Isa 52:13–53:12 in 12:1–4: the role of the wise (משכילים, cf. Isa 52:13 ישכיל); their setting the multitude right (cf. 53:11); also perhaps their shining like stars (cf. 53:11 1QIsa[a]; Cavallin, *SEA* 37–38 [1972–73] 51); and the increase in דעת ("suffering" [see n. 12:4.b], cf. Isa 53:11; Allen, *Vox Evangelica* 1 [1962] 28). See also 10:8, the seer's face being disfigured (משחית, cf. Isa 52:14); 11:12 (נשא and ירום, cf. Isa 52:13); and 11:22, 28, 30, 32 for the use of "covenant" to refer to people (cf. Isa 42:6; 49:8) (Brownlee, *BASOR* 132 [1953] 12).

Other passages from the prophets and elsewhere also underlie the vision. Verse 11:20 contrasts with Zech 9:8; 11:21 with 1 Chr 29:25. The end awaiting its time (10:14; 11:27, 35; cf. 8:17) takes up Hab 2:3. The ships from the west (11:30) are those of the prophecy in Num 24:24. The account of the last northern king's end (11:40–45) is shaped as a whole as well as in specific detail by the OT tradition of the attack of a gentile foe who is defeated and killed near the gates of Jerusalem (e.g., Pss 2; 46; 48; 76), a tradition already reworked in prophetic passages such as Isa 10; 14:24–25; 31; Ezek 38–39; Joel 2:20; Zech 14 (Gese, "Geschichtsbild," 150–51), as well as by the prophetic portrayals of judgment on Egypt (Isa 19; Jer 43:8–13; 46; Ezek 29–32; and for the Libyans and Sudanese, e.g., Nah 3:9, but also Ezek 30:5 [see BHS]). In chap. 12, the time of trouble (v 1) recalls Jer 30:7. The awakening of some who sleep in the dust and the consigning of some to abhorrence (v 2) combines phrases from Isa 26:19 and 66:24; Isa 26:17–21 also includes the ideas of an experience of trouble and of the punishment of the wicked (Kossen, *NedTT* 10 [1955] 296–301). The hurrying to and fro during the time that God's words are hidden (v 4) takes up Amos 8:12.

Dan 10–12 is situational midrash rather than expository midrash. Its starting point is more the problems raised by present experience, which the interpreter seeks to address by means of Scripture, than problems raised by study of the text in its own right. Or perhaps we may say that it solves one problem, the apparent meaninglessness of present history, by first bringing to the surface a second, the apparent nonfulfillment of ancient prophecy. Both problems are then solved by being set alongside each other. The interpreter promises that the ancient word is to be fulfilled in a way that will restore meaning to present experience. So the anthologizing of Scripture that has been a feature of chaps. 7–9 becomes central in chaps. 10–12: it enables the seer to develop a systematic interpretation of past, present, and future as a whole that will enable his people to live with these.

The quasi-predictions begin this process by interpreting recent history in the light of Scripture. They are not indulging in mere theological apologetic, but in a radical theological necessity (Fishbane, *Interpretation,* 510–11 [and see 509–22 generally], against Hartman, "The Functions of Some So-called Apocalyptic Timetables," *NTS* 22 [1976] 1–14). Nor is it the case that the mere—pretended!—ability to predict the future in 11:2–39 gives grounds for believing the actual prophecy in 11:40–12:3. It is rather the quasi-predictions' ability to make sense of the past by relating it in the light of Scripture that implies grounds for trusting the actual prophecy's portrait of what the future will bring, painted in the light of the same Scripture. When they speak about the past, they do so on the basis of having historical data, and scriptural text as a means of interpretation. When they speak about the future, they have only scriptural text, and are providing an imaginary scenario, a possible embodiment of that text, which is not to be pressed to provide (or be judged by) historical data. Its object is not to provide historical data but to provide scriptural interpretation of what the events to come will mean.

The seer implicitly wishes to commend a certain form of behavior, namely, resistance to Seleucid/reformist pressures. His explicit focus, however, is a cognitive one. He aims to provide a way for conservative Jews to understand their present experience, looking at it in the light of various scriptural texts. The supernatural being provides this for the seer (10:1, 14); the "discerning" provide it for the multitude (11:33).

It is possible that aspects of the ideas of the "discerning" have a Persian background, but there are no clear pointers to this. According to Bertholet (*OrSt* 34–37) there is no Persian equivalent to the idea of heavenly beings identified with particular peoples, which is more likely a development of OT ideas (e.g., Deut 32:8). The picture of the celestial beings' activities in 10:13; 10:20–11:1, and that of the discerning joining them in 12:1–3, provides crucial insight on the "metaphysical backdrop" to current events (Collins, *Daniel* [FOTL] 102); it likely reflects visionary experience of the kind chaps. 10–12 testify to, building on scriptural reflection. The dualism of light and darkness, Michael and Belial, in Qumran literature represents a way of thinking that might more plausibly be reckoned to indicate Persian influence than Daniel does (Collins, *VT* 25 [1975] 604–11).

The promise of resurrection in chap. 12 conflates the prophetic eschatological hope and its stress on the realization of God's sovereignty in relation to Israel as a whole with the concern for the destiny of the individual characteristic of the wisdom tradition and the Psalms (Kleinknecht, *Leidende,* 78; Moore, *TZ* 39 [1983] 17–34). It does not require an explanation in terms of Persian influence (cf. Nötscher, *Auferstehungsglauben,* 173–261; against, e.g., Birkeland, *ST* 3 [1949–50] 75–78; Hultgård ["Judentum," 544–45] derives the idea of double reward from Persia). If extra-Israelite traditions appear here, they are old Canaanite ideas about human life being subsumed into the life of the celestial world (Spronk, *Afterlife,* 341–43). The evidence for Egyptian background for the portrait of Antiochus (Lebram, *VT* 25 [1975] 750–52) is rather circumstantial.

Structure

- 10:1 Narrative introduction and summary
- 10:2–19 Opening appearance of supernatural beings
  - 2–3 Seer's preparation
  - 4–19 Appearing and address of supernatural being
    - 4–6 Appearing
    - 7–9 Daniel's response
      - 7–8 to the sight
      - 9 to the sound
    - 10–11 Twofold elevation of Daniel
    - 12–14 Preliminary address by supernatural being
    - 15–17 Daniel's response to address
    - 18–19 Reassurance of Daniel
- 10:20–12:4 Main address by supernatural being
  - 10:20–11:2a Introduction
  - 11:2b–12:3 Announcement of events to come
    - 11:2b Persian kings
    - 11:3–4 A warrior king
    - 11:5–19 Conflicts of southern and northern kings
      - 5 The rise of the southern king's lieutenant
      - 6 An alliance between north and south
      - 7–8a Invasion by the southern king
      - 8b–9 Invasion by the northern king
      - 10–12 Further invasion by the northern kings
      - 13–15 Further invasion by the northern king
      - 16–19 The northern king's triumph and eventual fall
    - 11:20 A northern king who sends round an oppressor

11:21–45 The last northern king
21–24 His rise and success (until a certain time)
25–28 His invasion of the south and his attack on a covenant (but the end waits)
29–35 His further invasion and attacks (at the set moment; but the end still waits)
36–39 His attack on God (until wrath is complete)
40–45 His last invasion, attack, and fall (at the time of the end)
12:1–3 The deliverance of the faithful (at that time)
12:4 Conclusion
12:5–13 Closing appearance of supernatural beings
5 Appearing of supernatural beings
6–7 Seer overhears their conversation
8 Seer asks for explanation of it
9–13 Closing address by supernatural being
9 Command to seer and explanation
10–12 Summary announcements of events to come
13 Command to seer and promise

The narrative introduction and summary (10:1) emphasize the importance of this last vision; it is the first such third-person introduction since chap. 7. They also introduce an element of suspense into the section as they allusively hint at the content that will follow. The elaborate opening appearance of supernatural being(s) and the dialogue with the seer (10:2–19) further underline the supernatural authority and paramount significance of the content of his revelation. Daniel's apprehensiveness and reluctance on account of his sense of unworthiness parallel features of prophetic call narratives and thus imply that the revelation has prophetic authority (Anderson). The dialogue also opens up a key point of substance regarding the perspective on history to which the revelation invites its audience (v 13), and perhaps implies an anticipatory contrast with the last northern king of 11:20–45: he will seek to storm heaven and will be put down; heaven reaches down to Daniel and he hesitates to raise his head, but he is lifted up. There *is* contact between earth and heaven, in the experience of the seer and in the realities of his people's history.

The main address opens (10:20–11:2a) by recapitulating this point and by emphasizing the reliability of what is to follow. Its announcement of events to come begins with a series of kings who seem to have the capacity to achieve much, but eventually fail or fall (11:2b–9). There follows one—not clearly distinguished from his predecessors—whose two campaigns against the southern king, his being checked by a third force, his receiving support among Daniel's own people, and his campaigning in the fairest land foreshadow acts of the last northern king (11:10–19). Before that another northern king foreshadows a different aspect of the last king's activity, his violation of the Jerusalem temple. He, too, then falls (11:20). The main address comes to a climax with a lengthy description of the last northern king (11:21–45), whose career thus follows that of his foreshadowing types, but goes beyond it—acting "as his fathers did not"—in his achievement, his intrigues, his campaigns, his unconscious fulfillment of Scripture, his dealings with a covenant people and their sanctuary, his god-like and god-defying assertiveness, his plunder, and his fall. The momentousness as well as the divine determination of his reign is marked by recurrent references to waiting for the "set moment." (On chap. 11, see Clifford, *BASOR* 220 [1975] 24–25.) The "rise" of a quite different leader, with the deliverance of the faithful who have been under attack during the last king's reign, completes the announcement of events to come (12:1–3). These verses manifest features of poetry (rhythm, parallelism, metaphor, simile), which emphasize their significance at the high point of the main address, as happens with the other visions. The main address is closed off with words to the seer (12:4). The vision then returns to the dialogue between seer and supernatural figures with which it began (12:5–13); the function of this further dialogue is to add reassurance regarding the limits set to the events that have been presaged, and to stiffen the resolve of those who will be put under pressure by them.

Chaps. 10–12 are again written in idiosyncratic Hebrew influenced by Aramaic and perhaps translated from Aramaic (see conveniently Hartman). Chaps. 10–12 include a number of instances of casus pendens followed by *waw* (11:5, 7 [n. 7.b], 17), emphatic *waw* (11:6, 15), and the combining of עשה and another verb in hendiadys (11:7, 30, 32, cf 28). At the same time, chap. 11 in particular is characterized by the use of a variety of terms within certain fields of meaning that help to give it a particular cast: terms to do with royal authority and power (√מלך, √משל, תקף, יד, כח, זרוע), with its acts and achievements (עשה [כרצון], חזק, בשלוה, עשר, ירום לבבו, גדל, רב, שים פנים, חלקלקות), with the rise and fall of kings and their empires ([על כנו] עמד, כשל, נפל, שבר, נתש, חצה, כח, עצר), with military matters (חיל, המון, שר, מבצר, מעוז, אף, מלחמה) and with military action, victory, and defeat (. . . ב בא, נלחם, עור, גרה, סלל, שטף, מעוז, שבר, נתן, נשא), and with movement more generally (בא, יצא, שוב). Family words are drawn in, often in the context of the making of alliances (בת, הילדה, אבות, אחרית, זרע, חבר, [מ]ישרים), as are religious terms such as words for God, gods, idols, and sacred vessels, and expressions for time (עת, שנים, קץ, מועד). Several words appear with particular frequency: עמד ("arise"/"stand"/"raise," sixteen times), בא ("come"/"attack"/"bring," twelve times), שוב ("turn"/"return"/"do again," twelve times), עשה ("make"/"act"/"do," ten times). These verbal phenomena contribute to the drawing of patterns in history such as we have noted above: for example, kings who seem to have the power to do as they will but who are then frustrated and fall (vv 3, 16, 36); kings who seek to seal alliances by means of marriages, and fail (vv 6, 17); more generally, the ceaseless movement and warring between north and south, the unending rise and fall of rulers and empires with their awesome power and authority yet their less acknowledged constraints and transience. Some of the terms are taken up from chap. 10 into chap. 11 or carried on from chap. 11 into chap. 12 (e.g., עמד; חזק and other terms for strength [Barth, *Diesseits,* 86]); they thus establish links and contrasts between the different forms of strength and authority that these chapters portray.

On the basis of overlaps, repetitions, and unevennesses, it has been suggested that an earlier form of the section lacked some of 10:1; 10:20–11:1; 12:5–13, in whole or in part (see, e.g., Hasslberger, *Hoffnung,* 135–41; Davies, 63–65), and some explanatory phrases such as "the northern king" in 11:11

(BHS) and the explicit reference in Egypt in 11:8 (Charles). Carroll looks at the sequence of estimated periods in 12:7, 11–12 in the light of Festinger's studies of how groups cope with nonfulfillment of prophecies (see *Bibliography*).

Setting

Hengel (*Judentum,* 8–107 [ET 1:6–55]) describes the Hellenistic period as one of secularization, materialism, economic activity, exploitation, and militarization, and more of this is visible as the background of chaps. 10–12 than was the case with earlier chapters. While Greek rule has had a profound influence on Palestine, Baʿal Šamem is a Syrian god; the Antiochene period is one of an identity crisis for Judaism both in relation to Eastern religions and in relationship to Hellenism (Lampe, "Apocalyptiker," 64). The chapters' specific historical setting at the point where quasi-prophecy gives way to actual prophecy lies after the outbreak of resistance to Antiochus IV some time between 167 and 164 B.C. It reflects the beliefs and pressures of conservative Jews, the "hasidim" of 1 Macc 2:42. These can later be divided into more and less militarist groups; here this division is possible but not certain. Although they may be characterized as a transformationist sect set over against reformist Jews (see chap. 7 *Setting*), their emphasis on the multitude, the main body of the community, indicates that they had a vision for the people as a whole; in this sense their mentality was not sectarian (Reid, 214–15, contrasting *1 Enoch*). They are anti-Seleucid but not explicitly anti-Hellenistic or pro-Ptolemaic. 10:2–3 suggests that the group respected mantic activity. Stylistic differences may indicate a different author from that of previous chapters (so, e.g., Hasslberger, *Hoffnung,* 145–58), but if so, the author comes from the same group.

Chaps. 10–12 are given special emphasis by their length and their location at the end of the book. The introduction to the prophecy is particularly complex and awesome, with a number of celestial beings involved. It provides a particularly concrete "metaphysical backdrop" to the quasi-prophecy in chap. 11 (Collins, *Vision,* 103–4). The latter, following on the symbolic dream and vision of chaps. 7 and 8 and the still cryptic scriptural exposition of chap. 9, then offers the plainest and most clear-cut of the quasi-prophecies, explaining and decoding what precedes (Szold, "Eleventh Chapter," 53). The account of the End complements the earlier portrait of the lasting reign of the holy ones, the vindication of the temple, and the downfall of the desolater, by working out some of their implications for people whom death seems to rob of the chance to see or share in them. The links between the visions are pointed up by links of vocabulary (e.g., cf. 10:1 with 8:27; 9:23 [Baldwin]). The repeated concluding instructions (12:4, 9, 13) enhance a sense of closure in chap. 12 (Collins, *Daniel* [FOTL] 98).

This closing section of Daniel links back to its opening chapter. 10:1 introduces chaps. 10–12 as a story *about* Daniel like chaps. 1–6, uses the name Belteshazzar, refers to Cyrus, and relates an incident in the king's third year (cf. 1:1, 7, 21). 10:2–3 recalls 1:8–16 as well as 9:3. We are to read a vision received by the hero portrayed in chaps. 1–6 (Anderson). It is a vision relating to leaders experiencing the same afflictions as are described in chaps. 1–6—sword (2:6, 12–13), fire (chap. 3), exile (chap. 1), and becoming prey (chap.

6): see 11:33. They are confronting an overweening king like those of chaps. 4–5: see 11:36; if he does not turn like the first, he will fall like the second. They are challenged to acknowledge their God and offer firm resistance (cf. chaps. 3; 6) and to purify themselves (cf. chap. 1): see 11:32, 35; 12:10. They are to be steadfast in sharing the fruits of their discernment (cf. chaps. 1–2; 4–5, especially the use of שכל and בין in 1:4, 17, 20): see 11:33.

Comment

10:1 The opening verse summarizes chaps. 10–12 as a whole, introducing the motifs of the reliability of the revelation Daniel is given, the conflicts chap. 11 describes, and the understanding Daniel is given. The date "in the third year of Cyrus" fits the pattern of other Danielic dates (see 1:1 *Comment,* 2:1 *Comment*) but it may be significant in its own right: it takes us beyond the first year of Cyrus mentioned in 1:21, which should herald the fulfillment of Jeremiah's seventy-years prophecy and the restoration of the temple as the exiles are free to return to Jerusalem (Ezra 1:1–3), into and apparently beyond "the second year of their arrival" (Ezra 3:8), when they were able to begin the restoration but were soon caused to give up (Ezra 4:24). The disappointment associated with the beginning of Israel's restoration from exile is countered by a promise of final restoration (12:1–3) (Plöger).

10:2–3 The date of v 1 thus provides the background to the "mourning" of vv 2–3, which emerges from a context parallel to that of 9:1–2 and has similar significance to Daniel's seeking God in 9:3 (see 9:3–23 *Comment* [h]). Mourning (אבל) is the response to the state of Jerusalem in Isa 66:10; cf. also 60:20; 61:2–3; Neh 1:4; 8:9. There is less ground here than in chap. 9 for taking the mourning to denote penance (against JB). As in chap. 9, mourning expresses itself in fasting in the sense of abstaining from festal food and even from the everyday grooming of a respectable person (2 Sam 12:20; 14:2; Qoh 9:7–10; Jdt 10:3). The three-week period will be explained by v 13; there is also perhaps an implication that Daniel's self-affliction goes far beyond the three-*day* periods of Exod 19:10–16; Esth 4:16 (Lacocque).

10:4 The date suggests that Daniel's fast will have included the feasts of Passover and Unleavened Bread, which Antiochus "turned into mourning" as he made them impossible of proper observance (1 Macc 1:39, 45). Daniel shares in anticipation in this "mourning." Twenty-four days also equals 3½ weeks: Burgmann (*RevQ* 10 [1979–81] 71) takes this to indicate that the vision comes halfway through a week of years.

10:5–19 The appearing of the man in linen (vv 5–6) reflects that of the supernatural beings in Ezek 1; 9–10 (see *Form*). Linen is the garb of a priest; here as in Ezek 9–10 the servants of the heavenly temple concern themselves with the affairs of its earthly equivalent. The details of the description in v 6, as in Ezek 1, combine to suggest the impression of the dazzling brightness and awesome splendor of a heavenly being.

This effect continues in vv 7–19, which describe the dismayed reactions of his companions and of Daniel himself to the sight and sound reported in vv 4–6, and the stages by which Daniel is restored. The man in linen is not described as a "holy one," but the verses illustrate "the idea of the holy" as suggesting fundamentally a splendor that inspires awe rather than a purity that evokes an awareness of sin (Gammie); they portray someone almost seeing God and hearing God, and almost losing his life as a consequence (see Exod 33:20; Deut 4:33; Judg 6:22–23) (cf. Anderson). We are told successively how his companions fled in terror, how Daniel was overcome by weakness, and how he fell into a trance (see 8:18 *Comment*). We are then told successively how he was touched and raised to his hands and knees, then to a standing but bowed position, then touched and enabled to voice his weakness, then touched and encouraged to listen to the messenger. It is perhaps significant that he is now addressed as "*man* held in high regard" (v 11, contrast 9:23): he has been devastated, then given the life of an animal on all fours, then restored to his human standing (cf. chap. 7) (Lacocque).

It is not clear how many supernatural beings are involved in the scene. In 12:5–6 there are two others apart from the man in linen, and so it may also be here, but the seer does not make it explicit. The man in linen (vv 5–6) may be Michael and the subsequent speaker Gabriel, though—if so—it is odd that the names are not actually applied to the figures, nor are the links noted (contrast 9:21); nor does the reference to Michael in 11:1 mention the fact that he is present. The man in linen is described in more awesome terms than have been used of Gabriel previously, like those used of God himself in Ezek 1. But they need not indicate that the person *is* God, or represents God (like the messenger of Yahweh, e.g., Gen 16), only that the passages have this literary connection (Heaton; contrast, e.g., H. Haag, *TWAT* ". . . בן-אדם"; R. D. Rowe, "Is Daniel's 'Son of Man' Messianic?" in *Christ the Lord* FS D. Guthrie, ed. H. H. Rowdon [Leicester/Downers Grove, IL: IVP, 1982] 90–91). He might be the one who spoke with Gabriel in 8:16 (Bampfylde, *JSJ* 14 [1983] 129–30). The figure in v 11 has the task of speaking, not acting, and the description of his role in v 12 corresponds to that of Gabriel in 9:20–23; so also v 14. Whether or not he *is* Gabriel, he has a role like Gabriel's. There is no reason to link any of the figures here specifically with the humanlike figure of 7:13. Like chap. 7, the scene has the allusiveness that often characterizes vision reports and the visionary experience itself, and exegesis must preserve this allusiveness. It heightens the awesomeness of what is described.

Like other ancient Near Eastern writings, the OT assumes that the results of battles on earth reflect the involvement of heaven. Usually the picture is of heavenly forces aiding Israel and enabling them to win against otherwise overwhelming earthly forces. Yahweh and his armies fight with Israel's armies: hence Israel's victories against impossible odds (Num 10:35–36; Deut 33:2–3; Judg 5:19–20; cf. 1QM 12; Hab 3; Ps 68). There is a certain parallel between the structure of heaven as Canaanite myths see it and as the OT sees it, but in the latter the "gods" are merely the servants of the one Yahweh. The exodus story gives Yahweh's messenger a key role regarding Israel's victorious progress (Exod 14:19; 23:20, 23; 32:34; 33:2); the conquest story pictures the involvement of the commander of Yahweh's armies (Josh 5:14–15). Where Israel loses, the presupposition will be that he fights against them. Other heavenly powers still act as his servants (cf. Deut 29:26; 32:8 4QDeut, LXX; Sir 17:17). A few passages, however, suggest that there are heavenly armies that oppose Yahweh, so that earthly battles reflect battles in heaven; whichever side wins in heaven, its equivalent wins on earth. Heavenly beings who oppose Yahweh are destined for punishment (Isa 24:21; Ezek 28, if the prince of Tyre is the heavenly figure who is identified with Tyre; Ps 82, if the "gods" are supernatural beings; *1 Enoch* 89–90; 2 Macc 5).

It is not quite clear how the description of affairs in heaven in 10:13 and 10:20–11:1 is to be "placed" in relation to this broader OT material. The description is again equivocal, though perhaps for reasons different from those that apply to the figure(s) appearing in the vision. Here it may be that seer and audience could presuppose a frame of reference that clarified what is now unclear to us.

The conflict referred to here may be a verbal/legal one with the representative of Persia, as in the scenes in Zech 3 and Job 1–2 (Jerome), or one involving a warrior seeking to halt a messenger (Plöger), or a "physical" struggle between supernatural armies (Collins, *Vision,* 135): cf. the appearance in the heavenly scene of the Persian kings, presumably heavenly equivalents of the earthly kings who appear in 11:2. The background to the Persian representative's opposing the messenger may be the earthly conflicts described in Ezra 4 (Keil), or it may be those to be announced in chap. 11: the Persian representative, then, wishes to avoid the declaring and thus the implementing of a message that begins with the fall of the Persian empire, an event associated with the end of the era (v 14) (Plöger).

Michael (מיכאל, "who is like God") is an ordinary OT name (e.g., Ezra 8:8). Michael, like Gabriel, is one of the senior angels in *1 Enoch* (e.g., 9.1; 20.5; 71.9).

10:20–11:2a Three comments about the messenger's purpose in coming and his intention with regard to the message (the opening of 10:20, of 10:21, and of 11:2) are interwoven with two sayings about his conflicts (the bulk of 10:20 and of 10:21–11:1) in an a-b-a-b-a arrangement; cf. the a-b-a arrangement of similar material in 10:12–14. The effect is to tie the delivering of the earthly message and the reality of the heavenly conflicts closely together, and to underline in yet another way the importance of the message, if its delivery was worth the turning of the messenger's attention away from such crucial conflicts. The sayings about his conflicts are longer and in that sense more prominent.

In v 20, the details of expression are again allusive, but the picture is apparently of the messenger returning to resume the fight to ensure that Persia continues to be restrained from adversely affecting God's purpose (especially for Israel), but then of the Greeks in turn taking up their attempt to implement their own will, which also threatens that purpose. It is not implied that the nations oppose Israel in particular; Israel just happens to be in their way. The same picture is implied in chap. 11. There is not the direct concern of imperial nations with Israel that is presupposed elsewhere when the nations are God's agents in executing his wrath on Israel. The conflict between Persia or Greece and Israel is a political, not a religious one (Collins, *VT* 25 [1975] 601). It is the heavenly correspondents of these earthly powers that the messenger opposes, supported only by Michael (v 21b)—not surprisingly, because the interests that the messenger is concerned about, which focus on the purpose of God himself, are also the interests of Michael's own people, because they are central to that purpose. There is thus a common interest between the messenger and Michael, which made it appropriate also for the messenger to support Michael on another occasion (11:1). This might refer to the fall of Babylon to the Medes, an earlier historical event of key importance for Israel (see 6:1 [5:31] *Comment*), or to the angelic deliverance of Daniel (see chap. 6), or to the angelic message in chap. 9 (see 9:1).

The "nevertheless" of v 21 indicates that the messenger is prepared to delay resuming his battles in order to deliver the revelation that follows. For the notion of a book detailing a program of events to take place, cf. the heavenly tablets of *1 Enoch* 81; 93 (see Russell, *Apocalyptic,* 107–8); regarding the individual, Ps 139:16.

11:2b–39 The content of the message combines a considerable amount of historical information on the Persian and Greek periods, especially the reigns of Antiochus III and IV, with interpretation by means of a considerable number of allusions to passages from Scripture (see *Form*). These may portray the history of the period as a recapitulation of crises in earlier centuries, so that typologically the earlier Assyrian enemy from the north stands for the Syrians, Sargon for Antiochus . . . (Fishbane, *Interpretation*). Or they may portray this period as a fulfillment of biblical prophecies from Isaiah, Habakkuk, Numbers, and elsewhere, in the manner of 1QpHab (Seeligmann, VTSup 1 [1953] 171). Or they may simply illuminate the period without the chapter presupposing the nature of the hermeneutical link between them and the events. Our chief sources for the history of the events on which chap. 11 focuses, apart from Daniel itself, are the second-century B.C. Greek historian Polybius, 1 and 2 Maccabees, Diodorus Siculus (first century B.C.), the Roman historian Livy (c. 59 B.C.—A.D. 17), Josephus, Appian (second century A.D.), and Porphyry as quoted by Jerome (see *CAH* vii, 1:1–22).

Like narrative history, quasi-predictive history must select and present its material on some principle, such as an interest in political or social or military or religious affairs, or in the achievements of great individuals. The focus of Dan 11 is the career of Antiochus IV. He is portrayed as a second-century B.C. instance of the arrogant gentile warrior attacking the people of God (see *Form, Structure*). The historical facts that are included are ones that illustrate this; the generalizations relate to the "type" that Antiochus is believed to fulfill, so that descriptions of his cleverness or deceitfulness should not be taken as attempts to characterize his personal individuality.

One aspect of the pattern of history as chap. 11 sees it emerges immediately. It is the story of the exercise of power, but the exercise of power leads only to external conflict (v 2b), internal dissolution (vv 3–4), or eclipse by a more powerful entity (v 5). It is the nature of kings not to recognize this; they always aspire to that elusive final victory. They seek it by marriage alliances, but fail (v 6). More commonly they seek it by the use of force, but that also fails (vv 8b–9). It may win famous victories, but these always turn out to be temporary (vv 7–8a, 10–12). A first climax to the portrayal of history by this pattern comes in vv 13–19, where most of the individual features of vv

2b–12 come together. A final victory of north over south seems possible, but in the end the northern king is stopped in his tracks by another power altogether. The talk of his standing as others are unable to stand before him (vv 15–16) is replaced by talk of his plan's not standing and of his stumbling and falling (vv 17, 19). The account of the relationship between Seleucid and Ptolemaic empires is not primarily concerned with making moral judgments. As it describes kings obtaining wealth and power, being in a position of unchallengeable authority, using marriage as a means of cementing dynastic relationships, invading the holy land, or involved in ceaseless invasion and warmongering, it is reflecting the fact that such conflicts are built into history.

When the seer reaches his goal, the reign of Antiochus, he structures his portrayal by means of a series of time expressions, mostly reusing terms that appeared in 8:17, 19 (see *Comment*). The repetition of קץ ("end," vv 27, 35, 40, cf. 45; also 12:4, 6, 9, 13) underlines the punctiliar, definitive actuality and finality of the reversal Daniel promises. The less punctiliar term אחרית ("latter part," "last stage": see on 2:28) comes only in 10:14; 11:4 (where it is not a temporal term), and 12:8 (where EVV do not take it in a temporal sense). The repetition of מועד ("set time," vv 27, 29, 35; cf. 12:7) underlines the divine control and purpose at work even in the abominations and the suffering of the Antiochene period. These are acknowledged by referring to it as a time of wrath (זעם, v 36), as a time of unprecedented trouble (עת צרה, 12:1), and a time of awesome events (הפלאות, 12:6); but the idea of wrath being "complete" (11:36) implies that it cannot go on without limit. In chaps. 10–12, the focus is more exclusively on the Hellenistic period than was the case in earlier chapters. While the time of wrath *may* be the period that began with the exile, there are fewer pointers to this than was the case in 8:19. Exegetically, it makes best sense to refer all the indications of time to the same moment. Antiochus's purposes are frustrated at a particular juncture because "an end will yet await the set time" (v 27), and some of the discerning later fall for the same reason (v 35). It is that moment which will arrive with the last battle between the two kings (v 40), and that moment which will see Michael arising (12:1). It is until that moment that Daniel's book is to be sealed (12:4, 9), that moment which will come after a set time (12:6), and—probably—that moment when Daniel will arise to his destiny (12:13).

11:2b "Three further kings . . .": the Achaemenid kings were Cyrus (560/59–530 B.C.), Cambyses (530–522), Smerdis (522), Darius I (522–486), Xerxes I (486–465), Artaxerxes I (465–424), Xerxes II (424), Sogdianos (424–423), Darius II (423–405/4), Artaxerxes II (405/4–359/58), Artaxerxes III (359/58–338/37), Artaxerxes IV (338/37–336), Darius III (336–330) (Cook, *Persian Empire,* 266). If the assertion that "the fourth king will be far wealthier than anyone" is to be pressed, it has to allude to Xerxes I, who invaded Greece to be defeated at Salamis in 480. Strictly, there was no one Greek empire until the time of Philip of Macedon. The reference of v 2b as a whole is thus to the four kings who followed Cyrus. But the prophecy then has to leap over a century from Xerxes to Alexander. Further, the reference to the four Persian kings recalls the four heads of 7:6, while "three . . . and the fourth" recalls wisdom's "graduated numerical saying" in, for example,

Prov 30 and Amos 1–2 (see H. W. Wolff, *Dodekapropheton* 2 [BKAT xiv, 2 (1969, 2nd ed. 1975) = *Joel and Amos* (tr. W. Janzen et al.; Hermeneia [1977])] in loc. and references). Thus the figure "four" may need not to be pressed, nor the kings specifically identified; the phrase may denote the Achemenids as a whole—perhaps represented by the kings mentioned in the OT, Cyrus, Darius I, Xerxes I, Artaxerxes I, and the Darius of Neh 12:22 if that is Darius II or III, and if "the fourth" means the fourth of the total number, not a fourth after Cyrus. The wealth of the last is then the presumed accumulated wealth of the last Persian king ([Hartman and] Di Lella), as the hostility to Greece denotes that of the empire as a whole.

11:3–4 "Then a warrior-king . . . will rule a great realm." Alexander the Great came to the throne of Macedon in 336 B.C.; he invaded and conquered the territory from Turkey to India and thus came to rule the largest empire the world had yet known. "But as soon as he arises, his empire will break up . . .": Alexander reigned over this empire less than a decade. He died of a fever in 323 B.C. and his empire shattered. It will "divide toward the four winds of the heavens": four major units eventually emerged from Alexander's fragmented empire, centered on Macedon and Greece, Thrace, Syria and the east, and Egypt. To speak of the empire dividing toward the four winds of the heavens is to use a figurative expression for this fragmentation (cf. the four horns of 8:8): the division did not correspond at all closely to the points of the compass. "It will not belong to his surviving family": Alexander's half-brother Philip III and his son Alexander IV were nominal rulers of the empire until their deaths in 317 and 311 (or 305: see Wacholder, "Seleucid Era," 183–211), but central administrative power was held by Alexander's prime minister, Perdiccas, until his assassination in 321. In any case the united Macedonian empire immediately became a fiction. Alexander's real "heirs" (*diadochoi*) were the generals who ruled different satrapies of his empire. Among these were Ptolemy, who was allocated Egypt, Antigonus, whose area included much of Turkey and later Syria and the east, and Seleucus, who became satrap of Babylonia in 321.

11:5 In chap. 11 "the southern king" and "the northern king" are generic terms to refer to the current occupants—whoever they may be—of the Ptolemaic throne in Egypt and the Seleucid throne in Syria and Babylonia. The two realms lie either side of Palestine and thus directly concern Judea, and are the two most powerful of the Hellenistic monarchies. Chap. 11 shows that the outline of the history of the Syrian and Egyptian empires was quite well known to the author. He alludes to thirteen of their kings, noted in the following outline of the period (all dates are B.C.):

Ptolemy I Soter, son of Lagus, 322–285 (v 5a)	Seleucus I Nicator, 312–280 (v 5b)
Ptolemy II Philadelphus, 285–246 (v 6)	Antiochus I Soter, 280–261
	Antiochus II Theos, 261–246 (v 6)
Ptolemy III Euergetes, 246–221 (vv 7–9)	Seleucus II Callinicus, 246–226 (vv 7–9)
	Seleucus III Soter Ceraunus 226–223 (v 10)
Ptolemy IV Philopator, 221–203 (vv 10–12)	Antiochus III Magnus, 223–187 (vv 10–19)

Ptolemy V Epiphanes, 203–181 (vv 14–17)	Seleucus IV Philopator, 187–175 (v 20)
Ptolemy VI Philometor, 181–146 (vv 25–28)	Antiochus IV Epiphanes, 175–163 (vv 21–45)
	Antiochus V Eupator, 163–162
	Demetrius I Soter, 162–150

The first southern king is Ptolemy I. Though he ruled Egypt from 322 B.C., he declared himself king only c. 305. "One of his officers will be more powerful than he . . .": Seleucus I. Antigonus had expanded his empire in Asia and had attacked Babylonia in 316; Seleucus had fled to Egypt and become one of Ptolemy's generals. Ptolemy and Seleucus defeated Antigonus's army at Gaza in 312. Subsequently Seleucus not only recovered Babylon but also gradually won control of the rest of Antigonus's empire, until after Antigonus's death at the battle of Ipsus in 301 Seleucus ruled "a greater realm than his [Ptolemy's]"—indeed, the largest of the post-Alexander empires. Its significance in the ancient world is reflected in the fact that the Seleucid era provided a new basis for chronology (see 1 Maccabees). The Ptolemies, however, controlled Palestine itself through the third century; this was a source of conflict between the Ptolemaic and Seleucid empires.

11:6 "After some years an alliance will be made . . ." About 250 B.C., half a century later, Ptolemy II attempted to mend relationships with the Seleucid empire, whose capital was now at Antioch, by marrying his daughter Berenice to Antiochus II, who divorced his first wife, Laodice, and excluded their sons Seleucus and Antiochus from succeeding him. "But she will not be able to hold onto her power. . . ." After two years, Antiochus II apparently went back to Laodice, who then had him killed, along with his son by Berenice (thus clearing the way for her own son Seleucus), Berenice herself, and a number of her Egyptian attendants. Berenice's father also died in the same year.

11:7–9 "One of the shoots from her roots . . .": Berenice's brother, Ptolemy III, succeeded to their father's throne in Egypt. "He will attack the army . . .": in connection with this violent sequence of events involving his sister, his nephew, and his kingdom's subjects, Ptolemy III invaded the Seleucid empire, gained control of considerable areas of Syria (including Antioch and Seleucia, its fortified port on the Mediterranean) and of the lands further east, avenged his sister by having Laodice killed, and took much booty back to Egypt. Taking a nation's gods was a sign of subjugation and the exercise of power. Despite his huge successes, Ptolemy did not press on to total conquest of the Seleucid empire. In the end he had to leave the throne there to Seleucus II (son of Antiochus II by Laodice) and return to Egypt to deal with an uprising at home. "Although he will then keep away from the northern king . . .": for two years there was no conflict between the two empires; then in 242 Seleucus II attempted to invade Egypt, but had to retreat, his army decimated.

11:10–12 "His sons will commit themselves to war . . .": Seleucus II was succeeded by his sons, Seleucus III (226–223) and—on his murder during a campaign in Turkey—Antiochus III (223–187). The latter attempted to turn the tide of aggressive power between the Seleucids and the Ptolemies, beginning in 219 by recapturing Seleucia. He invaded Palestine and conquered a large part of it. "But the southern king . . .": Ptolemy IV (221–203) in due course sent an army to engage with Antiochus III at Raphia, the Egyptian stronghold on the border with Palestine, in 217. According to Polybius (*Histories* 5.79), Antiochus took 62,000 infantry, 6,000 cavalry, and 102 elephants into battle against Ptolemy's 70,000 infantry, 5,000 cavalry, and 73 elephants. Antiochus lost over 14,000 men in defeat, but Ptolemy, despite the encouragement, still lacked his father's instinct for warmaking. He was content with victory and the regaining of Palestine and Phoenicia, and did not press his advantage, making peace with Antiochus.

11:13–15 "The northern king will return and raise a larger horde . . .": over the next fourteen years Antiochus campaigned in Turkey and the east and regained much of the old Seleucid empire, winning for himself the title "the Great." Then he raised an even larger army in alliance with Philip V of Macedon to invade the Ptolemaic kingdom. "During those times many will rise up against the southern king . . .": there were native Egyptian rebellions against Ptolemaic rule from 207 (a consequence, Polybius [5.107] suggests, of the encouragement of native Egyptian morale by the Egyptian victory over Antiochus), and Ptolemy IV died in mysterious circumstances, to be succeeded by his infant son Ptolemy V (203–181). The country was actually ruled by Agathocles, a chief minister under Ptolemy IV; his oppressive regency provoked insurrection in Egypt, and his assassination. But the "many" may also refer to the soldiers of Antiochus and Philip.

"Wild men among your people . . .": the period was one of strife within the Jewish community itself. The high priest held supreme authority in both political and religious affairs, but Onias II had been forced to share de facto political power with his brother-in-law Tobias, and the Tobiads became significant political forces in Jerusalem. The Oniads were inclined to be anti-Egyptian, the Tobiads to be pro-Egyptian, though there was also conflict over policy within the Tobiad family (see Schäfer, "Hellenistic and Maccabaean Periods," 571–78). The assertiveness of the "wild men" (בני פריצים) has often been taken to refer to Jews—presumably Oniads—joining in that resistance to the southern king which v 14a refers to. But it is odd to say that they failed or "fell." Apart from one short-lived victory on the part of the Egyptian general Scopas, the story of events from 201–198 B.C. is of Antiochus's triumphant conquest of Palestine. More likely the unsuccessful wild men are Tobiads (Toll, *OrSuec* 21 [1972] 73–86). Schlatter suggested Daniel was referring to their involvement in anti-Seleucid resistance (*ZAW* 14 [1894] 147–51). But "wild men" is actually a term used to suggest violation of the holy rather than merely violence. There is no polemic against violent action here.

Their acts of violation take place "in fulfillment of a vision." Reference to a "vision" recalls chap. 8, where the word occurs more frequently than in any other chapter in the OT; the violators might be seen as unintentionally fulfilling Daniel's revelation. But that would be true of many other aspects of chap. 11; it is not obvious why this particular motif in chap. 11 should be described thus. Nor is it likely that Daniel would use the term in the rather modern sense of the people's political vision or policy (against Plöger).

The vision might be one received within the community (cf. Ezek 13:6), or a passage from the prophets (cf. 9:24; also Ezek 12:22–27; Hab 2:2–3). OG assumes Amos 9:11 (see van der Kooij, "Reinterpretation," 75); Jerome suggests Isa 19:19, connecting the passage with Onias's building of a temple at Leontopolis (so, recently, Keil, *ZAW* 97 [1985] 228, though this involves taking the apparent reference to Onias's death in Dan 11:22 as an unhistorical gloss). Daniel would be implying a conscious or unconscious attempt to bring about the fulfillment of God's plan expressed in these scriptures, but one that fails, because God's time has not yet come; the present vision goes on to indicate the further events that must take place before that End (cf. Täubler, *JQR* 37 [1946–47] 1–30; J. C. H. Lebram, "Apokalyptiek als keerpunt in het joodse denken," *NedTT* 30 [1976] 273–75).

But the reference to a vision is one of the passage's points of contact with Ezek 7 (v 26; see *Form*), where it refers to people in Jerusalem seeking some vision to encourage them. More likely, then, the vision is this passage in Ezek 7, which the violators unconsciously fulfill, and fall because God brings judgment on them as he warned there.

"Then the northern king will advance . . .": in 199 B.C. Antiochus defeated Scopas at Paneas (Caesarea Philippi), followed him to Sidon, an Egyptian fortified city, and laid siege to it. In 198 Scopas and his troops, along with reinforcements sent from Egypt to relieve him, had to surrender.

11:16–19 "His attacker will thus be able to act as he pleases . . .": Antiochus thus gained firm control of Palestine and Phoenicia, including Judea, and also captured some of the areas on the coast of Asia Minor that had been subject to Egyptian rule: Cilicia, Lycia, and Caria. He was in a position to invade Egypt itself and destroy the Ptolemaic empire, but he feared Roman intervention. Instead he made peace with Egypt in 197, betrothing his daughter Cleopatra to Ptolemy V. He hoped to further his designs on Egypt through her, but she (Egypt's first Cleopatra) became perfectly loyal to her husband and new homeland and encouraged an Egyptian alliance with Rome, which frustrated Antiochus's continuing designs on the Ptolemaic area of the old empire of Alexander.

"So he will turn his attention to the sea lands . . ." (v 18): in the meantime, Antiochus resumed his attacks on Egyptian-held areas of Asia Minor and went on to invade Macedon, Thrace, and Greece itself. But in 191 the Romans defeated him at Thermopylae, and again decisively at Magnesia near Smyrna a year later, ending his pretensions to power in the west. Antiochus became a vassal of Rome and his younger son, the later Antiochus IV, was taken to Rome as a hostage. "So he will turn his attention to the strongholds in his own land . . ." (v 19): Antiochus thus returned to Syria; he was assassinated at Elymais in 187 while attempting to pillage the treasury of Bel, one of his own gods, to pay the tribute imposed on him by the Romans after their victory.

11:20 "There will arise in his place . . .": his successor, Seleucus IV, was an unfortunate and unpopular ruler whose main concern had to be paying the tribute imposed on his father. The oppressor he sent round in this connection was his finance minister Heliodorus, whose acts included attempting to pillage the treasury of the temple at Jerusalem. This was *the* event of Seleucus's reign not merely because of its unexpected thwarting (2 Macc 3) but because of its being an anti-fulfillment of an OT prophecy (see *Form*). Seleucus died in 175. According to Appian, *Wars* 11.8 [45], he was assassinated in a plot engineered by Heliodorus in which Seleucus's younger brother Antiochus—now on his way back from Rome—may also have been involved (see on 7:24). There is perhaps a slur in the comment on his ignominious death, "not in the heat of battle."

11:21–24 The most prominent feature of the prophecy, the career of the last northern king, forms a series of episodes, marked by time references (cf. in part Hanhart, "Übersetzungstechnik," 136–57): vv 21–24 (". . . until a certain time"), vv 25–28 (". . . an end will yet await the set time . . ."), vv 29–35 ("At the set time . . . until the time of the end—for it will still await the set moment"), vv 36–39 (". . . until wrath is complete . . ."; and see beginning of v 40), and vv 40–45 ("at the time of the end . . ."); cf. 12:1–3 ("at that time . . . to all eternity").

The prophecy begins with an account of the last northern king's extraordinary rise to power, remarkable for its shrewdness. "There will arise in his place a despised man . . .": Antiochus IV (175–164). The description, like the epithet Epimanes, Madman (Polybius 26.1a [10]), contrasts with the claim expressed in his title [Theos] Epiphanes, [God] Manifest. There had been no reason to regard the exiled Antiochus as a potential successor to his brother Seleucus IV. His heir was his eldest son, eventually to reign as Demetrius I, but in 175 he had been sent to Rome to replace Antiochus as hostage there.

The details of Antiochus's rise to power are uncertain. A plausible reconstruction is that while staying at Athens on his way home he heard that his brother had died and that Heliodorus was seeking to consolidate a position as regent, with Seleucus's younger son, also called Antiochus, as puppet king. He hastened homewards. On the basis of being uncle to Seleucus's son—and thus a safeguard against usurpers from outside the dynasty—he gained the support of King Eumenes of Pergamum and Attalus his brother, removed Heliodorus, and took power as guardian to and co-regent with the young Antiochus. "Overwhelming forces . . ." (v 22): perhaps rivals to the throne; but one of these was Ptolemy VI of Egypt, son of Seleucus's and Antiochus's sister Cleopatra, and the language here suggests a reference to the conflict with Egypt that is a main feature of Antiochus's reign as vv 21–45 as a whole describe it, and a main feature of the Hellenistic period as chap. 11 as a whole describes it. The removal of "a covenant prince" belongs in the same context, if the phrase refers to the high priest Onias III (cf. 9:26), replaced because of his Egyptian sympathies (cf. 2 Macc 4) by Jason from the aristocratic, pro-Syrian Tobiad party, as part of a logical policy on Antiochus's part of putting his own nominees in key governmental positions within his empire (Bunge, *Historia* 23 [1974] 61; Lebram, *VT* 25 [1975] 751–52; less likely it denotes Ptolemy [Calvin] or the young Antiochus [Rowley, *ExpT* 55 (1943–44) 24–27]).

Thus while Antiochus began with only the support of "a small group" (v 23), in Judea he won over the "powerful ones of a province," the Tobiads and Jason, Onias's brother. They furthered his cause in Jerusalem; he made it possible for them to hold both civil and religious power there; and it is presumably they who are the beneficiaries of his well-known liberality on the basis of plunder (v 24; cf. Macc 3:28–31).

The Tobiad family takes its name from a Tobias who originally came from across the Jordan. Whether gentilized Jews or Judaizing Gentiles, he and his family were not people of conservative attitude to the Torah. The account of events in 1 Macc 1 and 2 Macc 4 reveals that Jason and his associates also proposed to Antiochus that they should establish a Hellenistic-style community in Jerusalem. The sequence of events and the significance of the Antiochene measures affecting Jerusalem are disputed (see further Bickermann; Hengel; Tcherikover; Mørkholm; Goldstein [see *Main Bibliography*]; Fischer, *Seleukiden*). It seems best to see the events not as part of a cultural or religious concern for the Hellenization of Judea or the broader empire but in connection with Antiochus's political concern to exercise effective control of his empire and with the Tobiads' concern for power in Jerusalem.

Since Artaxerxes' decree in 458 B.C., the Torah had been the law of the land in Judea, a situation confirmed by Antiochus III when he made the Jews a people with internal self-government on the basis of their own laws (Josephus, *Ant.* 12.3.3 [12.135]). In accordance with the Torah, then, the government was in the hands of the priesthood, and the high priest was the means of implementing the king's authority. He was thus naturally appointed—from a priestly family—by the king. He had to see that Jewish affairs were conducted in accordance with the Torah, because the king said so, as well as because God said so; he would need the king's permission to introduce practices differing from those in the Torah, because of the Torah's place in the constitution approved by the king. The implication of 1 Macc 1 and 2 Macc 4, then, is that on Antiochus's accession the authorities in Jerusalem petitioned him for a constitutional change whereby Jerusalem ceased to be the center of a community governing itself in accordance with its own law and became a Hellenistic city-state whose citizenship would comprise those who accepted a Hellenistic way of life. From Antiochus's perspective, the proposal would be welcome because such Hellenistic city-states provided a means of controlling his empire, and the Jerusalem leadership presumably saw it as a wise move to conform their city's constitution and life more to the imperial norm. To do this would involve no necessary contravention of the central tenets of Jewish religion, though by conservative Jews it would be seen as an abandonment of the Torah and of the terms it set for the covenant relationship with Yahweh, which exclude covenants with other peoples. It would be quite in keeping with Daniel's portrayal of events, however, if initiative for the establishment of the city-state came from Antiochus himself (so Goldstein, *I Maccabees,* 111–21). While one might have expected Dan 11 to make this explicit, since it is inclined to emphasize Antiochus's responsibility for events, equally one might have expected Daniel to mention the fact if the reformist Jews were responsible.

11:25–28 There now begins a more detailed account of Antiochus's involvement with Egypt. "He will assert his strength . . .": in 170 B.C. an Egyptian army set off to attempt to recapture Palestine. According to 2 Macc 4:21–22 Antiochus became aware of the need to defend Palestine; indeed, according to 1 Macc 1:16 he had designs on Egypt that mirrored Ptolemy's on the

Seleucid realm. Antiochus defeated the Egyptian army, captured the border fortress of Pelusium, entered Egypt, took his nephew Ptolemy VI prisoner, and occupied much of the country (1 Macc 1:17–19). "Plans will be devised against him: people who eat his provisions will break him": in some sense Ptolemy was the victim of treachery. Perhaps the reference is to people who betrayed Pelusium to Antiochus, or perhaps to Ptolemy's advisers who brought about the Egyptian defeat by urging the attack on Palestine, his capture by urging him to flee from Antiochus, and his deposition by then crowning his brother as Ptolemy VII in Alexandria in 169 B.C. "The two kings . . ." (v 27): Antiochus and Ptolemy VI were now united in desiring to regain the throne for the latter, as Antiochus's puppet. Both are declared to be serving their own interests and deceiving each other but not achieving their conflicting ultimate purposes.

"He will act with determination against a holy covenant" (v 28); there are differences between the sources over events in Jerusalem and over Antiochus's visit(s) there after his two Egyptian campaigns (see Schäfer, "Hellenistic and Maccabaean Periods," 564–66). Dan 11 is more allusive than 1 Macc 1; 2 Macc 5; or Josephus, *Ant.* 12.5 [12.239–50]; *War* 1.1 [1.31–33] and not too exposed to the charge of finding prophecy difficult even after the event. It may be that Antiochus indeed took action against Jerusalem in both 169 and 168 (cf. vv 28 and 30) but that on the latter occasion he acted via Apollonius (cf. 1 Macc 1; 2 Macc 5 then conflates the two sets of events into a personal visit in 168). In 169, however, he personally visited Jerusalem and appropriated part of the temple treasury, which functioned as bank and state exchequer, probably viewing it as tribute (cf. Mørkholm, *Antiochus,* 143) and acting thus because he simply needed the money. The "holy covenant" is a new phrase, here denoting the covenant people (cf. v 30a; 1 Macc 1:15, 63; Jaubert, *Alliance,* 83; it hardly refers to the priesthood in this context [against Lebram, *VT* 20 (1970) 512–13]). It perhaps takes up the "holy ones" of chap. 7 (especially v 27); cf. also the "holy people" of 12:7 and the "covenant prince" of v 22. They are the people who are endowed with a covenant relationship with God; there need be no suggestion of an anthropocentric view of the covenant as depending essentially on its human possessor and guardians (against Eichrodt, *Theologie* 1:23 [ET 1:64]).

11:29–31 "At the set time": the momentous, then painful, then horrifying events to follow are all marked as within the control of God. "He will again invade the south . . .": after Antiochus's departure from Egypt the two Ptolemies had made peace and agreed to reign jointly. In 168 Antiochus invaded again, but this time with disastrous results. "Ships from the west . . ." (v 30): Gaius Popillius Laenas, heading a delegation from Rome—to which Egypt had appealed in connection with the events of 169—intercepted Antiochus on his way to Alexandria and ordered him off Egyptian territory (Appian 11.11 [66]). It was a turning point in Roman history, a mark of the extent to which internationally the period from 200 to 150 is the story of the extension of Roman dominion in the Hellenistic empire (Mørkholm, *Antiochus,* 11).

Following on a rumor that Antiochus had been killed in Egypt, Jason—whom Antiochus had removed from the high-priesthood—returned to Jerusalem and led a violent rebellion against his successor Menelaus and the Tobiad ruling party (2 Macc 5:5–10), and presumably against the Syrian governor (2 Macc 5:21–23a). Conservative Jews may have supported his action; he was a less objectionable person than Menelaus, who had cooperated with Antiochus's looting of the temple the previous year. To Antiochus Jason's action amounted to an attempt to overthrow the government he had appointed and replace it by one that could be presumed to be pro-Egyptian if it was anti-Syrian. Hence he had to "take harsh action against a holy covenant" (v 30) to put down this rebellion (2 Macc 5:11–14), sending Apollonius, the commander of his mercenaries from Mysia in Asia Minor, to Jerusalem (2 Macc 5:23b–27; 1 Macc 1:29–32). "He will pay heed to such as have abandoned a holy covenant": Antiochus thus reestablished the authority of the Tobiad leadership.

"Forces of his will take their stand" (v 31): Antiochus took steps to strengthen his position in Palestine in the context of the conflict with Egypt and/or the resistance in Jerusalem by developing "the stronghold" from which his forces and members of the Hellenistic city-state could oversee temple and city. It will have been near the temple mount: cf. that referred to in Neh 2:8, and the later Antonia Fortress (cf. Goldstein, *I Maccabees,* 213–19; Schäfer, "Hellenistic and Maccabaean Periods," 555–56; Tsafrir, *RB* 82 [1975] 501–21; see 1 Macc 1:29–40). The introduction of the Hellenistic city-state in 175 B.C. would have been an affront to conservative Jews, but it had not affected the temple. The imposition of this garrison, however, implies its desecration. The fortress would be a base from which gentile as well as Jewish "citizens" could enter the shrine in "their" city, which is effectively taken away from Jews who do not belong to the Hellenistic community (cf. 2 Macc 11:24–25, which records its return to conservative Jews; Tcherikover, *Civilization,* 194–95; Lebram, *VT* 20 [1970] 508–9). The former would naturally introduce the worship of their god Baʿal Šamem, the Syrian equivalent to Zeus and—as they would see it—to Yahweh (cf. 2 Macc 6; see *Comment* on 8:13).

"They will remove the daily offering . . .": to judge from 1 Macc 1:41–64, the suspension of the sacrificial system was a separate event from the desecration of the temple by the introduction of the "desolating abomination" just noted. This may imply that conservative Jewish resistance to Antiochene/Tobiad rule and the effects of the gentile garrison's presence continued and spurred Antiochus into this further action, the actual ban on the distinctive feature of Jewish religion. The reasoning behind the ban seems thus to be local and political. Evidence from elsewhere does not suggest that Antiochus tried to abolish the various religions of his empire to make everyone worship Zeus, despite 1 Macc 1:41–42.

11:32–35 "Such as have acted wickedly in relation to a covenant he will turn into apostates . . .": the sources do not say that the Jews who had sought the establishment of a Hellenistic community actually desired the abolition of the external distinctives of Jewish religion; 1 Macc 1 implies that they found themselves drawn into cooperation with a policy that had gone beyond their original expectations. The "people that acknowledges its God" comprises those who insist on still expressing their commitment to Yahweh in the ways specified by the Torah, the ḥasidim or "committed" of 1 Macc 2:42. Their "firm resistance" presumably included active attempts to prevent the implementing of Antiochus's edict. "The discerning" (משכילים, v 33: see n. 33.a) are conservative leaders who possess that wisdom which consists in awed submission to Yahweh, that understanding which has reflected deeply on his ways in history, and that insight which perceives how his cause will ultimately triumph (Kosmala, *JANESCU* 5 [1973] 235–39). They use this to "enlighten the multitude." The verb (בין) is a common word in Daniel, generally denoting insight into the meaning of dreams, visions, or prophecies (cf. Williams, *Death,* 60–61). It suggests that the ministry of the discerning is not teaching in general or exhortation to faithfulness but the interpretation of the prophetic scriptures—and no doubt of these Danielic visions—for the persecuted community. "The multitude" suggests the body of the community as a whole (see on 9:27) and seems to imply that the majority resisted Antiochus; only the Tobiads and the Hellenistic community accepted the edict. In Daniel's thinking it is "the discerning" and "the multitude" who make up "the people" (vv 32, 33; Hasslberger, *Hoffnung*). "Though they will stumble . . .": the martyrdom of some of the discerning comes in v 35; but many ordinary people went through the experiences described in v 33, "sword" (1 Macc 2:9, 31–38), "fire" (2 Macc 6:11; 7:1–41), "captivity" (1 Macc 3:41), "prey" (1 Macc 1:31), and other afflictions (cf. 1 Macc 1:60–64). The terms *the discerning* and *the multitude* hint at the idea that the calling of the servant of Yahweh described in Isa 52:13–53:12 (see *Form*) is being fulfilled here, not only by the leadership but by the people as a whole who also suffer (Brownlee, *BASOR* 132 [1953] 12–13).

"When they stumble, they will receive a little help" (v 34): not the Romans helping the ḥasidim, which only happened later (against Buchanan, *Hebrews,* 47–48); possibly the discerning encouraging the martyrs (Hasslberger, *Hoffnung*) or other Jews coming to share the martyrs' commitment (Collins, *Daniel* [FOTL] 101), if either would count as "help"; but more likely the successes of the first Judean activists (1 Macc 2–4). This is "a little help" compared with the ultimate victory, deliverance, awakening, and exaltation to come at "the set moment" (v 35): see 11:40–12:3. One need not infer that the seer dissociates himself from the active resistance of the Maccabees (cf. v 14 *Comment*). The ḥasidim did fight (1 Macc 2:40–44), but this does not mean that they relied on human hands rather than on the acts of God (see 1 Macc 3:16–22, 52–53, 58–60; 4:8–11, 30–33). We have no evidence for a pacifist group among them. To describe the achievement of the Maccabees as merely a little help might seem odd; it was they who achieved Judean independence. But Fischer speaks of the rebellion as ending in failure in 157 B.C. (*Seleukiden,* 193), and it was the Maccabean stance that was taken up by the Zealots two centuries later. Life for Judaism came rather from the faith that Daniel was commending.

"Many will join them with empty words": people whose commitment to the resistance movement could not be trusted in the long run. Some may have joined out of fear of the Maccabees' own ruthlessness (cf. 1 Macc 2:44; 3:5–8; 6:18–24). "Some of the discerning will stumble": their martyrdom tests how real was the commitment of people who had joined the resistance movement perhaps too lightly. That their "stumbling" is the means of their learning that violent resistance is a false path is hardly implied by vv 32–35 (against Lebram, "Piety," 182–83); in vv 14 and 19 "stumble" (כשל) does suggest the undoing of people who were on the wrong path, but not in vv 33, 34, 35, 41.

11:36–39 The quasi-prophecy closes with an evaluative summary of Antiochus's religious attitudes as king. It moves from the earthly plane of attacks on people and sanctuary to the heavenly plane of attacks on God himself, though the language of chaps. 9 and 11 is less mythical than that of chaps. 7 and 8 in this connection (Joubert [198] in critique of Collins, *Vision*, 135–36). A general statement comes in v 36, more detail in vv 37–39.

"The king will act as he pleases": the standard description of apparently unchallengeable authority (8:4; 11:3, 16) presages unexpected disaster, or at least frustration and failure, and thus adds to the sense of expectancy that Antiochus's success cannot continue. The reference has been taken to be to Antichrist, but the paragraph begins resumptively (not even "the *northern* king") and there is no hint that the subject might be different from that in vv 21–35. The sense of expectancy is encouraged by the phrase that follows, he "will exalt himself and magnify himself": the seer uses verbs applied in the OT only to God and to one who impiously asserts himself against God and has judgment declared upon him (Isa 10:15; 33:15). There may be an allusion to his title Epiphanes, "[God] Manifest," to his use on coins of the title Θεός "God" and of divine symbols, and to his plundering of temples and suppressing of other religions. None of this was peculiar to Antiochus (see v 5 *Comment*); it was characteristic of Hellenistic kings to associate themselves closely with religion in various ways, to support their position (see Walbank, *CAH* vii, 1:84–99). They thus stood under the protection of particular deities, sometimes assimilated themselves to them, and sometimes encouraged worship of themselves. But others did not come into such sharp conflict with the "God of gods" concerning whom Antiochus uttered his "awesome statements"—presumably the edicts that suppressed worship of Yahweh. If Antiochus seems to have taken his divinity more seriously than most, the reason may again be political: it helped to bind his empire together and to him. For him, as for other kings, religion was the servant of his political position. He *is* more important than any god.

"Thus he will pay no heed to the god of his fathers" (v 37): Antiochus replaced Apollo by Zeus as *the* god of the Seleucid dynasty, apparently again for political reasons: it provided religious support for the irregularity involved in his accession. "The one women love" is then plausibly taken as a god especially favored in Egypt, Adonis or Dionysus, who was slighted by Antiochus through his various encroachments on the southern kingdom. The reference to Tammuz as one worshiped by women in Ezek 8:14 seems less relevant. The point is that Antiochus had shown contempt for the key gods of both the Seleucid and the Ptolemaic dynasties (Bunge, *JSJ* 4 [1973] 169–82, with Lebram's comment, *VT* 25 [1975] 755). Possibly the critique presupposes the conviction that Yahweh himself allocated the nations their gods (Deut 32:8–9), so that Antiochus overreaches himself in changing them (Clifford, *BASOR* 220 [1975] 25). But the seer may simply be expressing a theological distaste for what he sees as Antiochus's subservience of religion to politics.

"In his place he will honor a stronghold god . . ." (v 38): further reference to Apollo's replacement by Zeus, worshipped as Baʿal Šamem by the Syrian garrison. Zeus could also be identified with Jupiter, Herakles, or Yahweh, but this seems less relevant (against, e.g., Charles; Morgenstern, *VT* 10 [1960] 167; Goldstein, *I Maccabees*, 157). "So he will deal with a most secure stronghold . . ." (v 39): further reference to the development of the citadel near the temple (see on v 31). "Those he regards . . .": the Tobiad leadership, favored by Antiochus (see on v 24).

11:40–45 The "him" again presupposes that "the northern king" is the same person as that in vv 21–39. There is no hint of a transition to Antichrist or Antiochus V (Fischer, *Seleukiden*, 155) or Pompey and his associates (Gurney), while the phrase "at the time of the end" (contrast v 35) seems to preclude our taking the verses as a résumé of Antiochus's career as a whole. Porphyry assumed that the quasi-predictive historical account of Antiochus's career continues in these verses. But vv 40–45 cannot be correlated with actual events as vv 21–39 can; further, in vv 40–45 the utilization of scriptural phraseology becomes more systematic than was the case earlier (see *Form*). These facts suggest that v 40 marks the transition from quasi-prediction based on historical facts to actual prediction based on Scripture and on the pattern of earlier events; this continues into 12:1–3. These predictions, then, are not to be read as if they were mere anticipatory announcements of fixed future events; like the promises and warnings of the prophets, they paint an imaginative scenario of the *kind* of issue that must come from present events. The fact that their portrayal does not correspond to actual events in the 160s B.C. compares with the fact that the Christ event does not correspond to other OT prophecies of future redemption (e.g., Isa 9:1–6 [2–7]). It is not the nature of biblical prophecy to give a literal account of events before they take place.

In vv 40–43, then, the seer imagines Antiochus's deeds reaching even beyond anything we have already read. He attempts that ultimate victory over the Ptolemaic king which has been denied so many of his predecessors, and breaks the shackles of the constraint north and south have exercised on each other (v 40; Newsom, "Past," 43). In doing so, he is recapitulating Nebuchadnezzar's invasion, once again sparing the old enemies who had taken advantage of Israel then (v 41; cf. Ezek 25). He goes on to fulfill the prophecies that envisaged Nebuchadnezzar's final defeat of Egypt itself—hence the actual naming of Egypt and other southern countries, as in those prophecies; the southern king is unmasked as old Egypt, the northern king as Israel's ancient Mesopotamian foe from the north (vv 42–43). But the moment of triumph again heralds downfall, as so often in chap. 11. Disturbing reports alarm the northern king—another motif from Ezek 7. His victory heralds the last great battle of this supreme world power against shady foes beyond the orbit of the Mesopotamia-Egypt axis (v 44). This final battle takes place, as it must, at the midpoint of that axis, at the center of the world, at the place where the Scriptures had therefore long expected the final conflict; it signifies the end of this apparently unassailable earthly power (v 45). He schemes against an unsuspecting and vulnerable people but finds himself God's victim (Davies, 97).

12:1 "At that time . . .": the phrase again indicates continuity with what precedes and excludes the idea that the seer is moving to some far future moment. The reference to Michael and his description take up 10:13, 21 (see *Comment*). The threefold "that time" in v 1 reinforces the impression that the whole verse is resumptive, as do the allusions to "the discerning" and "the multitude" in v 3. The "time of trouble" is thus a resumptive summary reference to the troubles of 11:40–45, not a new event; it would in any case seem implausible to suggest that the seer writing from the midst of terrible suffering (11:21–39) offers people not only one (11:40–45) but a second further scenario of affliction. Like the descriptions beginning in 11:25 and 11:36, this one also overlaps with the one that precedes it. Chap. 11 has made clear how the time of trouble is "such as has not occurred since they became a nation until that time," for Antiochus was seeking to terminate the worship of the true God and to annihilate his people.

Verse 12:1a, then, reveals the event that underlies the defeat of the northern king in 11:45, the heavenly side to that earthly event (Collins, *JBL* 93 [1974] 57). Each nation has a representative in the heavenly court who fights its battles, legal and military. Michael is thus the one who "stands by those who belong to your people"—by which he means Israel insofar as it resists the pressure of Antiochus and the reformists, who hardly now count as Israel (cf. 11:32). He is "the supreme leader," perhaps by implication the most powerful of those heavenly figures, as Israel is the most significant of the nations, the one whose destiny is guaranteed. So he stands up in court, as in *T. Dan* 6.2 and Jude 9 (Nickelsburg, *Resurrection*, 11–27), to fight for Israel, and his victory there over Antiochus's heavenly representative means that Antiochus is defeated on earth and that "your people will escape." Michael will take up their cause and point out that their names "can be found written in the Book"—not the "reliable book" of 10:21, which included the future acts of the wicked as well as those of the people of God, nor one of the "books" mentioned in 7:10, which recorded the past basis for God's judgment, but a list of those who belong to God's people, the citizen list of the true Jerusalem: cf. the lists referred to in Ezra 2; Neh 7. This becomes a metaphor in Isa 4:3; Ezek 13:9; Ps 87:6, and a mythic motif in Exod 32:32; Isa 48:19; Ps 69:29 [28]. Michael's intervention establishes that they belong to the people of God and have no business to be cast precipitously into the realm of death. This may mean they "escape" from the annihilation referred to in 11:44, avoiding death, unlike the martyrs of 11:33–35, or it may mean that they "escape" from the realm of death by breaking out from it, as v 2 will elaborate; for comparable usage of מלט, see Isa 49:24–25; Ps 116:3–4 (where צרה "trouble" also occurs); 4Q Words of the Luminaries (which also refers to people whose names are written in the book of life [Nickelsburg, *Resurrection*, 161]).

12:2 The meaning of v 2 has been much disputed, partly because its context has not been kept in mind. Its exegesis must be approached via what precedes it, not via the formulated doctrine of resurrection later developed by groups such as the Pharisees and adopted by Christians. Indeed, we must avoid treating it as a piece of theological "teaching": it is a vision or a flight of the imagination, not a "fully developed" belief in resurrection (against Gese, *Theologie*, 52 [ET 57]). The seer continues to portray the future on the basis of Scripture, especially Isaiah (see *Form*); his imaginative portrayal should not necessarily be taken as an attempt at literal prediction. Further, its message connects with the historical events related in its literary context in 11:21–12:3. Thus an awakening of the dead of nations other than Israel is hardly within the concern of v 2 (against Gese, loc. cit.). Nor is its concern the eschatological restoration of the covenant people (against Preuss, " 'Auferstehung,' " 133, referring to J. Kammerer, *Die Auferstehung der Toten im Alten Testament als Element der eschatologischen Restauration des Bundesvolkes Israel* [Diss., Vienna, 1968]), if this implies an eschatological future distinct from a present context. Nor is it concerned with "the transcendence of death" in itself; if this is the distinguishing mark of apocalyptic eschatology (Collins, *CBQ* 36 [1974] 30), then Daniel fails this test—even in chap. 12—as it fails others. Erling ("Ezekiel 38–39," in *Ex orbe religionum* 1:113–14) draws a contrast between the historically contextual resurrection idea of Ezek 37, which is characteristically prophetic, and the resurrection idea here, which reflects apocalyptic's withdrawal from history with its constraints because Yahweh did not now seem to be acting there. Actually Daniel's resurrection idea is as clearly historical as Ezekiel's (though more covertly)—and more so than Ezek 38–39.

The OT's standard way of envisaging dying and coming back to life is by speaking of lying down and sleeping, then of waking and getting up. The former is an extreme form of the latter, which thus provides the metaphor for it (2 Kgs 4:31; 13:21; Isa 26:19; Jer 51:39, 57; Job 14:12). Further, dying means lying down with one's ancestors in the family tomb, with its nonmaterial equivalent, Sheol; so coming back to life would mean leaving such a "land of earth" (cf. also Pss 49; 73). The image presupposes a restoring to life of the whole person with its spiritual and material aspects.

But what does the image of the renewing of earthly life refer to? The seer could be promising a revival of the nation after the Antiochene persecution (cf. e.g., Ezek 37). But the revival is to "lasting life," which suggests more than that, as does the reference to the destiny of "others." These whose destiny is rather "utter shame" and "lasting abhorrence" are presumably the apostate, the persecutors, and the blasphemers of 11:30–45. The promise of vv 1–2, then, corresponds to motifs from the Psalms (e.g., 6; 69; 79). There supplicants may pray for their own vindication and rescue from the realm of death, and for the exposure and punishment of people who have attacked them; the response to such a double prayer is a double promise. So here the seer promises renewal of life and the exposure of the wicked. There is both a community and an individual aspect to this awakening, as in the Psalms. Part of the sufferers' affliction is that one way or another it deprives them of a place in the people of God; their awakening restores them to that. Dan 12 promises the awakening of people individually, but with a view to their sharing a corporate destiny (Martin-Achard, "Trois remarques sur la résurrection," 315–17). It is an expression of what W. Brueggemann has called the movement "From Dust to Kingship" (*ZAW* 84 [1972] 1–18, especially 11–12) spoken of in passages such as 1 Sam 2:6–8; 1 Kgs 16:2; Ps 22:16 [15]; 44:26 [25]; 113:7, that great reversal in history when the powerful are put down and the nobodies are given power.

Like the motif of awakening to renewed life, the motif of the exposure of the wicked has a this-worldly connotation. This was so in Isa 66:24, which v 2 takes up: its picture of people in Jerusalem looking at the corpses of the wicked decomposing in the Valley of Hinnom suggests a metaphor for a feature even of the new Jerusalem. Vindication and exposure after this life cannot be literally described, as vindication and exposure in this life such as the Psalms seek can be, so the latter becomes a metaphor for the former.

The reference to the exposure of the wicked brings out how vv 1–3 as a whole are concerned with restoration to life not for its own sake or for the sake of communion with God, but as part of and as a means to vindication (Charles, *Eschatology,* 137–38; 211–13; Nickelsburg; Kleinknecht [see *Bibliography*]). It is for this reason that the seer speaks of *many* being awakened, not all: those who were faithful but who lost their lives awake for vindication, those who were wicked but who seemed to triumph awake for condemnation—the regular mass of faithful Israel apparently remaining in Sheol. Or it may be that the groups raised are the faithful in general and the unpunished wicked, only the already punished wicked remaining in Sheol (Kaiser, *Tod*); while the people of God as a whole is outside the focus of v 2 just as the gentile world is, v 13 points to a resurrection of more than the martyrs. But we need to keep in mind that the passage is handling a specific problem. The threefold division suggested by the metaphor must not be pressed to yield a coherent total doctrine of the afterlife.

12:3 "The discerning" who "set the multitude right" had had their teaching despised, and some of them had lost their lives. Their position, then, will also be reversed, not merely by restoring them to life, but by giving them a position of pre-eminent honor. They "will shine as bright as the sky, . . . shine like the stars to all eternity." The stars can be taken to represent celestial beings: cf. 8:10; also Judg 5:20; Job 38:7; *1 Enoch* 104; *T. Moses* 10.9; *2 Apoc. Bar.* 51. It is difficult to tell how literal and how metaphorical these passages are. In the light of 8:10, "the stars" here may well indicate celestial beings. "Like the stars" then *compares* the discerning with these, but does not necessarily thereby suggest that they will be located among them, still less will *become* stars/angels. It may point in the opposite direction (Nickelsburg, *Resurrection,* 26; contrast Collins, *Vision,* 136–38). A poetic couplet echoing an earlier scriptural passage (Isa 52:13; 53:11) within a visionary flight into the future cannot be pressed.

But what is the significance of comparing the discerning to stars or locating them among the celestial beings? In earlier OT thought the king has been spoken of in these terms (Num 24:17; 1 Sam 29:9; 2 Sam 14:17, 20; Isa 9:5 [6]), against the background of an assumed correspondence or other linking between heaven and earth, heavenly powers and earthly powers, such as we have noted in connection with Dan 10. The last northern king had himself sought to storm heaven's gates. In 12:3 such notions are not quite democratized, but they are applied more broadly to the "discerning" leaders of the community: cf. the designation of prophets as Yahweh's messengers/angels (מלאכים)? It is these "discerning" who partake of the honor of a place in Yahweh's council (see Wifall, "The Status of 'Man' as Resurrection," *ZAW* 90 [1978] 382–94). They receive the honor the last northern king wrongly and vainly sought. Here, too, we should not be literalistic in interpreting the poetry of vv 1–3: the vision is of life on earth lived by beings who are still human. But neither should we be prosaic in our understanding: it envisages a life of a heavenly character, the life of eternity. The discerning share in the theophanic glory of the new Jerusalem (Cavallin, *Life,* 27; Martin-Achard, *RHPR* 59 [1979] 449; Nickelsburg, *Resurrection,* 26).

12:4 Though "these words" and "the book" that records them denote the message(s) of the man in linen recorded in 10:11–12:3, placing this vision at the end of Daniel hints at applying them to the book as a whole. Daniel is to "close up" and "seal" them: the expressions suggest not merely conserving them but withholding them (cf. 8:26). This is confirmed by the next words: because they are withheld, "many will hurry to and fro," unable to find a word from God: see Amos 8:11–12. When Daniel's book is unsealed, during the Antiochene crisis, that famine ends (Lindenberger, *Int* 39 [1985] 184).

12:5–10 The scene returns to that of 10:2–18; again there is some unclarity over how many persons Daniel sees, and about their relationship to the persons in chap. 10. The "two other figures" of v 5 connect with 8:13–14 rather than Deut 19:15 (Hasslberger, *Hoffnung*). The anonymous—presumably celestial—questioner's "how long . . . ?" (v 6) once more takes up that of Israel's laments (see on 8:13–14). The "awesome events" (פלאות) of which he enquires are those that came to a climax in 11:29–12:3, involving Antiochus's laying his hand on the realm of God (cf. 8:24 as well as 11:36).

Raising one's hand to heaven in taking an oath (v 7) no doubt acknowledges God as witness: cf. Gen 14:22, though elsewhere the expression is used only of God himself (e.g., Ezek 20:5–6). The doubling of the hands further underlines the undertaking's solemnity. On the 3½ "set periods" (מועד here, not עדן), see on 7:25. "The shattering of the power of the holy people" is presumably the events of 11:21–45, or perhaps the whole period from the exile; there is no particular reason to refer it to the crushing of Judas's rebellion in 160 B.C., and the context goes against this (against Goldstein, *I Maccabees,* 43).

Daniel's own puzzled question (v 8), natural for one set in the exile, facilitates a further restatement of what we have been told (vv 9–10), which also comes nearest to an explicit exhortation regarding conduct under the affliction that has been described. The faithful have no scope for action that will change history. Daniel is told simply to go his way; contrast chaps. 1–6. The faithful are to keep themselves pure, however, in the context of the pressures of history.

12:11–12 The "how long?" receives a further answer giving temporal precision to the more symbolic expression of v 7, in terms of a number of days—indeed two numbers, both different from that in 8:14. Here the figures probably have some calendrical significance.

Various calendars were in use in the seer's day. The Babylonians used a lunar calendar that produced a year of 354 days, the Essenes a solar calendar of 364 days, the Hellenistic regimes a luni-solar one of 360 days; in each case the calendar was corrected to the true length of the solar year—just over 365 days—by intercalating months. Evidence of familiarity with all three calendars has been found in the OT. The question of the right calendar was overtly a subject of dispute in the second and first centuries B.C. (see on 7:23–25), and Daniel's periods of days have been seen as reflections of this dispute. They most straightforwardly fit the luni-solar calendar (e.g., Beckwith, *RevQ* 10 [1979–81] 377–78), but they can be understood in the light of the other systems. When allowance is made for intercalation, 1290 days can represent 3½ lunar years (e.g., C. H. Cornill, "Die siebzig Jahrwochen Daniels," *Theologische Studien und Skizzen aus Ostpreussen* 2 [1889] 29–30) or 3½ solar years (Burgmann, *ZAW* 86 [1974] 545–46); 1335 days can also be reckoned to comprise 3½ solar years (W. Eiss, "Der Kalender des nachexilischen Judentums," *WO* 3 [1964] 44–47).

As Daniel's figures can be related to several calendars, so they can be related to several sets of events between 168 and 164 B.C. The beginning point of v 11 could be the time of one of Antiochus's edicts, the actual desecration of the temple, or the enforcement of the ban on the regular sacrificial order (11:31–33). The beginning point of v 12 could be one of these, or an earlier event such as Apollonius's mission, though more likely vv 11–12 begin with the same event and v 12 terminates later, suggesting that the promised release will have successive stages during which a continuing faithful expectancy is required. Thus vv 11–12 could terminate with Judas's victories, the temple rededication, Antiochus's death, the arrival of news of his death, or the further events envisaged by 11:45–12:3. 1 Macc 1:59; 4:52–53 makes the period from the first pagan sacrifice to the altar's rededication exactly three years.

12:13 The concern of vv 1–3 was the resurrection of people in the seer's day, not figures from the past such as an exilic Daniel. Yet behind the latter is the seer himself who belonged to the group who might well lose their lives, so the man in linen's encouragement to face both life ("go your way") and death ("and rest") with equanimity relates directly to the calling of the discerning. The picture of death as rest (cf. Isa 57:2; Job 3:13, 17) and of coming back to life as rising from sleep picks up the imagery of v 2. "Destiny" (גורל) appears frequently in the Qumran literature as a term for the community's fellowship with the holy ones (1QS 11.7; 1QH 11.11), but even there the word is used with other meanings (e.g., 1QS 1.10).

Presumably "the final day" (קץ הימין, "the end of the days") is the same time as "the time of the end" (עת קץ) in v 4. It is not a technical term for the End: cf. similar expressions in 1:18; 11:6, 13; Neh 13:6 (Jones, 208–11).

Explanation

In retrospect, Daniel might have drawn our attention to six main affirmations in his final vision.

(a) The message itself came by divine revelation. The main point of the narrative in 10:1–11:2a was to encourage my hearers to receive the message in 11:2b–12:3 (and in 10:13, 20; 12:7–13) as a revelation from heaven. The overt basis on which it did so was the nature of the experience I related, an experience like Ezekiel's that implied that my message could be accepted as Ezekiel's was. Heavenly beings—so impressive and awesome that one of them might have been God himself—had been in touch with me. Their appearing may highlight the real gulf between earth and heaven, which makes it necessary for revelation to be sought and granted, but it also highlights the real contact between earth and heaven, because revelation *was* sought and granted (Joubert).

I do not necessarily imply that either I or my audience took this to be a conclusive argument. First, even if I believed my message to have come by divine gift, I of course knew, and at least some of my contemporaries knew, that it was not received by the exilic Daniel in the way I described it. Second, even if I was inviting people to believe that the message was received through a revelatory experience, "translated" into—or experienced as—an experience of the exilic Daniel, I and they also knew that a claim to revelatory experience is not to be accepted purely on the basis of the claim (cf. Jer 23:15–32).

But my account implicitly offers several other reasons for accepting the message as a God-given revelation. First, I could present it as an experience of a man of proved discernment and faithfulness. In chaps. 1–6 these qualities appear in Daniel; in chaps. 10–12 they also appear when we as the actual recipients of these visions become fleetingly visible (11:32–35; 12:10). Second, my message was presented not as a quite new revelation but in large part as a piece of scriptural exposition (see *Form*). Biblical prophecy and not merely personal insight provided the categories for my understanding of the events of Hellenistic history.

Of course not everything in my vision was expressed in terms that are anticipated earlier in the OT; the revelation concerning the involvement of heavenly figures behind earthly events is an important exception, even though it has theological links with earlier scriptures. And in any case, the use of Scripture no more makes a message biblical and true than an account of an experience like that in chap. 10 makes a message a divine revelation. I was *re*applying Scripture to Antiochus and the promised destiny of conservative Jews. And I was not the only person who was doing that: others were, in the cause of expounding different perspectives on the Antiochene crisis in 1 Maccabees, 2 Maccabees, and *1 Enoch;* some reformist Jews believed they had Scripture on their side, too (cf. 11:14?). Canons of exegesis cannot prove that my use of Isaiah reflects the spirit of Isaiah.

Another obvious criterion for deciding whether a prophecy comes from God is whether it comes true (Deut 18:22). I might seem to fail that test. People such as my community may live with apparently unfulfilled prophecies by reinterpreting the events that they experience (emphasizing that *something* did happen) or reinterpreting the prophecy's time reference (it hasn't been fulfilled *yet*) or reinterpreting the prophecy itself (it didn't really refer to an actual event), though in thus acquitting prophecies of failure they risk emptying them of cognitive content (see Carroll utilizing the work of Festinger [see *Bibliography*]). It might also be said that while I was offering people a way of seeing order in the cosmos by promising that things would work out, it was a high-risk enterprise: it could put the total order at risk in the long run (Fishbane, *Interpretation,* 510–11).

All three moves I have just noted have been found in my visions themselves. The words of the OT prophets, who sometimes fail the test of fulfillment, commonly receive what people could see as a partial fulfillment, and perhaps it is this that encouraged the community to hold onto words that were not fulfilled—these must also have come from God and must offer illumination for the future. My community, too, might not have preserved my words if they had experienced no spectacular deliverance in 164–163 B.C. Hanukkah celebrates the fact that proleptically my words were fulfilled and that I did not prophesy falsely (Gese, "Geschichtsbild," 152). Second, though 12:11–12 have been seen as successive reinterpretations of the prophecy's time reference, in general I can claim that I avoided giving the impression that the End was imminent even if I did sound interested in calculating its time (Lebram, "Piety," 183). Third, some prophecies are intended "mythically." They involve that "intersection of the ideal and the circumstantial" which features in the royal psalms; they are not purely eschatological (Carroll, *ZAW* 92 [1980] 113, quoting J. H. Eaton, *Kingship and the Psalms* [SBT ii, 32 (1976)] 134). Even my quasi-prophecies, after all, offered not an objective historical account of Antiochus but an interpretative portrait of what he stood for, painted in the light of scriptural archetypes. The actual prophecies, which also do something newly creative with old words from Scripture, are then more promise than prediction; 12:1–3, for instance, was a flight of my imagination comparable to Job's (e.g., 19:23–27). The encouragement they offer can survive apparent literal disconfirmation, and subsequent generations can feel that they directly address them in different but analogous crises in which the End approaches them as threat but in their light can become promise.

That suggests another way of establishing whether my message was a divine revelation. Does it look like one that can be lived with? At least some people in the second century B.C. found it so, preserved it, and shared it with subsequent generations, so that it found a place among those scriptures that shaped the identity of Jews and Christians of all shades of belief and gave them the perspectives with which to view analogous crises.

(b) Heavenly powers share in shaping the events of earthly history. I spoke of a struggle involving the leader of Israel, Michael, and the unnamed leaders of Persia and Greece, a struggle over whether God's purpose for history should be revealed and also a struggle over whether it should thereby be put into effect. That does not mean that we should think about history in a dualistic way. I am quite clear that God is sovereign in heaven and on earth; there is no other power to rival him (I refer to no Satan). His purpose can be opposed and delayed, but not frustrated. I did not suggest a dualism of ultimate powers. Nor did I imply that the real decisions about history are made in heaven, so that human acts make no difference to what happens. My revelation concerning Hellenistic history made clear that human beings are responsible for history. Armies have to fight as if the battle on the earthly plane alone counted. On the other hand, monistic thinking about history is an oversimplification. I do not see history as the outworking of human decisions alone. Not only do free human decisions unwittingly contribute to the working out of God's purpose (chap. 2 *Explanation*); what I said about the activity of the princes of the nations (10:13; 10:20–11:1) presupposed that the purposes of kings and nations are more than merely the decisions of particular human beings. Something in the realm of the spirit lies behind them.

Compared with *1 Enoch* I only made rather allusive reference to such heavenly beings, though I allowed more for this way of thinking than 1 Maccabees. I said little or nothing about their nature or origin, about how many of them there are or how they are ordered, or about distinctions between good and evil beings among them (cf. Barth, *Dogmatik* iii, 3:477 [ET 410–11]). What I did say indicates that consideration of them requires more than jest or sentimentalism. They are not dainty figures in dresses, but figures whose very names draw attention to the uniqueness and the might of God, which they mediate.

Historically, the leaders of the nations developed from the many gods of polytheistic religions. We always knew that Yahweh was uniquely God; even Michael's name draws attention to there being no one like God even in heaven (Barth, *Dogmatik* iii, 3:532 [ET 456]). But we also knew that the life of heaven was more complex than might be implied by a bare affirmation that Yahweh alone was God. The idea of the leaders of the nations provided a way of thinking about history as we actually experienced it. History involves conflicts between peoples that seem to reflect more than merely human factors—for instance, it involves unexpected defeats and unexpected victories. This conflict is sometimes one that seems to have more than merely human significance, yet on other occasions it is one in which the hand of God cannot be discerned nor promises such as those of Ps 2 be seen to be effective. The power of the leader of Persia reflects Persia's actual political power. The idea of the heavenly leaders of the nations is a way of expressing the fact that there is more to history and to reality than we can see: both individuals and states are more than merely themselves as historical realities (K. Koch, "Vom profetischen zum apokalyptischen Visionsbericht," in *Apocalypticism,* ed. D. Hellholm, 438). The leaders must somehow be under God's control, and they are not his demonic opponents, but neither are they simply his heavenly obedient servants. The job of the leader of Persia is to represent Persian interests in a world in conflict; "it has a right to contest for the best interests of the Persian empire narrowly defined." The leaders are not "idealized personifications" of their nations; "they represent the actual spirituality and possibilities of actual entities" (Wink, *Unmasking,* 89).

Not only does one miss the hand of God in history; one often misses the hand of the nations themselves. Events work out despite their intentions rather than through them. I have a vision of a day when the United States and the Soviet Union have reached an agreement in principle on the control of medium-range nuclear weapons such as could not have been dreamed of two years before, given the then posturing of both governments; but in that same week I foresee an escalation of Iranian-American hostilities in the Gulf War despite the apparent desire of both governments for disengagement. What nations do, for good or ill, is not always what they were planning to do. It is as if some power other than the powers themselves influences the shaping of their destiny.

Another theological issue underlies this idea, or at least emerges from it. In referring to the figures who appeared to me, I did not use words such as "angel" that apply only to supernatural beings. I called them by phrases such as "a manlike being," or—without qualification—"a man in linen." I emphasized that there was something special about these figures, but my language also stressed their kinship with humanity. I used the ordinary word "leader," too, without qualification, both for celestial beings and for earthly ones (10:13, 20, 21; 11:5; 12:1; cf. 1:7–11, 18; 8:11, 25; 9:6, 8), and the ordinary word for "king" in 10:13 in a context where I was talking about supernatural figures.

The NT uses the equivalent Greek words for "leader" for both material and spiritual/heavenly powers (e.g., ἄρχων, Th's equivalent for שר in Dan, in Rom 13:3; 1 Cor 2:6, 8; the more common related noun ἀρχή, e.g., Rom 8:38; Eph 6:12; Col 1:16). Both the Hebrew and the Greek words generally denote human leaders, but sometimes denote spiritual/heavenly ones, and sometimes are ambiguous (cf. Dan 10:13). Perhaps the fluidity and the ambiguity in such usage reflects a duality about all entities that embody power (Wink, *Naming; Unmasking*). There is something human, earthly, structural, political, and visible about them. There is also something heavenly, invisible, suprahuman, immaterial, and spiritual. The powers have an inner and an outer aspect, an outer form and an inner driving spirit. They are not merely metaphors for structures of power within the nation itself, but neither do they exist in themselves, as independent persons or disembodied spirits. They have no profile of their own; their significance is only as agents of God and/or foci of human societies.

Nations as such have personalities and vocations (Wink, *Unmasking,* 93–94). But even in a democracy power becomes embodied in individuals. "It is the fortuitous conjunction of a powerful personality in a powerful office that makes a powerful leader" (Wink, *Naming,* 66). "Leaders," human and heavenly, both focus that personality and vocation.

Col 1:16–20 reaffirms what I presupposed, that all power in its visible and invisible aspects was created by God and exists for God. Overwhelmed by the significance of Christ, it further affirms that all such power was created in Christ, through Christ, and for Christ. "They only have their being because of him; they are upheld, even in their defections, by him. They exist to serve the purpose of the whole creation as it comes to its focus in him. . . . Try as they will to become autonomous and set up their own interests as the highest good, the Powers must inevitably come to terms with the Power of the Powers" (Wink, *Naming,* 64). In a context such as that of Dan 1–6, it is our task to call them back to their origins and destiny. In a context such as that of Dan 7–12, when there seems no likelihood that they will respond to such a call, my vision implies that it is still our task to pray for them, for that is still our way of confronting the spiritual realities of which the political is an embodiment. Presumably it is no coincidence that my period of prayer and the leaders' period of conflict were coterminous. It implies that prayer can play a role in opening up the possibility of God's purpose being fulfilled when human purposes conflict with it. My cry "opened an aperture for God to act in concert with human freedom. It inaugurated war in heaven. It opened a way through the impenetrable spirituality of a foreign hegemony in order to declare a new and real divine possibility" (Wink, *Unmasking,* 91). My vision did not provide a rationale for how this is so, but it expresses in narrative form the conviction that it *is* so.

(c) The details of Israel's history are within the control of God. My vision pictured a heavenly being revealing in the exile events to take place over the coming four centuries up to the End, from the contents of "a reliable book" (10:21). To say that history was pre-written was to affirm the belief that it is under control. It may also seem to imply that history is an imposed destiny, fixed independently of the wills of its participants; the march of the kingdoms is the march of toy soldiers programmed by God (so Towner). If this were so, even I might have reckoned that God could have programmed it better. To speak in terms of history's being pre-written is not incompatible with speaking of God's giving people free will so that they choose whether to walk in his way (cf. *1 Enoch*). The stories of Nebuchadnezzar and Belshazzar (Dan 4–5) similarly treat heathen kings both as standing beneath an overarching determination of God and as responsible to him and to themselves for their destinies. In understanding the significance of the book image, you need to keep reminding yourself that the vast bulk of the history that I described as pre-written I was only declaring to be so afterwards. I was describing events as inevitable (11:14, 27, 36) when they *were* inevitable, after they had happened. To describe them so at that point need not imply a more mechanical view of history than the prophets', as if history is fixed and predetermined or self-imposing as it happens. It would be inappropriate to be literalistic in interpreting my visions, as if my message was other than a *quasi*-prophecy. The significance of describing what is actually *past* history as pre-written is to declare that God is somehow in control even of the inexplicabilities of history—the successes of the godless and the sufferings of the faithful—and even at moments when evil is asserting itself in a particularly oppressive way. Given the difficulty of viewing history as it actually unfolds as the direct will of God, the books declare that it was foreknown by God and in some sense willed by him. It is part of some pattern and purpose, rather than being random and meaningless.

The really future events that are read out of God's books are ones associated with the End, with the final defeat of evil and the final establishment of God's rule in the world. That is part of the purpose for human history that God is determined to achieve. There *is* a fixed inevitability about history; human beings cannot frustrate God's ultimate purpose, and in that sense cannot alter what has been determined by God's will. But the detailed portrayal of how the End will come is an imaginative scenario drawn in the light of Scripture, rather than a forecast of how things actually must be (see [a] above).

(d) The details of Persian and Hellenistic history have no positive theological significance.

> Tomorrow, and tomorrow, and tomorrow,
> creeps in this petty pace from day to day,
> to the last syllable of recorded time:
> . . . . a tale
> told by an idiot, full of sound and fury,
> signifying nothing.
>
> (*Macbeth*, 5.5.18–20, 25–27)

> I am unable to find any meaning in history.
>
> (H. A. L. Fisher, quoted by Philip)

My vision anticipates such judgments on history. It is an interpretation very different from that which predominates among OT historians, prophets, and psalmists. It constitutes an exposition of profane history, in contrast with the outline of sacred history in 9:24–27; it gives history more space than any other chapter in the book, but renders it essentially meaningless (see Hanhart, *Fourth WCJS Papers* 1:82; Towner). Events unfold as a pointless sequence of invasions, battles, schemes, and frustrations. Military power and political maneuvering are central themes; but military issues are not always settled by the size of an army, and political schemes come to nothing, whether pursued by means of battle or by means of alliance (Joubert, 191–92). It is a tale of selfishness, irrationality, and chance. Human beings formulate far-reaching plans but keep being frustrated by each other. Neither power nor politics take people anywhere. History is not the outworking of a just purpose, nor is the hand of God directly visible in it; God, indeed, for the most part remains in the gallery, only watching—though no doubt noting the parallels in this history to earlier events involving Assyria and Babylon as the prophet commented on these, and committed to bringing upon it a corresponding judgment. Yet I was not suggesting that history was always hell-bent on the disaster that emerges at the end of chap. 11. I was not negative about Alexander and the Hellenistic empires in general (contrast 1 Macc 1). Even the eventual disaster, though it comes as determined, is a result of chance collocations of people and events. History is going nowhere. The interpretation of history that I was offering will turn out to match the way people experience history in more secular centuries.

Not that the outworking of this history is quite incapable of theological interpretation. While the four great empires contained one another by each terminating the rule of the last, the Seleucids and the Ptolemies mutually contained each other by frustrating each other's aspirations to wider empire over a period of centuries, thus protecting each other from reaching the ultimate arrogance that must provoke God to intervene (Newsom, "Past," 48; Lebram, "Piety," 183). That provocation is also offered when war and politics become interwoven with religion. Generally I was not concerned to offer any ethical judgment on history, though I did imply a negative judgment based on the imperial powers' involvement—for their political reasons—in religious matters.

Nor was I concerned to comment on Israel's own involvement in history. Later works such as 1 and 2 Macc would do that, but they came from a period when there was the history of an independent Jewish state to reflect on. They revived in different ways a historical perspective like that of Kings, valuing the activism of the Maccabees, though presupposing two different evaluations of martyrdom, miracle, prophecy, belief in resurrection, and of the Hasmonean monarchy (see Goldstein, *I Maccabees*, 3–36). Whether or not people took a quietist stance rather than resisting Antiochus by military means, I wanted to put the emphasis on the activity of God, not on what our own acts could achieve in themselves. On the other hand, I did not want people to blame themselves for the Antiochene crisis—though neither did I want to put the responsibility on some cosmic act of rebellion near the beginning of world history, as if people in our day were not responsible for their acts. The reformist Jews had been irresponsible fools, but they had played into the hands of the person who was my real scapegoat, Antiochus.

(e) The destiny of the faithful—and of the wicked—is secure. My quasi-prophecy continued to be shaped by Scripture through chap. 11. The Assyrians provided one model for my portrait of the Seleucids: thus as the former fell, so would the latter. The temple desecration was like that during the exile: thus as that had been reversed, so would this one be. The affliction was like that of Yahweh's servant in Isaiah: thus in this case, too, it would give way to triumph.

As chap. 10 speaks of celestial figures who are the embodiments of earthly institutions, so chap. 11 speaks of earthly figures who are the embodiments of spiritual principles. Admittedly there is no such figure who embodies the fulfillment of God's positive purpose—no messiah. Nor is there any indication in my vision that at some point it moves from talking about Antiochus to talking about Antichrist or Satan, or begins to speak in words that refer both to Antiochus and to Antichrist. But in the way I spoke of Antiochus I was suggesting that he—like the King of Babylon in Isa 14 or Gog in Ezek 38–was the very embodiment of godless wickedness, so that the language used of him could be used of Antichrist or Satan. The passage could be treated typologically in this way: this is a way of using the passage to throw light on Antichrist or Satan, but not a way of approaching the passage exegetically.

I have hinted already that the trouble with Antiochus was that he treated religious questions as subordinate to political ones. Nationhood and kingship are not wholly evil, but they do have an irresistible tendency to self-idolatry. Whatever is the right interpretation of his motivation in his relationships with Jerusalem, what counted for him was the stability of the Seleucid empire and its ability to play the international role for which it seemed to be destined. The state, or Hellenism, or he himself, had highest importance: it was God (see Wink, *Unmasking,* 87–88, 95–96).

Hope for the living lay in the downfall of the one who epitomized godlessness and the vindication of those who resisted him. What of those for whom this vindication would come too late? In my vision I saw them brought back to life to resume the life they had wrongly lost, while those who led them in the way of faithfulness shine like stars.

One version of the myth of the overweening king, which underlies the portrait of Antiochus, describes him—ironically, in the end—as wiser than Danel/Daniel. But I was the one who was granted an audience with heavenly beings, who was addressed as held in high regard by God (a royal epithet), who actually had by God's grace the wisdom the king was supposed to possess. As the king and his kind come to their end and know shame and abhorrence instead of the place among the stars to which they aspired, those who were people of discernment and faithfulness leave the land of dust that is the overweening king's destiny and rise to an inheritance, to lasting life, and to our own place among the stars. Like the vision in Isa 52:13–53:12, my vision affirmed a kingship ideal in the context of radically reshaping it by presupposing that the way to royal glory is the way of martyrdom. It brings to a climax the ambivalent aspects to the portrayal of kingship that run through my story and my visions. Real power is recognized and can be affirmed, but in practice it tends to encourage a vainglorious arrogance that has to be turned to shame. Only those can enjoy royal glory who have already come to terms with shame.

These images came to have more literal meaning for the Qumran community, who saw themselves—in Johannine fashion—as already enjoying the life of heaven in the company of the angels. But my vision was not that prosaic in its implications. I was speaking the language of hope, speaking of a future resurrection, not of a transition to a new sphere of life now (against Collins, *CBQ* 36 [1974] 34–37); though it is, of course, the case that those who wait for Yahweh's new act find new strength, and in a sense new life, even now (Isa 40:31).

The reasoning that leads to affirmation of a resurrection is also worth noting. Its background is not the conviction that life once given can hardly simply fizzle out, or that suffering must be compensated for by bliss (so *1 Enoch* 102–3). It is the conviction that God will see that truth, commitment, and faithfulness are vindicated. Linked with that is the conviction that resurrection is not an individual experience. Belief in personal life after death does not replace belief in the final corporate and cosmic achievement of God's purpose. The resurrection of which I spoke (and of which Paul spoke) is one of the events associated with this final achievement of God's cosmic purpose. It happens to individuals, but it does not happen to them individually, in the meantime. It happens to individuals, yet it is not the means of their enjoying individual bliss, but of their having a share in the new life and glory of the people of God. My concern was nationalist rather than individualist. It was also nationalist rather than universalist; other peoples are not within my concern. And in my own mind, it was nationalist rather than sectarian. I viewed reformist Jews as having lost their soul through their involvement with the gentile powers and as having forfeited their place within the true Israel; that is an implicitly sectarian attitude, yet my vision was for the true Israel and the empirical Israel to be coterminous (Collins, *VT* 25 [1975] 603).

It is striking that other peoples began to formulate mythic solutions to the problem of death quite early on in their history, whereas we did that explicitly only after some centuries (Kellermann, *ZTK* 73 [1976] 261–62). Such moves had to be wrested from us. Our affirmation of this life sat in tension with the pie-in-the-sky beliefs of other peoples. They were wrested from us through experiences that made the affirmation of this life difficult for people whose experience was not of life in fullness.

But is this only an example of how "blissful illusions, such as those of Job and Daniel, not seldom prove to be effective opiates for patients whose condition is beyond rational cure"—illusions opposed by realists like the writer of Ecclesiastes (so Pfeiffer, *ZAW* 52 [1934] 101)? As the earlier history of the Near Eastern empires shaped my understanding of Antiochus and the fate he would experience, so my vision of the awakening and vindication of the holy and discerning martyr shaped the perceptions of Jesus, for Jesus himself and for his followers. It thus proved it had an anticipatory relationship with the event that more than any other brought a realization within history of realities that belong to the End; and by a feedback process this Christ event turned out to be the vindication of my own vision. Setting my vision in the context of the NT suggests that one martyr indeed awoke to such vindication. If you are called to walk the way that the discerning and holy of the Antiochene and the Roman period walked, you are promised that his experience is your key and your hope as you do so.

I must say something about the destiny of the wicked. My vision of resurrection also implied that for the wicked to die the same death as the righteous is not enough. What it promised for them was not eternal physical pain but eternal shame. And that promise has been fulfilled, both for reformist Jews and for Antiochus and his empire. They have not been forgotten, like most of the dead. Wherever the gospel of Daniel has been preached through the whole world, what these men did has been spoken of and has perpetuated their memory. Scholarship's difficulty in attaining a more objective historical understanding of Antiochus and the reformist Jews is unconscious testimony to the fulfillment of Dan 12:2.

(f) The faithful are challenged to steadfastness. So what was the purpose of offering people all this quasi- and actual information about the future? Information as such does do people some good (the gnostics were not wholly wrong!). It helps them formulate a mind on the issues that confront them. But I also wanted to influence their behavior. I wanted to encourage the discerning to be steadfast in their faithfulness, and to encourage others to join them. I went as near as I could to saying as much when I described the faithfulness of conservative Jews and the positive significance our affliction can have. I did not say that suffering was redemptive or atoning or a means of provoking God to act on our behalf (contrast Revelation: see Yarbro Collins, *JBL* 96 [1977] 241–56). I could see that it had a refining effect on the community. It forces people to make up their mind which side they are on. I did not need to encourage loyalist Jews to fight for the cause if necessary. If anything, they needed to be wary of overestimating what can be achieved through fighting. You would have thought our story over the centuries would have taught them that, but it had not, and the believing communities since have not been very good at learning it, either. But what I actually wanted to emphasize was the responsibility of the conservative leadership to teach people: to do what I was trying to do myself, passing on to people what I believe God was revealing to us about the way he looked at past and present and future, and encouraging them in the light of that to refuse to collaborate with Antiochus and the reformist Jews. I wanted them to fight in that sense, and stand their ground to the end if necessary (cf. Eph 6:10–18). I saw myself as having a position rather like Daniel's, and I wanted the rest of the leadership to be Daniel-like, too—indeed, I wanted the whole people to be Daniel-like. That is why I ended the way I did.

Conclusion

The Book's Form

The distinctive formal feature of Daniel is its combining in nearly equal proportions a series of stories about Daniel and his friends and a series of visions attributed to Daniel.

It is the second of these features that usually determines how scholars define Daniel's form: Daniel is an apocalypse. The word comes from the Greek term used of *the* Apocalypse in Rev 1:1. Apocalypse as a genre of writing is now usefully distinguished from apocalyptic eschatology, a particular form of eschatological belief that can appear in writings of various literary forms, and from apocalypticism, a form of religious faith that can arise in particular social contexts and in which apocalyptic eschatology has a prominent place (e.g., Hanson, *IDBSup* 27; cf. Barker, *ExpT* 89 [1977–78] 324–29, noting that Daniel lacks most of the features of apocalyptic thought). In Rev 1:1 an apocalypse is a revelation by God through an intermediary to a seer concerning realities in heaven and events to come associated with the End, accompanied by parenesis that prepares the hearers to be open to the visions that occupy the main part of the book. Developing this understanding, an influential current definition takes apocalypse as "a genre of revelatory literature with a narrative framework, in which a revelation is mediated by an otherworldly being to a human recipient, disclosing a transcendent reality which is both temporal, insofar as it envisages eschatological salvation, and spatial, insofar as it involves another, supernatural world" (Collins, *Apocalypse,* 9). Another stream of current study notes that apocalypses are not merely concerned with things to come, as the connection with eschatology suggests, but with things above (heaven), as is the case with Revelation, things below (Sheol), and things behind (the past) (Rowland, *Heaven*). Daniel is of course concerned with things to come, and with things above (see especially chap. 10); while telling us little about things below, each of the visions shows considerable interest in what is past from the actual perspective of seer and audience, giving much space to interpretations of past historical events from the exile to the second century. As a visionary work, Daniel is thus illuminated by each of these definitions.

Each definition also contains pointers to the significance of the stories. First, preceding the bulk of the revelatory material, they may be seen as equivalent to the parenesis of Rev 2–3 (cf. Koch, *Buch Daniel,* 25). Revelation incorporates parenesis in its visions; Daniel presents its parenesis in story form, in keeping with OT precedents. The stories implicitly urge upon their hearers the life of trust and faithfulness that will be difficult but vital in the circumstances to which the visions speak, but which the stories, relating as they do to pressures similar to those of the second century (see on 11:33), also show to be possible because it is undergirded by the faithfulness and power of God himself. Second, the stories comprise the bulk of the visions' narrative framework. They introduce the visionary with his qualities of discernment and faithfulness which help to establish his authority and give him the right to urge faithfulness on others. Third, the stories, like the visions, portray a God who rules in heaven who is also sovereign over the realm of death, who is active in the past and trustworthy for the future.

The space the stories occupy, however, warns against interpreting them as wholly subordinate to the visions. The apocalypse may be an example of a genre that becomes simpler as it develops, and the subsequent development of the apocalypse form must not obscure for us the nature of this early example. It is a mixed form, as much a series of short stories to which visions are attached as a series of visions prefaced by some stories.

The stories reflect historical experiences and events. But they are not historiography. It is not merely that features such as the portrait of Nebuchadnezzar, the Median empire located between the Babylonian and the Persian, and the existence of Darius the Mede differ from what we otherwise know of the period and suggest that the stories may be attempts at history that failed. Daniel hardly raises more historical problems than books such as Chronicles, and even if all such features *are* unhistorical, it is not this that indicates that the stories are not historiographical. The pointers to this are that they manifest the positive features of romance and legend, genres that make use of fictional features as well as historical ones in order to achieve their aim of telling an edifying story. To imply that they are at fault if they contain unhistorical features is to judge them on alien criteria; to defend them by seeking to establish that at such points they are factual after all is to collude with such a false starting point.

Similarly, the visions are for the most part quasi-prophecy rather than actual prophecy, and they are pseudonymous; we do not know who these visionaries were. The reasons for this conclusion are formal and theological rather than philosophical. It is not that prediction of second-century events in the sixth century would be impossible; let its possibility be granted. Formally, it is not essential to or distinctive of apocalypses to be pseudonymous or quasi-prophetic. Both features are missing from Revelation and present in works of other genres. But ancient Near Eastern parallels to visions such as these—there being no OT parallels—are all pseudonymous quasi-prophecies, not actual prophecies of known authorship. This also suggests that there is no reason to assume that the authors would necessarily have intended—or hoped—to deceive their hearers regarding the visions' origin; the latter would have known how to hear them. The theological support for this formal point is that the God of the Bible characteristically speaks contextually, into situations rather than independently of them. He reveals key truths about the End that are relevant to people's present lives. He declines to give information about the future of a concrete or dated kind, insisting that people live by faith. It is difficult to see how the God of the Bible would reveal detailed events of the second century to people living in the sixth, even though he could do so (cf. Goldingay, *Them* 2 [1976–77] 49).

Stories and visions share a midrashic aspect. Both presuppose the existence of some scriptures and make these one of their starting points. Indeed, it may be that the best way to understand the visions' pseudonymity is to take it as a reflection of the midrashic mentality (Niditch, "Visionary," 157–58). Stories and visions also share an explicit stress on interpretation, in connection with dreams, portents, and visions, as well as with Scripture. Daniel is the mediator of interpretation in chaps. 1–6, its recipient in chaps. 7–12. In each case there is a divine revelation whose meaning, however, is a mystery (רז, chap. 2). It cannot be made to yield clear sense except by divine gift of insight (בינה, a key word in Daniel [Beek, *Studia,* 20–21]), though this can be sought and prepared for; that it has this origin is reflected in the fact that the interpretation (פשר) stands on its own rather than emerging directly from the revelation in any obvious way (Mertens, 115–20).

Stories and visions are also characterized by repetition. Chaps. 1, 3, and 6 relate the testing of the exiles and God's faithfulness; chaps. 2, 4, and 5 Daniel's skill in interpretation and his revelations concerning the fall of kings; chaps. 2 and 7 a vision of a sequence of four empires; chaps. 7, 8, 9, and 10–12 a quasi-prophecy of events up to the Antiochene crisis and a promise of its end. The effect of such repetition is both to highlight common features of each set of chapters and thus to emphasize these, and to draw attention to distinctive features of each member of a set, those that make it stand out from its fellows, and thus to emphasize these (e.g., the different fates of Nebuchadnezzar and Belshazzar or the visions that come by God's initiative or by Daniel's seeking). In the terms of information theory, "verbal repetition increases predictability, creates expectations, eliminates noise, persuades, and reduces alternative interpretations." It "teaches the implied reader how to 'read' the text" (Anderson, *Semeia* 31 [1985] 84; cf. Collins, *Vision,* 116–17).

Stories and visions also communicate in complementary ways (Davies, 125–26). In neither do the authors speak directly, as happens with prophecy; they stand behind the narrator in the stories and the persons of Daniel and of heavenly beings in the visions. Also in contrast with prophecy, neither address the reader directly, though the visions come nearer to doing this. In the stories, the relationship between authors and second-century hearers is particularly indirect: anonymous authors tell stories to unidentified hearers about another time and another place. The visions, however, speak—if cryptically—about the situation in which authors and hearers live, and more explicitly draw them into identification with Daniel himself.

There is no indication that the book has been shaped in order to function as a canonical document (Koch, *Int* 39 [1985] 128–30, against Childs, *Introduction,* 613–22). On the other hand, the canonizing of Daniel may presuppose a reading of the book that differed from the authors'. If the authors believed they were providing the date(s!) of an imminent End that did not come about as they expected, the canonizers apparently read it in some more open way (Bauckham, *EvQ* 59 [1987] 165).

Streams of Tradition behind Daniel

We have noted the midrashic aspect to Daniel as a whole. It has specific links with a variety of streams of tradition in the OT and elsewhere.

It begins with a virtual quotation from Chronicles, and suggests links with Israelite historiography (Davies, *JSOT* 5 [1978] 15–28). The stories' working through a sequence of reigns while willing to incorporate legendary/didactic material also recalls this tradition. The same link is suggested by the accounts of postexilic history in quasi-prophetic form in the visions, especially chap. 11. The periodizing of history in chaps. 2 and 7 parallels the periodizing of P.

Daniel's contacts with the historiographic approach of P and the Chronicler hints at a background in cultic traditions, which is also suggested by the psalmlike passages at key points in the stories, by the stress on prayer, and by the visions' concern with worship and their longing for the cleansing of the temple, defiled by Antiochus (Chary, *Prophètes,* 236–74). Such a background might also explain the mythic features of chaps. 7 and 10–12 that make it possible to speak of remythologizing as a feature of Daniel (Delcor; Frost; F. M. Cross [see *Main Bibliography*]). Neither stories nor visions are preoccupied with details of obedience to Torah—though chap. 1 presupposes the importance of diet and chap. 9 has links with D—but with concerns it shares with other parts of the OT such as faithfulness to the one God. There is no mention of proscription of circumcision or sabbath observance, enforced eating of pork, or burning of Torah scrolls (contrast 1 Maccabees). Daniel *is* concerned about worship; there is no hint of hostility to the temple in Daniel (contrast *1 Enoch* 89.73).

Daniel's mythic background might alternatively suggest links with the learning of the scribes, who were likely also responsible for Israel's historiography. A connection with the scribes coheres with indications that Daniel has links with Israelite wisdom (Heaton; von Rad, *Theologie;* Gammie, *JBL* 93 [1974] 356–85, on "spatial and ethical dualism" in wisdom and the apocalypses; J. Z. Smith, "Wisdom," describing apocalyptic as a scribal phenomenon). Chap. 1 hints at practical wisdom as an Israelite royal ideal. The visions reflect speculative wisdom's concern for an understanding of the whole, its conviction that God's knowledge and activity undergird all, and its sometimes pessimistic view of humanity (cf. Qoh 3:11), which in Daniel appears as a concern with the possibility of grasping history on a large scale and by means of a grand scheme, if not the whole of history. Speculative wisdom has room for visions (Job!). Even Daniel's concern with the End appears in the Wisdom of Solomon, though not its sense of the world's being out of joint and of discontinuity between this age and the age to come (Collins, *HR* 17 [1977] 121–42).

There are some prophetic features to the stories, though Daniel is not termed a prophet. But as a man held in high regard, in whom the divine spirit dwells, and to whom such extraordinary revelations are given, he may be more than a prophet rather than less (Koch, *Int* 39 [1985] 124). He confronts Nebuchadnezzar and Belshazzar, speaking of sin and judgment in the manner of a preexilic prophet; the stories of these confrontations recall some prophetic stories in Kings. The visions with their symbolism recall those of prophets such as Zechariah. Gruenwald (*Mysticism,* 29–32) stresses the mystical aspect they have in common with, for example, Ezek 1. They manifest prophecy's concern with the interpretation of present history and with coming decisive events that will bring God's judgment on pagan kings who have resisted God's will, and the historical dualism—the contrast between this age and an age that God will bring about—of prophecy such as Isa 40–55 and Ezek 38–39 (e.g., Rowley; Frost; Osten-Sacken; Hanson [see *Main Bibliography*]). Concern with the purity of the temple is also a theme of postexilic prophecy

(G. Wanke, "Prophecy and Psalms in the Persian Period," *CHJ* 1:180–83, noting also eschatological expectation, messianic hope, and concern about the destiny of the nations). On the other hand, unlike the stories they do not confront people with a challenge to turn and thereby avert the judgment that threatens them. The hearers are not responsible for history; history itself seems to be predetermined rather than open, and God's purpose is only effected in it negatively, not positively (Buber, "Prophecy").

The link with prophecy leads to a consideration of Daniel's links with divination or mantic wisdom in the OT and elsewhere (Müller, VTSup 22:268–93; *TWAT* "חכם . . ."; VanderKam, "Origins"; Collins, *Vision*, 80–87). Daniel parallels Joseph in embodying the combination of prudential wisdom and mantic wisdom. As a sage who interprets dreams and omens with the apparent conviction that the future is predetermined, he operates in the same area and on the same basis as the Babylonian diviners. The book's symbolism has this mantic background (P. A. Porter, *Metaphors and Monsters* [ConB OT Series 20 (1983)]). Quasi-prophecy has its background in Akkadian prophecies that are influenced by Mesopotamian divination (VanderKam, *Enoch*, 62–69).

Babylonian, Persian, and Hellenistic thinking, the first two in part already incorporated within the last, are also the likely source of some features of Daniel that are not evidenced elsewhere in the OT. These may include the four-empire scheme, the concept of revelation, pseudepigraphy, and quasi-prophecy. OT ideas regarding angels and the various forms of dualism develop as they do in line with Hellenistic thought (see Hengel; Eddy [see *Main Bibliography*]); Betz sees Jewish apocalypticism in general as a fruit of Hellenistic syncretism (*ZTK* 63 [1966] 409, ET 155). It is, however, difficult to point to *distinctively* Hellenistic features in Daniel. Wacholder (*Dawn*) sees the dominant culture of Jerusalem up till Antiochus's time as still Persian—though even the distinctively Persian features are few. Indeed, aspects of the visions parallel *anti*-Hellenistic writings and traditions of Egypt and the East. The Antiochene crisis is part of widespread anti-Hellenistic reaction in the Middle East that contributed to the downfall of the Hellenistic empires, though Daniel is more specifically anti-Antiochene than anti-Hellenistic in principle (Lebram, *VT* 25 [1975] 737–72; Collins, *BASOR* 220 [1975] 27–36).

During the postexilic period there was a variety of streams of tradition in Judaism. Like Chronicles, Daniel represents a creative amalgam of many of these (cf. Hall, 221). It is not distinctively linked with one of them.

The Book's Structure

In discussing the setting of each chapter of the book, we have noted a number of links between them. There are a number of ways of understanding the structure of the book as a whole. We cannot say whether any was in the mind of an author, but each enables us to perceive aspects of the book.

In English, Daniel most obviously divides into a series of stories and a series of visions. The former also involve three other young men, while in the latter Daniel alone features. The former include a series of messages from God to kings, with Daniel interpreting them, the latter a series of messages given to Daniel, with a celestial being interpreting them. These series comprise chronological sequences corresponding to the schemes of four reigns, as we have interpreted these in the commentary:

1–4	Nebuchadnezzar	7–8	Babylon
5	Belshazzar	9	Media
6	Darius	10	Persia
6:29 [28]	Cyrus	11–12	Greece

To the person who reads Daniel in the original, another distinction is especially striking, that between sections in different languages:

1–2:4a Hebrew
2:4b–7:28 Aramaic
8–12 Hebrew

On such chiastic structures in ancient Near Eastern works, see J. W. Welch, "Chiasmus in Ugaritic," *UF* 6 (1974) 425–28. This linguistic distinction does not correspond to the literary one; the effect is that linguistic continuity binds the book where distinction of form might divide it, while conversely formal continuity binds the book where distinction of language might divide it. Such structural features underline diversity in unity as an important feature of the book (cf. also the distinction between material that speaks about Daniel and the friends [1:1–7:1; 10:1] and material in which Daniel speaks [the remainder]). They also draw attention to chap. 7 as the center of the book, belonging as it does to the first part by language, to the second by form.

Lenglet (*Bib* 53 [1972] 169–90) noted the chiasm formed by chaps. 2–7. This pattern holds together yet another sequence of chapters and further strengthens the bonds that hold together the diversity in the book. It may be that the rest of the book can be seen as structured around this chiasm:

1 Exile and the questions it raises: story
2 A vision of four empires
3 A trial of faithfulness and a marvelous deliverance
4 An omen interpreted and a king challenged and chastised
5 An omen interpreted and a king challenged and deposed
6 A trial of faithfulness and a marvelous deliverance
7 A vision of four empires
8 Aspects of this vision developed
9 Exile and the questions it raises: vision
10–12 Aspects of this vision developed

Gooding's tracing of a structure balancing chaps. 1–5 and 6–12 (*TynB* 32 [1981] 43–79) is less convincing.

In several ways the stories develop toward a climax. Nebuchadnezzar acknowledges Daniel's brilliance (chap. 1), then prostrates himself to him (chap. 2); he acknowledges the God of the exiles as uniquely able to deliver (chap. 3), then as ruling through all ages (chap. 4); Belshazzar finds that this God cannot be defied (chap. 5), then Darius requires that the whole empire acknowledge him (chap. 6). The four men progress from being the most insightful sages (chap. 1) via being responsible for provincial affairs and active at court (chap. 2) to the three friends' being promoted in Babylon (chap. 3) and Daniel's being the only interpreter in whom the spirit of deity dwells (chap. 4), and on to Daniel's being Deputy in the realm (chap. 5) and ultimately the most distinguished of the three most senior ministers of state (chap. 6). Their confession moves from private abstinence (chap. 1) through discreet revelation (chap. 2) and discreet noncooperation (chap. 3) to straight challenge (chaps. 4–5) and open defiance (chap. 6).

The relationship between the visions may be expressed schematically.

	Chap. 7	*Chap. 8*	*Chap. 9*	*Chaps. 10–12*
focus:	kingdom	temple	temple	persecution
following on:	Apollonius	desecration	desecration	resistance begins
	dream	vision	audition	audition
	myth	allegory	midrash	oracle in code
Babylon	lion/eagle		7 times 7 weeks	
Media/Persia	bear, then leopard	ram with two horns	7	four/five kings
Greece:			times	
(a) Alexander	horned animal	goat with big horn	62	mighty king of Greece
(b) Hellenistic empires	ten horns	four horns	weeks	breaking of his kingship
(c) Antiochus	small horn	small horn	final week of horror	north-south battles
God's act:				
(a) judgment	beast killed	last king broken		northern king dies
(b) restoration	new kingship	temple vindicated		faithful delivered

The Book's Origin

The book's two halves offer contrary indicators regarding their origin. The stories suggest a setting in the eastern dispersion in the Persian period where there are specific pressures on Jewish faith but the possibility of not only survival but success (Humphreys, *JBL* 92 [1973] 217–23). The visions presuppose a setting in Jerusalem in the 160s B.C. where power lies in the hands of constitutionally hostile gentile authorities and a compliant Jewish leadership that has cooperated with the subversion and outlawing of traditional Jewish faith. It is natural to ask whether the visions have a pre-second-century B.C. history, and specific indication of this has been found in chap. 7 and elsewhere, but we have noted that the arguments for identifying earlier strata are not compelling.

It is natural to ask conversely whether despite appearances the stories were actually composed in a similar period to the visions or were edited then. Specific indication of this has been found in 2:41–43, but intermarriage was a common phenomenon; we cannot infer that these verses refer to a particular instance. The chiasm formed by chaps. 2–7 presumably came into existence in the second century B.C. Aspects of the stories would be very relevant in the second century B.C., but the stories would not have come into existence in this form then (Ginsberg, against Rowley [see *Main Bibliography*]). This is not to imply that the stories and the visions were produced independently of each other and later combined (against Hartman). The stories contribute important features to the visions, such as the person of Daniel himself and thus the feature of pseudonymity, the four empires, and the characterization of Babylon as a lion. The visions were written in the light of the stories: they have been seen as a pesher or actualization of earlier Aramaic material now comprising chaps. 2–7 (e.g., Szörényi, VTSup 15 [1966] 278–94).

Can we go behind the story cycle as we know it? One of the various attempts to trace (for example) a three-stage process in the development of the stories may be right, but these are hardly compelling. A plausible and currently popular reconstruction of the development of the whole envisages some process such as the following whereby material collected around the "magic name[s] of Nebuchadnezzar [and Daniel]" (Oppenheim, *Mesopotamia,* 163): chaps. 1–6 are based on traditions concerning a legendary/mythic wise Daniel/Danel, concerning a Jew who ministered to the Babylonian king (cf. PrNab), concerning three men who stood firm in Babylon, and concerning a Jewish sage called Belteshazzar, all but the first originally reflecting the reign of Nabonidus; chap. 3 is the older of the confessor stories, chaps. 4–5 the oldest of the court-sage stories, chaps. 2 and 6 being developed in the light of chaps. 4–5 and 3, and chap. 1 coming into being last to introduce and unify the sequence as a whole. (See, e.g., von Soden, *ZAW* 53 [1935] 81–89; Eissfeldt, *ZAW* 72 [1960] 134–48; Dommershausen, *Nabonid;* Müller, *UF* 1 [1969] 85–88; Davies, 40–45.)

As for the development of the vision cycle, we have noted that the chapters are chronologically sequential and that, as well as deriving features from the stories, each refers back to one or more of its predecessors. They manifest a generally consistent viewpoint, though this need not suggest common authorship, which Hasslberger (*Hoffnung*) has contested on stylistic grounds. Diversity of authorship might be one of the reasons for diversity of language; perhaps Hebrew-writing authors added chaps. 8, 9, and 10–12 to the Aramaic chiasm (cf. Collins, *Vision,* 15–19). Although in their period one might have expected an introduction that was less friendly to foreign powers (Gammie, *JBL* 95 [1976] 195), they may also have been responsible for chap. 1. As well as introducing the chapters that make up the chiasm, it is also Hebrew, and has in common with chaps. 10–12 the term "discerning," the visionaries' self-designation, and a number of linguistic parallels with Gen 41.

The development of the book as a whole might then be pictured as follows (cf. Müller, just cited):

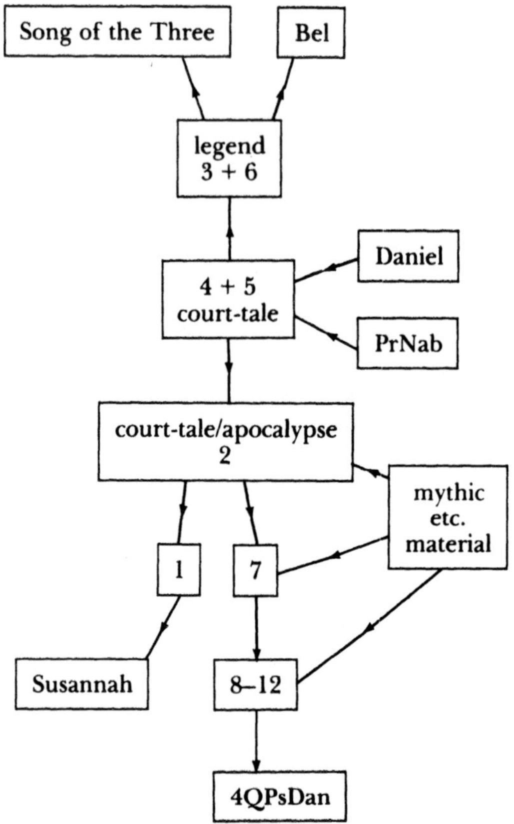

The Book's Authors

We have no direct information concerning what circles might have generated these stories and visions. What follows is conjecture based on the unproved assumption that the information may lie between the lines of the work itself.

The stories concern life at court in the dispersion and speak directly to Jews with leadership positions there. They presuppose a situation in which Jews can do well in dispersion (E. J. Bickerman, "The Babylonian Captivity," *CHJ* 1:346–48). A suspicious hermeneutic might view them as an upper-class text designed to justify the authors' collaboration in exile. But they are stories of a popular kind and may be designed to speak to Jews as an ethnic and religious minority more generally, the implicit argument being that if people like Daniel and his friends in their positions remained faithful and proved the faithfulness of God, ordinary people can do so too.

The visions presuppose a quite different audience, in second-century B.C. Jerusalem. In themselves neither apocalypse as a form nor apocalypticism as a phenomenon need suggest a situation of persecution or alienation; the one can exist without the other, in the ancient and in the modern world

(Burridge, *Semeia* 21 (1981) 100, commenting on Wilson, *Sem* 21 (1981) 84–86—with which cf. Hanson, *IDBSup* 27–31). In Daniel's case, however, authors and audience seem to be people who feel ousted from power in their own community, which is divided into people who support the foreign government and people who oppose it. They are persecuted by these foreign overlords and puzzled at their God's failure to act in response to attacks on his sphere—his shrine, its priesthood, its worship, its people. They are people who attach particular importance to such cultic matters; the authors could have belonged to priestly circles, though their concern about the temple need not imply that. They feel themselves clearly distinguishable from the more liberal Judaism of people prepared to cooperate with and share some of the ways of the Hellenistic imperial authorities, even though Daniel suggests no polemic against Hellenistic culture or lifestyle as such.

If the authors appear in the book, they are presumably the "discerning" of 11:33–35—and of 1:4, where they stand behind the figures of Daniel and his friends. They see themselves as called to a ministry of teaching and encouragement among the people inclined to faithfulness but pressed to apostatize. Although the visions are less popular, more learned works than the stories, here, too, it would be unwise to infer that the audience envisaged was confined to such circles: more likely the visions, too, were intended for the faithful as a whole in their time of testing, the means of the discerning teachers fulfilling their ministry. The authors will have belonged to the hasidim if we take that term to denote people committed to faithfulness to traditional Judaism, though 1 Macc 2:42; 7:12–13; 2 Macc 14:6 use the term with particular reference to people who fought for the right to maintain that faithfulness. While the visions may not oppose that, the particular calling of the "discerning" is to teach, not to fight (see Davies, *JJS* 28 [1977] 127–40, on the hasidim, against Plöger, *Theokratie;* Hengel, *Judentum* 319–94 [ET 1:175–218]). Within conservative Judaism, the "discerning" might be connected with circles that produced other "speculative wisdom," such as the Enoch literature (rather than the Torah-related wisdom of Sirach and the "scribes"). This interest seems to have developed in the dispersion; hence perhaps the linking of dispersion stories and visionary material of this kind, and thus the bringing of the former as well as the latter to Jerusalem (see Collins, *Vision,* 54–59; Davies, 122–25; VanderKam, *Enoch*).

The Book's Theological Significance

The points of difference—indeed, of tension—between the stories and the visions are also a key to considering the theological significance of Daniel as a whole. Readings that begin from one or from the other will suggest different understandings of God's relationship with the world and our life in it. The significance of the book depends on the interaction between them (Davies, 81).

(a) The book suggests varying perspectives on God's relationships with people and his involvement in the world. It does this against the background of a consistent portrait of God as powerful, sovereign, and almighty: the special name Yahweh all but disappears in favor of terms that make explicit that he is not merely a peculiarly Jewish god but the God in/of heaven, King/ Lord of heaven, God of gods, Lord of Lords, great God, living God, Most High, august, awesome, and fiery. He controls history and can therefore reveal history. Myriads of heavenly aides fulfill and reveal his will in the world. There is no need to infer that this makes him remote: he is also our God, my God, your God, the God of the covenant, the fathers' God, one who is compassionate and forgiving. Story and vision portray him as the hearer of prayer who is quite accessible to people even in dispersion, and as the personal giver of revelations whose spirit indwells the servant he holds in high regard. While such revelations are transmitted via his heavenly messengers, the faithful are not confined to approaching these messengers: they approach God himself. While the revelations are expressed mysteriously and communicated pseudonymously, this carries no implication regarding the remoteness of the God who reveals himself to the anonymous seer (against Collins, *Vision,* 75).

The difference between story and vision relates to his acts rather than to his revelations. In the stories he is involved as the God of mercy and grace in the lives of the faithful, in person or through his aides. The God of Daniel is always there when you least expect him—in a stone, in a crematorium oven, on a whitewashed wall, in a pit of ferocious beasts (Lacocque, 108). In the latter his involvement in the present is harder to see. Nevertheless, "it was the same God of the three youths who was the God of the Maccabees. The former escaped fire, the latter were executed by fires; but both will conquer in the eternal God" (Augustine, Sermon xxxii 15 on Ps 15, as quoted by Bickermann, *God,* v).

(b) The theme that is central to Daniel as it is to no other book in the OT is the kingdom of God (Boehmer, 16–17). The book as a whole concerns how the rule of God becomes a reality of this world in contexts where Jews as such lack political power but where the Gentiles who do exercise political power are assumed to have a religious responsibility (Joubert, 211–12). The purpose of God is to be realized on earth, but by the transcendent power of heaven (Hall, 224–25).

The stories portray it doing so via the heathen ruler, who receives his kingly power from God and is responsible to act as his viceregent in his world, but they recognize that often the heathen ruler fails to exercise his power in a way that reflects this understanding of his calling. They picture the leaders of the people of God then challenging him to do so, sometimes with success, sometimes not. But they close with him acknowledging that lasting dominion indeed belongs to God. The stories invite us to use their portrayal of this rule of God becoming reality to interpret the history for which we must accept responsibility. They imply that the cynicism and the deceit that often seem to characterize politics will not have the last word. The incompetence and stupidity that often seem to characterize our leaders will not have their way. Believers under pressure can stand by their convictions sure that the powers that be will ultimately acknowledge where true power lies and who is its witness. The stories invite us to set Daniel's experience and testimony alongside the stories that emerge from our political experience and see what happens.

The way kings exercise their rule as the visions describe it keeps the rule of God from becoming reality. Only an act from heaven can bring God's rule. The visions offer an alternative portrayal of how God's rule becomes reality, one designed to help us live with history when we cannot control it. They begin (chap. 7) with God's lasting dominion: rule is taken away from heathen rulers and given to the people of the holy ones on high. But that rule is still to be exercised on earth. Even the judgment by the venerable figure of chap. 7 takes place on earth and is implemented here, while the restoration to life of chap. 12 is a restoration to earthly life of whole people, not of disembodied spirits in heaven. The millenarian movements were not unfaithful to Daniel in looking for a salvation that was collective, terrestrial, imminent, total, and miraculous (N. Cohn, *The Pursuit of the Millennium* [rev. ed.; London/New York: Temple Smith/OUP, 1970] 13).

The whole book looks for the realization of the reign of God on earth; but apparently there is a time when we can see this coming through earthly rulers and through us, in this age, and at a time when that can be neither seen nor envisaged, only hoped for as the direct act of God, which brings a transition from this age to another age (Barth, *Diesseits*). There is a time when the present can only be understood in the light of the past and the future. There is a time when the people of God experience conflict with the world, and a time when behind that they perceive a conflict with supernatural powers (Philip). The focus on the future in chaps. 7–12 insists on our being critical of the present, in the conviction that the promise of God demands a fulfillment that cannot be identified with this present; the focus on the present in chaps. 1–6 forbids us to be escapist, and insists we face the force of the observation that "apocalyptic is full of promises, but it has never kept one of them" (R. Trevors Herford: see Kreuziger, *Apocalypse,* 149 [quoting Koch], and further, e.g., 78–79, 158–62, 176). Between them they affirm both present and promise. Political powers stand between the perspective of chaps. 1–6 and that of chaps. 7–12, choosing which is applicable to them, and believers involved in politics have to discern which choice they are making. Subject to them, ordinary believers live as children of this age, but also as children of an age to come. It is the conviction that the new age has come in Jesus that makes apocalyptic "the mother of all Christian theology" (Käsemann, *ZTK* 57 [1960] 180, ET 40).

(c) The book thus suggests two understandings of the meaningfulness or otherwise of political history. It begins with a God involved in history, giving the Judean king into the power of Babylon. He controls historical eras and removes and sets up kings. He rules human kingdoms and gives power to whomever he wishes. He evaluates the rule of kings and puts them down when they fail his assessment. The process of history thus has meaning; it sees the outworking of God's grace, mercy, purposefulness, justice, and zeal, even if it is not always clear *how* events reflect these. The prophets concern themselves with international history insofar as it affects the history of Israel; Daniel is closer to having a philosophy of international history in itself.

In the visions the origins of human empires are more ambiguous: they arise out of the world itself, rather than by the gift of God, and resemble strange animals emerging from the sea—even if it is a supernatural wind that stirs that sea. God has been active in Israel's history in revelation, in grace, and in judgment, and can be urged to be active there in mercy and in restoration (chap. 9); he is active in the nations' history only by bringing an End to it. He is in control of their history, but in the manner of the prison governor who still controls the prison during a riot in the sense that the prisoners can only go so far (the visions' quasi-prophetic form should not mislead us into thinking that Daniel sees God predetermining this history). Even in heaven there are conflicts between the agents of God's will who personify earthly powers in conflict with each other. The details of history have little intrinsic meaning; meaning belongs to the End, not to the process. Daniel thus differs from 1 and 2 Maccabees, which in different ways rework the classic attitude to history of books such as Kings and Chronicles, and it differs from *1 Enoch,* which extends its historical perspective back to embrace creation so that it extends from Beginning to End, and—like some Christian thinking, though not the OT or the NT—sees conflicts in heaven and in history as resulting from the rebellion of heavenly beings near the beginning.

Neither stories nor visions see history as a whole or see it as progressing toward a goal; the standard descriptions of the apocalyptic view of history do not apply to Daniel. The difference between stories and visions suggests that there are times when the hand of God can be detected in the processes of history and times when it has to be looked for at the End.

(d) The book offers two paradigms of the leadership of the faithful in community life. In the stories it is a matter of involvement in the life of government, which presupposes an affirming of those who exercise authority. By the will of God himself and by the nature of his commission to earthly rulers, human beings have a responsibility for urging them to fulfill that calling as before God; they can realistically be challenged to fulfill such a responsibility. The perspective matches that of Rom 13.

The perspective of the visions compares rather with that of Rev 13. They cannot see God's activity in history. Jews back in Jerusalem in the second-century B.C. experience, paradoxically, something more like exile with its meaninglessness (see especially chap. 9) than did their brothers and sisters in dispersion in the Persian period. Faithfulness to God, which, in the context presupposed by the stories, demanded participation in politics, now itself demands critique of the governing authorities and rules out involvement in government (Joubert, 212). The visions are not specific about lines of action they expect of the faithful (military action? passive resistance? continuing obedience to the Torah? withdrawal from temple worship?). Further, history is portrayed as closed and fixed, though this is a way of assuring people that history that is difficult to recognize as the act of God has nevertheless been under his control. The possibility of leadership is to instruct the believing community on the significance of history, past, present, and future.

Throughout the book the calling of the leadership is to pray, to the God who controls and reveals history. But apparently there is a time to be involved in the present and a time to teach about the End. The stories invite believers who live under oppressive regimes to allow for and to be encouraged by the possibility that there are contexts where one can be involved in the affairs of state without compromise. The visions invite believers in easier times than theirs to an empathetic act of identification—perhaps of deed, not just of word—if they are to enter into the pain of those who live under oppressive regimes and thus to be able to share the real meaning of their visions and not just the words.

(e) The book has a vision for both life in dispersion and life in Jerusalem. The stories see dispersion life as the result of the act of God; it is neither meaningless nor the reflection of the greater power of other gods. Neither is it explicitly the result of an act of God in punishment for the sin of Jews. It is simply his will. That in itself lays the foundation for the possibility that it is possible to be a good Jew in dispersion. A Jew will remain distinctive, will remain faithful, and will continue to pray toward Jerusalem, but he will do that in a dispersion setting, and will prove that this can be the way to a successful life. There is no suggestion of "next year in Jerusalem."

The visions almost ignore dispersion life. Their concern is with the restoration of the city of Jerusalem, its sanctuary, its worship, and its priesthood. Tellingly, the dispersion explicitly features only once, and there it is the result of sin (chap. 9). North and south are the origins of enemies rather than the location of brothers and sisters. Jerusalem is the only natural Jewish place to live. They offer their own challenge to faithfulness, yet not one accompanied by an implicit promise that faithfulness will be rewarded by worldly success and promotion. The stories of the dispersion heroes both illustrate Jews being willing for faithfulness to be its own reward, and remind their hearers of the power and the faithfulness of God himself who will see that faithfulness receives its reward in the age to come if not in this age (Joubert, 210).

In the book's portrayal, Jewish life is precarious and Jewish faithfulness is under pressure wherever it is lived. Both Babylon and Jerusalem are experiences of "desolation," the latter a protraction of the former, of which it can thus be a paradigm, and people dealing with the former can be prototypes of people dealing with the latter (Davies, 13). One might have expected it to be obvious that dispersion was a place of pressure: actually the pressures there are usually more subtle. One might have expected Jerusalem to be a place of safety: actually the pressures there are—to the seers at least—very clear. Neither dispersion nor Jerusalem is without danger. Each brings its challenge. Neither is called to judge the other.

(f) The book suggests two different overall thrusts, summed up by its being located by the synagogue among the Writings and by the church among the Prophets (cf. Koch, *Int* 39 [1985] 127). That encourages two alternative readings of Daniel, as wisdom or as prophecy, as pedagogics or as eschatology, as halakah or as haggadah.

Both story and vision exist to render a world. Story renders a world that is clearly one with our world, even though it points to signals of transcendence that suggest something beyond our world. It served the needs of the dispersion well. In the second-century B.C. crisis "the time of narrative must now leave room for the time of vision" (Lacocque, *BR* 26 [1981] 8). Vision creates a radically different world that makes continuing life in this world possible on the basis of its not being the only world, or in the End the most important one. Daniel's work is preserved even though the End of which he spoke did not come, because in another sense that End did come. His vision brought the End of an old order's power to lord it over his fellows, because it opened up an alternative world that people were prepared to believe would endure as the old order would not, a world in which what seemed at present to be weakness was revealed to be true power and what looked like death was revealed to be the gateway to life (Barr, *Int* 38 [1984] 39–50; cf. Schlüssler Fiorenza, "Early Christian Apocalyptic," 295–316). Daniel as a whole invites us to live this life in the light of such convictions about that life.

Index of Authors Cited

Index of Principal Subjects

Index of Biblical and Other Ancient Sources

A. Old Testament

B. New Testament

C. Other Jewish Writings

D. Other Christian Writings

The indices were compiled by Clarence Rickard

CPSIA information can be obtained at www.ICGtesting.com
Printed in the USA
LVOW06*0651220215

427713LV00002B/2/P

9 780310 521921